REFLECTIONS ON THE UN DECLARATION ON THE RIGHTS OF INDIGENOUS PEOPLES

The adoption of the Declaration on the Rights of Indigenous Peoples by the United Nations General Assembly on 13 September 2007 was acclaimed as a major success for the United Nations system given the extent to which it consolidates and develops the international corpus of indigenous rights. This is the first in-depth academic analysis of this far-reaching instrument. Indigenous representatives have argued that the rights contained in the Declaration, and the processes by which it was formulated, obligate affected States to accept the validity of its provisions and its interpretation of contested concepts (such as 'culture', 'land', 'ownership' and 'self-determination'). This edited collection contains essays written by the main protagonists in the development of the Declaration; indigenous representatives; and leading academics in the field. It offers a comprehensive institutional, thematic and regional analysis of the Declaration. In particular, it explores the Declaration's normative resonance for international law and considers the ways in which this international instrument could catalyse institutional action and influence the development of national laws and policies on indigenous issues.

Volume 30 in the series Studies in International Law

Studies in International Law

Volume 1: Between Light and Shadow: The World Bank, the International Monetary Fund and International Human Rights Law
Mac Darrow

Volume 2: Toxics and Transnational Law: International and European Regulation of Toxic Substances as Legal Symbolism
Marc Pallemaerts

Volume 3: The Chapter VII Powers of the United Nations Security Council
Erika de Wet

Volume 4: Enforcing International Law Norms Against Terrorism
Edited by Andrea Bianchi

Volume 5: The Permanent International Criminal Court
Edited by Dominic McGoldrick, Peter Rowe and Eric Donnelly

Volume 6: Regional Organisations and the Development of Collective Security
Ademola Abass

Volume 7: Islamic State Practices, International Law and the Threat from Terrorism: A Critique of the 'Clash of Civilizations' in the New World Order
Javaid Rehman

Volume 8: Predictablity and Flexibility in the Law of Maritime Delimitation
Yoshifumi Tanaka

Volume 9: Biotechnology and International Law
Edited by Francesco Francioni and Tullio Scovazzi

Volume 10: The Development of Human Rights Law by the Judges of the International Court of Justice
Shiv Bedi

Volume 11: The Environmental Accountability of the World Bank to Third Party Non-State Actors
Alix Gowlland-Gualtieri

Volume 12: Transnational Corporations and Human Rights
Edited by Olivier De Schutter

Volume 13: Biotechnologies and International Human Rights
Edited by Francesco Francioni

Volume 14: Human Security and International Law: Prospects and Problems
Barbara Von Tigerstrom

Volume 15: The Arms Trade and International Law
Zeray Yihdego

Volume 16: Africa: Mapping New Boundaries in International Law
Edited by Jeremy Levitt

Volume 17: Forced Migration, Human Rights and Security
Edited by Jane McAdam

Volume 18: The Use of Nuclear Weapons and the Protection of the Environment during International Armed Conflict
Erik Koppe

Volume 19: The Shifting Allocation of Authority in International Law: Considering Sovereignty, Supremacy and Subsidiarity
Edited by Tomer Broude and Yuval Shany

Volume 20: Counterterrorism: Democracy's Challenge
Edited by Andrea Bianchi and Alexis Keller

Volume 21: Amnesty, Human Rights and Political Transitions
Louise Mallinder

Volume 22: Property Rights and Natural Resources
Richard Barnes

Volume 23: Human Dignity and the Foundations of International Law
Patrick Capps

Volume 24: Sovereignty and the Stateless Nation: Gibraltar in the Modern Legal Context
Keith Azopardi

Volume 25: The International Court of Justice and Self-Defence in International Law
James A Green

Volume 26: State Liability in Investment Treaty Arbitration: Global Constitutional and Administrative Law in the BIT Generation
Santiago Montt

Volume 27: Reappraising the Resort to Force: International Law, Jus ad Bellum and the War on Terror
Lindsay Moir

Volume 28: International Law and Dispute Settlement: New Problems and Techniques
Edited by Duncan French, Matthew Saul and Nigel White

Volume 29: The Democratic Legitimacy of International Law
Steven Wheatley

Volume 30: Reflections on the UN Declaration on the Rights of Indigenous Peoples
Edited by Stephen Allen and Alexandra Xanthaki

Reflections on the UN Declaration on the Rights of Indigenous Peoples

Edited by

Stephen Allen

and

Alexandra Xanthaki

• HART •
PUBLISHING

OXFORD AND PORTLAND, OREGON

2011

Published in the United Kingdom by Hart Publishing Ltd
16C Worcester Place, Oxford, OX1 2JW
Telephone: +44 (0)1865 517530
Fax: +44 (0)1865 510710
E-mail: mail@hartpub.co.uk
Website: http://www.hartpub.co.uk

Published in North America (US and Canada) by
Hart Publishing
c/o International Specialized Book Services
920 NE 58th Avenue, Suite 300
Portland, OR 97213-3786
USA
Tel: +1 503 287 3093 or toll-free: (1) 800 944 6190
Fax: +1 503 280 8832
E-mail: orders@isbs.com
Website: http://www.isbs.com

British Library Cataloguing in Publication Data
Data Available

ISBN: 978-1-84113-878-7

Typeset by Compuscript Ltd, Shannon
Printed and bound in Great Britain by
TJ International Ltd, Padstow, Cornwall

Contents

SECTION C: SUBSTANTIVE PERSPECTIVES

SECTION D: REGIONAL PERSPECTIVES

Biographies

Stephen Allen Lecturer in Law, Brunel University, UK

Clive Baldwin Human Rights Watch

Julian Burger Head of the Indigenous Peoples' Programme, Office of the United Nations High Commissioner

Joshua Castellino Professor of Law, Head of Law Department, Middlesex University, UK

Erica Irene Daes Former Chairperson of the UN Working Group on Indigenous Populations. She has also served repeatedly as a UN Special Rapporteur

Cathal Doyle PhD, Fellow in Law, Middlesex University, UK; Researcher on behalf of the Philippines Indigenous Peoples Links, UK

Dalee Sambo Dorough PhD, Assistant Professor, Political Science, University of Alaska Anchorage; Alaskan Member of the ICC Advisory Committee on UN Issues; Member of the ILA Committee on Rights of Indigenous Peoples

Andrew Erueti Coordinator, Human Rights of Indigenous Peoples, Amnesty International, International Secretariat; SJD candidate, Faculty of Law, University of Toronto

Stefania Errico Observer, UN Working Group on the Draft Declaration on the Rights of Indigenous Peoples

Malgosia Fitzmaurice Professor of Public International Law, Faculty of Law, Queen Mary, University of London, UK

H Patrick Glenn Peter M Laing Professor of Law, Faculty of Law & Institute of Comparative Law, McGill University, Canada

Jérémie Gilbert Senior Lecturer in Law, Middlesex University, UK

Johanna Gibson Herchel Smith Professor of Intellectual Property Law, Queen Mary Intellectual Property Research Institute, Centre for Commercial Law Studies, Queen Mary, University of London

Will Kymlicka Canada Research Chair in Political Philosophy, Queen's University, Kingston, Canada

Cynthia Morel Open Society Justice Initiative

Rachel Murray Professor of International Human Rights Law, Bristol University, UK

Helen Quane Senior Lecturer in Law, Swansea University, UK

Javaid Rehman Professor of International Law and Head of Brunel Law School, Brunel University, UK

Luis Rodríguez-Piñero Ramón y Cajal Researcher, Law Department, University of Seville, Spain

Elsa Stamatopoulou Chief of the Secretariat of the United Nations Permanent Forum on Indigenous Issues

Rodolfo Stavenhagen Professor of Sociology, El Colegio de México; former Deputy Director General of UNESCO; former UN Special Rapporteur on the situation of human rights and fundamental freedoms of indigenous people

Patrick Thornberry Professor of International Law, Member of UN Committee on the Elimination of All Forms of Discrimination, Visiting Fellow of Kellogg College, University of Oxford, UK

Emmanuel Voyiakis Lecturer in Law, Brunel University, UK

Alexandra Xanthaki Reader in Law, Brunel Law School, UK

Introduction

STEPHEN ALLEN AND ALEXANDRA XANTHAKI

THE ADOPTION OF the Declaration on the Rights of Indigenous Peoples by the UN General Assembly in September 2007 has been widely viewed as a momentous occasion for indigenous peoples, for the United Nations system and for international law in general. The Declaration was the product of over 20 years of focused debate and negotiation between indigenous representatives, States, UN officials and other institutional actors. In 1982, the UN Economic and Social Council established the UN Working Group on Indigenous Populations (WGIP) as a subsidiary organ of the Sub-Commission on Prevention of Discrimination and Protection of Minorities (now the Sub-Commission on the Protection and Promotion of Human Rights). The WGIP was charged with the task of developing international standards on indigenous rights. It produced a draft declaration in 1993, which was subsequently adopted by the Sub-Commission in 1994;[1] and referred to the Commission on Human Rights. The Commission established an Inter-sessional Working Group for the purpose of reviewing the draft.[2] This Group meticulously scrutinised the draft over 11 annual sessions. In 2006, a compromise text was recommended to the Human Rights Council, the Commission's successor. The Council endorsed the draft Declaration and recommended it to the General Assembly with a view to adoption.[3] Concerns expressed by certain States meant that it was not adopted by this body at the first opportunity. After a further period of institutional activity, the Declaration was adopted on 13 September 2007.[4] One hundred and forty-three States voted in favour of the Declaration. The USA, Canada, Australia and New Zealand voted against, and there were 11 abstentions.

The Declaration is more comprehensive in substance and more extensive in scope than any other existing international instrument specifically dedicated to indigenous issues. It recognises (inter alia): the right

[1] Resolution 1994/45.
[2] Commission on Human Rights Resolution 1995/32.
[3] Human Rights Council Resolution 2006/2.
[4] General Assembly Resolution 61/295.

to self-determination; land/resource rights; the right to restitution; cultural rights; the right to separate political institutions and systems; the right of indigenous peoples to participate in governmental decision-making processes that affect them (including the right to prior, free and informed consent); intellectual property rights; the right to development; and the right to treaty recognition. Further, by elaborating the above rights the Declaration has bolstered the concept of collective rights and many of its articles demonstrate the ways in which individual and collective rights interrelate to protect and promote indigenous identities.

This collection of essays resulted from a perceived need to examine the Declaration critically and to situate it within the context of international law. The passionate claims advanced by the transnational indigenous movement during the processes which led to the Declaration's adoption and the normative analysis offered by international lawyers along the way have neglected—perhaps justifiably—some difficult questions regarding the content and the status of the Declaration in international law. This collection has been written on the premise that it is now time to engage with these issues, given the confidence that the Declaration's adoption has afforded. It is suggested that such a process of critical reflection is the only way that this ground-breaking instrument can become a vehicle for palpable change and global justice.

Against this background, the book explores the Declaration's normative resonance for international law and considers the ways in which it could be used to prompt and shape institutional action and influence the development of national laws and policies on indigenous issues. It contains essays written by the main protagonists in the Declaration's development; indigenous representatives; and field-leading academics. It offers comprehensive institutional, thematic and regional analysis of the instrument. Moreover, the book seeks to examine in depth a number of fundamental questions raised by the Declaration, and to reflect upon the wider challenges that confront the realisation of the rights of indigenous peoples in a variety of settings. In this respect, the collection addresses some crosscutting questions, which include:

- What is the status of the Declaration (and its provisions) as a matter of international law? What are the implications of achieving international legal recognition?
- How do the Declaration's provisions contribute to development of the substantive rights proclaimed in the instrument?
- How will the Declaration influence other areas of international human rights law and the work of United Nations treaty-based bodies?
- How can the Declaration's provisions be implemented?

- What will be the impact of the Declaration in different regions and national settings and how can best practice on indigenous issues be shared in this regard?
- What are the implications of the Declaration for other sub-State societal groups?
- What are the consequences for the structures and processes of international institutions given the unprecedented levels of indigenous participation in the Declaration's development?
- What is the significance of the Declaration for the internal structures of governance of States and for the institution of the State itself?
- Has the Declaration advanced the cause of global governance?
- Has the Declaration contributed to the re-orientation of international law away from its Eurocentric origins?

The first part of the collection discusses the emergence of the Declaration from the United Nations system while exploring its impact on the existing mechanisms and international instruments that have focused on indigenous rights. The first chapter provides a comprehensive overview of the United Nations system's engagement with the Declaration, written by the main driving force behind the instrument, Erica-Irene Daes. In her essay, Daes highlights a range of important instruments and discussions within key United Nations bodies that pushed the Declaration towards adoption. In the next chapter, Julian Burger, who headed the Indigenous Peoples' Programme at the Office of the United Nations High Commissioner for Human Rights (1991–2009), discusses how United Nations bodies can help the Declaration to become an engine for change, particularly at the national level. Specifically, he shows how the Declaration has been shaped by indigenous experiences and he analyses the Declaration's twin pillars: the principles of non-discrimination and self-determination.

In his essay, Patrick Thornberry, a member of United Nations Committee on the Elimination of All Forms of Racial Discrimination, shows how that Committee has internalised indigenous rights into its mandate with considerable success. Accordingly, he argues that the International Convention on the Elimination of All Forms of Racial Discrimination has achieved a generally symbiotic relationship with the Declaration. Thornberry emphasises United Nations treaty bodies' pivotal role in interpreting this Declaration and prompting its implementation given the absence of a fully equipped monitoring body for the instrument. In the light of its pioneering role in the development of international standards concerning indigenous issues, the work of the International Labour Organization (ILO) is profoundly important to the emergence and consolidation of the Declaration. In Chapter 4, Andrew Erueti discusses the ILO's contribution to the internationalisation of the Declaration and more generally, the challenges that internationalisation confronts in terms of goals of indigenous peoples and the underlying justifications for indigenous rights recognised in different regions of the world. In particular, he argues that the use of the concept of 'cultural difference' to support emerging indigenous movements has provided a means of connecting indigenous peoples to the global indigenous movement.

Clive Baldwin and Cynthia Morel's chapter provides an in-depth analysis of a number of legal cases (particularly the *Endorois* case, the Chagos Islanders litigation and the claims made by the Tasmanian Aboriginal Centre) in order to demonstrate that litigation offers a useful means of grounding the Declaration. Further, they show that litigation allows the interpretation of general human rights instruments in ways that draw upon the content of the Declaration and clarify and consolidate the rights of indigenous peoples.

The second part of the collection is dedicated to thematic analysis of the Declaration. The issues of status and implementation have dominated debates about the Declaration in the aftermath of adoption. Rodolfo Stavenhagen addresses the latter issue. Drawing upon his experience as the Special Rapporteur on the Situation of Human Rights and Fundamental Freedoms of Indigenous People between 2001 and 2008, he believes that the Declaration provides an opportunity to link the global and the local, through a process of 'glocalisation', and he views the Declaration as a 'statement of redress' as well as a 'map of action'. In contrast, H Patrick Glenn identifies the conventional ironies embedded in the Declaration: it advances indigenous law by harnessing 'the profoundly western notion of international law', a source responsible for the dispossession and subjugation of indigenous peoples throughout the world; it uses the idiom of western 'culture theory' to advance different world views; and finally, Glenn notes the formal opposition to the Declaration by those States that have been among the most active in developing municipal laws for the benefit of indigenous peoples. However, Glenn believes that these ironies can reveal the extent to which normative interdependence has occurred. Will Kymlicka is also critical of the Declaration. Although he considers the Declaration's value to be a precedent for other culturally distinct sub-State groups and an important example of the 'multicultural model of political ordering', Kymlicka suggests that the Declaration's precedential significance for national minorities might be much more limited in practice, as indigenous rights claims have been endorsed by the international community on the tacit understanding that they have no conceptual or legal implications for such minorities.

The collection moves on to address the question of the Declaration's status. Emmanuel Voyiakis accepts that resolutions can provide the inspiration for the development of customary international law but his interest lies in what resolutions tell us about the attitudes of those States participating in the General Assembly's voting procedures and their significance in relation to the creation of customary international law. In particular, he considers whether the proper interpretation of a State's vote in this context should be determined by its intentions as expressed by the exercise of its vote and its subsequent practice. In his chapter, Stephen Allen questions the techniques used by some indigenous activists and international lawyers supportive of indigenous rights to promote the significance of the Declaration for international law. The essay argues that the Declaration's significance stems from the political legitimacy it embodies rather than its claimed international legal character and reiterates the importance of indigenous political engagement at a national level to close the existing 'implementation gap'.

The third part of the collection considers the Declaration's substantive provisions. Undoubtedly, the most important issue for indigenous peoples remains the right to self-determination. Helen Quane examines the Declaration's provisions on self-determination and participation and asks whether they are indicative of a new direction for international law. Quane considers whether the right to self-determination and rights of participation could coalesce to form a meta-right of effective participation in public life, thereby signalling a shift away from the troubled discourse of self-determination and towards more pragmatic approaches which combine explicit legal and political considerations.

The next series of essays concentrate upon specific manifestations of the right to self-determination for many indigenous peoples. Jeremie Gilbert and Cathal Doyle discuss the growing body of international human rights law concerning indigenous peoples' land/territorial rights. After considering the procedural doctrine of free, prior and informed consent, they argue that not only does the Declaration represent an integral component of the normative framework on indigenous land rights, it also provides the conceptual means for the elaboration and realisation of such rights in the foreseeable future. In her chapter, Stefania Errico examines the doctrine of free, prior and informed consent with respect to natural resources. She argues that while that States can dispose of sub-soil resources located in indigenous lands, the Declaration establishes a specific framework within which any extractive activity must be carried out and requires that States engage with indigenous peoples effectively in connection with projects for exploitation of natural resources to be carried out in their lands. Joshua Castellino considered the relationship between the right to self-determination and the right of development. Against a background of the general struggle to realise economic and social rights, he advances a holistic interpretation of this right of development and analyses the extent to which the Declaration's provisions contribute to its normative evolution. In addition, Castellino assesses the

Declaration's capacity to bring about the practical aim of securing a more equitable redistribution of economic and social resources for indigenous peoples despite the instrument's soft law status and the aspirational nature of the rights it proclaims.

The collection then turns to questions of identity and culture. Elsa Stamatopoulou, Chief of the Secretariat of the Permanent Forum on Indigenous Issues, maps the path towards the recognition of indigenous cultural rights and situates the Declaration's provisions concerning these rights within a wider international legal framework. The adoption of the Declaration, she argues, has unleashed tremendous potential for positive change in mending historical injustices and it represents a significant shift towards more inclusive, poly-cultural societies. Alexandra Xanthaki focuses on the challenges that such poly-cultural societies may face and, specifically, the possible conflicts between indigenous rights as confirmed in the Declaration and women's rights. She argues that now—following the adoption of the Declaration—is the time to discuss such difficult issues in order to address them, and highlights ways in which the Declaration and international law must resolve such conflicts. Another challenging issue is that of indigenous rights to heritage, which Johanna Gibson examines in her chapter. Gibson argues that current international law provides the foundations for deference to customary law with respect to community knowledge, as recognised in the Declaration, but she cautions that the sui generis protection of indigenous heritage rights may be an unobtainable goal in the foreseeable future.

The final part of the collection reflects upon the impact of the Declaration in specific regions. The book has sought to give priority to regions that have not been the focus of the literature on indigenous rights to date. Nevertheless, such a collection would not be complete without discussing the link between the Declaration and the Inter-American system. In his chapter, Luis Rodríguez-Piñero explains how the groundbreaking jurisprudence on indigenous rights of the Inter-American system interrelates with the Declaration via the eclectic processes of normative cross-fertilisation, as demonstrated by the *Awas Tigni* case. At the same time, the Inter-American system provides the institutional apparatus for implementing the Declaration's provisions within the adjudicative context, as evidenced by the recent case of *Saramaka People v Suriname*. The collection then turns to Africa. Despite not being materially involved in the elaboration of the Declaration, many African States refused to endorse the instrument when it first came before the United Nations General Assembly in the 2006 session. Rachel Murray's essay discusses the reasons behind this and the African Union's response to the Declaration in the aftermath of this session. In particular, she examines the extent to which the African Commission on Human and Peoples'

Rights' Working Group on Indigenous Populations/Communities (supported by a number of non-governmental organisations) managed to influence the position of African States on indigenous issues, which led to the decision of many African States to endorse the Declaration at the General Assembly meeting in September 2007.

Dalee Sambo Dorough, one of the most active indigenous representatives at the international level and a protagonist in the emergence of the Declaration, uses the Inuit example to demonstrate how the Declaration is important in counter-balancing the asymmetrical nature of negotiations between States and indigenous peoples. Dorough discusses several developments in the Arctic countries that have been important in giving indigenous peoples control over their affairs. She believes that the Declaration has the capacity to make an important contribution to Inuit lives. In the following chapter, Malgosia Fitzmaurice focuses on the 2005 Norwegian Finnmark Act and the 2005 Draft Saami Convention, a draft treaty between Finland, Norway and Sweden. Fitzmaurice uses these sources in order to highlight the extent to which the Declaration has influenced developments in these regions and, in turn, how such regional developments have the capacity to bring about the Declaration's implementation. Finally, Javaid Rehman analyses a very topical—albeit unexplored—issue with reference to Asia: the branding of indigenous peoples as suspects of terrorism by States in an attempt to curtail their rights. Rehman uses the situations of the Pachtuns and Beluchis in Pakistan in order to discuss whether the Declaration as a norm of international law can effectively help such cases; his conclusion coincides with the voices emphasising the political nature of the Declaration.

The adoption of the Declaration is perceived by the editors of this volume to be the beginning of a new phase in the debate on indigenous rights. Having focused on the coherence of indigenous claims within current international law, discussions should now turn to the challenges that the Declaration faces as well as the ones that the Declaration poses. We hope that this collection contributes to this debate. We would like to thank Richard Hart for giving us the platform for this volume and Rachel Turner for her support throughout its development. We would also like to thank Patrick Thornberry for pushing us in the right direction, Gudmundur Alfredsson for standing beside us in our first tentative steps on this journey, and, of course, all the contributors to this volume for their enthusiasm, their patience and, most of all, their ideas and for giving us an insight into their vision for indigenous rights.

Section A

Institutional Perspectives

1

The UN Declaration on the Rights of Indigenous Peoples: Background and Appraisal

ERICA-IRENE DAES

THE WORLD'S INDIGENOUS peoples will forever remember 13 September 2007, which marked the date of the proclamation by the General Assembly of the United Nations Declaration on the Rights of Indigenous Peoples ('the Declaration').[1] This historic event signified the beginning of the realisation of the vision, aspirations and basic rights of indigenous peoples living in all parts of the globe. In this regard, it is considered useful to present in short some of the principal points that relate to the background to the Declaration and the procedure that led to its adoption, and finally to offer an appraisal of its success.

INTRODUCTORY REMARKS

Before 1969, the problems and needs of indigenous peoples had not been on the agenda of the human rights organs and bodies of the United Nations (UN). That year, the former Sub-Commission on the Prevention of Discrimination and Protection of Minorities ('the Commission') had before it a Special Study on Racial Discrimination in the Political, Economic, Social and Cultural Spheres, which included a chapter on measures taken in connection with the protection of indigenous peoples.[2] Based on this chapter, a process of discussion started within the Sub-Commission which led to its recommending in 1970 that a comprehensive study be mounted on the problem of discrimination against indigenous populations.[3] The recommendation was

[1] UN GA Resolution 61/295 of 13 September 2007.
[2] UN Doc E/CN.4 Sub-Commission 2/301.
[3] Resolution 4B (XXIII) of 26 August 1970.

passed to the Commission on Human Rights ('the Commission') and was finally taken up by the Economic and Social Council (ECOSOC). ECOSOC adopted Resolution 1589 (L) of 21 of May 1971 in which it authorised the elaboration of such a study. Later in 1971, Mr José Martinez Cobo was appointed Special Rapporteur for the preparation of a Study on the Problem of Discrimination against Indigenous Populations.[4] The study was finally completed between the years 1981 and 1984 and contains a number of important conclusions and recommendations.[5]

Already though, even before this study was finalised, the concern that it had raised regarding the plight of indigenous peoples had caused the Sub-Commission to propose in 1981 the establishment of a Working Group on Indigenous Populations (WGIP).[6] The proposal was endorsed by the Commission and in 1982 ECOSOC authorised the Sub-Commission to create the WGIP. The WGIP held its first meeting in 1982 and its second one in 1983 under the able chairmanship of Mr Asbjorn Eide. In 1984, I was elected Chairperson-Rapporteur of the WGIP and served in this capacity until 2001.

According to its mandate, the WGIP would review current developments affecting the rights of indigenous populations and would specifically draft standards concerning the rights of indigenous peoples. Under this mandate of the WGIP on drafting standards concerning the rights of indigenous peoples and in my capacity as Chairperson-Rapporteur of the WGIP, I collected information and data for the elaboration of a draft declaration on the rights of indigenous peoples ('the draft declaration').

In September 1984, I was invited to represent the WGIP at the General Assembly of the World Council of Indigenous Peoples in Panama. I met with hundreds of indigenous peoples from various places around the globe who demanded that the UN formally recognise and protect their basic rights and fundamental freedoms. In particular, the Saami people, under the very able leadership of the late Sara from Kautokeino, insisted that a declaration or even a convention should be proposed for adoption by the UN. Following long and painful consultations, the following 17 principles were adopted for the purpose of constituting, the basis of a declaration.

[4] Resolution B (XXIV) of 10 August 1971.

[5] The conclusions and recommendations are contained in Vol V of the study, UN Doc E/CN.4/Sub.2/1986/7/Add.4.

[6] Resolution 2 (XXXIV) of 8 September 1981.

1984 DECLARATION OF PRINCIPLES

In September 1984, a Declaration of Principles was adopted by the Fourth General Assembly of the World Council of Indigenous Peoples in Panama.[7] It read:

> Principle 1: All indigenous peoples have the right to self-determination. By virtue of this right they may freely determine their political status and freely pursue their economic, social religious and cultural development.
>
> Principle 2: All States within which an indigenous people lives shall recognize the population, territory and institutions of the indigenous people.
>
> Principle 3: The cultures of the indigenous peoples are part of the cultural heritage of mankind.
>
> Principle 4: The traditions and customs of indigenous peoples must be respected by the States, and recognized as a fundamental source of law.
>
> Principle 5: All indigenous peoples have the right to determine the person or group of persons who are included within the population.
>
> Principle 6: Each indigenous people has the right to determine the form, structure and authority of its institutions.
>
> Principle 7: The institutions of indigenous peoples and their decisions, like those of States, must be in conformity with internationally accepted human rights both collective and individual.
>
> Principle 8: Indigenous peoples and their members are entitled to participate in the political life of the State.
>
> Principle 9: Indigenous peoples shall have exclusive rights to their traditional lands and its resources, where the lands and resources of the indigenous peoples have been taken away without their free and informed consent such lands and resources should be returned.
>
> Principle 10: The land rights of an indigenous people include surface and subsurface rights, full rights to interior and coastal waters and rights to adequate and exclusive coastal economic zones within the limits of international law.
>
> Principle 11: All indigenous peoples may, for their own needs, freely use their natural wealth and resources in accordance with Principles 9 and 10.
>
> Principle 12: No action or course of conduct may be undertaken which, directly or indirectly, may result in the destruction of land, air, water, sea ice, wildlife, habitat or natural resources without the free and informed consent of the indigenous peoples affected.

[7] Report of the WGIP on its fourth session, Chairman-Rapporteur: Mrs Erica-Irene Daes, UN Doc E/CN.4/Sub.2/1985/22 of 27 August 1985, Annex III, pp 1 and 2.

Principle 13: The original rights to their material culture, including archeological sites, artifacts, designs, technology and works of art, lie with the indigenous people.

Principle 14: The indigenous peoples have the right to receive education in their own language or to establish their own educational institutions. The languages of the indigenous peoples are to be respected by the States in all dealings between the indigenous people and the State on the basis of equality and non-discrimination.

Principle 15: Indigenous peoples have the right, in accordance with their traditions, to move and conduct traditional activities and maintain friendship relations across international boundaries.

Principle 16: The indigenous peoples and their authorities have the right to be previously consulted and to authorize the realization of all technological and scientific investigations to be conducted within their territories and to have full access to the results of the investigation.

Principle 17: Treaties between indigenous nations or peoples and representatives of States freely entered into, shall be given full effect under national and international law.

These principles constitute the minimum standards which States shall respect and implement.

1985 DECLARATION OF PRINCIPLES

The next year, another important draft text—another Declaration of Principles—was submitted to the 4th session of the WGIP by the Indian Law Resource Center, the Four Directions Council, the National Aboriginal and Islander Legal Service, the National Indian Youth Council, the Inuit Circumpolar Conference and the International Indian Treaty Council.[8] It was adopted by the participants at an Assembly of Indigenous Working Group in Geneva in July 1985 and read:

1. Indigenous nations and peoples have in common with all humanity, the right to life, and to freedom from oppression, discrimination, and aggression.
2. All indigenous nations and peoples have the right to self-determination, by virtue of which they have the right to whatever degree of autonomy or self-government they choose. This includes the right to freely determine their political status, freely pursue their own economic, social, religious and cultural development, and determine their own membership and/or citizenship, without external interference.

[8] Ibid.

3. No State shall assert any jurisdiction over an indigenous nation or people, or its territory, except in accordance with the freely expressed wishes of the nation or people concerned.

4. Indigenous nations and peoples are entitled to the permanent control and enjoyment of their aboriginal ancestral-historical territories. This includes surface and subsurface rights, inland and coastal waters, renewable and non-renewable resources, and the economies based on these resources.

5. Rights to share and use land, subject to the underlying and inalienable title of the indigenous nation or people, may be granted by their free and informed consent, as evidenced in a valid treaty or agreement.

6. Discovery, conquest, settlement on a theory of terra nullius and unilateral legislation are never legitimate bases for States to claim or retain the territories of indigenous nations or peoples.

7. In cases where lands taken in violation of these principles have already been settled, the indigenous nation or people concerned is entitled to immediate restitution, including compensation for the loss of use, without extinction of original title. Indigenous peoples' desire to regain possession and control of sacred sites must always be respected.

8. No State shall participate financially or militarily in the involuntary displacement of indigenous populations, or in the subsequent economic exploitation or military use of their territory.

9. The laws and customs of indigenous nations and peoples must be recognized by States' legislative, administrative and judicial institutions and, in case of conflicts with State laws, shall take precedence.

10. No State shall deny an indigenous nation, community, or people residing within its borders the right to participate in the life of the State in whatever manner and to whatever degree they may choose. This includes the right to participate in other forms of collective action and expression.

11. Indigenous nations and peoples continue to own and control their material culture, including archeological, historical and sacred sites, artifacts, designs, knowledge, and works of art. They have the right to regain items of major cultural significance and, in all cases, to the return of the human remains of their ancestors for burial in accordance with their traditions.

12. Indigenous nations and peoples have the right to be educated and conduct business with States in their own languages, and to establish their own educational institutions.

13. No technical, scientific or social investigations, including archeological excavations, shall take place in relation to indigenous nations or peoples, or their lands, without their prior authorization, and their continuing ownership and control.

14. The religious practices of indigenous nations and peoples shall be fully respected and protected by laws of States and by international law.

Indigenous nations and peoples shall always enjoy unrestricted access to, and enjoyment of sacred sites in accordance with their own laws and customs, including the right of privacy.

15. Indigenous nations and peoples are subjects of international law.
16. Treaties and other agreements freely made with indigenous nations or peoples shall be recognized and applied in the same manner and according to the same international laws and principles of treaties and agreements entered into with other States.
17. Disputes regarding the jurisdiction, territories and institutions of an indigenous nation or people are a proper concern of international law, and must be resolved by mutual agreement or valid treaty.
18. Indigenous nations and peoples may engage in self-defense against State actions in conflict with their right to self-determination.
19. Indigenous nations and peoples have the right freely to travel, and to maintain economic, social, cultural and religious relations with each other across State borders.
20. In addition to these rights, indigenous nations and peoples are entitled to the enjoyment of all the human rights and fundamental freedoms enumerated in the International Bill of Human Rights and other United Nations instruments. In no circumstances shall they be subjected to adverse discrimination.

Preparatory Work and General Comments concerning the Elaboration of a Draft Declaration (1985)

In my opening statement to that year's session (1985) of the WGIP as its Chairperson-Rapporteur, I drew attention to that part of the mandate of the WGIP relating to standard-setting activities.[9] I stressed, inter alia, that a starting point for meeting some of the serious problems facing indigenous peoples in both the international and national contexts would be to set appropriate standards directed to their needs and rights, and I underlined that this was not going to be an easy task. I was confident that despite the difficulties, international standards could be drafted. I emphasised that indigenous peoples were the largest and most disadvantaged group not yet addressed by UN standards at that time. Indigenous peoples have been subjected to great neglect and discrimination in contemporary society and too often they have been the first victims of gross and systematic violations of their human rights. It was on these, among

[9] Ibid, p 14.

other kinds of challenges, that the WGIP should focus, I argued. Finally, I pointed out that the two abovementioned sets of important drafts of principles for a declaration on indigenous rights should constitute the basis for drafting the new instrument, because they succinctly reflected the needs, rights and aspirations of the word's indigenous peoples.

The other members of the WGIP expressed support for the emphasis I had placed on the standard-setting activities of the WGIP and stated that the time had come to begin the elaboration of a draft instrument.[10] Similarly, statements made by various governmental observers, representatives of indigenous peoples and their organisations and other non-governmental organisations (NGOs) indicated general agreement with the drafting mandate and the need for and expectation of the preparation of new standards and norms on indigenous rights. One member of the WGIP noted that while many international instruments related to the human rights of indigenous peoples, their special needs required new standards so as to provide fresh impetus and a new emphasis on addressing and remedying the underlying problems facing indigenous peoples, including the frequent alienation of indigenous populations and nations by States. The view that existing instruments did not adequately respond to the needs of indigenous peoples was endorsed by most speakers, including various governmental observers. WGIP participants also stressed the need for implementation of the relevant provisions of the existing human rights instruments for the protection of indigenous peoples.

Several representatives of the hundreds of indigenous peoples attending the WGIP as observers also stressed the need for special indigenous standards. They argued that inequality and oppression had been suffered for centuries: ethnocidal practices—notwithstanding lofty statutes and policies—and a lack of understanding and knowledge of indigenous peoples' cultures all reflected accusations of backwardness and primitiveness. They brought up forced assimilation and integration by majority populations as reasons underlining the need for new standards concerning indigenous rights and freedoms,[11] and expressed the hope that concrete new international standards would bring into line national constitutional reforms and legislation, along with other measures. The more specific reason behind the need for a new instrument that was most often mentioned was the deprival of territorial base and land rights, including all the surface and sub-surface resources which come with land and which form such an essential basis of indigenous peoples' way of life.[12]

[10] Ibid, p 14, para 58.
[11] Ibid, p 14, para 61.
[12] Ibid, p 14, para 61.

One member of the WGIP hesitated, as he noted, to use the term 'indigenous peoples', as he said that the term 'peoples', as used in the UN Charter, related to all peoples, and new criteria establishing two different kinds of peoples should preferably not be introduced into international law. With a unified approach to the term 'peoples', he argued, there was no need to specify special rights for indigenous peoples. Most indigenous peoples could be treated as minorities and any attempt at distinguishing between the two was nothing more than an artificial dilemma. He noted that the minority concept was a well-known concept in constitutional and international law and claimed that, taking into account the reality and historical political processes, it would be illusory to expect from the WGIP any recognition and definition of 'indigenous peoples' in this regard. This member of the working group also argued that the right to land was important for every human being and group, and that emphasising indigenous peoples' land rights was a misunderstanding, as there was no specific need for ownership of land to maintain cultural or ethnic identities. It was more important to clarify the functions of land in different societies. He concluded by saying that the WGIP needed more time for further clarification of concepts before it could begin drafting standards in this field.[13]

Another member of the WGIP also spoke against the use of the term 'indigenous peoples'. He pointed out that the UN had managed for 40 years without a definition of the term 'peoples' and that a definition of 'indigenous peoples' was unnecessary, at least for the purposes of the present standard-setting activities, especially as there were ample international precedents of the usage of the latter term. The reality of the situation was also reflected by the presence in the conference room in which the WGIP held its meetings of a large number of persons who considered themselves to be indigenous and who attached basic values to this identification. He stressed that the task of the WGIP should not be further complicated by an attempt to define the beneficiaries; rather, the difficulties associated with defining the term 'minority' should serve as a warning signal to the WGIP. Additionally, the WGIP member reminded those present that the right of peoples to self-determination should not automatically be associated with independence.

Another member of the WGIP stated that the working party should draw inspiration from the influence that the Declaration on the Granting of Independence to Colonial Countries and Peoples[14] had on the decolonisation process. It was his belief that the recognition and restoration of basic rights to indigenous peoples would be hastened if an appropriate

[13] Ibid, p 15, para 63.
[14] UN GA Resolution 1514 (XV) of 14 December 1960.

declaration could be drawn up by the WGIP with the cooperation of all parties concerned, bearing in mind that any future set of principles could only be adopted with the support of governments.

The concept of indigenous peoples as opposed to minority groups occupied the WGIP. The expert member for China agreed that, historically speaking, the concept of indigenous populations was associated with colonialism and aggression by foreign nations and powers, and warned that there should be no confusion between indigenous populations on the one hand and ethnic minorities in certain countries and regions on the other. Issues relating to multinational States with populations of varying origin should be dealt with in other fora. She also said that in order to ensure success in the WGIP's work, indigenous peoples should be placed on an equal footing with all nationalities and individuals of all nations, but with clear protection of special rights.[15]

A great number of indigenous observers pointed out that the term 'indigenous populations' in the title of the WGIP should be changed to 'indigenous peoples', which in their opinion more accurately reflected reality. They insisted that they represented peoples and nations and did not wish to be considered mere populations or minorities subject to outside definitions.

Various governmental observers pointed out that the standards had to be drafted in such a way that the document would cover all indigenous groups: a task, they said, that would prove particularly difficult because of the factual diversities and different political demands involved. One set of solutions would not serve the needs of all aboriginal groups, even within a single State. Overly ambitious targets would also jeopardise the depth and seriousness of the analysis needed for the content and implications of the various substantive rights.

The discussion in that session of the WGIP also focused on the rights that the declaration should mention. According to one member of the WGIP, in addition to fundamental and civil rights laid down in other applicable instruments, the following rights should be mentioned in the draft declaration: the rights to life, physical freedom and security; the right to land and natural resources possessed by indigenous populations, the deprivation of which could in their case amount to deprivation of the right to life; and the right to appropriate political self-rule.[16]

Several governmental observers argued, in varying terms, that indigenous peoples' rights to land, religion, education and culture and respect for other aspects of their own life and for their own economic and political situation should be properly reflected in the new

[15] Report of the WGIP on its fourth session (n 7) pp 15 and 16, para 66.
[16] Ibid, p 17, para 72.

standards.[17] In accordance with the Plan of Action of the WGIP for 1985, specific suggestions were made with regard to the cultural, linguistic, educational and religious rights of indigenous peoples. Indigenous representatives emphasised the urgency of maintaining and securing their cultural identity, heritage and traditions in the broadest sense, including their cultural and religious value systems. It was stressed that education should be provided by and for themselves, in their own language and with their own curriculum. Some of them mentioned in this regard the need for intercultural education and ensuring that the larger national societies also learn about indigenous cultures. Further, the fullest regard for indigenous religious beliefs and religious sites was required when drafting the relevant articles of the new standards. With regard to the principles concerning the education and culture of indigenous populations, one governmental observer raised a number of issues. Among them was the question how best to preserve and enhance indigenous cultures, languages and religions within larger societies; and also what measures were appropriate to overcome the cultural losses experienced by many indigenous populations through history.[18]

Indigenous representatives also focused on the inalienable right to self-determination and rights to land, territories and natural resources. They underlined how important ancestral land and the territorial base were to all other rights of indigenous populations. Collective rights and peaceful possession of the surface and sub-surface of these lands, they argued, should be covered by the new standards, especially those connected to the indigenous way of life and activities relating to renewable resources, such as fishing, whaling, hunting, harvesting, gathering and trapping. They also stated that without corresponding rights to adequate surface and ground waters, indigenous land rights would be rendered meaningless. The representatives stressed further that the right to earth, land and natural resources was considered essential by indigenous peoples because of the many forms of dispossession they had suffered. The forms had become more prevalent in modern times due to transmigration and technological advances, reflected, inter alia, in increased pollution, dam construction, mining operations, military activities and other environmental contamination. Indigenous peoples reminded the WGIP that they had never had problems with conservation of the environment or the extinction of species.

The right to self-determination was the main subject of many indigenous representatives' statements. While some spoke in this context of autonomy or self-government as necessary for their control over land as

[17] Ibid, p 17, para 74.
[18] Ibid, p 17, para 76.

well as their economic, social and cultural systems, others spoke of the right in a broader sense prohibiting discovery, conquest, the concept of terra nullius, and occupation as means of depriving them of sovereignty. They also emphasised the need to respect treaties freely concluded between indigenous peoples and States, in accordance with the principle of pacta sunt servanda, which should be reiterated in the new standards.

Other principles and rights were also suggested: the right to peace, human dignity and justice; the right to life, physical integrity and security; the right to determine one's own membership or citizenship; political rights; family rights; the right to move across State boundaries in order to conduct traditional activities; the right to humanitarian treatment of indigenous refugees; the right not to be subjected to relocation; and the right to prior authorisation by indigenous populations of technological, scientific and social investigations.[19]

Indigenous representatives also emphasised the need to establish remedies. They requested that the instrument establish the responsibility of States to respect populations in accordance with the UN Charter and to protect peoples against private and public encroachment. They also referred to the right of indigenous peoples, as a last resort, to defend themselves against violations of their rights.

Indigenous NGOs stressed the duty of indigenous communities and Member States to engage in good-faith dispute resolution with respect to their differences.[20] Such disputes should be resolved by agreement between the parties. If good-faith negotiations failed, the two parties might wish to continue their negotiations with the assistance of a mediator, or they might wish to make efforts to establish a process whereby matters could be decided by an impartial third party. The WGIP, in fulfilling its mandate, should be able to hear information regarding such negotiations and monitor their progress.[21]

The observer for Canada expressed concern over proposals relating to the right to self-determination and the status of indigenous populations as subjects of international law, as spelled out in the abovementioned draft declarations of principles.[22] He agreed that indigenous populations might wish to organise their own lives autonomously and to have their own institutions, and reminded his listeners that this was the case in his state. However, the proposed text went much further, he claimed, and included the right of indigenous peoples to determine their political status and citizenship. Reference to the right to self-determination, he

[19] Ibid, p 17, para 80.
[20] UN Doc E/CN.4/Sub.2/AC.4/1985/WP.4 and Annex IV to this report.
[21] Ibid, p 19, para 82.
[22] Ibid, notes 2 and 3.

argued, would imply a right of secession, which governments would not be in a position to accept. He also questioned the assertion that indigenous peoples and nations are subjects of international law. International law was created by States, through agreement or practice, and there were no indications that States recognised indigenous peoples and nations as subjects of international law. In his view, therefore, it would be incorrect to include in the declaration something that was not, in fact, supported in international law.[23]

TYPE OF INSTRUMENT

There was more or less general agreement on all sides that the WGIP should in the first instance produce a declaration, eventually to be adopted by the UN General Assembly (GA). The possibility of a convention was also mentioned, but there seemed to be general agreement that this kind of instrument would emerge further down the road, possibly inspired by the declaration.

Having considered the abovementioned comments, along with information and data submitted mainly by governments and indigenous organisations and in particular the draft declarations of principles, presented by a number of indigenous NGOs,[24] I formally proposed to the WGIP that it produce a draft declaration on indigenous rights, to be adopted by the GA. It was clear to me that the WGIP, in addition to the abovementioned sets of principles, should also take due account of the international instruments already existing within the UN system. The WGIP agreed with my proposal and authorised me to prepare as a first step a draft containing some relevant important principles.

THE FIRST PRINCIPLES FOR A DRAFT DECLARATION

In accordance with the decision of the WGIP, I elaborated and submitted to the WGIP the following draft principles in 1985, to be used as the basis for discussion regarding the proposed draft declaration, so that it would include:

1. The right to the full and effective enjoyment of the fundamental rights and freedoms universally recognized in existing international instruments, particularly in the Charter of the United Nations and the International Bill of Human Rights.

[23] Ibid, p 19, para 83.
[24] Ibid, notes 2 and 3.

2. The right to be free and equal to all other human beings in dignity and rights, and to be free of discrimination of any kind.
3. The collective right to exist and to be protected against genocide, as well as the individual right to life, physical integrity, liberty, and security of person.
4. The right to manifest, teach, practice and observe their own religious, traditions and ceremonies, and to maintain, protect, and have access to sites for these purposes.
5. The right to all forms of education, including the right to have access to education in their own languages, and to establish their own educational institutions.
6. The right to preserve their culture identity and traditions, and to pursue their own cultural development.
7. The right to promote intercultural information and education, recognizing the dignity and diversity of their cultures.

These draft principles, together with the relevant recommendations of the WGIP, were submitted to its parent body the Sub-Commission, the former Commission and ECOSOC. Consequently, the systematic and substantive work of drafting standards relating to the recognition and protection of the rights and freedoms of the world's indigenous peoples began in 1985.[25]

The Drafting of Standards (1987–1993)

In 1987, in order to further facilitate the process of drafting standards, the WGIP recommended that I be entrusted with the preparation of a working paper containing a full set of preambular paragraphs and principles for insertion into the declaration. This recommendation was submitted to the Sub-Commission. Bearing in mind that the Commission in its Resolution 1987/34 of 10 March 1987 urged the WGIP to intensify its efforts to continue the elaboration of international standards in this field, the body 'expressed its appreciation to the WGIP and especially to its Chairman/Rapporteur Mrs Erica-Irene Daes for the progress made at its 5th session in carrying out its mandate, particularly in its standard-setting activities', and endorsed 'the recommendation that the WGIP make every effort to complete a draft declaration on indigenous rights as soon as possible'.

[25] Report of the WGIP on its fourth session (n 7) pp 14–19; Annex II, p 1; Annexes III and IV, pp 1 and 2.

At the opening of the 5th session (1987) of the WGIP, I recalled that at its 1985 session the WGIP had adopted the preliminary version of seven draft principles[26] and decided, as a first step, to elaborate a draft declaration on indigenous rights. The emphasis on standard-setting was previously also endorsed both by the Sub-Commission (Resolution 1985/22) and the Commission (Resolutions 1986/27 and 1987/34). Useful and constructive comments on the draft principles were submitted by the Governments of Australia, Canada and Norway.[27]

During the NGO-sponsored Workshop held in Geneva in September 1986, in which I participated together with another member of the WGIP, three additional draft principles in preliminary form were elaborated.[28] There, I also drew attention to GA Resolution 41/120 of 4 December 1986, entitled 'Setting international standards in the field of human rights'. The guidelines and requirements established by that draft resolution were quite relevant to the work of the WGIP. Criteria for every new standard included, inter alia, consistency with human rights law, sufficient precision, and realistic and effective implementation machinery.[29] At all meetings of this session a constructive dialogue took place between all the participants and a number of important proposals relating to the elaboration of a draft declaration were made. A government representative pointed out that the declaration should include collective rights. In this respect, he found the relevance of the Declaration on the Right to Development[30] of paramount importance and asked it to be taken into account by the WGIP in its future work. The further view was expressed that the following two elements should be met in a declaration of principles: (a) the principles should be applicable to all States in which there are indigenous populations; and (b) they should be acceptable to governments and thus be of a realistic nature.

In providing an overview of his thoughts on indigenous standard-setting, one expert member of the WGIP pointed out that this was a complex task which required a great deal of conceptual clarification and 'confidence-building' prior to the adoption of standards by the political bodies of the UN. In that connection, he identified three areas to be addressed: (a) the position of group rights in the context of UN human rights activities; (b) issues relating to autonomy; and (c) the possible relevance of new concepts, such as the right to development, to indigenous populations. With regard to the concept of group rights, he stated that the rights of minorities, historically the first type of

26 E/CN.4/Sub.2/1985/22, Annex II.
27 UN Doc E/CN.4/Sub.2/AC.4/1987/WP.1/Add.1, Annexes 2, 3 and 4.
28 Ibid, Annex 1.
29 See the GA Resolution in Annex III, UN Doc E/CN.4/Sub.2/1987/22, pp 25 and 26.
30 GA Resolution 41/128 of 4 December 1986.

group to receive human rights protection, had so far been addressed at the UN through 'the individualistic approach'; in other words, the focus had been on the protection of individual members belonging to minorities, rather than minorities as groups. The rights of peoples and the debates on self-determination had largely been concentrated on decolonisation and other political issues, such as foreign occupation. In his view the following group rights could be envisaged: (a) the right to maintain and develop group characteristics and identity; (b) the right to be protected against attempts to destroy group identity, including propaganda directed against a group; (c) the right to equality with other groups as regards respect for and development of their specific characteristics; (d) the duty of the territorial State to grant groups—within the resources available—the necessary assistance for maintenance of their identity and their development; and (e) groups' right to have their specific character reflected in the legal system and in the political institutions of their country, including cultural autonomy as well as administrative autonomy, wherever feasible. Alongside these general and common rights, each group would be entitled to more specific rights. For instance, the land rights of indigenous peoples constitute a specific category of rights necessary for their development. He emphasised that none of the group rights could be construed in such a way as to justify any violation of the universally recognised human rights of individuals or to impair the territorial integrity of those sovereign States that are conducting themselves in compliance with the principles of international law concerning friendly relations and cooperation among States in accordance with the Charter of the UN.[31]

The Indigenous Preparatory Meeting held in Geneva from 27 to 31 July 1987 considered again the 1985 Declaration of Principles.[32] Two new principles had been added: the right to be free from military conscription, and rights relating to health, social services and housing. The aforementioned Declaration had met with consensus among the participants at the 1987 Preparatory Meeting, including indigenous leaders and representatives who had not been present at the 1985 session.[33] The WGIP agreed that I should prepare a full draft text prior to the WGIP's 6th session in 1988.

[31] Declaration of Principles of International Law Concerning Friendly Relations and Cooperation among States in accordance with the Charter of the United Nations, GA Resolution 2625 (XXV) GAOR: Twenty-Fifth session, Suppl No 8 /A/ 80287, B.121: UN Yearbook 1970, p 788.

[32] UN Doc E.CN.4/Sub.2/1985/22, Annex IV.

[33] Attached to the Report of the WGIP on its fifth session, UN Doc E/CN.4/Sub.2/1987 22, Annex V, pp 30–32.

In accordance with this mandate I elaborated the first draft declaration, entitled 'Draft Universal Declaration on Indigenous Rights', tabled in August 1988 and composed of 12 preambular paragraphs and six main parts.

Article 3 of the draft dealt specifically with the first important issue for indigenous peoples: survival. It provided them with 'the collective right to exist and to be protected against genocide, as well as the individual rights to life, physical integrity, liberty and security of person'.

A second issue was equality. Indigenous peoples have frequently been denied legal equality with other members of the State. Article 1 of the draft provided that 'indigenous peoples are entitled to universally recognized rights and freedoms, implicitly asserting a right to equality'.

A third issue was cultural survival. It was considered that equality rights alone would not protect indigenous peoples against assimilationist State policies. Articles 4 and 11 dealt with cultural rights, including an affirmative obligation on States under Article 7 to ensure that indigenous collectivities receive state support for the maintenance of their identity.

A fourth issue is economic rights. The most fundamental aspect of the economic issue was the right of ownership of traditional lands and natural resources, a matter of ongoing dispute between States and indigenous peoples in many parts of the globe. In this respect, Article 12 provided for 'the right [of indigenous peoples] of ownership and possession of the lands which they have traditionally occupied. The lands may only be taken away from them with their free and informed consent as witnessed by a treaty or agreement.'

Issues regarding indigenous peoples' rights to commercial fishing were advanced in the United States, Canada and New Zealand. The *Kitok* decision of the Human Rights Committee recognised the legitimacy of special rights of the Saami people in relation to the reindeer breeding industry in Saami land (Northern Scandinavia).[34] Article 18 recognised these rights to traditional economic activities and its second and third paragraphs expressly provided that 'in no case may an indigenous people be deprived of its means of subsistence'. It also provided for the right to 'just and fair compensation, if they have been so deprived'.

A fifth issue for indigenous peoples was political rights. This issue was debated and views were expressed by a great number of participants, in particular by representatives of the observer governments concerning terminology. The use of the term 'populations' as opposed to 'peoples' and the right to 'self-determination' were again discussed. Canada and

[34] *Kitok v Sweden*, Communication No 197/1985, Report of the Human Rights Committee, 43rd session, UN GAOR Supp (No 40), UN Doc A/43/40, Annex 7 (G) 1988, Views adopted 27 July 1988.

Sweden specifically made submissions to the Human Rights Committee asserting, amongst other things, that Indian and Saami collectivities are not 'peoples' with a right to self-determination under Article 1 of the Covenant on Civil and Political Rights. However, there was consensus among members of the WGIP that the term 'peoples' was the more appropriate term. In addition, the other members of the WGIP supported my opinion that indigenous peoples do not wish to have or to exercise a right of secession.

Self-determination for indigenous peoples is assumed, among other meanings, to require a degree of autonomy involving cultural, economic and political rights within the structures of recognised States.[35] The draft declaration dealt with two self-determination issues. It recognised a right to political participation in the institutions of state in Articles 21 and 22, while Articles 23, 24 and 25 provided for indigenous autonomy within the state. Thus, Article 23 guaranteed indigenous peoples 'the collective right to autonomy in matters relating to their own internal affairs, including education, information, culture, religion, health housing, social welfare, traditional and other economic activities, land and resources administration and the environment, as well as internal taxation for financing those autonomous functions'.[36]

This draft declaration addressed the basic issues relating to the recognition and protection of the rights and freedoms of the world's indigenous peoples. For the first time in the UN's history, substantive discussion of these important issues had been launched in its fora, with hundreds of indigenous representatives recognised as active participants. On the basis of the comments I received, I elaborated a revised draft declaration,[37] which was presented at the 11th session of the WGIP.

At the first meeting of this session of the WGIP, I tried to accelerate the drafting of the declaration and clarified that the revised draft declaration contained, inter alia, the draft proposals prepared by the three informal drafting groups established during the 8th session of the WGIP as well as suggestions made by governments, indigenous organisations, other international organisations and interested parties.

Prior to the discussion of specific provisions of the draft declaration, a number of general statements were made regarding the draft declaration as a whole. The observer for New Zealand stated that the WGIP

[35] Daes, 'An overview of the history of indigenous peoples self-determination and the United Nations', (2008) 21 *Cambridge Review of International Affairs*, 7.

[36] Erica-Irene Daes, 'Discrimination against Indigenous Peoples, A Working Paper', containing a set of draft preambular paragraphs and principles for insertion into a universal declaration of indigenous rights, cwis.org/fwdp/International/draft88.txt.

[37] Sub-Commission Resolution 1991/36 on the 'Draft Universal Declaration on the Rights of Indigenous Peoples', UN Doc E/CN.4/Sub.2/1991/65, pp 66–69.

was now in a position to make substantial progress and emphasised a number of general points regarding the draft declaration. In particular, he underscored the necessity that the declaration be sufficiently precise for it to be easily understood and effectively implemented. The observer for the Government of Brazil referred to Commission Resolution 1990/62, which stressed that international standards must be developed on the basis of the diverse realities of indigenous peoples in all parts of the world. He drew attention to the positive aspects of the existing draft, including the protection of the cultural identity and economic structures of indigenous communities, but cautioned against the adoption of texts which are ambiguous or politically unacceptable to governments.

A representative of the Ainu people expressed her people's gratitude to the international community for its attempts to abolish oppression of indigenous peoples. The representative of the International Labour Organization reiterated the need for a new international instrument in this field to be compatible with those already in existence, but also indicated that the WGIP was in a position to produce a text that would also reflect the aspirations of indigenous peoples. Mr Ted Moses, Chief of the Grand Council of the Crees of Quebec, suggested that the drafting process should take into account the results of the Seminar on the Effects of Racism and Racial Discrimination on the Social and Economic Relations between Indigenous Peoples and States.[38] He also stated that the inalienable rights of indigenous peoples could not be negotiated or bargained away. Further, the representative of the International Organization of Indigenous Resource Development expressed the desire for a declaration which would explicitly recognise indigenous people as 'peoples' and provide practical remedies for ongoing problems without compromising existing rights. The representative of the Indian Council of South America stated that the draft declaration should be universal in its scope and that States participating in the work of the WGIP should use their political skill to assist in finding universally acceptable provisions. Another suggestion, made by the representative of the Mohawk nation, stressed that early treaties between indigenous peoples and Europeans were based on agreements among equals and that this notion should be incorporated into the draft declaration. In addition, a number of observers representing governments, indigenous peoples and others at the WGIP emphasised the need for the draft declaration to be both

[38] Report of the United Nations Seminar on the Effects of Racism and Racial Discrimination on the Social and Economic Relations between Indigenous Peoples and States, UN Doc E/CN.4/1989, Annex II, pp 19–23. See also Erica-Irene Daes, 'On the Relations between Indigenous Peoples and States' (1989) II(2) *Without Prejudice: The EAFORD International Review of Racial Discrimination*, Special Issue on Indigenous Peoples and the Law, 41–52.

consistent within itself, especially regarding terminology and substance, and consistent with existing international human rights instruments.

Subsequently, I submitted the draft declaration for its first reading[39] and requested that the WGIP proceed by considering the paragraphs of the draft declaration one by one. This exercise was extremely difficult, taking into account the great number of participants—over 700—and their different legal backgrounds and cultures.

During the discussion of certain provisions, various important issues were tackled. Several indigenous representatives stressed that the draft declaration should reflect the unqualified right of indigenous peoples to self-determination. However, some governmental observers indicated that it might be necessary to qualify at least the application of this right in order to make the text acceptable to governments, which would have to implement it. Other governmental observers expressed strong opposition to the inclusion of a reference to self-determination.

It was stated by certain indigenous representatives that indigenous peoples are entitled to the recovery, restoration, restitution of and/or adequate compensation for their lands and resources which have been taken without their consent, and asked for this right to be adequately expressed in the draft declaration. The question of control over the occupation and/or use of their lands and resources was highlighted as being of special concern to indigenous peoples. They particularly sought to exercise control over the use of their lands and resources for military purposes, the dumping of toxic waste and developmental and other projects that affect them. In this connection, the traditional role of indigenous peoples as custodians of the environment was brought to the attention of the WGIP.

I invited the WGIP to commence the second reading of the draft declaration, and several amendments were suggested. The new revised draft was presented at the fifth meeting of its 11th session on 21 July 1993. At this meeting, it was agreed that the word 'articles' rather than 'paragraphs' would in future be used in the draft declaration.

The UN Goodwill Ambassador, Ms Rigoberta Menchű Tum, addressed the 1993 meeting. She stated, inter alia, that the draft declaration would have to be an instrument which eased the struggle of all indigenous peoples.[40] During the prolonged and often contentious debate on specific provisions of the draft declaration, many important and complex issues relating to 'collective rights' were raised, in particular the issue of individual versus group rights in international human rights development. In this regard, the observer for the United States stated that 'the draft Declaration is largely a list of collective rights to which indigenous

[39] UN Doc E/CN.4/Sub.2/1991/40/Rev.1, pp 30–37.
[40] Statement by Rigoberta Menchu Tum in UN Doc E/CN.4/Sub.2/1993/29, p 15.

peoples are entitled'. She expressed concern about the fact that those references went far beyond the limited collective rights recognised in international law or the practice of States.[41] Many other governmental observers stressed that the approach to the question of 'collective rights' in the revised draft declaration was fundamentally inconsistent with existing international human rights instruments. This interpretation was opposed by all indigenous representatives, who supported an extension of the traditional Western understanding of human rights—that is, the right of individuals to be free from oppression by the State—to a broader recognition of the rights of peoples to exist as collectives and to be secure in their collective integrity from intrusions by the State or other threatening forces.

Observers for some governments expressed concern that the draft declaration did not contain a definition of 'indigenous peoples'. The representative for Japan expressed concern that this might give rise to subjective interpretations as to which groups were entitled to the rights contained in the declaration. I had always maintained that for the purposes of the draft declaration, the working definition of 'indigenous peoples' contained in the study by Martinez Cobo[42] should be applied. Further, several representatives of indigenous peoples commented on the need to use the term 'peoples', in the plural, both in the draft declaration and in other documents because the singular form was perceived by indigenous peoples to be discriminatory, denying them rights available to other peoples. Also, following a request for clarification of the terms 'cultural genocide' and 'ethnocide', it was explained that cultural genocide referred to the destruction of the physical aspects of a culture, while ethnocide referred to the elimination of an entire 'ethnos'.

Again, the majority of governmental observers expressed reservations regarding the issue of self-determination. The observer for Canada repeated at this session that his country supported the principle that indigenous peoples qualified for the right to self-determination in international law on the same basis as non-indigenous peoples. In all other cases 'self-determination' for indigenous peoples had to be granted within the framework of existing Nation States. The notion of 'self-determination' as used in the draft declaration implied the right of indigenous peoples to unilaterally determine their political, economic and social status within the existing State. However, according to him, it was not clear how the concepts of self-determination, self-government and autonomy, which were addressed in Articles 3 and 29 of the draft, interrelated and what

[41] UN Doc E/CN.4/Sub.2/1993/29, p 20, para 68.

[42] Study on the Problem of Discrimination Against Indigenous Populations, UN Doc E/CN.4/Sub.2/1986/Add.4)

the range of powers of indigenous governments would be and how they would relate to the jurisdiction of existing States.[43]

However, the observer for Finland stated that his country was in favour of the use of the concept of self-determination in the draft declaration.[44] In addition, the observer for Denmark stated that the exercise of the right to self-determination was a precondition for any full realisation of human rights for indigenous peoples. His country supported the formulation in the draft declaration that indigenous peoples had the right to autonomy and self-government in matters relating to their internal and local affairs. The enjoyment of the right to autonomy and self-government constituted the minimum standard for the survival and well-being of the world's indigenous peoples.[45] The observer for the Russian Federation said that when discussing the issue of self-determination it must be borne in mind that indigenous peoples live in very different regions of the world and that they might require totally different aspects of self-government. She felt that paragraph 29 did not cover all aspects that fell within the notions of self-determination and self-government and suggested that the declaration should contain only the general principle.[46]

The observer for Brazil also pointed out that some of the concepts proposed in the draft would encounter difficulty in being accepted by many governments, in particular those relating to self-determination as defined by existing international law, the extent of property rights over indigenous lands, demilitarisation of indigenous lands, and the impossibility of removal of indigenous populations from their lands.

Furthermore, the observer for New Zealand stated that a distinction could be made between the right to self-determination as it currently existed in international law, a right which developed essentially in the post-Second World War era and which carried with it a right of secession, and a proposed modern interpretation of self-determination within the bounds of a Nation State, covering a wide range of situations but relating essentially to the right of a people to participate in the political, economic and cultural affairs of a State on terms which meet their aspirations and which enable them to take control of their own lives. He suggested seeking language on self-determination which committed governments to working with indigenous peoples in a process of empowerment within the State in which they lived.[47]

The prevailing opinion of the indigenous peoples was expressed by Mr Moana Jackson, who reported on the conclusions reached in

[43] Ibid, p 16, para 50.
[44] Ibid, p 16, para 51.
[45] Ibid.
[46] Ibid, p 17, para 54.
[47] Ibid, p 17, para 52.

the informal meeting held by those representatives. The indigenous representatives were worried about attempts to limit the concept of self-determination to the conduct of internal affairs. He stated that, contrary to the arguments of the observer for New Zealand, the right to self-determination was not primarily a post-Second World War concept but had existed since time immemorial and was not dependent exclusively on international law for its understanding. Indigenous peoples claimed for themselves a right to a subjective definition of the right to self-determination. In addition to the general statement, a number of representatives of indigenous peoples expressed the view that the right to self-determination was the pillar on which all the other provisions of the draft declaration rested and the concept on which its integrity depended. Many representatives of indigenous peoples emphasised that the draft declaration must express the right to self-determination without any limitations or qualifications.

The observer for the Nordic Saami Council proposed that the issue of self-determination, in view of its importance, should be dealt with in the first operative paragraph or article and that the exact wording of Article 1 of the two International Covenants on Human Rights should be used. The observer for the Haudenosaunee Nation delivered a joint statement on behalf of the indigenous representatives of Australia of similar content, while Ms Lowitjia O'Donogue, Chairperson of the Aboriginal and Torres Strait Islander Commission at the time, stressed the fact that for Australia's indigenous peoples, 'self-determination' meant the right to seek increasing autonomy in terms of self-management and self-government and was not understood as a mandate for secession. Therefore, she argued, there was no need to stress the territorial integrity of States in the draft declaration.[48] Professor Anaya argued that the right to self-determination was a longstanding idea and noted the distinction between constitutive and ongoing self-determination. He also added that secession was not usually desirable and could in many cases prove to be detrimental to the interests of indigenous peoples.[49]

Another issue that reared its head in that meeting was the use of the term 'indigenous peoples'. Many representatives of indigenous peoples stressed that the term 'people' had primarily historical implications for them. Mr Ted Moses, Chief of the Grand Council of the Crees, for example, pointed out that indigenous peoples had defined themselves as peoples since time immemorial. Others emphasised that only the use of the term 'peoples' would reflect the notion of collectivity on which

[48] UN Doc E/CN.4/Sub.2/1993/29, p 18, para 59.

[49] A Summary of the intervention made can be found in UN Doc E/CN.4/Sub.2/1993/29, p 19.

indigenous life was based. The term 'indigenous people' or 'populations' signified only a group of individuals and therefore denied them their collective identity.[50]

On the question of 'land rights', the observer for Canada stated that the draft declaration drew no distinction between 'lands' and 'territories', nor was it clear whether these terms were intended to mean only those lands and territories where indigenous people had or could establish legal title to all lands and territories that they claimed. The provision in Article 24 of the draft declaration provided that indigenous peoples 'have the right to own, control and use their lands and territories'; in combination with the statement in Article 23 that 'lands and territories are those that have been traditionally owed or otherwise occupied or used' the notion of such rights was given far-reaching effect. Furthermore, Article 25, which established the principle of restitution of land, was problematic for Canada, which had devised a system of negotiated settlements (comprehensive land claim agreements) with indigenous peoples. Canada asked that a 'reasonable limits' clause be introduced in the declaration in order to enable more governments to support it.

The observer for Sweden stressed the importance of 'usufruct'—a strongly protected legal right to use land—as an alternative concept. Indeed, the Swedish Supreme Court has recognised the right of 'usufruct' of the Saami population on a large piece of the land on which they live.

Finally, the WGIP acceded to the requests of the representatives of indigenous peoples and adopted unanimously as Article 3 of the draft declaration the language that incorporates common Article 1 of the two International Covenants on Human Rights, now Article 3 of the Declaration. This WGIP's decision was greeted with a standing ovation from indigenous participants and a conciliatory response from many of the governments.[51]

Following careful consideration of comments and amendments, the WGIP agreed on a final text, entitled 'Draft Declaration as Agreed upon by the Members of the Working Group at its Eleventh Session', and submitted it for adoption to the Sub-Commission at its 45th session.[52]

Various amendments to the Sub-Commission's Resolution E/CN.4/Sub.2/1993/L.47, contained in Doc E/CN.4/Sub.2/1993/L.54, were submitted by me; mainly the renaming of the draft as 'United Nations Declaration on the Rights of Indigenous Peoples' and also the continuing, full and effective participation of indigenous representatives

[50] Ibid, p 20.

[51] Ibid, fn 12.

[52] UN Doc E/CN.4/Sub.2/1993/29, pp 50–60. Ms Attah stressed the need for the draft declaration to be adopted by the Sub-Commission in 1993, because that was the concern of the indigenous peoples.

irrespective of their consultative status during the elaboration of the draft United Nations Declaration. The Sub-Commission adopted unanimously those amendments and, following close consideration of the abovementioned revised draft declaration, decided unanimously to submit it to the Commission on Human Rights for consideration and adoption by the GA during the International Decade of the World's Indigenous People.[53]

Post-WGIP Work

The Commission established an open-ended inter-sessional Working Group (CDWG) with the sole purpose of elaborating a draft declaration. Unfortunately, despite the efforts of the Chairman, Luis-Enrique Savez, the working group did not succeed in completing the drafting of the declaration within the First International Decade of the World's Indigenous People, mainly because of delays on the part of certain delegations of Member States and various representatives of indigenous peoples. Finally, the 11th session of the CDWG adopted the draft declaration and submitted it to the Human Rights Council.[54] Following extensive discussions, the Council adopted the draft UN declaration by its Resolution 1/2 of 29 June 2006, the annex of which contained the text of the declaration.

The Council submitted its Resolution with the declaration to the 61st session of the General Assembly. At its 53rd meeting on 28 November 2006, the Third Committee of the General Assembly had before it a revised draft resolution submitted by a great number of Member States.[55] At the same meeting, the representative of Namibia introduced amendments to the draft resolution.[56] The Third Committee adopted the amendments by a recorded vote of 82 to 67, with 25 abstentions.[57] Accordingly, at its 54th meeting, on 30 November, the Third Committee, at the proposal of its Chairman, adopted Resolution 61/178 by which it adopted the draft declaration and (a) took note of the recommendation of the Human Rights Council contained in its Resolution 1/2 of 29 June 2006, by which the Council adopted the text of the United Nations Declaration on the Rights of Indigenous Peoples; (b) decided to defer consideration and action on the United Nations consultations thereon; and (c) decided to conclude its consideration of the declaration, as contained in the annex to the abovementioned resolution, before the end of its 61st session.[58]

[53] Sub-Commission Resolution 1994/45 of 26 August 1994.
[54] E/CN.4/2006/79 (Chairman's summary-proposal as Annex 1).
[55] A/C.3/61/L.18/Rev.1.
[56] A/C.3/61/L.57/Rev.1.
[57] Ibid.
[58] A/61/448, p 25.

Subsequently, on 10 May 2007, 67 Member States submitted a comprehensive letter to the President of the GA, Mrs Sheikha Haya Rashed Al Khalifa, underlining that reopening the text of the declaration might lead to yet another lengthy process with an uncertain outcome. They expressed the belief that this had not been the intention of the GA when it decided to postpone its consideration of the declaration. Further, in a spirit of compromise they enclosed a copy of a first draft for a new resolution that was prepared among the co-sponsors of a draft resolution A/C.3/61/L.18 and expressed their readiness to engage with concerned countries to discuss this proposal, which they hoped would pave the way towards the adoption of the declaration.[59]

The President of the GA appointed as facilitator Hilario G Davide Jr, the Permanent Representative of the Philippines to the UN, to undertake on her behalf further consultations on the Declaration on the Rights of Indigenous Peoples. Ambassador Davide conducted open and inclusive consultations. The President requested that he report back to her on the outcome of the consultations as soon as possible, and not later than mid-July 2007. Within his mandate, Ambassador Davide convened open-ended informal consultations of the plenary on the draft declaration on 29 June 2007 in order to focus discussion on a more tangible and concrete approach that would provide some middle ground for the major positions on the draft declaration. He submitted his first report to the President on 13 July 2007.

In response to the abovementioned report, the Permanent Missions of eight Member States sent a letter to Ambassador Davide, dated 18 July 2007,[60] arguing amongst other things that only through amendments to the text of the declaration, addressing their most significant concerns, would it be possible for them to consider supporting the declaration. They reiterated their support for a limited re-opening of the text, based on a thematic approach and with the objective of achieving an irreducible minimal number of amendments. They attached to the letter Non-Paper of 29 June 2007, which outlined a thematic approach reflecting their concerns. They considered that such an approach would provide the necessary flexibility for interested parties to achieve an irreducible minimum. In an effort to alleviate concerns, amendments were discussed in eight areas with regard to 16 articles: these were self-determination, self-government and indigenous institutions (Arts 3, 4, 5 and 33); lands, territories and resources (Arts 26 and 29); redress (Arts 11, 27 and 28); free, prior and informed consent (Arts 19, 32(2)); rights

[59] Copy of letter on file with author.

[60] Australia, Canada, Colombia, Guyana, New Zealand, Russian Federation, and Suriname.

of third parties (Art 46); intellectual property rights (Arts 11 and 31); military issues (Arts 10 and 30); and education (Art 14). They stated that these amendments to the declaration were necessary to render it consistent with international law.

Subsequently, the President of the GA addressed a letter to the Permanent Representatives, dated 23 July 2007, attaching the report of Ambassador Davide, dated 1 July 2007, as well as his supplementary report dated 20 July 2007 regarding the process of consultation undertaken up to 23 July 2007. She underlined, inter alia, that the reports outlined a proposed way forward which would enable all parties concerned to implement the mandate of the GA and adopt the draft declaration before the end of the 61st session. She also expressed the hope that the Permanent Representatives would consider the proposed way forward in a flexible and constructive manner, and encouraged them to reach a swift common understanding in order to enable the GA to make a decision on this very important issue during the first week of September 2007.[61]

PROCLAMATION OF THE UN DECLARATION ON THE RIGHTS OF INDIGENOUS PEOPLES

The General Assembly of the UN, taking note of the recommendation of the Human Rights Council contained in its Resolution 1/2 of 29 June 2006, by which the Council adopted the text of the United Nations Declaration, proclaimed by its historic Resolution A/61/295 on 13 September 2007 the United Nations Declaration on the Rights of Indigenous Peoples. It was adopted by an overwhelming affirmative vote of 143; four States were against (Australia, Canada, New Zealand and the United States) and 11 abstained.

In order to reach the consensus that led to the proclamation of the Declaration, consultations had continued among all parties concerned, and in particular between the Friends of the Declaration and the African Group, almost up to the last day. Many compromises were made concerning various articles of the Declaration.

The constructive role played by HE the President of the General Assembly, Ambassador Sheikha Haya Rashed Al Khalifa of Bahrain, should be mentioned: her tireless efforts and her important and timely consultations, decisions and action within her mandate, contributed decisively to the adoption of the Declaration. The international community, and in particular the world's indigenous peoples, are grateful to her.

[61] Copy of letter on file with author.

In spite of the efforts of certain governments, Article 3 of the Declaration was not in the event amended. Instead, Article 46 was revised. Paragraph 1 states:

> Nothing in this Declaration may be interpreted as implying for any State, people, group or person any right to engage in any activity or to perform any act contrary to the Charter of the United Nations or construed as authorizing or encouraging any action which would dismember or impair, totally or in part, the territorial integrity or political unity of sovereign and independent States.

As I stated to the Third Committee of the 62nd session of the UN General Assembly, the right to self-determination provided by Article 3 of the Declaration expresses the aspirations and vision of the world's indigenous peoples. It is a right of cardinal importance to them, because it is a sacred right to which they have been entitled since time immemorial.[62] The right to self-determination, as it is set out in the aforementioned Article 3, does not in my opinion carry with it a right to secession. Instead, as already mentioned, respect for the principles of territorial integrity and political unity of sovereign and independent States is provided and protected *expressis verbis* by Article 46 of the Declaration. It should also be emphasised that the Declaration is a declaration of human rights and it is universally understood in the law of nations that human rights obligations are not subject to contrary domestic legislation. Human rights law prevails over national law. The rights provided by the Declaration should be exercised by indigenous peoples with respect for the rights of others and are subject only to limitations contained in Article 46 and other legitimate restrictions established by international human rights law.

Effective implementation of the Declaration will prove the commitment of States and the entire international community to recognising, respecting and fulfilling indigenous peoples' collective and individual rights and such States' sincere wish to move towards a fair reconciliation with indigenous peoples. It is significant that national courts have already begun to respect and implement the provisions of the Declaration. In this respect, mention should be made of the very important judgment of the Supreme Court of Belize in Claim No 171 of 2007. The court stated: '[I]mportant in this regard is the recent Declaration on the Rights of Indigenous Peoples, adopted by the GA of the UN on 13 September 2007 … Of course, unlike resolutions of the Security Council, General Assembly resolutions are not ordinarily binding on member states. But where these resolutions or Declarations contain principles of general international law, states are not expected to disregard them.'[63]

[62] Erica-Irene Daes, 'Statement on item 69a of the Agenda: Indigenous Issues', UN Third Committee General Assembly, NY 22 October 2007, on file with author.

[63] Supreme Court of Belize, Claim No 171 of 2007, para 131.

APPRAISAL

The United Nations Declaration on the Rights of Indigenous Peoples constitutes the most important development concerning the recognition and protection of the basic rights and fundamental freedoms of the world's indigenous peoples to date. It is the product of many years' work by many people, including in particular many hundreds of indigenous people from all parts of the world. Its text was determined by an extraordinarily liberal, transparent and democratic procedure before the WGIP that encouraged broad and unified indigenous input. The members of the WGIP and I made every effort to incorporate primary indigenous peoples' aspirations, and also took into account several substantive comments and amendments proposed by various States. It should be noted that no other United Nations human rights instrument has been elaborated with so much direct involvement and active participation by its intended beneficiaries. Finally, the original text as it was drafted by myself and approved by the WGIP—and its final version—focused on issues of special concern to indigenous peoples in the exercise of their rights to equality, self-determination, lands and natural resources and collective identity. In broad terms the Declaration deals with aspects of strengthening the distinctiveness of indigenous societies within the institutional frameworks of existing States.

The Declaration now constitutes a normative instrument of the UN that memorialises, and simultaneously extends, international consensus regarding the individual and collective rights of indigenous peoples as previously set out in several international instruments, including, first and foremost, ILO Convention 169. The fact that the Declaration's provisions are not legally binding does not detract from their potential for driving cultural and political transformations, which often run deeper than legal change. In fact, the Declaration's normative—as opposed to legal—nature enables indigenous peoples to focus on invoking the many provisions that help them while continuing to critique those that harm them, for instance preambular paragraph 16, and Articles 30 and 46.

In connection with the normative substance of the Declaration, the following should be noted:

(a) Self-determination: Because this broadest of all human rights legitimises the other rights that indigenous peoples have fought for, they will vehemently defend its scope. In defending the realisation of this right, indigenous peoples clearly insist that they are among the 'peoples' of whom Article 1 of both International Covenants on Human Rights speaks.

(b) Territorial integrity of States: Some States rely on Article 46(1) of the Declaration to claim that the right to self-determination provided by Article 3 is limited by the duty of indigenous peoples to respect the territorial integrity and political unity of States. To date, international law continues to respect this principle, authoritatively set out in the Declaration of Principles of International Law Concerning Friendly Relations and Co-operation among States in accordance with the United Nations,[64] only regarding States vis-a-vis other States. The Declaration lacks the authority to mandate change in the existing international law framework on this matter.

(c) Human rights and collective rights: Some States indicate that, perhaps with the exception of the right to self-determination, they do not recognise that collective rights are human rights. Individual human rights, they state, are universal, whereas collective rights provided by the Declaration are particular to indigenous peoples. Moreover, since individual human rights supersede collective rights, whether those of the State or those of indigenous peoples, it would unsettle this hierarchy if collective rights were considered human rights. International law can recognise a new subset of collective human rights that do not trump international individual human rights. In any event, once adopted, international collective rights supersede domestic law.

The most important provisions of the Declaration relating to its implementation must also be noted.

— Preambular paragraph 7 of the Declaration calls on States to play a pivotal role in promoting and protecting—that is, operationalising—the rights contained in the Declaration. This paragraph correctly captures the close connection that exists between indigenous peoples' culture and their territory. That is, where indigenous peoples remain constituted as localised communities, they engage in everyday enactments and elaborations of knowledge, philosophy and spirituality on their lands and territories.
— Preambular paragraph 18 of the Declaration anticipates 'harmonious and cooperative relations between State and indigenous peoples'. Such relations will require the active involvement of indigenous communities, authorities and organisations as befits their role as primary actors in the actualisation of the rights of their peoples. Accordingly, the Declaration imposes positive obligations not only on States but also on the right-holders themselves.
— Under preambular paragraph 20 of the Declaration the UN system itself bears a broad and weighty responsibility for promoting and implementing its provisions. The UN has already begun to

[64] GA Resolution 2625, 24 October 1970, UN GAOR, 25th session, Supp No 28, 121.

operationalise this mandate through the creation of the following entities for this and other relevant purposes: the Permanent Forum on Indigenous Issues, which has already produced excellent work within its general mandate and recently by implementing Article 42 of the Declaration; the Expert Mechanism on the Rights of Indigenous Peoples, which has commenced substantive work under the able Chairmanship of Mr John Henriksen; and the roving office of Special Rapporteur on the situation of human rights and fundamental freedoms of indigenous people. The Special Rapporteur is Professor S James Anaya, whose depth of knowledge and experience of indigenous issues guarantees fruitful results.

— Article 37 of the Declaration includes a mandate to States to honour treaties, agreements and other constructive arrangements that they have concluded with indigenous peoples. Further, it should be stressed that operationalising the Declaration at the national level will require in certain cases the revision of various constitutional provisions or the adoption of new laws or amendments to existing laws as provided for by Article 38 of the Declaration. It should be stressed that the Declaration will be also used effectively for peaceful negotiations and reconciliation between States and indigenous peoples.

It is my sincere wish that in defending their basic rights and fundamental freedoms, as set out in the United Nations Declaration on the Rights of Indigenous Peoples, the world's indigenous peoples will not be compelled to rebel as a last resort against any kind of oppression, and in particular that the inalienable right to self-determination, as it is defined in Article 3 of the Declaration, will be duly implemented by all concerned to facilitate harmonious and constructive relations between indigenous peoples and the States in which they live.

2

The UN Declaration on the Rights of Indigenous Peoples: From Advocacy to Implementation

JULIAN BURGER*

IT WAS A long haul for many, but the Declaration on the Rights of Indigenous Peoples ('the Declaration') was finally adopted on 13 September 2007. It is the first universally acclaimed standard to set out the rights of indigenous peoples in the 60-year plus life of the United Nations. Many indigenous peoples would claim that it represents an historic advance, and in many ways it breaks new ground by recognising the past and present injustices done to indigenous peoples and identifying the rights and measures needed to address them. But like other human rights instruments that invoke respect by States, there is a yawning gap between the words on paper and their application. In particular, there is a clear tension between the rights established through international negotiation and supposed exigencies of national development that prioritise access to and exploitation of resources found on indigenous peoples' lands.

The present article identifies the rights that are recognised in the Declaration and considers the concerns that they try to address. It looks at some of the obstacles that may impede their realisation and suggests some directions for advancing implementation.

SOME COMMENTS ON THE ORIGINS OF THE DECLARATION

The Declaration on the Rights of Indigenous Peoples contains rights that indigenous peoples consider vital for their survival and development. From the moment the United Nations first considered the drafting

* The views expressed in this article are not necessarily those of the United Nations.

of a declaration, as early as 1982,[1] to its final adoption by the General Assembly in September 2007, many thousands of representatives of indigenous nations, peoples and communities participated in a process of elaboration, giving examples of violations of rights that they faced and providing proposals as to how new standards might address them. The content of the Declaration and the principles that it recognises emerged from this direct involvement of indigenous peoples.

There are other examples of international law-making that include substantial non-governmental participation, such as those relating to the (1990) Convention on the Rights of the Child and the (2008) Convention on the Rights of Persons with Disability, but there has never been such diverse and geographically broad-based participation of beneficiaries of the rights as proved to be the case with the Declaration on the Rights of Indigenous Peoples. The Declaration owes its existence and its content to the advocacy of indigenous peoples, rather than the considered goodwill of States. Indeed, there is only one article of the Declaration that depended for its inclusion on governments and that is Article 46, which serves to reassure States that the Declaration may not be interpreted as implying any action that would threaten their territorial integrity. Having said that, it should be noted that the Declaration is not an indigenous document either, since experts elaborated the draft that formed the basis of discussions with governments. The final version of the Declaration constitutes, therefore, a compromise between the text solicited by indigenous peoples on the basis of the draft prepared by experts and that finally accepted by States.

One of the observations that can be made is that the group of indigenous activists that engaged in the negotiating process feel a strong attachment to the document, because they struggled for 10 years with human rights experts to ensure inclusion of their core concerns, and a further 12 years with governments to maintain to the extent possible these principles. In considering the future implementation of the Declaration, it may be this very strong sense of ownership that will serve as the best catalyst for accommodation of these rights in national laws and policies.

A general comment that can be made is that the Declaration is not an abstract document. It responds to the real-life problems that threaten the existence of indigenous peoples as identified by indigenous peoples themselves. One of the remarkable features of the Working Group on

[1] While 1985 is the date that the formal drafting of the declaration began, in particular by elaborating several key principles, already at the inaugural session of the Working Group on Indigenous Populations in 1982 there was discussion about the desirability of such an instrument.

Indigenous Populations[2] was that the rights proposed were garnered from specific experiences, expressed in the language of the elder, community leader, woman or youth activist. How else could the recognition of indigenous peoples' spiritual relationship with their lands be included in an international human rights instrument, if not through countless stories of this non-materialist and harmonious bond between humankind and nature? This contributed to a practical orientation of the Declaration. As will be discussed below, the Declaration not only provides a listing of indigenous peoples' rights, it also offers a pragmatic and flexible framework for dialogue on national policies.

The Declaration contains two core rights that run in parallel through the entire document. These are the right to self-determination and the right not to be discriminated against. These rights have an historic base since the first action taken by the colonising States was to dispossess indigenous peoples of their lands and resources, dismantle their political, economic and spiritual authorities and effectively deny them their right to self-determination. The second action was to assimilate indigenous peoples, deny them equal treatment and reduce them to dependency. The legacy of this colonial approach continues to be present in practice today in many parts of the world. The Declaration seeks to address the desire of indigenous peoples to maintain and strengthen their institutions, cultures and traditions in accordance with their aspirations and needs.[3] It also requires states to ensure non-discrimination of indigenous peoples in areas such as health, housing, education and employment, discrimination which is manifest in nearly all socio-economic data available.[4]

Given that large numbers of indigenous peoples still live on their traditional lands with varying degrees of de facto autonomy and access to resources, the exercise of self-determination can be implemented by consolidating and enhancing their control over and ownership of their lands, territories and resources and through recognition in law and in practice of their self-governing institutions. However, there are also significant numbers of indigenous peoples—more than 50 per cent in some countries—living in urban environments for whom the problem of

[2] The Working Group on Indigenous Populations held 23 official sessions between 1982 and 2005 and one informal session in 1986, when due to financial restraints the Working Group met with the support of non-UN resources.

[3] See preambular para 10.

[4] An eloquent example of the disparities between indigenous peoples and broade[r] can be found in the report of Australia's Aboriginal and Torres Strait Islander C[...] of 2 July 2009 entitled *Overcoming Indigenous Disadvantage*, which sh[...] standing gap in living standards has worsened in some areas. The re[...] 50 key areas and found no improvement in 80% of them. In some ca[...] worsened. For example, in 2008 indigenous adults were 13 times more [...] oned than non-indigenous adults, compared to 10 times in 2000.

discrimination remains a daily reality. In such cases, the exercise of the right to self-determination calls for other mechanisms, which may take the form of decision-making with regard to the kinds of services that are delivered to the communities and to the resources that are necessary for their functioning.

In general, socio-economic data on indigenous peoples demonstrates that in all areas—whether it is health, education, employment, housing or life expectancy—indigenous peoples are disproportionately disadvantaged. One of the principal objectives of the Declaration is to set out measures to address that discrimination and ensure that indigenous peoples have equal rights to others and that their material conditions improve accordingly. The practical realisation of both indigenous peoples' right to self-determination and their right to live free from discrimination constitute considerable challenges notwithstanding that they are both well-established principles of international law.

THE PRACTICAL APPLICATION OF THE RIGHT TO SELF-DETERMINATION

One of the most difficult areas of negotiation during the discussions on the draft declaration revolved around the question of self-determination as it applied to indigenous peoples. This had also been the case at the expert meeting to review ILO Convention 107 on Indigenous and Tribal Populations of 1957 held in 1986. It led in the end to the inclusion of a qualification in the body of the new Convention on Indigenous and Tribal Peoples of 1989, namely that 'the use of the term peoples … shall not be construed as having any implications as regards the rights which may attach to the term in international law'. The ILO Convention of 1989 neither affirms nor denies indigenous peoples' right to self-determination; it simply considers the matter a political question that needed to be deferred to the United Nations itself. Some indigenous peoples were not satisfied with the solution found by the ILO, and it is true that during most of the years of negotiation over the draft indigenous declaration held with governments, a certain number of States insisted on the inclusion of a similar formulation to qualify the use of the term 'peoples', in particular in annual reports of the sessions.[5] The question of whether indigenous peoples were 'peoples' as understood in common Article 1 of the two international

[5] For many years the annual reports of the working group of the Commission on Human Rights on the draft declaration included the following type of formulation: 'This report is solely a record of the debate and does not imply acceptance of the usage of either the expression "indigenous peoples" or "indigenous people" by all Governments. In this report both terms are used without prejudice to the positions of particular delegations …' See eg E/CN.4/2002/98, para 4.

human rights conventions dogged discussions despite the insistence of indigenous peoples that their interests were not to form new States, but to live within the current States as self-determining peoples.

Much was done by the United Nations to place the discussions on self-determination in a more realistic framework, and, as early as 1991, the then Centre for Human Rights held an expert seminar on self-government and indigenous peoples in Nuuk, Greenland precisely to provide living examples of such arrangements.[6] As pointed out on many occasions by indigenous and governmental delegations, there is no right to political independence, but there were a growing number of experiences in which indigenous peoples enjoyed differing degrees and kinds of self-governing, autonomous or self-managing arrangements, thus giving practical application to the principle of self-determination.[7]

A number of the world's indigenous peoples enjoy some form of self-determination either because there is formal 'devolution' of competences to the communities through national legislation or de facto, because the communities themselves continue to take a large range of decisions, including notably in the administration of justice, at the community level and in accordance with their traditions and cultures. Far from being a divisive element, the discussions around the practical application of the right to self-determination need to be placed much more within the debates about how to broaden 'democratic' processes and improve social justice and equity for all citizens of a given country. It always seemed like something of a red herring for some of the most militarily enhanced nations to express worry about the supposed aspirations of statehood of numerically small and poor indigenous peoples.

Indeed there are sufficient examples of indigenous peoples' self-determination to offer a diversity of templates to governments entering into agreements with their own indigenous peoples. Greenland provides an example of self-rule as close to complete political independence as is possible, but there are also statutory advisory bodies such as the Saami Parliaments in the Nordic countries or even the 85-year-old 'Comarca' autonomous region of the Kuna in Panama that suggest that there are as many solutions as there are indigenous peoples.[8] In countries where

[6] E/CN.4/1992/42.

[7] Indigenous peoples did not specifically rule out the possibility of independence as an option and recent developments in Greenland in particular point to the possibility that the country may separate from Denmark within a mutually agreed framework.

[8] Greenland is a self-governing region within the Danish realm, having held a referendum in November 2008 to increase its authority. According to the Act on Greenland Self-Government of 2009, the country can declare its independence whenever it decides to do so. The Saami people are represented by three Saami Parliaments, in Sweden, Norway and Finland. The Parliaments work as elected bodies representing Saami interests. The Comarca of the Kuna of Panama is one of the earliest examples of the exercise of self-determination and dates from the 1920s.

indigenous peoples are geographically dispersed, such as Australia, the setting up of indigenous-run governmental departments to deliver services may be seen as one means of exercising the right of self-determination, provided, of course, that they emerge from discussions between the parties.[9]

The Declaration (Article 4) recognises indigenous peoples' right to 'autonomy or self-government in matters relating to their internal and local affairs as well as ways and means for financing their autonomous functions' as one means of exercising the right to self-determination. Article 18 elaborates further by acknowledging the right of indigenous peoples to 'participate in decision-making in matters which would affect their rights, through representatives chosen by themselves in accordance with their own procedures, as well as to maintain their own decision-making institutions'.[10] The implementation of these rights is in line with other measures that might be taken to ensure greater public participation in a democratic society. There is no special privilege being bestowed on indigenous peoples because they are given the right to decide upon policies, programmes and activities that impact upon their communities in a way that complies with their traditions. In practice, however, these institutions are not given either the recognition or the authority they require or as envisaged in the Declaration. Furthermore, as may be seen from the very low level of indigenous representation, in general, in national parliaments and local authorities, mechanisms are not in place in many countries to allow for good faith and effective participation of indigenous peoples in decision-making affecting them.[11]

Implementation of the right to self-determination revolves around discussions over the competences that will be afforded indigenous peoples' institutions as well as agreement on ways and means of participating

[9] In Australia, the Labour Government established the Aboriginal and Torres Strait Islander Commission in 1995 as an elected body composed of elected indigenous commissioners with the mandate to determine allocations of budgets for services and oversee implementation. ATSIC came under criticism from both the Government and Aboriginal peoples themselves for not living up to its commitments. It was abolished in 2005.

[10] It has been noted that the articles of the Declaration are not always clustered logically, and this is the case with those dealing with self-determination and self-government. In the course of the inter-governmental discussions on the draft declaration, perhaps regrettably, no request was made to the UN secretariat to undertake a technical review, a measure that may well have helped to ensure a more logical placement of the articles and avoided some repetition.

[11] A conference organised by the Inter-parliamentary Union on the Inclusion of Indigenous Peoples in Parliaments is to be held in Mexico in 2010. For further information see http://www.ipu.org/english/strcture/splzdocs/chiapas10.htm. However, in recent years indigenous representatives have increasingly been winning seats in Parliament in certain Latin American countries. The election of Evo Morales as the first indigenous President of Bolivia may be seen as symbolising a breakthrough for indigenous peoples after 500 years of occupation.

in national, regional and local decision-making. While the Declaration establishes the right of indigenous peoples to maintain and develop their own institutions, it also underlines the right of indigenous peoples to participate fully in the political, economic, social and cultural life of the State (Article 5).

PROMOTING THE RIGHTS TO PARTICIPATION AND THE PRINCIPLE OF FREE, PRIOR AND INFORMED CONSENT

The question of participation of indigenous peoples is not a new one. A number of States established formal mechanisms for indigenous participation in political life, most notably through reserved seats in parliament or government service. This is the case, for example, in New Zealand, in India for its scheduled tribes, and in Burundi, whose Constitution guarantees three seats for Batwa in both chambers of the National Assembly.[12] Access to education, housing, employment, health and other socio-economic benefits are facilitated by some States through special measures, such as educational scholarships for indigenous peoples, subventions for cultural activities, housing or dedicated health clinics. The implementation of the general principle of participation of indigenous peoples, however, is generally quite absent in most contexts given that historically such peoples were marginalised and held little economic and political power. The inclusion of indigenous peoples in decision-making represents a cultural challenge as much as a legislative one.[13] It may require changing habits that are founded on prejudices and privileges which themselves can only be modified by education and awareness-building.

The Declaration is focused emphatically on the application of the right of indigenous peoples to participate. Article 38 notes, for example, that States 'in consultation and cooperation with indigenous peoples' shall take measures to achieve the ends of the Declaration. Similar rights are contained in Article 17 relating to labour laws, Articles 14 and 15 on education and public information, Articles 11 and 12 on intellectual property and spiritual and religious traditions, as well as various other articles. The

[12] As early as 1867, four parliamentary seats were established for Maori in New Zealand (today there are seven designated Maori seats) and in India the scheduled tribes have reserved positions in government departments and services and separate constituencies to ensure their political participation. By contrast, Australia technically denied the vote to Aboriginal peoples until 1967.

[13] Involving indigenous peoples in the formulation, implementation and evaluation of programmes affecting them has also been acknowledged to be a challenge for the UN system; in order to encourage staff to consult with indigenous peoples fully, guidelines were produced by the United Nations Development Group, which coordinates the world body's development activities. See www2.ohchr.org/english/issues/indigenous/docs/guidelines.pdf.

insistence in the Declaration on the right to be consulted on all relevant matters stems from the tragic experience of colonisation, including such modern forms of colonisation as land and resource expropriation in the name of development, in which indigenous peoples were and often continue to be ignored and at worst seen as impediments to progress.[14]

In the course of discussions preceding the Declaration, much time was devoted to the notions of participation, consultation and consent. Indigenous peoples observed that governments and others often paid lip-service to consultation, hosting meetings where information was cursory and the decisions taken in advance. To address this concern, the ILO in its Convention 169 commented that consultations should be undertaken 'in good faith and in a form appropriate to the circumstances, with the objective of achieving the agreement or consent to the proposed measure'.[15] In the case of relocations of indigenous peoples, the ILO requires that relocation 'take place only with their free and informed consent. Where their consent cannot be obtained, such relocation shall take place only following appropriate procedures established by national laws and regulations, including public enquiries where appropriate, which provide the opportunity for effective representation of the peoples concerned.'[16] The ILO, thus, establishes as many constraints as it can on the arbitrary action of governments and provides specific procedures to give indigenous peoples every opportunity to resist a measure that it might find contrary to their interests.

The draft declaration adopted by the Sub-Commission of experts in 1994, like ILO Convention 169, uses on several occasions the term 'free and informed consent'—the inclusion of 'prior' being a later addition—seeking to strengthen still further indigenous peoples' control over State activities that might impact upon them. The final negotiated texts relating to free, prior and informed consent in the Declaration re-affirm the main thrust of the ILO Convention, namely that the purpose of consultations should be to reach agreement with the indigenous peoples concerned. Article 19 of the Declaration requires States to consult and cooperate in good faith with indigenous peoples 'in order to obtain their free, prior and informed consent before implementing legislative or administrative measures that may affect them'. On the critical issue of development, Article

[14] There are a number of landmark works on the impact of so-called development on indigenous peoples, including J Bodley, *Victims of Progress*, 4th edn (California, Mayfield Publishing Co, 1999); S Davis, *Victims of the Miracle: Development and the Indians of Brazil* (California, Californian University Press, 1977); J Burger, *Report from the Frontier: The State of the World's Indigenous Peoples* (London, Zed Books, 1987), as well as more recent critiques such as J Mander and V Tauli-Corpuz (eds), *Paradigm Wars: Indigenous Peoples' Resistance to Globalization* (California, Sierra Club, 2006).

[15] Art 2.

[16] Art 16(2).

32 uses the same formulation in relation to 'the approval of any project affecting indigenous peoples' lands or territories and other resources, particularly in connection with the development, utilization or exploitation of mineral, water or other resources'.

The practical application of this important principle faces at least two important obstacles. The first relates to the processes that may need to be established to bring about an agreement. Mechanisms for full and good faith consultations with indigenous peoples are largely not in place in many States, neither on the government side nor on that of indigenous peoples themselves. Establishing formal spaces for dialogue between States and indigenous peoples is certainly one of the principal challenges, and one whose implementation will determine whether or not the Declaration serves to advance the well-being of indigenous peoples or remains dead in the water.

The Declaration together with ILO Convention 169 sets out a framework for successful negotiations, and as such these two instruments contribute to conflict prevention. Both texts insist that the consultations need to be with indigenous peoples' own representative institutions using appropriate and therefore culturally sensitive procedures. The purpose of the use of the formulation 'free' is to ensure that no coercion or manipulation is used in the course of negotiations, an admonition that unfortunately is often absent in the discussions between unequal partners. The eventual inclusion of the term 'prior' acknowledges the importance of allowing time to indigenous peoples to fully review proposals respecting the time required for achieving consensus in many indigenous communities. It also anticipates the reality that decisions, especially those relating to major investments in development, are often taken in advance of discussions with indigenous peoples and other local communities. This, the Declaration implies, is not in keeping with the commitments set out in its provisions. Finally, the notion of 'informed' consent reflects the growing acceptance that environmental and social impact assessments are a pre-requisite for any negotiation process and allow all parties to make balanced decisions.[17]

There is, however, a second obstacle to the implementation of the principle of free, prior and informed consent, and it is one observed by the former Special Rapporteur on the situation of human rights and fundamental freedoms of indigenous people. He points to many factors that contribute to an 'implementation gap', including inconsistencies between laws within States and between international law and domestic

[17] A fuller discussion of the principle of free, prior and informed consent can be found in the report of the former Working Group on Indigenous Populations (E/CN.4/Sub.2/AC.4/2003/3) and of the Permanent Forum on Indigenous Issues (E/C.19/2005/3).

legislation.[18] In certain respects, conflicts between the rights established for indigenous peoples and laws on a wide range of other matters such as mines, environment, water and forest management or even finance constitute structural impediments to the realisation of the provisions of the Declaration. Many contemporary disputes revolve around these ambiguities. Typically, one Ministry may grant concessions to extractive industry on indigenous peoples' lands while another may invoke State obligations arising from ratification of ILO Convention 169. While it is fine to have a national commitment to bilingual education for indigenous peoples, implementation becomes a dead letter if the human and financial resources are not made available by the Ministry of Finance. Such contradictions are at the root of most disputes between indigenous peoples and governments and, of course, give rise to allegations of human rights violations.

Generally speaking, external human rights monitoring bodies and sometimes domestic courts will consider that the commitment made by States with regard to human rights should prevail.[19] Indeed, judgments of these bodies have been universally supportive of indigenous peoples' rights and were referred to as relevant jurisprudence during negotiations on the Declaration. But obtaining positive recommendations, judgments or decisions from human rights monitoring bodies or even domestic courts is not in itself a guarantee that indigenous peoples' rights will be implemented. In the case of the Inter-American Court of Human Rights decision in the *Awas Tingni* case, it took some six years before indigenous lands were titled, and the decision of the Supreme Court of Belize of 2007 in a land rights case involving Maya communities has not yet been respected by the government of that country.[20] This is not to say that such monitoring and judicial procedures do not have a critical role to play, but rather to observe that effective promotion of indigenous peoples' rights

[18] See Report of the Special Rapporteur on the situation of human rights and fundamental freedoms of indigenous people (Rodolfo Stavenhagen) (E/CN.4/2006/78, particularly paras 14–79).

[19] There are number of examples of the human rights treaty bodies taking this position. In 2001, for example, the Committee on Economic, Social and Cultural Rights urged Colombia to 'consult and seek the consent of the indigenous peoples concerned prior to the implementation of timber, soil or sub-soil mining projects or on any public policy affecting them' (E7/C.12/1/Add.74, §33). The Inter-American Court of Human Rights has ruled on a number of cases relating to indigenous peoples' lands, most notably that of the Mayanga (Sumo) Awas Tingni of Nicaragua; see *Mayagna (Sumo) Awas Tingni Community v Nicaragua* (Series C No 79) [2001] IACHR 9 (31 August 2001). The judgment of the Belize Supreme Court in 2007 in relation to claims made by a Maya community (claim Nos 171 and 172) constitutes a landmark decision because it considered that the State had obligations to comply with the Declaration even though it was not technically binding.

[20] For further information relating to the progress of these two cases see the website of the University of Arizona: www.law.arizona.edu/depts/iplp/advocacy/index.cfm?page=advoc.

requires strong national legislation, effective administrative procedures for its implementation, adequate financing and independent bodies that inspire confidence to adjudicate disputes.

IMPLEMENTING RIGHTS TO LANDS, TERRITORIES AND RESOURCES

The cluster of articles relating to lands and resources, principally Articles 25–30 and Article 32, recognise indigenous peoples' spiritual attachment to their lands and resources, provide a right of ownership and use, identify processes for recognition and adjudication in relation to lands and resources, address restitution and compensation in cases of loss of lands, give indigenous peoples rights over conservation of their lands, limit military activities, and give indigenous peoples the right to determine development priorities.

In addition to these specific articles, other provisions of the Declaration address critical issues related to land. Article 8(b) calls on States to provide effective mechanisms for prevention of and redress for any action that has the aim or effect of dispossessing indigenous peoples of their lands, territories or resources. Article 10 states that indigenous peoples shall not be forcibly removed from their lands or territories and that no relocation should take place without the free, prior and informed consent of the peoples concerned. Article 12 protects indigenous peoples' right to have access to their religious and cultural sites. Article 20 guarantees indigenous peoples' enjoyment of their own means of subsistence and development and to engage freely in their traditional and other economic activities. Article 24, referring to traditional health, protects the conservation of vital medicinal plants, animals and minerals. Article 36 gives indigenous peoples rights to maintain activities across borders with traditional lands that traverse modern frontiers. Finally, Articles 3, 4, 5, 18 and 19 provide rights relating to self-determination, participation, consultation and consent that are fundamental to ensuring that indigenous peoples are free to participate in and take decisions affecting their lands and resources. In all, 19 of the 46 Articles of the Declaration relate to the question of land rights, underlining the huge importance of the question for the survival of indigenous peoples and its manifold manifestations.

Articles 25–30 and 32 reflect to a high degree Articles 13–19 of ILO Convention 169, although there are elements of difference that are worth identifying insofar as they underline the value of treating the two documents in a complementary and mutually-reinforcing fashion. The ILO Convention, in Article 15, addresses the question of sub-surface resources that, it notes, may be owned by States. In cases where mineral exploration and exploitation on indigenous peoples' lands is under consideration, States are required to establish procedures of consultation to evaluate impacts and determine benefits and compensation for the community. Many States, including all States in the Latin America region, retain ownership over mineral resources and it is not difficult to infer that, while the Declaration makes no specific reference to ownership of sub-surface resources, it does clearly state that States have obligations towards indigenous peoples in such cases. Article 32 of the Declaration, as noted earlier, calls upon States to seek to obtain the free, prior and informed consent of the indigenous peoples concerned prior to the approval of any project affecting indigenous peoples' lands or territories and other resources, 'particularly in connection with the development, utilization or exploitation of mineral, water or other resources'. Article 7 of the ILO Convention is less explicit and guarantees that indigenous peoples shall 'exercise control, to the extent possible, over their own economic, social and cultural development'. 'In addition,' the article goes on, indigenous peoples have the right to 'participate in the formulation, implementation and evaluation of plans and programmes for national and regional development which may affect them.' Although the article appears less constraining on governments than the relevant article in the Declaration, it should be noted that Article 7(2) of the Convention gives an understanding of how its provisions relating to consultation should be understood and specifically states that consultations should be held 'in good faith' and have 'the objective of achieving agreement or consent to the proposed measures', making the two instruments complementary on this point.

It may be useful to further consider the practical implications of the articles contained in the two instruments, since the most serious confrontations between indigenous peoples and States revolve around conflicts over resources. Respect for the relevant provisions relating to land rights appears to clash at times with the realities confronting States and what they consider to be their development needs. When Alan Garcia, President of Peru, met resistance in granting exploration rights to oil and logging companies in the Amazon region in May 2009, he put it like this: 'We have to understand [that] when there are resources like oil, gas and timber they don't belong to the people that had the good fortune to be born there.'[21] In the neighbouring country of Ecuador, which has what is seen as a popular government, indigenous Kichwa peoples of Sarayaku learnt in May 2009 that the Ministry of Mines and Petrol had re-authorised exploration and exploitation of hydrocarbons on their lands, despite the country's ratification of ILO Convention 169, its support for the Declaration, and decisions in favour of indigenous peoples given by the Inter-American Court of Human Rights and Ecuador's own Constitutional Tribunal.[22]

[21] Reported by the BBC on 17 May 2009.
[22] Source: Agencia de Noticias Plurinacional del Ecuador.

In this fundamental area of indigenous peoples' rights to lands and resources, there has been a marked evolution in the attitudes and practice of States. Whereas in the 1980s invoking national development to ride roughshod over indigenous peoples' land rights went relatively unremarked except by indigenous peoples themselves and a handful of campaigning organisations, today indigenous peoples find support from formal international, regional and national juridical bodies and can draw upon much stronger national legislation. Pronouncements of the human rights treaty bodies and judgments of the Inter-American Court of Human Rights, in particular, strongly indicate that the articles of the Declaration relating to land and resources need to be understood as State obligations, not mere guidelines.

Indeed, the Special Rapporteur on the situation of human rights and fundamental freedoms of indigenous people specifically used the Declaration to engage the Government of Panama in dialogue in relation to the hydroelectric dam Chan-75 that was being built across the Changuinola River and which affected the Ngobé homeland in January 2009.[23] In his report to the Human Rights Council, he pointed out that the indigenous communities impacted by the project were not consulted, contrary to two specific articles of the Declaration. He recommended that the Government review the project and initiate a new process of dialogue with the indigenous peoples. What is innovatory about the action taken by the Special Rapporteur is that he was able to make an official visit in order to contribute to the resolution of a specific human rights issue and, in so doing, used the Declaration as the tool for dispute resolution in a situation involving different governmental ministries, the private sector and civil society.

The approach adopted by the Special Rapporteur, very much akin to the kinds of interventions undertaken by the Inter-American Commission of Human Rights, suggests a potential for the practical application of the Declaration as a framework for negotiations in these far too common stand-offs between governments and indigenous communities over lands and resources. Interestingly, the pattern of resistance of many indigenous peoples is to invoke international law, specifically the Declaration and ILO Convention 169, and make use of available human rights mechanisms in order to accumulate pressure on governments to enter into direct negotiations. In the case of Panama, the argument is made by the Special Rapporteur that the good faith character of the consultations was not respected, since the affected communities claimed that, while they were invited to participate in meetings, they were not consulted with a view to obtaining their consent in line with the procedures established in the

[23] See UN Report A/HRC/12/34/Add.4.

Declaration. The Special Rapporteur also extended his recommendations beyond the Government to propose that the company concerned develop a code of conduct based on relevant international norms to guide its activities in relation to the planning and implementation of projects affecting indigenous peoples.[24] The purpose of citing this example is to draw attention to the ways in which the rights of indigenous peoples can be advanced through the creation of spaces for dialogue among contesting parties. In this case, indigenous peoples used domestic channels of protest as well as an international human rights mechanism to draw attention to the prevailing norms concerning consultation, land and resource rights, forced displacement and redress. The fact that the Government invited the Special Rapporteur to conduct an investigation and that he also engaged in dialogue with the company involved, must be seen as a positive development given the history of such confrontations in the past. Whether these forms of intervention lead in time to mutually acceptable results for all parties remains open at this time.

Of interest is the response of the Government, which argues that the hydro-electric project is of vital public interest and will provide a source of renewable energy benefiting millions of people and contributing to national development. Without the project, the Government states, it will need to increase dependence on fossil fuels with the consequent impact on climate change. In one respect it is ironic that States—for Panama is not the only government that argues on these lines—should suggest that indigenous peoples and their demands for the implementation of their rights are holding back improvements in the living conditions of millions of people and are contributing to global warming, given that indigenous peoples have least benefited from national development and have a way of life that has no impact on climate change. But as the struggle for recognition of indigenous peoples' rights advances, such arguments will find favour with governments pursuing development agendas based on the extraction of natural resources.

CONCLUSIONS

The Declaration, even in its draft form, served as a source for law-makers in certain instances, and now that it has been adopted as an international human rights instrument its role has been considerably enhanced.[25]

[24] A/HRC/12/34/Add.4, para 68. It may be noted that, at the time of writing, Panama is not a signatory to ILO Convention 169, although it has ratified ILO Convention 107 (1957) on Indigenous and Tribal Populations.

[25] The Indigenous Peoples Rights Act of the Philippines of 1997 is one such example of national law-making being influenced by the draft declaration.

There is some debate about whether the Declaration is customary law or merely aspirational.[26] It is certain that the Declaration is not binding on States, as it is not an international human rights treaty and is not open to ratification and independent monitoring. However, the basic principles that run through the Declaration are themselves binding on States and the Declaration may be understood to provide guidance to those bodies responsible for the monitoring of these treaties insofar as their provisions affect indigenous peoples.[27] Furthermore, it is important to note that decisions and recommendations arising from cases considered by the Inter-American Court of Human Rights, the Inter-American Commission on Human Rights and the international human rights treaty bodies have in recent years recognised that States have obligations towards indigenous peoples in relation to matters such as land and resource rights and the principle of free, prior and informed consent. To this extent, the Declaration and particularly its provisions relating to indigenous peoples' rights over their lands and resources are increasingly accepted as being of universal application.

The challenge ahead is to see the rights contained in the Declaration implemented and bring about positive changes among indigenous communities that remain the most marginalised. For the last 20 years or more, indigenous peoples have been united around a common goal—to win recognition of their rights by the United Nations. To get these rights established in national laws, used in domestic courts, and given practical meaning through administrative measures and budgetary allocations, the focus of attention needs to move from the international to national and local arenas.

International and regional human rights mechanisms will be important insofar as they validate and give support to national processes of reconciliation. It is to be welcomed, therefore, that the Special Rapporteur on the situation of human rights and fundamental freedoms of indigenous people, the Permanent Forum on Indigenous Issues and the Expert Mechanism on the Rights of Indigenous People have committed to using the Declaration as the framework in implementing their mandates.[28] Other international human rights mechanisms, in particular the human rights treaty bodies and the so-called special procedures

[26] See eg the interesting article 'Instrumentos sobre los derechos de los pueblos indígenas' by Bartolomé Clavero, member of the Permanent Forum on Indigenous Issues, available on his website: clavero.derechosindigenas.org/wp-content/uploads/2009/04/prologo-ddpi-169.pdf.

[27] See Annex to the Report of the Permanent Forum on Indigenous Issues at its 8th session, for a comment on the legal character of the Declaration, E/CN.19/2009/14.

[28] See eg the statement of the Chairperson of the Permanent Forum on Indigenous Issues.

of the Human Rights Council, have a good track record of helping to define State obligations in relation to indigenous peoples through their recommendations to States and general observations.[29] The treaty bodies have also begun to use the Declaration as a guide to interpreting State obligations, as was the case, for example, with General Comment No 11 on indigenous children and their rights under the Convention of the Committee on the Rights of the Child.[30] The Inter-American Commission on Human Rights has broadly interpreted its mandate in line with the principles of the Declaration notwithstanding the continuing negotiations within the Organization of American States on the draft American declaration on the rights of indigenous peoples, and the African Commission on Human and Peoples' Rights formally stated its support for the Declaration through an Advisory Opinion.[31] A continuing need for advocacy is still required at the Human Rights Council's Universal Periodic Review (UPR) procedure, where to date the Declaration has had little influence in relation to both monitoring and recommendations for action.[32]

At the national level there are several areas where the Declaration can play a role and contribute to the implementation of indigenous rights.

Constitutional reforms and national law-making: The establishment of universally accepted rights for indigenous peoples through the adoption of the Declaration has opened the way for their incorporation into the processes of constitutional reform and national law-making. A notable example was the discussions of the Constituent Assembly leading up to the adoption of the new Constitution of Bolivia and the decision of the President of that country, in November 2007, to integrate the Declaration into national legislation. Constitutional reforms in Ecuador and Nepal also drew upon the Declaration as a source for the elaboration of relevant articles relating to indigenous peoples. As States move towards accommodating the concerns and rights of indigenous peoples, the Declaration provides both the broad agenda and the fundamental principles that can serve as the basis for the development of legislation. This is particularly

[29] Excellent reviews of the evolving jurisprudence of the treaty bodies is contained in the reports prepared by Fergus MacKay for the Forest Peoples Programme, available at www.forestpeoples.org/documents/law_hr/un_jurisprudence_comp_vol3_07_08_eng.pdf.

[30] See General Comment No 11 on Indigenous children and their rights under the convention of the Committee on the Rights of the Child of January 2009 (UN Doc C/CRC/GC/11).

[31] Advisory Opinion of the African Commission on Human and Peoples' Rights on the UN Declaration on the Rights of Indigenous Peoples, 41st Ordinary Session, Accra, Ghana, May 2007.

[32] The UPR is a procedure of the Human Rights Council whereby all States' human rights practices are periodically reviewed. Information can be submitted by civil society but is confined to a report of 10 pages. Further information can be found on the website of the Office of the High Commissioner for Human Rights (OHCHR): www.ohchr.org.

important in Asia and Africa, where the rights of indigenous peoples are generally not reflected in existing Constitutions.[33] One area of increasing concern is the incompatibility of national laws, decrees or concessions, notably relating to mining, environment or resource development, that contradict established legislation protecting indigenous peoples' lands and territories.

Courts and the justice system: Reference has been made to the judgment of the Supreme Court of Belize that cited the Declaration as a source of guidance in the case of a dispute between the Government and indigenous Maya communities over land rights. Importantly, the Court underlined the obligations of the State with regard to the implementation of the Declaration, stating: 'I therefore venture to think that the defendants would be unwilling, or even loath to take any action that would detract from the provisions of this Declaration importing as it does, in my view, significant obligations for the State of Belize in so far as the indigenous Maya rights to their land and resources are concerned.' It should be expected that courts, in dealing with disputes relating to indigenous peoples' rights, take into account the Declaration in particular if the State concerned voted in favour in the General Assembly. Implementation of the Declaration will depend on the willingness of well-informed courts to apply these established international standards in domestic disputes. While the present chapter has not dealt with the question of administration of justice and particularly Articles 13 and 34, a number of countries have shown a growing interest in recognising indigenous customary law and incorporating it into mainstream systems. Furthermore, the Declaration merely acknowledges the right of indigenous peoples to maintain and develop their judicial system, and there is therefore opportunity for engagement by ministries of justice, legal professionals and indigenous peoples to develop appropriate forms of legal pluralism.

Administrative measures and budgetary allocations: Even where there is adequate protection of indigenous peoples' rights and there are well-established laws to combat discrimination, appropriate administrative measures may not be in place to ensure their application in practice. The former Special Rapporteur referred to this as the implementation gap.[34] Giving effect to national laws also demands adjustments to budgetary allocations. Providing for the teaching of indigenous languages

[33] India provides specific constitutional protection of the rights of its scheduled tribes, and legislation recognises rights for indigenous peoples in the Philippines (see above, n 27). In Africa, Burundi is one of the few States that guarantees specific rights to the Twa ethnic group.

[34] See A/HRC/4/32. The Special Rapporteur notes that, '[w]hile there has been progress in the adoption of standards that recognize the rights of indigenous people, the gap when it comes to implementing those standards still remains'.

through legislative measures, for example, will be of little avail if the corresponding budget for qualified teachers is not there. The Declaration recognises indigenous peoples' right to redress in cases where lands have been taken from them, and certain States are committed to setting aside land or even buying land for indigenous communities, but the physical demarcation of these lands or the purchase of land from third parties can severely limit the impact of these positive measures.

Little has been said in this article about the role of the United Nations system in implementing the Declaration, and that is because it is national governments and indigenous peoples and civil society in those countries that are the driving force behind implementation. International cooperation can, nonetheless, contribute. This is the sense behind the establishment of the Permanent Forum on Indigenous Issues that is mandated to advise UN organisations and agencies. In response, the UN system has developed its own inter-agency cooperation strategies .[35] Coinciding with the adoption of the Declaration, the United Nations Development Group (UNDG) endorsed guidelines for mainstreaming indigenous issues into UN country programmes.[36] Since then, a number of UN agencies have committed to training their own staff on indigenous issues, familiarising them with the Declaration and the implications for programme planning, implementation and evaluation.[37]

The international financial institutions, including the World Bank, International Finance Corporation, Inter-American Development Bank (IDB) and others, have adopted operational guidelines relating to indigenous peoples.[38] These guidelines pre-date the Declaration and in certain aspects do not reflect the rights established under the new instrument, which is a cause of concern to indigenous peoples. Specifically, the Banks incorporate requirements for consultation with indigenous peoples but

[35] The Inter-Agency Group on Indigenous Peoples' Issues was established in 2000 at the initiative of the OHCHR and ILO to bring the UN system together in a more formal way to discuss better integration of indigenous issues into the work of the UN and contribute to the preparations for the 1st session of the Permanent Forum on Indigenous Issues and subsequently give support to the mandate.

[36] The UNDG is the high-level coordinating body of the UN for development issues and therefore plays a critical role in harmonising the UN's country-level policies and programmes.

[37] The ILO and OHCHR have held training sessions for staff for several years. In 2009, the Permanent Forum secretariat in cooperation with other UN agencies and organisations began training of UN country staff. Nevertheless, in many countries the UN system's own staff remain unfamiliar with developments relating to indigenous peoples' rights and in particular are not ensuring that indigenous peoples' representatives participate in programme design, as recommended by the UNDG guidelines.

[38] The IDB operational policy (OP-765) was adopted by the Bank in February 2006; the World Bank's operational policy on indigenous peoples (OP-4.10) was adopted by the Bank in July 2005; and the IFC's Performance Standard No 7 on indigenous peoples was adopted in April 2006.

do not recognise the principle of free, prior and informed consent. Thus, these policies require adjustments to ensure their compatibility with international standards.

The Declaration is a culmination of an extraordinary international effort on the part of indigenous peoples to gain international recognition, and, as both the proponents and the beneficiaries of these standards, they are the driving force behind their implementation. However, while the Declaration is a significant achievement, it comes at a time when indigenous peoples' lands and resources are subject to threats as potentially destructive as the process of historical colonialism. The accelerating search for resources and the pressures on land and living spaces due to global warming puts indigenous peoples at the front line. While this represents an ever-present danger, it also offers an unprecedented opportunity for indigenous peoples to link up with proponents of a more benign and equitable form of development.

3

Integrating the UN Declaration on the Rights of Indigenous Peoples into CERD Practice

PATRICK THORNBERRY

'If we could once achieve a synthesis of the archaic and the entirely new ...'[1]

INTRODUCTION

THE CANON OF human rights standards is increasingly multifarious. Normative integration remains an important aspiration, and progress towards it will lower the risk of sending out contradictory signals to the carriers of human rights responsibilities. UN General Assembly Resolution 41/120[2] invites States and UN bodies to bear in mind that new human rights instruments that are developed should, inter alia, be consistent with the existing body of human rights law, be of fundamental character and derive from the inherent dignity and worth of the human person, and be sufficiently precise to give rise to identifiable and predictable human rights obligations.[3] The other side of the coin is that the existing standards are open to the influence of the newer instruments, and monitoring bodies enhance their standing by burnishing their awareness of changing human rights frameworks.

The UN Declaration on the Rights of Indigenous Peoples ('the Declaration')[4] represents a substantial addition to the corpus of human rights, and the International Convention on the Elimination of All Forms of Racial Discrimination ('ICERD', or 'the Convention'),[5] the oldest of

[1] D Mahon, 'The Dawn Chorus' in *Collected Poems* (Oldcastle, County Meath, Gallery Press, 1999) 123.

[2] Adopted on 4 December 1986.

[3] The Resolution also adds the desiderata of realistic implementation machinery and broad international support.

[4] A/RES/61/295, 13 September 2007.

[5] Adopted by UN General Assembly Resolution 2106A (XX), 21 December 1965.

the UN 'core' human rights treaties,[6] occupies a substantial space in 'the existing body' of human rights. Improving normative synthesis in the field of human rights is not a simple process. Standards have been developed at different times and in light of different assumptions throughout the UN era—'the age of rights'.[7] This is nowhere more true than in the articulation of indigenous rights, which have moved since 1945 through discourses of integration and assimilation that showed scant respect for the claims of indigenous peoples to survive and flourish, towards the Declaration's lapidary statement of the principle of indigenous self-determination,[8] with sundry conceptual halting places in between.[9] The human rights mantra expressed in the Vienna Declaration and Programme of Action of the World Conference on Human Rights is one of indivisibility, interdependence, etc.[10] This anti-hierarchical, holistic stance on human rights strongly suggests an integrated approach to the ongoing application of norms, but may also serve to conceal differences and even tensions within the canon. The following glance at the normative register of the two instruments—the Convention and the Declaration—serves to highlight potential synergies as well as diverging conceptual pathways.

THE CONVENTION

The Charter of the United Nations prohibits distinctions in the enjoyment of human rights based on 'race, sex, language or religion'. The inclusion in the Charter of a proscription of racial discrimination contrasts with the silence of the Covenant of the League of Nations, despite the efforts of Japan to insert a provision therein on the equality of nations and peoples,[11] a silence which suggests that 'hierarchical'

[6] www2.ohchr.org/english/law—there are nine such 'core' treaties at present.

[7] Two books with this title were published in 1990: N Bobbio, *L'età dei diritti* (Torino, Einaudi); and L Henkin, *The Age of Rights* (New York, Columbia University Press). The book by Bobbio was later published in translation as *The Age of Rights* (Cambridge, Polity Press, 1996).

[8] 'Indigenous peoples have the right to self-determination. By virtue of that right they freely determine their political status and freely pursue their economic, social and cultural development' (Art 3). The principle is developed further in Art 4 of the Declaration and is also referred to in paras 16 and 17 of the preamble.

[9] On discourse development regarding indigenous peoples, see P Thornberry, *Indigenous Peoples and Human Rights* (Manchester University Press, 2002), Part I; L Rodríguez-Piñero, *Indigenous Peoples, Postcolonialism, and International Law* (Oxford University Press, 2005), *passim*; A Xanthaki, *Indigenous Rights and United Nations Standards: Self-Determination, Culture and Land* (Cambridge University Press, 2007).

[10] A/CONF.157/23, 12 July 1993. Paragraph 5 of the Vienna Declaration and Programme of Action (VDPOA) reads in part: 'All human rights are universal, indivisible and interdependent and interrelated.' The VDPOA is acknowledged in preambular para 16 of the Declaration in the context of the right to self-determination.

[11] WA McKean, *Equality and Discrimination under International Law* (Oxford University Press, 1983) 16–19.

thinking about peoples and nations was not uncongenial in the early twentieth century, dominated as it was by the corralling of large segments of humanity into vast colonial systems.[12] The proscription of racial discrimination represented a qualitative upgrade in international legal endeavours. The United Nations Sub-Commission on the Prevention of Discrimination and Protection of Minorities conceptualised the 'prevention of discrimination' limb of its mandate as 'the prevention of any action which denies to individuals or groups equality of treatment which they may wish'.[13] A memorandum of the Secretary-General added that, '[t]o prevent discrimination, therefore, some means had to be found to suppress or eliminate inequality of treatment which may have harmful results, aiming to prevent any act or conduct which implies that an unfavourable distinction is made between individuals solely because they belong to certain categories or groups in society'.[14] On this interpretation, equality is to be achieved by suppressing or eliminating certain forms of conduct, rather than through a positive 'politics of difference'.[15]

The Convention comprises only seven substantive rights articles. Article 1 provides a definition of racial discrimination:

> In this Convention, the term 'racial discrimination' shall mean any distinction, exclusion, restriction or preference based on race, colour, descent, or national or ethnic origin which has the purpose or effect of nullifying or impairing the recognition, enjoyment or exercise, on an equal footing, of human rights and fundamental freedoms in the political, economic, social, cultural or any other field of public life.

The governing term is 'racial discrimination'; there is no further elaboration of the controversial term 'race'.[16] Neither minorities nor indigenous peoples are specifically mentioned in the text of the Convention. The Convention reaches beyond formal equality towards equality in fact

[12] B Boxill (ed), *Race and Racism* (Oxford University Press, 2001).

[13] E/CN.4/52, Section V.

[14] *The Main Types and Causes of Discrimination*, UN Sales No 49.XIV.3, paras 6 and 7.

[15] IM Young, *Justice and the Politics of Difference* (Princeton University Press, 1990).

[16] Hence the reluctance of some governments to deploy the term 'race' in their legislation. One example is provided by the report of Norway explaining the absence of the term in its Anti-Discrimination Act: 'the Government has supported the view that the concept of race should not be used ... The reason for this is that the concept of race is based on biological, hereditary characteristics, grounded in theories that have no justifiable scientific basis or content. Moreover, the concept has strong negative connotations ... The Government therefore sees no need to use the term "race" in the text of the statute', CERD/C/497/Add.1, para 10. CERD nonetheless recommended—A/61/18, para 334—that Norway ensures that discrimination on the ground of race is adequately covered by the legislation. The Committee's response could be read as implying that the term as such could be avoided provided that this did not leave a substantive gap in protection against discrimination, which was also the contention of the State party.

or substantive equality.[17] On the core notion of discrimination, General Recommendation 14 observes that 'differentiation of treatment will not constitute discrimination if the criteria for such differentiation, judged against the objectives and purposes of the Convention, are legitimate'.[18] The term 'non-discrimination' itself does not signify the necessity of uniform treatment if there are significant differences in situation between one person or group and another,[19] or, in other words, if there is 'an objective and reasonable justification for differential treatment'.[20] Further nuance is provided in the Committee's observation that the principle of non-discrimination requires that the characteristics of ethnic groups be taken into consideration.[21] Perhaps it is also worth labouring another obvious point on the non-discrimination principle as expressed in ICERD and elsewhere: it addresses denial of equality in the recognition, enjoyment or exercise of *human rights*,[22] making it crucial to determine what counts as a human right.

The basic account of non-discrimination in further elaborated in Article 1.4:

> Special measures taken for the sole purpose of securing adequate advancement of certain racial or ethnic groups or individuals requiring such protection as may be necessary in order to ensure such groups or individuals equal enjoyment or exercise of human rights and fundamental freedoms shall not be deemed racial discrimination, provided, however, that such measures do not, as a consequence, lead to the maintenance of separate rights for different racial groups and that they shall not be continued after the objectives for which they were taken have been achieved.

Article 2.2 continues this theme, making it mandatory for States parties to take such special measures, 'when the circumstances so warrant'.[23]

[17] W Vandenhole, *Non-Discrimination and Equality in the View of the UN Human Rights Treaty Bodies* (Antwerp, Intersentia, 2005) 37–43. The general principle of equality is helpfully reviewed in AHE Morawa, 'The Evolving Human Right to Equality' (2001/2) 2 *European Yearbook on Minority Issues* 157–205.

[18] A/48/18, chapter VIII B.

[19] P Thornberry, 'Confronting Racial Discrimination: A CERD Perspective' (2005) 5 *Human Rights Law Review* 239–69.

[20] Concluding observations on the thirteenth and fourteenth periodic reports of Australia, A/60/18, para 35. In the case of the Czech Republic, the Committee, recalling its General Recommendation 30 on non-citizens, stated, in further elaboration of principle, that 'differential treatment based on citizenship constitutes discrimination if the criteria for such differentiation, judged in the light of the objectives and purposes of the Convention, are not applied pursuant to a legitimate aim, and are not proportional to the achievement of this aim': A/62/18, para 112.

[21] Concluding observations on Namibia, A/63/18, para 305.

[22] Present author's emphasis.

[23] CERD has often insisted on the mandatory nature of measures in question. For example, the concluding observations of the Committee with regard to the USA noted with concern 'the position taken by the State party that the provisions of the Convention permit, but do not require States parties to adopt affirmative action measures to ensure the adequate

The requirement that special measures do not lead to the maintenance of separate rights for the different racial groups and they are not continued after the objectives for which they were taken have been achieved may be misunderstood in the context of indigenous rights, recognition and respect for which will require more than temporary measures—this question is pursued further below in discussing the relationship between 'special measures' and indigenous rights.

It is not necessary here to review all the articles of the Convention. Suffice it to say that the responsibility of the State is engaged not simply by acts of public institutions, etc, but extends to acts of 'racial discrimination by any persons, group or organization'.[24] The Convention takes a resolute stance on racial segregation,[25] on racist propaganda and organisations—on 'hate speech',[26] on remedies for racial discrimination,[27] and envisages 'immediate and effective measures' being taken by State authorities particularly in teaching, education, culture, etc, to combat prejudice and promote understanding and tolerance 'among nations and racial or ethnical groups'.[28]

Among the lengthier articles of the Convention, Article 5 provides a non-exhaustive list of human rights to which the non-discrimination principle applies, and notably includes economic, social and cultural as well as civil and political rights. In current practice, a full range of human rights engages the Committee, which devotes a considerable amount of attention to economic, social and cultural rights, as well as civil and political rights, so that some or other question of economic, social and cultural rights figures in most of the concluding observations. There is support for the view that the 'unclosed' nature of the list of rights in Article 5, coupled with the promise of the Convention to eliminate 'all forms' of racial discrimination, means that 'Article 5, both alone and in conjunction with Article 2, addresses the enjoyment of all rights regardless of source'.[29]

development and protection of certain racial, ethnic or national groups. The Committee emphasizes that the adoption of special measures by States parties when the circumstances so warrant, such as in the case of persistent disparities, *is an obligation* stemming from article 2, para 2, of the Convention', A/56/18, para 399 (emphasis added). The USA attempted to clarify its position in its report examined by the Committee in 2008, acknowledging that, while Art 2.2 'requires States parties to take special measures "when circumstances so warrant"', the decision 'concerning when such measures are in fact warranted is left to the judgment and discretion of each State party' and the special measures 'may or may not in themselves be race-based': CERD/C/USA/6 (2007), para 127. For the response of CERD, see the concluding observations of 2008, A/63/18, para 486.

[24] Art 2.1(d).

[25] Art 3.

[26] Art 4.

[27] Art 6.

[28] Art 7.

[29] M O'Flaherty, 'Substantive Provisions of the International Convention on the Elimination of All Forms of Racial Discrimination' in S Pritchard (ed), *Indigenous Peoples, the United Nations and Human Rights* (London and Leichhardt NSW, Zed Books and the Federation Press, 1998) 162 at 179.

While the Convention lists rights, it does not define them—thus opening out the text to wider developments in the human rights canon.

CERD AND ITS PROCEDURES

The International Convention on the Elimination of Racial Discrimination has attracted 173 States parties, of which 53 have accepted the individual communications procedure under Article 14.[30] Per annum, the Committee (CERD) examines, in two sessions, some 20 or so 'regular' State reports, plus an indeterminate number of 'review' countries, perhaps 10 cases under the 'early warning and urgent action procedure' (numbers are increasing), as well as individual communications, the number of which rarely rises above three per session. The 18-member Committee works principally by analysing and commenting on reports by States which are obliged, according to Article 9.1 of the Convention, to report '(a) within one year after the entry into force of the Convention for the State concerned; and (b) every two years and whenever the Committee so requests. The Committee may request further information from the States Parties.' Each dialogue with a State party is followed by a set of concluding observations by the Committee that contains elements of praise, statements of concern and recommendations for further action. The system utilises individual members of the Committee as country rapporteurs who take responsibility for leading the dialogue with the reporting government. CERD sessions are normally held in Geneva: country visits are not part of its regular modus operandi. States that are five years or more overdue with their reports may be subjected to the 'review' procedure, under which CERD may decide to examine a country situation in the absence of a report. Mention of a review usually brings forth either a report or a reason for not submitting one. The Committee has recently added a follow-up procedure to check on implementation of selected recommendations.[31] Additional to the main dialogues, CERD 'summarises' its views and practice on particular issues relating to racial discrimination in General Recommendations, 33 of which have been issued in the life of the Committee.[32]

[30] A/63/18, p 1.

[31] See Rule 65.2 of the rules of procedure, and Guidelines on follow-up to concluding observations and recommendations, A/61/18, Annex VI.

[32] The Compilation of General Comments and General Recommendations adopted by Human Rights Treaty Bodies, HRI/GEN/1/Rev.9, 27 May 2008 lists 31 such recommendations. Two further General Recommendations were adopted by CERD at its 75th session in 2009: General Recommendation 32 on the meaning and scope of special measures; and General Recommendation 33 on the follow-up to the Durban Review Conference.

Two complaints systems are envisaged in the Convention. The first of these, the inter-State complaints procedure in Articles 11–13 of the Convention, has not been activated. The communications procedure for 'individuals or groups of individuals ... claiming to be victims of a violation' is set out in Article 14 of the Convention. Communications under Article 14 have not occupied the Committee to the same extent as analogous procedures under for example the International Covenant on Civil and Political Rights 1966 (ICCPR). The case law is, in consequence, sparse, focusing on a basic understanding of the concepts, structures and norms to address discrimination. A follow-up procedure has also been instituted for CERD's case law.[33] The further procedure provided for in Article 22, whereby disputes relating to 'the interpretation or application of this Convention' can be referred to the International Court of Justice, has been engaged by Georgia against the Russian Federation.[34]

CERD adopted early warning and urgent action guidelines in 1993[35] and refined them in 2007.[36] The 2007 guidelines are presented as a revision of the 1993 paper 'in the light of the practice of the Committee since 1993 and of the current needs and recent developments'.[37] In view of their overall preventive ethos, the guidelines make explicit linkage to the prevention of genocide in their recalling the 2004 'Stockholm' speech of the Secretary-General on prevention of genocide,[38] in reference to persistent patterns of racial discrimination 'in some cases with genocidal dimensions',[39] and to the Special Adviser of the Secretary-General on the prevention of genocide.[40] Most situations dealt with by the Committee reflect allegations of serious racial discrimination which do not approach the dimensions of genocide.

THE DECLARATION, EQUALITY, AND NON-DISCRIMINATION

The Declaration was drafted in light of the existence of the Convention as well as the raft of contemporary human rights standards enshrining

33 A/61/18, chapter VII.
34 International Court of Justice press release 2008/23, 12 August 2008.
35 A/48/18, Annex III (early warning guidelines). For a review of the early operation of the procedure, see T van Boven, 'Prevention, Early-Warning and Urgent Procedures; A New Approach by the Committee on the Elimination of Racial Discrimination' in E Denters and N Schrijver (eds), *Reflections on International Law from the Low Countries* (The Hague, Kluwer Law International, 1998) 165–82.
36 A/62/18, Annex III (revised early warning guidelines).
37 Ibid, para 3.
38 Ibid, para 4.
39 Ibid, para 7.
40 Ibid, para 14.

principles of non-discrimination.[41] The Declaration is also complemented by texts specific to indigenous peoples, notably ILO Convention 169 on Indigenous and Tribal Peoples adopted by the International Labour Conference in 1989.[42] The complex, 24 paragraph preamble to the Declaration affirms the principle of equality of indigenous peoples with other peoples,[43] reaffirms the freedom of indigenous peoples from discrimination in the exercise of rights,[44] and adapts and expands the Convention's condemnation of doctrines or theories of racial, etc superiority.[45] It also recognises and reaffirms 'that indigenous individuals are entitled without discrimination to all human rights recognized in international law',[46] exhorts indigenous organisations to bring an end to 'all forms of discrimination',[47] and expresses its conviction that harmonious relations between indigenous peoples and States, based, inter alia, on the principle of non-discrimination, will be enhanced by recognition of indigenous rights.[48] The operative articles include a general reference to international human rights law,[49] and restate principles of equality and non-discrimination in specific fields including community membership,[50] education,[51] media,[52] employment and economic and social conditions generally,[53] protection of women and children against violence,[54] in health services,[55] etc. The principle of non-discrimination is mandatory in terms of any limitations in the exercise of rights,[56] and the Declaration concludes with a portmanteau flourish, requiring that its provisions 'shall be interpreted in accordance with the principles of justice, democracy, respect for human rights, equality, non-discrimination, good governance and

[41] Thornberry (n 9) ch 15.
[42] Ibid, part IV.
[43] Preambular para 2.
[44] Preambular para 5.
[45] Preambular para 4: '*Affirming further* that all doctrines, policies and practices based on or advocating superiority of peoples or individuals on the basis of national origin or racial, religious, ethnic or cultural differences are racist, scientifically false, legally invalid, morally condemnable and socially unjust.' This may be compared with the statement in the preamble to the Convention: '*Convinced* that any doctrine of superiority based on racial differentiation is scientifically false, morally condemnable, socially unjust and dangerous', and the follow-up to this sentiment in Art 4 of the Convention.
[46] Preambular para 22.
[47] Preambular para 9.
[48] Preambular para 18.
[49] Art 1.
[50] Art 9.
[51] Arts 14 and 15.
[52] Art 16.
[53] Art 21.
[54] Art 22.
[55] Art 24.
[56] Art 46(2).

good faith'.[57] A range of 'mechanisms' circulate around the Declaration,[58] and a stimulus to institutionalisation of the Declaration is provided by Article 42 which provides that the 'United Nations, its bodies, including the Permanent Forum on Indigenous Issues, and specialized agencies, including at the country level, and States shall promote respect for and full application of the provisions of this Declaration and follow up the effectiveness of this Declaration'. Further normative development of indigenous rights is foreseen by Articles 43 and 45.[59]

The Convention on the other hand was drafted without benefit of the Declaration. The integration of principles on indigenous rights is one among many challenges facing the Committee in its ongoing task of monitoring the implementation of the Convention by States parties. A superficial reading of the Convention and the Declaration suggests that the two instruments are radically different in their focus, pedigree, philosophy, structure and content. The Convention makes reference not to indigenous peoples, but to discrimination on five general 'grounds'. The Convention emerged from internationalised struggles against colonialism, anti-Semitism and Apartheid in an inter-State framework, while the Declaration, finally accepted by the General Assembly within this framework, was largely built on the efforts of indigenous groups themselves. The philosophy of the Declaration could broadly be described as autonomist, whereas the Convention is commonly read as a paean to integration. The Declaration incorporates the principle of non-discrimination and applies it along with a rich elaboration of freshly minted standards. The Convention, unlike the Declaration, is not structured as a positive statement of rights but as a prohibition of discrimination in the enjoyment of rights. The Convention does not replicate the clear commitment of the Declaration to collective rights in the sense of rights inhering in the collective as such. On the surface, therefore, it might appear difficult to 'work' the two instruments together.

However, while the backgrounds and modes of presenting their substance are different in the two instruments, they are alike in that they are strong in humanitarian inspiration, and suggest complementary

[57] Art 46(3).

[58] Among the mechanisms, the current mandate of the Special Rapporteur on the situation of human rights and fundamental freedoms of indigenous people includes promotion of the Declaration: Human Rights Council Resolution 6/12 (28 September 2007), operative para (g), whereas the preamble to the mandate of the Expert mechanism on the rights of indigenous peoples recalls the Declaration: Human Rights Council Resolution 6/36, 14 December 2007.

[59] Art 43 provides that 'The rights recognized herein constitute the minimum standards for the survival, dignity and well-being of the indigenous peoples of the world'; and Art 45 provides simply that 'Nothing in this Declaration may be construed as diminishing or extinguishing the rights indigenous peoples have now or may acquire in the future.'

methodologies for upholding human dignity. Part of their ethos is also that they seek—zealously—to rectify some of the injustices of colonialism, while laying the ground for present and future social justice beyond the colonial paradigm. It should also be recalled that the groundbreaking Martinez Cobo study of indigenous rights, a consciousness-raising exercise which facilitated the emergence of the Declaration, was a study of *discrimination* against indigenous peoples.[60] Further, the 'integrationist' understanding of the Convention is a perennial matter of nuance and development: 'integration' should be interpreted as being based on respect for rights and not as a programme of artificial, particularity-destroying assimilation.[61] While the Convention does not match the articulation of self-determination in the Declaration, the self-determination-shaping Colonial Declaration of 1960 is referred to in the preamble to the Convention,[62] and Article 15 of the Convention addresses some of the residue of colonialism.[63] Finally, the essence of the protection provided by the Convention is for persons who 'stand for' the groups, targeted because of their affiliations, real or imagined, with real or imagined communities.

The current practice of the Committee demonstrates elaborate and regular engagement with indigenous questions, making it clear that indigenous peoples are among the primary groups entitled to protection from racial discrimination. Besides indigenous peoples, CERD recurrently addresses questions regarding minorities in general, non-citizens, caste/descent groups, as well as discrimination against those whose identities 'intersect' with the principal grounds set out in Article 1, notably women and members of religious minorities.[64] Taking only the Committee's report on the 2008 sessions to the UN General Assembly as a sample of work,[65]

[60] J Martinez Cobo, *Study of the Problem of Discrimination against Indigenous Populations*, E/CN.4/Sub.2/1986/7 and Add.1–4 (present author's emphasis).

[61] In its concluding observations on Namibia, A/63/18, para 305, CERD urged the State party 'to ensure that its integration policies and programmes respect and protect the cultural identities of persons belonging to national or ethnic minorities within its territory', an observation that would apply, a fortiori, to indigenous peoples.

[62] General Assembly Resolution 1514 (XV).

[63] Art 15.2 provides: '(a) The Committee established under article 8, paragraph 1, of this Convention shall receive copies of the petitions from, and submit expressions of opinion and recommendations on these petitions to, the bodies of the United Nations which deal with matters directly related to the principles and objectives of this Convention in their consideration of petitions from the inhabitants of Trust and Non-Self-Governing Territories and all other territories to which General Assembly Resolution 1514 (XV) applies, relating to matters covered by this Convention which are before these bodies; (b) The Committee shall receive from the competent bodies of the United Nations copies of the reports concerning the legislative, judicial, administrative or other measures directly related to the principles and objectives of this Convention applied by the administering Powers within the Territories mentioned in subparagraph (a) of this paragraph, and shall express opinions and make recommendations to these bodies.'

[64] Thornberry (n 19) 257–66.

[65] A/63/18.

its concluding observations on the reports submitted by Ecuador, Fiji, Namibia, Nicaragua, Russian Federation, Sweden, Togo and the USA, all make reference to indigenous peoples. Further, in the chapter on prevention of discrimination including early warning and urgent action,[66] indigenous issues are addressed in connection with Belize, Brazil, Chile, Peru, the Philippines, Canada, India and Panama. Matters raised in connection with the periodic reports and urgent procedures—some examples of which are commented on further in the present chapter—include securing the collective rights of indigenous peoples,[67] community justice and the use of indigenous languages in judicial proceedings (or more accurately the absence of such),[68] the impact of oil, logging and mining operations and gas pipelines on indigenous lands,[69] removal of trespassers from indigenous territories,[70] bilingual intercultural education,[71] the concept of indigenous peoples and the nature of the indigenous connection with land,[72] obstacles to the pursuit of traditional ways of life occasioned by the creation and management of national parks,[73] poverty among marginalised indigenous groups, recommending accession to ILO Convention 169 on Indigenous and Tribal Peoples[74] (as well as support for the Declaration),[75] indigenous political representation,[76] the burden of establishing indigenous rights,[77] and sundry environmental and health issues arising from the storage of toxic waste and other industrial processes, and nuclear testing.[78] These and allied questions are part of the staple diet of CERD and have been so for many years.[79]

CERD AND INDIGENOUS PEOPLES: THE INITIATION OF CONCERN

The history of how CERD factored indigenous peoples into the non-discrimination nexus can illuminate the prospects of further harmonisation of indigenous rights and non-discrimination discourses. The present

[66] Chapter II of the report.
[67] A/63/18, para 137 (Ecuador).
[68] Ibid, para 139 (Ecuador); para 334 (Nicaragua).
[69] Ibid, para 141 (Ecuador).
[70] Ibid, para 336 (Nicaragua).
[71] Ibid, para 147 (Ecuador).
[72] Ibid, paras 168 and 177 (Fiji).
[73] Ibid, para 300 (Namibia).
[74] Ibid, para 344 (Nicaragua); para 408 (Sweden).
[75] Ibid, para 500 (USA): 'the Committee … recommends that the declaration be used as a guide to interpret the State party's obligations under the Convention relating to indigenous peoples.'
[76] Ibid, para 370 (Russian Federation).
[77] Ibid, paras 407 and 407 (Sweden).
[78] Ibid, para 500 (USA).
[79] For an earlier review of the work of CERD on indigenous questions, see Thornberry (n 9) ch 8.

chapter does not attempt a learned disquisition on whether a declaration or other 'soft law' instrument can be used to interpret a treaty or vice versa, but focuses on CERD praxis to show by a species of 'reverse engineering' or simple induction that what is done, can be validly done.

The integration of indigenous peoples into racial discrimination discourses did not get off to a promising start, if the drafting and early operation of ICERD is taken as a relevant measure. Sporadic attention was paid to indigenous or aboriginal groups in a drafting process which was dominated by the *topoi* of denunciation of colonialism, Apartheid and racial segregation, and polemics over proposals to include specific references to anti-Semitism—proposals which were not successful.[80] Indigenous matters arising on the draft Convention at the level of the Sub-Commission on the Prevention of Discrimination and Protection of Minorities elicited statements of concern as well as care on the part of the experts. Abram implicitly brought indigenous peoples into focus in his appreciation of the scope of discrimination, counselling sternly that 'all forms of discrimination which deprive ... an ethnic group of the means of continuing its culture and maintaining its traditions ... should be made an offence under the Convention'.[81] Referring to a proposal by Latin American countries, Cuevas Cancino maintained that 'the protection of certain groups [does] not constitute discrimination'.[82] Others warned of the dangers of introducing group rights into the text. A proposal by Ivanov to insert a reference to the right of racial, national and ethnic groups of the population to take part in the work of legislative and executive bodies[83] prompted an objection by Ferguson, who argued that this might give rise to serious difficulties because 'the proposal depart[s] from the sphere of individual rights and might lead to discrimination in reverse'.[84]

At the level of the Commission on Human Rights, the link between the limitations on special measures in what became Articles 1.4 and 2.2 of the Convention was explained by Chile as embodying concern 'for the protection of aboriginal communities and, more specifically, in order to prevent the separate development of various communities being frozen into

[80] The drafting history of the Convention is accounted for extensively in N Lerner, *The UN Convention on the Elimination of All Forms of Racial Discrimination* (Alphen aan den Rijn, Sijthoff and Noordhoff, 1980).

[81] E/CN.4/Sub.2/SR.411, p 5.

[82] Ibid, p 9.

[83] E/CN.4/Sub.2/SR.423, pp 5–6.

[84] Ibid, p 7. He added, ibid, that the Sub-Commission draft 'should confine itself to the individual and define everything which might harm the rights of the individual'. Among other objections, it was felt by Calvocoressi that 'by introducing the idea of the rights of groups [the] proposal might involve the Sub-Commission in a prolonged debate', E/CN.4/Sub.2/SR.423, p 7. In withdrawing the proposal, Ivanov considered nonetheless that 'those groups [have] the right to take part in the work of legislative and executive organs', E/CN.4/Sub.2/424, p 6.

permanency'.[85] Chile later returned to this topic to contend that 'the apparently privileged treatment' meted out to a substantial group of indigenous inhabitants was not racial discrimination, rather it 'was merely intended to ensure the integrated development of the population as a whole and to avoid the perpetuation of certain divisions'.[86] Latin American countries, it was averred before the Third Committee, were countries 'whose peoples had always enjoyed complete integration'.[87] These and allied sentiments contribute to the shorthand description of the Convention as an integrationist instrument. Indigenous peoples, it may be observed, had a largely negative experience of the workings of 'integration' before and through an earlier age of international standard-setting represented by ILO Convention 107 on Indigenous and Tribal Populations.[88] The perception of indigenous peoples as distinctive groups surfaced occasionally in discussions. Thus, Ecuador argued before the Commission that, in international law, 'the emphasis ha[s] shifted over the years from the individual ... to the group ... In Latin America there [is] a large indigenous population, the members of which [are] more aware of their existence as members of a group than of their existence as individuals.'[89]

Consciousness of indigenous issues developed over the first 20 years or so of CERD activity. Banton points out the slowness of some States parties to ICERD to accept that the racial discrimination paradigm applied to indigenous peoples within their jurisdiction.[90] In the case of Latin American States, he suggests that this was because of their understanding that racial discrimination related essentially to the situation in the USA and South Africa.[91] Initial comments of States parties evidently travelled on the same conceptual track as in the drafting phases of the Convention. The Committee worked over the years to tease out information on the policies of States towards indigenous peoples, and on the impact of policies on their supposed beneficiaries. Lines to be drawn between integration and assimilation, and between segregation and autonomy, were also the subject of the Committee's explorations.[92] Some governments resisted the Committee's questions on indigenous issues, linking those

[85] E/CN.4/SR.785, p 4.
[86] E/CN.4/SR.787, p 5.
[87] A/C.3/SR.1300, para 28.
[88] Thornberry (n 9) chs 13 and 14.
[89] E/CN.4/SR.784, p 10.
[90] M Banton, *International Action against Racial Discrimination* (Oxford, Clarendon Press, 1996) esp 230ff.
[91] Ibid, 230.
[92] Banton (ibid, 232) cites a reply of the representative of Argentina to the Committee in 1982, that 'it was very difficult to promote development without integration and the danger was ever present of segregating people on the pretext of autonomy'.

questions with a claim based on their impressions that 'Western European' standards were being applied in the Committee.[93] Diverse opinions within the Committee were also in evidence, with some members favouring assimilationist policies towards the indigenous, and, it may be added, towards minorities.[94] State reports evinced—slowly and under pressure from CERD amongst others—a growing awareness of the ethnic complexity of their societies, reducing the number of instances where the demographics were guarded as 'secretly as a thought in a dark mind'.[95] Many States moved towards a politics of recognising diversity, including indigenous peoples, and away from the ideology of homogeneous single identities, despite arguments about the lack of physical distinctions between the indigenous and others, and the categorisation of indigenous issues as essentially resulting from problems of unequal development.

The argument of homogeneity is heard less often at CERD, but may still arise through the reluctance of States to either accept the complexity of their populations or accept the term 'indigenous peoples'. Recent responses of CERD to such claims in the indigenous context include its recommendation to the Lao People's Democratic Republic that, despite the State party's reluctance to do so, it should 'recognise the rights of persons belonging to minorities and indigenous peoples as set out in international law, regardless of the name given to such groups in domestic law',[96] and to Botswana, that it 'review its policy regarding indigenous peoples and, to that end … take into consideration the way in which the groups concerned perceive and define themselves'.[97] The Committee critiqued the report of El Salvador, noting once again 'the discrepancy between the assessment made by the State party, according to which society in El Salvador is ethnically homogeneous, and reliable reports indicating that indigenous peoples … live in the country';[98] the Committee accordingly requested disaggregated statistics on the ethnic composition of the population.[99] Committee recommendations and requests in this area display an increasing scepticism towards claims by States to ethnic homogeneity.[100] Scepticism may deepen in the face of State claims that what the Committee sees as indigenous or tribal

[93] Ibid, 233.

[94] P Thornberry, *International Law and the Rights of Minorities* (Oxford, Clarendon Press, 1991) part V.

[95] RS Thomas, 'The Ancients of the World' in *Collected Poems of RS Thomas 1945–90* (London, JM Dent, 1993).

[96] A/60/18, para 169.

[97] A61/18, para 58.

[98] Ibid, para 84.

[99] Ibid.

[100] Thornberry (n 19) 241, fn 12, gives further examples of deniers of complexity or deniers of racial discrimination in their territories.

groups, whatever name is employed to describe them by the State party, are not covered by the Convention.[101] Two General Recommendations in particular form part of CERD's conceptual apparatus for recognising groups and members thereof. General Recommendation 8 privileges the notion of self-identification with a group as the 'recognition of membership' criterion to be adopted, if 'no justification exists to the contrary'.[102] General Recommendation 24 states that, in terms of recognition of ethnic groups or indigenous peoples, '[c]ertain criteria should be uniformly applied to all groups',[103] and that the application of non-objective criteria, leading to the recognition of some groups and refusal to recognise others, can raise an issue of discrimination. The recommendation also states the Committee's view in relation to 'ethnic groups or indigenous peoples' that 'there is an international standard concerning the specific rights of people belonging to such groups'.

SHAPING THE CERD PROFILE ON INDIGENOUS RIGHTS

The further process of shaping of CERD's profile on indigenous questions suggests that the Committee profited from a set of Kairotic moments[104] to develop its views. The following markers of discourse and procedural development (by no means an exhaustive list) are worthy of particular note: General Recommendation 23, the enhanced integration of indigenous questions into CERD's early warning and urgent action procedure, and ongoing debates concerning special measures and indigenous rights. In these cases, developments in indigenous rights have left their imprint, and the Declaration is capable of providing further benchmarks for the development of the Convention.

General Recommendation 23

The recommendation, adopted at the 51st session of the Committee in 1997, represents the broadest statement of indigenous rights made by the Committee. General Recommendation 23 enjoys the continuing confidence of the Committee, and is regularly re-evoked when circumstances

[101] In the case of India, the Committee noted with concern that 'the State party does not recognize its tribal peoples as distinct groups entitled to special protection under the Convention': A/62/18, para 168. This was followed, ibid, by a recommendation that the tribal peoples be formally recognised 'as distinct groups entitled to special protection under national and international law'.

[102] A/45/18, chapter VII.1.

[103] A/54/18, Annex V.

[104] From the Greek *Kairos*: the opportune moment, the sense of which is also captured in the Latin 'carpe diem'.

demand. Importantly, in light of comments on the Declaration, it broaches the issue of 'informed consent'. In 1997, the Declaration was in the process of being drafted,[105] and ILO Convention 169 had entered into force. Concluding observations of CERD had been adopted as the collective opinion of the Committee only since 1991. Since that time, they had become more elaborate and reflected the enhanced consciousness of the situation of indigenous peoples brought about by Convention 169 and the draft declaration. States were commended by CERD for ratifying Convention 169,[106] and encouraged to consider doing so if they had not.[107] The practice of recommending ratification of ILO 169 became common practice,[108] and continues to this day. In General Recommendation 23, interest attaches in particular to paragraph 4(d) whereby States parties are called upon in particular to ensure that 'members of indigenous peoples have equal rights in respect of effective participation in public life and that no decisions directly relating to their rights and interests are taken without their informed consent'; and paragraph 5, wherein:

> The Committee especially calls upon States parties to recognize and protect the rights of indigenous peoples to own, develop, control and use their communal lands, territories and resources and, where they have been deprived of their lands and territories traditionally owned or otherwise inhabited or used without their free and informed consent, to take steps to return those lands and territories. Only when this is for factual reasons not possible, the right to restitution should be substituted by the right to just, fair and prompt compensation. Such compensation should as far as possible take the form of lands and territories.

The provisions in the recommendation on informed consent were a particular focus of discussion. Some members recalled the limitations in ILO Convention 169[109] on informed consent—ie that the Convention did not imply a right of veto on the part of indigenous peoples.[110] CERD member Diaconu raised the point that 'the idea of consent implie[s] the right

[105] The Working Group on Indigenous Populations had agreed a text in July 1993, and the Sub-Commission on the Prevention of Discrimination and Protection of Minorities adopted the text in 1994: E/CN.4/1995/2; E/CN.4/Sub.2/1994/56, p 105.

[106] Norway was an early example, being the first State to ratify ILO Convention 169: A/49/18, para 251. Peru was another country commended for ratifying: A50/18, para 196. Countries were also questioned in terms of the rights set out in Convention 169—Australia was one example: A/49/18, paras 512–51.

[107] An early example is in the concluding observations on Guatemala, A/50/18, para 317.

[108] See eg the concluding observations in A/51/18, para 189 (Finland), and para 310 (Brazil); A/52/18, para 355 (Panama); A/53/18, para 46 (Russian Federation).

[109] Arts 6 and 7 of Convention 169 are particularly relevant here, establishing modalities for 'consultation' and 'participation of indigenous peoples in applying the principles of the Convention'.

[110] See also M Tomei and L Swepston, *Indigenous and Tribal Peoples: A Guide to ILO Convention No 169* (Geneva, International Labour Office, 1996) 8–9.

to veto, which [is] not in conformity with the spirit of ILO Convention 169, which [is] based, rather, on the idea of consultation through the appropriate channels. In some cases ... there [is] cause to insist on prior consensus but there [are] many other cases where a small community could hinder the taking of decisions that would be of benefit to all citizens. The Committee should be careful not to innovate in that regard.'[111] Other members took a stronger line in favour of the principle of informed consent.[112] On the substance of the recommendation, it seems clear enough that members were influenced by the (then) draft UN Declaration on the Rights of Indigenous Peoples, as well as developments in Latin America.[113]

Paragraph 4 distinguishes between a 'general' right of effective participation in public life and a narrower principle insisting on informed consent when 'decisions' directly relating to the rights and interests of indigenous peoples are concerned.[114] 'Informed consent' was expressly preferred to 'informed participation'.[115] In concrete cases, the Committee has not always rigorously insisted on principles of informed consent, even in cases where there was a clear opportunity to follow this principle and General Recommendation 23 was recalled.[116] However, the principle of informed consent is now 'standard', and is factored into concluding observations when members of CERD sense that an issue has arisen. Committee references to the necessity of informed consent are usually coupled with a recall of General Recommendation 23, though in some

[111] CERD/C/SR.1235, paras 69 and 78. Caution was also expressed by members Ahmadu (para 70), Shahi (para 73), and Van Boven (para 71).

[112] The notion of a right to veto was supported specifically by CERD members Aboul-Nasr (SR/1235, para 72), Valencia Rodriguez (para 77), Wolfrum, (paras 67, 74, 80) and Garvalov (para 82). According to Garvalov (CERD/C/SR.1235, para 82), 'the two terms "consent" and "participation" mean ... entirely different things. If indigenous peoples [are] to give their "consent" they must agree to the proposal; they [may] "participate" and express their approval or disapproval, without actually having any power over the final decision. [I prefer] the word "consent".'

[113] Wolfrum, SR.1235, para 93. For a review of such, see JM Pasqualucci, 'The Evolution of International Indigenous Rights in the Inter-American Human Rights System' (2006) 6(2) *Human Rights Law Review* 281–322.

[114] See comments by Wolfrum, SR.1235, paras 67, 74 and 75; and Aboul-Nasr, ibid, para 72.

[115] CERD/C/SR.1235, para 60 (Wolfrum, referring to a proposal by Diaconu).

[116] For example in relation to Suriname, the Committee, noting the State party's assertion that 'there are mechanisms guaranteeing that indigenous and tribal peoples are notified and consulted before any forestry and or mining concessions within their lands are awarded', expressed concern that 'consultation of that kind is rare'. It invited the authorities 'to check that established mechanisms for notifying and consulting the indigenous and tribal peoples are working, and recommended that Suriname strive to reach agreements with the peoples concerned ... before awarding concessions': A/59/18, para 192. While General Recommendation 23 is recalled in the observations, we note the absence of reference to informed consent in the observations.

cases they float free of any anchoring point. Of particular interest in this last respect is the 2007 recommendation to India urging the State party to 'seek the prior informed consent' of communities affected by the construction of dams in the North-East, and provide adequate compensation and alternative land and housing to those communities.[117] The Committee's approach to the issue of consent is in line with the Declaration in its draft and finally adopted versions. The potential ramifications of 'free, prior and informed consent' figured among the catalogue of concerns relating to the Declaration raised by some States in the General Assembly.[118]

Indigenous Peoples, Early Warning and Urgent Action

Although neither the Declaration nor CERD has definitively reconnoitred the whole ground covered by the term 'indigenous peoples', CERD's appreciation of indigenous peoples as *whole and distinct societies* has gained considerable coherence under the Committee's early warning and urgent action procedure. The initial (1993) working paper of the Committee on early warning and urgent action was prompted by post-Cold War developments in the field of ethnic conflict. The context for fresh enhancement of a preventive approach on the part of CERD included the report of the UN Secretary-General, *An Agenda for Peace*,[119] and his report to the UN General Assembly for 1992.[120] As summarised in subsequent annual reports of the Committee, Committee efforts to prevent serious violations would include the following:

> *Early-warning measures*: ... criteria for early warning would include ... the lack of an adequate legislative basis for defining and criminalizing all forms of racial discrimination ... inadequate implementation of enforcement mechanisms... the presence of a pattern of escalating racial hatred and violence, or racist propaganda or appeals to racial intolerance by persons, groups or organizations, notably by elected or other officials; a significant pattern of racial discrimination evidenced in social and economic indicators; and significant flows of refugees or displaced persons resulting from a pattern of racial discrimination or encroachment on the lands of minority communities; *Urgent procedures*: these would aim at responding to problems requiring immediate attention ... Possible criteria for initiating an urgent procedure could include the presence of a serious, massive or persistent pattern of racial discrimination; or that the situation is serious and there is a risk of further racial discrimination.

[117] A/62/18, para 177. See also para 178.

[118] See in particular the speeches of the representatives of Australia and Canada, A/61/PV/107, pp 11–13.

[119] A/47/277-S/24111, in particular paras 15, 18, 20 and 23.

[120] A/47/1.

CERD adopted new guidelines at its 71st session in 2007 which merge the former 'procedures' into one early warning and urgent action 'procedure'.[121] The 2007 guidelines are more explicit than those of 1993 in making reference to indigenous peoples, who were subsumed in the 1993 paper under 'minorities', 'minority communities' or 'racial minorities'. Indicators for triggering the procedure include the important qualification that, since such indicators 'may be present in situations not requiring immediate attention to prevent and limit serious violations of the Convention, the Committee shall assess their significance *in light of the gravity and scale of the situation*,[122] including the escalation of violence or irreparable harm that may be caused to victims of discrimination'.[123] The 'gravity and scale' aspect of the guidelines is of particular importance in the indigenous context since threats that would not disturb the equilibrium of large societies might have disastrous effects on societies constructed on a smaller scale. The list of indicators[124] triggering the procedure includes significant and persistent patterns of racial discrimination, etc, with a specific reference to encroachment 'on the traditional lands of indigenous peoples or forced removal of these peoples from their lands, in particular for the purpose of exploitation of natural resources', as well as 'polluting or hazardous activities that reflect a pattern of racial discrimination with substantial harm to specific groups'. As observed, the 1993 'encroachment' reference is the less specific 'lands of minority communities'. The most outstanding of the indigenous cases under the early warning rules have concerned Australia's Native Title Amendment Act 1998,[125] New Zealand's Seabed and Foreshore Act 2004,[126] and the actions of the authorities in the USA towards the Western Shoshone.[127] Cases have involved Committee decisions, the texts of which are included in their annual reports, and letters from the Chairman to States parties. Recent sessions of the Committee have also utilised the reporting follow-up procedure if available—if there has been a recent report of the State party.[128]

[121] A/62/18, Annex III.

[122] Present author's emphasis.

[123] 2007 guidelines, para 12. Further comment on the importance of the early warning criteria to indigenous peoples is offered below.

[124] Ibid.

[125] CERD decisions 1 (53), A/53/18, Chapter II B; 2 (54), A/54/18, Chapter II A, and 2 (55), Chapter II C. See also the concluding observations of the Committee under the periodic report system, A/55/18, paras 23–43, and A/60/18, paras 21–48.

[126] Decision 1 (66), A60/18, Chapter II; and concluding observations on New Zealand, A/62/18, paras 434–66, para 452. See also A Erueti and C Charters (eds), *Māori Property Rights and the Foreshore and Seabed: The Last Frontier* (Wellington, Victoria University Press, 2007).

[127] Decision 1 (68), A61/18, Chapter II A. See also concluding observations on the report of the USA, A/63/18, paras 472–517, para 490.

[128] A/63/18, chapter II.

The Committee's regular consideration under the early warning and 'regular' reporting procedures of the effects of mining, logging and related activities by public or corporate bodies on indigenous lands may lead in time to a General Recommendation to clarify responsibilities. The Declaration's provisions on lands, territories and resources can provide more specific guidance than hitherto for any such venture. The proposition that business corporations should respect State laws on racial discrimination is implicit in CERD recommendations, though the question of how such responsibility intersects with the principle of State responsibility is relatively undeveloped. Elaborations of principle have recently been made in connection with indigenous peoples in cases including those of Canada and the United States. In concluding observations on Canada, CERD combined an observation on transnational corporations with an observation on 'extraterritoriality', recommending that 'the State party explore ways to hold transnational corporations registered in Canada accountable', requesting information in its next periodic report 'on the effects of activities of transnational corporations registered in Canada on indigenous peoples abroad and on any measures taken'.[129] The principles were further elaborated in concluding observations on the United States: 'the Committee encourages the State party to take appropriate legislative or administrative measures to prevent acts of transnational corporations registered in the State party which negatively impact on the enjoyment of rights of indigenous peoples in territories outside the United States. In particular, the Committee recommends that the State party explore ways to hold transnational corporations in the United States accountable.'[130]

Special Measures and Indigenous Rights

Indigenous groups and minorities enjoy their own rights in international law that stand independently of Convention provisions on special measures—the Declaration solidifies this situation forcefully. The Committee does not always distinguish cases of 'recognition of specific minority/indigenous rights' from 'special measures', but recommendations to States parties concerning indigenous groups may be made within and without the special measures paradigm.[131] A renewed surge of interest in the concept of special measures and how it relates to minority and

[129] A/62/18, para 78.
[130] A/63/18, para 501.
[131] See eg the Concluding Observations on Bangladesh on special measures—A/56/18, para 66. For a more wide-ranging set of recommendations, including many not confined to a 'special measures' or 'affirmative action' framework, see A/57/18, paras 315–43—Concluding Observations on Canada.

indigenous rights is evident from Committee discussion of the 17th periodic report of New Zealand.[132] The report incorporated an extensive section on special measures in accordance with Article 2.2 of the Convention which included a range of information on, inter alia, Maori fisheries, the Foreshore and Seabed Act, the Maori Land Act, Maori and Pasifika education, Maori language, etc.[133] The extent of the materials included under special measures provoked a question by the country rapporteur on why the State party considered that historical treaty settlements constituted special measures.[134] The issue was pressed by other Committee members who argued that distinctions should be drawn between such special measures and indigenous and minority rights, notably that special measures under Article 2.2 were exceptional and temporary in nature whereas indigenous and minority rights were to be enjoyed when the communities in question enjoyed a presence in the State party.[135] A statement by the New Zealand Race Relations Commissioner supported the members' critique in this respect—the Commissioner had 'made it clear that special measures should not be confused with the Government's treaty obligations, indigenous rights, or general social and economic measures tailored to particular ethnic groups'.[136] The response of the New Zealand delegation suggested that, in light of comments by Committee members on the scope of special measures, the matter could be reconsidered.[137]

The concerns of the Committee related in part to the potential fragility of historical settlements (including the Treaty of Waitangi) if included, even implicitly, as a temporary measure, a perception advanced by Maori groups in their submissions to the Committee.[138] In its concluding observations on New Zealand the Committee stated its concern that 'in the report of the State party, historical treaty settlements have been categorized as special measures for the adequate development and protection of Maori', while noting that 'the statement made by the delegation that such categorization should indeed be reconsidered'. Accordingly, the Committee drew the attention of the State party 'to the distinction to be drawn between special and temporary measures for the advancement

[132] Fifteenth, sixteenth and seventeenth reports of New Zealand, submitted as one document, CERD/C/NZL/17, 18 July 2006.

[133] CERD/C/NZL/17, paras 51–172.

[134] Sicilianos, CERD/C/SR.1821, para 38.

[135] Discussions at the 1,821st and 1,822nd meetings, 31 July and 2 August 2007.

[136] Statement by Joris de Bres, Race Relations Commissioner, New Zealand Human Rights Commission (on file with author). See also 'Guidelines on Measures to Ensure Equality', prepared by the New Zealand Human Rights Commission (undated, on file with author).

[137] CERD/C/SR.1822, para 21.

[138] Treaty Tribes Coalition, Aotearoa Indigenous Rights Trust, Maori Party, Te Wh nau-a-Apanui, and Peace Movement Aotearoa.

of ethnic groups on the one hand and permanent rights of indigenous peoples on the other hand'.[139]

The Committee held a thematic discussion on special measures in August 2008, and, as noted above, adopted a General Recommendation on special measures in August 2009. The recommendation robustly consolidates CERD practice in distinguishing permanent rights from special measures:

> Special measures should not be confused with specific rights pertaining to certain categories of person or community, such as ... the rights of indigenous peoples, including rights to lands traditionally occupied by them ... States parties should carefully observe distinctions between special measures and permanent human rights in their law and practice. The distinction between special measures and permanent rights implies that those entitled to permanent rights may also enjoy the benefits of special measures.[140]

The recommendation also states that 'special measures should clearly benefit groups and individuals in their enjoyment of human rights',[141] as well as counselling that States parties 'should ensure that special measures are designed and implemented on the basis of prior consultations with affected communities and the active participation of such communities'[142]—a provision that assists communities in securing genuine benefit from the measures in terms that they understand and accept. The accumulation of cautions suggests that not every domestic description of laws, policies or practices as 'special measures' will necessarily equate to special measures under the Convention.

The Convention and the Declaration: Symbiosis—And a Hint of Antibiosis?

The principle of non-discrimination aspires to hold the balance between the persons and communities that make up the fabric of society,[143] trying to ensure that a general equity prevails, so that the ascription of rights to some does not deny rights to others: respect for human rights should not be reduced to a zero sum game. The principle is rigid on the unacceptability of unequal treatment, while its understanding of equality is flexible and nuanced. The Convention does not however identify Ordnance

[139] CERD/C/NZL/CO/17, 15 August 2007, para 15.

[140] CERD/C/75/Misc.7/Rev.2, para 15 (unedited version, on file with the OHCHR Secretariat).

[141] Ibid, para 33.

[142] Ibid, para 18.

[143] Relevant versions of this principle include the account in general comment 23 of the Human Rights Committee, CCPR/C/21/Rev.1/Add.5 (1994).

Survey pathways to the flourishing of identities as in the Declaration but offers broad and open-ended statements of rights. The Convention in this sense is a 'bare bones' instrument, and the richness of detail in CERD engagement with the specifics of indigenous rights clearly owes a debt to post-Convention developments.

The introduction to the present paper referred to the ostensible differences and similarities between the programme of the Convention and the programme of the Declaration. The quantum leaps described above were instances where the non-discrimination principle gained specificity through CERD internalisation of indigenous rights. Harder questions for normative integration as well as general understanding are identified here: the identification of 'indigenous peoples' and the limits to be placed on the enjoyment of indigenous rights, approaches to self-determination, and the relationship between individual and collective rights.

On the first two of these, in refining its ideas concerning indigenous peoples, CERD has recognised indigenous societies as holistic societies with a particular 'take' on human rights, frequently denied full enjoyment of those rights.[144] This implies respect for their rights as developed through the specific instruments as well as more general statements. The canvas on which indigenous rights are portrayed is global: the terminology has been applied to all continents, and includes both the products of colonialism and the actions of post-colonial elites in marginalising groups within their societies. Reference has already been made to CERD's endorsement of the self-identification principle as applied in General Recommendation 8. It will be recalled that the recommendation places self-identification as a member of a racial or ethnic group in pole position 'if no justification exists to the contrary', an important qualification in order to defeat absurd claims of 'belonging' by those without community connection or acceptance. With this last qualification, CERD's understanding of *who is indigenous* prefers self-definition to more historically determined approaches or outsider-determined approaches, including those often preferred by the public administrations of States.[145] There has also, it seems, been an intuition at work in CERD practice associating

[144] For a reflection on the concept 'indigenous peoples' see Thornberry (n 9) ch 2.

[145] The stance of the Declaration is rather curious in this respect. Self-identification was explicitly referred to in early drafts but does not figure in the final text, Art 9 of which provides (in a formulation that is not a model of clarity) that 'Indigenous peoples and nations have the right to belong to an indigenous community or nation, in accordance with the traditions and customs of the community or nation concerned.' Community input into identity decisions is confirmed by Art 33: 'Indigenous peoples have the right to determine their own identity or membership in accordance with their customs and traditions.' The significance of dropping the self-identification phrase is well discussed in J Gilbert, 'Indigenous Rights in the Making: The United Nations Declaration on the Rights of Indigenous Peoples' (2007) 14 *International Journal on Minority and Group Rights* 207–30.

'indigenousness' with a vulnerable position in the State.[146] In the absence of structured definitional formulae or a fully affirmed epistemology, the status of claiming groups (or claiming governments) is necessarily appraised in context.

The question of who counts as indigenous has recently been raised in the case of Fiji.[147] The population balance between indigenous Fijians and indo-Fijians is almost even, and indigenous Fijians control the land base and are the dominant group as regards the institutions of state. The Committee, as it had done in relation to a previous report of Fiji,[148] coupled the 'who is indigenous?' question with a question on how the enjoyment of indigenous rights affected the enjoyment of human rights by everyone in the State. The Committee thus recommended that:

> The State party reflect further on how the concept of 'indigenous' Fijians relates to the understanding of indigenous peoples in international law, in particular as reflected in [ILO] Convention 169 and the 2007 United Nations Declaration on the Rights of Indigenous Peoples. Furthermore, the State party is invited to explain how the concept of indigenous Fijians is applied in law and practice and its impact on the enjoyment of human rights by everyone in Fiji.[149]

In pressing questions to the State party, members of the Committee queried the use of the term 'indigenous people',[150] or asked for further explanations regarding its use in this context.[151] Questions were also asked regarding the nature of the relationship between the indigenous communities and their lands on the basis, inter alia, of the concern that 'the current status of land distribution on the State party inhibits the economic

146 The reference to the scale and gravity of threats to indigenous peoples under the 2007 guidelines for CERD's early warning system also bears out this perception.

147 See also the discussion by M Scheinin, 'What are Indigenous Peoples?' in N Ghanea and A Xanthaki (eds), *Minorities, Peoples and Self-Determination* (Leiden, Martinus Nijhoff, 2005) 3–13.

148 'The Committee welcomes the commitment of the State party to ensure the social and economic development as well as the right to cultural identity of the indigenous Fijian community. None of these programmes, however, should abrogate or diminish the enjoyment of human rights for all', A/58/18, para 84. See ME Salomon, 'Masking Inequality in the Name of Rights: The Examination of Fiji's State Report under the International Convention on the Elimination of All Forms of Discrimination' (2003) 4 *Asia-Pacific Journal on Human Rights and the Law* 52–85.

149 A/63/18, para 168.

150 Lindgren Alves recalled that 'it [is] odd to apply the term "indigenous people" to the majority group in power since it normally refer[s] to persecuted minority groups', CERD/C/SR/1850, para 36.

151 Thornberry stated that it is 'an unusual situation when an indigenous people [is] in a dominant position in a State ... that raise[s] questions about the definition of the term "indigenous peoples". The Declaration on the Rights of Indigenous Peoples [does] not offer such a definition, though it [does] place some limitations on indigenous rights. That issue illustrate[s] the fact that much thought still need[s] to be given to the relationship between the norms of the Declaration and those of ICERD and other human rights instruments', CERD/C/SR.1850, para 41.

development of non-indigenous communities'.[152] Fiji, it may be noted, is a party to ILO Convention 169, and assured the Committee that the State constitution 'was formulated to comply with the Draft Declaration [on the rights of Indigenous Peoples], even though this instrument has yet to come into force'.[153]

Fiji may not be the only State where such questions will arise, and CERD may need to sharpen its conceptual tools and provide clearer conclusions. The point is less about majorities[154] than about dominant groups, an aspect of what is, in Scheinin's terms, the 'relational' aspect of indigenousness—when a group has attained power in the Nation State.[155] In the analogous area of minority rights, 'non-dominance' has been offered as a qualifying criterion for the recognition of minorities.[156] Concerning indigenous populations, the African Commission on Human Rights factors into its conceptualisation the notion of 'a state of subjugation, marginalisation, dispossession, exclusion, or discrimination because these peoples may have different cultures, ways of life or modes of production than the national hegemonic and dominant model'.[157] It should be observed that marginalisation is only one of a cluster of factors in this recognition strategy:[158] others include self-identification and cultural attachment to land,[159] and even 'marginalisation' itself is bound up with culture and ways of life. This is important in light of arguments that a group in a dominant position would lose the protection of indigenous rights.[160] Such a conclusion cannot be arrived at easily. In the

[152] Ibid, para 177.

[153] CERD/C/FJI/17, para 20. In discussions with the Committee, the representative of Fiji observed in relation to Convention 169 that the Government was aware that, 'under Article 1(3) of that Convention, the term "peoples" should not be interpreted in any way that could affect individuals' rights under international law', CERD/C/SR.1850, para 3.

[154] There are ostensible indigenous majorities in eg Bolivia and Guatemala and this has not inhibited the recognition of indigenous peoples therein by CERD and other bodies: see concluding observations on Bolivia, A/58/18, paras 327–50, and Guatemala, A/61/18, paras 101–28.

[155] Scheinin (n 147) 12.

[156] The *locus classicus* is the study of Capotorti on the Rights of Persons Belonging to Ethnic, Religious and Linguistic Minorities, UN Sales No E.91.XIV.2 (New York, United Nations, 1991) para 568. See also the Opinion of the Venice Commission (European Commission on Democracy through Law) on possible groups in Belgium to which the Framework Convention on National Minorities could apply, CDL-AD (2002) 001.

[157] Advisory Opinion of the African Commission on Human and Peoples' Rights on the United Nations Declaration on the Rights of Indigenous Peoples, adopted at its 41st ordinary session in May 2007, para 12(c).

[158] See also Thornberry (n 9) ch 2.

[159] The land issue is elaborated as: 'A special attachment to and use of their traditional land whereby their ancestral land and territory have a fundamental importance for their collective physical and cultural survival as peoples', *African Commission Advisory Opinion*, para 12(b).

[160] Scheinin (n 147, 12) draws the conclusion that the situation of indigenous dominance in Fiji may 'in the future' lead to the non-applicability of minority rights in the sense of

first place there will be a wide spectrum of group situations between 'non-marginalisation' and 'State dominance', and all relevant descriptors of situations are likely to need further conceptual unpacking. The argument also downgrades the 'cluster of factors' approach to recognition through *a contrario* reliance on a single factor. In the interests of conceptual clarity, we need to be wary of conflating the conceptualisation of indigenousness with the rights strategy employed by a group to secure its existence as a discrete entity.

The Declaration recalls oppression and victimisation of indigenous peoples, but its governing concepts are those of self-determination and inherent rights of indigenous peoples deriving from, in the words of the preamble, 'their political, economic and social structures and from their cultures, spiritual traditions, histories and philosophies, especially their rights to their lands, territories and resources'.[161] Perhaps the real point is not an argument about who is indigenous but that a State dominant group is unlikely to have the greatest need for the protections accorded by indigenous rights, though the manner in which it exercises rights may still be guided by the Declaration. The further CERD observation to Fiji about indigenous rights not overbearing the rights of others simply marks out the role for the non-discrimination principle as holding a balance between groups. As noted above, the non-discrimination principle is already extensively accounted for in the Declaration so that in principle, Declaration and Convention sing from the same hymn-sheet.

Concerning *self-determination*, one of the most important *topoi* in the Declaration, the Committee's account of this principle in General Recommendation 21[162] does not make specific reference to indigenous peoples; the closest it comes is in references to ethnic or religious groups and minorities. The summary records of the Committee do not greatly illuminate the extent to which the draft might have been influenced by developments in indigenous rights. The normative referents in discussions are to the UN Charter, the Declaration on Friendly Relations of 1970,[163] Article 27 of the ICCPR, and the UN Declaration on the Rights of Persons Belonging to Minorities.[164] The situations in Kosovo and Chechnya are also referred to.[165] The recommendation distinguishes

ART 27 of the Covenant on Civil and Political Rights and of the protection accorded by ILO Convention 169. On the other hand, he argues, ibid, that the indigenous people coming into power 'retains its status as a people'.

[161] Preambular para 7.

[162] A/51/18, Annex VIII B.

[163] General Assembly Resolution 2625 (XXV), 24 October 1970.

[164] Adopted by General Assembly 47/135, 18 December 1992.

[165] The draft was introduced by CERD member Wolfrum, CERD/C/SR.1084, para 72. A reasonably substantial discussion is recorded in CERD/C/SR.1147, paras 23–43.

between 'internal' and 'external' self-determination, links the rights of peoples with respect for individual human rights, and robustly declares that, in the view of the Committee, 'international law has not recognized a general right of peoples unilaterally to declare secession from a State'.[166] The recommendation nonetheless assumes that self-determination is a continuing right,[167] and reads it to underpin sensitivity towards the rights of minorities and their rights to engage in activities 'which are particularly relevant to the preservation of their identity'. An anti-secessionist ethos as regards minorities within States animated much of the discussions, and some CERD members expressed an awareness that minorities and peoples are not clearly distinguished in international law.

In view of CERD's citation of the Declaration as a guide to States in the implementation of indigenous policies, it is presumptively the case that the Committee's understanding of self-determination is broadly in line with its expression in the Declaration.[168] This would, *ex facie*, imply assent to the propositions in the preamble to the Declaration such as that 'indigenous peoples are equal to all other peoples'. The equality of peoples propositions in the operative articles are equally forthright, and the now famous Article 3 offers a ringing endorsement of the principle of self-determination to indigenous peoples.[169] The evocation by the Committee of internal and external self-determination finds its echo in the territorial integrity protecting Article 46(1) of the Declaration. The acceptance of indigenous self-determination by States has often been on the basis that it does not disturb territorial integrity and that it is specific to the indigenous. Hence for example the explanation of support by Japan for the adopted Declaration:

> The revised version of article 46[170] correctly clarifies that the right of self-determination does not give indigenous peoples the right to be separate and independent from their country of residence and that that right shall not be invoked for the purpose of impairing a State's sovereignty, national and

[166] The annual report of CERD, A/51/18, confusingly runs together General Recommendations 20 and 21. The above citation is listed in the report as para 11, but is in fact para 6 of General Recommendation 21.

[167] Comments of van Boven, CERD/C/SR.1147, para 27.

[168] Among current treatments of indigenous self-determination, see Xanthaki (n 9); P Aikio and M Scheinin (eds), *Operationalizing the Right of Indigenous Peoples to Self-Determination* (Turku/Åbo, Institute for Human Rights, Åbo Akademi University, 2000).

[169] Above, n 8.

[170] Art 46(1) of the Declaration provides that nothing therein 'may be interpreted as implying for any state, people, group or person any right to engage in any activity or perform any act contrary to the Charter of the United Nations or construed as authorizing or encouraging any action which would dismember or impair, totally or in part, the territorial integrity or political unity of sovereign States.'

political unity or territorial integrity. The Government of Japan shares that understanding of that right and we welcome the revision.[171]

CERD's continuing line on self-determination is likely to follow this cautious approach, and it remains to be seen to what extent the Committee will choose to evoke the principle of self-determination when generic references to the Declaration would suffice. And even in its excursus into 'big' self-determination in General Recommendation 21, the principle is largely read therein as a kind of meta-concept, subsuming within its embrace a range of specific human rights essential to the survival of diverse cultures. In practice, CERD is generally concerned with the smaller field, the minutiae of human rights, and its approach to indigenous peoples reflects this perspective. CERD does not always need self-determination language to express its concerns for the vindication of indigenous rights.

Beyond self-determination, CERD regularly endorses the *collective rights* of indigenous peoples in a variety of contexts and has not been in the habit of stressing the incompatibility of categories of rights. The Committee commonly places collective and individual rights together in a common recommendation,[172] or employs generic terms such as 'communal ownership',[173] or phrases specific to a people such as 'Saami rights'.[174] The Committee must be referring, at least in some cases, to collective rights where the right inheres in the community as such so that it could in principle be invoked against members of the community.[175] If such a question is highlighted before the Committee, perhaps a 'balancing' metaphor, such as that employed in the *Lovelace* case by the Human Rights Committee,[176] would be regarded as appropriate, though CERD's focus on discrimination could set the bar even higher against any asserted primacy of collective rights over those of individuals. On the other hand, the perception of communities at risk would itself tip the

[171] A/61/PV.107, p 20. The text may be compared with that adopted by the Human Rights Council in June 2006, Art 46(1) of which read: 'Nothing in this Declaration may be interpreted as implying for any State, people, group or person any right to engage in any activity or to perform any act contrary to the Charter of the United Nations.' The observations of Japan were echoed in a range of comments by States at the adoption of the Declaration. As far as self-determination is concerned the State comments are at something of a tangent to indigenous understandings of the principle, which are, in general, unconcerned with questions of secession and independence.

[172] Concluding observations on India, A/62/18, para 177.

[173] Concluding observations on Ecuador, A/63/18, para 144.

[174] Among many such references, see concluding observations on Sweden, A/63/18, para 406.

[175] Among many contributions to debates, see P Jones, 'Human Rights, Group Rights, and Peoples' Rights' (1999) 21 *Human Rights Quarterly* 80–107; M Jovanovic, 'Recognizing Minority Identities through Collective Rights' (2005) 27 *Human Rights Quarterly* 625–51.

[176] *Lovelace v Canada*, Communication No 24/1977, A/36/40.

scales in favour of community survival, perhaps deferring the issue of the perfect balancing of norms. In terms of discrimination, that principle is not inflexible, within and without the application of special measures to especially serious situations. There is, however, potential in CERD's endorsement of the Declaration for further clarification of relationships between individual and collective rights in light of—to take only one example—Article 35 of the Declaration, according to which indigenous peoples 'have the right to determine the responsibilities of individuals to their communities'.[177]

The prominence accorded to collective rights in the Declaration is not unexpected in a text largely addressed to peoples who may have an etiolated concept of the individual and a strong concept of the collective, and who support collective rights as an essential aspect of community defence,[178] reflecting what Gray describes as 'transitive' and 'intransitive' aspects of communal existence.[179] Such defence may be undermined by strident assertions by States that 'only' individual rights may be regarded as human rights.[180] This approach is not consistent with the recognition of 'collective' self-determination as a human right within the Covenants, nor does it appear consistent with ILO Convention 169 and general CERD

[177] Beyond the above brief comments, the present chapter does not intend to review 'double discrimination' affecting (particularly) the rights of women through intra-community discrimination as well as discrimination by State authorities. CERD has made many comments regarding the negative effects of traditional practices which may overlap with issues of individual and collective rights. These should, however, not be marked out as specific to indigenous peoples but suggest questions about the reach of human rights and intercultural compatibility that spill over into broader discussions. For further reflection on gender 'intersectionality' in the CERD context, see Thornberry (n 19) 265–69, and on the broader cultural context, S Mullally, 'The UN, Minority Rights and Gender Equality: Setting Limits to Collective Claims' (2007) 14(2/3) *International Journal on Minority and Group Rights* 263–83; L Volpp, 'Feminism versus Multiculturalism' (2001) 101 *Columbia Law Review* 1181–1218.

[178] A Gray, *Indigenous Rights and Development: Self-Determination in an Amazonian Community* (Providence and Oxford, Berghahn Books, 1997) ch 4.

[179] The 'intransitive' aspect of self-determination 'refers to ... control over social and cultural life, economic production, access to resources, and political status'; the intransitive aspect of self-determination 'operates in relation to ... outsiders to the community', Gray, ibid, 305.

[180] Hence the (rather unclear) statement of Slovakia, A/61/PV.108, p 5: 'Slovakia ... does not accept the concept of collective human rights in international law that has been integrated into the text. We would like to point out the distinction ... in the preamble to the Declaration. It clearly distinguishes between the individual character of the human rights of indigenous individuals and the collective rights indispensable for their existence', etc. The statement at once denies the character of collective rights as human rights but appears to accept that collective human rights have been integrated into the text. The statement of the representative of the United Kingdom, A/61/PV.107, p 21, put the argument succinctly: 'With the exception of the right to self-determination, we ... do not accept the concept of collective human rights in international law. Of course, certain human rights can be exercised collectively, in community with others.' The concession to self-determination is illuminating and leads to the possible contradiction if, as suggested above, self-determination is taken as a meta-concept, subsuming other human rights.

practice. If the collective rights are not human rights, they may amount to little more than a grant by States, which could in principle be withdrawn. The approach is allegedly based on the antepenultimate paragraph of the preamble to the Declaration,[181] but such a reading appears itself incompatible with Article 1 of the Declaration, as well as with the tenor of the text as a whole, including affirmations of the collective right to existence and to be free from genocide. Human rights are an unfinished project. One message of the Declaration is that ways of seeing human rights may be subject to change and expansion away from the political vision and dominant epistemologies of those who have hitherto 'controlled' both the concept and its implementation. In a contemporary blurring of perspectives, 'the circumference' appears to have shifted closer to 'the centre'.

CONVENTION AND DECLARATION: KEEPING COMPANY

The history of the application of the Convention on the Elimination of All Forms of Racial Discrimination by its monitoring committee, CERD, is a history of increasing recognition of group diversity in which the recognition of indigenous peoples and the endorsement of indigenous rights have played a pivotal role. The application of the principle of non-discrimination to indigenous contexts is an established part of CERD's repertoire. The Committee's reflection on the rights of indigenous peoples has expanded the potential of the Convention to address a wide range of human situations and served to clarify the nature of discrimination and difference, the reading of key norms including those in the field of property, and principles such as special measures or affirmative action. The approval of indigenous rights by CERD reaches a kind of apotheosis in recommending the Declaration as a guide to State practice. However, through such endorsement, CERD may require further refinements in its approach to matters that include the recognition of indigenous peoples, the limits of indigenous rights in relation to the rights of others and the implications of collective rights for human rights in general.

In the absence of a wholly dedicated monitoring body for the Declaration, the work of the treaty bodies assumes importance in providing a necessary edge to secure the application of its principles in State practice. As the Declaration influences treaty body practice, so will CERD and other treaty body practice impact on the interpretation of the Declaration. As indigenous rights continue to inform the inter-

[181] 'Recognizing and affirming that indigenous individuals are entitled without discrimination to all human rights recognized in international law, and that indigenous peoples possess collective rights which are indispensable for their existence, well-being and integral development as peoples.'

pretation of the Convention, so can the focus on anti-discrimination assist in discouraging a zealotry in the pursuit of indigenous rights that would produce only reverse injustice. The instruments are fated to live together for the foreseeable future; like cultures they are 'involved with one another; none is single and pure'.[182]

Developments in indigenous rights have set a challenge to existing human rights bodies to take account of fresh perceptions of where oppression is located, to listen to voices that have long been silenced, and resolve into human shape what may have been only their 'dim and undetermined sense of unknown modes of being'.[183] The Declaration is the culmination of a remarkable series of developments in the field of indigenous rights, including ILO Convention 169, which have expanded the frame of international law to render it truer to the aspirations of a wider range of groups. Despite its charisma, it is not without problems in the mildly chaotic nature of its text and its employment of challenging concepts. But the Declaration is as much a fact in the world as tables and chairs and carries within itself the contours of a re-imagined justice for the benefit of distinctive human communities.

[182] EW Said, *Culture and Imperialism* (London, Vintage Books, 1994) xxix.

[183] W Wordsworth, 'Boat-Stealing' in *The Prelude*, Book 1 (1805), cited in S Heaney and T Hughes (eds), *The Rattle Bag* (London, Faber and Faber, 1982) 84.

4

The International Labour Organization and the Internationalisation of the Concept of Indigenous Peoples

ANDREW ERUETI*

INTRODUCTION

THIS CHAPTER CONSIDERS the influence of the International Labour Organization (ILO) in the conceptualisation of contemporary definitions of indigenous peoples in international law. I argue (i) that the ILO played an important role in the growth and legitimacy of indigenous social movements beyond the Americas and Australasia—where the international movement first emerged; and (ii) that the ILO's original definition of Indigenous and Tribal Populations in Convention 107, with its emphasis on cultural difference to limit the domestic scope of the Convention, had a strong influence on contemporary understandings of what it means to be an indigenous people for the purposes of implementation of the United Nations Declaration on the Rights of Indigenous Peoples ('the Declaration') and related international norms (particularly in the context of Asia and Africa).

The chapter begins by looking at the ILO's efforts in the 1950s to draft a convention setting out standards for 'indigenous farmer communities' and 'forest peoples' in Latin America. The goal was to elevate these poor and marginalised communities so that they could contribute to nation-building. Quickly the ILO saw parallels between these groups and others in former European colonies of the East and South and extended its project to them as well. In so doing, the ILO became the first international body to establish international standards for 'indigenous peoples', though its use of cultural difference as a defining attribute of indigeneity severely limited the Convention's effectiveness.

* The views expressed by the author in this essay are his own. They are not the views of Amnesty International.

Secondly, the chapter considers the ILO's role in internationalising indigenous peoples' rights for the purposes of the contemporary international indigenous movement (from about 1975 to the present). This work commenced in the ILO itself during the 1970s and 1980s, through its monitoring mechanism, and was continued through its submissions to the UN Working Group on Indigenous Populations (WGIP). It was within the WGIP that the first version Declaration was drafted between 1985 and 1993 with input provided directly by indigenous peoples' organisations (IPOs) and other non-governmental organisations (NGOs) in the form of written and oral 'interventions' to the expert members of the WGIP at each annual session.[1] Within the WGIP, the ILO played an important function in generating general acceptance of extending the Declaration to hill-tribal peoples in Asia. Later, an Africa lobby sought the inclusion of African nomadic and hunter-gatherer peoples in the Declaration.

Finally, the chapter explores potential problems that result from the internationalisation of the Declaration, particularly the obfuscation of differences in terms of goals and underlying justifications attached to indigenous peoples from different regions of the globe, and the issues that arise with the continued use of the concept of cultural difference to support emerging indigenous movements. Cultural difference has been the vital hinge providing access to the international movement for these groups, particularly indigenous peoples in Africa. But it also threatens to undermine them.

ILO CONVENTION 107: AN INTERNATIONAL TREATY FOR 'PRIMITIVE' PEOPLES

During the early 1950s, the ILO directed its attention to drafting labour standards for broadly described communities of indigenous farmers or sedentary communities and forest dwellers in the Americas. This was to be a tripartite process—in keeping with the ILO's standard procedure for drafting conventions—involving all three bodies of the ILO: the ILO, state members, and workers' union members. The ILO was motivated by concern for the protection and well-being of these communities[2]—there was recognition of racial discrimination, the exploitation of indigenous peoples' labour and property rights, and denial of rights available to other

[1] For insightful comment on indigenous participation in the WGIP, see K Knop, *Diversity and Self-Determination in International Law,* Cambridge Studies in International and Comparative Law (Cambridge University Press, 2002) 248–74.

[2] See the preambular paragraphs of Convention 107: 'Considering it desirable both for humanitarian reasons and in the interests of the countries concerned to promote continued action to improve the living and working conditions of these populations …'

workers.[3] But the overriding policy was economics. According to the prevailing perception, equal opportunities would lead to indigenous people becoming productive members of society. Indigenous communities were viewed as an important source of labour and a more productive and efficient use of their resources would lead to greater economic prosperity for each nation and promote national solidarity.[4]

While initially the ILO's concern was directed at these communities in Latin America, it recognised also the broad parallels between them and communities in other countries of Asia, Africa and the Middle East. The ILO knew that indigenous peoples in the Americas had 'historical antecedents' as first peoples, and that this had normative value within many Latin American states; however, it also wanted to extend the convention to 'other tribal and semi-tribal groups as well who, without being "indigenous" in the historical sense, live in social and economic conditions comparable to those of [Latin American indigenous peoples]'.[5]

Many of these states in Asia, Africa and the Middle East were also newly independent former colonies and many more were on the cusp of acquiring independence. The first ILO report to seriously address the idea of a convention was entitled *Indigenous Peoples—Living and Working Conditions of Aboriginal Populations*, which was published in 1953 ('ILO 1953 Report').[6] The bulk of the report was directed at South and Central America, and to a lesser extent North America and Australasia. But it also referred to several Southeast Asian states, specifically Burma, Ceylon, India, Indonesia, Pakistan, the Philippines and Thailand. In these regions the focus was on hill-tribal peoples gathered in mountains, such as the Cordillera peoples of the Philippines.

By 1956, the scope of the project had expanded even further. The ILO's preliminary report, entitled *Living and Working Conditions of Indigenous Populations in Independent Countries* ('ILO 1956 Report'), covered many more states.[7] It referred to the 'tribal and semi-tribal' population groups of Southeast Asia, but also to the nomadic tribes and bushmen in Africa and the 'Near and Middle East'—Kurds, Bakhtiari and Baluchi. The report

[3] See ILO, *Indigenous Peoples—Living and Working Conditions of Aboriginal Populations in Independent Countries* (Geneva, ILO, 1953) (ILO 1953 Report); also, ILO, *Living and Working Conditions of Indigenous Populations in Independent Countries*, Report VIII(1), International Labour Conference, 39th session, Geneva, 1956 (ILO 1956 Report VIII(1)); and ILO, *Living and Working Conditions of Indigenous Populations in Independent Countries*, Report VIII(2), International Labour Conference, 39th session, Geneva, 1956 (ILO 1956 Report VIII(2)) 107.

[4] See ibid, ILO 1953 Report; 1956 Report VIII(1) (Ch III Basic Problems of Life and Work).

[5] See ILO 1956 Report VIII(2) (n 3) 107.

[6] See n 3.

[7] See ILO 1956 Report VIII(1) (n 3).

saw its target group as falling across a wide spectrum, and ranked them according to their degree of sedentarianism and cultural difference. At one end of the spectrum were the indigenous farmer communities, at the other the forest dwellers of Southeast Asia and the Amazon:

> As regards types, a clear distinction should be drawn between long established sedentary communities and nomadic or semi-nomadic groups; the latter group should be further broken down into forest dwellers and desert nomads. This distinction is particularly important if these groups are considered ... in terms of their greater or less degree of integration into the national community. Forest-dwelling groups, in particular, are characterised by the isolation in which they live, by their primitive tribal existence and by a number of cultural features which place them in a position of even greater inferiority than traditional sedentary communities (eg the *comunidades, resguardos* and *reducciones* of Latin America and the reservations in Australia, Canada and the United States), with the result that they are cut off from enjoying the rights enjoyed under national laws by the citizenship at large.[8]

A clearer idea of the forest dweller was provided in another ILO report that was circulated during this period:

> The expression 'forest dwelling aborigines' is taken to mean nomadic, semi-nomadic or settled aborigines living under a *tribal system* in virgin forest (primary) wooded savannah, bush etc (secondary) or other forest regions, and subsisting on a *simple, traditional* economy based mainly on the use of natural resources, whether directly (by hunting, fishing or gathering wild fruit) or indirectly (by *primitive* agriculture or elementary stockbreeding) and any other aboriginal population which can be likened to them by reason of its *simple* economic structure.[9]

A distinction was to be drawn between the forest dwellers and, due to their adherence to the Moslem faith of the nation, the more acculturated nomadic desert tribes of the Near and Middle East:

> As regards nomadic desert tribes in the Near and Middle East, such tribes are differentiated from forest-dwelling groups not only by their environment but by their close cultural kinship with the sedentary populations in the countries to which they belong. This kinship is due primarily to the influence exerted upon them by the Moslem religion.[10]

These types of communities would of course determine the types of interests that needed standards of protection in the new convention. The most civilised and sedentary communities would require radically different

[8] Ibid, 49.

[9] See ILO Questionnaire on aboriginal forest-dwelling populations, ILO Doc D.1.1952, undated, ILO archives 51/1001, 1, as cited in L Rodríguez-Piñero, *Indigenous Peoples, Post-Colonialism and International Law: The ILO Regime* (Oxford University Press, 2005) 155 fn 46.

[10] ILO 1956 Report VIII(1) (n 3) 49.

measures from the forest dwellers. And within sedentary communities, there were evident differences between, say, the *comunidades, resguardos* and *reducciones* of Latin America and the reservations of Canada and the United States. Given the broad reach of the community described in the ILO's 1953 and 1956 Reports, this was a highly ambitious project.

What problems and interests were identified, then? The standards in the ILO reflected the perceived problems encountered in the daily life and work of indigenous peoples. At the top of the list was 'the protection of the rights of indigenous peoples with respect to the ownership and use of the lands they occupy and to the economic development of these lands'.[11] The ILO recognised that those most exposed to outside contact were the first to be deprived of an adequate land-base. The loss of land had either put them in a semi-feudal relationship with large landowners—where workers were forced to provide labour, say, for the use of a plot of land—or reduced them to landless agricultural labourers forced to search for work in commercial plantations and cities. For more remote forest dwellers, the problem was protecting them from unwanted intrusions and loss of land.

For the indigenous sedentary communities, the ILO would seek to advance their interests by requiring states to delineate and title the lands that they occupied[12]—which would facilitate credit for long-term improvement of the land—and training them to use their lands more efficiently, through technical advice on fertilisation, crop rotation and so on. This would liberate them from their dependence on large landholders. The ILO could foresee a time when indigenous communities could be highly productive farmer communities.[13] But this was to be an 'elastic defence'.[14] The land rights were seen as a temporary measure before these

[11] Ibid, 63.

[12] Art 11. It is interesting that there was acceptance from the ILO that 'traditional occupation' was to be read with 'due regard to customary law'. Indigenous peoples' traditionally occupied lands would include not only cultivated land, but also 'uncultivated land which will cover the needs of coming generations, as well as land which at present may not be cultivated but which, in the course of shifting cultivation, may be put into use subsequently'. See ILO 1956 Report VIII(1) (n 3) 67.

[13] The ILO Report's comments on land promoted strong Lockean ideas about the need for land to be used effectively. John Locke and other classical scholars argued that uncultivated land in North America was not occupied and therefore free to be acquired by European settlers. See J Locke, *Two Treatises of Government* (P Laslett ed, Cambridge University Press, 1988) (1690); see also the Australian decision of *Milirrpum v Nabalco Party Ltd* (1971) 17 FLR 141, ruling that a colony could be considered uninhabited, or terra nullius, at the time of sovereignty if its occupants were nomadic or had no settled law. For an illuminating discussion of the medieval origins of these theories and their extension to the Americas, see generally RA Williams, Jr, *The American Indian in Western Legal Thought: The Discourses of Conquest* (Oxford University Press, 1990).

[14] For the ILO discussion on lands rights, see ILO 1956 Report VIII(1) (n 3) Chapter III, Basic Problems of Life and Work, 63.

tribal groups were integrated into western civilisation.[15] Segregation, say, in the form of reservation lands, was to be discouraged.

> Such a system may not only maintain these groups in a permanent state of social and economic inferiority but also render impossible their fruitful collaboration with other sections of the population for economic and social development of the national community as a whole.[16]

For tenant-labourers and those forced to leave their communities and search for work, ILO Convention 107 offered recruitment and employment protections[17] and vocational training.[18] The goal of eventual integration of indigenous peoples required that they acquire the skills to survive in cities and other centres of work. All indigenous peoples would also be provided with 'adequate health services',[19] access to social security,[20] and education at all levels on an equal footing with others.[21] Also, there was recognition of the need to respect indigenous values, institutions and language, though only to the extent that they did not undermine the project of integration.[22]

This broad agenda at first blush seemed to reach far beyond the traditional mandate of the ILO. It had created several conventions on labour rights for vulnerable workers in European colonies, but it was clear that the ILO wanted something far more ambitious in content and scope. States were obviously concerned about its potential application in their territories. In addition, many states had concerns regarding the normative implications of the term 'indigenous'. In both the 1953 and 1956 ILO Reports, 'indigenous' was merely an adjective attached to the perception of certain communities as culturally backward to varying degrees and in need of assistance. But states were worried about its close association with the decolonisation movement and historically prior rights to lands and sovereignty.[23] For states in Asia, Africa and the Middle East—many of which had

[15] See ILO 1956 Report VIII(2) (n 3) 160.
[16] See ILO 1956 Report VIII(1) (n 3) 68.
[17] Art 15.
[18] Arts 16–18.
[19] Art 20.
[20] Art 19.
[21] Arts 21–26.
[22] While tradition was generally to be respected, if it obstructed economic development it had to be 'gradually eliminated' or 'at least adapted to the economic and social needs of the communities concerned'. See ILO 1956 Report VIII(1) (n 3) 69.
[23] See eg ILO, *Protection and Integration of Indigenous and Other Tribal and Semi-Tribal Populations in Independent Countries*, Report VI(1), International Labour Conference, 40th session, Geneva, 1956, 8. ('The Indonesian Government member informed the Committee that the policy of his country was to abolish all differentiation between the various elements in its population. Moreover, all the national laws of his country applied to all the sectors of the population. In these conditions, it was not appropriate to consider that certain tribal or semi-tribal groups were indigenous, as the Office had done in the descriptive part of Report

recently acquired independence—indigenous populations or communities meant all of the 'original inhabitants' of dependent European colonies (eg Ethiopia, India, etc) that were entitled to the right to decolonise. Use of the term 'indigenous populations', therefore, suggested that there were internal groupings that were also entitled to decolonisation and independence. The Latin American states had similar concerns and sought to avoid the convention by arguing that there were no longer indigenous populations as such in their countries but rather *mestizo* peoples who were nearly or fully integrated into society. Additionally, states would have baulked at the notion of the ILO holding them to account for their minorities, when they had just obtained their own independence from western colonising powers. This resistance to the word 'indigenous' foreshadowed later controversy over its use in the context of drafting the Declaration three decades later given its connection to the right of all 'peoples to self-determination' in the international covenants[24] and also the normative power of first peoples and the robust rights set out in the Declaration.

In 1957, when ILO Convention 107 was adopted, the definition finally settled upon in the convention contained an umbrella concept of '*tribal* populations'—the use of 'indigenous populations' as the umbrella concept was dropped because of its normative implications. '*Tribal* populations' referred to two separate categories:

(a) members of tribal or semi-tribal populations in independent countries whose social and economic conditions are at a less advanced stage than the stage reached by the other sections of the national community, and whose status is regulated wholly or partially by their own customs or traditions or by special laws or regulations;
(b) members of tribal or semi-tribal populations in independent countries which are regarded as indigenous on account of their descent from the populations which inhabited the country, or a geographical region to which the country belongs, at the time of conquest or colonisation and which, irrespective of their legal status, live more in conformity with the social, economic and cultural institutions of that time than with the institutions of the nation to which they belong.[25]

The first category was aimed at 'tribal populations' in Asia, the Middle East and Africa. The second category was aimed at indigenous peoples

VIII(1). A broadly similar point was made by other speakers among the Government group, including those of Egypt, Syria and Liberia, who explained that the term "indigenous" itself could have an undesirable connotation in certain areas.')

[24] States in the WGIP, therefore, argued that the Declaration should refer to 'indigenous people', without the 's', to avoid the connection with the right of peoples to self-determination.

[25] Art 1(1).

in the Americas and Australasia (Latin America principally). The term 'semi-tribal' was defined to include groups 'in the process of losing their tribal characteristics' but who were not 'yet integrated into the national community'.[26] Creating a tribal population category separate from the indigenous category helped to address the concerns of the Asian, African and Middle Eastern states with regard to the normative implications of the word 'indigenous'.[27] On the recommendation of India, all references to 'indigenous', 'non-indigenous' and 'peoples' were removed and replaced with references throughout the text to 'tribal', 'semi-tribal' and 'the populations concerned'.[28]

Central to the definition was cultural difference as expressed in terms of tribal and semi-tribal, and the notion of indigenous peoples living in conformity with pre-conquest institutions. It allowed the ILO to determine the parameters of the category, and particularly to shut out certain *mestizo* groups in the interests of the practicalities of implementation. This was the ILO's goal: to limit the target group to those it saw as most in need of its integration programme for culturally distinctive communities. For the ILO, such an approach was seen as simply practical, given the problems with determining the practical boundaries of Convention 107 in the Latin American context:

> [T]he 'tribal or semi-tribal' criterion appears to be decisive since, in its absence, the proposed instrument would be so all-embracing that it would lose much of its effectiveness ... Were this criterion not embodied in the definition, the scope of the instrument would become so vast and indefinite that it might in a number of countries cover the majority of the rural population and even certain non-indigenous urban groups.[29]

This was understandable. But there were unfortunate consequences. While the ILO reports clearly contemplated Convention 107's application to indigenous sedentary communities, the broad reference to cultural difference could be used in a narrow manner by states to exclude these groups and to confine the scope of Convention 107 to the smaller category of forest-dwelling tribes. Several states, pointing to the definition, argued that such 'backward' peoples no longer existed in their countries due to racial amalgamation, or, if they existed, they were a small, inconsequential pool of people. New Zealand, Australia, Canada and

[26] Art 1(2).

[27] See Rodríguez-Piñero (n 9) 170 (noting that this second category 'became a good escape valve for the deadlock created by the opposition of African and Asian states to the express use of the term Indigenous Peoples evoking historical precedence').

[28] See ILO, *Protection and Integration of Indigenous and Other Tribal and Semi-Tribal Populations in Independent Countries*, Report VI(2), International Labour Conference, 40th session, Geneva, 1957, 4.

[29] ILO 1956 Report VIII(2) (n 3) 105.

the United States had throughout the drafting process pointed to the limitations of the definition for them, noting that indigenous populations within their borders were at an advanced stage of integration.[30] None of these states ratified the Convention. Ghana, the first African state to ratify, argued in its first report to the ILO that it had no indigenous populations.[31] Several Latin American and Asian states proffered similar arguments[32] or argued that indigenous peoples were limited to the more marginal element of forest peoples.[33] That glossed over the clearly identified problem of the discrimination and poverty suffered by indigenous sedentary communities in these countries. While the goal of the ILO had been the steady integration of these communities into national life, Convention 107 offered strong standards for these communities. Furthermore, State compliance with the standards would be monitored by the ILO. Eventually, 27 States would come to ratify ILO Convention 107—four from Africa,[34] four from the Middle East,[35] 14 from Latin America,[36] two from Europe[37] and three from Asia.[38] But there was little enthusiasm for it until many years

[30] See Rodríguez-Piñero (n 9) 166, fn 106.

[31] See ILO, International Labour Conference, 45th session, Report of the Committee of Experts on Application of Conventions and Recommendations, Report III (Part I): Summary of Reports on Ratified Conventions (1961) 128.

[32] El Salvador argued that no indigenous peoples existed in the state ('There are no population groups in El Salvador which may be considered as indigenous, tribal or semi-tribal. The majority of the population belongs to the mestizo (cross-breed) and white races ... [E]ven though the characteristics of an indigenous race are more marked in the population of certain parts of the country, this fact is of no importance as concerns their legal, social and economic position, since these inhabitants speak the same language, practise the same religion, enjoy the same rights and have the same opportunities as their fellow citizens ...', ibid). Argentina and Costa Rica also noted that the 'Indian problem' had already been solved in their countries. See Rodríguez-Piñero (n 9) 236, fn 98. The United Arab Republic (Egypt) ignored the ILO's repeated requests for information on the Bedouin. See ILO, International Labour Conference, 53rd session, Report of the Committee of Experts on Application of Conventions and Recommendations, Report III (Part IV): Summary of Reports on Ratified Conventions (1969) 124–25. In relation to the Middle Eastern states that ratified the Convention—Egypt, Syria and Tunisia—the ILO had by the mid-1970s accepted their governments' official position that the issue of nomadism was no longer an issue as these peoples had successfully been settled. See Rodríguez-Piñero (n 9) 237, fn 102.

[33] Brazil for example consistently argued during the drafting of the Convention and after its adoption that within Brazil it applied 'only to forest-dwellers—the only indigenous peoples living on the territory of Brazil'. See ILO 1956 Report VIII(2) (n 3) 4. Several Latin American states failed to ratify Convention 107. Honduras, Venezuela, Belize and Nicaragua did not ratify Convention 107, and of these four states only Honduras ratified Convention 169 in 1995.

[34] Ghana ratified in 1958; Guinea-Bissau in 1997; Malawi in 1965; and Angola in 1976.

[35] Iraq ratified in 1986; Syrian Arab Republic in 1959; Tunisia in 1962; and Egypt in 1959.

[36] Argentina ratified in 1960; Bolivia and Brazil in 1965; Colombia, Paraguay and Ecuador in 1969; Costa Rica and Mexico in 1959; Cuba in 1958; Dominican Republic in 1958; El Salvador and Haiti in 1958; Panama in 1971; and Peru in 1960.

[37] Belgium ratified in 1958; and Portugal in 1960.

[38] Bangladesh ratified in 1972; India in 1958; and Pakistan in 1960.

later, when international NGOs co-opted it to promote their human rights work in Southeast Asia and Latin America.

THE ILO'S ROLE IN THE INTERNATIONALISATION OF THE DECLARATION

ILO Convention 107 had a global goal: to integrate tribal and indigenous peoples into mainstream society. But the international indigenous movement—which emerged in the 1970s with its centre of gravity in the developed states of North America and Australasia—had radically different plans, centred around claims to self-determination based on historical arguments and denial of their right as 'peoples' to decolonise. The international indigenous movement emerged to a large degree from within 'western' states—Canada, Australia, New Zealand and the United States—with the recognition there by indigenous activists of the potential benefits of establishing an international advocacy network for first peoples.[39] This was a highly effective movement and it culminated in the UN commitment in 1982 to establish the UN Working Group on the Rights of Indigenous Populations (WGIP).[40] When the WGIP first met in the early 1980s, it was filled with groups from these regions.[41] That can be contrasted with international meetings today, in particular the UN Permanent Forum on Indigenous Issues (PFII), which is always full of indigenous activists from all regions of the globe. Within the international movement, indigenous activists from Asian and African states now play an active and important role. Meanwhile, most of the Asian and African states resist or reject the concept of 'indigenous peoples', arguing that it relates only to the descendants of those colonised by Europeans in the Americas/Australasia.[42]

[39] See DE Sanders, 'The Formation of the World Council of Indigenous Peoples', Copenhagen, 1977, IWGIA document no 29; also DE Sanders, 'The UN Working Group on Indigenous Populations' (1989) 11 *Human Rights Quarterly* 405, 428–29. For the role of Saami activists and Nordic states in these early years see H Minde, 'The Making of an International Movement of Indigenous Peoples' (1996) 3 *Scandinavian Journal of History* 221–46; and H Minde, 'The Destination and the Journey: Indigenous Peoples and the United Nations from the 1960s through 1985' in 'The UN Declaration on the Rights of Indigenous Peoples: What Made it Possible? The Work and Process Beyond the Final Adoption' (2007) 4 *Gáldu Čála—Journal of Indigenous Peoples' Rights* 9.

[40] Commission on Human Rights Resolution 1982/10 (March 2010).

[41] The NGOs and IPOs recorded in attendance at the WGIP in 1982 included the North America-based International Indian Treaty Council, Metis Native Council of Canada, Nishnawbe-Aski Nation, Indian Law Resource Centre, and World Council of Indigenous Peoples.

[42] See eg the statement of India when voting for the Declaration in the General Assembly: 'While the Declaration did not define what constituted Indigenous Peoples, the issue of Indigenous rights pertained to peoples in independent countries who were regarded as Indigenous on account of their descent from the populations which inhabited the country, or a geographical region to which the country belonged, at the time of conquest or the

Indeed, the inclusion and acceptance of indigenous activists from outside of the Americas/Australasia was gradual. The first few years of the WGIP were critical for promoting the idea of a truly global movement and declaration. One of the foundation IPOs with an international agenda, the Canadian-based World Council of Indigenous Peoples, had tried to contact groups in Russia, China and other parts of Asia in its early years and had strong ties with the Saami movement.[43] On the other hand, when the WGIP discussed definitions of indigenous peoples—which of course it had to as a preliminary issue—frequent reference was made by WGIP participants to the working definition in the report of UN Special Rapporteur Martinez Cobo. This report, which sought to set out the contemporary living conditions of indigenous peoples, played an integral role in the decision to establish the WGIP. But its working definition of indigenous peoples seemed to contemplate only indigenous peoples of Australasia and the Americas since it referred to indigenous peoples as 'those ... having a historical continuity with pre-invasion and pre-colonial societies that developed on their territories'.[44]

Frequently, IPOs referred to the right of indigenous peoples to self-identify as such. This was a response to years of being categorised and defined by the state and the narrowing of definitions to facilitate indigenous peoples' integration into the dominant culture. Gradually, during the tenure of the WGIP, the WGIP experts and participants came to accept the idea of the Declaration applying to peoples within specific Southeast Asian states, and then later, pastoral and nomadic communities in African states. Throughout this process, Asian states objected strongly that the Declaration ought to address the specific problems of western states and argued that the Declaration needed a definition to make clear that it applied only to indigenous communities occupying the Americas and Australasia. Asian states stressed the specific history and experience of these peoples as first peoples overwhelmed by settlers from a foreign country:

> The Chinese Government believes that the question of indigenous peoples is the product of European countries' recent pursuit of colonial policies in other parts of the world. Because of these policies, many indigenous peoples were

establishment of present state boundaries and who, irrespective of their legal status, retained some or all of their socio-economic, cultural and political institutions.' Here, India is simply using the definition of 'indigenous peoples' set out in ILO Convention 169. See UN press release, 'General Assembly Adopts Declaration on Rights of Indigenous Peoples: Major Step Forward towards Human Rights for All, Says President' (2007). See also the comments of Indonesia, noting that the Declaration did not apply in the context of Indonesia, ibid.

[43] Sanders, 'The Formation of the World Council of Indigenous Peoples' (n 39).

[44] Mr Jose R Martinez Cobo, 'Study of the Problem of Discrimination against Indigenous Populations', UN Doc E/CN.4/Sub.2/1986/Add.4, paras 379–80.

> dispossessed of their ancestral homes and lands, brutally oppressed, exploited and murdered, and in some cases even deliberately exterminated. To this day, many indigenous peoples still suffer from discrimination and diminished status … As in the majority of Asian countries, the various nationalities in China have all lived for aeons on Chinese territory. Although there is no indigenous peoples question in China, the Chinese Government and people have every sympathy with indigenous peoples' historical woes and historical plight. China believes it absolutely essential to draft an international instrument to protect their rights and interests … The special historical misfortunes of indigenous peoples set them apart from minority nationalities and ethnic groups in the ordinary sense. For this reason, the draft declaration must clearly define what indigenous peoples are, in order to guarantee that the special rights it establishes are accurately targeted at genuine communities of indigenous people and are not distorted, arbitrarily extended or muddled.[45]

Asian states also pointed to the particular vulnerability of indigenous peoples in Latin America given recent decades of intense violence; to ignore these regions, they suggested, was irresponsible. Some also stressed that their cultures were so diverse, resulting from a melting pot of identities, that it was impossible to identify distinct peoples. Later, African states would raise similar arguments. At the same time, many Asian and African states have always officially recognised tribal communities and ascribed names to them—such as 'aboriginals', 'bushmen', 'hill tribes', 'minority nationalities', 'scheduled tribes' and 'tribal groups'—and have included them in development plans and programmes. These states, like others in the Americas and Australasia, were concerned about the normative connotations of 'indigenous' with its association with historical priority, claims to lands and self determination—all issues that were at the forefront of the debate within the WGIP sessions.

But within the WGIP and later within the Working Group on the Draft Declaration on the Rights of Indigenous Peoples (WGDD), Asian states encountered a strong lobby group made up of states from the west—keen to spread responsibility for indigenous peoples beyond their borders and so remove the focus on them. Another particularly strong lobby group was the ILO and international NGOs which used the ILO monitoring mechanism and the WGIP to highlight commonalities between indigenous peoples in Latin America and tribal peoples in parts of Southeast Asia.

Although Convention 107 was ratified by over 20 states in the 1960s and 1970s, for many years the Convention was neglected. This neglect can be traced to several factors, including states' argument that the Convention was not relevant (even though they may have ratified it) because their

[45] Consideration of a Draft United Nations Declaration on the Rights of Indigenous Peoples, UN Doc E/CN.4/WG.15/2 (1995).

indigenous and tribal populations were now fully integrated into the national society; the lack of useful information provided by states to the ILO; the absence of technical expertise within the ILO; and the general lack of enthusiasm for and interest in the Convention from the ILO and workers' and employers' organisations.[46]

It was not until the mid-1970s that the ILO took a more proactive interest in the rights of indigenous peoples, prompted by international NGOs such as Anti-Slavery International and Survival International. These NGOs were active during the 1970s, highlighting human rights abuses of indigenous peoples in repressive regimes in the Southeast Asian and Latin American regions. In the minds of these NGOs, there was a clear link between the situation of the Chittagong Hill Tract tribes of Bangladesh and the scheduled tribes of India and indigenous peoples in the Latin American states of Guatemala, Nicaragua and Brazil. They were culturally distinct communities, often with different religions from the mainstream, highly vulnerable and poor, and subject to severe human rights abuses. The most significant instrument at the time was ILO Convention 107, because it contained useful standards in relation to land rights and forced relocation and had been ratified by many Latin American states as well as India and Bangladesh (all sites of conflict at the time). Additionally, Convention 107 was a binding convention with a comprehensive monitoring process, whereby states were required to file annual reports to an ILO Committee of Experts. The Anti-Slavery Society, for example, invoked the monitoring process of the ILO under Convention 107 to shine a light on human rights abuses in Bangladesh and India—Bangladesh, particularly, was the site of well-known atrocities and political repression—while also speaking of similar repressive practices in Brazil, Guatemala and Nicaragua.[47] These were fundamental human rights issues—the right to life and security. Still, the other unifying factor was cultural difference, particularly the fragile land rights of these peoples. International NGOs noted the plight of the thousands of Adivasis forcibly removed by the Sardar Sarover Dam and Power Project in India and also the forced removal of indigenous peoples from traditional lands in Guatemala. Additionally, they sought to apply a contemporary 'progressive' perspective to these land rights

[46] See Rodríguez-Piñero (n 9) 244–48. Note also the ILO's futile attempts throughout the 1960s to provide technical assistance to African and Asian states with regard to the integration of tribal and indigenous peoples. Rodríguez-Piñero notes (at 216–33) that these efforts failed for many reasons, including confusion over the target group; tensions created by identity politics in the post-colonial states; and the inexperience of the ILO in terms of the local issues in these regions.

[47] See eg the Anti-Slavery reports to the WGIP on the Republic of the Philippines, WGIP 82/SEA.PHL/1; Bangladesh, WGIP 82/SAS.BDG/1; India, WGIP 84/SAS.IND/1.

commensurate with the philosophy of the emerging international indigenous movement (centred in the WGIP).[48] They argued that secure land rights were not a temporary measure on the road to integration, but necessary for the continued survival of these communities and their way of life. The ILO responded with enthusiasm and strongly criticized these states.[49]

During the first four years of the WGIP, the same international NGOs that had appeared before the ILO now appeared before the WGIP and again spoke in the same breath of the struggle of Asian indigenous peoples and those in Latin America.[50] These NGOs framed the issues of Asian indigenous peoples in such a way that their historical and contemporary circumstances mirrored that of indigenous peoples in the Americas and Australasia. They were effectively forced to adopt this position due to the insistence of Asian states that the WGIP was concerned with colonisation of the Americas and Australasia.[51]

[48] See Rodríguez-Piñero (n 9) 251 (referring to a second phase of implementation of the Convention from 1975 to 1989 whereby the 'interaction between the international NGO movement and the organisation's supervisory system gradually fostered an interpretation of Convention 107 as an instrument for the defence of indigenous rights, opening the most active phase thus far of the international protection of the rights of Indigenous Peoples by the ILO'). The ILO's gradual shift from integration towards rights protection coincided with several other important and influential initiatives, including the indigenous lobby within the UN and the growth of the international human rights network generally. See ME Keck and K Sikkink, *Activists beyond Borders: Advocacy Networks in International Politics* (Ithaca, Cornell University Press, 1998). The Anti-Slavery Society and other international NGOs were all part of the new dynamic of NGOs using international fora to gain leverage in their efforts to shame states into halting their abuses of vulnerable peoples. Effectively, they subverted the original intention of Convention 107 to their goals of securing indefinite (not temporary) land rights for indigenous peoples and raising public awareness of the fundamental human rights abuses occurring in Latin America and Asia.

[49] See eg the observation of the ILO Committee of Experts on the Application of Conventions and Recommendations (CEACR) in relation to India and the Sardar Hydro Project, 1988 Report 3 (Part 4A) (75th session), noting that recent occupation of government-owned lands did not mean that tribal populations had no land rights.

[50] See eg the Anti-Slavery Society report to the WGIP in 1984 referring to the Chittagong Hill Tracts (CHT) in Bangladesh, Guatemala, West Papua and the Philippines; see E/CN.4/Sub.2/AC.4/1984/4/Add.2.

[51] For example, in response to the claim by Bangladesh that the Anti-Slavery Society should focus on indigenous peoples in Australasia where 'a colonizing and racially distinct people coming from overseas established settlements and entered into conflict with the autochthon population', the Anti-Slavery Society outlines the parallels between the situation of Australian aboriginal peoples and those of the CHT: 'The Chittagong Hill Tracts have been inhabited since "time immemorial" by hill tribes different in race, religion and culture from the Muslim Bengali majority of Bangladesh. They retained their autonomy during Mughal and British occupation of the region. Until the 1950s more than 90 per cent of the population was tribal. Bengalis from the plains have only begun to settle in the hill tracts in the last two decades.' See E/CN.4/Sub.2/AC.4/1984/4/Add.2, p 2. See also the report for 1984 to the WGIP, WGIP 84/SAS.IND/1.

The ILO also consistently argued for a global inquiry to be commenced by the WGIP. In the 1991 session of the WGIP, the ILO argued that the efforts to draft a UN indigenous-specific declaration needed to include Asian, African and Middle Eastern indigenous peoples or risk falling short of the standards set by Convention 107.[52] The ILO criticised the limited scope of the Martinez Cobo definition, with its reference to historical continuity with first peoples, and argued that if the ILO Conventions applied globally then the WGIP should also ensure that the Declaration applied to all of these marginalised peoples. For the ILO, the 'tribal peoples' of Asia and Africa were 'indistinguishable in all respects from indigenous peoples except as concerns their historical relationship to the place in which they live'.[53] The ILO was conscious that the WGIP had been established largely due to the indigenous lobby from North America and expressed concern that this lobby might dominate the process and overlook the pressing concerns of tribal peoples from other regions. The IPOs of the Americas and Australasia could have sought a definition that made clear that the Declaration was for them, but this conflicted with their claims to self-determination and their argument that it was for indigenous peoples only to determine their membership and status (see below). At least in terms of the fundamental rights at stake, it was difficult for all present at the WGIP sessions to ignore the similarities between indigenous peoples of Latin America and the Chittagong Hill Tribes etc in Asia. By the year 1987, only five years after the WGIP held its first meeting, Asian indigenous activists themselves began to attend WGIP meetings in increasing numbers, and the presence of the Anti-Slavery Society and other NGOs went into decline. The momentum that indigenous activism had built up was maintained when the ILO made the decision in the mid-1980s to revise ILO Convention 107, so that its emphasis would shift from integration to autonomy (again, in keeping with the contemporary philosophy). Again, the ILO stressed that the

[52] See the comments of the ILO's Coordinator for Human Rights, Lee Swepston, at the WGIP meeting in 1991 (WGIP 91 UN/UNI/8). Referring to the Martinez Cobo definition, Swepston notes: 'There is a certain concern, however, that the use of this definition might restrict the coverage of the declaration which you are considering to only a portion of the Indigenous and tribal peoples around the world. The use of the term "Indigenous" alone implies those with historical precedence in the region. The ILO Conventions—and its operational programmes in this area—extend both to Indigenous and tribal peoples. I am sure it is not the Working Group's intention to exclude the San of the Kalahari, the Bedouin and Tuareg of north Africa, or the tribal peoples of the Indian sub-continent, none of whom have any special claim to historical precedence in those areas. Questions arise as well concerning other tribally-organised peoples as the Romany or Gypsy peoples, who might in some respects be considered to be within the coverage of the ILO Convention—this had not been explicitly dealt with for now—but who are not Indigenous in any strict sense.'

[53] Ibid.

revised Convention needed to continue to apply globally to all distinctive and marginalised peoples.[54]

INDIGENOUS PEOPLES' SOCIAL MOVEMENT(S)

At the same time, the bringing together of these groups from different regions of the globe under the rubric of 'indigenous peoples' obscured some quite fundamental differences in terms of their historical experience, their priorities (which could conflict at a fundamental level), and the realities of their social, economic and political situation in their home states. This may be conceived of as a struggle of several independent yet interrelated regional social movements focused, first, on the history of the European colonisation of North America and Australasia; secondly, on the Saami indigenous movement from the Nordic states; thirdly, on the movement within the Latin American regions (Mexico, and Central and South America); and fourthly, on the politics of what were commonly known as 'tribal peoples' or the 'hill tribes' of Asia (and by logical extension the pastoral and hunter-gatherer tribes of Africa).[55] (Africa's indigenous peoples movement would not emerge fully until towards the end of the Declaration drafting process.) Of course, more of these movements can be referred to and they can be broken down further.[56] Within regions and states there were indigenous movements with their own particular histories, arguments, aims, and internal tensions.[57] Still, within the four regional movements, on a broad level, and in the context of the drafting of the Declaration, there were shared justifications, priorities and political, social and cultural circumstances.

[54] See also the academic work of Benedict Kingsbury arguing that the orthodox justifications for indigenous norms (historical sovereignty, first occupation, etc) are too restrictive and should be extended to include a broader range of justifications so that the international concept of indigenous peoples can accommodate tribal peoples of Asia, say, who share many common characteristics with indigenous peoples. B Kingsbury, '"Indigenous Peoples" in International Law: A Constructivist Approach to the Asian Controversy' (1998) 92 *American Journal of International Law* 414.

[55] Parallels can be drawn here with other similar social movements, such as the women's suffrage movement that emerged within and utilised the experience of the anti-slavery movement. See Keck and Sikkink (n 48).

[56] See KB Warren and JE Jackson, *Indigenous Movements, Self-Representation, and the State in Latin America* (Austin, University of Texas Press, 2002) 11: '[M]ovements rarely emerge in the singular and most often come in the highly contested plural. Rarely are indigenous movements as standardized in vision or coherent in organisation as their supporters suggest. Their heterogeneity may be an asset in some situations and a liability in others.'

[57] See eg the tension between urban-based indigenous movements and rural, traditional tribal organisations in New Zealand. See K Gover and N Baird, 'Identifying the Maori Treaty Partner' (2002) 52 *University of Toronto Law Journal* 39; and A Sharp 'Blood, Custom and Consent: Three Kinds of Maori Groups in New Zealand and Challenges they Present to Government and the Constitution' (2002) 51 *University of Toronto Law Journal* 9.

However, there were important differences in terms of their justifications for the recognition of indigenous rights. IPOs from North America and Australasia framed their issues in terms of *history* and denial of the right to decolonise.[58] They were 'first peoples'—the very original inhabitants of the land—who had been stripped of their rights to autonomy and territory by European colonising powers. In many cases, these IPOs could refer to colonial court decisions and international treaties/proclamations made with the colonising state that affirmed their prior occupation and nationhood. Despite a history of discrimination and marginalisation, they were still a distinctive and coherent community of peoples, connected to their lands and one another in a unique way. When the process of decolonisation was taking place in the post-World War II years, they had been denied their right as peoples to self-determination and decolonisation. Their priorities were the recognition of their international treaty rights as independent nations; their right to self-determination; the right to self-identify as indigenous peoples; their free, prior and informed consent; and the return of their traditional lands. IPOs from the Asian region, on the other hand, found it more difficult to advance the same historical-based justifications used by IPOs from the Americas/Australasia. Historically, after millennia of migration of ethnic groups, it was difficult to use the 'first peoples' argument and few could point to treaties affirming their original rights. In addition, many Asian states had just recently experienced decolonisation and by extension so had internal groups of Asian indigenous peoples. This was the very point stressed repeatedly by the Asian states in the working groups: that the situation of indigenous peoples in the Americas and Australasia was unique and that it was this particular experience that the UN working groups should be addressing.[59]

Furthermore, Asian IPOs' priorities tended to differ from those of indigenous peoples from North America/Australasia. Throughout the WGIP meetings—during the most critical years in terms of framing the key issues for the Declaration—indigenous activists from the Asian regions tended to speak more about fundamental human rights (right to life and security) and cultural difference (particularly traditional land rights). This was a continuation for the most part of the themes used by the international NGOs before the ILO monitoring bodies and the WGIP to emphasise the commonalities between Asian and Latin American indigenous peoples.

[58] Clear expression of their early concerns—fulfilment of treaty promises, return of lands and political control over their communities—can be found in a declaration issued by the indigenous activists who attended the International NGO Conference on Discrimination against Indigenous Populations in the Americas, held in Geneva in 1977. Reproduced in Martinez Cobo (n 44).

[59] See eg the statement of China in the WGIP above, n 45.

This approach also addressed the concerns of Asian states regarding the claims to self-determination in the WGIP made by the indigenous movements of North America and Australasia. Given the staunch resistance of Asian states to their inclusion in the work of the WGIP, they needed to be cautious about claiming more ambitious rights to self-determination and historical remedies. Self-determination in the Asian (and later African) context was particularly sensitive given the drive by these new, post-colonial states to promote unity and cohesion and implement plans for development that might conflict with indigenous land rights.

Indigenous activists in Latin America faced similar problems. While Latin American indigenous peoples could use historical-based justifications, in their home states there was little room for making claims to self-determination when indigenous peoples were dealing with serious security issues. Their priorities were the right to life and security, access to basic goods and services, and secure land rights. The international indigenous movement was important for Asian and Latin American IPOs because it shone a light on these fundamental human rights abuses.

This tension between the priorities and justifications of different indigenous movements was clearly illustrated by the ILO Convention 107 review process, which would result ultimately in ILO Convention 169.[60] In contrast to the Convention 107 process, the presence and active participation of indigenous peoples was seen as essential to the legitimacy of the revision exercise and there were now many IPOs actively participating in the WGIP and could speak to their specific problems. Several of these IPOs—most of them originating from North America—had drafted their own statements and declarations on indigenous peoples' rights and the ILO was well aware of their content and particularly their focus on issues of self-determination and self-government. But the tripartite process, particularly in comparison to the relatively open process of the WGIP, did not allow them ready access to present their arguments to the ILO conference.[61] In any event, the ILO described claims to self-determination etc as

[60] For commentary on the revision process, see L Swepston, 'Indigenous and Tribal Peoples and International Law: Recent Developments' (1989) 30(2) *Current Anthropology* 259–64; L Swepston, 'A New Step in International Law on Indigenous and Tribal Peoples: ILO Convention No 169 of 1989' (1990) 15 *Oklahoma City University Law Review* 677; L Swepston, 'The Adoption of the Indigenous and Tribal Peoples Convention, 1989 (No 169)' (1990) 5 *Law and Anthropology* 221-35; and L Swepston, 'Indigenous and Tribal Populations: A Return to Centre Stage' (1987) 126(4) *International Labour Review* 447–455.

[61] For discussion on the ILO drafting process and the problems IPOs encountered in participating in the process see Knop (n 1) 223–37 (process); and SH Venne, *Our Elders Understand Our Rights: Evolving International Law Regarding Indigenous Rights* (British Columbia, Theytus Books, 1988) 88–90.

'political aspects' of indigenous peoples' rights falling outside the scope of the revision process.[62] The ILO needed to adopt a 'realistic' approach if it wanted broad support for the revised Convention. There would be stronger land rights. The protection against removal of indigenous peoples from the lands they occupied was strengthened and the right to ownership of traditional lands retained. A brief provision requiring states to establish 'adequate procedures' to resolve land claims was inserted, but only after much heated debate about whether to also include a reference to treaties. The refusal of the ILO to incorporate more ambitious rights did not deny the legitimacy of the claims made by IPOs from North America and Australasia; the ILO repeatedly stressed that its more limited perspective should not jeopardise the framing of more ambitious norms in the UN.[63] But these issues were not for the ILO. Its task was to protect 'basic rights' or 'fundamental rights', not 'rights that cannot be implemented in law and practice'. The die had effectively been cast back in the 1950s with the ILO's original fixation on 'tribal peoples' in the Amazon and Asia etc. However, it was not simply the scope or the political nature of these claims that persuaded the ILO to leave out self-determination. The ILO also saw these claims as limited to the traditional tribes of the west, tribes like the Navajo and Cree and so on. Referring to the principles enshrined in the declarations produced by the World Council of Indigenous Peoples and other foundation IPOs based in North America, the ILO noted that 'many reflect the interests and concerns of the most homogenous and articulate of the Indigenous Peoples Organizations':[64]

> The populations they represent have well defined territories, they have in the past entered into treaty relations with colonising powers, they are familiar with international law, and many of them are now seeking to bring about radical changes in the nature of their relationship with the governments of the states in which they reside. It must be remembered there are many other indigenous and tribal groups and organizations which also seek to protect their economic, social, cultural and civil and political rights against abuse by the state and other encroachers but whose primary concerns are local autonomy and self-fulfillment, rather than the more ambitious declaration of principle adopted by certain international indigenous organizations.[65]

The ILO also saw the organisations of these other peoples, particularly groups in 'Africa and Continental Asia', as being at an 'embryonic stage'

[62] See ILO, Partial Revision of the Indigenous and Tribal Populations Convention, 1957 (No 107) Report VI(1), International Labour Office, 75th session, Geneva, 1988, 15.

[63] Ibid, 30: 'Issues of self-determination, and the exact definition of the meaning of this term, must be left to the highest political organs of the United Nations and cannot be debated in the ILO.'

[64] Ibid, 15.

[65] Ibid.

or yet to be formed.[66] The claims of IPOs from Canada and the United States were contrasted with those in Latin America, where most indigenous organisations had been set up in the last decade and were yet to achieve significant influence. The Latin American IPOs represented 'peasant communities and tribal groups' with far less ambitious interests, including 'the defence of their cultural identity and land ownership' and 'managing the expansion or improvement of public services and the individual rights of their members'.[67] The indigenous peoples of Latin America and Asia were being denied their most fundamental human rights. IPOs of North America, it was intimated, were more privileged sub-national groups, promoting their own 'radical' interests ahead of less well-off groups. For the ILO, there was also a sense that the WGIP drafting of the Declaration was more in tune with their aims because the process was dominated by discussion of claims to self-determination and historical remedies. The focus of the new Convention 169 thus remained on protecting the rights of the global community of culturally distinctive tribal peoples.

THE INCLUSION OF AFRICAN INDIGENOUS PEOPLES IN THE CONTEMPORARY INDIGENOUS MOVEMENT

More recently, the difficulties presented by the internationalisation of the indigenous movement in terms of differences in priorities, justifications and local social, economic and political circumstances were brought into sharp focus by the rise of the African indigenous movement. The relatively recent participation in the international movement of indigenous peoples from parts of the African region—eg the Batwa and San—was based largely on the concept of their cultural difference relative to other peoples in the same state and their 'indigenous priorities'—claims to lands and traditional knowledge.

Only months before it was hoped that the Declaration would be adopted by the UN General Assembly, some African states opposed it. The concerns of these states mirrored those of Asian states participating in the WGIP and WGDD. African states in general, however, had not participated regularly in either working group. This was partly because the indigenous peoples' movement in Africa had come to participate in the international movement in a meaningful manner at a relatively late

[66] Ibid, 16.

[67] Ibid. For these points, the ILO relied on a report prepared by the International Labour Office: *Rural Development, Taking into Account the Problems of the Indigenous Populations as well as the Drift of the Rural Population to the Cities and its Integration in the Urban Informal Sector*, Report II, 12th Conference of American States Members of the ILO, Montreal, 1986.

stage of the Declaration's drafting process, but also because of African states' lack of experience of the international movement and its potential application to the continent.

African concerns were directed at the potential instability that the Declaration could create for their states, given that it offered no definition of 'indigenous peoples', leaving its precise scope uncertain, as well as the fact that it contained controversial rights to self-determination, autonomy and lands that could be exploited by any group with separatist ambitions. Africa was said to be 'still recovering from the effects of ethnic based conflicts' and the absence of a definition would 'create tensions amongst ethnic groups and instability within sovereign States'.[68] To counter this resistance, indigenous activists emphasised that the concept of indigenous peoples in Africa was different from that in the Americas and Australasia. In a report issued in March 2007 by a group of experts on African indigenous peoples,[69] care was taken to demonstrate that the concept of indigenous peoples had a different meaning in the context of Africa compared with the west and that African claims to indigenous rights related to unique claims and were supported by a different set of historical justifications:

> [I]n Africa, the term 'indigenous peoples' does not mean first inhabitants as opposed to foreigners or communities that came from elsewhere. This specific meaning distinguishes Africa from other continents such as America and Australia, where native communities were virtually exterminated by foreigners who took their lands. Consequently, African states do not have any heavy past on their consciences that might justify reticence with regard to the Declaration.[70]

Instead, 'indigenous peoples' in the African context meant those peoples that had been 'left behind' by the colonisation process, peoples who had consistently suffered discrimination on the basis of their difference from the mainstream culture. The demand for post-colonial development programmes and projects had meant that the rights of these peoples were overlooked for the sake of the broader interests of the state. Given their unique status, African indigenous demands were said to be different to those of indigenous peoples of the Americas and Australasia. The brutal effects of colonisation in the west implied robust remedies for them, special rights, even possibly the right to secession. That was a problem for western, not African, states. The priorities for African indigenous peoples

[68] United Nations Declaration on the Rights of Indigenous Peoples, Draft Aide Memoire, African Group (2006) New York, para 2.2.

[69] Response Note to Draft Aide Memoire of the African Group on the UN Declaration on the Rights of Indigenous Peoples, presented by an African group of Experts, 21 March 2007.

[70] Ibid, 2.

were the fundamental human rights enjoyed by all African peoples and denied to them because of their cultural differences. It was not correct to talk about indigenous rights leading to tribalism and ethnic conflicts in Africa. African-indigenous claims to self-determination did not mean secession, but robust forms of political participation.[71] Additionally, in response to claims that African indigenous peoples could not be readily identified, it was argued that their numbers were small and they were readily identifiable by states as disadvantaged, isolated, culturally distinctive communities of 'hunter-gatherers and nomadic pastoralists'.

> [I]n Africa indigenous communities are clearly identified or identifiable by the rest of their fellow citizens and governments. These peoples or communities are largely hunter-gatherers and nomadic pastoralists whose methods of occupation and use of the land have not been legally recognised and protected. They include, among others, the 'Pygmies' of the African tropical forests, the San or 'Bushmen' of southern Africa, the Hadzabe, Akie, Ogiek, Yaaku, Sengwer and other hunter-gatherer groups in East Africa, various pastoralist groups in eastern, western and northern Africa such as the Maasai, Samburu, Turkana, Barabaig, Mbororo, Toubou, Tuareg etc. Since colonial times, these communities have remained in a disadvantaged position, primarily because of the prejudice and negative stereotyping to which they are victim, their geographical isolation, their high levels of poverty twinned with illiteracy, and their ways of life considered to be uneconomic, uncivilised and unproductive for national economies.[72]

While the African states' opposition to the Declaration threatened to scupper the adoption process, ultimately, all of the African states voted for the Declaration in the UN General Assembly. Changes had to be made to the Declaration to gain their approval, including a statement noting that the situation of indigenous peoples in different states will vary according to local and historical circumstances.[73] Also, African states

[71] Ibid, 5. See also IPACC, 'Statement on the UN General Assembly decisions to postpone the vote on the UN Declaration on the Rights of Indigenous Peoples', Press Release of the Indigenous Peoples of Africa Co-ordinating Committee (2006): 'The African group "aide memoire" repeatedly refers to the threat of secession. As most indigenous peoples in Africa number only a few thousand and live outside the cash economy, the assertion that so-called "Pygmies", "Dorobo" or San are going to separate from the state is blown out of proportion, fails to comprehend that no single African indigenous community claims statehood and there brings into question the "good faith" of the objections. Repeatedly in IPACC statements, African indigenous peoples have asked for greater inclusion in the State system, to have identity documents, citizenship, the right to vote, the right of access to schools and clinics, to be recognised by government and to be part of the nation's political economy. These are of course internal aspects of the right to self-determination, which should be differentiated from its external aspects leading to secessionism and statehood.'

[72] Response Note (n 69) 2.

[73] See the preambular paragraph of the Declaration: '*Recognising* that the situation of Indigenous Peoples varies from region to region and country to country and that the significance of national and regional particularities and various historical and cultural backgrounds should be taken into consideration ...'

continue to resist local application of the rights set out in the Declaration. But their participation in the process at such a critical stage and the resulting amendments suggests that the Declaration applies throughout Africa. Cultural difference, then, was a strong factor in the argument that African indigenous peoples should fall within the scope of the Declaration. As with the Asian indigenous movement, this was a matter of necessity. It was not possible for African IPOs to refer to the historical-based arguments of North America and Australasia. The 'first peoples', treaties and denial of the right to decolonisation justifications cannot be readily deployed in the African context. It was easier for African IPOs to emphasise other criteria that resonated with the international indigenous movement—cultural difference, particularly an association with traditional land, traditional knowledge, a history of marginalisation and poverty. These justifications also feed into their stated priorities of rights to lands and participation in decision-making.

Gradually, with time and perseverance, the indigenous movement in Africa might be able to move beyond these relatively modest priorities,[74] but the process is likely to be piecemeal and will vary according to local political and social contexts. In Asia, for example, indigenous peoples in some states have been able to be more assertive in their claims to rights to autonomy and free, prior and informed consent. Their claims and priorities have gradually converged with those of the indigenous peoples of North America and Australasia. In Latin America also, steps towards democracy and the resulting security for indigenous rights defenders have enabled them to be more assertive with their claims. But in all states progress remains slow and states continue to resist indigenous rights. So far though, despite some pessimism about the potential of an international indigenous rights movement, the movement has been remarkably effective.

THE CONCEPT OF INDIGENOUS PEOPLES AND CULTURAL DIFFERENCE

The use of cultural difference as a criterion for recognition of indigenous status raises obvious complications. States use cultural difference to limit their obligations to indigenous peoples, and particularly the powerful norms attached to the concept. The central role of cultural difference in (recent) African indigenist discourse threatens to limit the scope of their rights and lock out groups that fail to conform to the local image

[74] Note the report of March 2007 by the group of experts on African indigenous peoples claiming 'aspects of the right to self-determination that do not threaten national boundaries, including … the right to local self-government'.

of indigenous peoples. Sylvain, for example, writing about the problem in Southern Africa, notes how the emphasis on tradition has overlooked those San who were not able to maintain a measure of separateness because they were removed from their lands and as a result had become a permanent underclass working as farmhands.[75] In relation to the domestic African indigenous movement, anthropology scholars have been locked in debate for several years over the relative merits of cultural difference as a tool for identification. Kuper, the strongest critic, has likened the African indigenous movement's focus on originality and culture to the *blod* and *brocht* arguments of Nazi Germany.[76] For him, 'the conventional lines of argument currently used to justify "indigenous" land claims rely on obsolete anthropological notions and on romantic and false ethnographic visions'.[77] Also, the criteria have never worked well for indigenous peoples in the developed states of Australasia and North America. An important reason for the opposition of some of these indigenous activists to the introduction of a definition in the Declaration was concern that it would focus too much on cultural difference and not acknowledge their experience of resisting decades of assimilation policies.

But at the same time cultural difference has proven to be an essential tool for the Asian and African indigenous movements by (i) finding common cause with the international indigenous movement, particularly in Latin America; and (ii) closing the category of indigenous peoples within states, and assuring states that their priorities are reasonable and, therefore, less of a threat to the state. For example, African and Asian IPOs use cultural difference to assure states that the indigenous concept poses no threat of political instability in these regions because it excludes other ethnic minorities—sometimes known as 'communal contenders' or 'ethnonationalists'—with more ambitious aims than indigenous peoples, such as greater autonomy and sometimes secession from the state. Often these minorities were contenders but losers in the post-independence/decolonisation process of state formation. Indigenous peoples, on the other hand, were considered too backward and remote to participate in modern state formation. In the Democratic Republic of Congo, therefore, the concept of 'indigenous peoples' includes the Batwa but not the Bantu-speaking tribes. Similarly, in Mindanao, the Philippines, 'indigenous peoples' includes the Lumad peoples, but not the Moro Islamic peoples; in Sri Lanka, the Veddah but not the Tamil peoples. Cultural difference is also

[75] See R Sylvain, '"Land, Water and Truth": San Identity and Global Indigenism' (2002) 104 *American Anthropologist* 1074–85; and DL Hodgson, 'Precarious Alliances: The Cultural Politics and Structural Predicaments of the Indigenous Rights Movement in Tanzania' (2002) 104(4) *American Anthropologist* 1086–97.

[76] A Kuper, 'The Return of the Native' (2003) 3 *Current Anthropology* 395.

[77] Ibid.

used to draw a line between indigenous peoples and more acculturated, adjacent communities of 'peasant farmers', for example the *criollo/mestizo* in parts of Latin America. The difference between many of these groups is far from clear, of course, and there continues to be contestation and flux within states over who might qualify as indigenous.[78] Furthermore, the idea conflicts with the conventional wisdom that self-identification is the key criterion. But for now, the criterion of cultural difference has been remarkably effective in establishing indigenous movements outside of the Americas and Australasia. This is particularly critical in the context of Africa and Asia, because there are no robust human rights protections for sub-national groups, such as the San and the Cordillera peoples, and the situation is unlikely to change in the near future. The international movement, especially the rights set out in the Declaration, therefore provides a de facto human rights instrument for the protection of these peoples. In the Americas and Australasia too, IPOs have appealed to international concern for the preservation of original cultures, and cultural knowledge of their environs. Also, the idea of continuity of culturally distinctive community supported their argument that indigenous peoples are cohesive, distinctive 'peoples' entitled to self-determination. But these IPOs have also had to resist efforts by states to use cultural difference to limit the nature of their rights. The use of cultural difference in Australian and New Zealand native title litigation to limit indigenous rights to 'use rights' and not exclusive titles is an example of this dynamic. For the international indigenous movement, then, cultural difference arguments contain a paradox. It is an essential justification for recognition of indigenous rights, while at the same time it places significant obstacles on the path towards the recognition of indigenous rights.

THE INTERNATIONAL INDIGENOUS MOVEMENT—FUTURE ISSUES

Still, there are difficult times ahead. The use of cultural difference arguments in international meetings to gain traction for local indigenous movements will continue to undermine the efforts of many, while at the same time advancing their cause. States will continue to use cultural difference to limit both the scope of indigenous rights and the potential beneficiaries of such rights. Additionally, states in Asia and Africa are aware and have consistently argued that the campaign to internationalise

[78] See eg the conflation between indigenous rights and Afro-Caribbean rights to lands in the Inter-American Human Rights Court decisions of *Community of Moiwana v Suriname* (Series C No 124) [2005] IACHR 5 (15 June 2005); and *Case of the Saramaka People v Suriname* (Series C No 172) [2007] IACHR 5 (28 November 2007).

indigenous rights has obscured differences between the movements, particularly in terms of their respective justifications for the recognition of indigenous rights. These states will continue to use these differences to resist the application of the Declaration in their states.

The limiting effects of the use of cultural difference arguments and the differences in terms of justifications can best be kept in check through the efforts of supporters of the movement at the international and domestic levels. Much progress will depend on the skill of international NGOs and IPOs using the international and domestic framework to best effect through a continuous process of argument and persuasion—a largely constructivist approach. So far, international organisations—UN agencies, NGOs, IPOs, international financial institutions and international organisations—are mobilising behind the universal implementation of the Declaration. The PFII has made clear that it will promote respect for and full application of the Declaration—as it is asked to do in the Declaration[79]—and integrate the Declaration into its recommendations and regular work. One of its key roles is to coordinate, monitor and evaluate the activities of the UN agencies working with indigenous peoples. Moreover, the PFII has signalled that it wishes to play a monitoring-type role regarding the Declaration's implementation by states:

> In addition to integrating the [Declaration] into its regular work, the [PFII] will have to promote its implementation and follow up its effectiveness. It will have to promote a constructive dialogue with Governments on the challenges, achievements and priorities that indigenous issues require in each country. Such dialogue would take place periodically and enlist the participation of indigenous organizations and the United Nations system. The discussion and the role of the [PFII] would create an enabling environment of partnership and cooperation at the national and international levels, aiming at practical results on the ground. The example of a number of United Nations bodies in the human rights area provides a good guideline in that regard.[80]

A brief glance at the PFII's website reveals the reports filed by the international organisations with the PFII each year respecting their efforts to promote implementation of the Declaration. Many of these bodies, such as the United Nations Development Programme (UNDP) and the Office of the United Nations High Commissioner for Human Rights (OHCHR),

[79] See Art 42 of the Declaration: 'The United Nations, its bodies, including the Permanent Forum on Indigenous Issues, and specialized agencies, including at the country level, and States, shall promote respect for and full application of the provisions of this Declaration and follow up the effectiveness of this Declaration.'

[80] 'Structures, Procedures and Mechanisms that currently exist or that might be established to effectively address the human rights situation of indigenous peoples', paper prepared by two members of the Permanent Forum on Indigenous Issues, E/C.19/2008/2 (19 December 2007), para 38.

have offices scattered around the globe with people on the ground engaged with local communities and states. In African and Asian states, it is clear that these UN agencies struggle with the typical local sensitivities attached to the concept 'indigenous peoples' and there are reports that agencies disguise policies directed at indigenous peoples; or attach a less volatile label to the target group to avoid upsetting local governments.[81] Within the UN agencies themselves, there can be resistance to indigenous peoples' rights. With the UN focus on millennium development goals, there is the ever-present risk of the claims of indigenous peoples being lost amongst the emphasis placed on their *development* rights. This is a continuation of the old theme of development applied by the ILO, international agencies and states during the post-war years. Some poverty reduction initiatives—such as road construction to rural areas or investment and commercialisation programmes—can pose a threat to *indigenous* peoples. And indigenous peoples can face a struggle to differentiate their claims from those of similarly situated groups that do not identify as indigenous (eg Afro-Caribbean, *mestizo*, or peasant farmer claims to land rights). There are also the common problems of communicating with indigenous peoples—some agencies struggle to identify the representatives of indigenous communities, or find it easier to deal with intermediaries instead. Still, despite these challenges a review of the reports of the agencies reveals significant progress.[82] In particular, the ILO continues to direct its energies towards the promotion of indigenous peoples' rights in Asia, Africa and Latin American states. The ILO, having played a key role in the internationalisation of the indigenous movement, now has a responsibility to ensure that it does not falter. The ILO's technical arm will play an important function here, as will effective use of its monitoring mechanisms in relation to Conventions 107 and 169. If the ILO was ready during the 1970s and 1980s to adapt Convention 107 to the new philosophy of the emerging international indigenous movement, then there is hope that it may adapt Convention 169 to the new philosophy contained in the Declaration. Ultimately, however, the major responsibility for maintaining the momentum of international indigenous movements

[81] See M Ooft, *UNDP and Indigenous Peoples: Towards Effective Partnerships for Human Rights and Development*, UNDP Oslo Governance Centre, Democratic Governance Fellowship Programme, 2006: 'There are few projects or programmes in UNDP that are focused specifically on IPs and even fewer on IPs' rights. Generally the focus of those interventions is on increased participation of IPs in national policy dialogue and capacity strengthening for dealing with issues affecting them.'

[82] For example, the UNDP has established the Regional Initiative on Indigenous Peoples' Rights and Development (RIIPRD) in the Asia Pacific, which is aimed at building the capacity of Asian indigenous peoples. The Food and Agriculture Organisation (FAO) is engaged in activities aimed at improving the tenure security of the 'rural poor' in sub-Saharan Africa, and has supported demarcation initiatives in Angola and Chile.

and implementation of the Declaration lies with NGOs and IPOs. That leaves us with the question of the potential for the Declaration in North America/Australasia. All of these states voted against the Declaration, but Australia has recently supported it and it is hoped that the remaining three states will follow suit. But again, the support of these states and implementation will turn in large part on the skill and determination of the international indigenous movement.

CONCLUSIONS

Now, three years after the adoption of the Declaration by the UN General Assembly, we have a vibrant and energised international indigenous movement. The use of the concept of cultural difference played an important function in the realisation of this. The international movement has traction in regions—Asia and Africa—where there are no robust remedies for sub-national peoples and where such groups are frequently vulnerable to human rights violations. The ILO can take some of the credit for this. The challenge for the immediate future lies with the ILO and other key participants in the international indigenous movement—international NGOs, IPOs, etc—to engage in a continual process of exchange and persuasion with states.

5

Using the United Nations Declaration on the Rights of Indigenous Peoples in Litigation

CLIVE BALDWIN AND CYNTHIA MOREL

INTRODUCTION

THE ADOPTION OF the Declaration on the Rights of Indigenous Peoples ('the Declaration') by the United Nations General Assembly represents a major step forward in the development and articulation of the rights of indigenous peoples, at least in terms of achieving rights on paper. Thirty-nine Articles of the Declaration set out, in more precise language than in any previous global document, indigenous peoples' rights on many specific issues. As is the case with the new UN Convention on the Rights of Persons with Disabilities, adopted in 2006, the Declaration demonstrates a new type of international law-making where the people concerned have had very significant input, leading to a comprehensive document setting out their rights. However, if the rights set out at such length in the Declaration are actually to be secured and implemented, litigation will be required in order to give concrete effect to the rights in question. In this chapter, we, as litigators, will look at how a non-binding declaration can be used to achieve the actual implementation of the rights through both national and international courts.

Litigation has been increasingly important in securing indigenous rights in the last few decades. In both domestic courts and international jurisdictions, indigenous peoples have persuaded courts to recognise certain of their key rights, setting precedents that have been used by other indigenous groups around the world. There appears to be a trend towards increased strategic litigation on indigenous issues, as affected communities become more familiar with their rights and avenues for vindicating them.

The new, comprehensive and global Declaration therefore arrives at what could be a very opportune time in indigenous rights litigation. However, it is the manner in which activists and legal practitioners use the Declaration over the next decade that will largely determine whether it will eventually be regarded as the standard reference for indigenous rights law; or as a useful guide; or simply as an aspirational document of little or no consequence for change in the lives of indigenous peoples requiring its protection.

In this chapter, we shall first look at the legal status of the Declaration, both in international law and in terms of its possibilities at the domestic level, including how it has already been used in litigation and judgments. We shall look specifically at the closely related issues of whether the lack of a definition of the term 'indigenous peoples' matters in terms of litigation and also whether the Declaration itself will help the recognition of specific indigenous groups. Finally, we shall examine briefly how the Declaration could be used to further strengthen protection of key indigenous rights that have already been the subject of significant litigation, such as land rights and historic injustices. Any bias towards the African experience is due to our work in preparing and arguing the first indigenous land case before the African Commission on Human and Peoples' Rights—the *Endorois* case.[1]

LEGAL STATUS OF THE DECLARATION

For the Declaration to be used by lawyers, activists and most importantly judges, it will need to actually be accepted as an instrument having an impact on international or domestic law. More specifically, the Declaration will need to be perceived as an authoritative document for effectively addressing indigenous issues. At first glance, it may not be likely to be viewed as such on the basis of it being a declaration, rather than a legally binding treaty. In this regard, no one will be able to invoke the Declaration before a court specifically entrusted with its interpretation and enforcement. Furthermore, unlike the UN human rights treaties, the Declaration will lack its own specialist 'treaty' body to rule on violations, or to provide thorough guidance on its interpretation through General Comments.

However, the Declaration could still become a vital source for guidance on law. At the very least, the end product of a many years of discussion represents a consolidation of the law affecting indigenous peoples in a universal framework. As such, it has unparalleled legitimacy as a reference for any litigation affecting them. As former UN Special Rapporteur Rodolfo Stavenhagen put it in a report in February 2007, prior to the Declaration's adoption by the General Assembly:

> Having been adopted by the Human Rights Council, the Declaration is now an essential frame of reference for actions both by the Council itself and the

[1] *Minority Rights Group International and CEMIRIDE (on behalf of the Endorois Community) v Kenya*, Communication 276/2003. The ruling of the African Commission on Human and Peoples' Rights was made public in February 2010.

Office of the United Nations High Commissioner for Human Rights, and by other United Nations agencies. The Declaration will also serve as a guide for the actions of the international human rights treaty bodies. The Declaration must be a fundamental part of the discussion about future international standards relating to indigenous peoples, not only at the international level, but also in regional or specialized areas. Its adoption also gives a strong impetus to the clarification of emerging customary law concerning indigenous rights at the international level, and should similarly energize the processes of legislative reform and domestic court proceedings.[2]

The Declaration in Law

As the former Special Rapporteur noted, the Declaration will help to clarify the emergence of customary international law. Customary law, as is well known, is demonstrated by evidence of a 'general practice accepted as law'.[3] General acceptance of the principles set out in the Declaration is confirmed by the fact that after much discussion, 143 states voted in favour of the Declaration, with only four voting against[4] and 11 abstaining. Supporters of the Declaration came from every part of the globe. This is particularly significant given that the concept of indigenous peoples, and the acceptance that such peoples have specific rights, has often been portrayed as only applying to a few specific locations (notably in the Americas) and of not being a term that could be used in most of the world.[5] The Declaration marks a significant step in the right direction given that, to date, the only existing treaties to specifically address indigenous peoples' rights were the flawed International Labour Organization (ILO) Convention 107, and ILO Convention 169, which had secured only 19 ratifications by the time the Declaration was approved.[6]

[2] United Nations, Report of the Special Rapporteur on the situation of human rights and fundamental freedoms of indigenous people (Rodolfo Stavenhagen), UN Doc A/HRC/4/32 (2007), para 79,. daccess-ods.un.org/TMP/3658674.html

[3] Statute of the International Court of Justice, Art 38.

[4] Australia, one of the four opponents, announced its support for the Declaration on 3 April 2009 as did New Zealand in April 2010 The two remaining opponents Canada and the USA have stated that they are reviewing their positions with regard to the Declaration.

[5] See eg the Draft Aide Memoire, African Group, United Nations Declaration on the Rights of Indigenous Peoples, 9 November 2006, www.ipacc.org.za/uploads/docs/Africanaidememoire.pdf.

[6] ILO Convention 107 was widely rejected by indigenous peoples around the world, who called for the adoption of new standards that would recognise indigenous peoples' rights to exist as separate, distinct peoples. The International Labour Conference adopted a new Convention, ILO 169, in 1989 which revised ILO 107. This means that the latter is no longer open to further ratifications; but it is still in force in those countries which ratified it and have not yet ratified ILO 169.

Opinio juris is notoriously difficult to assess, but in favour of the Declaration being customary law is the fact that it is drafted in positive legal language, rather than in the form of mere exhortation. It is also free of caveats such as that found in Article 1(3) of ILO Convention 169. Another factor suggesting that the Declaration was seen by states as having at least some legal effect is the diligence accorded by states to the drafting process, along with the fact that those few states that objected to its adoption appeared to do so through fear that by accepting, they would be accepting some form of legal commitment. In addition, the action of governments and courts in countries such as Japan, Bolivia and Belize in the short time since the Declaration was agreed shows how some countries (or domestic courts) have already perceived the Declaration as establishing requirements for action.

This call for action is enshrined in Article 42 of the Declaration, which calls upon states to 'promote respect for and full application of the provisions of this Declaration and follow up the effectiveness of this Declaration'. Bolivia has been most explicit in addressing this provision by incorporating the Declaration into domestic law on 7 November 2007.[7] Litigation in that country will now clearly be able to rely directly on the Declaration. Further, the Supreme Court of Belize has confirmed that the Declaration can equally be relied upon at the highest levels of domestic courts even in countries that have not formally incorporated its content into domestic legislation. In the spirit of Article 42, which imposes duties on governments to promote respect for and full application of the provisions of the Declaration, the Supreme Court of Belize has demonstrated how the articles of the Declaration could have binding effect in its domestic law. This was demonstrated in the case of *Cal v Attorney General of Belize*,[8] where the Supreme Court of Belize held that, on the basis of having voted for the Declaration, Belize had an obligation to respect the right to property of indigenous peoples, as set out in the Declaration. The Court held that, because the property provisions of the Declaration embodied 'general principles of international law', those articles of the Declaration had the same force as would articles of a treaty.

Cal represents the strongest judgment to date on the binding nature of the Declaration. Still, it is clear that the Declaration can and has been used as a source of law and for guidance in interpreting relevant domestic laws (or articles in human rights treaties) by domestic and interna-

[7] Adopted as National Law 3760 on the Rights of Indigenous Peoples. The wording of the law is an exact copy of the Declaration.

[8] *Aurelio Cal and the Maya Village of Santa Cruz v Attorney General of Belize; and Manuel Coy and Maya Village of Conejo v Attorney General of Belize*, (Consolidated) Claim Nos 171 & 172, 2007, Supreme Court of Belize (18 October 2007).

tional courts, and in the drafting of laws in many different parts of the world. In the first judgment on an indigenous rights case at the international level since the adoption of the Declaration, *Saramaka People v Suriname*, the Inter-American Court of Human Rights explicitly used the Declaration as a source in addressing the issue of the need for a community to give prior and informed consent to the use of its land.[9] The Court drew attention to the fact that, in voting for the Declaration, Suriname had expressly supported its Article 32, which showed that 'consultation should not be viewed as an end in of itself, but should serve the purpose of respecting the interest of those who used the land'.[10] The Colombian Constitutional Court drew heavily on the principles of the then-draft Declaration, in a case in 2003 relating to the issue of prior and informed consent.[11] In a subsequent case in the same court inin 2006 further express reference to the (still draft) Declaration was made in relation to the right to prior and informed consent, and the rights related to demarcation of land, as well as exploitation of natural resources.[12]

Despite the previous limited acceptance of indigenous rights in Africa, there has also been reference to and support for the Declaration in that continent. At the regional level, this has been most evident in the African Commission on Human and Peoples' Rights' adoption of an Advisory Opinion on the Declaration.[13] Its active lobbying of the African Union (AU) in a bid to reverse the AU's initial rejection of the Declaration is also significant, coming as it did from the African regional system's guardian of human rights. These significant steps forward subsequently paved the way for the first indigenous land rights case to be successful before the African Commission, and adopted by the AU, in February 2010.[14] The African Commission drew extensively on the Declaration's provisions to support its findings of violations in relation to the Endorois Community's rights to land and natural resources, their cultural and religious rights, and their right to development.

This landmark precedent builds on initial references to the principles of the draft Declaration in domestic jurisdictions in Africa as early as 2006, as evidenced in a Kenyan High Court case dealing with public

[9] *Case of the Saramaka People v Suriname* (Series C No 172) [2007] IACHR 5 (28 November 2007), para 131.

[10] Ibid. See fn 131 of the judgment.

[11] Constitutional Court of Colombia, Judgment SU.383/03, Indigenous Community on prior consultation, right to ethnic and cultural integrity (Comunidad Indigena—Consulta previa, acción de tutela, derecho a la integridad étnica y cultural de la comunidad indigena).

[12] Constitutional Court of Colombia, Judgment T-880/2006.

[13] Advisory Opinion of the African Commission on Human and Peoples' Rights on the UN Declaration on the Rights of Indigenous Peoples, 41st Ordinary Session, Accra, Ghana, May 2007.

[14] *Endorois* case (n 1).

participation.[15] Similarly, the San's decisive Botswana High Court victory on a case involving their land rights[16] resulted in a judgment heavily reliant on several of the principles of the Declaration, including the obligation of governments to respect indigenous systems of land rights and the intrinsic link between the preservation of indigenous culture and the right to life of indigenous peoples. It is remarkable that such reliance on the Declaration's principles occurred in a judgment preceding its adoption. Additional evidence of courts in Africa applying the principles enshrined in the Declaration can be found in the South Africa Constitutional Court ruling in the *Richtersveld* case, where it was found that South African law could recognise rights over land for an indigenous community, with the Court recognising the traditional laws and practices of that community.[17]

Asia provides limited positive examples to date on the implementation of indigenous rights. The Philippines counts as one notable exception at least on paper through the adoption of the Indigenous Peoples Rights Act (IPRA) in 1997.[18] Though fraught with obstacles which ultimately frustrate its effective implementation, it is worth noting that from a purely normative standpoint, the IPRA is consistent with many of the standards set out in the Declaration. In fact, express reference is made to the 'Universal Declaration of Indigenous Peoples Rights', which presumably is meant to read as the UN Declaration on the Rights of Indigenous Peoples, even if at the time of adoption the Declaration only existed in draft form.[19] Though reliance on the Declaration for the promotion and protection of indigenous rights has yet to take root in Asia, Japan's marked shift in attitude towards the concept of indigenous peoples on its territory, described further below, certainly confirms its potential impact at government and other policy-making levels. If governments recognise the Declaration, then their courts should too.

Minimum Standards

Article 43 of the Declaration states that the Declaration establishes minimum standards of rights. The meaning of this is linked to Article 1, which

[15] *Rangal Lemeiguran v Attorney General* [2006] High Court of Nairobi, 18 December 2006, www.kenyalaw.org. The judgment, delivered prior to the adoption of the Declaration on the Rights of Indigenous Peoples, cited Arts 3 (on equality) and 7 (on free, prior and informed consent) of ILO Convention 169. Art 3 corresponds to the Declaration's Art 2. Art 7 corresponds to the Declaration's Arts 10, 11(2), 19, 28(1), 29(2) and 32(2).

[16] *Sesana v Attorney General* (52/2002) [2006] BWHC 1 (13 December 2006).

[17] *Alexkor Ltd v Richtersveld Community*, Constitutional Court of South Africa, October 2003.

[18] Rules and regulations implementing Republic Act No 8371, otherwise known as the (1997) Indigenous Peoples' Rights Act.

[19] The reference is made under Rule VI, Section 10, dealing with intellectual property rights, which echoes Art 31 of the Declaration.

states that indigenous peoples have the right to the full enjoyment, as a collective or as individuals, of all human rights and fundamental freedoms as set out in international law. Therefore, countries remain bound to protect indigenous rights on the basis of international treaties they have signed, customary law, or domestic practice that already matches or exceeds the protections afforded under the Declaration. The Declaration can explain or supplement these rights, especially by adding the collective dimension. It certainly cannot be used to take away any rights from indigenous peoples.[20] In terms of binding international standards of equal or higher value, signatories to ILO Convention 169 remain bound to maintain that Convention as a minimum standard to be upheld, which if undertaken in 'good faith' requires a level of protection comparable to the provisions set out in the Declaration, with the notable exception of the right to self-determination.[21]

Using the Declaration in International Litigation—UN Bodies

The Declaration therefore can and should be used when litigating on any rights issue that affects indigenous peoples, which is addressed by at least one of its articles. For the UN treaty bodies, where litigation is often possible using the complaints procedures, the starting point should be the requirement in Article 42 of the Declaration that '[t]he United Nations, its bodies, including the Permanent Forum on Indigenous Issues, and specialized agencies, including at the country level, and states shall promote respect for and full application of the provisions of this Declaration and follow up the effectiveness of this Declaration'. One could infer from this provision that treaty bodies, and any other UN judicial body, should produce decisions consistent with the Declaration.

Whilst the International Covenant on Civil and Political Rights (ICCPR) does not enshrine an express provision on indigenous rights, a wealth of case law on indigenous rights has been generated under Article 27.[22]

[20] Arts 37 and 45 of the Declaration. See also Art 53 of the European Convention on Human Rights: 'Nothing in this Convention shall be construed as limiting or derogating from any of the human rights and fundamental freedoms which may be ensured under the laws of any High Contracting Party or under any other agreement to which it is a Party', and the American Convention on Human Rights, Art 28(3)(b): 'No provision of this Convention shall be interpreted as … (b) restricting the enjoyment or exercise of any right or freedom recognized by virtue of the laws of any State Party or by virtue of another convention to which one of the said states is a party.'

[21] This reverts back to the caveat set out under Art 1(3), which strips the rights holders under ILO Convention 169 of any rights associated with 'peoples' under international law. The primary right associated with peoples under international law is of course that of (internal) self-determination.

[22] See eg *Lubicon Lake Band v Canada*, HRC Communication No 167/1984 (26 March 1990); *Länsman v Finland*, HRC Communication No 511/1992 (14 October 1993); and *Apirana Mahuika v New Zealand*, HRC Communication No 547/1993 (27 October 2000).

These cases touch on public participation, representation, community rights and land rights. The Declaration can and should be used from now on as a guide to interpreting these rights as they apply to indigenous peoples. Most notably, however, Article 1 of both the ICCPR and its twin Covenant, the International Covenant on Economic, Social and Cultural Rights (ICESCR), upholds the right to self-determination—a right of fundamental importance to indigenous peoples. In assessing whether the Declaration will assist in litigation on self-determination, one must first understand the two fundamental obstacles that have prevented indigenous peoples from having any rights under the common Article 1 secured by litigation.

First, the Optional Protocol to the ICCPR, which allows for victims of human rights violations to take petitions to the Human Rights Committee, has been limited by the Committee to petitions on behalf of individuals, rather than groups. While some indigenous communities have successfully applied as collectives, communications to this body otherwise generally consist of individual claims, or claims of individuals affected by a similar issue in community with others. However, the Committee has maintained that it cannot address complaints alleging violations of Article 1, even when submitted by an identifiable people.[23] In this context, the only indigenous rights cases to be successfully litigated under Article 27 have been those where the Committee has accepted the litigants , as individuals, living in community with others.

The second obstacle lies in the fact that the right to self-determination under Article 1 of the ICCPR is reserved for 'peoples' under international law. Unlike ILO Convention 169, which effectively strips indigenous peoples of the rights afforded to 'peoples' under international law in Article 1(3), the ICCPR is silent as to who may or may not qualify as the holders of the right to self-determination. The Human Rights Committee (HRC) has said that as Article 1 is not an issue to be considered under the Optional Protocol—ie in litigation before the Committee—the Committee will not rule on who constitutes 'a people'.[24] The new Optional Protocol to the ICESCR, for its part, is silent on whether communications (i.e. litigation under the Covenant) can include possible violations of its Article 1. Nevertheless, the final version of the Protocol is an improvement on earlier drafts that had specifically excluded Article 1 for consideration by the Committee on Economic, Social and Cultural Rights (CESCR) in communications with the opposition to such inclusion coming from the United Kingdom and

[23] *Lubicon*, ibid, para 32.
[24] Ibid.

other countries.[25] The adoption of the Declaration represents an opportunity for the Human Rights Committee and CESCR to allow the right to self-determination to be litigated. In particular, the fact that most states in the world have accepted that indigenous peoples are indeed 'peoples' and therefore have a right to self-determination ought to mean that the application of that right in individual cases should be considered. As one of the most widely ratified human rights instruments,[26] use of the ICCPR in particular would make it possible for any strengthened jurisprudence and protection of the right to self-determination to extend to the widest possible geographic scope.

Regional Tribunals

We have already seen how the Inter-American Court has interpreted its regional human rights treaty to recognise and address key rights of indigenous peoples, most notably in relation to property, despite the lack of mention of indigenous peoples or a collective right to property within the wording of the American Convention on Human Rights. Given that it has already used the Declaration in its judgment in *Saramka v Suriname*, it seems likely that this regional Court will be a key body in terms of the development and application of the Declaration in legal cases.[27]

As previously stated, the African Commission on Human and Peoples' Rights has recently joined the Inter-American system in expressly relying upon the Declaration in its ruling in the *Endorois* case, a case for which we served as co-counsel, along with Korir Singo'ei from Nairobi-based CEMIRIDE.[28] In relation to restitution, the African Commission drew heavily on the principles of the Declaration, starting by making specific reference to Article 27 which states that:

> Indigenous peoples have the right to restitution of the lands, territories and resources which they have traditionally owned or otherwise occupied or used; and which have been confiscated, occupied, used or damaged without their free and informed consent. Where this is not possible, they have the right to just and fair compensation. Unless otherwise freely agreed upon by the peoples

[25] United Nations, Report of the Open-Ended Working Group on an Optional Protocol to the International Covenant on Economic, Social and Cultural Rights on its 5th session, UN Doc A/HRC/8/7 (2008).

[26] There are 162 nations party to the ICCPR—70 others are signatories to the Convention. treaties.un.org/Pages/ViewDetails.aspx?src=TREATY&mtdsg_no=IV-4&chapter=4&lang=en

[27] *Saramaka People v Suriname* (n 9) para 131.

[28] *Endorois* case (n 1).

> concerned, compensation shall take the form of lands, territories and resources equal in quality, size and legal status.[29]

The African Commission further drew on the principles of the Declaration for defining the content and meaning of restitution. In this regard, it drew on a number of provisions to support its finding that:

> The jurisprudence under international law bestows the right of ownership rather than mere access. The African Commission notes that if international law were to grant access only, indigenous peoples would remain vulnerable to further violations/dispossession by the State or third parties. Ownership ensures that indigenous peoples can engage with the state and third parties as active stakeholders rather than as passive beneficiaries.[30]

Sub-regional inter-governmental groupings, such as the Economic Community of West African States (ECOWAS) and the Southern African Development Community (SADC), perhaps also have a role to play in increasing effective protection of indigenous peoples through the scope and content of the Declaration, given the space accorded to human rights (however modest) within their mandates. In terms of litigation, the Community Court of Justice of the Economic Community of West African States (ECOWAS Court) has already proven its potential for providing expedient hearings and its openness to ruling on human rights issues. This was demonstrated in the case of *Hadijatou v Niger*, submitted to the ECOWAS Court in September 2007, and culminating in a hearing on admissibility by April 2008. A final judgment was delivered on 27 October 2008.[31] It remains to be seen whether indigenous issues could be equally successful before this body; such bodies' primary focus on economic integration supposes that cases touching on land rights or natural resources may prove particularly contentious.

As signatories to a variety of treaties, a vast number of states are governed by an increasingly interdependent network of standards for the promotion and protection of indigenous peoples' rights. It is an interdependence strengthened by virtue of the duty of supervisory bodies to rely on the wider body of international law when interpreting the application of their respective covenants, conventions and charters.[32] The

[29] Ibid, para 232, citing Art 27 of the Declaration on the Rights of Indigenous Peoples, E/CN.4/Sub.2/1994/2/Add.1 (1994).

[30] Ibid, para 204, citing Arts 8(2)(b), 10, 25, 26 and 27 of the UN Declaration on the Rights of Indigenous Peoples.

[31] Case supported by the Niger-based anti-slavery association, Timidria, and London-based Anti-Slavery International. The ECOWAS Court, which has authority across most of West Africa, found Niger to be in breach of its own laws and international obligations to protect its citizens from slavery. The Court has made clear that Niger is obliged to take positive measures to protect its citizens from slavery.

[32] Eg as guaranteed in Art 60 of the African Charter of Human and Peoples' Rights.

adoption of the Declaration serves to raise the minimum threshold, as a universal benchmark, to be upheld by these bodies and the states parties to their respective treaties. It is the very interdependence that characterises these bodies that will help to sharpen the scope and application of the Declaration's provisions. Lawyers have a strong role to play in mapping out the best possible test cases to help make this possible, with the outcome of these cases heavily dependent on the extent of their creativity in using the Declaration to form their arguments. Most important is that courts, and other judicial bodies, at both the domestic and the international level, give real meanings to the rights.

Application in Domestic Courts

What is the practical scope of the legal application of the Declaration for domestic litigators? This depends to a degree on how domestic courts will use such international instruments as the Declaration. Looking at whether international law may be 'invoked' begs the question of what such 'invocation' entails, as the term may refer to the use of international law as a guide to interpretation, or as the substantive basis of a legal remedy.[33] Given that the Declaration is not an international treaty, whether the state's courts formally adopt a monist or dualist approach to international treaties in domestic law is not of great significance in terms of how its courts can use and apply the Declaration. Whatever the legal tradition in a given state, international law creates a legal space, within a domestic jurisdiction, to influence the adoption (or improvement) of domestic legislation on the legal principles involved. The Declaration can therefore be referred to by domestic courts, as has already happened in the cases set out above. Actions such as that already taken in Bolivia in formally incorporating the Declaration into domestic law will make it particularly easy in some countries to use the Declaration in litigation. As was shown in *Cal*, domestic courts may and can interpret this Declaration as giving rise to legal rights directly in national law, even without any specific domestic 'adoption' of the document.[34] Further, we believe that the Declaration can be used as a guide to interpreting the relevant law in any case, regardless of the jurisdiction, where indigenous peoples' rights are an issue.

It should also be noted that by ratifying human rights treaties, whether at the UN or regional level, states are required to ensure that their

[33] See F Viljoen, *Human Rights in Africa: National and International Protection* (Oxford University Press, 2007) 18.

[34] For a more general examination of domestic courts and international law, see Viljoen, ibid, 533–34.

domestic system provides available, effective and sufficient remedies.[35] The Declaration itself requires this of states, for both individual and collective rights, in Article 40. If the Declaration is used, as it should be, as a guide in the interpretation of any relevant human right, indigenous peoples can argue at the domestic level that states are under an obligation to ensure that they can secure their rights in domestic courts, and that courts need to interpret the domestic law to allow their rights to be considered. This would include, most notably, their rights as 'peoples', and all rights in their individual and collective dimensions. Where states, including domestic courts, refuse to allow indigenous rights to be determined and secured domestically, indigenous peoples will have strong grounds to bring their cases to international tribunals on the basis that their domestic system does not provide available, effective and sufficient remedies.

A key issue will be whether domestic courts can and do recognise collective rights. In the *Endorois* case, the Kenyan High Court's reliance on the protection of property rights as individual rights only in the Kenyan Bill of Rights was pivotal to the applicants' success in proving exhaustion of domestic remedies. The African Commission agreed that such narrow restrictions on the right to property under Kenyan law resulted in there being no available, effective and sufficient remedies to safeguard the collective land rights sought by the Endorois Community. The Declaration makes it even clearer that governments can and should give recognition to collective rights at the domestic level—and that a failure to grant this recognition would ultimately pave the way for access to international courts, as no effective remedy at the domestic level could be successfully argued.

DEFINITIONS AND RECOGNITION

The term 'indigenous peoples' is not defined in the Declaration. This could be a major limitation on the Declaration's usefulness in litigation. A criticism often articulated on this issue is that it would be very difficult to conduct litigation, which requires precision, when the rights holders themselves are not clearly identified. Concerns relating to this issue were articulated in a Draft Aide Memoire put forward by the African Group at the UN in early 2007, which emphasised that the adoption of the

[35] A remedy is only effective if it offers a prospect of success (*Akdivar v Turkey*, ECHR App No 21893/93, para 65; *Aksoy v Turkey*, ECHR App No 21987/93, para 51); and it is sufficient if it is capable of redressing the complaint (*X v Portugal*, ECHR App No 11660/85). A remedy that is not available, effective and sufficient need not be exhausted. A 'remedy' is not 'available' where the avenue is incapable of redressing the applicant's complaints (*Akdivar*, para 65).

Declaration without a definition would be 'legally incorrect', and that the lack of a definition was likely to 'create tensions amongst ethnic groups and instability within sovereign States'.[36]

With respect to the claim that it is 'legally incorrect' to adopt a Declaration without a definition, the Declaration is far from being alone in not defining its basic terms. Few treaties that contain the word actually define 'peoples'; one example of an instrument that fails to do so is the African Charter on Human and Peoples' Rights. Similarly, the 1992 Declaration on the Rights of Persons Belonging to National or Ethnic, Religious or Linguistic Minorities contains no definition of 'minorities'. This issue is little different from the arguments about definitions of other key human rights terms, such as 'arbitrary detention' or even 'religion'. As in those cases, the absence of a straight-jacket definition should not be viewed as a liability, but instead as an opportunity to afford the flexibility necessary to accommodate the various expressions and characteristics of indigenous peoples worldwide.[37] A degree of understanding as to who is and is not an indigenous people has been emerging through guidance of experts—and in time, key cases will emerge and assist.

It is important to note also that definitions for indigenous peoples already exist, set out by UN and regional bodies, which provide guidance on what approaches may be adopted and how much flexibility is possible within an overall understanding. In the authors' opinion, the most comprehensive definition to date has been developed by Erica-Irene Daes, the chairperson of the United Working Group on Indigenous Populations.[38] Criteria used in determining the existence of an indigenous people include the occupation and use of a specific territory; the voluntary perpetuation of cultural distinctiveness; self-identification as a distinct collectivity, as well as recognition by other groups; and finally, an experience of subjugation, marginalisation, dispossession, exclusion or discrimination. The Declaration supports these criteria. On self-identification, Article 33 of the Declaration confirms the right of indigenous peoples to 'determine their identity or membership in accordance to their customs and traditions'. In that regard, the Declaration itself will be a useful guide on the question of definition. Paragraphs 4, 5, 6 and 10 of the preamble also leave little doubt as to what groups the Declaration is intended to protect. Also noteworthy is that fact the Declaration has abstained from making

[36] *Draft Aide Memoire of the African Group: A Brief Commentary*, Indigenous Peoples of Africa Coordinating Committee, 16 January 2007, www.converge.org.nz/pma/indig.htm.

[37] Numerous expert bodies concur on this point, including the African Commission on Human and Peoples' Rights, as confirmed in its Advisory Opinion (n 13) paras 9–13.

[38] See eg E-I Daes, 'Indigenous Peoples' Rights to Land and Natural Resources' in N Ghanea and A Xanthaki (eds), *Minorities, Peoples and Self-Determination: Essays in Honour of Patrick Thornberry* (Leiden, Martinus Nijhoff, 2005) 75–91.

undermining caveats analogous to Article 1(3) of ILO Convention 169, which had firmly excluded the use of the term 'peoples' in that Convention as being construed to have 'any implications as regards the rights which may attach to the term under international law'. By refraining from making such a statement, the Declaration makes it clear that indigenous peoples are to be treated in a similar way to all other peoples (and therefore should be defined in the same way, at least as regards the word 'peoples').

Americas

At the regional level, the most advanced level of recognition exists in the Americas. While the concept of indigenousness may be most evidently clear on this continent, the Inter-American Court of Human Rights has embraced the flexibility encouraged by the UN Working Group on Indigenous Populations in instances where protection was required by communities of African descent who demonstrated an ancestral and spiritual relationship with their land in the Americas; shared this land collectively; and proved that the use of this land was central to their traditional social and economic way of life. This approach was first adopted in the case of *Moiwana Village v Suriname* (2005), which acknowledged the obligation of the Surinamese government to properly investigate the massacre of the residents of a Maroon village in part because of the spiritual and cultural connection of the villagers to their land.[39] It was reiterated in *Saramaka People v Suriname,* decided after the adoption of the Declaration, which affirmed the rights of descendants of escaped African slaves to have their traditional property rights protected by the state. In *Saramaka,* the Court acknowledged that the community were not indigenous to the area, but as a 'tribal' people they had developed a strong connection to the land and therefore indigenous rights applied, including collective rights and the necessity for prior and informed consent. On this, the Court referred specifically to the Declaration, including the fact that Suriname had supported it at the UN General Assembly.[40]

Africa

Until very recently, the concept of indigenousness in Africa was widely rejected. African governments across the continent strenuously argued

[39] *Community of Moiwana v Suriname* (Series C No 124) [2005] IACHR 5 (15 June 2005).
[40] *Saramaka People v Suriname* (n 9) para 131.

that all Africans are indigenous to Africa. This, however, has been increasingly acknowledged as too simplistic an idea, with there being many distinct groups across the continent that fit the existing definition. It has been recognised, by numerous African governments and civil society alike, that labelling all Africans as indigenous would mean that it would not be possible to litigate or otherwise secure indigenous rights in Africa, as no distinct indigenous groups could be found. In this respect, the Working Group on Indigenous Populations/Communities (WGIPC), created by the African Commission on Human and Peoples' Rights, warned that if the concept of *indigenous* was exclusively linked with a colonial situation, it would leave no suitable concept for analysing internal structural relationships of inequality that have persisted after liberation from colonial dominance.[41]

Accordingly, the WGIPC has stressed that in Africa, as elsewhere, an understanding of who is indigenous can be found through recent approaches elsewhere in the world that rely on *self-identification* as distinctly different from other groups within a state; on a *special attachment to and use of their traditional land* whereby the ancestral land and territory of the group is of fundamental importance to their collective physical and cultural survival as peoples; and on an experience of *subjugation, marginalisation, dispossession, exclusion or discrimination* because these peoples have different cultures, ways of life or modes of production from the national hegemonic and dominant model.[42] The WGIPC's significant research and advocacy efforts since 2005 were instrumental in shifting opinions to recognise that indigenous peoples' socio-economic and cultural survival which depends on access to their ancestral lands warrant special forms of protection.[43] The synergies between the WGIPC and the wider advocacy process surrounding the adoption of the Declaration makes clear that that such bodies can play a vital role in strengthening the scope and application of indigenous peoples' rights at the regional level.

Any remaining doubt about the status of indigenous peoples in Africa will have been allayed by the very clear ruling on this issue by the African Commission in the *Endorois* case. Noting that the term 'indigenous peoples' was a 'contested term' with 'no universal and unambiguous

[41] WGIPC report 2005, submitted in accordance with the Resolution on the Rights of Indigenous Populations/Communities in Africa, adopted by the African Commission on Human and Peoples' Rights at its 28th ordinary session, p 92.

[42] Ibid, pp 92–93.

[43] See Report of the African Commission's Working Group of Experts on Indigenous Populations/Communities (2005), submitted in accordance with the Resolution on the Rights of Indigenous Populations/Communities in Africa, adopted by the African Commission on Human and Peoples' Rights at its 28th ordinary session. See also *Indigenous Peoples in Africa: The Forgotten Peoples? The African Commission's Work on Indigenous Peoples in Africa* (International Work Group for Indigenous Affairs, 2006).

definition', it went on to state that the African Charter places special emphasis on the rights of peoples, and that the term 'indigenous' is 'not intended to create a special class of citizens, but rather to address historical and present-day injustices and inequalities'. With respect to the Endorois, the Commission stressed the importance of their sacred relationship with the land, and self-identification in determining whether they were an indigenous people. It ruled:

> From all the evidence (both oral and written and video testimony) submitted to the African Commission, the African Commission agrees that the Endorois are an indigenous community and that they fulfil the criterion of 'distinctiveness'. The African Commission agrees that the Endorois consider themselves to be a distinct people, sharing a common history, culture and religion. The African Commission is satisfied that the Endorois are a 'people', a status that entitles them to benefit from provisions of the African Charter that protect collective rights. The African Commission is of the view that the alleged violations of the African Charter are those that go to the heart of indigenous rights—the right to preserve one's identity through identification with ancestral lands.

Asia

A 2007 report of the Special Rapporteur on indigenous peoples confirmed that the situation of indigenous peoples in Asia, who consist of tens of millions of individuals across the continent and are present in virtually all the countries of the region, has long been neglected and has only recently begun to be considered at the international level. The Special Rapporteur cited that one reason for the lack of a comprehensive analysis of the human rights problems faced by these peoples is the history of differences between Asian states in terms of how their laws and public policies refer to these peoples and define their legal status.[44]

The Special Rapporteur noted that:

> While States such as Cambodia, Nepal and the Philippines explicitly use the term 'indigenous', which is now used in international discourse on the subject, other countries have traditionally used different expressions, such as 'tribal peoples' and 'hill tribes', as well as similar expressions in local languages, such as Adivasis or Orang Asli, which refer to the idea of aboriginality. In other countries the legal and constitutional treatment of these peoples is not noticeably different from that of other minority groups; rather, they are subsumed under the category of 'ethnic minorities' or 'national minorities'.[45]

[44] Report of the Special Rapporteur on the situation of human rights and fundamental freedoms of indigenous people, A/62/286, 21 August 2007, para 44.

[45] Ibid, para 44.

Irrespective of these variations, the Special Rapporteur stressed the commonalities between these peoples and indigenous peoples in other parts of the world, that is, 'a set of cultural, social and economic characteristics that make them particularly vulnerable to marginalization and discrimination by majority sectors of the population in the countries they inhabit, exclude them from decision-making processes at all levels in their own countries and make them victims of systematic human rights violations'.[46]

Commonalities or not, what remains is that without some form of recognition or official legal status, indigenous peoples will generally fail in their attempt to secure their rights. Certainly the absence of a regional mechanism in Asia has reduced the scope for indigenous peoples in that region to actively use international law in order to overcome their pervasive invisibility. The vacuum of regional standards therefore perhaps explains why one of the Declaration's greatest impacts thus far—in terms of fostering recognition—has taken place in Japan. On 23 May 2008, during discussions in Parliament on Ainu rights, which would ultimately be passed in the Diet, Chief Cabinet Secretary Nobutaka Machimura publicly stated that:

> The response will be decided after looking at the draft Diet resolution. However, there is the important fact that the UN General Assembly adopted the Declaration (on the rights of indigenous peoples) in September last year, and that Japan supported this. So I believe this should be examined in a positive light.[47]

The significance of this statement is immense given Japan's longstanding official position that it is a mono-ethnic state, devoid of minorities or indigenous peoples.

In sum, whether at the UN or the regional level, all working definitions echo the key principles advanced by Rodolfo Stavenhagen, former Special Rapporteur on the situation of human rights and fundamental freedoms of indigenous people, who emphasised that '[f]rom a human rights perspective, the question is not who came first but the shared experiences of dispossession and marginalisation. The term "indigenous" is not intended to create a special class of citizens, but rather to address historical and present-day injustices and inequalities.'[48] Therefore the Declaration, far from being stymied by the apparent lack of a definition, can actually assist in making clear who are the indigenous peoples to whom the rights apply, especially in regions of the world such as Africa

[46] Ibid, para 45.

[47] Quoted in *Yomiuri* newspaper, 23 May 2008.

[48] Fifth Report of the Special Rapporteur on the situation of human rig[illegible] freedoms of indigenous people (Rodolfo Stavenhagen), UN Doc E/CN.4,

and Asia, where there has been reluctance even to accept the existence of indigenous peoples.

SPECIFIC ISSUES—LITIGATING LAND AND HISTORIC INJUSTICES

Land

The key right for many indigenous peoples is that of land. This has been and will continue to be one of the centrepieces of litigation on indigenous issues. Deciding on who the rightful owners of lands are and whether land should be returned to the peoples who originally owned it, whether they should be compensated, or the extent of other rights, such as access and use, are all legal issues that will require judicial or other legal determination[49]. Where, as in most of the world, these issues are far from having been resolved on the ground, litigation—and especially test cases—will be needed to determine and confirm the basic principles in action.

Litigation on indigenous land issues goes back centuries in some states, such as the United States. Famously, the US Supreme Court found in favour of the Cherokee in *Worcester v Georgia* in 1832.[50] However, the judgment was then effectively ignored by President Andrew Jackson and the Georgia state authorities, with the Cherokee being evicted from their land very shortly afterwards, in the Trial of Tears. However, in recent decades a series of precedent-setting decisions have begun to address the issue of indigenous peoples' right to land, both land they still occupy and land they have lost in the past. Notably, courts in such cases have used laws that do not refer specifically to indigenous peoples, but have started to graft indigenous rights onto them. To mention just three of the most famous cases, in *Mabo*[51] the High Court of Australia used the common law, as applied in Australia, to both recognise a concept of 'native title' connected to traditional occupation or other connection to the land, and reject the idea that Australia was terra nullius. In *Awas Tingni*,[52] the Inter-American Court of Human Rights interpreted the protection of property

[49] See also the June 2010 disclosure rules of the Hong Kong Stock Exchange, which require mineral companies to disclose 'any claims that may exist over the land on which exploration or mining activity is being carried out, including any ancestral or native claims.' www.revenuewatch.org/news/news-article/china/hong-kong-stock-exchange-require-greater-transparency

[50] *Worcester v Georgia*, 31 US (6 Pet) 515 (1832). The actual judgment ruled that only the US federal government and Congress could infringe the rights of sovereign tribes, and the state authorities (eg Georgia) had no right to do so.

[51] *Mabo v Queensland (No 2)* [1992] HCA 23; (1992) 175 CLR 1.

[52] *Mayagna (Sumo) Awas Tingni Community v Nicaragua* (Series C No 79) [2001] IACHR 9 (31 August 2001).

rights under the American Convention on Human Rights[53] to include the rights of indigenous peoples to their customary land, and also required states to ensure that these rights were adequately protected (including from unwanted resource extraction). In *Richtersveld,* the South African Constitutional Court used its new land law on righting racially discriminatory land transfers to recognise the historic land rights of an indigenous people. In these and other cases, courts were forced to draw on a limited resource of comparable jurisprudence from around the world.

For the foreseeable future, litigation on indigenous peoples' land issues will centre on resolving a few basic questions. These will include: who are the indigenous peoples themselves who are making a claim and whether or not they are able to have their rights recognised in law as a collectivity; to what degree their historic occupation or other use of a land should establish current land rights; to what degree other rights, especially religion and culture, should include special rights of access or ownership to sacred land; and how historic claims should be resolved for peoples who were expelled many years ago, including whether and how land should be returned, and to whom, and, if compensation is to be paid, how much and to whom.

On all these issues the Declaration can serve as a new source. Article 8 clearly prohibits the dispossession of 'land, territory or resources' and forced population transfer. Article 10 makes clear that removal without free, prior and informed consent is prohibited. Articles 26–28 urge states to recognise the traditional occupation, ownership and use of land, and, where indigenous land has been taken away or damaged, to either restore or provide just and fair compensation through equivalent land or money. No time limit is put on this. Other rights set out in the Declaration will also be critical in determining the protection of indigenous land. The rights to culture, religion and health are critical, while Article 31 requires respect for traditional medicine, seeds and flora and fauna. Together, these will almost invariably be linked to traditional land.

Critically, the preamble and Article 33 stress the importance to indigenous people of the right to development 'in accordance with their aspirations and needs'. This recognises that indigenous peoples must decide what sort of development they want on their land and not the state in attempts to 'civilise' them. The *Endorois* case, cited above, constitutes the first case in an international tribunal where the right to development has been

[53] Art 21: Right to Property: '1. Everyone has the right to the use and enjoyment of his property. The law may subordinate such use and enjoyment to the interest of society. 2. No one shall be deprived of his property except upon payment of just compensation, for reasons of public utility or social interest, and in the cases and according to the forms established by law. 3. Usury and any other form of exploitation of man by man shall be prohibited by law.'

adjudicated. In the context of a forced eviction without prior informed consent or adequate compensation, the African Commission stressed that:

> [T]he Respondent State bears the burden for creating conditions favourable to a people's development.[54] ... The Respondent State is obligated to ensure that the Endorois are not left out of the development process or benefits. The African Commission agrees that the failure to provide adequate compensation and benefits, or provide suitable land for grazing indicates that the Respondent State did not adequately provide for the Endorois in the development process. It finds against the Respondent State that the Endorois community has suffered a violation of Article 22 of the Charter.[55]

In reaching this decision, the Commission did not expressly draw on the Declaration on the Rights of Indigenous Peoples per se, but relied more broadly on guidelines established by the UN Special Rapporteur on the situation of human rights and fundamental freedoms of indigenous people and the UN Committee on the Elimination of Discrimination. In the future the Declaration on the Rights of Indigenous Peoples can be used specifically in rulings on the right to development, especially when coupled with the wealth of supporting and interdependent UN mandates and mechanisms.

Finally, Article 37 sets out how indigenous peoples will still be able to claim the rights under any treaty or similar document that may have been signed in the past. The Declaration does not take away any of these rights. These provisions caused Canada to oppose the Declaration down to the final vote, arguing that it will create uncertainty with regard to existing treaties. This position has been widely condemned.[56]

HISTORIC INJUSTICES

As the preamble to the Declaration notes, indigenous peoples have suffered immense historic injustices. It may still be possible to reverse some of these through litigation. As previously stated, the Declaration recognises, without any time limit, indigenous peoples' right to restoration and/or compensation for land that was taken or damaged without. It also confirms the continuing application of treaties that may have recognised or granted other rights to indigenous peoples. The Declaration further

[54] *Endorois* case (n 1) para 298, citing the UN Declaration on the Right to Development, Art 3.

[55] Ibid.

[56] See the Open Letter of 1 May 2008 by 101 legal experts in Canada calling the Canadian position on the Declaration 'misleading', www.itk.ca/system/files/Open-Letter-On-UN-Declaration.pdf. native-rights-news.blogspot.com/2008/06/legal-scholars-and-experts-urge-canada.html

sets out in Articles 11 and 12 the right to restoration of cultural, intellectual, religious and spiritual property and of ceremonial objects and human remains. This of course goes far beyond the issue of land.

In resolving the issue of historic injustices, the Declaration clarifies that any comprehensive settlement must be reached with the full participation and agreement of indigenous peoples themselves, using, where possible, indigenous mechanisms. The Declaration does not, of course, prevent or discourage unilateral apologies to indigenous peoples. In fact, the first such apology following the adoption of the Declaration took place in Australia under the newly-elected Rudd government in February 2008, particularly significant for a country that had been one of only four to officially oppose the Declaration at the General Assembly. But implementing the Declaration would mean that such apologies would be only a starting point in ensuring that the wrongs done historically can be righted.

In terms of righting past wrongs, it is particularly important that the Declaration is universal, and in particular that it applies to the former colonising states (largely but not exclusively European) who were responsible for many of these injustices. Specifically, these states may still hold indigenous property or remains in their territory, including in museums; furthermore, states that still rule imperial territories may still govern indigenous peoples and will thus need to secure rights for these peoples. Such states may also be liable to compensate for the major rights violations they have committed in the past. The Declaration says nothing about time limits, but the setting out of clear principles on the basic rights of restoration or compensation certainly makes the basis for such types of litigation or settlement easier.

Effective Litigation

The Declaration makes clear that resolving violations of indigenous peoples' rights should be done in a way that engages the full participation of the affected indigenous communities, and, as much as possible, reflects indigenous representative institutions.[57] However, the history of indigenous rights shows that litigation will be inevitable. When this happens, the Declaration actually appears to require that states provide assistance to the indigenous peoples to conduct the litigation effectively. Article 40 states that:

> Indigenous peoples have the right to access to and prompt decision through just and fair procedures for the resolution of conflicts and disputes with States or other parties, as well as to effective remedies for all infringements of their individual and collective rights.

[57] See Declaration on the Rights of Indigenous Peoples, Art 19.

This actually goes into more detail than most international human rights instruments on the need for effective remedies, which clearly must include any judicial remedies. In fact, the need for 'prompt decision through just and fair procedures' requires that states create justice systems that are able to deal with indigenous peoples' complaints, for example by addressing collective and historic complaints. Article 13 of the Declaration specifically requires that legal systems are able to deal with indigenous languages. In fact, there is a very strong argument that a 'just and fair' procedure for indigenous peoples requires the provision of financial and other assistance to bring claims, not just legal assistance (where the law and procedure are sufficiently complex), but also assistance in the process of gathering the necessary evidence and in ensuring that the entire people are involved.[58]

CONCLUSIONS

Viewing the Declaration from the perspective of litigators highlights the need for clarity in the actual content and meaning of the rights that indigenous peoples actually have. To take just three cases in which we have been involved, first, for the Endorois at the African Commission on Human and Peoples' Rights, the Declaration served as a clear benchmark for interpreting the provisions of the African Charter with respect to property, resources, culture, religion and the right to development. The Declaration played a valuable role in making clear that the Endorois, although African, are nevertheless a distinct indigenous people who are entitled to rights to restoration and compensation for having been expelled from their ancestral land.

Second, for the Chagossians, a people expelled en masse by the British from their ancestral lands in the 1970s to make way for a US military base, the Declaration should make it clear that they are also an indigenous people as the original inhabitants of the land and as a distinct people. Therefore the issues at the heart of their litigation should be seen through the rights that the Declaration recognises. Not least that under Article 30, military activities should only be conducted on indigenous peoples' land with their consent.

Finally, for the Tasmanian Aboriginal Centre, which was forced in 2007 to take the Natural History Museum in London to court in connection

[58] As an analogy see the European Court of Human Rights judgments in cases such as *Steel and Morris v United Kingdom* (2005) 41 EHRR 22 and *Airey v Ireland* (1979) 2 EHRR 305, in which that Court has made it clear that the right to a fair trial can include the duty to provide legal aid, when the law or procedure is complex enough that without legal assistance a litigant would not have a fair hearing.

with the return of ancestral remains, the Declaration represented a very clear statement of what international law actually is, clearly requiring the return of such remains. It is hoped that any museum housing indigenous ancestral remains or indigenous property or sacred objects will be aware of the Declaration and return such property without need for any further litigation. In this particular case, the Declaration, in its clarity, proved sufficiently persuasive for the Museum to swiftly resort to the offer of a friendly settlement that was satisfactory to the applicants, rather than enter into full scale litigation.

Litigation will be a crucial part of ensuring that the Declaration takes root, but of course it is only one part of the struggle. It will give indigenous peoples a tool, but even winning a case will only be the start of further negotiations, as the *Mabo* and *Awas Tingni* cases show. Strategic litigation efforts that systematically seek to explore opportunities for dialogue with authorities generally comprise the best strategies for implementation and enforcement of international human rights law domestically. Litigation needs to be part of a well executed campaign and advocacy strategy. The Declaration makes clear, as never before, the range (and global scope) of indigenous peoples' rights. If made widely known and used effectively, it will become an invaluable tool for litigation, and for ultimately converting that litigation into effective protection of indigenous peoples where it counts the most—on the ground and in their everyday lives.

Section B

Thematic Perspectives

6

Making the Declaration on the Rights of Indigenous Peoples Work: The Challenge Ahead

RODOLFO STAVENHAGEN

THE 'SOLEMN PROCLAMATION' of the Declaration on the Rights of Indigenous Peoples ('the Declaration') by the General Assembly of the United Nations in September 2007, following 20 years of negotiation, marks a major step forward in the consolidation of the international human rights structure that the United Nations has been painstakingly building over the last 60 years. Not until well into the twentieth century were indigenous peoples recognised progressively as citizens of their respective countries, and remaining restrictions and limitations on the full exercise of their rights and freedoms removed.

The structural inequalities that led historically to the dispossession of the rights, sovereignty and dignity of indigenous peoples are deep-rooted in contemporary society, and their effects continue to exist and determine the lives of indigenous individuals and communities. In the Declaration's preamble the General Assembly expresses its concern 'that indigenous peoples have suffered from historic injustices as a result of, inter alia, their colonisation and dispossession of their lands, territories and resources, thus preventing them from exercising, in particular, their right to development in accordance with their own needs and interests'.[1] It also recognises the urgent need to respect and promote the inherent rights of indigenous peoples which derive from their political, economic and social structures and from their cultures, spiritual traditions, histories and philosophies, especially their rights to their lands, territories and resources.[2] Considering the persistent patterns of political exclusion, social marginalisation, economic exploitation and cultural discrimination that indigenous peoples

[1] UN Declaration on the Rights of Indigenous Peoples, para 6.
[2] Ibid, para 7.

suffered during the era of national state construction, it is noteworthy that beginning in the 1980s a number of states adopted legal reforms that for the first time incorporated indigenous peoples into existing constitutional structures.

THE NEW MULTICULTURALISM AND THE UNITED NATIONS

Numerous countries now recognise themselves as multicultural or multiethnic; indigenous cultures and languages have been designated as deserving of respect and state protection, indigenous communities have been given legal status, their lands and territories have sometimes been recognised and in some cases indigenous peoples have been acknowledged as collective and individual holders of specific rights. At the same time, these reforms have spelled out the responsibilities and obligations of states regarding, among others, the preservation of indigenous lands and territories, multicultural and intercultural education, respect for traditional customs, social organisation and forms of governance, and special attention has been given to the social needs of indigenous communities, for example in the field of health delivery and educational services. In some instances, the specific rights of indigenous peoples became enshrined in national constitutions or in major legislation.

The progress thus achieved in many countries over the last quarter century or so is due to various factors, including the struggles of indigenous peoples and their organisations, the democratisation of national polities, and the increasing relevance of international human rights instruments in the construction of more open, inclusive and just societies. Indigenous peoples have not only become socially and culturally more visible, they are also in the process of becoming major political actors in a number of countries.

Despite these gains, a major gap between legislation and practice still exists. Not only are there serious contradictions in the laws themselves which make their application enormously complex and difficult, but we can also detect an increasing gap between legal framework and public policy. Consequently, with few exceptions the new legislation is not in fact being implemented as it should be. No wonder indigenous organisations are increasingly disappointed and often show their frustration through direct action such as street protests, sit-ins, land occupations and the like.

Furthermore, available evidence suggests that in terms of development indicators and living standards (such as the UN Human Development Index and similar measures), indigenous peoples find themselves consistently below national averages and behind other more privileged sectors of society. Since the creation of the mandate on the human rights and fundamental freedoms of indigenous people by the UN Human Rights Commission in 2001, the Special Rapporteur has provided the Commission (now Human Rights Council) with data from many countries showing this to be the case.[3]

In the 1980s, even as they became increasingly organised and militant in their own countries, some of the few indigenous peoples' organisations that existed at the time were able to send delegations to the United Nations to lobby for their cause within the framework of the human rights mechanisms that were daintily being sewn together by the Commission on Human Rights. With the support of a number of international non-governmental organisations and donor agencies, they met at the sessions of the Working Group on Indigenous Populations with fellow delegates from other parts of the world and diplomatic representatives of the member states, and together they began to hammer out the first drafts of the Declaration.[4] The debates in the annual sessions of the Working Group were open to the participation of indigenous people, much to the amazement and discomfort of the traditional diplomatic elite that takes its seats at such gatherings.

For the first time, the United Nations opened the doors of its meeting rooms to the Indians of the American continent, the Aborigines of Australia, the Inuit and Saami of the Arctic, the tribals of Southeast Asia, the natives of the Pacific Islands, and the Bushmen, Pygmies and nomadic herders of Africa. The sessions of the Working Group, which continued for over 20 years, soon turned into something akin to public hearings that were extensively covered by the international media and helped to sensitise public opinion to the plight of indigenous peoples worldwide. In the end the Human Rights Council adopted the Draft Declaration on the Rights of Indigenous Peoples in June 2006, and transmitted it for adoption to the General Assembly, the highest organ of the United Nations, which proclaimed it on 13 September 2007.[5]

Like all other international human rights instruments, the Declaration is the result of ideological debates, diplomatic negotiations, geopolitics, various group interests and personal relations. It needs to be seen in

[3] See the Special Rapporteur's annual reports to the Human Rights Council at www2.ohchr.org/english/issues/indigenous/rapporteur/reports.htm.

[4] The UN Working Group on Indigenous Populations met for over 20 years under the successive chairmanship of Asbjorn Eide (Norway), Erica-Irene Daes (Greece) and Miguel Alfonso Martínez (Cuba). The dialogue between states and indigenous representatives benefited for many years from the guidance of UN official Augusto Willemsen Díaz (Guatemala). For a good introduction to indigenous peoples and international law see J Anaya, *Indigenous Peoples in International Law* (Oxford University Press, 2004).

[5] The story of how this came about, written by many of the concerned actors, is told in R Stavenhagen and C Charters (eds), *Making the Declaration Work* (Copenhagen, IWGIA, 2009).

the wider context from which it emerges and in connection with the geopolitical controversies that have characterised the United Nations human rights debates since the beginning of the indigenous discussions. While some indigenous representatives who were involved in the negotiating process at several levels insisted on a stronger text, and some states did not want a declaration at all, other government representatives would have preferred a weaker, more traditional declaration along the lines of the (1992) Declaration on the Rights of Persons Belonging to National or Ethnic, Religious and Linguistic Minorities. The dispute between the maximalists and the minimalists continues to this day.

What we have now is surely a novelty in the annals of the United Nations human rights field, to the extent that the states that adopted the Declaration took into account the needs, arguments and desires of a highly vocal, assertive and organised collection of peoples who had been demanding the recognition of their identities and rights for several generations at both the domestic and the international levels.[6] Moreover, the Declaration clearly distinguishes between the individual rights that indigenous persons share with all other persons according to the United Nations human rights instruments, and the specific rights enjoyed by indigenous peoples collectively as a result of their specific identities. Although effective protection mechanisms for the rights of indigenous peoples are still few and weak in the United Nations system, the Declaration has opened the door to indigenous peoples as new world citizens.

THE CHALLENGE: HOW TO MAKE THE DECLARATION WORK

To be sure, the Declaration on the Rights of Indigenous Peoples does not actually establish any new rights and freedoms that do not exist in other UN human rights instruments, but it spells out how these rights must relate to the specific conditions of indigenous peoples. Given the historical circumstances under which indigenous human rights have been violated or ignored for so long in so many countries, the Declaration is not only a long awaited *statement of redress* for indigenous peoples, it must also be considered a *map of action* for human rights policies that need to be undertaken by governments, civil society and indigenous peoples themselves if their rights are actually to be guaranteed, respected and protected. *How to make the Declaration work* is the challenge that we now face. The adoption of the Declaration marks the closing of a cycle of

[6] The first delegation of American Indians demanding their rights sought to address the nascent League of Nations in the 1920s, but was rebuffed. A Maori chief was equally unsuccessful.

great historical significance, even as it opens at the same time a new cycle relating to its implementation.

If the long-term struggle of indigenous peoples for their rights helps explain the background of the Declaration, the next stage will determine how the Declaration relates to other international human rights legislation and, more importantly, in what ways it will be implemented at the national level. Of immediate concern is the fact that governments do not consider the Declaration to be legally binding, because it is not an international convention that requires ratification. Many indigenous people and human rights activists ask themselves what good is a Declaration if it is not legally binding and therefore will not bring hard legal results. Similarly, state officials may consider that signing the Declaration is certainly a gesture of goodwill, but does not carry any real obligations for the governments concerned, and even less for those states that did not bother to sign the Declaration or actually voted against it in the General Assembly (Australia, Canada, New Zealand, the United States).[7] At best, the Declaration is considered to be 'soft law' which can be ignored at will, particularly as it does not include enforcement mechanisms.

This debate has opened up a new space for strong action by those who believe that the Declaration does represent an important step forward in the promotion and protection of human rights. On the one hand there is the opportunity, indeed the need, to begin working on a future convention on the rights of indigenous peoples. This has been the strategy in the United Nations before: the Universal Declaration of Human Rights (1948) was followed by the two international human rights covenants 20 years later (1966), and they did not enter into force until 1976. Much the same happened with other specific declarations/covenants (women, children, racial discrimination), but the waiting period here was shorter. While a number of indigenous and human rights organisations favour this route, others are more skeptical and feel that given the controversial nature of indigenous rights, it is unlikely that a UN convention on the topic could be produced any time soon, if at all. They also point to ILO Convention 169 concerning Indigenous and Tribal Peoples in Independent Countries, which has so far been ratified by only 20 states. Consequently, they are searching for other, more effective strategies.

The strongest argument for the Declaration is that it was adopted by an overwhelming majority of 143 states, from all the world's regions, and that as a universal human rights instrument it morally and politically binds all of the UN member states to comply fully with its contents. Just as the Universal Declaration of Human Rights has become customary international law, so can this Declaration become customary international

[7] Australia has since adhered to the Declaration.

law over time as well, if—as is possible and likely—national, regional and international jurisprudence and practice can be nudged in the right direction. Just as with good wine, given a favourable environment, the passing of time can improve the flavour of the Declaration.

One of the preambular paragraphs of the Declaration recognises 'that the situation of indigenous peoples varies from region to region and from country to country and that the significance of national and regional particularities and various historical and cultural backgrounds should be taken into consideration'.[8] While some observers might argue that the intention of this paragraph is to detract from the universality of the rights set out in the Declaration, a more constructive reading would lead one to conclude that it is precisely at the regional and country levels that the rights of the Declaration must be made to apply. And this requires interpreting every right within a particular context that may be national or regional. For example, the political right to vote will be exercised in one way through the ballot box, where registered political parties compete in elections, and in another way where a village assembly appoints its representatives by consensus. Both are equally valid procedures as long as the freely expressed will of the people concerned is respected. The question of how to implement the political right to vote in different contexts requires careful institutional management in each situation, as well as overall, and of course there may be a number of other alternatives available. Thus, according to Article 18 of the Declaration: 'Indigenous peoples have the right to participate in decision-making in matters which would affect their rights, through representatives chosen by themselves in accordance with their own procedures, as well as to maintain and develop their own indigenous decision-making institutions.'

Another example, in the area of economic, social and cultural rights, might refer to Articles 23 and 32, which state that indigenous peoples have the right to determine and develop priorities and strategies for exercising their right to development and for the development or use of their lands or territories and other resources. This important right cannot simply be applied mechanically in any circumstance. It refers, in fact, to two interlocking rights—the right to development as defined in other UN instruments and the right of indigenous peoples to 'determine and develop priorities and strategies' in order to best exercise that right, particularly with regard to their lands, territories and resources. Here it will be necessary to use the various tools of the social sciences in order to come up with the right answers to myriad problems involved in setting priorities, building and applying strategies, conceptualising development, focusing on objectives, and measuring and evaluating processes

[8] para 23.

and results, let alone defining lands, territories and resources. To the extent that these issues are not carefully defined in the Declaration, they need to be addressed and interpreted at other levels and in other frameworks.

Approaches to these complex issues will vary according to region and country. States must consult and cooperate in good faith with the indigenous peoples concerned, as Article 32 proclaims, through their own representative institutions, in order to obtain their free and informed consent prior to the approval of any project affecting their lands or territories and other resources. Assuming that all government authorities everywhere are equally endowed with good faith, these issues become enormously complicated in practice. I have received numerous complaints, in my capacity as Special Rapporteur, concerning allegedly rigged consultations carried out by officials whose good faith was being questioned. In other cases the members of a given indigenous community may be divided on the issue that is being put before them, and the exercise of the right referred to in Article 32 ends up as part of a wider political negotiation, or perhaps in a stalemate.

Here, as in other issues, the rights in the Declaration can be seen as a frame of reference, a point of departure leading perhaps, among other things, to new legislation, to a different kind of judicial practice, to institution building and also, whenever necessary, to a different political culture (from authoritarian to democratic, from technocratic to participative) and a different citizenship regime (say from corporatist to neoliberal to multicultural).[9] Each of the articles in the Declaration must be analysed not only in terms of its origins and provenance, nor solely in terms of its fit within the general structure of the UN human rights edifice, but particularly with regard to its possibilities as a foundation upon which a new kind of relationship between indigenous peoples and states can be built. Besides methodology and skills, this requires imagination and will. The Declaration must be wielded by indigenous peoples and their advocates in government and civil society as an instrument for the pursuit and achievement of their rights.

The Declaration provides an opportunity to link the global and local levels, in a process of *glocalisation*. At the beginning of this historical cycle many of the people who came to the United Nations to contribute to the debates surrounding the draft declaration followed the rule, 'think locally and act globally'. Now this rule can be turned around into thinking

[9] On indigenous peoples and citizenship regimes in Latin America see D Yashar, *Contesting Citizenship in Latin America: The Rise of Indigenous Movements and the Postliberal Challenge* (Cambridge University Press, 2005). Also W Kymlicka, *Multicultural Citizenship: A Liberal Theory of Minority Rights,* (Oxford, Clarendon Press, 1995).

globally (the Declaration) and acting locally (the implementation process). In fact, as most everybody might agree, the major obstacle to the full operation of the United Nations human rights mechanisms (declarations, treaties, treaty bodies, resolutions, etc) is their lack of effective implementation and absence of enforcement mechanisms.

When human rights declarations are followed by a convention, their chances of effective implementation may increase slightly, but basically the issue has to do with national and local level political processes. At this stage the Declaration on the Rights of Indigenous Peoples carries sufficient momentum so that serious efforts to push for its implementation at the national level may produce short-term results, but these will surely vary greatly from case to case. Within two months of its adoption at the UN, the national congress of Bolivia voted to incorporate the Declaration into national legislation, and it is now ensconced in the new Bolivian Constitution (2008), but the Government recognises that to make it effective additional implementing and regulating legislation will be required. The Supreme Court of Belize cited the Declaration in support of its finding in favour of an indigenous community involved in a land law case.[10] In June 2008 the Japanese Diet voted unanimously to recognise the Ainu as an indigenous people, calling on the government to refer to the UN Declaration on the Rights of Indigenous Peoples and take comprehensive steps to advance Ainu policies.[11] On 8 April 2008 the Canadian House of Commons passed a Motion that the Government (which had voted against the Declaration) endorse the United Nations Declaration on the Rights of Indigenous Peoples as adopted by the UN General Assembly, and also instructed that Parliament and the Government of Canada fully implement the standards contained therein.

Nevertheless, the potential impact of the Declaration is also being recognised by those whose interests may be affected by its implementation. A prominent and powerful member of the congress of Brazil proposed that the Government withdraw its signature from the Declaration because it was contrary to Brazil's national interest to have voted for its adoption at the General Assembly. As they have been for so long, the battle lines surrounding the Declaration continue to be drawn. The worst thing that could happen now to the Declaration, in my opinion, is that it may be ignored, even by the governments that affixed their signature to it. And this can only be avoided by employing adequate strategies for its implementation at the national and local levels and support for it at the international level.

[10] Supreme Court of Belize, Claim Nos 171 and 172 (Consolidated) (19 October 2007).
[11] *Japan Times Online*, 7 June 2008.

A TEST FOR THE UNITED NATIONS SYSTEM

Another window of opportunity for the implementation of the Declaration has opened within the United Nations system itself. In the preamble it is clearly stated that this Declaration is an important step forward for the recognition, promotion and protection of the rights and freedoms of indigenous peoples and in the development of relevant activities of the United Nations system in this field, and that the United Nations has an important and continuing role to play in promoting and protecting the rights of indigenous peoples. The first responsibility lies within the human rights structure, the Human Rights Council, the treaty bodies, commissions and sub-commissions and expert groups, the Economic and Social Council (ECOSOC), and the General Assembly's Third Commission, which should not simply sit back and feel that their job is done. The Special Rapporteur on the situation of human rights and fundamental freedoms of indigenous people was instructed by the Human Rights Council to promote the Declaration, which means that the mandate has to work with governments and other relevant actors on the best strategies to promote the implementation of the Declaration.[12] By Resolution 6/36 of December 2007, the Human Rights Council decided, 'in order to assist the Human Rights Council in the implementation of its mandate, to establish a subsidiary expert mechanism to provide the Council with thematic expertise on the rights of indigenous peoples in the manner and form requested by the Council'. It is to be hoped that this new mechanism will build upon the work of the former Working Group on Indigenous Populations and devise ways and means to promote and implement the Declaration.

The next responsibility lies within the structure of the Secretariat, where different departments and units, particularly within economic, social and cultural affairs, can generate numerous activities involving the principles set out in the Declaration. In fact the Declaration 'calls upon the United Nations, its bodies, including the Permanent Forum on Indigenous Issues, and specialised agencies, including at the country level, as well as States to promote respect for and full application of the provisions of this Declaration and follow up the effectiveness of this Declaration' (Article 42). This is a major task that requires the full commitment of the Secretariat at all levels, including the field of technical cooperation where UNDP country teams carry a particular responsibility. At the country team level national and international civil society organisations have often proved extremely helpful in their support of a robust human rights

[12] The US delegate at the General Assembly in October 2007 stated his government's astonishing view that the Special Rapporteur was not authorised to promote the Declaration in countries that had voted against it.

agenda for indigenous peoples. In February 2008 the UN Development Group (UNDG) approved the Guidelines on Indigenous Peoples' Issues, following up on the ongoing work of the Inter-Agency Support Group on Indigenous Issues (IASG). The UNDG Guidelines have been agreed upon at the highest level of management of the UN system and recommend the integration of indigenous peoples' rights and issues into all UN country programmes. The Declaration can now serve as a beacon to improve coordination between numerous UN agencies and non-governmental organisations, and promote the support of international donor agencies where required.

An important call has been sent out by the General Assembly to the UN specialised agencies, many of which have over the years developed their own programmes in support of the rights of indigenous peoples (with special emphasis on women and children). But much more can and should be done, especially now with the Declaration as the major legislative authority, to prompt the specialised agencies to do much more in promoting and protecting the rights of indigenous peoples. In recent years, the UN has adopted a human rights-based approach to development, recognising that there can be no real development that excludes the human rights of target populations. This is certainly the case for indigenous peoples, who are often the object of specific programmes in which the various specialised agencies of the UN play an important part.

A number of these agencies have been active over the years in promoting indigenous rights; such activities can now be strengthened and improved in light of the Declaration. The International Labour Organization adopted Convention 169 in 1989. Even though only 20 states had ratified this convention by 2009, there is much scope for increasing the ILO's role in the protection of indigenous rights. Similarly, UNESCO's rather weak Convention on the Protection and Promotion of the Diversity of Cultural Expressions (2005) urges states parties to encourage individuals and social groups to create, produce, disseminate, distribute and have access to their own cultural expressions, paying due attention to the special circumstances and needs of women as well as various social groups, including persons belonging to minorities and indigenous peoples. Other agencies have also adopted relevant policies in their respective fields concerning indigenous peoples. The Declaration now provides an overall framework for the work of all the agencies in the UN system.

HOW SHALL RIGHTS BE IMPLEMENTED?

The Declaration is linked, on the one hand, to the emergence of the worldwide social and political movements of indigenous peoples in the second half of the twentieth century, and on the other, to the widening debate in the international community concerning civil, political, economic, social and cultural rights. While much has been written about these topics, there are many unresolved issues that the new Declaration addresses.

In the literature on the rights of indigenous peoples we can identify several perspectives that were clearly present in the process leading up to the Declaration, and which have become important issues of concern in a number of countries. The first perspective is grounded in the classic tradition of universal individual human rights. The preamble to the Declaration states that 'indigenous individuals are entitled without discrimination to all human rights recognised in international law'.[13] On this basis, many people and governments have asked why there should be a need for a specific declaration on indigenous peoples at all, if indeed they have the same rights as everybody else.[14]

One answer to this question is the extensive evidence showing that the universal human rights of indigenous peoples are not fully or actually respected in many circumstances. During 2001–08, I documented for the United Nations Human Rights Council the human rights violations of indigenous peoples in various parts of the world. Whereas their plight is generally acknowledged, the widely held idea that it can be solved by simply improving existing implementation mechanisms is less than satisfactory. States are indeed expected to deploy stronger efforts to ensure compliance with all human rights, whereas civil society as well as the international protection mechanisms (such as human rights committees and other monitoring bodies) need to become more effective in making States duly *accountable* in this regard.

The fact is, however, that indigenous people continue to suffer a serious human rights deficit. They do not in practice enjoy all their civil, political, economic, social and cultural rights in the same measure as other members of society. I provided evidence of this in my 11 country reports to the Human Rights Council.[15] The differential compliance with the human rights discourse points from the start to a situation of *inequality* between indigenous and non-indigenous peoples, which results from a pattern of *differential and unequal access* to these rights. While the *inefficiency* of human rights implementation mechanisms is surely one factor in this situation, other factors are the *inadequacy* of human rights policies, the *obstacles* that indigenous peoples encounter when they wish to exercise their rights, and the various forms of *discrimination* that indigenous peoples continue to suffer around the world. In many countries public authorities are well

[13] para 22.

[14] We have heard the same argument regarding the rights of women, and yet not only was there a declaration at the UN but also an international convention on the rights of women, which it took decades to achieve.

[15] See the reports of the Special Rapporteur (n 3).

aware of these issues, though in some parts they tend to deny them. And yet, even when there is awareness, remedial action is absent or insufficient or too late and too little. A widespread response to all of this is the belief that *'improving human rights protection mechanisms'* will turn the trick. In fact, however, the impulse to improve human rights protection mechanisms may entail all sorts of different actions and it is easier said than done. Numerous obstacles may be encountered in the attempt to improve human rights protection mechanisms, such as the inertia of bureaucratic systems, particularly the judiciary where attention to the specific needs of indigenous peoples is not usually of the highest priority.

One extra-judicial institution that at least in some countries has been called upon increasingly to concern itself with indigenous rights is the public human rights protection agency, or *ombudsman*. Frequently, national human rights institutions are thinly staffed and lack the necessary skills to provide protection to indigenous people: usually, their priorities are elsewhere. But even more serious is the widespread practice of corruption in poor societies with great inequalities. Indigenous peoples are often the victims of corruption, and sometimes they become partners in corruption as well. Unless we work out the nuts and bolts of improving human rights mechanisms, this will remain an empty phrase and it has to do with existing institutional structures, legal systems and power relationships, which in turn relate to the wider social system in which indigenous peoples are the historical victims of human rights violations to begin with. Improving access to the courts, establishing an ombudsman office with special regard to indigenous peoples, setting up special monitoring agencies, and adopting regulatory measures and new legislation may all point in the right direction, but unless the core issues are addressed directly, progress will be slow at best.

If the classic human rights protection mechanisms (equal access to the courts, impartial justice, efficient ombudsmen) have not worked or at least not worked well for indigenous peoples, then we must look at other causes of inequality which are not formally institutional, but are more deeply embedded in the history and social structures of national society. The underlying root here is ethnic racism and discrimination against indigenous peoples as expressed in the context of specific social processes and at many different levels. Because discrimination is a catchall term that in fact refers to complex and multidimensional phenomena, in human rights terms it must be dealt with specifically at distinct levels.

Indigenous peoples are the victims of racial and cultural discrimination which is not only based on biological attributes, is not only a matter of inter-personal relations involving prejudice, and exists at many different levels. We have institutional discrimination when social service agencies are so designed to provide services mainly to certain sectors of the population, and exclude entirely or partially, or deliver services of lesser quality to, other sectors such as indigenous communities. We see this in most countries, where a higher concentration of services is available for higher income people in urban areas, and lesser services reach outlying rural communities. I documented these inequalities extensively in my country mission reports, showing—mostly on the basis of official indicators and statistics—that indigenous peoples are victims of discrimination in the distribution of socially valued goods, general social services necessary to maintain or improve adequate standards of living in health, education, housing, leisure, environment, benefits, employment, income, etc. The World Bank has documented that institutional discrimination against indigenous peoples in some Latin American countries has not changed much over the last 10 years.[16]

The importance of counting with adequate quantitative information and reliable indicators cannot be overstated, because they are necessary to formulate the right kind of public policies and target the neediest populations. Surprisingly, in most countries such information is lacking regarding indigenous peoples. They are most often lumped together with a general category of 'the poor', or 'isolated communities', or the 'rural sector' or the lowest 'decile' of an income scale, a practice that tends to ignore the cultural specificities of indigenous peoples and simply locates them in relation to national or regional averages, medians or minimums. It is amazing how little information about the actual situation and conditions of indigenous populations public officials in many country possess—a lack of awareness that easily tends to inject anti-indigenous bias, very often unwittingly, in the design, operation and evaluation of social programmes of all kinds (health, nutrition, education, housing, welfare and so on). No wonder that indigenous organisations insist that such information be produced, used and made publicly available by the specialised agencies. The UN Permanent Forum on Indigenous Issues has insisted on this, and I have made numerous recommendations to governments in the same vein. A number of specialised UN agencies have now begun to work on these issues. In view of the importance of the problems involved, it is hard to explain why some governments still argue that generating such information disaggregated by ethnicity would be an 'act of racism', which they, being well-intentioned liberals, would want to avoid. I believe the shoe is on the other foot: not doing it means perpetuating institutional racism against indigenous peoples. We are dealing here not with a purely technical matter, but with basic human rights.

[16] G Hall and HA Patrinos (eds), *Indigenous Peoples, Poverty and Human Development in Latin America* (New York, Palgrave Macmillan, 2006).

Inter-personal discrimination can be attacked with legal measures (for example, outlawing hate speech, racist organisations etc) and with educational and communication campaigns in favour of tolerance, respect for cultural and physical differences and so on. Institutional discrimination, however, requires a major overhaul of public institutions in terms of objectives, priorities, budgets, administration, capacity building, evaluation, feedback and coordination, and therefore constitutes a major challenge for public policy and for the political power structure in any country. Why? Because political decisions in any democratic society express group concerns, economic interests and structured power systems, from which indigenous peoples are usually quite distant in geographical as well as in economic, social and cultural terms.

Thus, indigenous peoples face many obstacles, as individuals and as collectivities, before they can reach the equal enjoyment of all universal individual human rights. That is why the classic, liberal approach to human rights has so far been less than satisfactory for indigenous peoples. This does not mean, however, that the effort to improve human rights protection mechanisms for individual members of indigenous communities should not be pursued; on the contrary, it is a long neglected task that must be promoted and consolidated, according to Article 2 of the Declaration which states:

> Indigenous peoples and individuals are free and equal to all other peoples and individuals and have the right to be free from any kind of discrimination, in the exercise of their rights, in particular that based on their indigenous origin or identity.

Let me also add that even if indigenous people, as individuals, achieve full enjoyment of all universal individual rights which are guaranteed by international human rights instruments and in domestic law in most countries, some of the basic human rights issues that indigenous peoples have been struggling for over so many decades will not necessarily be resolved.

Common ideas on the effectiveness of international human rights instruments hold that human rights conventions must include the protection mechanisms that enable victims of human rights violations to seek legal remedies. Declarations, in contrast, have the drawback that they do not include such mechanisms, and therefore states are not obligated to provide legal remedies. As far as the rights of indigenous peoples are concerned, it may be argued that the prevention of human rights violations should be as much a matter of public policy as of existing legal remedies. And in that respect, the Declaration on the Rights of Indigenous Peoples points to the kind of obligations states have to protect these rights. That is why at this point strategies for the promotion and consolidation of the right kind of public policies must be added to the well-established recourse to judicial remedies in seeking redress for human rights violations.

Individual and Collective Rights

Whereas the Declaration reaffirms that indigenous individuals are entitled without discrimination to all human rights recognised in international law, indigenous peoples also possess collective rights which are indispensable for their existence, their well-being and their integral development as peoples. The main departure from other human rights instruments is that here the rights-holders are not only individual members of indigenous communities, but the collective unit, the group, indigenous peoples as living societies, cultures and communities.

Many states refused for a long time to consider indigenous peoples as collective human rights-holders, which is one of the reasons why the Declaration took such a long time to come to fruition. It is now slowly becoming a standard interpretation that there are certain individual human rights that can only be enjoyed 'in community with others', which means that for human rights purposes the group involved becomes a rights-holder in its own right. Take linguistic rights, for example. These refer not only to the individual's right to speak the language of her choice at home, but also to the right of a linguistic community to use its language in public communication at all levels, including education, the media, the judiciary and government. The use of language is not only a means of communication but a way to live one's culture. Non-discrimination is not only a negative liberty ('to have a right not to be discriminated against'), but requires a favourable public and institutional environment in which to be different is not a stigma but a right and an asset.

The issue of collective versus individual human rights is an old concern in the United Nations that became particularly controversial with regard to common Article 1 of both International Covenants, which recognises the right of all peoples to self-determination. A recent study of human rights in the UN observes, 'it was one of the most divisive human rights issues at the UN and nearly torpedoed the covenant … The self-determination debate affected the nature and composition of the United Nations itself and struck at the heart of the international system'.[17] It did so again in relation to the right to self-determination of indigenous peoples as stated in Article 3 of the Declaration, a divisive debate that had been foreshadowed during the drafting of ILO Convention 169.

[17] R Normand and S Zaidi, *Human Rights at the UN: The Political History of Universal Justice* (Bloomington, Indiana University Press, 2007) 212–13.

How can the Right to Self-Determination be Implemented?

In the theory and practice of the United Nations the right of peoples to self-determination has been strictly limited to the process of decolonisation, and it has been invoked more recently in a number of instances of secession. The 1960 General Assembly Declaration on the Granting of Independence to Colonial Countries and Peoples rejects 'any attempt aimed at the partial or total destruction of the national unity and the territorial integrity of a country', and Article 46 of the Declaration makes it clear that 'nothing in this Declaration may be … construed as authorizing or encouraging any action which would dismember or impair, totally or in part, the territorial integrity or political unity of sovereign and independent States'. ILO Convention 169 on Indigenous and Tribal Peoples stipulates in Article 1(3) that 'the use of the term peoples in this Convention shall not be construed as having any implications as regards the rights which may attach to the term under international law'. However, as a result of years of negotiations, and despite the opposition of a number of states, the Declaration also formally recognises that indigenous peoples have the right to self-determination, a right that the UN has not been willing to recognise in the case of ethnic and national minorities.[18]

The challenge now is to renew the usefulness of a people's right to self-determination in the era of democratic multiculturalism when indigenous peoples claim this right for themselves. Indigenous peoples and states must now work together on the interpretation and application of the various facets of the right to self-determination within the specific contexts of their countries. How can this right—and other collective rights in the Declaration—be defined in legal terms, how will it be interpreted and by whom, how is it to be implemented, how will it be protected? But even more importantly, how is the rights-holder of the collective right to self-determination to be determined? How will the bearer of this right (a people) be defined? The United Nations has never defined a 'people', although it may be generally agreed that the right to self-determination is mainly a territorial right and to a lesser degree a political right. On this controversial issue, indigenous peoples have challenged states, and more than one state representative at the UN has challenged indigenous peoples. I have encountered numerous public officials in many countries around the world who would still deny indigenous peoples the right to self-determination, fearing that the exercise of this right may lead to separatism or secessionist movements, which presumably would have serious

[18] The Declaration on the Rights of Persons Belonging to National or Ethnic, Religious and Linguistic Minorities was proclaimed by the General Assembly in 1992 in Resolution 47/135. It does not recognise any collective rights of minorities.

consequences for national unity, territorial sovereignty and democratic governance.

Most observers of this problematique appear to agree that in the context of the Declaration the right to self-determination should be interpreted as an internal right, that is, within the framework of an established independent state, especially when this state is democratic and respectful of human rights. The Declaration links the right to self-determination (Article 3) with the exercise of autonomy or self-government of indigenous peoples in matters relating to their internal and local affairs (Article 4). The external interpretation of self-determination would apply in case of secession or territorial separation from an existing State, and it has been said often enough that this is not what indigenous peoples have been demanding with regard to their claim to self-determination, though of course external self-determination cannot be excluded as a logical possibility.

Thus, attention must now be paid mainly to the various forms and problems of the exercise of internal self-determination. To the extent that the legal, territorial, social and political situation of indigenous peoples varies considerably around the world, so also the exercise of the right to (internal) self-determination (autonomy, self-government) will have to take these differences into account. In countries where indigenous identities have been closely linked to recognised territories (such as might be the case in the circumpolar area, the Amazon basin, the Andean highlands) the right to self-determination will tend to present certain characteristics peculiar to these environments. Another approach might be taken in those countries that have a history of treaties, or where legal territories were established such as reserves or reservations for indigenous peoples, which would be the case in Canada and the United States. Other perspectives will be required in those countries (such as in Latin America) that have a long history of social and cultural intermingling in rural and urban areas between indigenous peoples and the *mestizo* (mixed) populations. What are to be the scope and levels of autonomy arrangements? How will they be made legally and politically viable? There are many successful examples around the world, but also quite a few failures.

In contrast to an act of self-determination during the process of decolonisation, which usually implies a one-time referendum such as took place, for example, in East Timor or in Namibia, the right to self-determination of indigenous peoples can be seen as an ongoing, continuing process which must be exercised on a daily basis involving a multitude of human rights issues, most of which are included in the Declaration. Thus, Article 3 does not refer to a right which is different from the other rights in the Declaration, but rather to a general umbrella principle in the light of which the exercise of all other rights must be assessed. Let us take as an example the struggle of an indigenous community to preserve its communal territory against the onslaught of a hydro-electric development project that has government backing and international financing. The project may affect numerous specific collective and individual rights of the members of this community, and in each case perhaps specific remedies may be available. But the fundamental issue is much larger than a number of particular rights that are likely to be violated. Here the fundamental issue is the community's permanent collective right to self-determination, which encompasses all the other rights. To the extent that rights are never absolute, adequate human rights policies must be found to preserve the community´s right to self-determination and to take into account the wider implications of the national development process including the rights of third parties within a human rights framework. Such is one of the many challenges that the Declaration has laid before us.

The Need for Specific Human Rights Policies

It is likely that in the coming years the focus of attention of many indigenous peoples' organisations will shift from the international arena to more local concerns. While at the UN and elsewhere (the regional African and American systems for example) indigenous diplomacy will undoubtedly continue with increasing effectiveness, at the national level attention will have to centre on legislative and political activity, the formulation of social and economic policies, litigation in the courts, and varieties of local organising. A new generation of indigenous representatives and leadership will have to begin working with the Declaration at the national level, finding ways to introduce it in the courts, the legislative organs, the political parties, academic centres and the public media. Many of the indigenous activists who worked for the Declaration at the United Nations also have had practical experience in their own countries. Making the Declaration work at the national level will surely re-energise indigenous movements everywhere. The international networks and transnational cooperation that indigenous organisations were able to set up during the process leading up to the adoption of the Declaration will surely continue across the bureaucratic separators of the United Nations, perhaps shifting more into the development and conflict-resolution fields. Putting into practice the collective right to self-determination at the local level will also be a new experience for all parties concerned.

Governments will now have to pick up where the diplomats finished their task. How should states implement their obligations emanating from the Declaration? Numerous technical and operational branches of government will have to adjust their activities in order to align with the objectives of the Declaration and become accountable to indigenous peoples as well as the UN system. Not least, academic research institutions, social science and law departments and programmes are now challenged to incorporate the Declaration into their plans and activities.

A major victory for indigenous peoples are the articles in the Declaration referring to the rights to land, territories and resources, although perhaps not everybody is satisfied with the final text as this was approved by the General Assembly (Articles 25, 26, 27, 28, 29). Consequently these Articles also represent a major challenge to both indigenous peoples and states in terms of their adequate interpretation, practical application and effective implementation and may require new legislation, litigation in the courts and detailed political negotiations with different stakeholders. As observed in various Latin American and Southeast Asian countries, simply the question of mapping and delimiting traditional indigenous lands and territories, let alone the process of adjudication itself, requires careful, costly, conflictive and often drawn-out procedures.

Some years ago the Inter-American Court of Human Rights handed down a landmark case in which it recognised the collective property rights of the Awas Tingni community against the Nicaraguan state. But the lands in question had never been delimited or titled, as many other such indigenous territories, raising complex legal and technical issues between the government and the local population. Subsequently the Court found in favour of indigenous peoples' land rights in several other cases in Paraguay and Suriname.[19] In Brazil and Colombia the law recognises vast indigenous territories but there are no efficient mechanisms to protect these areas from invasion by outsiders. The same situation prevails regarding the territories set aside for uncontacted tribes (or rather, peoples in voluntary isolation) in the remote Amazonian regions of Ecuador and Peru, which are being coveted by international oil and timber companies (not to mention drug traffickers) and poor landless settlers from other areas. Similar processes are reported in Cambodia and Malaysia, among other Southeast Asian countries. Very often governments say they are protecting these indigenous lands on the one hand, but on the other they hand out concessions to transnational corporations for so-called development purposes in the same places. How can the Declaration, which is very clear on the collective territorial and land rights of indigenous peoples, be brought to bear in practice on the problems faced by indigenous communities in such circumstances?

The implementation of laws is one of the principal stumbling blocks in the long, painful process of getting human rights to work for people. This will be no different regarding the implementation of the Declaration. In one of my reports to the UN Human Rights Council I wrote about the 'implementation gap' between laws and practical reality, which I have

[19] These cases can be consulted at www.corteidh.or.cr.

observed in many countries.[20] This means that there may be good laws on the books (sometimes the result of lengthy lobbying efforts or carefully negotiated political deals), but then something happens and they fail to be implemented. Many people I talk to about this come up with a simple answer: 'there is no political will'. But what exactly does this mean? How can political will be made to appear if there is none?

At this level the full import of the collective rights of indigenous peoples can be brought to bear on their empowerment, the building of multicultural citizenship and their effective participation in national society and the polity. If this is to be achieved, it will require more than improving human rights protection mechanisms, it will require institutional, economic, political and judicial reform across the board. To be sure, this may sometimes lead to social confrontation of various kinds, as it has before, and therefore new policies and new spaces for dialogue and negotiation must be designed. This will be particularly urgent in relation to issues concerning land rights, natural resources and the environment.

The issue is more complex than the absence of political will to implement legislation. In fact, I have observed in some countries that human rights legislation may be adopted for any number of political, cultural, diplomatic or other reasons, even when there is no real intent to implement it, or when the legal and political system is sufficiently complex that its implementation is almost out of the question. In other words, politicians may be ready to adopt such legislation knowing full well that there is no real chance of it being implemented. A good case in point is a local state law passed in the state of Oaxaca, Mexico in the 1990s on the rights of the indigenous peoples (a majority in that state). It looks like a good law on the books, and many distinguished local indigenous leaders and intellectuals participated in its design and preparation. The state governor pushed hard for its passage. A decade later it is still waiting to be implemented. It turns out that most of the actors involved in the passage of this law had other objectives in mind, and were not really concerned about implementation from the very beginning.

The United Nations has in recent years put forward a new human rights-based approach to development. The basic principle underlying this approach is that the realisation of human rights should be the end goal of development, and that development should therefore be perceived as a relationship between rights-holders and the corresponding duty-bearers. All programmes designed in accordance with this approach incorporate human rights indicators for the purpose of monitoring and assessing the impact of development projects and programmes. The key to this approach lies in its explicit link to human rights norms and

[20] See United Nations Economic and Social Council Document E/CN.4/2006/78.

principles, which are used to identify the start-up situation and goals and to assess the development impact on indigenous peoples.[21]

A rights-based approach identifies indigenous peoples as full holders of human rights and sets the realisation of their rights as the primary objective of development. As documented in many best practices followed in different parts of the world, an endogenous and sustained development is possible when it is based on respect for the rights of indigenous peoples and undertakes to ensure their observance. Attested best practices in development based on the rights of indigenous peoples are to be found in social and political processes initiated by indigenous communities and organisations in exercising and defending their rights. These are empowerment processes which are predicated on the assumption by indigenous peoples of ownership of their rights and on strengthening the ability of these peoples to organise and demand the observance and exercise of their rights, and also their political participation. The rights-based approach brings with it a system of principles which may be used in formulating, applying and evaluating constructive policies and agreements between governments and indigenous peoples. With the recent adoption of the United Nations Declaration on the Rights of Indigenous Peoples, development stakeholders now have at their disposal a clearly formulated regulatory framework for development policies and actions that target them.

The human rights-based approach stems from a concept of development that identifies subjects of rights and not merely a population that is the object of public policies. Indigenous peoples must thus be identified as subjects of collective rights that complement the rights of their individual members. A human rights-based development approach is:

(a) Endogenous: it should originate with the indigenous peoples and communities themselves as a means of fulfilling their collective needs.
(b) Participatory: it should be based on the free and informed consent of the indigenous peoples and communities, who should be involved in all stages of development. No project should be imposed from outside.
(c) Socially responsible: it should respond to needs identified by the indigenous peoples and communities themselves and bolster their own development initiatives. At the same time, it should promote the empowerment of indigenous peoples, especially indigenous women.

[21] This section is based on my 2007 report to the Human Rights Council, A/HRC/6/15.

(d) Equitable: it should benefit all members equally, without discrimination, and help to reduce inequality and alleviate poverty.
(e) Self-sustaining: it should lay the foundations for a gradual long-term improvement in living standards for all members of the community.
(f) Sustainable and protective of environmental balance.
(g) Culturally appropriate in order to facilitate the human and cultural development of the persons involved.
(h) Self-managed: resources (economic, technical, institutional, political) should be managed by those concerned, using their own tried and tested forms of organisation and participation.
(i) Democratic: it should be supported by a democratic state that is committed to its population's well-being, respects multiculturality and has the political will to protect and promote the human rights of all its citizens, especially those of indigenous peoples.
(j) Accountable: the actors responsible for development must be able to render a clear account of their performance to the community and society in general.

CONCLUSIONS

It will be necessary for all stakeholders in the Declaration to set out strategies for its implementation at different levels. At the national level this must begin with the passing of domestic regulating legislation and continue with the harmonisation of all kinds of sectorial laws with the principles set out in the Declaration. In numerous countries this will be a complex process because distinct legislation may benefit or be of interest to powerful political groups, such as land, forestry, mining or environmental laws, that may be in conflict with indigenous human rights. This will necessarily have to be dealt with through different and probably difficult political negotiations.

A classic and trusted way to ensure implementation is through the courts. While the Declaration is not as yet legally binding in most countries where indigenous peoples urgently require protection, recourse to the judiciary has become an increasingly useful way for indigenous peoples to seek justice and redress in a number of fields in which human rights may be vulnerable, such as land rights, educational rights, linguistic rights and political rights. Whereas progress has been achieved in some countries where courts have ruled favourably for indigenous peoples, in others access to the judiciary is still more of a far-away promise than a living reality. Indigenous people must overcome numerous obstacles before they can achieve fair and equal access to the courts. The judicial system and the legal profession must be willing and able to develop their own strategies for the inclusion of indigenous rights in their treatment of human rights in general. Monitoring mechanisms should be established at an early date to evaluate progress in this field.

Even more urgent, particularly regarding economic, social and cultural rights, is the need to develop public policies addressing indigenous peoples, especially their collective rights that are set out in the Declaration. Numerous countries have social programmes for indigenous communities, but they are generally marginal to the main thrust of government concerns. Priorities in social and economic programming are usually set without considering the special needs and specific rights of such communities. Indigenous peoples are more often than not classed within a general category of 'lower than average' or vulnerable population segments and no particular attention is paid by government departments to their cultural context and the specific characteristics of their community life, nor their special relationship to the land as well as other issues that are dealt with in the Declaration. Following the adoption of the Declaration, this should now change. If governments are serious about implementing it, they will have to pay special attention to the requirements of indigenous peoples and reform not only particular public policies, but also the framework in which public policies are formulated. This must include, of course, the adequate budgeting that goes hand in hand with social and economic programmes. Consistent monitoring mechanisms and accountability must be factored into this reform process.

In many cases new public policies will also require the redesign of public institutions. When Evo Morales, an Aymara Indian leader, became President of Bolivia in 2005, he dismantled the ministry of Indian affairs on the ground that it represented a form of discrimination against the country's majority indigenous population. When the indigenous peoples of Nepal, in alliance with other political forces, abolished the Hindu monarchy in 2008, they demanded greater participation in major institutional changes in the structure of government. In countries that have not yet recognised themselves as multicultural and where assimilationist policies have long been favoured, certain public institutions such as ministries of education need to adopt not only a new face, but also new structures to be able to respond ably to the requirements of the Declaration and the social demand that indigenous peoples will surely bring to their attention.

Indigenous peoples, in turn, are already inspired by the rights that are now recognised as theirs in this new international human rights instrument. In certain instances they will proceed to implement some of these rights on their own, without waiting for new legislation or different public policies. In many Latin American countries indigenous communities have long practised their own forms of administration of justice, in a de facto situation of legal pluralism, and they will certainly want to consolidate the collective right to do so even before the necessary legal, administrative and political changes are put into practice.

Even if one swallow does not yet a summer make, the UN Declaration on the Rights of Indigenous Peoples is one more building block in the international protection structure of human rights that needs now to be put to work, and one more step in the construction of the full world citizenship of indigenous peoples globally. Falk has written that among the most improbable developments of the previous hundred years or so has been the spectacular rise of human rights to a position of prominence in world politics.[22] I would add that even more improbable was the adoption of the UN Declaration on the Rights of Indigenous Peoples. But that is precisely why it is so encouraging and why it has given rise to great expectations, which should not and must not be betrayed.

In the end, how the Declaration will be made to work depends on the political will and ability of all the actors involved in the human rights of indigenous peoples. In the future, governments will be held accountable for their performance regarding the implementation of the Declaration, as they have been in relation to other international human rights instruments. The distance covered since the idea of the Declaration was first floated at the United Nations a quarter of a century ago is a notable achievement and the road ahead is steep and long, but indigenous peoples have learned to say: 'yes, we can!'

[22] R Falk, *Human Rights Horizons: The Pursuit of Justice in a Globalizing World* (New York, Routledge, 2000).

7

The Three Ironies of the UN Declaration on the Rights of Indigenous Peoples

H PATRICK GLENN

INTRODUCTION

THE ADOPTION OF the Declaration on the Rights of Indigenous Peoples in 2007 ('the Declaration') was a major event, the culmination of many years of difficult negotiations and the product of great skill and patience on the part of all those involved in the process. It is a truly impressive document.[1] Beyond its specific content, however, and from a broad historical perspective, it is the ironies which underlie it that are its most striking feature. A prominent anthropologist thus recently wrote that the spokespersons of indigenous peoples 'demand recognition for alternative ways of understanding the world, but ironically enough they do so in the idiom of Western culture theory'.[2] This is a statement which demands further justification than the author provides, but there is a further, more evident irony, beyond the idiom of the Declaration, which resides in the underlying notion of law—the profoundly western notion of international law—which has been used as a means for its creation. And if these two ironies are in a sense upstream of the Declaration,

[1] SJ Anaya, 'Report of the Special Rapporteur on the situation of human rights and fundamental freedoms of indigenous peoples', http:/unsr.jamesanaya.org/PDFs/Annual2008.pdf; S Errico, 'The UN Declaration on the Rights of Indigenous Peoples is Adopted: An Overview' (2007) 7 *Human Rights Law Review* 756; CJ Fromherz, 'Indigenous Peoples' Courts: Egalitarian Juridical Pluralism, Self-Determination, and the United Nations Declaration on the Rights of Indigenous Peoples' (2008) 156 *University of Pennsylvania Law Review* 1341; J Gilbert, 'Indigenous Rights in the Making: The United Nations Declaration on the Rights of Indigenous Peoples' (2007) 14 *International Journal on Minority and Group Rights* 207; S Wiessner, 'Rights and Status of Indigenous Peoples: A Global Comparative and International Analysis' (1999) 12 *Harvard Human Rights Journal* 57, 101ff; A Xanthaki, *Indigenous Rights and United Nations Standards* (Cambridge University Press, 2007) 102ff.

[2] A Kuper, 'The Return of the Native' (2003) 44 *Current Anthropology* 389, 395.

conceptual or foundational elements in its articulation, a further irony lies downstream in the refusal of a major group of countries to vote in its favour, a group of countries which ironically have been in the vanguard of judicial affirmation of indigenous rights.

These three ironies would correspond, more or less, to the contemporary understanding of irony, explained by the Concise Oxford Dictionary as 'the expression of one's meaning by language of the opposite or a different tendency.' Using 'western culture theory' would thus be opposite to that which was sought to be expressed, as would use of international law as a means of sustaining indigenous law, or voting negatively on an international declaration when domestic law was largely positive. Irony thus implies some form of dissembling or contradiction. Beyond this usual sense of irony, however, there is a more subtle sense, which would consist of placing statements in relation to some kind of other 'truth' and therefore interrogating each truth by juxtaposing it with another.[3] This understanding of irony assumes the commensurability of the truths invoked, as well as the need for mutual interrogation and the possibility of mutual influence. Irony here would be both a means of understanding and a check on fundamentalist or apodictic understanding of given texts or sources of law. This form of irony, more than the first, is to be welcomed in an age of interdependence. It teaches the need for mutual understanding and broadly-based normative support.

To what extent, then, can the three ironies of the Declaration be understood not only in the usual sense of irony, but in this more subtle sense of interrogation, mutual understanding and interdependence? The largest historical irony is in the use of international law as a legal resource for indigenous peoples.

IRONY AND THE USE OF INTERNATIONAL LAW

Indigenous peoples have always had their own, unwritten law. It can be broadly described as chthonic, in its attachment to land, the earth, and the recycling of all things within a circular understanding of time.[4] Indigenous peoples have also come to know and use the law of the nation-state within which they reside, and each of these nation-states has developed its own

[3] S Prickett, *Narrative, Religion and Science: Fundamentalism versus Irony 1700–1999* (Cambridge University Press, 2002) 203, and see also 44 (irony as a voice 'whispering' in the ear).

[4] For an attempted explanation, with further references, see HP Glenn, *Legal Traditions of the World*, 4th edn (Oxford University Press, 2010) ch 3, notably n 6 for E Goldsmith, *The Way: An Ecological World View* (London, Rider, 1992) xvii ('the *chthonic* world-view … when people really knew how to live in harmony with the natural world'). The root is the Greek *kthonos*, or earth, in French *chthonien* or *chtonien*, as in *autochtone* (or in English the rarely used *autochthonous*).

means of reconciliation of state and indigenous law. Each western state also controlled, in some measure, the extension of its own law into new territory.[5] The primary legal justification for extension of western legal authority lay beyond the laws of individual states, however, and rested on a large, non-formal combination of papal authority, natural law reasoning and academic writing then known variously as the *ius gentium* or the *ius publicum commune*. This was to become the public international law of today. As a primary legal justification for the colonising process it is said to have 'played an important role in the destruction of indigenous cultures'.[6]

The role of what we know today as public international law was not exhausted, however, by initial justification of colonial endeavours. Understood as an ongoing means of regulating the relations of the collective identities known as states, public international law also defined its own field of application, and for centuries rigorously excluded from its domain all human groups that did not meet the formal requirements of statehood. In the case notably of indigenous peoples this was justified by the notorious 'standard of civilisation', which placed indigenous peoples in the lowest position on a Darwin-inspired scale of progressive evolution, the ultimate goal of 'civilisation' itself corresponding to the then position of the colonising powers.[7] Exclusion of indigenous peoples from the privileged circle of sovereign states implicitly validated 'imperial claims of sovereign power over indigenous peoples and territories'.[8] It also served to justify the conclusion that indigenous peoples had no law.[9]

[5] HP Glenn, *On Common Laws* (Oxford University Press, 2005).

[6] Gilbert (n 1) 230; and for international law as a 'major instrument for legitimizing European expansion and domination overseas', L Rodríguez-Piñero, *Indigenous Peoples, Postcolonialim, and International Law: The ILO Regime (1919–1989)* (New York, Oxford University Press, 2005) 3.

[7] B Bowden, 'The Colonial Origins of International Law: European Expansion and the Classical Standards of Civilization' (2005) 7 *Journal of the History of International Law* 1; SJ Anaya, *Indigenous Peoples in International Law*, 2nd edn (Oxford University Press, 2004) 27–31; and for Christian influence in the formulation of the standard, RS Horowitz, 'International Law and State Transformation in China, Siam, and the Ottoman Empire during the Nineteenth Century' (2004) 15 *Journal of World History* 445, 452–3 ('During the nineteenth century the natural law justification [of the state] disappeared and was replaced by a more parochial idea: that international law was Christian in its origins and that only those non-Christian states that had reached a comparable level of "civilization" could be treated as full participants in international law'). The legal consequences of 'civilisation' were also drawn in constitutional law. See eg L Duguit, *Traité de droit constitutionnel*, 2nd edn, vol II, *La théorie générale de l'État* (Paris, Boccard, 1923) 46 (modern civilised societies fixed on determined territories).

[8] P Macklem, 'Indigenous Recognition in International Law: Theoretical Observations' (2009) 30 *Michigan Journal of International Law* 177, at 185.

[9] PG McHugh, *Aboriginal Societies and the Common Law* (Oxford University Press, 2004) 151 (citing the argument that indigenous peoples have no habit of obedience to a given superior); and for complicity of anthropological science in the conclusion, Rodríguez-Piñero (n 6) 339 ('anthropology was more an instrument for the subjugation of indigenous peoples than for their liberation').

Contemporary use of international law in aid of indigenous peoples is thus ironic when this history is contemplated. For some the irony is ongoing, since even today international law would be best characterised by its 'homogenizing, universalizing' tendency towards Third World mass resistance.[10] It would remain 'trapped in a version of politics that is narrowly focussed on institutional practice', yielding 'an artificially narrow outlook'.[11] The irony is thus constituted by an outright contradiction between an international law which remains fixated on the state as sole, legitimate international actor and a Declaration which would purport to use the resources of international law to benefit indigenous peoples in some collective sense. The resort to international law might even appear as a form of dissembling to the most cynical. Whatever the content of the Declaration, international law could not be of significant assistance towards its realisation.

The more subtle sense of irony, however, would be more open to the recent history of public international law and more open to the theoretical significance of the Declaration itself. We would thus be in the presence of alternative truths, of mutual influence, and neither would be capable of remaining what it previously was, prior to the encounter. The Declaration would be situate in a broader movement of public international law, away from its original, founding purpose and more open to non-state priorities, a movement recently described as 'humanizing'.[12] The Declaration would move public international law even further in this direction and would represent not simply a use or application of international law, in novel circumstances, but a major shift in the nature and direction of international law itself. It thus comes to recognise non-state, non-incorporated *peoples*, and thus abandons centuries of what Amartya Sen has qualified as 'unique categorization', the insistence on a unique means of classification of the people of the world.[13] Unique categorisation, the refusal to consider anything other than one's own means of collective organisation, would be the 'intellectual background' to the much-discussed concept of a clash of civilisations, 'a sharply carpentered vision of one dominant and hardened divisiveness'.[14] Regardless of the idiom used in the body of the Declaration itself, it fundamentally changes international law not only through its recognition of indigenous peoples, after centuries of rejection,

[10] B Rajogapal, *International Law from Below: Development, Social Movements and Third World Resistance* (Cambridge University Press, 2003) 166.

[11] Ibid, 235.

[12] T Meron, *The Humanization of International Law* (Leiden, Martinus Nijhoff, 2006); R McCorquodale, 'An Inclusive International Legal System' (2004) 17 *Leiden Journal of International Law* 477.

[13] A Sen, *Identity and Violence* (New York, WW Norton, 2007) 10.

[14] Ibid.

but also through its abandonment of a unique categorisation of human relations.

The Declaration is also indicative, however, of a shift in the concept of indigenous peoples, and even of a new and different form of self-understanding on the part of indigenous peoples themselves. Bound together by unwritten forms of law and local practices, the identities of indigenous peoples have been closely linked to place and local practice. They have been profoundly chthonic. Some, like the Koori of Australia, have rejected the language of 'indigenous' or 'aborigine' as unremittingly colonial in character, in favour of their own name, in their own language. Local traditions would thus remain local, in practice and designation. There is, however, a new appreciation of the importance of orality in the world,[15] closely linked to contemporary means of communication, and the movement of indigenous peoples in the world has made strategic use of modern means of communication. Indigenous peoples across the world have thus become an 'epistemic community' like many others, linked together by common cause and by virtual and other networks of information.[16] The Declaration is thus indicative of a fundamental shift in public international law, but also of an equally fundamental shift in appreciation of the breadth and significance of the indigenous movement. No longer longer is it just local and particular; it is also global and general. There are differences within it, but like all global traditions it manages its own, internal differences. It does so in the name of overarching commonalities, which are those of ongoing, chthonic values and continued indigenous resistance to colonisation.

The irony of the use of international law thus goes well beyond the usual sense of irony as contradiction or dissembling and clearly extends to a much broader form of mutual understanding and reciprocal influence. It is irony in this subtler sense which is present and which may well extend to the actual content and idiom of the Declaration.

IRONY AND THE IDIOM OF THE DECLARATION

It would be ironic, in the usual sense of the expression, for indigenous peoples to be expressing their understanding of the world in the idiom of 'Western culture theory'.[17] Moreover, this would represent only one (anthropologist's) perspective of the still larger phenomenon of articulating guarantees for the ongoing existence of unwritten law in the language and form of written, international law. It is not 'culture theory' that is

[15] WJ Ong, *Orality and Literacy: The Technologizing of the Word* (London, Methuen, 1982).

[16] See in particular Xanthaki (n 1) 120 on the gradual expansion of the 'international legal personality' of indigenous peoples, notably as an 'entity separate from the state'.

[17] Kuper (n 2).

so evident and striking in the Declaration of the Rights of Indigenous Peoples, but the existence of a *written* declaration of *rights*. Neither writing nor rights have played a visible role in the hundreds of thousands of years of chthonic legal tradition prior to the colonial experience.

Some have seen in the adoption of the language and concepts of the coloniser an abandonment of that which is sought to be defended, and the '*ultimate* violence' of colonialism would be the constant temptation for the ruled to fight the rulers 'within the psychological limits set by the latter'.[18] There would be a process of 'mental colonisation'; the irony would be an oppressive one.[19] James Tully has thus written in salutary manner that if there is to be a 'post-imperial dialogue' it would be necessary for the participants to speak 'in their own languages and customary ways', without being constrained to speak 'within the institutions and traditions of interpretation of the imperial constitutions that have been imposed over them'.[20]

Is the Declaration therefore an imperialist instrument? There are indications to this effect. It assumes the existence of states and ongoing bodies of international and national law which would be essential to its implementation. The Declaration does speak in terms of culture, notably in its preambular paragraphs, and Articles 8 (the right not to be 'subjected to forced assimilation or destruction of the culture') and 34 (right to develop 'distinctive cultures'), and most notably in terms of rights. It guarantees, in Article 6, the right to a nationality, of a nation state.

Rights, of course, are means of resistance to the law of nation states, and have been seen as important means of empowerment. It is also the case, however, that the development and articulation of the concept of rights has largely paralleled that of the development of the modern state, and in the granting of rights to citizens and even more broadly to individuals (where that is the case), there has been a whittling away of identities other than that of citizenship. The state would exist in contrast to the individual, with no mediating associations other than those authorised by the state. Put more aggressively, the individual would exist alone before the state, deprived of all other associations and armed only with the rights that the state confers. Human rights thus emerge not in opposition to the state, or antagonistic to the state, but as the sole, approved means of resistance.[21]

[18] A Nandy, *The Intimate Enemy: Loss and Recovery of Self under Colonialism* (Delhi, Oxford University Press, 1983) 3 (emphasis in original); and see ME Turpel, 'Aboriginal Peoples and the *Canadian Charter*: Interpretive Monopolies, Cultural Differences' (1989–90) 6 *Canadian Human Rights Yearbook* 3, notably 4, 20 ('... simply making a claim requires accepting the dominant cultural and conceptual framework').

[19] H Trask, *From a Native Daughter: Colonialism and Sovereignty in Hawaii* (1993) 23, cited in McHugh (n 9) 56.

[20] J Tully, *Strange Multiplicity* (Cambridge University Press, 1995) 24.

[21] Rajogapal (n 10) 9–10, 165, 186.

Invocation of rights on behalf of indigenous peoples would therefore be entirely consistent with an ongoing, imperial constitutional structure.

The difficulty, however, in speaking only one's own language and using only one's own concepts is that of not being understood. This is compounded if in the precise circumstances one's language and concepts are local, though it is also the case with powerful and widespread languages if they are not known to the persons being addressed. So communication is necessary for dialogue to actually occur and translation *into* another language or conceptual scheme involves active use of both languages or conceptual schemes. This is necessary on both sides of the ongoing dialogue. James Tully thus speaks of the necessity of participants not being *constrained* to speak *within* the language of the other, and there is thus ample room for *use* of the language of the other in effectively communicating one's own concepts. Irony consists in different truths being placed in parallel for purposes of mutual interrogation and understanding.

Indigenous peoples on occasion in the past have chosen not to engage in dialogue, but on many occasions they have also become expert, even cosmopolitan, in the use of language and (legal) idioms other than their own. This is part of a pattern of resistance, to infiltrate and use the resources that are found. The indigenous people of what we now know as Mexico were adept at resorting to the justice of the distant Spanish Crown, when this was perceived as advantageous.[22] Tibetan pastoralists may make use of both traditional and governmental means of dispute resolution, seeing the latter as an additional and not exclusive source of decision making.[23] These are specific examples of what would be a world-wide process of deliberate choosing amongst available sources of law and legal institutions on the part of indigenous peoples, one in which constraint is difficult to perceive.[24] There is a similar process in the emergence of what has come to be known as 'indigenous diplomacy', the deliberate choice to engage in international legal processes, beyond both indigenous and national ones, in the effort to preserve indigenous traditions and ways of

[22] BP Owensby, *Empire of Law and Indian Justice in Colonial Mexico* (Stanford University Press, 2008) 1, 2, 4, 8; MT Sierra, 'Indian Rights and Customary Law in Mexico: A Study of the Nahuas in the Sierra de Puebla' (1995) 29 *Law and Society Review* 227; J González Galván, *Derecho nayerij* (Mexico, UNAM, 2001) 71 (on indigenous people choosing state courts only when dissatisfied with a non-state remedy).

[23] F Pirie, 'Legal Complexity on the Tibetan Plateau' (2006) 53–54 *Journal of Legal Pluralism* 77, notably 91.

[24] See WJ Mommsen and JA de Moor (eds), *European Expansion and Law: The Encounter of European and Indigenous Law in 19th-and 20th-Century Africa and Asia* (Oxford, Berg, 1992) notably 3–7 on 'interaction' and 'unequal bargains' between European and indigenous law; L Benton, *Law and Colonial Cultures* (Cambridge University Press, 2002) notably 8 ('rampant boundary crossing'), 14, 84 (picking and choosing law in India and the Americas), 81 (conquered peoples are not passively accepting roles assigned to them).

life.[25] This has provided leverage that is lacking at the national level, and contributed to the gathering cohesion of the indigenous peoples' movement at a global level.[26]

The Declaration thus uses (some of) the language of western national and international laws. It also profoundly influences them. This has already been seen in the influence of the Declaration on fundamental presuppositions of western international law.[27] It is also evident in the Declaration's effect on more general concepts of western substantive law, notably in its insistence on rights as capable of being collective in enjoyment, and its acceptance of the non-exclusivity of state law on state territory.

Rights have been seen as individual means of empowerment through almost all of their history. They were initially conceived in terms of an individually-possessed *potestas* or power and only gradually, with the emergence of the state, came to be seen as a legally protected interest. In either case, the beneficiary of the right was the individual, and individual rights could be authorised and accepted by the state because they were a necessary quid pro quo for the stripping away of other associational forms of legal identity, leaving in principle only the citizen.[28] The Declaration, however, is 'mainly framed' in terms of collective rights,[29] those of indigenous peoples. The preambular paragraphs of the Declaration speak persistently of the 'rights of indigenous peoples' and declare, even more provocatively, that 'indigenous peoples possess collective rights'. Not only does the Declaration thus challenge the 'unique categorization' of people as state citizens,[30] the non-state peoples that are recognised are declared to be holders of rights, and necessarily empowered as such.

As holders of rights, indigenous peoples are empowered in relation to the state, and an associational identity is thus recognised, mediating

[25] JY Henderson, *Indigenous Diplomacy and the Rights of Peoples: Achieving UN Recognition* (Saskatoon, Purich, 2008); Anaya (n 7) 56–58; Gilbert (n 1) 211–12; S Allen, 'The Consequences of Modernity for Indigenous Peoples: An International Appraisal' (2006) 13 *International Journal on Minority and Group Rights* 315, 320 (prior ILO Convention 169 was weakened by a lack of indigenous participation in development), 325–28 (on indigenous groups seeking to penetrate supra-national institutions, notably the UN Working Group on Indigenous Populations (WGIP), and the emergence from the 1960s of a new group of indigenes educated on the ways of societies that had encroached upon them).

[26] Above, text accompanying nn 15 and 16.

[27] See above under the heading 'Irony and the Use of International Law'.

[28] For the long history of this subjectivisation of law, see M Villey, 'La genèse du droit subjectif chez Guillaume d'Occam' (1964) 9 *Archives de philosophie du droit* 97; and more generally M Villey, *Pensée juridique moderne* (Paris, Montchrestien, 1975); B Tierney, *The Idea of Natural Rights: Studies on Natural Rights, Natural Law and Church Law* (Atlanta, Scholars Press, 1997) (identifying notions of subjective right in 12th century commentaries on Gratian).

[29] S Errico, 'The Draft UN Declaration on the Rights of Indigenous Peoples: An Overview' (2007) 7 *Human Rights Law Review* 741, 745; Gilbert (n 1) 210.

[30] Above, text accompanying nn 13 and 14.

between the individual and the state. It follows that the law of the state is reduced in significance in relation to indigenous peoples, and thus reduced in significance generally. There is recognition, in the written law, of unwritten law. Article 5 states explicitly that 'Indigenous peoples have the right to maintain and strengthen their distinct … legal … institutions' and Article 34 guarantees the collective right to distinctive 'traditions, procedures, practices and, in the cases where they exist, juridical systems or customs', all in conformity with international human rights standards. The language used here is that of western legal traditions in some measure, notably in speaking of 'customs', but it is language which ensures the ongoing existence of indigenous and chthonic legal traditions. If the language or idiom can be taxed as imperial, the same can scarcely be said of the result.

The language of 'incommensurability' has been used in speaking of the positions of government representatives and indigenous peoples.[31] The Declaration is itself, however, proof of commensurability. There is both comparability and compatibility. Participants in the negotiations understood one another; they were able to reconcile positions that might have been taken as incompatible. There is always a middle ground if the logic used is multivalent as opposed to binary.[32] The Chair of the Global Indigenous Caucus has stated that 'The Declaration does not represent the viewpoint of the United Nations, nor does it represent solely the viewpoint of the Indigenous Peoples'.[33] It has been described as a 'good balance'.[34] The irony that is here present is the subtle one of mutual interrogation and understanding and not that of contradiction or dissembling.

There remains the further irony of those states whose judges have most advanced the notion of indigenous rights voting against the Declaration.

IRONY AND OPPOSITION

Australia, Canada, New Zealand and the United States of America voted against the Declaration in the General Assembly. A total of 143 states voted in its favour and a further 11 abstained. There is no evident geographic pattern in the 11 abstentions, or in the remaining group of states absent from the vote. All the former colonising jurisdictions of Europe voted in

[31] P Thornberry, *Indigenous Peoples and Human Rights* (Manchester University Press, 2002) 10, though the statement is only that positions have 'seemed' incommensurable.
[32] For these notions, see Glenn (n 4) ch 10.
[33] L Malezer, Statement by the Chairman, Global Indigenous Caucus, 13 September 2007, www.arena.org.nz/unindig6.htm.
[34] Gilbert (n 1) 226.

favour of the Declaration. The group of Australia, Canada, New Zealand and the United States is striking because these have been the states whose judiciaries originated the current doctrines of aboriginal rights and title, now increasingly being heeded by other judiciaries in the world.[35] There have also been major efforts of reparation in these jurisdictions, though the process is clearly ongoing.[36] It therefore appears ironic, in the usual sense of the term, that the states in which aboriginal rights and title have received the most official support are those which have declared their formal opposition to the Declaration. There is contradiction between local support and formal, international opposition.

To the extent that the Declaration requires national, legislative means of implementation, these appear unlikely in the opposing states.[37] Formal opposition may thus be translatable into formal rejection of the Declaration as a ground for changes to positive, national law. The Declaration, however, does not have the status of a 'binding' international instrument and could in any event serve as no more than motivation for domestic implementation. National governments can fail to implement for many reasons, which may or may not include their own negative vote. They may also implement many measures of the Declaration in spite of such a negative vote. The contradiction between local support and formal, international opposition is thus less radical than it may initially appear. Refusal to sign and implement a *treaty* intended to create binding international obligations is much more easily understood in terms of a binary distinction between law and non-law. The significance of voting on a Declaration—and this includes positive votes as well as negative ones—is much more difficult to evaluate and describe. It is in all cases a question of governmental sentiments or attitudes.

[35] J Gilbert, 'Historical Indigenous Peoples' Land Claims: A Comparative and International Approach to the Common Law Doctrine on Indigenous Title' (2007) 56 *International and Comparative Law Quarterly* 583, notably 585, for judicial references to the 'common law doctrine of indigenous peoples' land rights' in Malaysia, Belize, South Africa, Botswana and Kenya.

[36] See the national reports in F Lenzerini, *Reparations for Indigenous Peoples* (Oxford University Press, 2008); and for large, recent judgments or settlements in the US, S Banner, *How the Indians Lost their Land* (Cambridge, MA, Harvard University Press, 2005) 291 ($248 million to Cayuga in New York; forty million acres and nearly $1 billion in Alaska). The Supreme Court of Canada has also declared that the Government of Canada has a fiduciary obligation towards indigenous peoples in Canada, and that the 'honour of the Crown' requires negotiation and accommodation with indigenous peoples prior to decisions that might affect as yet unproven aboriginal rights and title claims. See, for the fiduciary obligation, *R v Van der Peet* [1996] 2 SCR 507, and for the honour of the Crown, *Haida Nation v British Columbia (Minister of Forests)* [2004] 3 SCR 511.

[37] Art 38 of the Convention calls upon States, in consultation and cooperation with indigenous peoples, to take the appropriate measures, including legislative measures, to achieve the ends of the Declaration. For this 'pivotal role' falling to states, see Anaya (n 1) paras 44ff, and notably paras 56ff on 'mainstreaming and awareness-raising'.

The Declaration thus represents a form of persuasive authority in law. This is entirely compatible with the more subtle sense of irony, since the Declaration interrogates, and is meant to interrogate, national legislation that is inconsistent with its terms. The commensurability of the Declaration with national legislation is evident from its negotiation and content, so the possibilities of mutual understanding and mutual influence are evident. The status of the Declaration as persuasive authority is also compatible with the entire, transnational doctrine of indigenous rights and indigenous title. The origination of these concepts in national case law was not based on national legislation, and their increasing influence amongst national judiciaries in the world has not been due to international law but rather to an informal, and growing, judicial consensus. International law supports this consensus but has not imposed it.

Statements that the Declaration can serve as an interpretational tool, or a guide or model for subsequent treaties or national legislation,[38] should not therefore be seen as apologetic, or as an admission that the Declaration somehow falls short of what might have been. It may well act as a guide and model, but it already provides normative justification for the accommodation of indigenous law by state law. The modern state is not self-justifying. It lives off preconditions which it cannot itself guarantee, and the most important of such preconditions is the transnational, normative tradition justifying states and the exclusivity of their law.[39] The Declaration is thus already a change or variation in the legal tradition of the nation-state, which is now interrogated by a document receiving the support of some three-quarters of the nation-states of the world. Only four states in the world maintained the doctrinal position that state law is of exclusive application in its national territory. The consequences of this may well extend beyond the field of indigenous rights.

CONCLUSIONS

The three ironies of the Declaration on the Rights of Indigenous Peoples are best understood not in the traditional sense of contradiction or dissembling, but in the more subtle sense of placing different truths in juxtaposition with one another, leading to mutual interrogation, mutual

[38] See eg Errico (n 29) 747, 755; Gilbert (n 1) 229.

[39] EW Böckenforde, *Recht, Staat, Freiheit* (Frankfurt, Suhrkamp, 1991) 112 ('the liberal, secular state lives off the preconditions which it cannot itself guarantee'), as cited in J Murkens, 'The Future of *Staatsrecht*: Dominance, Demise or Demystification?' (2007) 70 *Modern Law Review* 731, 746; and see HP Glenn, 'The National Legal Tradition' in K Boele-Woelki and S van Erp, *General Reports of the XVIIth Congress of the International Academy of Comparative Law* (Brussels/Utrecht, Bruylant/Eleven International, 2007) 1, reproduced in (2007) 11(3) *Electronic Journal of Comparative Law*, www.ejcl.org.

understanding, and mutual influence. International law is thus juxtaposed with indigenous law; written, individual rights are juxtaposed with unwritten, collective enjoyment; and positive, charismatic acts of adherence or rejection are juxtaposed with gradual processes of influence over time. The Declaration is remarkable for both its adoption and its content. It is also remarkable for these ironic contributions to the coexistence of different types of law in the world.

8

Beyond the Indigenous/Minority Dichotomy?

WILL KYMLICKA

INTRODUCTION

THE ADOPTION OF the Declaration on the Rights of Indigenous Peoples by the UN General Assembly in 2007 is a major victory for one of the most oppressed groups in the world. It can also be seen as a victory for international law itself. As various commentators have noted, international law has not only historically supported the colonisation of indigenous peoples, it largely emerged precisely in order to facilitate European imperialism.[1] The Declaration suggests that international law has a capacity to overcome its imperial origins, and to become an instrument of justice. As James Anaya puts it, 'international law, although once an instrument of colonialism, has developed and continues to develop, however grudgingly and imperfectly, to support indigenous peoples' demands'.[2] If the Declaration helps to legitimise indigenous demands, it is equally true that the Declaration helps to re-legitimise international law itself in a post-colonial era.[3]

The detailed provisions of the Declaration, and the 'grudging and imperfect' support they provide to indigenous peoples, are discussed in other

[1] P Keal, *European Conquest and the Rights of Indigenous Peoples: The Moral Backwardness of International Society* (Cambridge University Press, 2003); A Anghie, *Imperialism, Sovereignty and the Making of International Law* (Cambridge University Press, 2004).

[2] SJ Anaya, *Indigenous Peoples in International Law* (Oxford University Press, 1996) 4. Similarly, Patrick Macklem argues that the Declaration can best be understood not as responding to some exogenous injustice out in the world, but rather as rectifying injustices that international law itself created: '[I]nternational indigenous rights mitigate some of the adverse consequences of how international law validates morally suspect colonization projects that participated in the production of the existing distribution of sovereign power.' P Macklem, 'Indigenous Recognition in International Law: Theoretical Observations' (2008) 30 *Michigan Journal of International Law* 177, 179.

[3] A Xanthaki, *Indigenous Rights and United Nations Standards: Self-Determination, Culture and Land* (Cambridge University Press, 2007) 6, 285.

chapters in this volume. My concern in this paper is with the Declaration's implications for other historically oppressed substate groups. My main focus will be on one particular type of group—namely 'national minorities', also sometimes known as 'stateless nations', 'captive nations', or 'sub-state nations'—such as the Scots, Catalans, Kurds, Chechens, Crimean Tatars, Kashmiris, Palestinians, and Tibetans. Like indigenous peoples, these are culturally distinct groups living on their traditional territory, who think of themselves as a distinct people or nation, and show a deep attachment to their cultural distinctiveness and to their homeland, which they have struggled to maintain despite being incorporated (often involuntarily) into a larger state. Such ethnonational groups are not typically seen as 'indigenous peoples', but they share many of the same concerns about cultural integrity, non-discrimination, and the right to govern themselves and their territory. Given the many similarities between indigenous peoples and stateless nations, I am interested in how developments regarding the former will affect the latter, and whether stateless nations can invoke international progress on indigenous rights as a precedent.

But national minorities are not the only type of group who might look to the Indigenous Declaration as a possible model. The Declaration could serve as a precedent for a wider range of subaltern groups, including the Roma, Afro-descendents, Dalits, and immigrants. Unlike both substate nations and indigenous peoples, these are not 'homeland groups' in the traditional sense—that is, they are not groups living on a historic homeland which was subsequently incorporated into a larger state as a result of conquest, colonisation or changes in state borders. Yet even if they do not have the same territorial claims, they certainly share the indigenous experience of suffering cultural oppression, political marginalisation and racial discrimination. As such, they may look to the Indigenous Declaration as evidence that international law can be enlisted to support their struggles for respect and emancipation.

In this paper, I want to explore whether such hopes are realistic. Will the Declaration be the first step towards a broader transformation of international law's treatment of substate groups, or will it prove to be a one-off exception, with few if any implications for the rights of other minorities?

Many commentators view the Declaration as a first step towards a more systematic strengthening of the international standing of substate minority groups. According to Stephen Allen, for example, the success of indigenous peoples at the UN can be seen as a 'foretaste' of the enhanced standing that other substate groups can expect to achieve 'in a mature international society'. It is particularly relevant, he suggests, for those national minorities seeking internal self-determination:

> [G]rowing support for the indigenous right to self-determination empowers the societal claims of other challenged minorities. By securing the right of self-determination, indigenous societies have opened up the prospect of the internal

> right being made available to other sub-State societal groups. Moreover, the widening of the conception of people-hood is consistent with the notion of fragmented popular sovereignty ... In particular, by dispelling the arbitrary distinction between 'minorities' and 'peoples', this development could contribute to the amelioration of ethnic tensions and, in turn, allay the fears of impending disintegration on the part of established States.[4]

On this view, indigenous peoples have opened the door for other 'challenged minorities' to make progress in international law.

At first glance, this seems an eminently reasonable expectation. After all, it is widely recognised that indigenous peoples and minorities are 'overlapping categories subject to common normative considerations', and that 'indigenous and minority rights issues intersect substantially'.[5] Given these shared concerns, it is also widely acknowledged that the difference between such national minorities and indigenous peoples 'is one of fuzzy edges rather than bright lines'.[6] This is reflected in the overlap in participation in the UN Working Group on Minorities and the UN Working Group on Indigenous Populations, and in the ongoing difficulties the two Working Groups have had in determining the principles on which groups should be categorised as indigenous or minorities.[7] Indeed, the former Chair of the UN's Working Group on Minorities, Asbjorn Eide, in a paper he co-authored with the Chair of the Working Group on Indigenous Populations (Erica-Irene Daes), acknowledged that:

> The usefulness of a clear-cut distinction between minorities and indigenous peoples is debatable. The Sub-Commission, including the two authors of this paper, have played a major role in separating the two tracks. The time may have come for the Sub-Commission to review the issue again.[8]

Given the overlapping nature of the underlying concerns, and the fuzzy nature of the categories themselves, it seems natural, even inevitable, that

[4] S Allen, 'The Consequences of Modernity for Indigenous Peoples: An International Appraisal' (2006) 13 *International Journal on Minority and Group Rights* 315, 335–36, 338.

[5] SJ Anaya, 'International Human Rights and Indigenous Peoples: The Move towards the Multicultural State' (2004) 21 *Arizona Journal of International and Comparative Law* 13, 21.

[6] P Thornberry, *Indigenous Peoples and Human Rights* (Manchester University Press, 2002) 54.

[7] See Tom Hadden's account of the Working Groups, noting that minorities and indigenous have 'broadly similar concerns', that there is 'a good deal of overlap' in representation in the two Working Groups, and that 'it is difficult to distinguish clearly' between indigenous and other sub-state ethnic groups. He suggests therefore that, in the future, the two could be combined. T Hadden, 'The United Nations Working Group on Minorities' (2007) 14 *International Journal on Minority and Group Rights* 285, 296.

[8] A Eide and E-I Daes, 'Working Paper on the Relationship and Distinction between the Rights of Persons Belonging to Minorities and those of Indigenous Peoples' (2000) prepared for the UN Sub-Commission on Promotion and Protection of Human Rights (UN Doc E/CN.4/Sub.2/2000/10), para 25. See also I Brownlie, 'The Rights of Peoples in Modern International Law' in J Crawford (ed), *The Rights of Peoples* (Oxford University Press, 1988) 1.

the adoption of an indigenous rights declaration should open the door for other minorities. Moreover, as Allen notes, the substantive provisions of the Declaration help to dispel many of the shibboleths that states have used historically to justify the oppression of minorities. The Indigenous Declaration has shown that sovereignty can be multiple and multi-level rather than unitary and homogenous; that international human rights law can recognise collective and group-differentiated rights and not just individual and universal rights; that self-determination can take many different forms, including internal autonomy; that cultural identities are worthy of respect and protection; that historic injustices should be rectified; and so on. In all of these respects, the Indigenous Declaration has been described by commentators as rooted in a broader 'multicultural outlook',[9] or 'multicultural model of political ordering',[10] that has implications for the treatment of other forms of ethnic and cultural diversity. This broader multicultural outlook endorses ideas of multiple loyalties, cultural diversity and dispersed sovereignty, and challenges outmoded ideas of national homogeneity, exclusive loyalty and monolithic sovereignty. For Xanthaki, the way in which international indigenous rights norms endorse this multicultural outlook is their 'most important contribution', relevant not just to indigenous peoples, but also to international human rights norms more generally.[11]

In short, by endorsing the legitimacy of concerns about cultural integrity and autonomy, and by endorsing a multiculturalist model of political ordering, the Indigenous Declaration sets a precedent that minorities can invoke to defend their struggles for strengthened rights in international law. Moreover, the very process of drafting the Declaration, with its innovative procedures for ensuring the full participation of indigenous peoples themselves, also can be seen as opening the door for other minorities. During the long history of negotiations over the Declaration, UN decision-making fora and procedures that had previously been restricted to state representatives were opened up to representatives of indigenous peoples. This can be seen as setting a precedent for a wide range of substate ethnocultural groups to participate in the creation and enforcement of international law.[12]

In both content and process, therefore, the Declaration seems to open the door for other minorities.[13] This optimistic view of the broader

[9] Xanthaki (n 3) 90.
[10] Anaya (n 5) 15.
[11] Xanthaki (n 3) 90.
[12] Ibid, 121, 282.
[13] Some commentators go even further and argue that the success of the indigenous rights movement at the UN provides an opening, not just for ethnocultural groups, but for a broad array of new social movements devoted to social justice and global democracy, including

transformative potential of the Indigenous Declaration is both intuitively plausible and normatively attractive. However, I believe that it is too optimistic. I see no evidence that the conceptual or procedural breakthroughs made by indigenous peoples are opening doors for minorities. On the contrary, as we will see, the dramatic enhancement of the rights of indigenous peoples over the past 15 years has coincided with a period of stagnation, even retrenchment, in the international status of minorities, and with growing international hostility to many minority rights claims. Indigenous peoples and minorities have been moving along very different, even opposite, trajectories at the UN.

Nor is this an accident. The success of the international indigenous movement to date has depended precisely on the assumption that progress for indigenous peoples need not, and will not, open the door to greater recognition or protection of other minorities. When Member States voted for the Indigenous Declaration, I believe they did so on the assumption that the UN can enhance the rights of indigenous peoples while simultaneously resisting the expansion of, or even diminishing, the rights of other minorities. In this sense, they presupposed what I call a 'firewall' model of the relationship between indigenous peoples and minorities. On this view, the rights of indigenous peoples are categorically distinct from, and have no conceptual or legal implications for, other minorities, and an ironclad barrier will prevent other minorities from walking through any doors that indigenous peoples have opened.

women's rights, environmental groups, and anti-poverty groups. This helps to explain the enormous interest in the international indigenous movement amongst scholars of new social movements and of 'counter-hegemonic globalisation' or 'globalisation from below'. These scholars hope and assume that the achievements of indigenous peoples at the UN are a precedent that other non-state actors can draw upon to help create a more just system of international law and a more mature international society. These achievements are transformative, not just of the status of indigenous peoples and minorities, but of international law and international organisations more generally, changing the very ground rules of the Westphalian order that had privileged state actors over non-state actors, and privileged state sovereignty over principles of justice and democratic inclusion. See eg A Muelbach, 'What Self in Self-Determination: Notes from the Frontiers of Transnational Indigenous Activism' (2003) 10 *Identities: Global Studies in Culture and Power* 241; F Passy, 'Supranational Political Opportunities as a Channel of Globalization of Political Conflicts: The Case of the Rights of Indigenous Peoples' in D della Porta, H Kriesi and D Rucht (eds), *Social Movements in a Globalizing World* (London, Macmillan, 1999) 148; A Feldman, 'Making Space at the Nations' Table: Mapping the Transformative Geographies of the International Indigenous Peoples' Movement' (2002) 1 *Social Movement Studies* 31; R Morgan, 'Advancing Indigenous Rights at the United Nations: Strategic Framing and its Impact on the Normative Development of International Law' (2004) 13 *Social and Legal Studies* 481; R Falk, 'The Rights of Peoples (in particular Indigenous Peoples) in Crawford (n 8) 17; R Falk, *On Humane Governance: Toward a New Global Politics* (Cambridge, Polity Press, 1995). However, my focus in this paper is on the impact of the Indigenous Declaration on other ethnocultural groups. Even if the international indigenous movement has opened the door for new social movements generally, I will argue that it has not done so for other ethnocultural groups.

The Declaration will not have broader transformative effects unless or until this firewall breaks down. And it is indeed possible that, over time, international law will need to acknowledge the overlapping categories and common concerns that connect indigenous and minority rights, and that the Declaration will thereby end up having transformative effects that Member States neither intended nor desired. However, I will argue that we should not underestimate the capacity and determination of UN Member States to prevent minorities from invoking the Indigenous Declaration as a precedent or model. Moreover, even if the firewall were to break down, acknowledging the overlap between minorities and indigenous peoples could have unpredictable effects. It could result in the status of minorities in international law being pulled up by the achievements of indigenous peoples. However, it is equally possible that support for the rights of indigenous peoples would be dragged down by international hostility to minority rights.

To my mind, this is one of the great uncertainties regarding the long-term effects of the Declaration. Will the core ideas of the Declaration—ideas of multicultural political ordering, multiple loyalties, cultural diversity, dispersed sovereignty and rectification of injustice—spread outwards to lift up other ethnocultural minorities? Or will state fears about the destabilising effects of such a spread gradually erode support for indigenous rights? Or will the firewall in fact prove stable over time, allowing the UN to continue to enhance indigenous rights while resisting minority rights?

Since the Declaration was only adopted in 2007, it is obviously too soon to make definitive predictions. However, we can identify some of the factors that are likely to determine the long-term relationship between indigenous rights and minority rights. I will begin by outlining the divergent trajectories of minorities and indigenous peoples over the past 20 years at the UN, and how these trajectories reveal the pervasiveness of the firewall view. I will then explain why the firewall may ultimately break down, but in ways that are as likely to erode indigenous rights as to strengthen minority rights. I will conclude with some thoughts about how the concepts and categories currently used in international law might need to change if the broader transformative potential of the Declaration is to be realised.

THE NEED FOR TARGETED INDIGENOUS RIGHTS

In order to see the shape of the problem here, we need to recall why indigenous peoples struggled to gain a dedicated declaration on indigenous rights, separate from the rights owed to minorities under the UN. After all, the International Bill of Rights does not neglect issues of cultural diversity. Article 27 of the International Covenant on Civil and Political Rights (ICCPR), in particular, enshrines a right to enjoy one's culture:

> In those States in which ethnic, religious or linguistic minorities exist, persons belonging to such minorities shall not be denied the right, in community with the other members of their group, to enjoy their own culture, to profess and practise their own religion, or to use their own language.[14]

This guarantee of a right to enjoy one's culture in community with co-members is clearly relevant to many concerns of indigenous peoples, and indeed Article 27 has been successfully invoked in a series of cases to help protect indigenous cultural practices that were threatened by state policies.[15]

However, while Article 27 has proven helpful, it has clear limitations as a framework for articulating indigenous claims. To oversimplify, Article 27 can be invoked to contest discrete laws or policies adopted by states, but it does not contest the structure of the state itself. It sets limits on how states govern their indigenous peoples, but it does not put in question the right of states to govern indigenous peoples and their territories. Yet it is precisely the structure of the state that is the central issue for many indigenous peoples. They do not simply want the state to govern them differently; rather, they want to govern themselves. They do not simply want to change *how* power is exercised over them, but *who* exercises that power. They seek self-government, not just because they see it as vital to their future well-being, but also because it is the core of the historic injustice inflicted upon them. The core injustice of colonialism was the assertion of claims to sovereignty over indigenous peoples and their territories by colonial settlers, and this was an injustice that was ratified by international law itself. By now affirming an indigenous right of self-government, international law can mitigate that injustice.

These sorts of claims cannot plausibly be handled under Article 27. Article 27 is a generic minority rights clause that seeks to articulate a rights-claim that all minorities can invoke, regardless of their particular historical relationship with the state. It therefore applies to newly arrived immigrants and refugees as well as to historically settled indigenous peoples or national groups. The members of all such groups—new or old, large or small, territorially concentrated or dispersed—have the right to enjoy their culture in community with their co-members. Indeed, the UN

[14] (1966) 999 UNTS 171.

[15] See *Lovelace v Canada*, 30 July 1981, HRC No 24/1977, A/36/40 (1981) UN Doc Supp No 40 (A/36/40) at 161; *Kitok v Sweden*, 27 July 1988, HRC No 197/1985, CCPR/C/33/D/197/1985; *Ominayak v Canada*, 26 March 1990, HRC No 167/1984, CCPR/C/38/D/167/1984; *Lansman v Finland*, 26 October 1994, HRC, No 511/1992, CCPR/C/58/D/617/1995; and *Hopu and Bessert v France*, 29 July 1997, HRC No 549/1993, UN Doc CCPR/C/60/D/549/1993.

Human Rights Committee has ruled that even visitors to a country should be able to claim an Article 27 right to enjoy their culture.[16]

This right to enjoy one's culture is a profoundly important human right. But precisely because it is a generic minority right, claimable by visitors as much as indigenous peoples, it cannot speak to issues raised by histories of colonisation and conquest, or to cases where the very right of the state to govern particular peoples or territories is in dispute. To deal with these issues and cases, a separate legal instrument is needed, focusing not on minorities in general, but on a narrower set of groups who share a particular pattern of injustice in their historical relationship to state power.

And this of course is the rationale and function of the Indigenous Declaration. It focuses not just on the right of individuals to enjoy their culture in community with co-ethnics, but on the structure of the state, the distribution of political power over peoples and territories, and on rectifying historic injustice in that distribution. This is reflected in the Declaration's core principle of self-determination, and in its provisions regarding internal autonomy, legal pluralism, and control over traditional territory.

It is precisely these principles and provisions that most clearly mark the Declaration as rooted in a 'multicultural model of political ordering'.[17] If Article 27 endorses a culturally sensitive model of *human rights*, the Indigenous Declaration endorses a multicultural model of *the state*. And this is why commentators have seen it as transformative. It doesn't just say that cultural identities are worthy of respect by the state. It also says that the state itself must be pluralised, accepting ideas of dispersed sovereignty, substate autonomies, legal pluralism and multiple loyalties, and acknowledging the injustices done when political authority was illegitimately claimed over indigenous peoples and territories.

CAN THE DECLARATION BE A PRECEDENT?

In my view, justice for indigenous peoples requires addressing these issues of political order, and so a separate legal instrument was indeed needed that went beyond the generic minority rights guarantees of Article 27. The adoption of the Declaration is therefore a genuine achievement for

[16] Human Rights Committee, General Comment No 23, 'Rights of Minorities (Article 27)', adopted 8 April 1994, CCPR/C/21/Rev.1/Add, paras 5.1 and 5.2. When Art 27 was first drafted, it was generally assumed that only long-standing historically settled groups would qualify as 'minorities', and not immigrants or refugees. However, the UN monitoring bodies have successfully pushed for a more inclusive definition of 'minorities'. See W Kymlicka, *Multicultural Odysseys: Navigating the New International Politics of Diversity* (Oxford University Press, 2007) 200–01.

[17] Anaya (n 5) 15.

indigenous peoples. My interest in this paper, however, is on its potential impact for other groups. In what ways, if any, can the Declaration serve as a model or precedent for other substate ethnocultural groups?

We can distinguish three different ways in which the Declaration could be seen as setting a precedent for other groups:

— First, at the level of substantive norms, the Declaration endorses a principle of (internal) self-determination for indigenous peoples. This principle is also central to the struggle of national minorities, and so the Declaration could be seen as setting a precedent for them, or for other groups who claim a sense of peoplehood or nationhood. As I noted earlier, Allen views this as the most obvious or likely effect of the Indigenous Declaration. As he puts it, 'by securing the right of self-determination, indigenous societies have opened up the prospect of the internal right being made available to other sub-State societal groups'.[18]
— Second, at a more formal level, the Declaration involves the articulation of 'targeted' rights. The Declaration rests on the premise that because of their distinctive history and relationship to the state, indigenous peoples require a separate legal instrument codifying rights that are specific to indigenous peoples, above and beyond the generic rights in Article 27 (and the 1992 UN Minorities Declaration) that accrue to all minorities. This idea of formulating targeted rights to deal with distinctive patterns of injustices is one that can be invoked by many types of substate groups, even if their substantive needs are different from those of indigenous peoples. The Roma, Afro-Latinos, Dalits and immigrants may not seek the same substantive norms as indigenous peoples (such as self-determination or territorial autonomy), but they too argue that they face distinctive patterns of injustice that are not adequately addressed by the generic Article 27 right to enjoy one's culture. The Indigenous Declaration could be seen, therefore, as a precedent for other sorts of targeted rights (eg a 'Charter of Romani Rights').
— Third, at a procedural level, the Indigenous Declaration emerged out of a process that included indigenous peoples themselves. Indigenous peoples argued that historically they have been the objects of international law, but were not active subjects in its formulation, and that international law will only be fair and legitimate if the peoples governed by it have a say in the development of its standards. This principle—that the objects of international law should also be its subjects—is one that can be invoked by many substate

[18] Allen (n 4) 335.

groups. While minorities have been the objects of international law dating back to the League of Nations, they have played virtually no role in the drafting of international minority rights norms, whether in the League's minority protection scheme, Article 27 of the ICCPR, or the 1992 UN Declaration on the Rights of Persons Belonging to National or Ethnic, Religious or Linguistic Minorities.[19] Minorities have been the object of international debate, but not active subjects in the debate. This was precisely the situation that indigenous peoples successfully contested,[20] and minorities could claim that they too have the right to participate in the formulation of new international standards.

In all of these ways, the Indigenous Declaration is potentially a model for other ethnocultural substate groups to seek enhanced recognition and rights. And indeed there have been efforts along all three of these lines: attempts to extend autonomy/self-determination to national minorities; attempts to formulate new types of targeted rights for a range of different types of groups; and attempts to develop mechanisms whereby minorities can participate in the formulation of new international standards. However, to date, none of these efforts has been a success, and we can learn important lessons from their failure.

Let me start with the first issue—the extension of rights of internal self-determination to national minorities. At the level of moral principle, this extension seems natural and obvious. All of the arguments I mentioned earlier for a separate Indigenous Declaration—in particular, the inadequacy of Article 27, and the need to address issues of historic injustice and contested state authority—can and have been raised by stateless nations like the Chechens, Kurds, Kashmiris, Tibetans, Basques and Palestinians. Like indigenous peoples, the members of these substate national groups do not simply seek the right to enjoy their culture with co-members. They also contest the authority of the state to govern them and their territories, seek acknowledgement of historic injustices, and seek to pluralise state structures through recognition of rights of self-determination or autonomy.

So if a powerful case can be made for having a separate Indigenous Declaration, above and beyond Article 27, it seems that a similar case can be made for drafting a separate Declaration on the rights of sub-state national groups. And indeed this has been proposed, both at the UN and within Europe. For example, in 1993—at the same time as the indigenous draft declaration was first adopted by the UN Working

[19] UN General Assembly Resolution 47/135, 18 December 1992.

[20] RL Barsh, 'Indigenous Peoples in the 1990s: From Object to Subject of International Law?' (1994) 7 *Harvard Human Rights Journal* 33.

Group—Liechtenstein submitted to the UN General Assembly a 'Draft Declaration on Self-Determination through Self-Administration'.[21] This draft declaration, like the indigenous draft declaration, affirmed the right of self-determination for all peoples, and recognised a right of internal autonomy as an expression of that right. It differed from the indigenous declaration, however, in understanding 'all peoples' to include sub-state nations as well as indigenous peoples.

A similar debate about the rights of national minorities to autonomy was occurring at the Council of Europe. In 1993, for example, the Council of Europe's Parliamentary Assembly adopted a recommendation stating that

> in the regions where they are a majority, the persons belonging to a national minority shall have the right to have at their disposal appropriate local or autonomous authorities or to have a special status, matching this specific historical and territorial situation and in accordance with the domestic legislation of the State.[22]

Unlike the Liechtenstein proposal, this recommendation did not explicitly endorse a right to 'self-determination' for national minorities. But it did endorse many of the same substantive rights and powers that are supposed to instantiate internal self-determination, in particular forms of regional autonomy, which many commentators viewed as implicitly drawing on norms of internal self-determination.

This recommendation was generalising a principle adopted two years earlier by the EU Commission regarding the recognition of independent states following the break-up of Yugoslavia. The Commission recommended that states seeking independence, like Croatia, should only receive international recognition if they grant 'a special status of autonomy' to areas populated by national minorities.[23] The Council of Europe's Parliamentary Assembly suggested that this principle be affirmed as part of a new European declaration on the rights of national minorities, and/or as an additional protocol to the European Convention of Human Rights.

[21] For the draft resolution submitted to the General Assembly, see UN A/C.3/48/L.17. The draft convention itself is reprinted (together with legal commentaries) as an appendix in W Danspeckgruber (ed), *The Self-Determination of Peoples: Community, Nation, and State in an Interdependent World* (Boulder, Lynne Reinner, 2002) 382. See also the discussion in G Welhengama, 'The Legitimacy of Minorities' Claim for Autonomy through the Right to Self-Determination' (1998) 68 *Nordic Journal of International Law* 413. When the draft convention was rebuffed at the UN, the Prince of Liechtenstein set up the 'Liechtenstein Institute on Self-Determination' at Princeton University, in the hope that it would generate greater public debate and academic analysis of the issues involved. See http://www.princeton.edu/~lisd/.

[22] Recommendation 1201, Art 11.

[23] For a discussion of this aspect of the European Commission Treaty Provisions for the Yugoslavia Draft Convention, see R Caplan, *Europe and the Recognition of New States in Yugoslavia* (Cambridge University Press, 2005).

For a brief moment in the early 1990s, therefore, we see a striking parallel between debates about indigenous peoples and debates about national minorities. In both cases, influential voices at the UN and in regional organisations were drafting new declarations that would enshrine rights to internal autonomy, based on a new 'multicultural model of political ordering'. And in both cases, the justifications for these claims had a similar dual structure. On the one hand, both indigenous peoples and national minorities appealed to facts of cultural distinctiveness, historical injustice, and contested legitimacy to ground their demands for self-government;[24] and on the other hand, both emphasised that the generic minority rights in Article 27 were 'fatally weak',[25] and 'completely inadequate ... to their needs'.[26]

For a moment, therefore, it seemed possible that international law would develop two sets of targeted rights that went beyond generic Article 27 minority rights to include rights to internal self-government or autonomy: one for indigenous peoples, and one for national minorities. The Working Group's 1993 draft declaration on indigenous rights differed in some respects from Liechtenstein's 1993 draft declaration on self-determination for national minorities, or the Parliamentary Assembly's 1993 recommendation on territorial autonomy for national minorities. For example, issues regarding sacred sites, the repatriation of cultural objects, and the use of customary law are all more relevant to indigenous peoples than to national minorities.[27] But the various declarations shared the core ideas of a multicultural model of political ordering, based on rights to self-government, and the renegotiation and dispersal of authority over peoples and territories. There was much talk at the time of 'the evolving right to autonomy' in both contexts, and of the need to develop new models of political order in a 'post-national world' that would accommodate both indigenous peoples and national minorities.[28]

This is a prime example of how indigenous rights might have interacted with minority rights in a mutually reinforcing way to help consolidate a new international commitment to a multicultural outlook. However, all of these proposals have come to naught. Liechtenstein's 1993 draft declaration at the UN received no support, not even the courtesy of being discussed and studied. While the UN has progressively come to support

[24] As Miriam Aukerman notes, indigenous peoples and national minorities 'share the goal of preserving their distinctive cultures, and justify their claims to group-differentiated rights with similar appeals to self-determination, equality, cultural diversity, history and vulnerability'. M Aukerman, 'Definitions and Justifications: Minority and Indigenous Rights in a Central/East European Context' (2000) 22 *Human Rights Quarterly* 1011, 1045.

[25] Barsh (n 20) 81.

[26] Aukerman (n 24) 1030.

[27] Xanthaki (n 3) 214–15.

[28] Ibid, 6.

autonomy for indigenous peoples, the idea that other substate national groups might have such rights remains anathema at the UN. Indeed, for reasons discussed below, opposition to that idea is more powerful today than in the mid-1990s. Similarly, when the Council of Europe finalised its Framework Convention on the Protection of National Minorities in 1995, it rejected the Parliamentary Assembly's recommendation 1201 on a right to autonomy. Indeed, it rejected any proposed articles that would have even hinted at the need for states to renegotiate the structure of state institutions, or the need to acknowledge the potential contestability of, and injustice in, state claims to authority over national minorities and their traditional territories.[29] In this sense, the European Framework Convention on national minorities is essentially a dressed-up version of Article 27. Like Article 27, it endorses a right to enjoy one's culture in community with others, and hence the legitimacy of cultural diversity, but refuses to address issues of state structure and contested claims to authority and territory.[30]

Consider now the second possible transformative effect of the Declaration: namely, creating increased space for claims to 'targeted rights'. Before the drafting of the Declaration, international law operated on the assumption that issues of diversity were best addressed by putting together all of the different types of minorities—ethnic, national, linguistic, immigrant, indigenous, etc—and according them all the same generic minority rights. The Indigenous Declaration carves out a clear exception to this pattern, acknowledging the need to differentiate amongst different types of substate groups. At present, this is a one-off exception, leaving all the other types of groups lumped together. But it can be seen as a precedent, rather than just an exception. Rather than a simple bifurcation of 'indigenous peoples' and 'minorities', we could instead have a 'multi-targeted' scheme of international norms, with separate legal instruments for indigenous peoples, national minorities, the Romani, Afro-descendents, Dalits, immigrants, or other types of groups in other regions of the world. All such groups would benefit from the generic Article 27 right to enjoy one's culture—which would remain a bedrock principle of any human rights regime—but each would also benefit from targeted rights that address the path-dependent injustices that have arisen from their particular histories of interaction with, and incorporation into, the state.

Inspired by the indigenous movement, other types of ethnocultural groups have indeed started to mobilise for targeted international rights.

[29] For a more detailed discussion of this shift in the Council of Europe (and other European organisations) from a commitment to substantive targeted rights for national minorities to more generic minority rights, see Kymlicka (n 16) ch 6.

[30] As I discuss below, the Advisory Committee that monitors the Framework Convention has tried to reintroduce some of these issues in their reports.

For example, there have been draft declarations on Romani rights,[31] as well as proposals for dedicated legal instruments regarding Afro-descendants in Latin America,[32] or the Dalits in Asia.[33] In each case, we see the same dynamic: groups are seeking targeted rights because the generic Article 27 right to enjoy one's culture is inadequate to address the distinctive needs arising from a distinctive history of (unjust) relations with the state. The detailed provisions of these proposals on Romani rights or Afro-Latino rights or Dalit rights are different from those of the Indigenous Declaration, but they share a common goal of envisaging new multicultural models of political order based on targeted norms that address distinctive patterns of injustice in relations with the state.

This is another way in which the Indigenous Declaration could help to consolidate a broader commitment to multiculturalism. However, here again, all of these proposals for targeted rights for other groups—whether for the Romani, Afro-Latinos, Dalits or immigrants—have gone nowhere. While all of these groups continue to benefit from their generic Article 27 right to enjoy one's culture, attempts to formulate more robust standards in light of their particular needs have failed.

Finally, let me turn to the third potential effect of the Declaration: namely, creating the precedent that the objects of international law should also be the subjects or co-authors of it, and should play a role in formulating its standards. The UN Working Group on Indigenous Populations is 'widely viewed as a great success of the UN system',[34] and as an 'extraordinary' model of 'human rights dynamism',[35] precisely because it helped to establish new standards. As a result, it has become the focal point of a vibrant transnational advocacy movement, leading to the creation of the higher-status Permanent Forum and the Expert Mechanism on the Rights of Indigenous Peoples.

Inspired by this example, minorities have also sought to gain 'a seat at the table' at the UN. And indeed for many years there was a UN Working Group on Minorities, working in parallel with the UN Working

[31] I Klimova-Alexander, 'Transnational Romani and Indigenous Non-Territorial Self-Determination Claims' (2007) 6 *Ethnopolitics* 395.

[32] C Lennox, 'The Changing International Protection Regimes for Minorities and Indigenous Peoples: Experiences from Latin America and Africa', paper presented to Annual Conference of International Studies Association, San Diego, March 2006.

[33] C Bob, '"Dalit Rights Are Human Rights": Caste Discrimination, International Activism, and the Construction of a New Human Rights Issue' (2007) 29 *Human Rights Quarterly* 167. See also the Parliamentary Assembly of the Council of Europe's recommendation for a declaration on immigrant rights: it 'recognises that immigrant populations whose members are citizens of the state in which they reside constitute special categories of minorities, and recommends that a specific Council of Europe instrument should be applied to them' (recommendation 1402).

[34] Xanthaki (n 3) 2.

[35] See Morgan (n 13).

Group on Indigenous Populations, which offered a forum for minorities to participate in Geneva. However, the two Working Groups could not have been more different. The Minorities Working Group had no mandate to draft new legal standards, or to monitor compliance with existing standards. As Tom Hadden notes, minority rights 'has always been the poor relation in the human rights family' at the UN, and the Working Group on Minorities was 'one of the weakest' of the human rights bodies.[36] The Working Group has now been replaced by the even weaker Forum on Minority Issues. Whereas the Indigenous Working Group has been intensively studied as a model of transnational activism and human rights dynamism, the minorities Working Group was virtually unknown outside a small circle of activists and experts coordinated by the Minority Rights Group, which has valiantly (but unsuccessfully) tried to make it a meaningful international forum. Without a mandate to draft new standards, and given the inadequacy of relying on the generic rights set out in Article 27 or the 1992 Declaration on Minorities, the Working Group on Minorities was unable to provide a meaningful forum for minorities to become subjects rather than objects of international law. While minorities have certainly made appeals at the international level—such as the pursuit of new targeted rights by national minorities, Roma, Dalits and Afro-Latinos—the Minorities Working Group had no mandate to draft such targeted rights, and so, unlike the Indigenous Working Group, it was largely unable to articulate the aspirations of its intended beneficiaries, and never became a focal point of mobilisation or enthusiasm.

In short, since 1993, the remarkable progress we have seen in the formulation of targeted norms for indigenous peoples has coincided with more or less complete failure in terms of formulating new standards for other substate groups. In this sense, Allen's claim that the UN's endorsement of the indigenous right to self-determination 'empowers the societal claims of other challenged minorities' seems overly-optimistic.[37]

I don't mean to imply that the international community has been silent or indifferent to the needs of other groups. Various UN bodies have commissioned studies of 'best practices' regarding national minorities, Roma, Dalits and Afro-Latinos; UN human rights committees often ask states to explain their polices towards such groups; and UN world conferences include references to the urgency of their respective situations. But all of this was also true of indigenous peoples before the Indigenous Declaration. For indigenous peoples, all of these studies, questions and expressions of concern were not enough—indeed, they are of little use if there are no relevant *standards* for evaluating state conduct. The point

[36] Hadden (n 7) 285.
[37] Allen (n 4) 335–36.

of drafting a declaration was precisely to turn vague expressions of international concern into tangible legal standards that could be internationally monitored. Indigenous advocates argued that the pre-existing international standard—namely, Article 27—was simply inadequate. Indeed, it was regarded as 'fatally weak'.[38] Without clearer and more robust standards that addressed the real problems in the relationship between states and indigenous peoples, vague expressions of international concern and/or lists of best practices had no bite, particularly in those states of greatest international concern. The formulation of new standards was an essential step in ensuring that international concern was effective, rather than just rhetorical or impotent.

And this is equally true, I believe, of other substate groups. The UN and other international organisations have expressed concern about national minorities, Roma, Dalits, immigrants and Afro-Latinos, and have commissioned studies of best practices. For example, many international organisations have published glowing reports about how well autonomy works for national minorities in, say, South Tyrol, Catalonia or the Åland Islands. But as we have seen, those same organisations have steadfastly resisted any proposal to make these 'best practices' a matter of legal right for national minorities. Similarly, there has been no willingness to turn best practices for the Roma, Dalits or Afro-Latinos into new legal standards. In none of these cases has the UN been able to formulate standards that make any appreciable progress on the generic minority rights and anti-discrimination rights that exist in the ICCPR or the International Covenant on the Elimination of all Forms of Racial Discrimination (ICERD).[39] And in the absence of strengthened standards, the expressions of international concern have been largely ineffective.[40] So while we have seen episodic endorsements of multicultural models in relation to a wide range of groups, it is only in relation to indigenous peoples that serious efforts have been made at formulating new rights, standards or entitlements.

[38] Barsh (n 20) 81.

[39] (1965) 660 UNTS 195. Some commentators argue that the 1992 UN Declaration on the Rights of Persons Belonging to National or Ethnic, Religious or Linguistic Minorities, and/or the 1995 Council of Europe Framework Convention on the Protection of National Minorities, make appreciable progress on Art 27. I disagree, for reasons explained in Kymlicka (n 16) ch 6. They are both fundamentally a restatement of generic Art 27 rights combined with a restatement of equally generic civil and political rights, leaving untouched the 'fatal weakness' that led indigenous peoples and other groups to seek more targeted rights.

[40] There are many different arenas within the UN and other international organisations where a (genuine) concern for minorities has been expressed, including concerted efforts at promoting multicultural models as 'best practices'. However, I believe that these efforts have been generally ineffective in the absence of appropriate standards, for reasons discussed in Kymlicka (n 6) chs 6–7.

In short, the groundbreaking achievements of indigenous peoples have not—to date at least—had transformative effects for other minorities. The Indigenous Declaration broke new ground: (i) in its substantive norms (such as self-determination, legal pluralism, autonomy); (ii) in its very form—namely, as a 'targeted' instrument that seeks to identify norms that are appropriate for a particular type of group, rather than relying exclusively on 'generic' minority rights norms that apply to all groups, such as Article 27 or the 1992 UN Minorities Declaration; and (iii) in its drafting process, which gave the objects of international law a chance to become its subjects. None of these breakthroughs has been replicated for other substate groups. Efforts by national minorities to appeal to the substantive norms of self-government and autonomy have been repudiated, as have efforts by other groups to seek targeted minority rights, and no comparable mechanisms have been created that would enable minorities to become subjects of international law.

These divergent trajectories of indigenous and minority rights clearly suggest that UN Member States are operating with a firewall view. They are assuming that it is possible to enhance the rights of indigenous peoples while resisting the rights of minorities; that it is possible to create targeted legal norms for indigenous peoples while relegating all other groups to generic minority rights; and that that it is possible to strengthen the standard-setting mandate of UN bodies dealing with indigenous issues, while weakening the mandate of UN bodies dealing with minority issues. In all of these ways, optimistic predictions about the broader transformative effects of the Indigenous Declaration have not acknowledged the capacity and determination of UN Member States to prevent minorities from taking advantage of indigenous achievements.

WILL THE FIREWALL ENDURE?

And yet, as I noted earlier, there are serious questions about whether this sort of firewall can endure indefinitely. Indeed, while Member States will cling as long as possible to the firewall, I suspect it will ultimately break down. I will focus in this section on the pressures that may require international law to acknowledge the commonalities and overlap between indigenous peoples and national minorities.

The attempt to create an inviolable hedge between indigenous peoples and national minorities is subject to multiple stresses, even contradictions. For one thing, the firewall creates moral inconsistencies, since whatever arguments exist for recognising rights of self-government for indigenous peoples also apply to national minorities. This is clear from the explanations given within the UN itself for the targeted indigenous track. Consider the paper co-authored by the Chair of the UN's Working

Group on Minorities (Asbjorn Eide) and the Chair of the UN Working Group on Indigenous Populations (Erica-Irene Daes) on the distinction between 'indigenous peoples' on the one hand, and 'national, ethnic, religious and linguistic minorities' on the other.[41] In explaining why indigenous peoples are entitled to targeted rights beyond those available to all minorities under the generic Article 27, the two Chairs identified three key differences: (a) whereas minorities seek institutional integration, indigenous peoples seek to preserve a degree of institutional separateness; (b) whereas minorities seek individual rights, indigenous peoples seek collectively exercised rights; (c) whereas minorities seek non-discrimination, indigenous peoples seek self-government. These are indeed relevant differences between different types of ethnocultural groups, but none of them distinguishes indigenous peoples from national minorities. On all three points national minorities fall on the same side of the ledger as indigenous peoples.

In an earlier document, Daes offered a somewhat different account. She stated that the distinguishing feature of indigenous peoples, compared to minorities in general, is that they have a strong attachment to a traditional territory. As she puts it, 'attachment to a homeland is nonetheless definitive of the identity and integrity of the [indigenous] group, socially and culturally. This may suggest a very narrow but precise definition of "indigenous", sufficient to be applied to any situation where the problem is one of distinguishing an indigenous people [from] the larger class of minorities.'[42] But this criterion—'attachment to a homeland'—applies to national minorities as well as indigenous peoples.

Or consider Xanthaki's account of why indigenous peoples are entitled to representation in the international legal sphere: namely, that 'indigenous peoples are not merely groups organized around particular issues, but long-standing communities with historically rooted cultures and distinct political and social institutions'.[43] Is this not equally true of the Basques, Kurds or Tibetans?

Some indigenous scholars accept that the underlying core principles apply equally to national minorities. According to James Anaya, for example, all substate nations or peoples have the same substantive rights to internal self-determination as indigenous peoples. The rationale for having international norms targeted specifically at indigenous peoples, on his view, is purely a remedial one: indigenous peoples are more likely

[41] Eide and Daes (n 8).

[42] E-I Daes, 'Working Paper on the Concept of "Indigenous People"', prepared for the UN Working Group on Indigenous Populations ((1996) UN Doc E/CN.4/Sub.2/AC.4/1996/2), para 39.

[43] Xanthaki (n 3) 4.

to have had their substantive rights violated in the past.[44] Indeed, it is widely acknowledged that the problems of indigenous peoples and national minorities 'are the same in principle',[45] that they raise 'broadly similar concerns',[46] and that they are subject to 'common normative considerations'.[47] As historically settled groups living on their homelands, both national minorities and indigenous peoples have legitimate interests with respect to the governance of their traditional territory, and to the expression of their language and culture within the public institutions of that territory, and hence to a restructuring of state power—and all of these shared interests and claims go beyond the generic minority rights accorded to all minorities.

Since the principles advanced within the UN for targeted indigenous rights also apply to national minorities, the sharp gulf in legal status between the two groups lacks any clear moral justification. There was, at first, an understandable justification for prioritising the rights of indigenous peoples. The subjugation of indigenous peoples by overseas European colonisers was typically a more brutal process than the subjugation of national minorities by their neighbouring societies, leaving indigenous peoples more vulnerable, and hence in more urgent need of international protection. As a result, there was a plausible moral argument for giving priority to indigenous peoples over national minorities in the codification of self-government rights in international law.

However, what began as a difference in relative urgency between the claims of indigenous peoples and national minorities has developed into a total rupture at the level of international law. Across a wide range of international documents, indigenous peoples have been distinguished from national minorities, and claims to autonomy or internal self-determination have been restricted to the former. National minorities are lumped together with visitors, immigrants and diasporas and accorded only generic minority rights, ignoring their distinctive needs and aspirations relating to historic settlement and territorial concentration. The distinction between indigenous peoples and other homeland minorities has thereby assumed significance within international law that is morally difficult to justify or sustain.

[44] See Anaya (n 2).

[45] Brownlie (n 8) 5. According to Brownlie, the 'heterogeneous terminology which has been used over the years—reference to "nationalities", "peoples", "minorities" and "indigenous populations"—involves essentially the same idea … the problems of the Lapps, the Inuit, Australian Aboriginals, the Welsh, the Quebecois, the Armenians, the Palestinians and so forth are the same in principle … the separation of the topic of indigenous populations from the question of self-determination and the treatment of minorities is not justified either as a matter of principle or by practical considerations' (16).

[46] Hadden (n 7).

[47] Anaya (n 5).

This inconsistency raises the question of why the international community has been so much more sympathetic to the claims of indigenous peoples than to national minorities. There are many reasons,[48] but the core of the problem is revealed in a passing comment by Erica-Irene Daes. In trying to diminish state opposition to indigenous claims to self-determination, she states that 'in view of their small size, limited resources and vulnerability' it is 'not realistic to fear indigenous peoples' exercise of the right to self-determination'.[49] The clear if unintended implication is that it *would* be realistic to fear the exercise of self-determination by groups that are not small, or that have sufficient resources (or allies) to credibly challenge state power. And this, of course, is precisely how states think of national minorities like the Kurds, Tibetans or Palestinians. They are seen, not as small, weak and peripheral, but as potential players or pawns in regional geo-political struggles that threaten the very existence of the state. Some of these fears about national minorities are paranoia, but not all. History shows that national minorities often have been recruited as proxies, collaborators or fifth-columns in struggles between neighbouring states or between rival regional powers. The assumption that national minorities are the potential cause of, or pretext for, geo-political conflict has been omnipresent in all of the international deliberations on national minorities, dating back to the League of Nations. As a result, discussions of national minority rights are heavily 'securitised', in a way that precludes recognition of, or even discussion of, the 'common normative considerations' that connect indigenous peoples and national minorities. Whereas humanitarian concerns and arguments of justice have driven UN debates on indigenous peoples, security concerns have driven the debate on national minorities.[50]

When Daes insisted that states should not fear the self-determination of indigenous peoples because of their small size and vulnerability, she was implicitly acknowledging the pervasiveness of state fears about the self-determination claims of larger national minorities. She was saying, in effect, that while the fear of self-determination by national minorities is understandable, states should draw a bright line between national minorities and indigenous peoples, and should not let their fear of the former erode their recognition of the latter.

In short, Daes was appealing to something like the firewall strategy. Aware of the depth of their anxiety about national minorities, she was asking state representatives to think of indigenous peoples not as sharing

48 See generally Kymlicka (n 16).

49 Daes (n 42) para 28.

50 For detailed discussion of this difference in the geo-political role of national minorities and indigenous peoples, and the resulting contrast between a humanitarian debate on indigenous peoples and a 'securitised' debate on national minorities, see Kymlicka (n 16) ch 7.

common normative concerns with national minorities, but as radically different from national minorities. Rather than emphasising the ways in which national minorities and indigenous peoples share experiences of unjust and involuntary incorporation into larger states, resulting in cultural oppression and loss of self-government, Daes instead emphasised that indigenous peoples are not as scary as national minorities, since they are numerically small, politically weak, geographically peripheral, and geo-politically innocent.

Given the securitisation of national minority issues, it was perhaps inevitable that advocates of indigenous rights would adopt this firewall strategy. UN Member States simply would not have endorsed the Declaration if they thought that it was opening the door for the self-determination of national minorities. So it was essential for advocates to downplay the possible normative commonalities between indigenous peoples and national minorities, and instead to emphasise their geo-political differences.

The firewall strategy has therefore served the interests of both indigenous advocates and Member States. Neither side in the struggle between indigenous peoples and states has had an interest in drawing attention to the moral inconsistencies involved in the diverging treatment of indigenous peoples and national minorities. This helps to explain why the firewall has been so pervasive and enduring at the UN.

If the only problem with the firewall strategy was its moral inconsistency, it could probably endure. But there is another, perhaps deeper, source of instability. Drawing a firewall between indigenous peoples and minorities is not only morally suspect; it is also conceptually unstable, as the very distinction is difficult to draw in much of the world. In the West, there is a relatively clear distinction to be drawn between European national minorities and New World indigenous peoples. Both are groups whose historic homeland has been incorporated into a larger state, but the former have been incorporated into a larger state dominated by a neighbouring people, whereas the latter have been colonised and settled by a distant colonial power. As I noted earlier, the latter process has typically been more brutal and disruptive, and this provides some reason for prioritising the international protection of indigenous peoples. However, it is less clear how we can draw this distinction in Africa, Asia or the Middle East.

In one sense, few if any groups in Africa, Asia or the Middle East fit the traditional profile of indigenous peoples.[51] Homeland minorities in these regions have been incorporated into larger states dominated by neighbouring groups, rather than being incorporated into settler states.

[51] Indigenous peoples in Taiwan are a possible exception, having been colonised by Chinese (and Japanese) settlers since the 17th century.

In that sense, they are all closer to the profile of European national minorities than to New World indigenous peoples. And for this reason, several Asian and African countries insist that none of their minorities should be designated as indigenous peoples. However, if targeted indigenous norms do not apply in Asia or Africa, then minorities are left with only the weak generic minority rights under Article 27, and these provide no protection for their legitimate interests in self-government and territorial autonomy.

In order to extend the protections of international law to some particularly vulnerable groups, therefore, the UN has attempted to re-conceptualise the category of indigenous peoples to cover at least some minorities in post-colonial states. On this view, we shouldn't focus on whether minorities are dominated by settlers from a distant colonial power as opposed to neighbouring peoples. What matters is simply the fact of domination and vulnerability, and finding appropriate means to remedy them. And so various international organisations have encouraged groups in Africa, Asia and the Middle East to identify themselves as 'indigenous peoples' in order to gain greater international protection.

This push to extend the category of indigenous peoples beyond its original New World setting is a logical result of the humanitarian motivation that led to the targeting of indigenous peoples in the first place. Insofar as the motivation for targeted rights was the distinctive vulnerability of indigenous peoples in New World settler states, it was natural to expand the category to include groups elsewhere in the world that share similar vulnerabilities, even if they were not subject to settler colonialism.

The difficult question however is how to identify *which* homeland groups in Africa, Asia or the Middle East should be designated as indigenous peoples under international law. Once we start down the road of applying the category of indigenous peoples beyond the core case of New World settler states, there is no obvious stopping point. Indeed, there are significant disagreements within IOs about how widely to apply the category of indigenous peoples in post-colonial states.[52] Some would limit it to isolated peoples, such as hill tribes or forest peoples in Southeast Asia, or pastoralists in Africa. Others would extend the category much more widely to encompass all historically subordinated

[52] B Kingsbury, '"Indigenous Peoples" as an International Legal Concept' in RH Barnes (ed), *Indigenous Peoples of Asia* (Ann Arbor, Association of Asian Studies, 1995) 13; '"Indigenous Peoples" in International Law: A Constructivist Approach to the Controversy' (1998) 92 *American Journal of International Law* 414; and 'The Applicability of the International Legal Concept of "Indigenous Peoples" in Asia' in J Bauer and D Bell (eds), *The East Asian Challenge for Human Rights* (Cambridge University Press, 1999) 336.

homeland minorities that suffer some combination of political exclusion and cultural vulnerability.

Under these circumstances, attempts to draw a sharp distinction between national minorities and indigenous peoples will seem arbitrary. Moreover, any such line will be politically unsustainable. The problem here is not simply that the category of indigenous peoples has grey areas and fuzzy boundaries—that is true of many categories in both domestic and international law. The problem, rather, is that too much depends on which side of the line groups fall on, and as a result, there is intense political pressure to change where the line is drawn, in ways that are politically unsustainable.

As should be clear by now, the current UN framework provides no incentive for any homeland minority to identify itself as a national minority, since national minorities can claim only generic minority rights. Instead, all homeland minorities have an incentive to (re)define themselves as 'indigenous peoples'. If they come to the UN under the heading of 'national minority', they get nothing other than generic Article 27 rights; if they come as 'indigenous peoples', they have the promise of land rights, control over natural resources, political autonomy, language rights, and legal pluralism.

Not surprisingly, an increasing number of homeland groups in Africa, Asia and the Middle East are adopting the indigenous label. Consider the Arab-speaking minority in the Ahwaz region of Iran, whose homeland has been subject to state policies of Persianisation, including the suppression of Arab language rights, renaming of towns and villages to erase evidence of their Arab history, and settlement policies that swamp the Ahwaz with Persian settlers. In the past, Ahwaz leaders have gone to the UN Working Group on Minorities to complain that their rights as a national minority in relation to their traditional territory are not respected. But since the UN does not recognise national minorities as having any distinctive rights in relation to their areas of historic settlement, the Ahwaz have re-labelled themselves as an indigenous people, and have attended the UN Working Group on Indigenous Populations instead. Similarly, various homeland minorities in Africa that once attended the Working Group on Minorities have re-branded themselves as indigenous peoples, primarily to gain protection for their land rights. Leaders amongst the Crimean Tatars, Roma, Afro-Latinos, Palestinians, Chechens, Dalits and Tibetans are now debating whether to self-identify as indigenous.[53] Even the Kurds—the textbook example of a 'captive nation' or stateless national minority—are

[53] See Lennox (n 32); Aukerman (n 24); Klimova-Alexander (n 31); and A Jamal, 'On the Morality of Arab Collective Rights in Israel' (April 2005), *Adalah Newsletter* 12: www.adalah.org.

debating this option. And if the Kurds, why not the Catalans or the Basques? Indeed, some advocates for the historic Frisian minority in the Netherlands have started to adopt the label 'indigenous people'.[54]

In all of these cases, national minorities are responding to the fact that the UN's generic minority rights are 'fatally weak', since they do not protect any claims based on historic settlement or territorial attachments. Given international law as it stands, recognition as an indigenous people is the only route to secure protection for these interests.

The availability of this back-door route for national minorities to gain targeted self-government rights may seem like a good thing. After all, the underlying moral logic should be to acknowledge the legitimate interests relating to historic settlement and territory shared by all homeland minorities, and expanding the category of indigenous people to cover national minorities is one possible way to do this.

Unfortunately, this is not a sustainable approach. The tendency of national minorities to adopt the label of indigenous peoples is likely to lead to the collapse of the international system of indigenous rights. As we have seen, the UN and other IOs have repeatedly rejected attempts to codify rights of self-government for powerful substate national groups, in part because of their geo-political security implications. They are not going to allow such groups to gain rights of self-government through the back door by redefining themselves as indigenous peoples. If more and more homeland groups adopt the indigenous label, the likely result is that IOs will retreat from the targeted indigenous rights track.

There are a number of ways in which this retreat could take place. One scenario would be for states to attempt to put sharp limits on which groups qualify as indigenous, so as to ensure that national minorities do not sneak in. For example, the category of indigenous peoples could be restricted to New World settler states, or to small groups, or to geographically isolated groups maintaining a subsistence economy. But I don't think such stipulative redefinitions will work, since they would rule out many of the most influential participants in (and indeed founders of) the international indigenous movement. For example, the Saami are not in the New World; the Quechua are not small; the Mohawks are not isolated or engaged in subsistence living, and so on. The category of indigenous peoples is therefore likely to continue to expand, including to groups that formerly were seen as national minorities. But we know that states will not extend rights of self-determination to national minorities in international law. The likely result, therefore, is that as the category of indigenous peoples expands, states will start to retreat from

[54] A Onsman, *Defining Indigeneity in the Twenty-First Century—A Case Study of the Frisians* (Lewiston, Edwin Mellen Press, 2004).

the substantive provisions of the Declaration. The Declaration's most transformative elements relating to political ordering will be downplayed or ignored, and focus shifted instead to the sorts of cultural recognition issues addressed by Article 27. We can already see signs of this in the way the World Bank interprets indigenous rights as a matter of culturally sensitive development policy, rather than as a matter of the political restructuring of the state. Whatever the technique, the result of such a retreat would be to undermine the major progress that has occurred to date in the indigenous track.[55]

This suggests that the long-term future of the UN's indigenous track is unclear. It is often cited as the clearest success story in developing international minority rights, but its success rests on shaky foundations. The UN has attempted to create a legal firewall between the rights of indigenous peoples and national minorities. This firewall was needed to get the indigenous track off the ground, but it is at odds with the moral logic of multiculturalism, and is politically unsustainable. A durable international framework will require a more coherent account of the relationship between indigenous peoples and national minorities, and a more consistent approach to self-government rights. And this in turn will require a dramatic rethinking of the underlying concepts and categories used in international law. We need to recognise that indigenous peoples aren't the only group in need of targeted rights—this is also true, in different ways, of national minorities, the Roma, Dalits, immigrants, and others. The idea of indigenous rights as just a one-off exception to the rule that minorities are a single category with generic minority rights is not sustainable, either morally or politically. This broader rethinking of categories is needed not only to achieve the broader transformative potential of the Indigenous Declaration for other groups, but also perhaps to prevent a retreat in support for indigenous peoples themselves.

Unfortunately, I am not optimistic that such a rethinking is likely in the foreseeable future. Security-based fears about national minorities are deeply entrenched in the international order, and neither states nor indigenous groups have much interest in questioning the current exclusion of

[55] For various expressions of this worry, see Aukerman (n 24) 1017 ('The very success of the indigenous peoples movement in developing an ambitious rights framework and in gaining an institutionalised presence at the United Nations through the working group threatens to undermine the fragile, unspoken standards of inclusion which have characterised the movement up until now'); Kingsbury 1998 (n 52) 419 ('There is an appreciable risk for the indigenous peoples' movement that the existing and highly functional international political distinction between indigenous peoples and ethnic and other minorities will erode, galvanizing opposition to claims of indigenous peoples'); and Barsh (n 20) 81–2 ('Indigenous organizations will have to choose between excluding these [national minority] groups from the movement and attracting the hostility of many states that have previously taken no interest in indigenous issues').

national minorities from the debate. Both states and indigenous peoples are likely therefore to continue to act on the assumption of a firewall, even amidst the growing signs of its dissolution. Sooner or later, however, we will need to address more systemic questions about the relationship between national minorities and indigenous peoples, between generic rights and targeted rights, and between normative principles of justice and geo-political security fears. Without a more coherent account of these relationships, the Indigenous Declaration rests on shifting sands.

9

Voting in the General Assembly as Evidence of Customary International Law?

EMMANUEL VOYIAKIS

INTRODUCTION

HERE IS A pair of statements one can safely make about the relationship between General Assembly (GA) Resolutions and customary international law. First, GA Resolutions can provide inspiration for the development of new customary international practices. Second, such Resolutions may often help to sharpen existing customary practices by encouraging—or challenging—States to take a stand on a particular formulation of what these practices require or allow. The common feature of both cases is that any change in customary international law comes as a result of practice *external* to the Resolution in question.[1] In other words, what makes an impact on international custom is not the GA Resolution itself, but the fact that States choose to 'take up' the propositions expressed in that Resolution in their conduct.

A much more controversial issue is whether the adoption of a GA Resolution in and of itself has an impact on the content of customary international law—I will call this the Resolution's 'intrinsic' impact. In particular, should we take the fact that a State has cast a vote in favour of a given Resolution as evidence that that State believes that the propositions expressed in the Resolution are or ought to become customary international law? By the same token, should we take a negative vote or an abstention to count against those propositions becoming customary law? These questions are controversial because there are good arguments for different answers. On the one hand, it seems sensible to take States'

[1] In Brownlie's terminology, here GA Resolutions function as 'material' rather than 'formal' sources of customary international law. I Brownlie, *Principles of Public International Law*, 7th edn (Oxford University Press, 2009) 12–13.

attitudes towards the propositions stated in a given Resolution as a defeasible indicator of whether they would accept those propositions as law. On the other hand, just as participation in a treaty does not necessarily allow inferences about the views of States parties regarding customary international law, we have some reason to doubt whether GA votes can tell us that much about the views of voting States on international custom.

These questions are no less pressing in practice than they are in theory. Should we consider the one hundred and forty-three States that voted in favour of the Declaration on the Rights of Indigenous Peoples ('the Declaration') as having a favourable attitude towards those rights becoming part of customary international law? Should we consider the four States that voted against the Declaration to oppose such a development? And what should we make of the position of the 11 States that abstained? On the one hand, it is true that these States were asked to take a position in respect of a Resolution that enumerates indigenous entitlements couched in the language of rights and duties. On the other hand, voting States were not expressly asked to take a view on the current status of those rights under customary law or on the desirability of those rights becoming part of customary law in the future. Under which conditions could we justify attributing to voting States certain favourable or unfavourable attitudes for the purposes of customary international law relating to indigenous peoples?

It is not hard to see that, their legal importance aside, our answers to these questions will carry important implications for the conduct of diplomacy both within and outside the GA context. States tend to calculate their actions before, during and after the adoption of any GA Resolution to ensure that their conduct, considered as a whole, will have the intended impact on customary international practice. Those States can reasonably want to know whether a positive (or negative) vote in the GA is enough to register their support for (or opposition to) a proposition of customary law, or whether they also need to manifest their position through collateral or subsequent practice. Conversely, for States to be able to assess the potential impact of their collateral or subsequent practice for the purposes of customary international law, it is important that they be able to know how much can be read into their GA votes in the first place.

The aim of this chapter is to outline what I take to be the main substantive ideas that shape how we think about the intrinsic impact of GA votes on customary international law and to assess how these ideas impact on the debate about the legal status of the Declaration.

Section 1 sets the scene for my discussion by considering the widely subscribed-to view that the proper interpretation of a State's vote in the GA context should be determined by that State's *intentions*, as expressed both through the actual vote and any collateral and subsequent practice of that State. I argue that, for all its surface plausibility, the appeal to intentions underdetermines the questions it is designed to address. Knowing that we should attend to the voting State's intentions is not enough; we also need to know *which* of various intentions that States have when voting is significant for the purposes of customary international law, and how much. The better view, I suggest, is that attributing content to a State's vote in the GA context requires us to confront a complex normative question about the value or values that GA decision-making is best understood as serving. It is those normative considerations that determine which intentions are paramount when interpreting any State's GA vote and how these intentions shape any contribution of that vote to customary international law.

Section 2 outlines and compares two different normative arguments about the contribution of GA voting to the customary law-making process. The first holds that the distinctive value of the GA decision-making process lies in its representativeness and strong egalitarian credentials. According to this argument, States' GA votes should be taken to have an impact on customary international law because the GA context provides superior safeguards of procedural and substantive equality compared to the normal circumstances of international diplomatic interaction. Most specifically, the GA provides a forum in which States with limited capacity to make representations on matters of international concern have the chance to make an impact on the content of international law. In that way, it is argued, taking GA votes as evidence of international custom can help to address the perceived 'legitimacy deficit' in the process of formation and identification of customary international law.

The second argument does not dispute the egalitarian credentials of GA decision-making. Rather, it holds that the attempt to redress the perceived legitimacy deficit of international custom by interpreting GA votes as evidence of customary law fails to register a *further* valuable function of GA decision-making, which—in terms familiar to international lawyers—I will refer to as the value of 'softness'. According to this view, States have a reasonable interest in being able to articulate standards of conduct without simultaneously committing themselves to those standards as a matter of international law. In fact, the more one appeals to States' GA votes as evidence of international custom, the more one risks driving negotiations and initiatives for the future development of the law outside the context of the GA. If this is correct, a more modest conception of the contribution of GA votes to international custom may actually be the best way of securing the GA's impact on the development of international law.

Rather than take sides between those two arguments, each of which has been ably defended in the literature, I submit that we should endorse an alternative that accommodates the values underpinning each under a single practical scheme. To that end, I put forward a suggestion that I believe can preserve the softness of the GA decision-making process, while allowing voting States the valuable option of using that process to make their contribution to the formation of customary international law.

Three caveats are in order. First, my discussion does not dwell on the possibility of treating GA Resolutions as practice of the United Nations (UN) for the purposes of customary international law. I take for granted that GA Resolutions can be regarded as evidence of UN practice and that UN practice can contribute to the content of customary international law. The question I am interested in is what, if anything, these Resolutions tell us about the attitudes of the *States* that participate in the voting procedure. Second, my discussion is limited to GA Resolutions that purport to express general standards of conduct, rather than Resolutions with a particular addressee or tied to a specific situation.[2] Third, I stake no claim as to whether voting in the GA context provides evidence of the practice of States or only evidence of their opinio juris.[3] In fact, part of the point of my discussion in the next section will be that this question is less consequential than it is often taken to be.

ATTRIBUTING CONTENT TO GA VOTING: THE RELEVANCE OF INTENTIONS

It is plausible to think that we regard GA Resolutions as evidence of customary international law because, or to the extent that, States' votes for or against such Resolutions tell us things about their beliefs or intentions regarding customary international law. The overall research aim, the idea goes, is to throw light on what States believe or intend for the purposes of international custom, and looking at States' voting choices in the GA context seems a straightforward way of achieving this.[4]

The International Court of Justice endorsed a particularly strong version of this idea in its decision in the *Nicaragua* case. As is well known, the Court had to satisfy itself that the prohibition on the use of force against

[2] For a discussion of the practical effectiveness of such Resolutions, see *South-West Africa (Voting Procedure) Advisory Opinion*, Separate Opinion of Judge Lauterpacht, [1955] ICJ Rep at 118–19.

[3] For a discussion of this point see International Law Association, *Statement of Principles Applicable to the Formation of General Customary International Law*, Report of the Sixty-Ninth Conference of the International Law Association (2000), 712, 764–75; M Villiger, *Customary International Law and Treaties*, 2nd edn (The Hague, Kluwer Law International, 1997) 20–21.

[4] Compare J Alvarez, *International Organizations and Law-Makers* (Oxford University Press, 2005) 592: 'International organizations provide shortcuts to finding international custom.'

the territorial integrity or political independence of a State, as expressed in Article 2(4) of the United Nations Charter, had also attained the status of customary international law. In that regard, the Court said:

> The Court has to be satisfied that there exists in customary international law an *opinio juris* as to the binding character of such an abstention [from the use of force]. This *opinio juris* may, though with all due caution, be deduced from, *inter alia*, the attitude of the Parties and the attitude of States towards certain General Assembly resolutions, and particularly resolution 2625 (XXV) entitled 'Declaration on Principles of International Law concerning Friendly Relations and Co-operation among States in accordance with the Charter of the United Nations'. The effect of consent to the text of such resolutions cannot be understood as merely that of a 'reiteration or elucidation' of the treaty commitment undertaken in the Charter. On the contrary, it may be understood as an acceptance of the validity of the rule or set of rules declared by the resolution by themselves ... It would therefore seem apparent that the attitude referred to expresses an *opinio juris* respecting such rule (or set of rules), to be thenceforth treated separately from the provisions, especially those of an institutional kind, to which it is subject on the treaty-law plane of the Charter.[5]

The Court's construction of GA voting for the purposes of international custom has been subject to significant criticism.[6] In particular, it has been noted that the *Nicaragua* methodology fails to note that States can support or oppose a given GA Resolution on different grounds and on the basis of very different views as to whether that Resolution reflects or ought to reflect customary international law. As the recent International Law Association (ILA) Statement of Principles on the Formation of Customary International Law puts it, 'delegations sometimes feel able to cast a positive vote precisely because they believe that General Assembly resolutions do *not* have any legal effect. Or again, whilst for some Members the resolution may be declaratory of existing law, for others it might be "merely" *lex ferenda*.'[7] This more restrained view also acknowledges the possibility that a State may have voted in favour of a Resolution without intending to commit itself to the propositions stated therein as a matter of international law, or even that a State may have voted against a Resolution as a matter of diplomatic tactics, even though it generally endorses its content. Furthermore, it is quite common for States to accompany their votes with collateral explanatory statements, or to follow them up with conduct

[5] *Military and Paramilitary Activities In and Against Nicaragua*, Judgment of 27 June 1986, [1986] ICJ Rep 99–100, para 188.

[6] M Mendelson, 'The Nicaragua Case and Customary Law' in W Butler (ed), *The Non-Use of Force in International Law* (Leiden, Martinus Nijhoff, 1989) 85; A D'Amato, 'Trashing Customary International Law' (1987) 81 *American Jouranl of International Law* 101.

[7] ILA *Statement of Principles* (n 3) p 58. See also C Chinkin, 'The Challenge of Soft Law: Development and Change in International Law' (1989) 38 *International and Comparative Law Quarterly* 850.

intended to clarify or qualify their original intentions with regard to the Resolution. Given that all these bits of information can be relevant in assessing the attitudes of voting States with regard to customary international law, one could not draw confident conclusions about a Resolution's contribution, if any, to international custom without trying to understand that information as a unified whole. On these grounds, the ILA Statement recommends that 'the circumstances of adoption need to be examined closely. It is necessary to examine, not just who voted for the resolution as a whole, but also the explanations or comments accompanying each vote and the paragraph by paragraph votes of States'.

At the same time, the Court's more basic suggestion that GA votes are legitimate indicators of voting States' attitudes with regard to customary international law has not been subject to much doubt. The Court's critics only dispute whether the Court was accurate in assessing the weight of that indicator alongside voting States' collateral statements and surrounding practice. This impression is further confirmed by the fact that most of the Court's critics appear to agree that, under certain very special conditions, the mere adoption of a GA Resolution can create 'instant' rules of customary international law.[8] For that to be the case, and regardless of how high one places the threshold for the creation of instant custom, one must proceed on the assumption that GA votes can function as legitimate indicators of the position of voting States regarding customary international law.

I want to suggest that, despite its apparent plausibility, the idea that GA Resolutions tell us things about States' intentions with regard to international custom needs much more careful defence. The problem is not that the voting States' intentions do not matter, but that we need some criterion that determines *which* of the various intentions States may have when voting in favour or against a GA Resolution are controlling for the purposes of customary international law.

My starting point is that inferences about the beliefs or intentions of States regarding international custom from their intentions when casting an affirmative or negative GA vote, or when choosing to abstain, must rely on some account of how the latter intentions are to be understood. In particular, such inferences must rely on some explanation of why it is legitimate to take a State's conduct in the particular institutional setting of the GA as a basis for attributing to that State certain intentions with regard to customary international law. Call the intentions that a State has when voting that State's 'voting intentions' and the intentions it has when

[8] ILA *Statement of Principles*, ibid, para 32; B Cheng, 'United Nations Resolutions on Outer Space: "Instant" Customary International Law?' (1965) 5 *Indian Journal of International Law* 23.

aiming to contribute to customary international practice its 'customary law intentions'. The question is when evidence of a State's voting intentions may also be considered evidence of its customary law intentions, or, to put it differently, when one may legitimately consider the two sets of intentions to overlap.

How, then, do we determine a State's voting intentions? Taking an affirmative GA vote as an example, it seems to me that there are at least three distinct intentions that one could legitimately attribute to a State casting a vote in favour of a GA Resolution:

— the intention to adopt a non-binding instrument (the *formal* intention);
— the intention to endorse or oppose the propositions contained in that instrument (the *substantive* intention);
— the intention to express endorsement or opposition before other States (the *publicity* intention).[9]

This multiplicity gives rise to a double challenge for anyone who thinks that GA votes can be regarded as legitimate indicators of voting States' customary law intentions. First, it requires one to explain which of the three sorts of voting intentions I have identified might be significant for the purposes of customary international law. Second, it calls for some account of how that sort of voting intention can be separated from the rest.

It is reasonably clear that the theorists who take affirmative GA votes as evidence of customary international law focus on States' substantive and publicity voting intentions. In examining the contribution of a given Resolution to customary law, they draw attention to the fact that States have endorsed the content of the Resolution in question and to the public character of that endorsement.[10] At the same time, those theorists are clearly committed to the claim that it is possible to *separate* those intentions from the formal intentions of voting States. The reason why such a separation is necessary for their position to add up is that one cannot infer an intention to endorse a proposition as a matter of

[9] Note that all three of those intentions are necessarily present in every GA Resolution, in the sense that we cannot conceive of a Resolution that is formless, empty or clandestine.

[10] Cf SJ Anaya, *Indigenous Peoples in International Law*, 2nd edn (Oxford University Press, 2004) 61–62. Writing on the effect of modern institutional settings on the formation of international custom, Anaya writes: 'With the advent of modern international intergovernmental institutions and enhanced communications media, states and other relevant actors increasingly engage in prescriptive dialogue. Especially in multilateral settings, explicit communication of this sort may itself bring about a convergence of understanding and expectation about rules, establishing in those rules a *pull towards compliance*.' The implicit assumption here is that we can legitimately use states' 'substantive' and 'publicity' intentions as a basis for inferring their intentions regarding customary international law.

binding law from the intention to endorse a non-binding instrument. Unless formal voting intentions are discounted, or otherwise shown to be of only marginal significance, any prospect of finding an overlap between voting and customary law intentions should be ruled out from the start.

Are the three kinds of intentions separable? If so, on what grounds? Although I have distinguished between them for the purpose of analysis, it is hard to see how any one of those intentions could be understood independently of the rest. This should not surprise us, given that all three sets of intentions are expressed through a singular act of voting. In practice, when voting in favour of a GA Resolution, States choose to publicly endorse the propositions contained in a non-binding instrument; the three intentions I have identified come as a package. If that is correct, the challenge for anyone who thinks that we can take voting intentions as an indicator of customary law intentions is to explain how it could be legitimate to 'split' the package and leave formal intentions out, without *also* changing the content of States' substantive and publicity intentions. Suppose that a State was told that its affirmative vote in favour of the Declaration on the Rights of Indigenous Peoples meant that, unless its surrounding practice gave a clear indication to the contrary, it also endorsed the propositions expressed in the Declaration as a matter of customary international law. Would it not be natural for that State to object to the propriety of that inference on the ground that, once we discount the formal element, we are taking its intentions very much out of context?

The challenge can be taken a step further. If one can legitimately separate formal voting intentions from substantive voting intentions, it might also be possible to discriminate between the various substantive intentions that voting States can have when supporting a given GA Resolution. The content of the Declaration offers a good case-study of how this extreme argument might be put into practice. On the one hand, the Resolution states that the Assembly 'solemnly proclaims' that the provisions of the Declaration should not be understood as binding legal norms but as 'as a standard of achievement to be pursued in a spirit of partnership and mutual respect'. On the other hand, the actual formulation of most Articles of the Declaration is strongly similar to human rights provisions in legally binding instruments. To take just two examples, Article 3 provides that 'indigenous peoples have the right to self-determination', while Article 26 provides that 'indigenous peoples have the right to the lands, territories and resources which they have traditionally owned, occupied or otherwise used or acquired'. Once we begin to discount some voting intentions, what is there to stop us from discounting States' substantive intention to adopt 'standards of achievement' rather than a legally binding code of conduct and focus exclusively on their substantive intention to endorse the rights stated in the rest of the Declaration?

I do not mean to suggest that theorists who think that voting intentions can be taken as evidence of customary law intentions will carry their view to that extreme. My point is that those theorists need to provide some explanation of how the various intentions States have when voting can be legitimately separated from one another and, assuming that some such separation is legitimate, which of those intentions is most significant for the purposes of international custom. And that explanation must appeal to something *other* than the intentions it is supposed to explain the significance of.

It is not hard to see that the challenge to the view that voting intentions can 'translate' into customary law intentions will be present no matter where one stands on the more particular question whether GA votes should be regarded as evidence of practice or evidence of opinio juris. No less than their counterparts, those who treat GA voting as evidence of practice still need to explain which aspects of that practice are significant for the purposes of international custom. They too need to appeal to criteria other than the practice itself and the intentions that accompany it.

Where should we look for such criteria? I have argued elsewhere that we can only hope to settle questions of this sort on *normative* grounds.[11] That is, we can only decide which, if any, voting intentions are significant for the purposes of customary international law in the light of what we take the respective values of GA decision-making and customary law-making to be. It is those values that tell us which intentions matter and how important they are.

Rather than defend this suggestion on theoretical grounds, I hope that my discussion in the next section will do enough to show that the most pressing and persistent debates about the contribution of GA Resolutions to customary international law are explicitly normative in character. In particular, I will suggest that what lies at the heart of those debates is a disagreement about the range of values that GA decision-making is best understood as serving.

CUSTOMARY LAW AND THE VALUE OF GA DECISION-MAKING

Antonio Cassese has argued that 'the unique opportunity afforded by the UN for practically all members of the world community to get together and exchange their views cannot fail to have had a strong impact on

[11] E Voyiakis, 'Access to Court v State Immunity' (2003) 52 *International and Comparative Law Quarterly* 297, 325–28 and 'Customary International Law and the Place of Normative Considerations' forthcoming in (2010) 55 *American Journal of Jurisprudence*.

the emergence or reshaping of customary rules'.[12] The idea seems very attractive and is shared by many international lawyers. How can we explain its appeal?

I think that the appeal of treating GA votes as evidence of customary international law derives from the intuition that this strategy can address two related normative problems of international law-making.

The first problem concerns the normatively paradoxical position of the GA in the UN system. Despite being the forum with the highest credentials of representativeness and overall political legitimacy, the Assembly has very limited decision-making powers and no general legislative capacity. Were we to say that GA Resolutions do not even make an intrinsic contribution to the formation of customary law, we would effectively be shutting the world's most representative and legitimate political forum out of international law-making.

The second problem concerns what has been called the 'legitimacy deficit' in customary international law. The conditions of international politics, it is alleged, have the effect of allowing a few powerful States to control customary international law-making. This occurs either because those States are able to use their power to make their practices—or their objections to others' practices—more 'visible' to international lawyers, or because those States are able to increase the cost for other States of protesting against their practices. Although it is not altogether immune to these distorting effects, the Assembly at least offers a model of decision-making with two important guarantees of inter-State equality: first, the procedural guarantee that the voice of weaker States can be heard alongside that of more powerful States; and second, the guarantee that power imbalances between individual States have no formal effect on the outcome of the decision-making process.[13] Were we to say that this decision-making model does not contribute to the formation of international custom, we would risk exacerbating lingering doubts about the political legitimacy of that source of law.

[12] A Cassese, *International Law in a Divided World*, 2nd edn (Oxford University Press, 2000) 193. Compare H Thirlway, *International Customary Law and Codification* (Leiden, Sijthoff, 1972) 65: 'It cannot be denied that when a resolution is formally adopted in so universal an organization as the United Nations, the resolution is something more than the consistent statements or wishes of the member States; that, in a sense, the whole is more than the sum of its parts.'

[13] Compare Alvarez (n 4) 592: 'Traditional custom was usually in fact made by a handful of interested (and generally powerful) states able and willing to make their practice visible to all. The modern resort to [international-organization]-generated forms of evidence for custom might be seen, therefore, as a relatively more egalitarian approach to finding this source of law, even if it comes, as critics charge is the case with respect to GA resolutions for example, at the expense of sometimes elevating the rhetoric of states over their deeds.'

The reason why the suggestion that we should take GA votes as evidence of customary international law is so appealing is that it presents us with some hope of addressing both normative problems simultaneously. On the one hand, it guarantees some role for the Assembly in the regulation of international affairs by allowing its Resolutions to make an intrinsic contribution to the customary law-making process. On the other hand, it uses the high legitimacy credentials of the GA to limit the exposure of customary international law to the unequal forces of international politics.[14]

Having said as much, it is not immediately clear how the values of representativeness and legitimacy allow us to discount formal intentions when we view States' GA votes as potential contributions to international custom. On the face of it, respect for representative and legitimate decision-making would seem to entail that we ought to give full weight to *all* intentions that decision-making agents express through the appropriate procedures. On what grounds could we say that discounting some of those intentions enhances rather than undermines representative and legitimate international political decisions?

It seems to me that an important assumption behind the normative case in favour of taking GA votes as evidence of customary law is that formal voting intentions can be discounted because they are *themselves* an unfortunate effect of an illegitimate distribution of decision-making competence in the context of the UN. The explanation of the Assembly's limited formal powers at the expense of the Security Council lies in the imbalance of power between a few States and the rest of the international community. Given that it is precisely that imbalance that offends against the values of representative and legitimate decision-making, the more weight we attribute to States' formal voting intentions, the more we exacerbate the effects of the UN's flawed institutional design. In fact, if we were to hold that States' formal voting intentions are significant for the purposes of international custom too, we would risk extending those effects beyond the confines of the UN and into general international law-making. That, I think, is the basic reason why the view I have outlined holds that discounting States' formal voting intentions from the impact of GA Resolutions on international custom would be consistent with the values of representativeness and political legitimacy.

14 See eg O Yasunaki, 'The ICJ: An Emperor Without Clothes?' in N Ando et al (eds), *Liber Amicorum Judge Shigeru Oda* (The Hague, Kluwer Law International, 2002) 191, 211–12, who argues that the legitimacy of traditional customary international law 'in terms of global participation of States in the creation of global norms, transparency and identification of the sovereign will of nations is far inferior to that of the general international law-creating process based on multilateral treaties or the universal nature of UN declarations'.

In the rest of the chapter, I will pursue two suggestions. First, for all its flaws, the current configuration of the Assembly's decision-making powers does serve a distinct and important value, well known to international lawyers as the value of legal 'softness'. Second, the proper accommodation of that value with those of representativeness and legitimacy points against taking GA votes to have an intrinsic impact on customary international law.

I take the first of those suggestions to be relatively uncontroversial. There is clearly value in States being able to agree on the content and formulation of certain standards of conduct without simultaneously committing themselves to those standards as a matter of international law. The vast literature on 'soft law' and its practical importance for the development of international law when no consensus can be easily achieved provide good evidence for this view.[15] More importantly for the present discussion, it is equally clear that the desired 'softness' can only be achieved on the condition that the outcome of the GA decision-making process does not commit participating States to the propositions stated in the Resolution in question. The reason is well stated in Thomas Franck's careful criticism of the *Nicaragua* judgment:

> The effect of an enlarged concept of the lawmaking force of General Assembly resolutions may well be to caution states to vote against 'aspirational' instruments if they do not intend to embrace them totally and at once, regardless of circumstance. That would be unfortunate. Aspirational resolutions have long occupied, however uncomfortably, a twilight zone between 'hard' treaty law and the normative void. Even if passed with a degree of cynicism, they still may have a bearing on the direction of normative evolution. By seeking to harden this 'soft' law prematurely, however, the Court advises prudent states to vote against such resolutions, or at least to abstain.[16]

To put the point differently, the more one treats the GA decision-making process as a source of binding obligation, the less willing States will be to use the GA as a forum for the articulation of common standards for the future development of international practice.

Now, there are reasons to suspect that this suggestion would not convince anyone who holds that GA votes have an intrinsic impact on customary international law. If serving the values of representativeness and legitimacy requires that we discount States' formal voting intentions for

[15] ME O'Connell, 'The Role of Soft Law in a Global Order' in D Shelton (ed), *Commitment and Compliance* (Oxford University Press, 2000) 110–15. See also A Schaefer, 'Resolving Deadlock: Why International Organizations Introduce Soft Law' (2006) 12 *European Law Journal* 198; K Abbott and D Snidal, 'Hard and Soft Law in International Governance' (2000) 54 *International Organization* 421.

[16] T Franck, 'Some Observations on the ICJ's Procedural and Substantive Innovations' (1987) 81 *American Journal of International Law* 116, 119.

the purposes of international custom, while serving the value of softness requires that we give full weight to those intentions, the two sets of values would seem to stand in practical conflict with each other. If that is correct, we would need to choose between the objective of enhancing the normative credentials of international custom and the objective of maintaining the softness that makes the GA a central forum for international debates about the development of international law. However that conflict of values might be resolved, it is hard to see a compelling argument why softness should take precedence.

I think that it would be a mistake to take our concerns about representativeness, legitimacy and the value of softness to stand in conflict with each other. At least, we should not endorse this idea unless we have first examined whether we can accommodate all three values in a way that safeguards both the softness of GA decision-making and its ability to make an impact on the formation of customary international law.

I believe that such an accommodation is in fact possible if we take care to differentiate between formal GA decision-making and the broader procedural context in which it takes place. In particular, I think we can serve the value of softness by holding that GA votes do not *in themselves* impact on customary international law and still enhance the representativeness and legitimacy of international custom by allowing that *collateral* statements by voting States do have such impact. Under the proposed scheme, the Assembly remains a forum in which States can articulate international standards of conduct without also committing themselves to those standards as a matter of international law. At the same time, the scheme allows States to use the GA context as a way of taking a position on the content and future development of customary international law. Any State that believes that the content of a given Resolution is, or ought to become, part of customary international law can exercise the option of making an impact on international custom by attaching a collateral statement to that effect in the explanation of its vote.

On the methodological front, the scheme I propose avoids the whole problem of having to explain how we can 'split' the package of States' voting intentions and the related difficulty of finding some plausible limits to the practice of parsing States' intentions into smaller and smaller bits. On the practical front, the main advantage of the proposed scheme is that it gives States the choice of restricting themselves to taking a position on the proposed GA Resolution, of expressing a view on the content and development of customary international law, or of doing both. Furthermore, the scheme does not make it more costly or cumbersome for weaker States to contribute actively to the formation of international custom, as it only requires them to express an intention to that effect in the explanation of their GA vote or in some other collateral statement within the reasonably egalitarian context of the Assembly.[17]

CONCLUSION: LESS CAN BE MORE

Many international lawyers have come to accept two propositions as safe indicators of the relationship between GA Resolutions and international custom. First, that GA votes can count as evidence of customary international law. Second, that the precise impact of GA votes on international custom can only be estimated when we take into account their collateral and subsequent practice. I have argued that both propositions rely on a plausible normative premise. Counting GA votes towards the formation of international custom not only allows the world's most representative and legitimate political institution to make an impact in the customary law-making process, but also infuses that process with its distinctly egalitarian ethos.

I have nevertheless argued that neither proposition is wholly accurate. On the one hand, the idea that we can take a State's vote in the GA context as expressing that State's attitude towards customary international law fails to register the importance of allowing States to articulate standards of conduct without committing themselves to those standards as a matter of international law. On the other hand, a proper accommodation of the applicable values of softness, representativeness and legitimacy requires us to separate the effects of a GA vote from the effects of a voting State's collateral and subsequent practice.

In practical terms, the scheme I have suggested entails that the adoption of Resolutions such as the Declaration on the Rights of Indigenous Peoples should not be taken to have an intrinsic impact on customary international law, but rather to function as an inspiration for future practice and as an occasion for individual States to make collateral statements that clarify their attitude with regard to the customary law of indigenous rights.

This conclusion may strike proponents and theorists of indigenous rights as overly conservative, as it entails that the Assembly's contribution to international law-making is more restricted than the bulk of international literature assumes. I believe that the charge is not warranted. Far from sidelining the Assembly for the purposes of the

[17] In fact, the assumption that weaker states would be willing to use the GA decision-making process in order to express their views about customary international law tends to underplay the fact that those states too have an interest in being able to distinguish between their contribution to GA decision-making and their contribution to the formation of international custom.

development of international law, a more modest conception of the impact of its Resolutions on international custom has the potential to defuse bitter disagreements of the sort that delayed the adoption of the Declaration by nearly a decade and to create conditions for the development of better substantive law.

10

*The UN Declaration on the Rights of Indigenous Peoples and the Limits of the International Legal Project**

STEPHEN ALLEN

But you must know that we are all in agreement, whatever we say.

Turba Philosophorum

INTRODUCTION

PROMINENT INDIGENOUS REPRESENTATIVES and sympathetic international lawyers/scholars have embraced the UN Declaration on the Rights of Indigenous Peoples ('the Declaration') on behalf of the international legal project, despite it being a non-binding international instrument. This essay questions the techniques used by some members of these constituencies to promote the significance of the Declaration for international law. In particular, it demonstrates the shortcomings of the version of the international legal project favoured by some indigenous rights advocates and the weaknesses in their specific legal arguments and rights theorising. Instead, this essay argues that the Declaration's significance stems from the political legitimacy it embodies rather than its claimed international legal character. It suggests that the Declaration should be viewed as a highly persuasive tool to be utilised in the political contests that determine municipal laws and policies within the arena of the State. Indigenous peoples must seize this internationally sponsored opportunity to (re)engage in national political processes in

* I would like to thank Emmanuel Voyiakis for his helpful comments on an earlier draft of this essay. However, the usual caveats apply.

order to make their particular cases for comprehensive municipal legal rights. The essay suggests that political engagement at a national level is more likely to generate the political will needed to operationalise indigenous rights (thereby closing the existing 'implementation gap') than the currently preferred route of trying to impose international standards on ambivalent States, a process which typically leads to the creation of paper rights that do little to protect indigenous peoples in their national settings.

INDIGENOUS PEOPLES AND THE INTERNATIONAL LEGAL PROJECT

David Kennedy has suggested that the latest generation of international lawyers and scholars are typically committed to a vision of 'the international' in which international law and its concomitant institutions are seen as forces for good.[1] In contrast, States are considered to be bad.[2] Their preferences need to be shaped;[3] they need to be prompted and pushed into doing the right thing. Consequently, proponents of this normatively muscular international legal project seek to promote the authority of international norms on a wide range of issues (especially on human rights) at the expense of the autonomy of national legal systems.[4] The project aims to alter the concept of sovereignty so that it reflects cosmopolitan rationality. Accordingly, it challenges the primacy of the State, claiming that it is being superseded by a web of institutions that promote and deliver global governance.

Given that the indigenous cause has invariably been thwarted at the national level, indigenous peoples have more reason to believe in this international legal project than most: in many cases, denying the existence of indigenous peoples was central to founding myths of settler States. While indigenous peoples have long resisted strategies of national assimilation, the cause for rights and recognition only gained broad coherence and momentum when they managed to internationalise their struggle by harnessing the institutional interest shown in the indigenous problem by the United Nations and the International Labour Organization.

[1] D Kennedy, 'A New World Order: Yesterday, Today, and Tomorrow' (1994) 4 *Transnational Law and Contemporary Legal Problems* 329, 335–36.

[2] This binary simplification of Kennedy's thesis was expressed in J Klabbers, 'The Undesirability of Soft Law' (1998) 67 *Nordic Journal of International Law* 381, 383.

[3] See eg M Finnemore, *National Interests and International Society* (Ithaca, NY, Cornell University Press, 1996) ch 1.

[4] Kennedy (n 1) 337.

They have used this interest to transform themselves from the objects of international law into its subjects.[5]

From the 1980s onwards, indigenous networks began to coalesce around key supranational institutions, not least the UN Working Group on Indigenous Populations (WGIP), and as more indigenous peoples began to find their voices they started to participate in the task of drafting international standards on indigenous rights.[6] The Declaration bears testament to indigenous peoples' commitment to this task. The instrument's adoption vindicates their international strategy and evidences the extent to which they have penetrated institutions that were previously reserved for States; in addition, it demonstrates their faith in the international legal project outlined above.

THE DECLARATION AND (CUSTOMARY) INTERNATIONAL LAW

State Views Regarding the Declaration's International Legal Status

Many indigenous representatives and sympathetic international lawyers/scholars have consistently claimed the Declaration on behalf of the international legal project (and States have remained mindful of these claims). To be sure, the Declaration's provisions are substantially informed by international law and they are couched in the unmistakable language of rights. Further, the protracted and painstaking process of developing and elaborating the text in a succession of UN fora was an indication of the potential ramifications that a final Declaration would have for international law and national legal systems.

In the UN General Assembly 143 States voted in favour of the Declaration, 11 abstained, and four States voted against its adoption (the USA, Canada, Australia and New Zealand). Nevertheless, the formal status of this international instrument was never in any doubt—it is not legally binding upon States as a matter of international law. This is clear from the statements made by States when voting on the Declaration's adoption.[7] However, this position still leaves open the possibility that

[5] See L Rodríguez-Piñero, *Indigenous Peoples, Postcolonialism and International Law: The ILO Regime (1919–1989)* (Oxford University Press, 2005) 116; and RL Barsh, 'Indigenous Peoples in the 1990s: From Objects to Subjects of International Law?' (1993) 7 *Harvard Human Rights Journal* 33.

[6] In 1982, the UN Economic and Social Council established the WGIP as subsidiary organ of the Sub-Commission on Prevention of Discrimination and Protection of Minorities (now the Sub-Commission on the Promotion and Protection of Human Rights). It was charged with the task of developing international standards on indigenous rights.

[7] 61st session of the UN General Assembly, 107th and 108th Plenary Meetings, GA/10612, 13 September 2007: see also the International Law Association's *Statement of Principles Applicable to the Formation of General Customary International Law* (2000), para 28.

particular rights contained in the Declaration could bind States as a matter of customary international law.

The doctrine of customary international law attaches considerable weight to the views and practices of those States that would be 'specially affected' by the formation of new customary norms.[8] Accordingly, it is worth considering the views of the USA, Canada, Australia and New Zealand in detail, given their substantial indigenous populations. The representative of the Australian government stated that:

> it was the clear intention of all States that it be an aspirational Declaration with political and moral force, but not legal force. The text contained recommendations regarding how States could promote the welfare of indigenous peoples, but was not in itself legally binding or reflective of international law. As the Declaration did not describe current State practice or actions considered themselves obligated to take as a matter of law, it could not be cited as evidence of the evolution of customary international law. The Declaration did not provide a proper basis for legal actions, complaints or other claims in any international, domestic or other proceedings.[9]

The representative of New Zealand said:

> The Declaration was explained by its supporters as being an aspirational document, intended to inspire rather than to have legal effect. New Zealand did not, however, accept that a State could responsibly take such a stance towards a document that purported to declare on the contents of the rights of indigenous peoples. The history of the negotiations on the Declaration and the divided manner in which it had been adopted demonstrated that the text did not state propositions that were reflected in State practice, or which would be recognized as general principles of law.[10]

Further, the representative of the USA government stated that:

> While the United States was voting against the Declaration, [it] would continue its efforts to promote indigenous rights domestically ... Under United States

[8] See *North Sea Continental Shelf Cases* [1969] ICJ Rep 3, paras 73–74.

[9] GA Meeting (n 7) 5. The Australian government officially endorsed the Declaration on 3 April 2009 following a change of government. Nevertheless, the new government expressed the view that the Declaration is an aspirational non-binding instrument designed for the achievement of inter-societal reconciliation.

[10] Ibid. On 19 April 2010, the New Zealand government changed its position and announced its support for the Declaration. However, as the New Zealand Prime-minster stated in the New Zealand Parliament on 20 April 2010:

> 'I think it is important to understand that the Declaration on the Rights of Indigenous Peoples is just that—it is a declaration. It is not a treaty, it is not a covenant, and one does not actually sign up to it. It is an expression of aspiration; it will have no impact on New Zealand law and no impact on the constitutional framework...' Volume 662; 10238, New Zealand Parliament, available at http://www.parliament.nz/en-NZ/PB/Business/QOA/8/3/d/49HansQ_20100420_00000001-1-UN-Declaration-on-the-Rights-of-Indigenous.htm.

> domestic law, the Government recognized Indian tribes as political entities with inherent powers of self-government as first peoples. In its legal system, the federal Government had a government-to-government relationship with Indian tribes. In that domestic context, that meant promoting tribal self-government over a broad range of internal and local affairs.[11]

The statements made by two States in the General Assembly appear to answer the question of whether States intended to create new rules of international law when voting in favour of the Declaration. First, Guyana, noted that 'the Declaration was political in character as opposed to being a legally binding document, though not without potential legal implications'.[12] Second, the representative of the government of Guatemala observed that:

> Great care had been taken to ensure that the Declaration was consistent with the principles of international law ... [It] did not create new rights, but reaffirmed the rights of indigenous peoples, recognizing the collective right to live in freedom, peace and security ... The Declaration was the expression of the international community's political will to respect the rights of indigenous peoples.[13]

Accordingly, it is clear that those States that voted in favour of the Declaration did not do so with the intention of creating (or declaring) rules of international law regarding indigenous rights.

Creative Interpretations

Interpretations of the content and scope of the international legal project vary, and the views of the most prominent indigenous rights advocates are not necessarily endorsed by all indigenous peoples and sympathetic lawyers/scholars. However, many of the advocates whose work is discussed in this essay are presently driving the (international) legal agenda on indigenous rights and, as such, their views deserve special attention.

[11] Ibid. On 20 April 2010, the USA announced its intention to endorse the Declaration. However, it did not consider the Declaration to have created international legal obligations for States. In the words of Susan E. Rice, the government's Permanent UN Representative:

> 'We recognize that, for many around the world, this Declaration provides a framework for addressing indigenous issues. During President Obama's first year in office, tribal leaders encouraged the United States to reexamine its position on the Declaration — an important recommendation that directly complements our commitment to work together with the international community on the many challenges that indigenous peoples face' (http://usun.state.gov/briefing/statements/2010/140600.htm).

[12] Ibid, 12.

[13] Ibid, 15.

For Anaya and Wiessner, the language of rights is the language of law.[14] Specifically, they are troubled by what they perceive as ambivalence in the USA's approach to indigenous rights. For them:

> The most interesting aspect of the US argument is, however, the at least implicit recognition that indigenous peoples do have a 'status,' that they enjoy 'special benefits and rights contained in the declaration' ... By participating in the process and the concern shown over the years for special rights and status of indigenous peoples on the international plane, the four opposing states have demonstrated an *opinio juris*, a willingness to be bound if the provisions as finally formulated were in line with their detailed policy preferences.[15]

This is a rather unconvincing argument. Participation in a standard-setting exercise should not be interpreted as evidence of consent to be bound by a final instrument. If this argument were to gain general favour, it may result in an unwillingness on the part of States to participate in standard-setting exercises in the future.[16] Nevertheless, Anaya shows the negative votes in their best possible light:

> While the explanatory statements of the four States that voted against adoption of the Declaration (Australia, Canada, New Zealand, and United States of America) showed disagreement with the wording of specific articles or concerns with the process of adoption, they also expressed a general acceptance of the core principles and values advanced by the Declaration.[17]

On an orthodox reading, it is possible to view the Declaration's adoption as satisfying the opinio juris requirement regarding many of the rights it proclaims (the *lex ferenda* approach). Consequently, certain of its provisions could crystallise into customary international law once they are supported by appropriate evidence of State practice. However, many indigenous representatives and their supporters believe that urgent action is required to operationalise the Declaration and, for them, the *lex ferenda* approach is not going to achieve sufficient gains in the foreseeable future. In the circumstances, they have pursued two other international

[14] SJ Anaya and S Wiessner, 'The UN Declaration on the Rights of Indigenous Peoples: Towards Re-empowerment', Jurist Forum, School of Law, University of Pittsburgh, 3 October 2007, 4, jurist.law.pitt.edu/forumy/2007/10/un-declaration-on-rights-of-indigenous.php. However, the authors do not make the important distinction between legal rights and moral rights in this context. To say that X has a right does not necessarily mean that X has a right as a matter of (international) law; for such a right to arise it must conform to a prescribed type of practice.

[15] Ibid, 4.

[16] This issue is explored in detail in Emanuel Voyiakis' essay in this volume.

[17] *The Human Rights of Indigenous Peoples, in the Light of the New Declaration, and the Challenge of Making Them Operative*, Report of the Special Rapporteur on the situation of human rights and fundamental freedoms of indigenous people (SJ Anaya), UN Doc A/HRC/9/9, 5 August 2008, para 35.

law strategies. The first argument does not involve direct reliance on customary international law concerning indigenous peoples; rather it adopts an interpretative approach, claiming that the Declaration created no sui generis rights or new rights for indigenous peoples. As Anaya explains:

> The Declaration does not affirm or create special rights separate from the fundamental human rights that are deemed of universal application, but rather elaborates upon fundamental rights in the specific cultural, historical, social and economic circumstances of indigenous peoples. These include the basic norms of equality and non-discrimination, as well as other generally applicable human rights in areas such as culture, health or property, which are recognized in other international instruments and are universally applicable.[18]

This approach was also advanced by Les Malezer, the Chairperson of the Global Indigenous Caucus, during the UN General Assembly meeting at which the Declaration was adopted. He said that the Declaration 'contained no new provisions of human rights. It was based on rights that had been approved by the United Nations system but which had somehow, over the years, been denied to indigenous peoples. It was a framework for States to protect and promote the rights of indigenous peoples without exclusion or discrimination.'[19]

This strategy promotes the idea that the Declaration is an interpretative mechanism through which to view and apply fundamental human rights. Accordingly, it matters not that the Declaration is not binding as a matter of (hard) international law, because as a soft source it can achieve the same result. On this view, the Declaration facilitates the application of general standards established either in customary international law or in treaty law in the indigenous context. However, this strategy presupposes that relevant decision-makers, be they States, courts or other institutions, are receptive to this interpretative argument.[20] Clearly, some institutions will be persuaded. But if the decision whether to take cognisance of international legal sources is solely a matter of interpretation, the international law relating to indigenous peoples will remain very fragile. And, as most indigenous representatives must surely appreciate, this interpretive argument is not going to be enough to operationalise the Declaration

[18] Ibid, para 40.

[19] GA Meeting (n 7) 2. This interpretation was echoed by the government of Guatemala, as noted above.

[20] While, in dualist jurisdictions, customary international law may be part of the municipal law in principle, typically there exist significant institutional barriers to the incorporation of a customary rule in any given case. In practice, much will depend on the extent to which the rule or principle accords with the judge's favoured interpretation of the domestic law in issue. Further, in such jurisdictions, treaties typically need to be incorporated into municipal law by primary legislation before they can be relied upon in domestic litigation.

in affected States.[21] Consequently, many indigenous rights advocates have adopted an additional (hard law) strategy—they claim that the Declaration's provisions strengthen pre-existing customary international law concerning the rights of indigenous peoples.[22]

This second strategy requires the adoption of elaborate techniques to survey and distil those fragments of opinio juris and State practice that enable some of the rights set out in the Declaration to have immediate and enhanced legal effect. Indeed, Anaya and Wiessner claim that a number of indigenous rights have already attained the status of customary international law, including the rights to 'demarcation, ownership, development, control and the use of lands they have traditionally owned or otherwise occupied and used'.[23] The evidence required to underpin this strategy is

> discernible from international instruments, reports and decisions by authoritative international bodies, such as the UN Commissions/Committees and those of regional human rights commissions and courts; states' assertions and communications at the international and national levels and the actions of states internationally and domestically.[24]

However, the strategy involves a good deal of double counting (whereby a piece of evidence is interpreted as representing both opinio juris and State practice), and this raises serious questions regarding the probative value of such evidence. As Dupuy observes:

> many scholars quite innocently cite the largest possible number of opinions, treaties, and recommendations in order to convince themselves that not only must a particular rule be recognized by states as compulsory, but also that

[21] It is clear from the work of Boyle and Chinkin that the soft law argument is a modest one. See C Chinkin, 'The Challenge of Soft Law: Development and Change in International Law' (1989) 38 *International and Comparative Law Quarterly* 850; A Boyle, 'Soft Law in International Law-Making' in MD Evans, *International Law*, 2nd edn (Oxford University Press, 2007) 141; A Boyle and C Chinkin, *The Making of International Law* (Oxford University Press, 2007) 225–29. For incisive analysis of the shortcomings of this argument see J d'Aspremont, 'Softness in International Law: A Self-Serving Quest for New Legal Materials' (2008) 19 *European Journal of International Law* 1075, 1077–87.

[22] See eg S Wiessner, 'Rights and Status of Indigenous Peoples: A Global Comparative and International Legal Analysis' (1999) 12 *Harvard Human Rights Journal* 57; S Wiessner, 'Indigenous Sovereignty: A Reassessment in Light of the UN Declaration on the Rights of Indigenous Peoples' (2008) 41 *Vanderbilt Journal of Transnational Law* 1141; SJ Anaya, *Indigenous Peoples in International Law*, 2nd edn (Oxford University Press, 2004) 62–72; and SJ Anaya and RA Williams Jnr, 'The Protection of Indigenous Peoples' Rights over Lands and Natural Resources Under the Inter-American Human Rights System' (2001) 14 *Harvard Human Rights Journal* 33.

[23] Anaya and Wiessner (n 14) 4.

[24] See *Aurelio Cal and the Maya Village of Santa Cruz v Attorney General of Belize; and Manuel Coy and Maya Village of Conejo v Attorney General of Belize*, (Consolidated) Claim Nos 171 & 172, 2007, Supreme Court of Belize (18 October 2007), Conteh CJ, para 128. The judgment referred specifically to Anaya (n 22) on this point.

such is effectively the case in their actual practice. However, mere reiteration in different international documents may well have to be dissociated from what a state actually considers to be binding law in a specific situation.[25]

The Radicalisation of Customary International Law

Because they possess universal moral significance, human rights exist beyond the realm of positive law. However, such rights can only attract legal validity once they have been sanctioned by a given legal system acting on behalf of its political community. A State can endorse a human right by enacting legislation which ensures that the right becomes a municipal legal right. Alternatively, States, acting together, can decide to recognise a human right via a multilateral treaty or by the formation of a new norm of customary international law (for the latter, State consent can be established either expressly or by implication). Nevertheless, in general, international human rights law is not enforced in the international realm; it is put into effect by municipal law. The application of customary international law is especially problematic in the domestic sphere. It is often difficult to identify when norms have crystallised, whether a given State is actually bound, and whether a particular norm has been incorporated into the municipal law of a particular State.

It is entirely possible that a customary norm may have been created without the involvement of a State that is bound by it.[26] Consequently, from the perspective of political legitimacy, a norm of customary international law concerning human rights may not have been endorsed by the national community which is directly responsible for its realisation and regardless of its binding force the norm will remain external to the national community. In contrast, a treaty would have been agreed by State representatives and, therefore, it would have been indirectly endorsed by that community, irrespective of whether it was directly enforceable in its municipal law.

Where a purported customary norm concerns indigenous peoples, evidence of State practice is inevitably drawn from the domestic laws and practices of affected States. But instead of adducing evidence of uniform or consistent behaviour regarding adherence to certain indigenous rights on the part of such States, many indigenous rights advocates marshal the best *particular* practice of the most 'enlightened' States on indigenous/

[25] PM Dupuy, 'Formation of Customary International Law and General Principles' in D Bodansky, J Brunnee and E Hey (eds), *The Oxford Handbook of International Environmental Law* (Oxford University Press, 2007) 449, 453.

[26] Unless the 'persistent objector' rule is invoked.

human rights issues.[27] This data is then presented as evidence of the *general* practice of affected States. This radical conception of customary international law licences indigenous rights advocates to find the most suitable examples of State practice, to present them in their best possible light, and to studiously ignore any practices to the contrary. Of course, the opinio juris requirement must also be satisfied as well but, as the ICJ indicated in the *Nicaragua* case, there is a difference 'between what States say and what they actually do'.[28]

Indigenous rights advocates are able to exercise an influential role in the creation and development of customary international law, one that they could not enjoy in relation to the evolution of treaty law. It may be that this advantage is primarily rhetorical but, as we shall see, effective presentation is an important aspect of the quest for rights. Accordingly, far from presenting an obstacle to the development of modern international law, the ambiguity inherent in the formation of customary international law seems to facilitate the cause of indigenous rights (but, as this essay argues, not their realisation). Thus while a particular customary norm could be classified as an external legal phenomenon, both because it is a norm of a different legal system and because it may not be reflected in the practice of a given State, nonetheless it has the potential to realise indigenous rights within that State. While this situation may also be true in relation to the orthodox operation of customary international law, it is central to the radical variant, in which customary international law is promoted as a legal source that transforms domestic conditions in all affected States rather than a relatively conservative source of international law that seeks to maintain a consistent level of general practice.

This radical version of customary international law has capacity to circumvent the democratic processes by which the political good is determined in affected States. It attempts to impose a vision of the national society that has not been sanctioned by the community in question. In the present context, indigenous representatives present the Declaration as a complete, non-negotiable code that must be given effect by affected States because it represents either the contextual elaboration of more general human rights which are grounded in customary international law or multilateral treaties (the interpretative argument) or because key parts of the Declaration constitute existing customary international law specific to indigenous peoples. However, the Declaration has not been subjected to the vagaries of political negotiation and compromise *within the national*

[27] See the sources cited above, n 22.

[28] Dupuy (n 25) 459. See *Case Concerning Military and Paramilitary Activities in and against Nicaragua* [1986] ICJ Rep 93, para 184. As demonstrated by the government positions in *Maya v Belize* (n 24); and *Case of the Saramaka People v Suriname* (Series C No 172) [2007] IACHR 5 (28 November 2007).

communities concerned, a process which confronts other models of the good society.[29] Of course, the Declaration was the subject of political negotiation and compromise within various UN fora but not with a view to its direct and automatic application within affected States. If this were the intention of participating States, they would have acknowledged that the Declaration represented international law.

THE DECLARATION AND THE RIGHTS DISCOURSE

The Sui Generis Quality of Indigenous Rights Claims

It is well known that the function of rights is to trump the political, to defy utilitarian and realist calculations about the good.[30] Rights, therefore, appear to be foundational, universal, unhistorical and unpolitical. However, in reality, they are particular, historically contingent and political in nature.[31] Claimants deflect attention away from the subjectivity of their particular interests by expressing them as objective rights.[32] The transformation of political claims into the language of (human) rights is possible because virtually anything can be the subject of a right.[33] Rights are a device to disguise focused political claims.

Nevertheless, there are other ways of thinking about human rights. For instance, Gunther considers the act of claiming a human right to be significant even if the claimant does not possess a right as a matter of positive law.[34] He suggests that propositional claims have important social (as opposed to legal) consequences because they allow claimants who may have been excluded from the rights discourse within a particular community to enter into the communicative public sphere.[35] For him, members of the community are required to listen to human rights claims arising out of instances of injustice, to weigh them and to decide whether the social practices in issue are unjust. If a claim is upheld by the community the unjust practice in question is prohibited by the recognition of a new human right and, in addition to regaining his or her voice, the victim

[29] This issue is discussed below.

[30] M Koskenniemi, 'The Effect of Rights on Political Culture' in P Alston (ed), *The EU and Human Rights* (Oxford University Press, 1999) 99, 101 (referring to the core thesis in R Dworkin, *Taking Rights Seriously* (Cambridge, MA, Harvard University Press, 1977)).

[31] Ibid, 100–101.

[32] Ibid, 101.

[33] Ibid. The present author would, however, disagree with Koskenniemi's suggestion that legal rights have no essential quality as they enable a claimant to call upon the political institutions of state in order to enforce such a right.

[34] K Gunther, 'The Legacies of Injustice and Fear: A European Approach to Human Rights and their Effects on Political Culture' in Alston (n 30) 117, 136.

[35] Ibid, 137.

regains his or her agency within that community.[36] This interpretation of the formation of new human rights should, in principle, appeal to indigenous peoples as they have been excluded from the rights discourse within modern States and therefore they invariably lack specifically applicable rights. Indigenous peoples' efforts to internationalise their struggle for rights could be seen as a search for voice, and their successful penetration of supranational institutions and the development of international standards demonstrate that indigenous peoples have moved from objects to subjects of the international community and thus have regained their agency (albeit at an international level).

Prominent indigenous representatives are sensitive to the sui generis quality of indigenous rights claims, as apparent from the statements of Anaya and Malezer above. In their view, not only does the Declaration not create special rights for indigenous peoples, it creates no new rights at all. This is an unusual tactic. The strategic reasons for denying that the Declaration creates new rights were discussed in the context of the interpretive argument above. The reasons for denying the sui generis character of certain indigenous rights claims are also political. Gunther suggests that claimants typically adopt a two stage strategy when making new human rights claims. First, they emphasise that part of the new right that reflects the generic characteristics of fundamental human rights (respect for human dignity, equality etc) and then they promote the right's new (particular) component.[37] In sharp contrast, indigenous representatives seek to replicate the first stage but they ignore the second, preferring to view the contextual elaboration of general human rights as an interpretative act rather than as a means for the creation of new rights.

This approach has two advantages in the indigenous context. First, it stresses the universal, unhistorical and unpolitical nature of the rights contained in the Declaration, thus hiding their particular, temporal and political characteristics. Second, it seeks to avoid stirring up identity politics. Specifically, if indigenous peoples claim special rights then, in principle, there is no reason why other sub-State societal groups (national minorities) could not claim similar rights. The recognition of special rights for such groups would be extremely problematic for nearly all States, and indigenous peoples' refusal to couch their demands in terms of special rights must be read as an acknowledgement that such claims would have jeopardised the Declaration's adoption, despite the fact that many indigenous rights manifest a sui generis quality.[38]

[36] Ibid, 134–35.

[37] Ibid, 137.

[38] Land rights are a prime example here (discussed in the next subsection). See Will Kymlicka's essay in this volume for detailed analysis of the problematic divide between indigenous peoples and minorities.

The interpretive argument (that indigenous rights are merely contextual manifestations of general human rights) is not an argument that is available to national minorities.[39] The distinction between indigenous peoples and national minorities in this regard only makes sense if the concept of indigenous sovereignty is embraced. The question of the contemporary significance of indigenous peoples' pre-colonial (historical) sovereignty is neatly captured by Anaya:

> Within this frame of argument indigenous groups have been referred to as 'nations' and identified as having attributes of 'sovereignty' that predate and, at least to some extent, should trump the sovereignty of states that now assert power over them. The rhetoric of nationhood is used to posit indigenous peoples as states, or something like states, within a post-Westphalian world of separate, mutually exclusive political communities. Advocates for indigenous peoples point to a history in which 'original' sovereignty of indigenous communities over defined territories has been illegitimately taken from them or suppressed.[40]

Nevertheless, Anaya appreciates that the historical sovereignty argument is no match for the concept of sovereignty conceived and exercised by modern States. He understands that assertions of original indigenous sovereignty will not result in a return to the status quo before the arrival of European colonialism. Instead, as he implicitly acknowledges, it is the ideological or rhetorical value (the symbolism) of indigenous sovereignty that remains important. In particular, the historical sovereignty argument underpins the endeavour to redeem indigenous sovereignty not as something directly competing with State-centred conceptions of sovereignty but as an attribute to be regained via the contemporary human rights discourse. Anaya, acting in his capacity as Special Rapporteur on the situation of human rights and fundamental freedoms of indigenous peoples, explains the connection between indigenous sovereignty, the Declaration and contemporary human rights claims:

> The basic normative justification of the Declaration is stated in the sixth preambular paragraph, which acknowledges that 'indigenous peoples have suffered from historic injustices as a result of, inter alia, their colonization and dispossession of their lands, territories and resources, thus preventing them from exercising, in particular, their right to development in accordance with their own needs and interests'. The Declaration's preamble stresses the essentially remedial purpose of the instrument. Far from affirming special rights per se, the Declaration aims at repairing the ongoing consequences of the historical

[39] For instance, they have long been denied the right to self-determination in international law. See R Higgins, 'Post-Modern Tribalism and the Right to Secession: Comments' in C Brolmann et al (eds), *Peoples and Minorities in International Law* (Dordrecht, Kluwer, 1993) 29, 32.

[40] Anaya (n 22) 6.

> denial of the right to self-determination and other basic human rights affirmed in international instruments of general applicability.[41]

The strategy of emphasising indigenous sovereignty and, therefore, the Declaration's corrective purpose has the additional benefit of distancing indigenous claims from those of other minority societal groups who also seek the right to self-determination (and other rights similar to those claimed by indigenous peoples). However, because national minorities converged with modernity (either before or after they were overwhelmed by dominant societal groups) they cannot establish the pre-modern cultural distinctiveness which necessarily underpins the indigenous sovereignty argument;[42] consequently, they cannot advance contemporary human rights claims in the same way.

Human rights approaches to problems of group discrimination have focused on affirmative action (special measures) as a means of promoting substantive equality. However, while the case for eliminating the contemporary discrimination suffered by indigenous peoples is undeniable, the extent to which international law should confer sui generis rights on such groups is problematic at the theoretical level. The ostensibly attractive 'cultural difference' argument has often been advanced by indigenous rights advocates to sustain indigenous claims for sui generis rights.[43] Clearly, past oppression based on cultural affiliation, which also manifests ongoing discriminatory effects, can provide a legitimate basis for contemporary rights claims. But, if past injustices are resolved (as far as possible) and current discriminatory practices are corrected, the case for permanent rights rooted in cultural affiliation collapses and any such entitlements must cease. Accordingly, the cultural difference argument has the theoretical capacity to undermine the case for special rights in the longer term.[44] Because indigenous peoples argue that they constitute distinctive societies in the absence of prejudice (and therefore their entitlements should

[41] Anaya (n 17) para 36.

[42] See S Allen, 'The Consequences of Modernity for Indigenous Peoples: An International Appraisal' (2006) 13 *International Journal on Minority and Group Rights* 315, 337.

[43] See D Ivison et al, 'Introduction' in D Ivison et al (eds), *Political Theory and the Rights of Indigenous Peoples* (Cambridge University Press, 2000) 9–11. For Xanthaki, sui generis rights are 'justified on the basis of past injustices that such peoples have suffered and the scale of their cultural differences measured against the populations living in the same state'. A Xanthaki, *Indigenous Rights and United Nations Standards: Self-Determination, Culture and Land* (Cambridge University Press, 2007) 4. For Gilbert, 'whereas indigenous peoples' rights are part of a larger fight against discrimination and thus rely on temporary affirmative action procedures, their territorial claims remain specific, or *sui generis*; therefore, the special measures that have to be put in place must also remain equally specific'. J Gilbert, *Indigenous Peoples' Land Rights under International Law: From Victims to Actors* (Ardsley, Transnational Publishers, 2006) 191.

[44] See W Kymlicka, *Politics in the Vernacular: Nationalism, Multiculturalism and Citizenship* (Oxford University Press, 1999) 121, 128–29.

not be constrained by a temporal dimension), the theoretical weaknesses in the cultural difference argument may have contributed to the decision of prominent indigenous rights advocates to avoid reference to the sui generis quality of indigenous rights claims.

The Declaration and the Natural Law Tradition

Gunther observes that claimants who make propositional claims invariably present them as though they have already acquired legal validity.[45] In part, this is a rhetorical device designed to compel a specific legal system to recognise a claim by exploiting its close resemblance to existing legal rights or by emphasising that the law ought to convert the claim into a legal right as a result of overwhelming moral considerations. In this respect, claims are being *presented* as rights. In addition, claimants often argue that a propositional claim has, in fact, already been legally sanctioned (typically by reference to natural law) and, as such, the claimed right is, in reality, an old (external) legal right that demands recognition within a given legal system. This strategy strengthens the case for positive legal rights by a using self-authorising manoeuvre in order to secure general authorisation.[46]

Against this background, it is perhaps unsurprising that Anaya seeks to co-opt natural law to support the indigenous cause. In his own words:

> International law, furthermore, has been made to include a burgeoning and influential transnational discourse concerned with achieving peace and a minimum of human suffering. This modern discourse of peace and human rights which tempers positivism in international law, represents in significant measure the re-emergence of classical-era naturalism, in which law was determined on the basis of visions of *what ought to be*, rather than simply on the basis of *what is*, and which contextualized the state as an instrument of humankind rather than its master.[47]

Natural law impliedly justifies some of the rights proclaimed in the Declaration. A good example of its influence is apparent in the provisions concerning reparations for the loss of lands, territories and natural resources. The Declaration recognises that indigenous peoples possess land/territorial rights but, in Article 26, it restricts these entitlements

[45] Gunther (n 34) 138.
[46] Ibid.
[47] Anaya (n 22) 50. For present purposes, I shall leave to one side the well-documented naturalistic fallacy of deriving an 'ought' from an 'is'. For a brief discussion see MDA Freeman (ed), *Lloyd's Introduction to Jurisprudence*, 8th edn (London, Sweet & Maxwell, 2008) 84–90.

to those lands/territories they currently own, occupy or use by reason of their traditional ownership/occupation/use.[48] Article 26 therefore interprets tradition as practice. It does not acknowledge that indigenous peoples hold rights to land/territories which they possessed in the pre-colonial era or even in the more recent past—it does not endorse tradition as history. Nonetheless, Article 28(1) recognises that indigenous peoples have the right to redress, which may include restitution, where 'lands, territories and resources which they have traditionally owned or otherwise occupied or used ... have been confiscated, taken, occupied, used or damaged without their free, prior and informed consent'.[49]

If Article 28(1) simply concerns prospective instances of dispossession, its application appears to be straightforward and uncontroversial. However, if the concept of reparations is meant to be applied retrospectively then it is much more problematic.[50] While a prospective interpretation would be consistent with a literal reading of the text, if the Declaration is a remedial instrument, reparations would seem to be central to its purpose. The case for reparations in situations where lands/territories were seized in violation of the law applicable at the time is highly persuasive. However, many of the key general human rights that prominent indigenous rights advocates seek to invoke have only been recognised in international law relatively recently and many indigenous peoples were deracinated long before such recognition occurred. Moreover, if many indigenous peoples were subjugated and dispossessed by European colonial powers without offending the principle of inter-temporal law,[51] as was the (self-serving)

[48] Art 26 provides: '1. Indigenous peoples have the right to the lands, territories and resources which they have traditionally owned, occupied or otherwise used or acquired. 2. Indigenous peoples have the right to own, use develop and control the lands, territories and resources that they possess by reason of traditional ownership or other traditional occupation or use, as well as those which they have otherwise acquired. 3. States shall give legal recognition and protection to these lands, territories and resources. Such recognition shall be conducted with due respect to the customs, traditions and land tenure systems of the indigenous peoples concerned.'

[49] See also Art 11(2), which provides: 'States shall provide through effective mechanisms, which may include restitution, developed in conjunction with indigenous peoples, with respect to their cultural, intellectual, religious and spiritual property taken without their free, prior and informed consent or in violation of their laws, traditions and customs.'

[50] The issue of reparations proved to be a major sticking point in the scrutiny/approval process and the original text of the draft declaration was significantly altered. See Report of the Eighth Session of the inter-sessional Working Group on the draft Declaration on the Rights of Indigenous Peoples, UN Commission on Human Rights (2003), UN Doc E/CN.4/2003/92; and the Report of the Ninth Session (2004) UN Doc E/CN.4/2004/81 (and the textual proposals contained in UN Doc E/CN.4/2004/WG.15/CRP.1 and UN Doc E/CN.4/2004/WG.15/CRP.7).

[51] Actions carried out in one period cannot be judged by the legal standards of another. See Huber J's interpretation of this principle in the *Island of Palmas Case* (1928) 2 RIAA 829, 845. See also J Gilbert (n 43) 141–64; and, generally, F Lenzerini (ed), *Reparations for Indigenous Peoples: International and Comparative Perspectives* (Oxford University Press, 2008).

view adopted by the international law of the time, the argument for reparations is substantially weakened.

The shortcomings of international law in the colonial context are usually blamed on clinical positivist approaches favoured during the late nineteenth century. However, Vitoria, one of the fathers of the discipline and an avowed exponent of natural law thinking, used classical naturalism to justify the international legal doctrine which subjugated and dispossessed indigenous peoples in the New World. He recognised that indigenous peoples possessed natural rights because they had the facility of reason and thus could access the universal natural law, which Vitoria conceived as being coterminous with *jus gentium* (early international law). According to Vitoria, the Spanish explorers had natural rights to travel and trade in indigenous territories, but not only were the Amerindians unable to deny these universal rights, any resistance would amount to an act of war justifying their subjugation and dispossession. Consequently, rather than being a universal normative code mandating societal equality and reciprocity, *jus gentium* 'naturalize[d] and legitimate[d] a [Spanish] system of commerce and Spanish penetration'.[52] Accordingly, 'an idealised version of the particular cultural practices of the Spanish assume[d] the guise of universality as a result of appearing to derive from the sphere of natural law'.[53] And '[t]he discrepancy between the ontologically "universal" Indian and the socially, historically, "particular" Indian must be remedied by the imposition of sanctions' so that the Indian could meet the universal (Spanish) standards required by *jus gentium* (natural law).[54]

Thus, while early international law may have accepted that indigenous peoples possessed certain natural rights, it rendered these rights highly contingent and practically meaningless. Against this background, the universal naturalism that Anaya seeks to resurrect is one that never actually existed.[55] Anaya's 'classical' naturalism is one that has been reflexively altered in the light of subsequent practice.[56] In effect, he is arguing that a version of universal naturalism which is consistent with contemporary human rights values should be projected back to a moment before the advent of European colonialism in order to recognise indigenous peoples'

[52] A Anghie, *Imperialism, Sovereignty and the Making of International Law* (Cambridge University Press, 2004) 21.

[53] Ibid, 21.

[54] Ibid.

[55] Anaya acknowledges the negative aspects of Vitoria's interpretation of natural law. However, instead of dwelling on these, he promotes the positive aspects of Vitoria's jurisprudence for indigenous peoples (ie the recognition that indigenous peoples have always possessed natural rights). See Anaya (n 22) 16–19.

[56] Reflexive practices refer to the way in which all human actions are reflexively monitored with the resultant knowledge conditioning future conduct. They are central to the process of systemic reproduction within modernity. See A Giddens, *The Consequences of Modernity* (Cambridge, Polity Press, 1990) 16–17.

sovereign rights, despite the fact that they were not recognised in any material sense by the natural law of that time. It is clear that Anaya is trying to ignore the temporal and contingent nature of international (and natural) law in order to reinstate a politically motivated universalism. Therefore, although it is possible to identify fragments of classical naturalism that endorse the indigenous sovereignty argument, there are powerful arguments that counter it. Accordingly, at best, the natural law tradition is ambivalent in its support of the indigenous sovereignty argument.

The Moral Foundations of Indigenous Rights Claims

Human rights are morally informed political claims. For instance, the right to self-determination has a high political quotient. Consequently, it is notoriously indeterminate, both in terms of the relevant unit for the purpose of exercising the right (which criteria should be used) and how the right is given effect (what organisational forms should it take).[57] From a moral perspective, all societal groups should be entitled to exercise autonomy in recognition of their equality. Nonetheless, international law has never endorsed the ethical basis for self-determination, not least because it would cause great inter-societal tension in many cases.[58] Indeed, it has always endeavoured to circumscribe the right's political significance in the interests of the international legal order. Unsurprisingly, the orthodox position remains that only 'peoples' can exercise the right to self-determination and the concept of 'people-hood' equates to the entire population of a sovereign State.[59]

Indigenous representatives have fashioned a political claim for the right to self-determination by reference to existing international legal standards.[60] In this respect, they have set themselves apart from other sub-State societal groups because they can demonstrate a comparable degree of sovereignty to that exercised by States.[61] Accordingly, indigenous peoples claim a status that distinguishes them from national

[57] M Koskenniemi, 'The Wonderful Artificiality of States' (1994) 88 *ASIL Proceedings* 22, 27. Admittedly, the former is clearer in the case of indigenous peoples than that of most societal groups.

[58] This is clearly why national minorities have not been recognised as possessing the right in modern international law.

[59] A Cassese, *Self-Determination of Peoples: A Legal Reappraisal* (Cambridge University Press, 1998) 59–62.

[60] Art 3 provides: 'Indigenous peoples have the right to self-determination. By virtue of that right they freely determine their political status and freely pursue their economic, social and cultural development.' It transposes the provisions of joint Art 1 of the International Covenant on Civil and Political Rights (1966, 999 UNTS 171) and the International Covenant on Economic, Social and Cultural Rights (1966, 993 UNTS 3) into the indigenous context.

[61] But perhaps a lesser kind of sovereignty; see Wiessner 2008 (n 22) 1170.

minorities, one that elevates them to quasi-States (or frustrated States). However, the claim cannot be based on equality: indigenous peoples seek the privileges of 'statehood' for themselves, not for all societal groups. In this respect, they are making a claim for special treatment.

Further, when prominent indigenous representatives claim territorial/land/natural resource rights they invoke the general canon of human rights law in order to justify such rights on the ground of societal equality.[62] However, the nature of such finite resources ensures that such rights claims have profound inter-societal implications and raise intricate issues of distributive justice that cannot be resolved at a distance or by reference to first principles.[63] While it would be wrong to argue that a rights claim can only be justified on the grounds of equality if it is claimed on behalf of all those who suffer discriminatory treatment, in advancing an equality claim it must at least be plausible, by reference to the logic of the claim, that all societal groups could make the same argument. However, it is clear that the case for many indigenous rights is justified on the basis of indigenous exceptionalism. This is not to suggest that claims to indigenous self-determination or resource rights are without merit, but it does show that the moral foundations for these claims are questionable. The same could be argued for the participatory and consultation rights contained in the Declaration.[64] Clearly, they are legitimate means through which indigenous peoples can exercise their substantive rights. But while they might be grounded in the rhetoric of equality, they are privileged rights when compared with the entitlements held and exercised by other sub-State societal groups.

THE DECLARATION AND THE DE-FORMALISATION OF INTERNATIONAL LAW

As noted previously, some of the Declaration's provisions have already been endorsed by a number of courts, and it has guided national processes concerning the protection and promotion of indigenous rights in

[62] Art 17 Universal Declaration on Human Rights (1948, UN Doc A/811) provides: (1) 'Everyone has the right to own property alone as well as in association with others'; and (2) 'No one shall be arbitrarily deprived of his property'.

[63] See eg J Waldron, 'Indigeneity: First Peoples and Last Occupancy' (2003) 1 *New Zealand Journal of Public and International Law* 55.

[64] For example, Art 18 provides: 'Indigenous peoples have the right to participate in decision-making in matters which would affect their rights, through representatives chosen by themselves in accordance with their own procedures, as well as to maintain and develop their own indigenous decision-making institutions.' Art 19 provides: 'States shall consult and cooperate in good faith with the indigenous peoples concerned through their own representative institutions in order to obtain their free, prior and informed consent before adopting and implementing legislative or administrative measures that may affect them.'

a number of States.[65] However, many sympathetic scholars have largely ignored questions concerning the Declaration's international legal significance.[66] Sources such as the Declaration clearly have the capacity to effect considerable normative cross-fertilisation for the benefit of indigenous peoples; but what is the significance of the Declaration for international law? First, regarding the use of international law by courts in domestic cases where it is not directly binding on a State party, the use of persuasive authority (both within the common law world and beyond it) supports the argument that courts can positivise laws that may not have been binding within a given jurisdiction before judgment was entered.[67] There are numerous examples of this practice,[68] and international lawyers and scholars are prone to seize them when they arise in an effort to demonstrate the trend towards the de-formalisation of international law.[69]

The de-formalisation argument is invariably made in relation to law that is binding in at least one jurisdiction, the material development being that it has been applied in another jurisdiction without having been incorporated into it by national legislation or constitutional provision. A non-binding international instrument, such as the Declaration, has never been binding as a matter of (international) law and so the argument has to confront a seemingly insurmountable obstacle. However, soft instruments, like the Declaration, take the de-formalisation argument one stage further because rather than referring to the de-formalisation of a particular legal source in a specific context, the enhanced argument necessitates the de-formalisation of international law itself.[70]

For those committed to the international legal project, the focus is on the effectiveness of human rights regimes rather than on the preoccupation with the binding quality of international law. International instruments which manifest (potential) legal implications have often been termed 'soft law' because the rights which they proclaim may possess a nascent legal quality. A popular viewpoint is that soft law is a useful

[65] See Anaya (n 17) paras 52–53.

[66] See eg Xanthaki (n 43) 281: 'Although when adopted by the UN General Assembly, it will not be strictly binding, it may generate political pressure on states to comply with its terms.'

[67] See HP Glenn, 'Persuasive Authority' (1987) 32 *McGill Law Journal* 261; and 'Transnational Common Laws' (2005) 29 *Fordham International Law Journal* 457.

[68] See eg *Minister for Immigration and Ethnic Affairs v Teoh* (1995) 128 ALR 353 (Australia); and *Baker v Canada* [1999] 2 SCR 817 (Canada). In the indigenous context, see *Mayagna (Sumo) Awas Tingni Community v Nicaragua* (Series C No 79) [2001] IACHR 9 (31 August 2001), Separate Opinion, Garcia-Ramirez J, para 7.

[69] See J Nijman and A Nollkaemper (eds), *New Perspectives on the Divide between National and International Law* (Oxford University Press, 2007). This collection does not consider the status of the Declaration.

[70] J Nijman and A Nollkaemper, 'Beyond the Divide' in ibid, 341, 352.

conceptual matrix through which to interpret and apply international law. While this approach has some merit, in that it recognises the role that non-binding standards can play within a formal legal universe, it is surely an inadequate response to the urgent challenges confronting humanity, especially for those who see international law as an emanicipatory project.

For many internationalists, contemporary international law is not primarily concerned with the regulation of inter-State relations. International institutions and the standards, recommendations, decisions and reports they produce are far more important for the development of significant international agendas than the self-interested and short-term views of States. The constitutional values embraced by such institutions, the transparent and impartial conditions under which they invariably operate, and the way they typically endeavour to ensure that stakeholders participate meaningfully in standard-setting exercises enhance the legitimacy of resulting institutional outcomes. While States remain major actors within international institutions, institutions often have independent executive bodies with agendas separate from those of their State members;[71] and where multilateral human rights treaties exist, monitoring or adjudicative bodies often perceive their empowering treaties as living instruments and their jurisprudence appears to develop in quite a different direction to the one foreseeable to States parties when ratification occurred.[72]

Alternatively, some international lawyers and scholars may question the reach of international law and thus the value to be ascribed to certain aspects of international law. While international law invariably works effectively at the inter-State level, that part of international law that concerns itself with State actions (and omissions) within their own domestic jurisdiction is typically more problematic. Moreover, the direct application of international law in national courts is also much more limited in practice than many international lawyers would care to admit. Thus, for some internationalists, if formal international law's capacity to address human rights obligations is so restricted then informal institutional means of realising universal values must be pursued. Against this background, they may feel justified in separating the authoritative quality of international law from the sphere of its formal application and applying it in a wider range of settings.

[71] Regarding the independent efforts of the ILO Secretariat on indigenous issues, see Rodríguez-Piñero (n 5).

[72] See eg the work of the Human Rights Committee and the Committee on the Elimination of Racial Discrimination in this respect. Regarding the latter, see Patrick Thornberry's essay in this volume.

However, despite such good intentions, the de-formalisation of international law is extremely problematic, as Nijman and Nollkaemper acknowledge:

> [It] redirects us to a meta-juridical level of analysis: who or what validates non-positive law sources of international law? What may grant (democratic) legitimacy to international law which is not only non-binding but by lacking the consent of States also lacks the (hypothetical) authority coming from the governed represented by their governments. After all, consent remains the main legitimacy-conferring power. Are there other ways of international representation of the governed and thus other kinds of authority?[73]

Nevertheless, according to them:

> Part of the answer is found in the fact that deformalization is a parallel development to the emergence of common values. International law does not (only) find its authority in binding rules and principles, ie in conformity with the positivist model but is in a way more substantive since it is grounded on international norms as keepers of universal common *values* rather than as binding rules of positive international law. In this role, (binding or non-binding) international norms have authority because of the values they represent and even if they are not binding they may be directive in the interpretation of national law on the same issues.[74]

The idea of law as the direct embodiment of values has many prominent adherents.[75] But not only does it fail to overcome the legitimacy deficit conceded by Nijman and Nollkaemper above, it cannot perform international law's operational function either. The common values in question (equality, dignity etc) are highly abstract and indeterminate (our interpretation of them is determined by our own particular social reality).[76] Accordingly, values cannot resolve concrete (legal) rights conflicts in a sustainable manner or reconcile the opposing political agendas that lie beneath the surface of their claimed universality. As Koskenniemi explains:

> We have recourse to legal rules precisely because organising social life directly on values turned out to be impossible: values are too general as policy guidelines when formulated so that all would agree. If transformed into concrete reforms, they will inevitably overrule some interests in favour of other interests and seem thus no longer reflective of the society as a whole.[77]

[73] Nijman and Nollkaemper (n 70) 353.
[74] Ibid.
[75] See eg R Higgins, *Problems & Processes: International Law and How We Use It* (Oxford, Clarendon Press, 1994). Anaya clearly subscribes to this (New Haven) school of thought.
[76] See M Koskenniemi, 'International Law in a Post-Realist Era' (1994) 16 *Australian Yearbook of International Law* 1, 8. Further, as Koskenniemi recognises, if we can organise ourselves directly by reference to our values, which we already know, then law becomes redundant. '"The Lady Doth Protest Too Much" Kosovo, and the Turn to Ethics in International Law' (2002) 65 *Modern Law Review* 159, 165.
[77] Ibid, 1994, 8.

Law provides an intermediate mechanism that mediates between the inherent complexity of our (modern) values and the particularity of our own social reality and it achieves this by maintaining its commitment to formalism.[78] Consequently, as the enhanced de-formalisation argument is irredeemably flawed, it cannot be used to justify the direct application of the non-binding international instruments, such as the Declaration, in municipal legal regimes.

INSTITUTIONALISING RIGHTS

The Global Legal Order and the Functional Decline of the State

The political nature of rights is a general phenomenon that becomes glaringly apparent when rights conflict with each other.[79] Such conflicts are not resolvable by reference to the rights in issue because their claimed absoluteness renders them incapable of mediation. As Gray explains:

> To make a political issue that is deeply morally contested a matter of basic rights is to make it non-negotiable, since rights … are unconditional entitlements, not susceptible to moderation. Because they are peremptory in this way, rights do not allow divisive issues to be settled by legislation [or adjudicative] compromise: they permit only unconditional victory or surrender.[80]

They can only be resolved from a point beyond rights where the relevant decision-maker has to choose which outcome (right) best fits the prevailing socio-political conditions.[81] Rights are shaped by background political interests that are constantly being renegotiated and reconfigured themselves. Consequently, rights do not trump political considerations as a matter of course.[82] They are reduced to minor policy directives that must be balanced along with utilitarian and realist calculations in order to produce politically acceptable decisions.[83]

Who can fulfil the role of determining conflicting rights claims? Clearly, the courts can perform this function if the rights in issue are

[78] Klabbers (n 2) 387. Of course, as this essay suggests, background values do have a role to play in the creation and interpretation of legal rules and principles. The disagreement here is about the position and weight of values in relation to law's function.

[79] Koskenniemi (n 30) 107–10.

[80] Ibid, 113, quoting from J Gray, *Enlightenment's Wake: Politics and Culture at the Close of the Modern Age* (London, Routledge, 1995) 22.

[81] Ibid, 109.

[82] Even Dworkin has never subscribed to the view that rights are absolute. In his view, 'The idea of rights as trumps is a *formal* idea: it fixes the general function of rights within any particular theory that uses the idea at all'. R Dworkin, 'A Reply by Ronald Dworkin' in M Cohen (ed), *Ronald Dworkin and Contemporary Jurisprudence* (Totowa, Rowman and Allanheld, 1983) 247, 281.

[83] Koskenniemi (n 30) 110.

(narrow) legal rights. However, processes of adjudication are limited by their ad hoc and reactive nature. Moreover, courts are not well equipped to make broad public policy decisions, not least because the judiciary lacks a democratic mandate.[84] Further, they now invariably lack the capacity to create new legal rights. For these tasks a more representative institution is required. Traditionally, the State has discharged these political functions.

Many of the proponents of the international legal project treat international law as a global legal order rather than as a law that principally regulates inter-State relations. Accordingly, for them, the State presents no bar to the quest for justice. It merely serves as one of a number of institutions involved in the process of managing and delivering global governance.[85] While they may concede that the State still possesses a privileged status in the new global legal order, many of these internationalists often claim that the fate of this historical aberration is sealed as it is being incrementally superseded by more dynamic transnational institutional processes. As Anaya explains:

> Notions of state sovereignty, although still very much alive in international law, are ever more yielding to an overarching normative trend defined by visions of world peace, stability, and human rights. This trend, promoted by modern international institutions and involving nonstate actors in multilateral settings, enhances international law's competency over matters at one time considered within states' exclusive domestic domain.[86]

The functional decline of the State is a narrative that appeals to indigenous representatives for at least two reasons. First, the idea of a global legal order justifies the internationalisation of the struggle for indigenous rights while endorsing the view that this order has a legitimate role in implementing international solutions within national settings. Second, the recalibration of the notion of sovereignty provides indigenous peoples with the opportunity to recast and promote their own parallel version of sovereignty. As Lenzerini argues (albeit in a highly qualified fashion):

> [T]he spread of contemporary practice favourable to the recognition of indigenous autonomy seems to demonstrate that, to a certain extent, the idea of indigenous sovereignty, as parallel to State sovereignty (that is to say that the territorial State, pursuant to international law, can, to a certain extent

[84] See B Santos, *Towards a New Legal Common Sense: Law, Globalization, and Emancipation*, 2nd edn (London, LexisNexis Butterworths, 2002) 336–7.

[85] See D Held and A McGrew, 'The Great Globalization Debate: Introduction' in D Held and A McGrew (eds), *The Global Transformations Reader*, 2nd edn (Cambridge, Polity Press, 2003) 11–13.

[86] Anaya (n 22) 53. See also S Sur, 'The State between Fragmentation and Globalization' (1997) 8 *European Journal of International Law* 421.

> regulate, but not preclude, its exercise), has emerged in the context of the international legal order, giving rise to a provision of customary law binding States to grant a reasonable degree of sovereignty to indigenous peoples. Although such sovereignty is to be exercised within the realm of the supreme sovereignty of the territorial State, it actually produces the result of shifting some aspects of State sovereignty, providing indigenous peoples with some significant sovereign prerogatives that previously belonged to the State and that, at least in principle, may be opposed to the State itself under general international law.[87]

However, the belief in the arrival of global governance places too much faith in the capacity of global/transnational institutions to govern effectively. Political authority may have become diffused across a wide range of institutions but the consequent process of institutional fragmentation has created profound organisational problems which threaten to undermine the governmental authority that these institutions seek to exercise. As Schacter observes:

> We can foresee that in a new, even more globalized world, markets and 'networks' based on functional rationality may partly take the place of state law. We may also foresee that local groups and enclaves will carry more of the burdens of governance, and that some transnational associations dedicated to higher values will be given public responsibility. All of these … have a growing role in the political and legal processes of contemporary society, but each one is partial, serving some interests, some groups. They do not ensure what the territorial state promises—an arena in which all in the defined territory have access to common institutions and the equal protection of law.[88]

There remains a need for an impartial institutional structure that can organise and exercise social power. In this respect, it is clear that the international legal project outlined in this essay underestimates the capacity of the State to adjust to the current realities of the world.[89]

The Juridical State

The State remains the only institutional structure capable of organising collective political goods into a coherent (if momentary) package. Only the State, in its juridical form, can mediate comprehensively between the conflicting political programmes that lie beneath the surface of rights claims, giving effect to those rights which reflect the community's agreed

[87] See F Lenzerini, 'Sovereignty Revisited: International Law and Parallel Sovereignty of Indigenous Peoples' (2006) 42 *Texas International Law Journal* 155, 189.

[88] O Schacter, 'The Decline of the Nation-State and its Implications for International Law' (1997) 36 *Columbia Journal of Transnational Law* 7, 22–23.

[89] S Marks, *The Riddle of All Constitutions* (Oxford University Press, 2000) 79–80.

political imperatives.[90] The State, therefore, provides the arena in which political discourse can be conducted by all citizens, participating on the basis of equality and dignity.[91] In the juridical State, competing political visions of the good society are reconciled by the creation of laws that reflect the political consensus arrived at through discourse.[92] The law may reflect this ad hoc consensus imperfectly, but it does represent a community's agreed political imperatives at a particular moment in time and, in that respect, the juridical State reflects, and gives effect to, social reality.[93] This (democratic) political process ensures that the State cannot be reduced to particular (vested) interests regardless of its history: because it reflects socio-political values and practices it remains receptive to the outcomes of the national discourse.[94]

Nevertheless, this model of the juridical State is premised on an inclusive reading of national political processes and so it appears to hold little significance for those individuals and societal groups that have been excluded from political discourse. In such circumstances, propositional rights claims (rights as voice) provide a means of accessing political discourse and thus are immensely important to the democratic enterprise. It is this essay's contention that the rights contained in the Declaration are best seen as propositional claims. These 'rights' are not positive or nascent international legal rights; they are focussed political claims, which have been infused with considerable political legitimacy derived from the extent to which they have been sanctioned by the international community and as a result of the processes by which the Declaration was developed. The fact that the Declaration adopts the language of rights in order to articulate its powerful aims heightens the persuasiveness of its provisions. Nonetheless, by not endorsing these rights as (international) legal rights, the international community has stopped short of trying to impose the Declaration on affected national communities. Instead, it has adopted an international instrument that has the normative capacity to influence and guide political discourse while leaving the ultimate political decisions to the national communities concerned.

The Juridical State and Communicative Ethics

Institutionalised dialogue between indigenous representatives and States has been incredibly significant in the evolution of indigenous rights (both

[90] Koskenniemi (n 57) 28 (relying upon various works by Kelsen).
[91] Ibid, 29.
[92] Ibid.
[93] Ibid, 28–29.
[94] Ibid, 29.

domestically and internationally) and its value has been championed by sympathetic international lawyers and scholars.[95] Indeed, it has led to the bold claim that indigenous peoples have moved beyond the age of rights into the age of negotiation.[96] Habermas' work on communicative ethics offers a number of attractions in this context and his discourse principle supports Kelsen's juridical conception of the State as well. This principle holds that the correctness of a particular normative claim can only be determined through discourse: 'only those norms are valid [legitimate] to which all affected persons could agree as participants in a practical discourse'.[97] Accordingly, such discourse enables the rationality of assertions to be challenged through dialogue and thus it provides claimants with the opportunity to justify their claims and persuade other participants of their normative validity.[98] The discourse principle operates on the assumption that participants can reach genuine consensus about the normative content of a given claim and that, ultimately, the force of the better ethical argument will prevail.[99] Habermas recognises the inability of traditional values and practices to organise social reality in modern conditions.[100] This insight strengthens the juridical conception of the State because it endorses the view that only law is able to organise and convert a national community's shared norms into the State's administrative power. This is achieved via the operation of the discourse principle, which is rendered effective by the community's democratic practices.[101]

Habermas' work addresses one of the weaknesses in Kelsen's juridical conception of the State. This conception assumes that the law directly reflects political consensus within a given society. Habermas, however, is sensitive to the ambiguity in law's relationship with social reality. He distinguishes between law's instrumental role as a mechanism of order and social control (law as medium) and law's reflective function (law as institution). The former 'is relieved of the problem of justification and is

[95] See eg B Kingsbury, 'Reconstructing Self-Determination: A Relational Approach' in P Aikio and M Scheinin (eds), *Operationalising the Right of Indigenous Peoples to Self-Determination* (Turku, Institute for Human Rights, 2000) 19.

[96] See Gilbert (n 43) 301.

[97] Habermas quoted in A Barron, 'Foucault and the Law', in J Penner et al (eds), *Jurisprudence & Legal Theory: Commentary and Materials* (London, LexisNexis Butterworths, 2002) 955, 1081.

[98] Ibid, 1081–82.

[99] Ibid, 1082. For a brief discussion of the empirical challenges confronting the discourse principle, see Lloyd (n 47) 871–72.

[100] Ibid, 1083.

[101] Ibid. Habermas' conception of the discourse principle is not restricted to formal institutional processes. Further, it has also been applied to the international field; however, in this context, it only seems to make sense in restricted institutional settings such as the UN Security Council, which hardly satisfies Habermas' premise of discourse without domination. Nevertheless, see I Johnstone, 'Security Council Deliberations: The Power of the Better Argument' (2003) 14 *European Journal of International Law* 477.

only connection through formal correct procedures with the body of law whose substance requires legitimation'.[102] Legitimacy is acquired through law's institutional capacity to reflect a community's shared background norms which are filtered through the discourse principle (facilitated by democratic practices).[103] Habermas does not claim that law (and thus the juridical State) consistently and directly reflects political consensus; rather he stresses law's capacity for giving effect to such a consensus. This interpretation promotes law's emancipatory function while acknowledging that law itself remains morally neutral. In Habermas' discourse principle what matters is access and equality of participation rather than status-based rights since the outcomes of practical discourse cannot be pre-determined.[104]

At one level, Habermas's work on communicative ethics seems ideally suited to the indigenous cause as indigenous peoples have achieved much in supranational institutions by emphasising the moral force of their arguments for recognition and extensive substantive and procedural (participatory) rights.[105] However, as this essay has shown, the ethical foundations of indigenous rights claims are contestable and it is suggested that this is mirrored in States' widespread reluctance to recognise the Declaration's provisions as international law. Indigenous peoples have gained considerable voice and leverage in international institutions. However, profoundly difficult issues remain concerning the realisation of indigenous rights within national settings, and these cannot be resolved at the global level. Relations between dominant societal groups and indigenous peoples are complex, fraught and scarred by history. But in order to secure the kind of municipal legal rights that will protect and promote their societal identities in concrete ways, indigenous peoples need to (re)engage in democratic political processes within *their* States. Their claims must be open to challenge and subject to negotiation and mediation within the political community in which they are to be given effect in the same way as other political claims. Indigenous peoples do not have all the best ethical arguments and, as noted above, the law will not always reflect the best ethical position. In any event, indigenous peoples may question the value of democratic practices given their histories of oppression and exclusion at the hands of dominant settler societies, but there is no alternative. In any event, democracy can take many forms and the rights of minority groups can

[102] Barron (n 97) 1082 (quoting J Habermas, 'Law as Medium and Institution' in G Teubner (ed), *Dilemmas of Law in the Welfare State* (Berlin, de Gruyter, 1985) 203, 213.

[103] Ibid, 1083.

[104] Ibid, 1084.

[105] See eg P Thornberry, *Indigenous Peoples and Human Rights* (Manchester University Press, 2002) 8.

be protected through a wide range of constitutional and consociational arrangements.[106]

THE IMPLEMENTATION GAP

A major problem in the context of protecting indigenous identities is not the absence of law but the failure of States to implement it.[107] The 'implementation gap' manifests itself in many ways, including: the failure to enact secondary legislation to give effect to pertinent constitutional provisions or broad principles enunciated in primary legislation; bureaucratic inertia or ignorance; wilful disregard or corruption on the part of public officials; uncoordinated and conflicting government policies; inadequate monitoring procedures; and insufficient indigenous consultation/participation in public decision-making processes.[108] These are significant national problems that must be solved if indigenous rights are to become operational. However, they are problems of political will and institutional effectiveness rather than problems that can be resolved by recourse to law.

International law has catalysed the general struggle for indigenous rights and it manifests the capability to prompt States to comply with its growing provision on indigenous issues.[109] Nevertheless, international law cannot solve the implementation problems identified above. In fact, international law has to battle with its own implementation gap. It is typically not directly effective in municipal legal regimes, and customary international law is particularly difficult to enforce in domestic cases. Consequently, by interpreting the Declaration's provisions as international law, indigenous rights advocates are adding another tier of law that will confront (heightened) implementation challenges and thus it will be unable to deliver effective reform.

The Declaration, however, does seek to remove many of the obstacles to the implementation of indigenous rights, especially in relation to participation, consultation and the issue of monitoring the realisation of indigenous rights.[110] Accordingly, the Declaration is able to contribute to

[106] The Declaration includes measures aimed at enhancing indigenous participation in national democratic decision-making processes. See eg Arts 18 and 19 (n 64).

[107] *Indigenous Issues*, Report of the Special Rapporteur on the situation of human rights and fundamental freedoms of indigenous people (R Stavenhagen), UN Doc E/CN.4/2006/78, 16 February 2006, para 5.

[108] Ibid, paras 80–91.

[109] See the jurisprudence of the Human Rights Committee and CERD in this regard in Thornberry (n 105).

[110] Regarding the latter, Art 42 provides: 'The United Nations, its bodies, including the Permanent Forum on Indigenous Issues, and specialized agencies, including at the country level, and States shall promote respect for the full application of the provisions of this Declaration and follow up the effectiveness of this Declaration.'

the job of closing the implementation gap. But this is not because of its claimed international legal character; rather its value in this context stems from its political resonance: the Declaration offers a route to building genuine national consensus on indigenous issues. It can be used to engage political discourse on indigenous issues within national settings and can strengthen the political will needed not only to create paper rights but to ensure that such rights are implemented properly as well.

THE DECLARATION AS A NATIONAL LEGAL PROJECT

The aims of the First International Decade of the World's Indigenous People (1995–2004) were:[111]

1. the finalisation of the Declaration and its adoption by the UN General Assembly during the period of the Decade;
2. the establishment of a distinct UN body to bring coherence to indigenous issues from an institutional perspective;[112] and
3. to take appropriate steps to encourage States to incorporate emerging international standards [ie, the Declaration] into their municipal legal systems.

From the above, it appears that the UN expected the Declaration's provisions to feed back into national settings as States incorporated them into their municipal legal regimes. From an institutional perspective, the Declaration was not developed with a view to creating international law. Instead, it was forged as a model for the legal regulation of indigenous issues at the municipal level.[113]

Further, the Declaration's text does not endorse the view that States considered it to have a positive legal character. For example, the last paragraph of the preamble 'solemnly proclaims the [Declaration] as a standard of achievement to be pursued in a spirit of partnership and mutual respect'. This creates the impression that the Declaration is hortatory in character. Guyana's statement neatly captures the Declaration's essential quality: it is 'political in character [but] not without potential legal implications'. However, as noted above, by using the language of rights the UN/States have ensured that the rights contained in the Declaration are potentially legally relevant without imbuing them with international legal status. Accordingly, the international community has acknowledged

[111] GA Res 48/163 (1993) and Res 50/157 (1995).

[112] The Permanent Forum on Indigenous Issues was created in 2002.

[113] This interpretation is confirmed in Art 38, which provides: 'States, in consultation and cooperation with indigenous peoples, shall take the appropriate measures, including legislative measures, to achieve the ends of this Declaration.'

the legitimacy of these rights while leaving the issue of their legal status and effect to concerned States.

Moreover, Article 46(2) of the Declaration provides:

> In the exercise of the rights enunciated in the present Declaration, human rights and fundamental rights of all shall be respected. The exercise of the rights set forth in this Declaration shall be subject only to such limitations as are determined by law and in accordance with international human rights obligations. Any such limitations shall be non-discriminatory and *strictly necessary solely for the purpose of securing due recognition and respect for the rights and freedoms of others and for meeting the just and most compelling requirements of a democratic society.*[114]

Arguably, this paragraph significantly weakens the rights contained in the Declaration by rendering them explicitly contingent both on other rights and on the rights of others (if these rights are interpreted as unconditional international legal rights). However, even if indigenous peoples manage to acquire municipal legal rights that are broadly consistent with the rights contained in the Declaration, as noted in the previous section, the question of how those rights are implemented remains a difficult issue. As discussed above, legal rights are not automatically effective and this is true of all such rights. They must be interpreted, balanced and/or shaped before they can be applied. This interpretative process renders legal rights susceptible to being overridden or marginalised in favour of other more politically significant rights or interests.[115] Just like other rights-holders, indigenous peoples must enter the marketplace of rights where all rights must be resolved within the political framework of the State.[116]

Interestingly, in their statements, the opposing States connected the Declaration's provisions to their own municipal laws. For instances, Australia said that it would interpret the Declaration's provisions on land/resource rights in keeping with its domestic laws.[117] The representative of the Canadian government drew attention to the extent to which Canada had already recognised the land and treaty rights of indigenous peoples within its constitution and municipal laws.[118] Further, the representative of New Zealand observed that it 'had been implementing most of the standards in the Declaration for many years'.[119] Anaya and Wiessner harness domestic jurisprudence in such States as evidence of the development of customary international law.[120] However, rather than

[114] Emphasis added.
[115] See Koskenniemi (n 30).
[116] PG McHugh, *Aboriginal Societies and the Common Law: A History of Sovereignty, Status and Self-Determination* (Oxford University Press, 2005) 538.
[117] GA Meeting (n 7) 5.
[118] Ibid, 6.
[119] Ibid, 7.
[120] Anaya and Wiessner (n 14) 4–5.

trying to link the Declaration to international law, in the circumstances it is preferable to interpret these domestic developments as either instances of good practice that have informed the Declaration's provisions or evidence of the Declaration's suitability for national application. To this end, even Australia and New Zealand recognise the Declaration's value as a means of establishing domestic standards concerning indigenous rights and as a measure by which to judge State relations with indigenous peoples.[121]

CONCLUSION

International law has played an important role in catalysing indigenous rights, but it is only capable of making a limited contribution to their realisation and this must be appreciated by indigenous rights advocates. This essay suggests that engaging in the national political processes in order to secure legal rights and to effect change in political and administrative culture is a more legitimate (and productive) strategy than attempts to inflate the rights contained in the Declaration and to impose them on affected national communities from the outside via international law. Now that the Declaration has been endorsed by the international community it is time for indigenous representatives to (re)engage in the political processes in affected States to generate the political consensus needed to secure not only municipal legal rights required to protect and promote indigenous identities but also to create the political will to ensure that such legal rights are properly implemented.

[121] GA Meeting (n 7) 6–7.

Section C

Substantive Perspectives

11

The UN Declaration on the Rights of Indigenous Peoples: New Directions for Self-Determination and Participatory Rights?

HELEN QUANE*

INTRODUCTION

THE UN DECLARATION on the Rights of Indigenous Peoples ('the Declaration') breaks new ground not only in terms of the rights of indigenous peoples but also in terms of international human rights law more generally. Its adoption by the General Assembly in September 2007 represented the culmination of a remarkable drafting process involving both States and indigenous peoples. Notwithstanding assertions that the Declaration contains no new rights,[1] it is anything but a codification of existing international law. Even a cursory glance at its provisions reveals significant innovations, particularly in the area of self-determination and participatory rights. Some of these innovations are self-evident, others less so, and both types merit detailed scrutiny as they open up the possibility of new directions for the development of both categories of rights.

The recognition of a right to self-determination for indigenous peoples is undoubtedly one of the most striking features of the Declaration. The adoption of the Declaration by 143 States[2] represents the first explicit and

* I would like to thank the members of the International and European Law Research Group of Swansea University for their helpful and insightful comments.

[1] See eg UN Docs A/61/PV.107 (Thailand); A/61/PV.108 (Guatemala and Namibia); and E/CN.4/1996/84, para 24 (representatives of several indigenous organisations).

[2] The Declaration was adopted by a vote of 143 in favour, four against (Australia, Canada, New Zealand and the United States) and 11 abstentions. It should be noted that the Canadian House of Representatives subsequently adopted a motion calling on its Parliament and Government to 'fully implement the standards' in the Declaration: see Press Release, 'UN

widespread recognition by States that the right to self-determination is not confined to colonial peoples or peoples organised as States but applies to a further category of peoples: indigenous peoples. In this respect, the Declaration may represent one of the most significant stages in the development of the right to self-determination since decolonisation. At the same time, one has to acknowledge that while many States voted in favour of the Declaration, it is far from clear what exactly they were accepting in terms of a right to self-determination for indigenous peoples.

The right to self-determination is a notoriously elusive concept, and this was evident during the drafting of the relevant provisions of the Declaration. In international law, self-determination is defined as the right of a people to freely determine their political status, to freely pursue their economic, social and cultural development, and to freely dispose of their natural wealth and resources.[3] Although not explicitly spelled out in the relevant international instruments, there is a consensus that self-determination has both internal and external dimensions.[4] Internal self-determination generally refers to the right of a people to choose their own system of government and develop their own policies, while external self-determination generally refers to the right of a people to determine their international status, for example by becoming an independent State or integrating or associating with an existing State. Once an entity is recognised as a people, the traditional position in international law is that they enjoy the full range of options in respect of both internal and external self-determination.[5] To date, peoples organised as States and colonial peoples have been recognised as having a right to self-determination, but the position in respect of other groups is far less certain. The tendency in State practice has been to adopt a territorial concept of a people

Experts Welcome Canadian House of Commons' Endorsement of the Declaration on the Rights of Indigenous Peoples', issued on 18 April 2008 by three UN Special Rapporteurs, www.ohchr.org. Australia has also changed its position on the Declaration. On 3 April 2009, the Australian Government announced its formal support for the Declaration: see, http://www.hreoc.gov.ac/about/media/media_releases/2009/21_09.html.

[3] See common Art 1 of the International Covenant on Civil and Political Rights and the International Covenant on Economic, Social and Cultural Rights.

[4] See eg A Cassese, *Self-Determination of Peoples: A Legal Reappraisal* (Cambridge University Press, 1995); R Higgins, *Problems and Process* (Oxford, Clarendon Press, 1994) ch 7; P Alston, 'Peoples' Rights: Their Rise and Fall' in P Alston (ed), *Peoples' Rights* (Oxford University Press, 2001), although this distinction has been questioned by several writers, eg SJ Anaya, *Indigenous Peoples in International Law* (Oxford University Press, 1996) 81.

[5] State practice reveals that controversies may surround the recognition of an entity as a people but once the entity is explicitly recognised as a people it is difficult to find many examples of a limitation being imposed on the range of self-determination options available to them. Further, there are no explicit references to any limitations on the right in the relevant international instruments. This position may be evolving with the increasing recognition that groups within States may have a right to some form of self-determination: see further, n 9 below. It is open to question, however, whether this has crystallized into customary international law.

whereby a people is defined as the entire population of a territory irrespective of ethnic, linguistic and religious differences.[6] Admittedly, there is considerable support in the literature for defining a people in more expansive terms so that distinct groups within States could claim a limited form of self-determination to ensure that their identity and legitimate interests are protected within the structures of government.[7] Indeed, several eminent international lawyers would go so far as to argue that such groups also have a right to external self-determination whenever they are subject to gross oppression or a *carence de souveraineté*.[8] While these views are significant in terms of current debates about self-determination and were influential during the drafting of the Declaration, until very recently they found little explicit support in State practice,[9] and consequently one has to be cautious about their status as part of customary international law.

[6] See eg the discussion of State practice in H Quane, 'The United Nations and the Evolving Right to Self-Determination' (1998) 47 *International and Comparative Law Quarterly* 537; and 'Rights in Conflict? The Rationale and Implications of Using Human Rights in Conflict Prevention Strategies' (2007) 47 *Virginia Journal of International Law* 463, 472–75 and 477–81.

[7] See eg Cassese (n 4); J Crawford, *The Creation of States in International Law*, 2nd edn (Oxford University Press, 2006) 126–27 and 141–42; and H Hannum, 'The Right of Self-Determination in the Twenty-First Century' (1998) 55 *Wash & Lee Law Review* 773, 776–77. There is also limited judicial support for the concept: see *Opinion No 2*, Arbitration Commission of the European Community Conference on Yugoslavia, reprinted in (1992) 31 *International Law Materials* 1488; and the Canadian Supreme Court's decision in *Reference re Secession of Quebec* [1988] 2 SCR 217 (Can). However, one has to be cautious about the legal significance of these cases not least due to the judicial reasoning they employ: see further Quane 2007 (n 6) 481–83.

[8] See eg Cassese (n 4) 118–20; and Crawford (n 7) 126–27. Further support for this form of self-determination can be found in the Separate Opinions of Judges A A Cancado Trindade and Yusuf to the ICJ's Advisory Opinion on the 'Accordance with International Law of the Unilateral Declaration of Independence By the Provisional Institutions of Self-Government of Kosovo': available at http://www.icj-cij.org/docket/index.php?p1=3&p2=4&k=21&case=141&code=kos&p3=1. While the Court did not consider it necessary to resolve the self-determination question, it did observe that this was a 'subject on which radically different views were expressed by those taking part in the proceedings and expressing a position on the question': see paras 82–83 of the Advisory Opinion. The absence of a consensus on this issue together with the paucity of State practice tends to undermine suggestions that such a right currently exists in customary international law.

[9] Excluding the adoption of the Declaration, State practice suggests a reluctance to recognize explicitly even a limited right to self-determination for groups within territorial borders. See eg the review undertaken by the present author of the State reports submitted by 118 States under Art 40 ICCPR on how they comply with the right to self-determination in the Covenant: Quane 2007 (n 6) 477–83. This position may be evolving. In 2009, 36 States submitted written statements during the course of the Advisory proceedings in the Kosovo case: see, http://www.icj-cij.org/docket/index.php?p1=3&p2=4&k=21&case=141&code=kos&p3=1. Of the States that addressed the issue of self-determination, approximately 12 States seemed to accept a right to some form of self-determination for groups within States: see Written Statements (April) of Estonia, Latvia, Finland, Germany, Netherlands, Poland, Slovenia, Denmark, Switzerland, Ireland and Written Statements (July) of Albania, Bolivia: ibid. At the same time, the geographically limited nature of the State practice, the recognition by some of these States that the 'implications of the right of self-determination are not fully developed in international practice' (see, eg, Denmark's Written Statement) and the

Given the existing contours of the right, one can understand its significance for indigenous peoples and why the question of its inclusion proved so contentious that it took over 20 years to draft the Declaration. For indigenous peoples, self-determination means the right to control their own destiny and preserve their way of life and identity. The right to freely dispose of their wealth and natural resources is an integral element of this right and is of vital significance to indigenous peoples given the importance of their ancestral lands and natural resources to preserving their way of life. The collective nature of the right is also significant. As the right is conferred on and exercised by an indigenous people as a group rather than individuals belonging to the group, it can help to preserve the communal dimension of indigenous identity. At the same time, these very aspects of the right help to explain why States were hesitant about including it in the Declaration, at least without some form of qualification or clarification. One of their key concerns was whether recognition of the right would impede the State's ability to govern in the interests of the entire population, and in particular its ability to exploit natural resources as part of national development plans. By far the central concern, however, was whether recognition of a right to self-determination for indigenous peoples would enable them to exercise the full range of self-determination options, including the right to secede from the State. Clearly stemming from the traditional interpretation of self-determination in international law, the question arises whether this interpretation accurately reflects the right to self-determination as set out in the Declaration.

The present chapter explores this and several related questions. It does so primarily in the light of the text of the Declaration, its drafting history and the statements made at the time it was adopted in the General Assembly. The emphasis throughout is on these original sources rather than the considerable body of literature that exists on indigenous peoples' right to self-determination.[10] The relationship between the right to self-determination in the Declaration and the right to self-determination in customary international law is analysed at the outset, followed by an examination of the meaning

divergence of opinion on the issue (see n 8 above) suggest that a cautious approach should be adopted to its significance in terms of the formation of general international law.

[10] See eg Anaya (n 4) chs 3 and 4; E-I Daes, 'The Concepts of Self-Determination and Autonomy of Indigenous Peoples in the Draft United Nations Declaration on the Rights of Indigenous Peoples' (2001–02) 14 *St Thomas Law Review* 259; A Xanthaki, *Indigenous Rights and United Nations Standards* (Cambridge University Press, 2007); P Aikio and M Scheinin (eds), *Operationalizing the Right of Indigenous Peoples to Self-Determination* (Turku/Abo, Institute for Human Rights, Abo Akademi University, 2000); and CE Foster, 'Articulating Self-Determination in the Draft Declaration on the Rights of Indigenous Peoples' (2001) 12 *European Journal of International Law* 141.

of self-determination in the Declaration and an exploration of its significance for indigenous peoples and for international human rights law generally. Initially, the emphasis is on those provisions that refer explicitly to self-determination. However, the chapter does not confine its analysis to these provisions. To do so would limit unnecessarily the scope of the enquiry and the possible insights it might provide. Instead, it broadens out the analysis to explore the interplay between the provisions explicitly linked to self-determination and those concerning the participatory rights of indigenous peoples.

Arguably, it is the relationship between self-determination and participation that is one of the more interesting and innovative aspects of the Declaration. The relationship between the two is undoubtedly a complex one. This is evident in the literature, where participation is described variously as a composite element or consequence of the right to self-determination for indigenous peoples,[11] an instrumental means of attaining it,[12] or a means to ensure its ongoing exercise.[13] This ambiguity was also evident during the drafting of the Declaration in the comments of several participants as well as the coupling and ultimate decoupling of some of the provisions on participation from those on self-determination.[14] Indeed, it is difficult to discern any clear consensus on the interplay between the two, and for this reason the present chapter develops a typology of the various ways in which the provisions on participation may be viewed.

The typology developed in this chapter suggests that the provisions on participation may be characterised as a form of self-determination or as an expansion of the right to participate in public life. The manner in which the provisions are classified can have significant implications of a doctrinal nature, raising questions about the nature and scope of both types of rights suggesting new directions or pathways for their possible development in the future. It also suggests that the manner in which one classifies these provisions can have important practical consequences not only for how they are implemented but also, perhaps, for their very prospects of implementation. Above all, the typology serves to highlight the complex and multidimensional character of the Declaration.

[11] See eg Foster (n 10) 148, 151, 153–54.

[12] See eg ME Turpel, 'Indigenous Peoples' Rights of Political Participation and Self-Determination: Recent International Legal Developments and the Continuing Struggle for Recognition' (1992) 25 *Cornell International Law Journal* 579, 593.

[13] See eg Higgins (n 4) 121, albeit in the context of a general discussion of self-determination.

[14] See further the discussion accompanying nn 62–64 below.

SELF-DETERMINATION IN THE DECLARATION: A NEW RIGHT FOR INDIGENOUS PEOPLES OR THE CODIFICATION OF AN EXISTING RIGHT IN INTERNATIONAL LAW?

While the issue of self-determination proved to be a major stumbling block during the drafting of the Declaration,[15] it was taken as given that its inclusion was necessary to address the legitimate concerns of indigenous peoples.[16] The possibility of omitting references to self-determination from the final draft of the Declaration was never broached during the later stages of the negotiations,[17] not even by those States that voted against the Declaration in the General Assembly.[18] Instead, discussions always centred on the nature and scope of the right for indigenous peoples. Ultimately, Article 3 of the Declaration asserts in unequivocal terms that:

> Indigenous Peoples have the right to self-determination. By virtue of that right they freely determine their political status and freely pursue their economic, social and cultural development.

In addition, Article 4 provides that:

> Indigenous Peoples, in exercising their right to self-determination, have the right to autonomy or self-government in matters relating to their internal and local affairs, as well as ways and means for financing their autonomous functions.

Notwithstanding the clarity of the language used in these articles, a host of questions are left unanswered. The first and most immediate question

[15] Concern was expressed with regard to the provisions on self-determination throughout the drafting process. As late as July 2007, it was noted that seven States (Australia, Canada, Colombia, Guyana, New Zealand, the Russian Federation and Suriname) had expressed concern about several issues in the draft declaration, including the provisions on self-determination, and stated that action on the draft declaration without any adjustments to address these concerns 'might result in wide-ranging polarization'; see Report to the President of the General Assembly on the Consultations on the Draft Declaration on the Rights of Indigenous Peoples, 13 July 2007, and Supplement to the Report of the Facilitator on the Draft Declaration on the Rights of Indigenous Peoples, 20 July 2007, www.un.org/ga/president/61/follow-up/indigenous.shtml. Notwithstanding this, the draft declaration was adopted by the General Assembly without any textual changes.

[16] See eg UN Doc E/CN.4/2000/84, paras 73 (Guatemala), 50 (Canada), 77 (France) and 84 (Chairperson-Rapporteur); Report of the International Workshop on the Draft UN Declaration on the Rights of Indigenous Peoples, Patzcuaro, Michoacan, Mexico, 26–30 September 2005, E/CN.4/2005/WG.15/CRP.1, at p 4.

[17] There is no record of any attempt to omit references to the right during the negotiations within the Working Group established in accordance with Commission on Human Rights Resolution 1995/32 of 3 March 1995. However, there were some attempts to exclude references to self-determination during the earlier discussions of the draft declaration in the UN Working Group on Indigenous Populations: see K Myntti, 'The Right of Indigenous Peoples to Self-Determination and Effective Participation' in Aikio and Scheinin (n 10) 85, 87–88.

[18] Although Australia expressed its 'dissatisfaction' with the references to self-determination throughout the drafting process: see UN Docs E/CN.4/2000/84, para 62; E/CN.4/2001/85, para 89; and A/61/PV.107. However, it now supports the Declaration: see n 2 above.

concerns the relationship between the right to self-determination in the Declaration and the right to self-determination in customary international law. If the former is simply a codification of the latter, then indigenous peoples have a legal right to self-determination and, significantly, one that is not subject to limitation.[19] This would have far-reaching implications, opening up the possibility of indigenous peoples seceding from existing States. The drafting of the Declaration might suggest some support for this interpretation, with its use of language almost identical to that used in common Article 1 on self-determination in the International Covenant on Economic, Social and Cultural Rights and the International Covenant on Civil and Political Rights (ICCPR).[20] Further support for this interpretation may be derived from the preamble, which acknowledges that the UN Charter, the International Covenants and the Vienna Declaration and Programme of Action affirm the fundamental importance of the right to self-determination of all peoples,[21] and that nothing in the Declaration may be used to deny any people their right to self-determination exercised in conformity with international law.[22] At the same time, one cannot overlook the significance of Article 46(1). It provides that 'Nothing in this Declaration may be interpreted as implying for any State, *people*, group or person any right to engage in any activity or to perform any act contrary to the Charter of the United Nations or construed as authorizing or encouraging any action which would dismember or impair, totally or in part, the territorial integrity or political unity of sovereign and independent States'.[23] At the very least, this provision suggests that the right to self-determination in the Declaration may be restricted to a form of internal self-determination which does not threaten the territorial integrity or political unity of existing States.

It is clear from the drafting history that indigenous peoples and States were divided on the nature and extent of the right to self-determination in the Declaration. Indigenous peoples took the view that they had a

[19] See above, n 5.

[20] Art 3 of the Declaration seems to have been based on the wording of common Art 1 of the two Covenants: see UN Doc E/CN.4/Sub.2/1994/2, para 30. Furthermore, some of the Concluding Observations and/or Recommendations of a number of the UN human rights treaty monitoring bodies suggest that common Art 1 already applies to indigenous peoples or is at least relevant to them: see UN Docs CCPR/C/CAN/CA/5 (Human Rights Committee (HRC), 2006) paras 8, 9; A/55/40, Vol I (HRC, 2000) para 507; CCPR/CO/82/FIN (HRC, 2004) para 17; E/C.12/1/Add.94 (Committee on Economic, Social and Cultural Rights (CESCR), 2003) paras 11, 39; CCPR/C/CHL/CO/5 (HRC, 2007) para 19; E/CN.4/2006/78/Add.3 (SR Indigenous, 2006) paras 80, 84, 102; CCPR/CO/74/SWE (HRC, 2002) para 15; CCPR/C/USA/CO/3 (HRC, 2006) para 37; concerning the reports of Canada, Australia, Finland, the Russian Federation, Chile, New Zealand, Sweden, and the United States respectively.

[21] Preambular para 17.

[22] Preambular para 18.

[23] Emphasis added.

right to self-determination under international law and that this right, which is not subject to limitation, is reflected in the final text of the Declaration.[24] Although in reality most indigenous peoples did not want to secede,[25] they were unwilling to accept any restrictions on their right to self-determination as a matter of principle. As no restrictions had been imposed on the right in the past, they argued that it would be discriminatory to impose them now.[26] States, for their part, were unwilling to countenance even a symbolic recognition of an unqualified right to self-determination given the potential implications for their territorial integrity and political unity. The general consensus among States seems to have been that while they were prepared to accept a right to self-determination for indigenous peoples, the right could not impair the territorial integrity of existing States.[27]

Ultimately Article 3 of the Declaration asserts in unequivocal terms that indigenous peoples have a right to self-determination. This, combined with the absence of any explicit reference to restrictions on the right, met the wishes of indigenous peoples. Nevertheless, this represents only one part of the overall picture. It is clear from the drafting history that a 'package deal approach' was adopted on the issue of self-determination.[28] It was in this context that numerous proposals imposing restrictions on the right[29] were dropped in favour of the use of more positive language stressing the benefits of cooperation between States and indigenous peoples in implementing the Declaration in a spirit of good faith.[30] It was also stressed that the right to self-determination in Article 3 had to be interpreted in the light of the other provisions,[31]

[24] See eg UN Docs E/CN.4/2003/92, para 24; E/CN.4/2001/85, paras 37, 39; and E/CN.4/2000/84, paras 57, 58.

[25] See eg UN Docs E/CN.4/1996/ 84, para 47; E/CN.4/1997/102, paras 323, 328; E/CN.4/1998/106, para 44(g); E/CN.4/1999/82, paras 21, 31, 33, 70; E/CN.4/2000/84, paras 68, 69, 45; E/CN.4/2001/85, para 63; and E/CN.4/2004/81, para 73.

[26] See eg UN Docs E/CN.4/2001/85, paras 71, 72, 74, 79, 84; E/CN.4/1996/84, paras 3, 47; and E/CN.4/1997/102, paras 326, 331, 342.

[27] See eg UN Docs E/CN.4/1998/106, para 44; E/CN.4/1997/102, paras 42 (Chile), 312 (Colombia), 314 (Philippines), 332 (Canada), 340 (Argentina); E/CN.4/1999/82, para 40 (United States); E/CN.4/2000/84, paras 53 (Brazil), 56 (Ecuador), 61 (Russian Federation), 63 (Argentina), 64 (Switzerland), 70 (Finland), 74 (Mexico), 80 (Venezuela), 81 (Norway); E/CN.4/2001/85, paras 70 (Cuba), 83 (Spain); E/CN.4/2003/92, para 11 (Guatemala); E/CN.4/2003/92, para 17 (New Zealand proposal); A/61/PV.107 (Argentina, Japan, Norway, Jordan, Mexico, Sweden, Thailand, Suriname); and A/61/PV.108 (Iran, Myanmar, Namibia, Nepal, Paraguay, Turkey, India, Philippines, Egypt, France, Guatemala).

[28] See eg UN Docs E/CN.4/2005/89, para 43; and A/61/PV.107 (Argentina).

[29] See eg UN Docs E/CN.4/2003/92, Annex (New Zealand proposal concerning Art 3); and E/CN.4/2006/79, Annex (summary of proposals concerning Art 3 and draft Art 31 which subsequently became Art 4).

[30] See eg preambular paras 18 and 24. See also UN Doc E/CN.4/2006/79; and Report of the International Workshop (n 16) 4.

[31] See eg UN Docs E/CN.4/2005/89, para 43; and E/CN.4/2006/79, para 20.

notably Article 46(1) which upholds the territorial integrity and political unity of States.[32] In this way, the Declaration addresses State concerns and effectively bridges the gap between States and indigenous peoples, allowing each to take refuge in the interpretation that best reflects their interests. At the same time, interpreting the Declaration in context and in the light of the drafting history makes it difficult to contend that it endorses anything but a limited right to internal self-determination for indigenous peoples.

By attaching limitations to the right, the Declaration effectively signals a break with the right to self-determination as traditionally understood in international law. This raises the question of how the right to self-determination in the Declaration relates to the existing right in international law. Few States appear to have given this issue much consideration, or at any rate only a small number were prepared to address the issue openly. In view of this, one has to be cautious about arriving at any definitive conclusions on this issue. The drafting history and the statements made at the time the Declaration was adopted suggest at least two possible interpretations.

The first is that the right to self-determination in the Declaration represents a development of the internal dimension to self-determination in international law. This aspect of self-determination, largely ignored during the decolonisation period, has evolved in the post-Cold War period to the point where it is possible to speak of a legal right to internal self-determination.[33] At present, the actual content of the right is formulated in quite general terms as the right of a people to choose its own system of government and determine its own political, social and economic policies.[34] There is some evidence to suggest that the right requires a representative and non-discriminatory system of government. On the basis of current State practice, it seems that this requirement is met whenever the government is elected in free and fair elections by universal suffrage and in a secret ballot.[35] Consequently, the right as currently formulated seems to endorse formal rather than substantive notions of 'representative and non-discriminatory' government. To this extent, it is arguably of limited use in addressing the legitimate concerns of indigenous peoples, as 'historical and contemporary marginalization and the often small numbers in society of indigenous peoples [means] that the normal operation of a democratic system of

[32] See eg UN Docs A/61/PV.107 (Chile); and E/CN.4/2005/WG.15/CRP.6. See also the tendency to group Arts 3 and 45 (subsequently Art 46) together during the drafting of the Declaration: UN Doc E/CN.4/2005/89, para 19.

[33] See further Quane 2007 (n 6) 488–91, and Annex, paras A–C.

[34] Ibid.

[35] Ibid.

government [does] not necessarily allow for adequate expression of indigenous perspectives'.[36]

Viewed in this light, the concept of self-determination in the Declaration can be seen as a development of the existing right to internal self-determination, one that can help make it more responsive to the needs and interests of indigenous peoples. This is evident especially in Article 4 of the Declaration with its references to autonomy and self-government as forms of indigenous self-determination. It goes beyond the existing, rather minimalist concept of internal self-determination and suggests that the right can be developed in a more flexible manner to meet the legitimate concerns of indigenous peoples. For some States at least, it seems that this development may not be confined in its application to indigenous peoples, but reflects the evolution of self-determination as an 'ongoing right which was expanding to include the concept of an internal right for *groups* living within existing States … which respected the territorial and political integrity of the State'.[37] This suggests that the Declaration may embody a variable or context-dependent right to self-determination that alters depending on the identity and legitimate aspirations of the people invoking it.

The second interpretation is a variation on the first. It also adheres to the view that the right of indigenous peoples to self-determination is limited to a form of internal self-determination. The principal difference, however, is that it does not view the right as a development of the existing right in international law but as a completely new right that is confined in its application to indigenous peoples. This suggests that there are different rights to self-determination operating in parallel to one another but also effectively insulated from one another. Undoubtedly motivated by a desire to limit the possible implications of the Declaration, several States expressly endorsed this interpretation of self-determination in the Declaration.[38] Viewed from this perspective, the Declaration's provisions on self-determination are innovative not only in terms of the rights of indigenous peoples but also in terms of international human rights

[36] UN Doc E/CN.4/1997/102, para 203 (the observer for the Aboriginal and Torres Strait Islander Commission). For further discussion of the concept of formal and substantive non-discrimination, see the discussion accompanying nn 95–101 below.

[37] UN Doc E/CN.4/1997/102, para 332 (Canada) (emphasis added). It is also evident in some of the views expressed during the International Workshop on the Draft UN Declaration on the Rights of Indigenous Peoples (n 16) 3–4.

[38] See UN Docs E/CN.4/2000/84, para 56, where Ecuador stated that the concept of self-determination in the draft declaration was 'not equivalent to the principle of international self-determination'; and A/61/PV.107, where the United Kingdom referred to Art 3 of the Declaration as 'promoting the development of a new and distinct right of self-determination specific to Indigenous Peoples' 'separate and different' from the right in common Art 1 of the International Covenants. A similar approach was adopted by Colombia at the regional level in the context of the Draft American Declaration on the Rights of Indigenous Peoples: see OAS Doc OEA/Ser.K/XVI, GT/DADIN/doc.276/06, 4 December 2006, 7.

law more generally by asserting the existence of distinct categories of self-determination rights.

Whichever interpretation is adopted, it seems that the Declaration represents an important stage in the development of the right to self-determination. At a minimum, if the second interpretation is adopted, the Declaration would appear to contribute to the development of a new right to internal self-determination.[39] If it constitutes a legal right, it would be significant in expanding the existing rights of indigenous peoples. Also, by introducing different categories of self-determination rights, it would represent an innovation in terms of the right to self-determination in international law and suggest new directions and possibilities for the right. Whether these new directions would be confined to indigenous peoples is open to question. At the very least, the Declaration may have a demonstration effect. If the Declaration proves to be a success, it may lessen State opposition to developing a more flexible approach to self-determination for other groups within States. In this regard, the full significance of the Declaration may only become apparent over time, in the light of subsequent State practice.

THE MEANING OF SELF-DETERMINATION IN THE DECLARATION

The meaning of the right to self-determination in international law is notoriously difficult to pin down, and the position is no different in the Declaration. Although the right is defined as the right of a people to 'freely determine their political status and freely pursue their economic, social and cultural development', there is little if any guidance as to what this means in actual practice. Much of the guidance that does exist derives largely from State practice during the decolonisation period, where self-determination invariably meant independence for the people in question. It is clear that a similar meaning does not attach to the right in the Declaration. By ruling out any action that would impair the territorial integrity of States, the Declaration effectively precludes a right to external self-determination for indigenous peoples and in its place asserts a more limited right to internal self-determination. The exact parameters of this more limited right, however, are far from certain.

[39] See also developments at the regional level: Art III of the Draft American Declaration on the Rights of Indigenous Peoples under consideration within the Organization of American States provides that '*Within the States,* the right to self-determination of the indigenous peoples is to be recognized, pursuant to which they can define their forms of organization and promote their economic, social and cultural development'. OAS Doc OEA/Ser.K/XVI, GT/DADIN/doc.301/07, 27 April 2007 (emphasis added).

Some guidance can be gleaned from the rationale underlying its inclusion in the Declaration. For some participants, self-determination was included to address the 'legitimate aspirations of Indigenous Peoples to enjoy more direct and meaningful participation in decision-making and political processes and greater autonomy over their own affairs'.[40] This is consistent with the idea of developing a new relationship between indigenous peoples and States based on a sense of partnership, which is evident in the drafting history as well as the preamble to the Declaration.[41] Indeed, one commentator who was associated with the drafting process suggested that the inclusion of self-determination would facilitate a form of 'belated state-building' whereby distinct peoples are incorporated into the fabric of the State on agreed terms.[42]

For some States, it seems that this underlying objective could be achieved through the granting of internal autonomy or self-government to indigenous peoples.[43] As to the meaning of internal autonomy or self-government, there was some guidance in the earlier drafts of the Declaration. Draft Article 31, which subsequently became Article 4 of the Declaration, provided that:

> Indigenous Peoples, as a specific form of exercising their right to self-determination, have the right to autonomy or self-government in matters relating to their internal and local affairs, including culture, religion, education, information, media, health, housing, employment, social welfare, economic activities, land and resources management, environment and entry by non-members, as well as ways and means for financing these autonomous functions.

This listing of the areas in which autonomy or self-government would apply was instructive but proved to be too controversial.[44] States tended to be wary of any listing which might fail to take account of variations in the circumstances of different indigenous peoples[45] and which might impose excessive restrictions on a State's management of natural resources and ability to govern in the interests of the entire population. Indigenous peoples had mixed views on draft Article 31, finding the explicit listing useful in helping to prevent States from reneging on their international commitments while at the same time wary of any perceived attempts to use the provision to limit their right to self-determination.[46] Ultimately,

[40] UN Doc E/CN.4/2000/84, para 62 (Australia).

[41] See preambular para 25; and Report of the International Workshop (n 16) 5.

[42] UN Docs E/CN.4/Sub.2/1993/26/Add.1, paras 26, 25, 29 (Erica-Irene Daes); and Report of the International Workshop (n 16) 3.

[43] See eg UN Docs E/CN.4/2000/84, paras 64 (Switzerland), 70 (Finland); E/CN.4/2001/85, para 64 (Mexico); E/CN.4/2003/92, para 11 (Guatemala); and A/61/PV.108 (India).

[44] See eg UN Doc E/CN.4/2004/81, paras 79–83.

[45] See eg UN Docs E/CN.4/1997/102, para 334 (Brazil); and A/61/PV.108 (Myanmar).

[46] See eg UN Docs E/CN.4/2003/92, para 25; and E/CN.4/2004/81, paras 83, 81, 80.

Article 4 omits any reference to the areas in which internal autonomy or self-government would apply, which suggests that a flexible and non-prescriptive approach should be adopted. Indeed, when one interprets this provision in context,[47] it seems that the meaning of self-government or internal autonomy is to be worked out at the national level through a process of negotiation between States and indigenous peoples.[48]

The idea that the right to self-determination should be implemented through a process of negotiation is hardly surprising and unquestionably pragmatic. Yet it does raise some interesting questions about the nature of the right in the Declaration and in international law more generally. In international law, the right has traditionally been formulated in absolute terms. According to this formulation, the will of the people is paramount and this means that they can freely determine their system of government as well as their economic, social and cultural development. The right to self-determination in the Declaration departs from this view of self-determination. By requiring negotiations to implement the provisions on self-determination, it suggests that the will of indigenous peoples is not paramount even if they are recognised as having a right to self-determination. In this respect, the Declaration places a further limit on their right to self-determination, one that suggests that internal self-determination is restricted to what can be agreed between indigenous peoples and the States in which they reside.

Beyond these rather general principles, the Declaration provides little explicit guidance on the meaning of self-determination for indigenous peoples. Nevertheless, by exploring some of the questions implicitly posed by the Declaration it may be possible to arrive at a more concrete understanding of the concept and its application. One of the most important questions concerns the relationship between the right to self-determination and the provisions on the right to participate in public life. Although these provisions do not refer explicitly to self-determination, the drafting history shows that for several States self-determination meant the right of indigenous peoples to participate fully in decisions affecting them.[49] Some States seemed to take the view that

[47] Preambular para 25 states that the Declaration is 'to be pursued in a spirit of partnership and mutual respect' while preambular para 24 recognises that the 'situation of indigenous peoples varies from region to region and from country to country and that the significance of national and regional particularities and various historical and cultural backgrounds should be taken into consideration'.

[48] This was also the view taken by several States: see, eg UN Docs E/CN.4/1996/102, para 332 (Canada); and E/CN.4/2001/85, para 62 (France). See also the references to 'negotiations' in the proposals concerning draft Art 31 (subsequently Art 4): UN Docs E/CN.4/2005/89/Add.2; E/CN.4/2006/79, Annex I; E/CN.4/2004/81, p 28; and E/CN.4/2003/92, p 18.

[49] See UN Docs E/CN.4/2000/84, paras 50 (Canada), 53 (Brazil), 81 (Norway); and E/CN.4/2001/85, para 90 (Russian Federation).

several of these provisions on participation formed part of the substance of the right to self-determination in the Declaration.[50] Indeed, a proposal by Australia, New Zealand and the United States would have defined the right to self-determination of indigenous peoples as the right '*to freely participate in*' determining their political status.[51] Arguably, it is this relationship between the provisions on participatory rights and the provisions on self-determination that highlights some of the truly innovative aspects of the Declaration.

THE RELATIONSHIP BETWEEN THE RIGHT TO SELF-DETERMINATION AND THE RIGHT TO PARTICIPATE IN PUBLIC LIFE AS SET OUT IN THE DECLARATION

The Declaration's provisions on participation are extensive in terms of both their number and scope. Just under a quarter of the provisions in the Declaration are concerned with participation.[52] As many extend beyond the scope of the existing right to participate in public life, the question arises as to how these provisions should be classified. Do they represent an expansion of the right to participate in public life as set out, for example, in Article 25 of the International Covenant on Civil and Political Rights?[53] Alternatively, are they a practical working out of the internal dimension to self-determination? The way in which these provisions are classified may suggest new directions for self-determination and participatory rights affecting not only the scope of these rights but also their very nature as individual or collective rights. On a practical level, it may also affect their prospects of implementation at the national level as

[50] See eg UN Doc A/61/PV.107 (Norway and Sweden).

[51] UN Doc E/CN.4/2006/79, Annex I to the Report of the Working Group (emphasis added). See also the proposals regarding the original Art 23: UN Doc E/CN.4/2004/81, p 24.

[52] See Arts 5, 13(2), 18, 19, 20(1), 23, 27, 30(2), 32, 36 and 38.

[53] Art 25 ICCPR provides:

Every citizen shall have the right and the opportunity, without any of the distinctions mentioned in Article 2 and without unreasonable restrictions:

(a) To take part in the conduct of public affairs, directly or through freely chosen representatives;
(b) To vote and to be elected at genuine periodic elections which shall be by universal and equal suffrage and which shall be held by secret ballot, guaranteeing the free expression of the will of the electors;
(c) To have access, on general terms of equality, to public service in his country.

According to the Human Rights Committee, the conduct of public affairs covers 'all aspects of public administration, and the formulation and implementation of policy at international, national, regional and local levels'; see General Comment XXV, The Right to Participate in Public Affairs, Voting and the Right of Equal Access to Public Service (Art 25), 12 July 1996, UN Doc CCPR/C/21/Rev.1/Add.7, para 5.

States may find it more palatable to implement the provisions if they are regarded as part of the right to effective participation rather than as part of the more politically sensitive right to self-determination.

Arguably, the Declaration's provisions on participation fall into four broad categories. The first category[54] is the least innovative: it simply reaffirms the right to participate fully in the political, economic, social and cultural life of the State, a right that is already recognised in numerous international human rights instruments.[55] The remaining categories go beyond the existing parameters of this right. The second category does so by recognising the right of indigenous peoples to maintain and develop their distinct political, legal, economic, social and cultural systems and institutions.[56] As a form of autonomy, it may be regarded as an expression of the right to self-determination but it may also be seen as a way of increasing participation in public life in much the same way as devolution or other autonomy arrangements have tried to do so in non-indigenous contexts.[57] The provisions in category three may reinforce this perception as they seem to envisage the indigenous institutions acting as a nexus between States and indigenous peoples, helping to facilitate the latter's more effective participation in public life as well as enabling them to exercise more effective control over their own affairs. For example, Article 19 stipulates that States shall consult with indigenous peoples 'through their own representative institutions' in order to obtain their free, prior and informed consent before adopting and implementing legislative or administrative measures that may affect them.[58] Article 18 recognises the right of indigenous peoples to participate in decision-making in matters which would affect their rights 'through representatives chosen by themselves in accordance with their own procedures.'[59] The formulation of these provisions suggests that they are genuinely groundbreaking. They suggest that new structures or modalities of participation are required by virtue of international human rights standards rather than, as is the current position, being dependent on the discretion of the State concerned. This is also evident in the fourth category of provisions, which provides that States shall establish 'in conjunction with indigenous peoples concerned' a 'fair, independent, impartial, open and transparent process'

[54] 54 See, Arts 5 and 41.

[55] See ICCPR, Art 25; American Convention on Human Rights, Art 23; African Charter on Human and Peoples' Rights, Art 13; and the European Convention on Human Rights, Protocol 1, Art 3.

[56] See Arts 5, 20 and 18.

[57] See eg the UK Government's White Paper, *A Voice for Wales* (1997) (Cm 3718), explaining the reasons for proposing devolution for Wales.

[58] See also Arts 30(2), 32(2), 23. On consultation more generally, see Arts 36(2) and 38.

[59] See also Arts 13(2), 27 and 41 concerning the participation of indigenous peoples with regard to issues affecting them.

to give due recognition to indigenous peoples' laws, customs and land tenure systems and to recognise and adjudicate the rights of indigenous peoples pertaining to their lands, territories and resources.[60] What is most striking about this category is that it envisages not only the participation of indigenous peoples in this new decision-making process but also their right to participate in its very creation.

Given the innovative nature of many of these provisions, one needs to consider their classification in terms of the existing rights to self-determination and participation. A useful starting point is the jurisprudence of the UN Human Rights Committee, a treaty body that monitors State compliance with the International Covenant on Civil and Political Rights. This Committee has consistently distinguished between the right to self-determination in Article 1 and the right to participate in public life in Article 25 of the Covenant. According to the Committee, the former determines the modalities of participation while the latter guarantees the right to participate in them without discrimination.[61] This perception of the relationship between these rights is widely accepted but it is one that may be called into question by the Declaration.

The drafting of the Declaration reveals that there was ambiguity as to the precise nature of the relationship between the provisions on participation and the right to self-determination. Several States, for example, noted a 'close relationship' between the two[62] while others went further and regarded the provisions as 'a form of realization' of the right to self-determination for indigenous peoples.[63] For a time, some of the provisions were organised thematically as relating to the right to self-determination but were subsequently decoupled from the right.[64] This raises the question of how the provisions on participation should be classified and what are the implications that flow from any such classification.

The present section develops a typology of three possible classifications of the provisions. It begins by classifying them as a form of self-determination. However, this raises the question of whose right to

[60] Art 27.

[61] See General Comment XXV (n 53) paras 2, 5; and *Mikmaq People v Canada*, Communication No 205/1986, para 5.4.

[62] See UN Docs E/CN.4/1997/102, paras 217 (Australia), 231 (Canada); and E/CN.4/2006/79, para 10(a).

[63] See eg UN Doc A/61/PV.107 (Sweden).

[64] A Norwegian proposal to re-cluster 'Articles 3, 31, 19–21, 30 and 36 of the draft declaration dealing with self-determination and autonomy' was 'welcomed' by government delegations and several indigenous peoples' representatives, and discussions on the right to self-determination proceeded on the basis of this re-clustering, at least for a time: see UN Docs E/CN.4/2003/92, paras 19–20; and E/CN.4/2004/81, para 67. This re-clustering was subsequently changed and the provisions on participatory rights were dropped from the organisation of work concerning self-determination: see UN Doc E/CN.4/2005/WG.15/CRP.6, para 12.

self-determination they embody: that of the entire population of the State or of indigenous peoples? The drafting history provides support for both interpretations. Each one is taken in turn, allowing a more in-depth exploration of the possible meaning and implications of the right to self-determination in the Declaration. The provisions are then classified in terms of the right to participate in public life and the possible consequences of this classification for the nature, scope and manner of implementation of the right are examined. Given the absence of an explicit consensus on the precise classification of the provisions during the drafting of the Declaration, the overriding objective of the typology is to map out the possible future directions or pathways suggested in the Declaration for the development of the right to self-determination and the right to participate in public life.

A typology of the provisions on participation in the Declaration

(1) The Provisions as an Expression of the Right to Self-Determination of the Entire Population of the State

The first way in which the provisions can be classified is as a reflection of the right to self-determination of the entire population of the State, in much the same way as the extensive rights granted to the Basques concerning self-government and effective participation are a reflection of the right to self-determination of the entire Spanish people.[65] This might appear to be a curious interpretation, but it is not without some supporting authority. It is implicit in the statements made by several States that the scope and exercise of the rights set out in the Declaration had to be determined by national law.[66] As national law is presumed to reflect the wishes of the entire population of the State, the clear implication is that any special participatory rights for indigenous peoples are dependent on the consent of the entire population of the State and, by implication, the manner in which they choose to exercise their right to self-determination.[67] This interpretation is also consistent with the approach traditionally adopted by the Human Rights Committee to the right to self-determination.[68]

[65] See eg fourth periodic report submitted by Spain under Art 40 ICCPR, UN Doc CCPR/C/95/Add.1, para 7.

[66] See eg UN Docs A/61/PV.108 (Myanmar, Namibia, Paraguay and France); and A/61/PV.107 (Mexico).

[67] Eg, by exercising their right to self-determination in establishing a unitary or federal State or by granting some form of territorial or functional autonomy to groups within the State.

[68] According to the Committee, the 'means by which individual citizens exercise the right to participate in the conduct of public affairs … should be established by the constitution and other laws' which, in turn, are determined by virtue of the right to self-determination: see General Comment XXV (n 53) paras 5 and 2.

Viewed in this light, the references to the 'right' of indigenous peoples to be consulted or to participate in certain processes must be interpreted in the Hohfeldian sense of 'privileges'[69] held at the discretion of the State and quite probably contingent on the fulfilment of certain responsibilities or duties to the State. This classification of the provisions suggests that the effective participation of indigenous peoples in public life is very much dependent on the consent of the State. In effect, it leaves the question of effective participation and the implementation of these provisions to the discretion of the State concerned, which is the current position. Interpreting the provisions in this way would deprive the Declaration of much of its value. It would also mean that the considerable amount of time and effort committed to drafting the Declaration on the part of both States and indigenous peoples resulted in simply confirming the existing status quo. Furthermore, it would be at odds with the idea of a new relationship between States and indigenous peoples implicit in the Declaration.[70] For all these reasons, it may be difficult to sustain this particular classification of the provisions on participation in the Declaration.

(2) The Provisions as an Expression of the Right to Self-Determination of Indigenous Peoples

According to the second classification, the provisions reflect the right to self-determination but in this instance it is the right to self-determination of the indigenous people rather than the entire population of the State in which they reside. This is evident in the statements made by indigenous peoples themselves during the drafting of the Declaration.[71] It is also evident in the view expressed by several States that indigenous people would exercise their right to self-determination by participating effectively in public life, including in decisions affecting them.[72] This classification raises a number of interesting issues of a doctrinal and practical nature. It should be noted, however, that irrespective of how these provisions are classified, these issues would arise in any event due to the explicit recognition of a right to self-determination for indigenous peoples in Articles 3 and 4 of the Declaration. Nevertheless, they are discussed in the present context as the drafting history of the provisions on participation provides useful insights into these issues.

[69] As Hohfeld noted, the term 'rights' tends to be used indiscriminately to cover what would in a given case be a 'privilege'. He observed that the dominant technical meaning of 'privilege' is 'negation of legal duty': see WN Hohfeld, 'Some Fundamental Legal Conceptions as Applied in Judicial Reasoning' (1913) 23 *Yale Law Journal* 16, 32–44.

[70] See eg Press Release issued by the three UN Special Rapporteurs (n 2).

[71] See eg UN Docs E/CN.4/1997/102, paras 198, 206, 323; and E/CN.4/1996/84, para 82.

[72] See eg UN Docs A/61/PV.107 (Norway and Sweden); and E/CN.4/2000/84, paras 50 (Canada), 53 (Brazil).

The first point to note is that classifying the provisions as a form of self-determination for an indigenous people, and indeed the very recognition that indigenous peoples have a right to self-determination, operates as an implied limitation on the right to self-determination of the entire population of the State in which they reside. It implies that the latter, in exercising their right to self-determination, must consider the concurrent right to self-determination of the indigenous people. In this respect, the Declaration seems to break new ground by suggesting that even in respect of peoples constituted as States there is now a difference in terms of the scope of their right to self-determination depending on whether or not there are indigenous peoples within their borders.

Related to this is the question of how to reconcile conflicts that might arise between the right to self-determination of an indigenous people and the right to self-determination of the entire population of the State in which they reside, especially concerning the exploitation of valuable natural resources on ancestral lands. As the first international instrument to recognise explicitly a right to self-determination for groups within States, the Declaration opens up the very real possibility of such conflicts occurring. Up until now, international law has not had to grapple with this issue as the right to self-determination was confined to the entire population of a State or colony, thereby obviating the possibility of this type of conflict occurring.[73] In this respect, the Declaration is very much in unknown territory. For this reason, it is perhaps not surprising that the Declaration fails to deal with the issue directly. At most, the preamble suggests that conflicts should be resolved through negotiation,[74] but it does not explain what happens in the event of such negotiations breaking down. A review of the drafting history reveals that some States,[75] and most indigenous peoples,[76] would resort to the traditional, absolutist concept of self-determination. This would be inappropriate and arguably ill-advised. It would simply allow each party to invoke their right to self-determination to claim that their wishes are paramount and should be respected. This would do little to resolve conflicts and could do much to inflame them by encouraging an intransigent, zero-sum approach to self-determination. In the present context, one needs to depart from this traditional perception

[73] See the review of State practice outlined in Quane 2007 (n 6) 478–79. Admittedly, some of the UN human rights treaty bodies would take a different view. See Committee on the Elimination of Racial Discrimination, General Recommendation 21, The Right to Self-Determination (Forty-eight session, 1996), UN Doc A/51/18, annex VII at 125 (1996); and some of the Concluding Observations and Recommendations of the Human Rights Committee and the Committee on Economic, Social and Cultural Rights (n 20).

[74] Preambular para 20.

[75] See UN Docs E/CN.4/2003/92, Annex, p 17; A/61/PV.108 (Paraguay, France and Egypt); and A/61/PV.107 (Mexico). See also UN Doc E/CN.4/2000/84, para 47.

[76] See eg UN Docs E/CN.4/2003/92, para 24; and E/CN.4/2005/89/Add.1, p 5.

of self-determination and develop a coherent, principled framework for resolving conflicts between competing self-determination claims.

In order to develop such a framework, States and indigenous peoples will have to confront difficult issues. For their part, indigenous peoples will have to engage with the right to self-determination of the entire population of the State in which they reside and the question of how their respective rights may be reconciled. This may involve indigenous peoples revisiting the issue of whether they must always give their consent prior to the application of any State laws and administrative practices to them and in respect of any State use of their land and natural resources. This issue overshadowed the drafting of many of the relevant provisions[77] with indigenous peoples claiming a veto over such matters[78] and States resisting such claims.[79] The implications of such a veto were clear, with many States arguing that it would have potentially far-reaching consequences, especially for their ability to manage national resources in the interests of the entire population[80] and the disruptive effect it could have on democratic political systems.[81] Ultimately, the provisions in question were redrafted in such a way as to temper the suggestion that indigenous peoples will always have a veto in such matters.[82] At the same time, one has to acknowledge that the current wording, although a somewhat diluted version of the original drafts, can still be interpreted in such a way as to suggest that indigenous peoples retain a veto. Indeed, concerns about this issue led several States to vote against,[83] or abstain from voting on,[84]

[77] See eg UN Doc E/CN.4/2005/89, para 35.

[78] See eg UN Docs E/CN.4/2005/89, para 57; and E/CN.4/1997/102, paras 53, 203, 275.

[79] See eg UN Docs A/61/PV.107 (Australia); E/CN.4/2003/92, para 46 (Canada); E/CN.4/1997/102, paras 209 (France), 280 (Brazil), 281 (United States), 283 (Japan); and E/CN.4/1996/84, para 81 (several unidentified States).

[80] See eg UN Doc E/CN.4/2003/92, para 46 (Canada).

[81] See eg UN Doc A/61/PV.107 (Australia and New Zealand).

[82] Compare eg the text of Art 19 with the text ultimately adopted. The original text provided that 'States shall obtain the free and informed consent of the peoples concerned before adopting and implementing' legislative or administrative measures that may affect them. The final text provides that 'States shall consult and cooperate in good faith with the indigenous peoples concerned … in order to obtain their free, prior and informed consent …' See UN Doc E/CN.4/2006/79, Annex I, proposals concerning Art 20 (subsequently Art 19). It suggests that the emphasis shifted to the need for consultation rather than granting indigenous peoples a veto over the relevant matters, and this would be consistent with the views expressed by several States during the drafting process that the emphasis was on consultation rather than the recognition of a veto: see eg UN Doc E/CN.4/1997/102, paras 208 (Malaysia), 214 (Brazil).

[83] See UN Doc A/61/PV.107 (Australia, Canada and New Zealand), although it was only one factor in their negative vote. See also *Non-Paper: United Nations Declaration on the Rights of Indigenous Peoples: Summary of Key Areas of Concern*, submitted by Australia, Canada, Colombia, Guyana, New Zealand, the Russian Federation and Suriname, Annex I to the Supplement to the Report of the Facilitator (n 15).

[84] See UN Docs A/61/PV.108 (Nigeria); and A/61/PV.107 (Colombia).

the General Assembly resolution to which the Declaration is annexed.[85] It seems that indigenous peoples have a choice either to adhere to an absolutist concept of self-determination,[86] or to participate in the development of a framework for reconciling competing self-determination claims that would allow the Declaration to yield tangible benefits for all the parties concerned. Realistically, their willingness to choose the latter may come down to the degree to which indigenous peoples trust their respective States. Arguably, historic injustices as well as the ongoing marginalisation and privations experienced by many indigenous peoples were factors in their adherence to an absolute concept of self-determination as a means of ensuring adequate protection for their rights and legitimate interests.

For their part, States need to adopt the necessary measures to avoid any perceived need to invoke such an uncompromising interpretation of self-determination and to generate the necessary goodwill to facilitate the effective implementation of the Declaration at the national level. There is a very real prospect that the parties will not be in complete agreement as to how to implement the right to self-determination in the Declaration, particularly when it impacts substantially on the right to self-determination of the entire population of the State. In these circumstances, in the absence of any clear guidelines on conflict resolution and given the respective bargaining power of States and indigenous peoples, the likelihood is that any conflict will be resolved primarily in favour of the right to self-determination of the entire population of the State, albeit perhaps with some modest concessions to indigenous peoples. This would be unhelpful if not positively harmful to the creation of the new sense of partnership between States and indigenous peoples envisaged in the Declaration. Indeed, by generating expectations that may not be fulfilled, the Declaration could simply contribute to a deterioration of relations between States and indigenous peoples.

For the Declaration to work, States must move beyond generalities. It is not enough to express a willingness to recognise a right to self-determination for indigenous peoples; States must spell out how they are going to reconcile the inevitable conflicts that will occur between competing self-determination rights. In this sense, it is unhelpful to leave the matter open-ended or to include vague references in the Declaration to the UN Charter or to the need to cooperate. A framework must be developed to limit the discretion of States in this area and to provide guidelines for a principled reconciliation of conflicting self-determination claims.

[85] Even States that voted in favour of the Declaration put on record their interpretation that the provisions should not be interpreted as granting a veto to indigenous peoples: see UN Doc A/61/PV.107 (Suriname).

[86] Implicit in the claim to exercise a veto over a wide range of matters.

In this regard, one can draw inspiration from international human rights law concerning the permissibility of restrictions on individual human rights.[87] If the right in question is one that can be subject to restrictions, then a restriction may be permitted provided that the restriction: (i) is prescribed by law; (ii) pursues a legitimate aim; (iii) is necessary to achieve that aim; and (iv) is not discriminatory. If a similar approach is adopted in the present context, any restriction on the right to self-determination of indigenous peoples must satisfy these four criteria in order for it to be permitted. This approach would have several advantages. First, it would provide a coherent framework for reconciling competing self-determination claims. Second, experience has shown that this approach can provide tangible protection for the rights of members of marginalised groups even when they appear to conflict with the rights and interests of the majority.[88] Third, and perhaps most importantly of all, this approach renders the State accountable for any interference with the right to self-determination of indigenous peoples.

Admittedly, such a framework is present in Article 46(2) of the Declaration. Inserted at a relatively late stage in the drafting process,[89] it provides that the rights set out in the Declaration shall be subject only to such limitations as are 'determined by law, and in accordance with international human rights standards … non-discriminatory and strictly necessary solely for the purpose of securing due recognition and respect for the rights and freedoms of others and for meeting the just and most compelling requirements of a democratic society.' It is important to note, however, that at no stage in the drafting process was there any suggestion that this provision applied to the right to self-determination of indigenous peoples. This is hardly surprising given the negotiating positions of the respective parties and especially of indigenous peoples, who would not countenance any limitation on their right to self-determination. While such an approach may have been understandable during the drafting process from a strategic perspective, it is questionable whether it is sustainable when it comes to actually implementing the Declaration. Arguably, it could do much to undermine the rights and interests of indigenous peoples. As previously noted, differences in bargaining power suggest that conflicts between self-determination claims will tend to be resolved in favour of the right to self-determination of the entire population of the State. Continued adherence to an unqualified right to self-determination will do little to address this situation and will leave

[87] See eg Arts 18(3), 19(3), 21 and 22(2) ICCPR.

[88] See eg *A v Secretary of State for the Home Department* [2005] 2 WLR 87, concerning the indefinite detention of suspected foreign terrorists without charge.

[89] One of the earliest references to it appeared in 2004 in a preambular para: see UN Doc E/CN.4/2004/81, p 20.

disagreements about the implementation of the right at a rather vague and abstract level. This could allow the State to evade the kind of detailed and transparent scrutiny associated with the framework for assessing the legality of restrictions on human rights developed in international human rights law and embodied in Article 46(2) of the Declaration. While it may be difficult as a matter of principle for indigenous peoples to depart from an absolute concept of self-determination, pragmatic considerations suggest that they may need to do so in order to obtain tangible benefits from the Declaration.

Recognition that the right to self-determination can be subject to restrictions would be a first step towards opening up a host of possibilities for a more creative and pragmatic interpretation and application of the right. At a minimum, it would mean that Article 46(2) could apply to any limitations on the right to self-determination and would ensure that these limitations, which invariably will occur, are subject to detailed scrutiny. It should also go some way to addressing State concerns that recognition of a right to self-determination for groups within its borders is a zero-sum process which will lead to secession or at the very least a serious impediment to it governing in the interests of the entire population of the State. By recognising a right to self-determination for indigenous peoples, the Declaration suggests new and exciting possibilities for a more constructive and flexible approach to self-determination.[90] Whether this potential will be realised depends on the willingness of States and indigenous peoples to engage with current realities, not least that the concept of self-determination as interpreted and applied in the past may not always be relevant or appropriate in the present.

(3) The Provisions as an Expansion of the Right to Participate in Public Life

The third classification of the provisions on participation locates them within the framework of the right to participate in public life but acknowledges that they represent a significant departure from the nature and content of that right as traditionally conceived.[91] From a practical perspective, this classification would have its advantages. By separating the provisions on effective participation from the more contentious issue of self-determination, it could make them more politically acceptable to States and possibly increase the prospects of successful implementation.

[90] There is some support for such an approach in the academic literature: see eg B Kingsbury, 'Claims by Non-State Groups in International Law' (1992) 25 *Cornell International Law Journal* 481.

[91] See General Comment XXV (n 53); and GH Fox, 'The Right to Political Participation in International Law' in GH Fox and BR Roth (eds), *Democratic Governance and International Law* (Cambridge University Press, 2000).

Although there are cogent reasons for not separating the two, it is possible to find some support for this classification in several international instruments concerning the rights of indigenous peoples.

Of particular interest in the present context is the International Labour Organization's Indigenous and Tribal Peoples Convention 169 of 1989 ('the ILO Convention').[92] It contains numerous provisions on participation that are quite similar in content to those set out in the Declaration. Article 6, for example, provides that in applying the provisions of the Convention, governments shall:

> (a) consult the peoples concerned … in particular through their representative institutions, whenever consideration is being given to legislative or administrative measures which may affect them directly; [and] … (c) establish means for the full development of these peoples' own institutions …

Further, Article 7(1) provides that indigenous peoples 'shall participate in the formulation, implementation and evaluation of plans and programmes for national and regional development which may affect them'.[93] Admittedly, these provisions do not go so far as granting indigenous peoples a veto over certain matters. Nevertheless, the similarity between the provisions is significant because the provisions in the ILO Convention are not linked either explicitly or implicitly with the right to self-determination.[94]

Classifying the provisions in the Declaration as an expansion of the right to participate in public life would suggest a fundamental rethinking of the nature and scope of this right. At the very least, by focusing on the modalities of participation and not simply the right to participate in existing modalities without discrimination, the provisions challenge the traditional dichotomy between self-determination and effective participation evident in the Human Rights Committee's General Comment on Article 25 ICCPR. Similarly, by conferring rights on indigenous peoples rather than persons belonging to indigenous peoples, they depart from the current position where the right to participate in public life is conferred on and exercised by individuals rather than groups. These observations may seem somewhat radical, but it is possible to reconcile them with the existing structure and underlying rationale of the right to participate in public life.

Central to the existing right is the concept of non-discriminatory participation in public life. To date, non-discrimination has tended to be interpreted in a formal sense as requiring all citizens to be given the same

[92] 72 ILO Official Bulletin 59.

[93] See also Arts 2(1), 5(c), 7(3), 15, and 17.

[94] It is significant, eg, that Art 1(3) provides that 'The use of the term "peoples" in this Convention shall not be construed as having any implications as regards the rights which may attach to the term under international law.'

rights and opportunities to participate. This is evident in the drafting of Article 25 ICCPR. It provides that every citizen has the right to take part in the conduct of public affairs, to vote and be elected at genuine periodic elections, and to have access on general terms of equality to public service without distinction of any kind. Similarly, the Human Rights Committee has stressed that where, for example, a mode of direct participation by citizens is established[95] 'no distinction should be made between citizens as regards their participation' on the grounds of race, national origin or other status.[96] It shows that, at present, no distinction may be drawn between citizens in terms of the *extent* of their rights and opportunities to participate in public life, although the *exercise* of these rights can be subject to conditions such as age or mental capacity provided they are based on objective and reasonable criteria. This may help to explain the concerns expressed by several States that some of the Declaration's provisions on participation were discriminatory since they conferred rights on indigenous peoples that were not conferred on the rest of the population.[97]

Arguably, one can address these concerns and reconcile the provisions with the existing right to participate in public life if one departs from a formal concept of non-discrimination. As the Permanent Court of International Justice noted in its Advisory Opinion on *Minority Schools in Albania*, it is possible to envisage 'cases in which equality of treatment of the majority and of the minority, whose situation and requirements are different, would result in inequality in fact'.[98] The Court observed that to achieve factual equality or non-discrimination, it may be necessary to accord 'different treatment in order to attain a result which establishes equilibrium between different situations'.[99] In the light of the political and economic inequalities often experienced by indigenous peoples,[100] the Declaration's provisions granting special participatory rights to such peoples may not be inherently discriminatory but simply a reflection of the factual or substantive concept of non-discrimination evident in the Advisory Opinion of the Court. The numerous references to the need to ensure the 'effective' participation of indigenous peoples during

[95] Direct participation would include citizens participating directly 'in bodies established to represent citizens in consultation with government': see General Comment XXV (n 53) para 6.

[96] Ibid.

[97] See eg UN Docs A/61/PV.107 (New Zealand and Suriname); and E/CN.4/1996/84, para 80.

[98] PCIJ (1935), Ser A/B, no 64, 19.

[99] Ibid.

[100] See eg Committee on the Elimination of Racial Discrimination, General Recommendation 23, Rights of Indigenous Peoples (Fifty-first session, 1997), UN Doc A/52/18, annex V at 122 (1997), para 3. See also UN Docs E/CN.4/Sub.2/2000/24, paras 24, 23, 28, 33, 34, 48, 58, 143, 147; A/61/PV.107 (United Kingdom); E/CN.4/Sub.2/1993/26/Add.1, para 24; and E/CN.4/1997/102, para 203.

the drafting of the relevant provisions suggests that this concept of substantive non-discrimination may have been endorsed by at least some of those involved in the drafting of the Declaration.[101]

Adopting this approach would also have practical implications, in the sense that it suggests that an overarching, unifying principle exists to guide implementation of the provisions. This is the principle of non-discrimination, which dictates that if there is a difference in treatment it must be capable of objective and reasonable justification otherwise the difference in treatment will be deemed to be discriminatory.[102] This means that there must be objective and reasonable justification for the special participatory rights granted to indigenous peoples that are not granted to the rest of the population. Given the inequalities usually experienced by indigenous peoples it should not be unduly difficult to provide such justification, at least at the level of general principle. The scope and duration of these special rights, however, will need to be worked out at the national level, taking into account the actual circumstances of the indigenous peoples concerned. In this respect, the non-discrimination principle can operate as a powerful constraint against potential abuses of these provisions by ensuring that a strong correlation exists between the granting of additional participatory rights and the objective need for them as an instrument to address the substantive inequalities experienced by indigenous peoples. Arguably, this point will be important in heading off criticisms that the provisions are discriminatory as well as any potential resentment that they could engender among the non-indigenous population. By requiring continual reflection on the need for these special participatory measures, this approach should ensure that they remain within justifiable limits and in this sense address the concerns of States and non-indigenous peoples. At the same time, this approach should also benefit indigenous peoples by ensuring that the situation is kept under review, thereby avoiding their ghettoisation and the adoption of a static approach to their role in public life.

[101] See eg UN Doc E/CN.4/1997/102, paras 199 (Canada), 202 (Sweden); statements by indigenous peoples that the Declaration 'sought to correct the fact that international standards had not been applied equally to all peoples' (UN Doc E/CN.4/1997/102, paras 62, 53); and the observations of States locating the provisions firmly within the context of facilitating the effective participation of indigenous peoples in public life (UN Docs E/CN.4/1997/102, paras 196 (Mexico), 205 (Argentina), 221 (United States), 227 (Norway); and E/CN.4/1996/84, para 79). See also the numerous references to using the Declaration to address the discrimination, marginalisation and inequalities experienced by indigenous peoples: UN Docs A/61/PV.108 (Namibia, Cuba, Bolivia, Guatemala and Ecuador); A/61/PV.107 (Republic of Korea and United Kingdom); and E/CN.4/2000/84, para 29 (representatives of indigenous organisations).

87 See eg *Diergaardt v Namibia*, Communication No 760/1997, UN Doc A/55/46, vol II (25 July 2000) 140, para 10.8.

[102] Ibid.

CONCLUSION

The Declaration is a complex and multidimensional document embodying a range of innovations concerning the rights of indigenous peoples. The explicit recognition that indigenous peoples have a right to self-determination is one of the most significant aspects of the Declaration. It acknowledges that the right is no longer confined to peoples organised as States or colonial peoples but now extends to an additional category of peoples. In doing so, it also challenges the territorial concept of a people in international law. Departing from this traditional concept of a people, the Declaration defines a people in terms of their distinct ethnic, cultural and religious identity. It echoes the concept of a people associated with the political principle of self-determination and, in this respect, blurs the distinction between the legal and the political principle of self-determination.

In theory, the adoption of a non-territorial concept of a people could have far-reaching consequences. It could lead to a wide range of groups claiming the right to self-determination, potentially fuelling secessionist claims, inter-communal violence and, given the risk of conflict spilling over into neighbouring States, threaten international peace and security. In reality, the Declaration avoids or at least limits these potential dangers in two ways. First, it is concerned solely with the right to self-determination of indigenous peoples, a relatively closed category of peoples. In this way, the Declaration is restricted in its sphere of application, although, as noted throughout this chapter, its implications may not be so limited either in terms of the general development of the right to self-determination or in terms of its impact on the exercise of that right by other categories of peoples. Second, by limiting the right of indigenous peoples to internal self-determination, the Declaration avoids some of the difficulties associated with external self-determination and secessionist claims.

This recognition of a limited right to self-determination is a further innovation in the Declaration. Admittedly the existence of a limited right to self-determination has been canvassed in the academic literature for some time, but it has not until now received clear, unequivocal endorsement in State practice. At the very least, it suggests that international law may be evolving to the point where there is either a variable/context-dependent right to self-determination or separate and clearly distinguishable rights to self-determination operating in parallel to one another while also being effectively insulated from each other.

The recognition of a limited right to self-determination brings with it new challenges as well as opportunities. In respect of the former, the most important is how to reconcile competing claims to self-determination by indigenous and non-indigenous peoples within a State. The Declaration is largely silent on this issue, although arguably it contains the seeds of a coherent and principled framework for reconciling these claims in Article 46(2). Like many international human rights instruments, Article 46(2) provides that any restrictions on a human right must be prescribed by law, non-discriminatory, pursue a legitimate aim and be necessary to achieve that aim. The use of this provision to reconcile competing self-determination claims would ensure not only close scrutiny of any balance struck between these claims but also coherence and internal consistency within the international human rights system more generally. Whether this occurs depends on the willingness of all parties to depart from the rather absolutist concept of self-determination which emerged in the past and embrace the possibilities offered by the Declaration to make self-determination responsive to the needs of the present.

These possibilities are very much in evidence in terms of the formulation of the right to self-determination. The Declaration clearly moves the concept of internal self-determination on from the rather abstract manner in which it has been interpreted to date. This is evident particularly in Article 4 with its references to autonomy and self-government as forms of indigenous self-determination. It fleshes out the content of the right in a way that helps to make it more responsive to the needs and legitimate interests of indigenous peoples. In this respect, the Declaration suggests new pathways for the development of the right. Whether they will be confined to indigenous peoples remains to be seen. If the Declaration proves to be a success, it may lessen State opposition to developing a more flexible approach to self-determination for other distinct groups within States. In this respect, the full significance of the Declaration may only become apparent over time in the light of subsequent State practice.

Related to the right to self-determination in the Declaration is the recognition of extensive participatory rights for indigenous peoples. The precise nature of this relationship, however, is far from clear. The drafting history suggests a variety of perspectives, with States and indigenous peoples viewing participatory rights as a form of indigenous self-determination, a means of attaining it, as having some indeterminate 'close' relationship to it, or as a permutation of all three. For this reason, the present chapter developed a typology to map out how the provisions on participation could be classified and to explore the consequences that attach to such classifications. What emerges from this typology is that the provisions can be categorised in two principal ways. The first is as a form of internal self-determination, building on Article 4 by providing further guidance on the meaning and implications of the right to self-determination in the Declaration. The second is as an expansion of the right to participate in public life which departs from the exclusively individualistic nature of the existing right. According to this second interpretation, the provisions require the adoption of new modalities of participation in order to achieve substantive or factual non-discriminatory participation. In this sense they stray into territory traditionally occupied by the self-determination principle and collapse, or at least challenge, the dichotomy that currently exists between self-determination and participatory rights.

In view of the ambiguity that surrounds the relationship between self-determination and participation in the Declaration, it is difficult to state with certainty which pathway the provisions on participation will ultimately follow. Nevertheless, the typology reveals the truly innovative potential of the Declaration in opening up new directions for a more creative and constructive development of self-determination and participatory rights.

12

A New Dawn over the Land: Shedding Light on Collective Ownership and Consent

JÉRÉMIE GILBERT AND CATHAL DOYLE

INTRODUCTION

IT IS NOW widely recognised that a profound cultural, social and spiritual relationship with their lands and territories is characteristic of indigenous peoples and fundamental to their survival. In spite of this fact, indigenous peoples have been and are repeatedly deprived of their lands, territories and resources.[1] Present day economic imperatives arising from globalisation are putting new strains on indigenous peoples' rights over their traditional territories.[2] Driven by the demands of an increasingly globalised economy and the opening up of markets in developing countries to foreign direct investment, activities such as mining, logging, dam construction and mono-cropping are becoming synonymous with violations of indigenous peoples' rights, resulting in ongoing tensions and conflicts between indigenous peoples, states and transnational corporations. Central to the realisation of indigenous peoples' land and self-determination rights is their ability to ensure recognition and enforcement of these rights.

In recent decades, owing to the difficulties encountered in relation to access to justice at the local level pertaining to the enforcement of their rights, many indigenous peoples have turned to international legal institutions.[3] This has resulted in the emergence of an important body

[1] See *Indigenous Peoples and their Relationship to Land*, Final Working Paper Prepared by the Special Rapporteur, E-I Daes, UN Doc E/CN.4/Sub.2/2001/21.

[2] For references, see M Stewart-Harawira, *The New Imperial Order: Indigenous Responses to Globalization* (London, Zed Books, 2005).

[3] The UN declared 1994–2004 the First World Decade on the Rights of Indigenous Peoples and 2005–15 the second decade; see GA Res A/RES/48/163 (1994) and Res A/RES/59/174 (2005). See also SJ Anaya, *Indigenous Peoples in International Law* (Oxford University Press, 2004).

of international human rights law relating to indigenous peoples' land rights.[4] However, this regime is still in its infancy and remains somewhat fragmented. Cognisant of this, indigenous peoples and the organisations that were involved in the negotiations for the adoption of the UN Declaration on the Rights of Indigenous Peoples ('the Declaration') placed great emphasis on the need for strongly worded and unambiguous language pertaining to their land, territory and resource and associated self-determination rights in this Declaration. Accordingly, it was expected that a universal declaration on the rights of indigenous peoples would reflect the importance of these rights for indigenous peoples.

The aim of this chapter is to evaluate the potential significance of the adoption of the Declaration in the development of international legal standards regarding indigenous peoples' land, territory and resource rights. Despite the expanding jurisprudence generated by the UN treaty monitoring bodies on indigenous peoples' rights,[5] questions remain as to the capacity of general international human rights law to successfully accommodate indigenous peoples' specific territorial claims at the local level. Given this context, this chapter aims to examine to what extent the Declaration can serve as a positive force to protect indigenous peoples' land, territory and resource rights by providing the basis for the development of a strong corpus of specific territorial and associated self-governance rights for indigenous peoples. The chapter is divided into three sections. The first section analyses the extent to which the Declaration plays an important role in affirming and recognising indigenous peoples' specific relationship with their lands and territories. The authors go on to examine how, in a context where many states have traditionally been reluctant to recognise collective rights, the Declaration articulates a collective right to lands, territories and resources.[6] The following section addresses the requirement that, in accordance with their right to self-determination, indigenous peoples' free, prior and informed consent is obtained in the context of developments that impact on their lands and territories, in particular in relation to resource exploitation. It examines the Declaration's potential to contribute to the realisation of this self-determination requirement in practice and to act as a platform for the affirmation of a right to free, prior and informed consent within the normative framework of indigenous peoples' rights. Drawing from

[4] J Gilbert, *Indigenous Peoples' Land Rights under International Law: From Victims to Actors* (New York, Transnational, 2006).

[5] See generally P Thornberry, *Indigenous Peoples and Human Rights* (Manchester University Press, 2002).

[6] D Sanders, 'Collective Rights' (1991) 13 *Human Rights Quarterly* 368; C Holder and J Corntassel, 'Indigenous Peoples and Multicultural Citizenship: Bridging Collective and Individual Rights' (2002) 24 *Human Rights Quarterly* 126.

their analysis, the authors conclude the chapter by arguing that the true significance of the Declaration can only be fully appreciated when viewed in its historical context as having emerged from the systematic denial of indigenous peoples' rights; its contemporary context as an integral component of the evolving normative framework pertaining to the rights of indigenous peoples; and its future context as a platform for the elaboration and realisation of these rights.

LAND RIGHTS AND CULTURAL IDENTITY

The United Nations Permanent Forum on Indigenous Issues (PFII) recently observed that 'Land is the foundation of the lives and cultures of indigenous peoples all over the world. Without access to and respect for their rights over their lands, territories and natural resources, the survival of indigenous peoples' particular distinct culture is threatened.'[7] For indigenous peoples, land is not only a source of economic livelihood but also the source of spiritual, cultural and social identity. From this perspective indigenous peoples' claims to land rights involve not only traditional property rights and claim to title to territory but also cultural, social and spiritual claims. It is this specificity that indigenous peoples wanted the Declaration to reflect. The recognition of indigenous peoples' specific claims to land in the Declaration was seen as an important step for international law as, historically, international law had been a major factor in the alienation of indigenous peoples' land rights.

The Origins: International Law and Dispossession

International institutions working with indigenous peoples have begun to acknowledge this specific connection between cultural identity and land rights for indigenous peoples, but this practice is recent. Traditionally, international law and legal institutions at the national level have played a significant role in the destruction of indigenous peoples' cultures by supporting acts of dispossession and legalising the colonisation of indigenous peoples' territories.[8] Justifications of such colonisation were invariably based on racist approaches towards indigenous cultures. Notions such as terra nullius and discovery assumed that indigenous peoples

[7] Permanent Forum on Indigenous Issues, Report on the Sixth Session (14–15 May 2007), Economic and Social Council Official Records Supplement No 23, UN Doc E/2007/43, E/C.19/2007/12, para 4.

[8] See generally L Robertson, *Conquest by Law* (Oxford University Press, 2005); RA Williams, Jr, *The American Indian in Western Legal Thought* (Oxford University Press, 1990).

were so uncivilised that they could be considered not to exist and that consequently their lands were open to conquest.[9] Ironically, the universalisation of international law was principally a consequence of the imperial expansion that took place in the past centuries, as one of the first doctrines of international law was the recognition of a right of conquest for the imperial powers.[10] Through such theory international law has affirmed the superiority of imperial colonial powers over indigenous communities. A clear distinction between the 'civilised' and the 'non-civilised' served to assert that international law applied only to the sovereign states that composed the so-called 'civilised family of nations'.[11] With the assumption of the superiority of 'civilised' states and the denial of the legal existence of so-called 'non-civilised communities', indigenous communities were refused ownership of their lands.

Probably the best summary of international law's approach to land rights during the colonial era comes from Lindley's famous book *The Acquisition of Backward Territory*, in which he describes how law was used as a justification for the dispossession of indigenous peoples.[12] Chronologically, international law legitimised the acquisition of indigenous territories in two different ways. The first epoch saw the recognition of indigenous territorial existence, with international law developing around the notion of the right to acquire these territories by conquest. The second epoch was based on a different approach whereby indigenous peoples were regarded as legally non-existent. Thus, indigenous communities and nations could not hold territorial rights and this legacy of non-existence facilitated the subsequent colonisation of all indigenous land. Without going into detail on the role of international law in such instances of dispossession, it is important to bear in mind that it was only in 1992 that the Australian High Court recognised that terra nullius was a 'racist fiction',[13] and it was only during the twentieth century that it became 'possible to argue that the right of conquest has ceased to be upheld by international law'.[14] Overall, international law has clearly been a crucial tool that justified the dispossession of indigenous peoples of

[9] See especially M Bedjaoui, *Terra nullius, 'droits' historiques et autodétermination* (La Haye, Exposés oraux prononcés devant la Cour Internationale de Justice en l'affaire du Sahara Occidental, 1975).

[10] See generally P Keal, *European Conquest and the Rights of Indigenous Peoples* (Cambridge University Press, 2003).

[11] See generally M Koskenniemi, *The Gentle Civilizer of Nations* (Cambridge University Press, 2001); A Anghie, *Imperialism, Sovereignty and the Making of International Law* (Cambridge University Press, 2004).

[12] MF Lindley, *The Acquisition and Government of Backward Territory in International Law* (Longmans, Green and Co, 1926, reprinted New York, Negro Universities Press, 1969) 11.

[13] *Mabo v Queensland (No 2)* (1992) 107 ALR 1.

[14] S Korman, *The Right of Conquest: The Acquisition of Territory by Force in International Law and Practice* (Oxford, Clarendon Press, 1996) 8.

their territories; hence, viewed from a historical perspective, international law was not considered a logical ally and friend to support indigenous peoples' land rights; rather it was seen as a foe. It was with this historical background in mind that in 1985 the UN Working Group on Indigenous Populations (WGIP) started work on the elaboration of an international declaration on the rights of indigenous peoples.[15] It is consequently not surprising that one of the first affirmations in the preamble to the Declaration is the acknowledgement that 'indigenous peoples have suffered from historic injustices as a result of, inter alia, their colonization and dispossession of their lands, territories and resources ...'.

The Holistic Approach to Land Rights

As highlighted above, historically international law failed to recognise indigenous peoples' specific attachment to land. Hence recent recognition of indigenous peoples' specific attachment to their territories is seen as an important step under international law. In their claims under international law, indigenous peoples have insisted on the need to acknowledge their specific approach to land rights. This is reflected in the International Labour Organization's (ILO) Convention 169 which affirms that, in applying the Convention, 'governments shall respect the special importance for the cultures and spiritual values of the peoples concerned of their relationship with the lands or territories, or both as applicable, which they occupy or otherwise use, and in particular the collective aspects of this relationship'.[16] Likewise, the World Bank operational policies on indigenous peoples also recognise that 'the identities and cultures of Indigenous Peoples are inextricably linked to the lands on which they live and the natural resources on which they depend'.[17] The African Commission on Human and Peoples' Rights (ACHPR) has also acknowledged the importance of recognising indigenous peoples' specific and fundamental attachment to their traditional territory. The ACHPR recognises that indigenous peoples have 'a special attachment to and use of their traditional land, whereby their ancestral land and territory have a fundamental importance for their collective physical and cultural survival as peoples'.[18] Overall,

[15] For an overview of the subsequent history of the draft declaration, see UN Doc E/CN.4/AC.4/1998/1/Add.1.

[16] Convention concerning Indigenous and Tribal Peoples in Independent Countries (ILO 169) (1989) 28 ILM 1382, Art 13.

[17] World Bank Operational Policy (OP) 4.10 on Indigenous Peoples (2005), para 2. See also World Bank, BP 4.10 (2005).

[18] Advisory Opinion of the African Commission on Human and Peoples' Rights on the UN Declaration on the Rights of Indigenous Peoples, 41st Ordinary Session, Accra, Ghana, May 2007.

looking at the development of international law with regard to indigenous peoples' rights to land, there is a clear evolution towards the recognition of indigenous peoples' specific relationship with their traditional territories. This recognition was seen as an important step and was reaffirmed during the drafting of the Declaration. As a result, Article 25 affirms that:

> Indigenous peoples have the right to maintain and strengthen their distinctive spiritual relationship with their traditionally owned or otherwise occupied and used lands, territories, waters and coastal seas and other resources and to uphold their responsibilities to future generations in this regard.[19]

In this Article, the Declaration recognises not only indigenous peoples' specific spiritual attachment to their lands but also their inter-generational approach to land rights. This inter-generational aspect is important as indigenous peoples have insisted that not only is land not a commodity but it also part of their heritage to be transmitted from generation to generation.[20] As summarised by Lars Andres Baer: 'Without the land and the knowledge that comes mainly from use of the land, we as indigenous peoples cannot survive.'[21] This specific cultural relationship to land is not only embedded in the present but is derived from the past and reaches into the future. Indigenous peoples' specific relationship with their land has three temporal dimensions to it:

(a) *Past*: indigenous peoples have a historical continuity with 'pre-invasion' and 'pre-colonial societies' that developed on their territories.
(b) *Present*: indigenous peoples live on these territories (or part of them).[22]
(c) *Future*: indigenous peoples are determined to transmit to future generations their ancestral territories.

The Declaration's recognition of the inter-generational facet of indigenous peoples' relationship to land can thus be seen as an important source of affirmation. Its reference to responsibilities towards future generations is perhaps indicative of international law's willingness to start addressing the relatively underdeveloped arena of the legal obligations and

[19] United Nations Declaration on the Rights of Indigenous Peoples, adopted by GA Res 61/295, 13 September 2007.

[20] J Gilbert, 'Seeking the Fair Land: Indigenous Peoples as Custodians of their Lands' in W Logan, M Langfield and M Mairead (eds), *Cultural Diversity, Heritage and Human Rights* (London, Routledge, 2009).

[21] Lars Anders Baer is a member of the United Nations Permanent Forum on Indigenous Issues, President of the Saami Parliament in Sweden, and a member of the Saami Council. See LA Baer, 'Protection of Rights of Holders of Traditional Knowledge, Indigenous and Local Communities' (2002) 12 *World Libraries* 17.

[22] UN Doc E/CN.4/Sub.2/1986/Add.4.

rights that flow from inter-generational considerations. Regarding the affirmation of indigenous peoples' specific cultural attachment to their lands, the preamble recognises 'the urgent need to respect and promote the inherent rights of indigenous peoples which derive from their political, economic and social structures and from their cultures, spiritual traditions, histories and philosophies, especially their rights to their lands, territories and resources'. The Declaration acknowledges that indigenous peoples' relationship with their lands and territories is to be treated specifically, in a way which recognises indigenous peoples' holistic approach to land rights.

Emphasising the importance of respecting indigenous peoples' holistic approach to land rights, Article 8 states that any action which has the aim or effect of dispossessing indigenous peoples of their lands falls within the category of forced assimilation or cultural destruction. This article is the result of intense negotiations on the meaning of genocide in the Declaration. The original text proposed by the Sub-Commission to the former Commission on Human Rights established a clear link between so-called 'cultural genocide' (or 'ethnocide)' and 'any action which has the aim or effect of dispossessing' indigenous peoples of their lands.[23] There was a clear attempt to link dispossession of land with acts of genocide. During the drafting process some indigenous representatives highlighted that 'land was a key component of indigenous culture and dispossession of land was paramount to ethnocide'.[24] Many indigenous representatives stated that their removal from their traditional territories often amounted to cultural genocide, as the practice of dispossession, forced relocation or population transfer amounted to the destruction of their community. The adoption of Article 7 of the draft declaration would have established a clear link between land dispossession and international criminal prosecution.[25] However, this connection between land dispossession and genocide (or cultural genocide/ethnocide) was strongly resisted by states and consequently the terms 'cultural genocide' and 'ethnocide' do not appear in the text adopted by the General Assembly. In many ways, Article 8 reflects a middle ground agreement by recognising that dispossession of land is a threat to indigenous peoples' cultures and could be akin to an act of forced assimilation but not an act of genocide per se. Hence, Article 8 recognises the crucial connection between indigenous peoples' survival and land rights but remains in conformity with international law on

[23] UN Doc E/CN.4/Sub.2/1994/56, UN draft declaration, Art 7.

[24] UN Doc E/CN.4/2002/98 paras 73 and 74 and page 33.

[25] Note that the draft declaration used the term 'aim or effect', a requirement which is less onerous than the 'specific intent' threshold. See especially J Gilbert, 'Environmental Degradation as a Threat to Life: A Question of Justice?' (2003) 6 *Trinity College Law Review* 81.

genocide, which does not recognise cultural genocide or ethnocide.[26] In addition, Article 10 of the Declaration adds that 'indigenous peoples shall not be forcibly removed from their lands or territories'. Overall, this part of the Declaration emphasises land as a key component of indigenous cultures, with dispossession consequently recognised as being paramount to cultural destruction.

COLLECTIVE LAND RIGHTS: CONTENT AND LIMITATIONS

One of the critical battles that took place during the prolonged drafting process of the Declaration was centred on the issue of collective rights. During one of the sessions of the United Nations Working Group on a Draft Declaration on the Rights of Indigenous Peoples (WGDD), indigenous representatives highlighted that 'exercise of our collective rights is not only critical to indigenous spirituality, but also [to] maintaining the inter-generational nature of all our social, cultural, economic and political rights'.[27] They also pointed out that 'a key element of indigenous collective rights is the profound social, cultural, economic and spiritual relationship of indigenous peoples with our lands, territories, resources and environment'.[28] On the other side several states, including the United Kingdom and France, insisted on the 'inexistence' of collective rights under international law. One of the anxieties concerned the potential difficulties that might emerge in cases of antagonism between individual and collective rights. As a result, the preamble to the Declaration recognises and affirms that 'indigenous individuals are entitled without discrimination to all human rights recognized in international law, and that indigenous peoples possess collective rights which are indispensable for their existence, well-being and integral development as peoples'. Article 1 also highlights that indigenous peoples have rights 'as a collective or as individuals'. While several articles in the Declaration make a distinction between indigenous peoples and indigenous individuals, the articles dealing with land rights do not make such a distinction. They recognise that when it comes to land rights the subjects of rights are indigenous peoples, not individuals.

Despite some states' arguments regarding the 'non-existence' of collective rights under international law, the recognition of collective rights to land for indigenous peoples is consistent with other existing legal standards. The

[26] For a discussion of the connection between genocide and land rights for indigenous peoples, see Gilbert (n 4) ch 3. More generally on the issue of genocide, see W Schabas, *Genocide in International Law: The Crimes of Crimes* (Cambridge University Press, 2000).

[27] Proposals by Indigenous Representatives, 7th session of the WGDD, UN Doc E/CN.4/2002/98, Annex II, 28.

[28] Ibid.

Inter-American Court of Human Rights (IACHR) in the *Awas Tingni* case clearly affirmed the right to property in lands for 'members of indigenous communities within the framework of commonality of possession'.[29] ILO Convention 169 also recognises the collective nature of property in lands for indigenous peoples, and the jurisprudence of the Human Rights Committee (HRC) and the Committee on the Elimination of All Forms of Racial Discrimination (CERD) also emphasises the collective nature of this connection.[30] Hence, on this issue, the Declaration conforms to other international standards, and all point towards the emergence of the recognition of indigenous peoples' collective rights to land. Moreover, it was important for the Declaration to recognise the need for greater protection of these collective rights as, to date, international law has been inadequate in the provision of this much-needed protection. In terms of the substance of such collective rights, it is worth analysing in detail the content of the Declaration, which makes some important contributions regarding notions of (1) ownership in the present tense; (2) recognition of indigenous peoples' traditional customary land laws; and (3) affirmation of rights to territories and lands as including natural resources.

Ownership: 'Past and Present'

In terms of the content of indigenous peoples' right to land, Article 26 affirms that 'Indigenous peoples have the right to own, use, develop and control the lands, territories and resources that they possess by reason of traditional ownership or other traditional occupation or use, as well as those which they have otherwise acquired'. In making this broad affirmation the Declaration does not get into the debate on what indigenous peoples' land rights do or do not constitute. Traditionally on this issue there has been some debate as to whether land rights for indigenous peoples means a right to ownership or a right to use the land.[31] The Declaration avoids such questions by adopting a broad approach to the content of a right to land, which means not only a right of ownership and use but also a right to develop and control. This is an important step, and one which rejects any narrow approach to land rights as meaning only a right to use, an approach sometimes favoured by states. Crucially, the Declaration recognises that with ownership comes control over developments undertaken in indigenous lands.

[29] *Mayagna (Sumo) Awas Tingni Community v Nicaragua* (Series C No 79) [2001] IACHR 9 (31 August 2001).

[30] CERD, General Comment XXIII (51) on the Rights of Indigenous Peoples (adopted at the Committee's 1235th meeting, 18 August 1997) para 5.

[31] Gilbert (n 4).

However, the recognition of indigenous peoples' right to 'own, use, develop and control' their lands comes at a price: it is limited to present day occupation. Article 26 makes a distinction between rights to lands 'presently' occupied by indigenous peoples and rights to land 'traditionally' occupied by indigenous peoples. This distinction is the result of intense negotiation in which some states were reluctant to recognise indigenous peoples' land rights to traditionally owned territories that are now out of indigenous peoples' control. Australia, for example, underlined that it could only support the text of Article 26 if it applied to lands that indigenous peoples currently owned or exclusively used.[32] As a result, Article 26 makes a distinction between traditional territories and land now in possession of indigenous peoples and those that are not. Under paragraph 1 indigenous peoples have 'the right to the lands, territories and resources which they have traditionally owned, occupied or otherwise used or acquired'; while under paragraph 2 they have 'the right to own, use, develop and control the lands, territories and resources that they possess by reason of traditional ownership or other traditional occupation or use, as well as those which they have otherwise acquired'. The content of the 'right' in paragraph 1 remains somewhat ambiguous as it mentions a 'right' to the lands but does not qualify whether it is a right to own, use, control or develop. The ambiguity associated with the right to land traditionally owned but no longer occupied by indigenous peoples could be seen as an 'ambiguous compromise': ambiguous because it will be up to national jurisdictions to interpret what rights indigenous peoples have to the lands that they have traditionally owned, occupied or used in the past; and a compromise because it does not adopt the position of those states which wanted to ensure that land rights were only recognised in terms of land presently occupied. Such 'ambiguous compromise' is not surprising as the issue of land rights over historical and traditional territories touches on the contentious issue of 'dealing with the past'. In many ways this relates to the issue of reparations for past wrongs, an issue with which, traditionally, international law has not been at ease.[33]

Article 26 is not the only article dealing with historical claims. The entire Declaration could be seen as an attempt to address the issue of reparation of past wrongs, as one of the overriding goals of the Declaration is reconciliation. The preamble recognises that 'indigenous peoples have suffered from historic injustices as a result of, inter alia, their colonisation and

[32] Report of the Working Group established in accordance with Commission on Human Rights Resolution 1995/32, UN Doc E/CN.4/2003/92 (6 January 2003), para 32.

[33] See generally G Ulrich and K Boserup (eds), *Reparations: Redressing Past Wrongs*, Human Rights in Development Yearbook (Oslo, Kluwer Law International, 2003); and E Barkan, *The Guilt of Nations: Restitution and Negotiating Historical Injustices* (Baltimore, Johns Hopkins University Press, 2000).

dispossession of their lands, territories and resources, thus preventing them from exercising, in particular, their right to development in accordance with their own needs and interests'. So not only does the Declaration recognise that indigenous peoples have suffered in the past, it also affirms that such historical dispossession still has some impact on indigenous peoples' lives nowadays. This underlines one of the philosophies behind the Declaration, which is to recognise past wrongs and to address present day situations by building a bridge between them. Land rights are the cornerstone of such a bridge. One of the difficult issues in the Declaration was the notion of reparations and remedies for past wrongs. Originally the draft declaration proposed by the former Sub-Commission referred to a right to restitution of lands in its Article 27.[34] Due to resistance on the part of some states towards the recognition of a right to restitution of lands, Article 28 of the Declaration develops a 'right to redress' instead.[35] It reads:

> Indigenous peoples have the right to redress, by means that can include restitution or, when this is not possible, just, fair and equitable compensation, for the lands, territories and resources which they have traditionally owned or otherwise occupied or used, and which have been confiscated, taken, occupied, used or damaged without their free, prior and informed consent.

Restitution of land becomes part of a larger right to redress, not the main principle. Yet, the Declaration affirms the rule that restitution should be the first principle, and only when it is not possible should other methods of compensation be contemplated. This approach reflects the position adopted by CERD in its General Comment XXIII, which states that 'only when this is for factual reasons not possible, the right to restitution should be substituted by the right to just, fair and prompt compensation. Such compensation should as far as possible take the form of lands and territories.'[36]

Overall, on the issue of collective land ownership, while the Declaration makes a distinction between lands presently occupied (right to own, use, develop and control) and lands historically occupied (a right to lands), such division is attenuated by the affirmation of a regime for remedies for past wrongs which includes a right to land restitution. The affirmation

[34] 'Indigenous peoples have the right to the restitution of the lands, territories and resources which they have traditionally owned or otherwise occupied or used, and which have been confiscated, occupied, used or damaged without their free and informed consent.' UN draft declaration, Art 27.

[35] J Gilbert, 'Indigenous Rights in the Making: The United Nations Declaration on the Rights of Indigenous Peoples' (2007) 14 *International Journal on Minority and Group Rights* 207.

[36] CERD, General Recommendation 23 Indigenous Peoples, UN Doc A/52/18, Annex V, para 5.

of a right to redress, and a right to restitution, is crucial as in many ways the question of land rights is often a question of restoring lands that were taken under a past discriminatory enterprise and linked to a continuing denial of indigenous peoples' rights. From this perspective, the recognition of an ambiguous 'right to lands' traditionally occupied has to be coupled with the affirmation of a right to redress and restitution. Moreover, regarding the link between past and present occupation, the Declaration also insists on the need for states to recognise that indigenous peoples' land rights derive from traditional occupation and indigenous laws and customs relating to land ownership. This may be seen as another positive step towards reconciliation between past practices, which rejected indigenous peoples' own customary land laws, and the present situation.

Laws, Traditions and Customs: Recognition and Adjudication

Regarding the content of a collective right to land for indigenous peoples, another crucial aspect of such a right concerns its source and origin. While most indigenous communities have elaborated traditional laws and customs regarding land rights, such laws are usually ignored, not recognised, or not respected by states' formalised legal systems.[37] This non-recognition of indigenous peoples' own laws regarding land rights is an important area of contention between states and indigenous peoples, which often result in the latter losing their rights to their lands. On this issue Article 26 of the Declaration affirms that when states give legal protection to indigenous peoples' land rights they should do so with 'due respect' for indigenous peoples' customary laws. More specifically, paragraph 3 of Article 26 affirms that 'States shall give legal recognition and protection to these lands, territories and resources. Such recognition shall be conducted with due respect to the customs, traditions and land tenure systems of the indigenous peoples concerned.' This is an important affirmation given that in most situations indigenous peoples are dispossessed of their lands as a result of state authorities' non-recognition of their traditional forms of land tenure systems. On this issue the Declaration goes even further by calling on states to recognise indigenous peoples' customary systems of laws when recognising and adjudicating land rights. Article 27 reads:

> States shall establish and implement, in conjunction with indigenous peoples concerned, a fair, independent, impartial, open and transparent process, giving due recognition to indigenous peoples' laws, traditions, customs and land tenure systems, to recognize and adjudicate the rights of indigenous peoples

[37] See generally D Roy, *Traditional Customary Laws and Indigenous Peoples in Asia* (Minority Rights Group International, March 2005).

pertaining to their lands, territories and resources, including those which were traditionally owned or otherwise occupied or used. Indigenous peoples shall have the right to participate in this process.

This article provides for a sort of 'guideline' or 'framework', inviting states to put in place a 'transparent process' at the national level that gives space to indigenous peoples' customary laws. The emphasis is on the need for states to establish a process that will recognise indigenous peoples' customary land laws. This part of the Declaration does not argue for a rejection of the formal state systems and for the application of indigenous peoples' own laws only; rather the aim is to encourage states to establish a process which will give 'due respect' to indigenous laws. It is important to highlight that such a process will play a role not only in the adjudication of land rights but also in the process of recognition of such rights. This provides more space for the recognition of indigenous peoples' rights based on their own traditional ownership rather than official state recognition of such rights—again an approach based on the idea of reconciliation between states' institutions and indigenous peoples.

Regarding the operationalistion of such recognition, one might find this part of the Declaration disappointing: while it supports the establishment of a 'transparent process' it does not provide details on how such a process should work. At this stage it is important to bear in mind that the aim of the Declaration is to set basic minimum international standards and to affirm the need to give due recognition to indigenous peoples' own laws. For centuries, legal institutions at the international and national levels have dismissed indigenous customary systems of laws as being 'backward' or 'uncivilised'.[38] The Declaration attempts to contribute to the redress of this injustice by calling on states to put in a place a 'transparent process' which gives space to indigenous peoples' systems of laws when it comes to recognition and adjudication of land rights. Regarding practical implementation of such an obligation, one of the only limitations is set out in Article 34 of the Declaration, which states that indigenous peoples' customs have to be in accordance with international human rights standards. This addresses one of the issues raised by some of the states involved in the drafting of the Declaration regarding potential conflicts between customary laws and human rights law, in particular the rights of women with regard to familial and inheritance rights. The Declaration, otherwise, provides the framework for states, in cooperation with indigenous peoples, to develop systems that will give some space for indigenous laws, traditions and customs. The processes employed to develop these systems are required to be open, participative and transparent.

[38] See generally Anghie (n 11); Keal (n 10); and L Benton, *Law and Colonial Cultures* (Cambridge University Press, 2002).

Rights over Natural Resources

Another important component of indigenous peoples' collective rights to their land is the recognition of their rights over the resources contained in those lands. Article 26 affirms that indigenous peoples' land rights (presently and traditionally occupied) refer to a right over lands, territories and resources. This recognition is particularly significant when viewed in the context of the increased global demand for primary natural resources, much of which are located within indigenous peoples' territories. Control over natural resources is an area of historical and ongoing conflict between states, indigenous peoples and other private actors such as transnational corporations that are increasingly encroaching on indigenous peoples' territories to exploit natural resources located therein. Hence, the recognition that land rights also means control over natural resources is an affirmation which has potentially profound implications for indigenous peoples. As with other potentially far-reaching provisions of the Declaration, this acknowledgement on the part of states is the result of prolonged debate during the drafting process, with some states, often notably those most active in the area of resource exploitation on indigenous peoples' lands both at home and abroad, reluctant to recognise rights over natural resources.

Moreover, it is worth noting that on this issue of ownership and control over natural resources ILO Convention 169 recognises a right to use such resources rather than a right of ownership.[39] During the drafting of ILO 169 there was intense debate as to whether land rights should include rights over natural resources. Several states argued that ownership of natural resources was exclusively reserved to states and that in most national legislations such resources could be granted to private individuals on a concessionary basis only.[40] Due to this insistence of states and arguably a reduced voice of indigenous peoples due to a less than inclusive drafting process, the ILO Convention makes a distinction between a right to own land and territories and a right to use natural resources. The Declaration, with its recognition of the right to own, use, control and develop resources, reflects the position of indigenous peoples and the contemporary challenges they face in relation to their cultural survival.

This recognition is part of a larger evolution of international law on the issue of indigenous peoples' rights in relation to natural resources.

[39] Art 15 states: 'The rights of the peoples concerned to the natural resources pertaining to their lands shall be specially safeguarded. These rights include the right of these peoples to participate in the use, management and conservation of these resources.'

[40] See especially the debates of the Working Party: International Labour Conference, Partial Revision of the Indigenous and Tribal Populations Convention, 1957 (No 107), Provisional Record 25, 76th session, Geneva, 1988.

The IACHR has been especially active in examining issues relating to the rights of indigenous peoples over natural resources. In the landmark decision of *Awas Tigni* the Court asserted that the term 'property' used in Article 21 of the American Convention includes 'those material things which can be possessed, as well as any right which may be part of a person's patrimony; that concept includes all movables and immovables, corporeal and incorporeal elements and any other intangible object capable of having value'.[41] Likewise, in the case of the Yakye Axa community the Court pointed out that 'the close ties of indigenous peoples with their traditional territories and the natural resources therein associated with their culture, as well as the components derived from them, must be safeguarded by Article 21 of the American Convention'.[42] More recently the Court confirmed and refined its position in the *Saramaka* case, stating:

> the right to use and enjoy their territory would be meaningless in the context of indigenous and tribal communities if said right were not connected to the natural resources that lie on and within the land. That is, the demand for collective land ownership by members of indigenous and tribal peoples derives from the need to ensure the security and permanence of their control and use of the natural resources, which in turn maintains their very way of life. This connectedness between the territory and the natural resources necessary for their physical and cultural survival is precisely what needs to be protected under Article 21 of the Convention in order to guarantee the members of indigenous and tribal communities' right to the use and enjoyment of their property. From this analysis, it follows that the natural resources found on and within indigenous and tribal people's territories that are protected under Article 21 are those natural resources traditionally used and necessary for the very survival, development and continuation of such people's way of life.[43]

This decision of the IACHR, highlighting that it would be 'meaningless' to recognise land rights for indigenous peoples without recognising their rights over natural resources, mirrors the rationale adopted in the UN Declaration linking control over natural resources with indigenous peoples' survival. This position is illustrative of the evolution in the recognition of indigenous peoples' land rights and an increased awareness of the profound impact that external forces, such as unwanted exploitation of natural recourses, can have on their cultural survival, which has occurred since the adoption of ILO Convention 169 some 20 years ago. To protect and give effect to these recognised rights to territories, lands and resources in the context of unwanted exploitation, the Declaration

[41] *Awas Tingni Community v Nicaragua* (n 29) para 144.

[42] *Yakye Axa Indigenous Community v Paraguay (Merits, Reparations and Costs), IACHR, judgment of 17 June 2005, Series C No 125 (2005).*

[43] *Case of the Saramaka People v Suriname* (Series C No 172) [2007] IACHR 5 (28 November 2007) para 122.

requires that states obtain indigenous peoples' free, prior and informed consent (FPIC).

THE REQUIREMENT TO OBTAIN FPIC: NATURAL EVOLUTION OR GROUNDBREAKING DEVELOPMENT?[44]

As discussed in the introduction to this chapter, activities such as mining, logging, dam construction and mono-cropping are becoming synonymous with violations of indigenous peoples' rights. These economic development projects, executed for the most part without the adequate participation of indigenous peoples, have had a serious impact on their well-being. The former Special Rapporteur on indigenous people and their relationship to land, Erica-Irene Daes, described the associated problem of expropriation of indigenous lands and resources without indigenous peoples' consent as 'growing and severe'.[45] This widespread phenomenon of imposing projects on indigenous peoples without their consent has come to be termed by indigenous peoples as 'development aggression'.[46] This is particularly pervasive in the extractive sector and its negative impact on indigenous peoples has been described as enormous.[47] The associated ongoing violations of indigenous peoples' rights, combined with increased demand and prices for minerals and the fact that much of the world's remaining mineral resources are located in indigenous territories,[48] has led many indigenous peoples to conclude that development aggression in the area of natural resource extraction poses a grave threat to their cultural survival.[49] Given this context, it is

[44] This section of the chapter is based on Cathal Doyle's doctoral thesis which addresses the operationalization of Free Prior and Informed Consent in the extractive sector. See also Doyle, Cathal, "Free, prior and informed consent: a universal norm and framework for consultation and benefit sharing in relation to indigenous peoples and the extractive sector", submission made to the UN OHCHR Workshop on Extractive Industries, Indigenous Peoples and Human Rights, Moscow in December 2008 Available at ww2.ohchr.org/english/issues/indigenous/resource_companies.htm.

[45] E-I Daes, *Indigenous Peoples' Permanent Sovereignty over Natural Resources*, E/CN.4/Sub.2/2004/30/Add.1, para 7.

[46] Permanent Forum on Indigenous Issues, 4th session, New York, 16–27 May 2005, Special Theme: Millennium Development Goals Information Received from the United Nations System, E/C.19/2005/4/Add.13, 28 March 2005, paras 3–6; see also Report of the Special Rapporteur on the situation of human rights and fundamental freedoms of indigenous people (R Stavenhagen), 21 January 2003, UN Doc E/CN.4/2003/90, para 28.

[47] J Ruggie, Interim Report of the Special Representative of the Secretary-General on the Issue of Human Rights and Transnational Corporations and Other Business Enterprises, UN Doc E/CN.4/2006/97, paras 25, 29.

[48] R Moody, *Rocks and Hard Places* (London, Zed Books, 2007) 10; see also AA Tujan, Jr and RB Guzman, *Globalizing Philippine Mining* (Manila IBON Foundation Inc Databank and Research Centre, IBON Books, 2002) 153.

[49] Report of the Special Rapporteur on the situation of human rights and fundamental freedoms of indigenous people (R Stavenhagen), Mission to Philippines (2002) UN Doc

hardly surprising that the unprecedented volume and scale of extractive projects currently being planned in indigenous territories is escalating tensions and conflict between indigenous peoples, states and transnational corporations.

International Human Rights Law and FPIC

The former UN Working Group on Indigenous Populations (WGIP) pointed to the ruling of the International Court of Justice (ICJ) in the *Western Sahara* case as evidence that consent has formed the basis of agreements between states and indigenous peoples since as far back as 1975.[50] Others point to the fact that consent as a principle in relation to dealings with indigenous peoples has been operational for hundreds of years, dating back to the original treaties negotiated with indigenous peoples by colonisers.[51] Regardless of when consent was initially established as a principle in relation to negotiations between states and indigenous peoples, it is clear that the adoption of FPIC as a general principle in negotiations with indigenous peoples has gained significant momentum in recent years. This momentum is reflected in the fact that FPIC is increasingly referenced in international instruments and fora ranging from general comments, recommendations and concluding observations of UN treaty bodies to jurisprudence of treaty bodies and regional courts, reports and analyses of UN special procedures and legislation, and jurisprudence emerging from national jurisdictions. In recognition of the importance of FPIC, the PFII and the WGIP worked on developing methodologies and legal frameworks aimed at promoting the principle of FPIC and assisting with its implementation.[52] ILO Convention 169, the only international

E/CN.4/2003/90/Add.3, para 63. See also Report of the Special Rapporteur (n 46) para 20, providing examples of developments that are threatening the existence of indigenous peoples in locations around the world.

[50] International Court of Justice, *Western Sahara: Advisory Opinion of 16 October 1975* [1975] ICJ Rep 12. The ICJ advisory opinion refers the 'freely expressed will and desire' of a people. See M Janis, 'The International Court of Justice: Advisory Opinion on the Western Sahara' (1976) 17 *Harvard International Law Journal* 609. For an analysis of the self-determination issue in the Western Sahara see J Castellino, *International Law and Self Determination: The Interplay of Politics of Territorial Possession with Formulations of Post-Colonial 'National' Identity* (Leiden, Martinus Nijhoff, 2000).

[51] M Colchester and F MacKay, 'In Search of Middle Ground: Indigenous Peoples, Collective Representation and the Right to Free, Prior and Informed Consent', Forest Peoples Programme, August 2004, www.forestpeoples.org.

[52] Report of the International Workshop on Methodologies regarding Free, Prior and Informed Consent, and Indigenous Peoples, New York, 17–19 January 2005, UN Doc E/C.19/2005/3; WGIP Standard-Setting Legal Commentary on the Concept of Free, Prior and Informed Consent, Expanded Working Paper submitted by AI Motoc, E/CN.4/Sub.2/AC.4/2005/WP.1, 14 July 2005.

treaty specifically dedicated to indigenous peoples, contains an explicit reference to indigenous peoples' informed consent in the context of relocation. It also recognises indigenous peoples' right to 'decide their own priorities for the process of development' and requires that states consult with them through their representative institution, 'with the objective of achieving agreement or consent to the proposed measures'.[53]

The HRC, the Committee on Economic Social and Cultural Rights (CESCR) and CERD have all clarified that the right to self-determination applies to indigenous peoples.[54] Consistent with this recognition of the right to self-determination these treaty bodies have pointed to state duty to seek and obtain FPIC in the context of activities impacting on indigenous peoples' rights and interests.[55] Both CERD and the CESCR have instructed states that indigenous peoples' consent is required in the context of extractive projects.[56] In 2009, in its ruling on the *Poma-Poma v Peru* case, the HRC stated that for indigenous participation in decision-making to be effective their FPIC was required and that 'mere consultation' was inadequate to ensure protection of their rights under Article 27 of the International Covenant on Civil and Political Rights (ICCPR).[57] This ruling was consistent with the HRC's 1994 decision in the case of *Lansman v Finland*, where it clarified that the scope of a state's freedom with regard to development on indigenous peoples' lands cannot be 'assessed by

[53] ILO Convention 169 (1989) Art 6. Art 15 requires consultation in the context of exploration or exploitation of subsoil resources.

[54] HRC: Australia UN Doc CCPR/C/69/AUS (2000) para 10, Mexico CCPR/C/79/Add.109 (1999) para 19, Canada CCPR/C/79/Add.105 (1999), paras 7 and 8, Sweden CCPR/C/74/SWE (2002) para 15, Norway CCPR/C/79/Add. 112 (1999) paras 10 and 17 and Denmark CCPR/C/70/DNK (2000) para 11. CESCR: Russian Federation UN doc E/C.12/1/Add.94 (2003), para 39; the Philippines UN Doc E/C.12/PHL/CO/4 (2008), para 16; Sweden E/C.12/SWE/CO/5 (2008) para 15. CERD General Comment XXI (1996) clarifies that self-determination applies to 'all peoples' Its General Comment XXIII on 'indigenous peoples' is an implicit recognition of this right to self-determination as 'peoples'.

[55] The terminology used by the treaty bodies relation to the requirement for consent varies from the weaker formulations of 'seek' / 'endeavour to obtain' FPIC, to the stronger formulations of 'obtain' / 'require' FPIC. For examples of the latter CERD Concluding observations to Ecuador CERD/C/ECU/CO/19 15 (2008); CERD's Early Warning Urgent Action letter to the Philippine Government (7 March 2008) and HRC *Poma-Poma v Peru* UN Doc CCPR/C/95/D/1457/2006 (24 April 2009).

[56] See CERD, General Comment XXIII (n 30). See also CERD, Concluding Observations on Ecuador, 2003, CERD/C/62/CO/2: 'as to the exploitation of subsoil resources located subjacent to the traditional lands of indigenous communities the Committee observes that mere consultation of these communities prior to exploitation falls short of meeting the requirements set out in General Comment XXIII on the Rights of Indigenous Peoples. The Committee therefore recommends that the prior informed consent of these communities be sought'; CESCR Concluding Observations on Ecuador, 32nd session, 26 April–14 May 2004, E/C.12/1/Add.100, paras 12 and 35; CESCR Concluding Observations on Colombia, 27th session, 12–30 November 2001, E/C.12/1/Add.74, paras 12 and 33.

[57] HRC *Poma Poma v Peru* (n 55) Paras 7.6 and 7.4. Complaint taken against Peru in 2006 under the Optional Protocol to the ICCPR.

reference to a margin of appreciation but by reference to the obligations it has undertaken in Article 27'.[58] To date CERD has been the most engaged and innovative international human rights body on the subject of FPIC. Its General Comment XXIII, issued in 1997, on the Rights of Indigenous Peoples states that 'no decisions directly relating to their rights and interests are to be taken without their informed consent'.[59] The focus of CERD's current work in relation to indigenous peoples is reflective of the increased emphasis being placed on FPIC following the adoption of the Declaration. In addition to an increased emphasis on the requirement to obtain FPIC in its concluding observations to states,[60] CERD is currently examining cases in countries including Brazil, Botswana, Canada, Niger, the Philippines, Peru, India and Indonesia in the context of its Early Warning Urgent Action procedure, and has asked those states' respective governments to respond to allegations regarding their failure to obtain the FPIC of the affected indigenous peoples.[61]

Support for the affirmation of a right to FPIC can also be found in reports and declarations of UN Special Rapporteurs. The former Special Rapporteur on the human rights and fundamental freedoms of indigenous people, Rodolfo Stavenhagen, emphasised the importance of the 'right to free prior and informed consent by indigenous peoples', which includes their 'right to say no', describing it as being of 'crucial concern' in relation to large-scale or major development projects and 'essential' for the protection of their human rights.[62]

The current Special Rapporteur, S James Anaya, has argued that we are witnessing the development of an international norm requiring the consent of indigenous peoples when their property rights are impacted by natural resource extraction.[63] The Rapporteur addressed the issue of FPIC in his 2009 annual report to the Human Rights Council and in communications

[58] *Lansman v Finland*, Communication No 511/1992, UN Doc CCPR/C/52/D/511/1992 (1994), para 9.4 the Committee clarified that 'measures whose impact amount to a denial of the right [to culture] will not be compatible with the obligations under article 27'.

[59] CERD, General Comment XXIII (n 30) para 4(d).

[60] Ecuador UN Doc CERD/C/ECU/CO/19 (2008), Russia UN Doc CERD/C/RUS/CO/19 20 (2008), and Philippines UN Doc CERD/C/PHL/CO/20, (2009) addressing FPIC for resource exploitation.

[61] See Early Warning Urgent Action letters sent following CERD's 73rd, 74th and 75th sessions, 2008–2010, http://www2.ohchr.org/english/bodies/cerd/early-warning.htm.

[62] Report of the Special Rapporteur (n 46) paras 13 and 66. He points out that FPIC is necessary as too many major developments do not respect the consultation and participation criteria that are laid out in ILO Convention 169.

[63] SJ Anaya, 'Indigenous Peoples' Participatory Rights in Relation to Decisions about Natural Resource Extraction' (2005) 22 *Arizona Journal of International and Comparative Law* 17: 'Where property rights are affected by natural resource extraction, the international norm is developing to also require actual consent by the indigenous peoples concerned.' See also F MacKay, 'Indigenous Peoples' Rights and Resource Exploitation' (2004) 12 *Philippines Natural Resources Law Journal* 58.

and statements to the Ecuadorian and Peruvian governments in 2008 and 2010 respectively.[64] In his comments on FPIC the Rapporteur cited the UN Declaration and the recent IACHR *Saramaka v Suriname* ruling,[65] holding that measures which have a potentially substantial impact on the basic physical and/or cultural well-being of an indigenous community should not proceed without their consent.[66] The Rapporteur proposed that the extent of the obligation to obtain consent be a function of the potential impact of a proposed measure on indigenous peoples' lives and territories, with significant and direct impacts leading to a 'strong presumption' of the requirement for consent. He further noted that this requirement could 'in certain contexts' 'harden into a prohibition of the measure or project in the absence of indigenous consent.'[67] In his 2010 statement to the Government of Peru the Rapporteur noted that the UN DRIP indicated that consent was a requirement, as opposed to merely an objective, under Article 32 for extractive projects which may have significant social, cultural or environmental impacts on indigenous peoples.[68]

The UN Expert Mechanism on the Rights of Indigenous Peoples (EMRIP), established by the Human Rights Council, is also in the process of addressing the right to FPIC. Having recommended at its 1st session in October 2008 that the Durban Declaration and Programme of Action 'should acknowledge that both the right to self determination and the principle of FPIC are now universally recognized through the adoption of the Declaration',[69] the EMRIP proceeded to examine the issue in more detail at its 3rd session in the context of its draft study on indigenous peoples' right

[64] In the case of Ecuador the Special Rapporteur addressed the requirement for FPIC in response to a request for advice regarding the drafting of its constitution. See Report of the Special Rapporteur on the situation of human rights and fundamental freedoms of indigenous people (S James Anaya), Addendum A/HRC/9/9/Add.1, 15 August 2008, Annex 1. In the case of Peru the Rapporteur addressed the requirement for consent in relation to legislative developments following his country visit, see 'Declaración pública del Relator Especial sobre los derechos humanos y libertades fundamentales de los indígenas, James Anaya, sobre la "Ley del derecho a la consulta previa a los pueblos indígenas u originarios reconocido en el Convenio No. 169 de la Organización Internacional de Trabajo" aprobada por el Congreso de la República del Perú' 7 de julio de 2010.

[65] Report of the Special Rapporteur 2008 (n 64). See also *Saramaka People v Suriname* (n 43).

[66] Report of the Special Rapporteur 2008 (n 64) para 39.

[67] Report of the Special Rapporteur on the situation of human rights and fundamental freedoms of indigenous people, James Anaya 15 July 2009 UN Doc A/HRC/12/34 Para 47.

[68] Declaración pública del Relator Especial (n 64) 'El Relator Especial agregaría además, como ejemplo en el que se requiere el consentimiento indígena, el caso de una propuesta de instalación de actividades de extracción de recursos naturales dentro de un territorio indígena cuando esas actividades tuviesen impactos sociales, culturales y ambientales significativos.' The Rapporteur also noted that consent was a requirement in the situations covered under Articles 10 (relocation) and 29 (disposal of hazardous materials) of the Declaration.

[69] Report of the expert mechanism on the rights of indigenous peoples on its first session A/HRC/10/56 (8 January 2009) 4.

to participate in decision making. The draft study notes that indigenous peoples view the right to FPIC as 'a requirement, prerequisite and manifestation of the exercise of their right to self-determination' and that particular emphasis is placed on FPIC in the context of large-scale natural resource extraction.[70] Likewise the PFII dedicated its 9th session in 2010 to the issue of development with culture and identity in accordance with Article 3 (self-determination) and Article 32 (development and FPIC) of the Declaration.

At the regional level the IACHR has recently reaffirmed the requirement for FPIC, citing Article 32 of the Declaration in its November 2007 ruling on the *Saramaka v Suriname* case. It stated: 'the Court considers that, regarding large-scale development or investment projects that would have a major impact within Saramaka territory, the state has a duty, not only to consult with the Saramaka, but also to obtain their free, prior, and informed consent, according to their customs and traditions.'[71] The Inter-American Court and Commission respectively, previously identified the requirement for consent in the cases of the *Awas Tingni v Nicaragua* and *Mary and Carrie Dann v The United States*.[72] In addition, the Proposed American Declaration on the Rights of Indigenous Peoples contains a similar clause to Article 32 of the UN Declaration, requiring FPIC for 'any plan, program or proposal affecting the rights or living conditions of indigenous peoples'.[73] The updated procedure of the working group responsible for the drafting of the American Declaration requires that the UN DRIP serve as 'a point of reference' for reaching agreement on those articles where consensus had not yet been reached. [74] This would appear to imply that a standard lower than the requirement to obtain FPIC, as recognized in the UN DRIP, would not be acceptable. In the 2009 case of *Kenya v Endorois* the ACHPR also affirmed the requirement for FPIC to be obtained in accordance with indigenous peoples' customs and traditions in the context of development projects that could have a major impact in their territories.[75]

[70] 'Progress report on the study on indigenous peoples and the right to participate in decision-making. Report of the Expert Mechanism on the Rights of Indigenous Peoples' UN Doc A/HRC/EMRIP/2010/2 (17 May 2010) para 34.

[71] *Saramaka People v Suriname* (n 43) para 134.

[72] *Awas Tingni Community v Nicaragua* (n 29) para 143 and *Mary and Carrie Dann v. United States*, Case 11.140, Report No. 75/02, Inter-Am. C.H.R., Doc. 5 rev. 1 at 860 (2002) para 165.

[73] 'Eleventh meeting of negotiations in the quest for points of consensus (United States, Washington D.C.—April 14 to 18, 2008) Record of the current status of the draft American Declaration on the Rights of Indigenous Peoples' OEA/Ser.K/XVI GT/DADIN/doc.334/08 (18 April 2008) Article XXIX 19.

[74] 'Report of the chair on the meeting for reflection on the meetings of negotiations in the quest for points of consensus' OEA/Ser.K/XVI GT/DADIN/doc.321/08 (14 January 2008) 4.

[75] African Commission on Human and Peoples Rights Case 276 / 2003—Centre for Minority Rights Development (Kenya) and Minority Rights Group International on behalf of Endorois Welfare Council v Kenya (2009) para 291.

At the national level a number of jurisdictions, including the Philippines, Australia's Northern Territory, Venezuela and Greenland have enacted legislation recognising the requirement to obtain indigenous peoples' informed consent prior to approving activities in their territories.[76] As a further reflection of evolving customary international law in the area of indigenous participation rights, a number of donor governments have also recognised the importance of FPIC as a key principle in safeguarding indigenous peoples' rights. These include the governments of Denmark and Spain, which, along with the European Commission, have incorporated the principle of FPIC of indigenous peoples into their development strategies.[77]

Jurisprudence at the national level has also recognised the duty to obtain indigenous peoples' FPIC. The Supreme Court of Canada in the *Delgamuukw v British Columbia* case clarified that where aboriginal people hold title to land, the government's duty to consult is 'in most cases … significantly deeper than mere consultation' and can require the 'full consent of an aboriginal nation'.[78] In its October 2007 landmark ruling in *Maya Villages of Santa Cruz and Conejo v The Attorney General of Belize and the Department of Environment and Natural Resources*, the Supreme Court of Belize referenced the FPIC requirements in both the Declaration and CERD's General Comment XXIII on the rights of indigenous peoples. The Court ordered that the state cease and abstain from any acts, including the granting of mining permits and the issuing of regulations concerning resource use, which impacted on the Mayan indigenous communities 'unless such acts are pursuant to their informed consent'.[79] In 2010 the Court reaffirmed the applicability of its 2007 ruling to all 'the Maya villages in the Toledo

[76] Philippines: Indigenous Peoples Rights Act (IPRA) Republic Act No 8371 (1997) Chapter III s 3g; Greenland: The Greenland Home Rule Act, Act No 577, (1978), Sect 8(1) which included 'a mutual right of veto' over mining projects. This Act was superseded by the Act on Greenland Self-Government adopted 19 May 2009, which transfers responsibility for the mineral resource area to Greenland's Self Government authorities; Venezuela: Ley Organica de Pueblos y comunidades Indígenas Gaceta Official de la Republica Bolivariana De Venezuela Numero 38,344 Caracas (2005) Chapter II Art 11–19; Australia: Aboriginal Land Rights (Northern Territory) Act An Act providing for the granting of Traditional Aboriginal Land in the Northern Territory for the benefit of Aboriginals, and for other purposes. (No 191 of 1976), Sect 42.

[77] The EC has included FPIC as the key principle in development cooperation: see 'The European Consensus on Development, Joint statement by the Council and the representatives of the governments of the Member States meeting within the Council, the European Parliament and the Commission on European Union Development Policy', Official Journal of the European Union 2006/C 46/01 paras 101 and 103. See also 'Strategy for Danish Support to Indigenous Peoples' (Danish Ministry of Foreign Affairs, Danida, May 2004) 11; and Report of the Government of Spain to the PFII 6th session, 21 February 2007, UN Doc E/C.19/2007/4 para 4.

[78] *Delgamuukw v British Columbia* [1997] 3 SCR 1010, para 168.

[79] *Aurelio Cal and the Maya Village of Santa Cruz v Attorney General of Belize; and Manuel Coy and Maya Village of Conejo v Attorney General of Belize*, (Consolidated) Claim Nos 171 & 172, 2007, Supreme Court of Belize (18 October 2007) para 136(d).

Districts'.[80] In the 2009 case of *Álvaro Bailarín y otros, contra los Ministerios del Interior y de Justicia; de Ambiente, Vivienda y Desarrollo Territorial; de Defensa; de Protección Social; y de Minas y Energía* the Constitutional Court of Colombia addressed the requirement to obtain FPIC in relation to the issuance of a concession for mining exploration.[81] The Court ruled that the state has a duty to obtain FPIC in accordance with indigenous peoples' customs and traditions where large scale investment or development plans may have a major impact within their territories.[82] These recent jurisprudential developments pertaining to FPIC illustrate the importance of the strongly worded and unambiguous language contained in the Declaration, particularly in relation to the development, utilisation and exploitation of resources. Despite the objections of some states to this language during the drafting and negotiating process, indigenous peoples' insistence that it not be compromised prevailed. The adoption of the Declaration, which contains no fewer than six references to the requirement to obtain FPIC, is an acknowledgement by states that FPIC is, in principle (if not yet in practice), a minimum standard to be respected 'for the survival, dignity and well-being of the indigenous peoples of the world'.[83]

Scope of Requirement to Obtain FPIC in the Declaration

The Declaration provides a normative framework for future engagement between indigenous peoples and states, the private sector or the UN system.[84] If implemented in good faith it provides an opportunity to address historical power imbalances between indigenous peoples and those wishing to access their lands and exploit their resources. In so doing, it affords a unique opportunity to significantly reduce the potential for further development aggression and to address existing conflicts. Fundamental to, and inseparable from, the Declaration's framework is respect for what indigenous peoples view as two of its core principles, namely self-determination and FPIC.[85] It has long

[80] *The Maya Leaders Alliance and the Toledo Alcaldes Association on behalf of the Maya Villages of Toledo District et al v The Attorney General of Belize and the Minister of Natural Resources* Environment Claim No. 366, 2008 Supreme Court Of Belize (28th June 2010) para 126 (i).

[81] Constitutional Court of Colombia Sentencia T-769/09 [2009], 36 (between n27 and 28).

[82] Ibid.

[83] Art 43.

[84] United Nations Development Group Guidelines on Indigenous Peoples' Issues, February 2008, p 10; see also Statement by the Chairman, Global Indigenous Caucus, Les Malezer, 13 September 2007.

[85] Art 3 states: 'Indigenous peoples have the right to self-determination. By virtue of that right they freely determine their political status and freely pursue their economic, social and cultural development.'

been argued by indigenous peoples that the fulfilment of their right to self-determination is dependent on the recognition of their rights to lands and territories and the resources contained therein.[86] According to Erica-Irene Daes, the modern concept of self-determination, in order to be meaningful, 'must logically and legally carry with it the essential right of permanent sovereignty over natural resources'.[87] This reasoning is reflected in the IACHR's *Saramaka v Suriname* ruling that indigenous peoples' land rights would be rendered meaningless 'if not connected to the natural resources that lie *on and within* the land'.[88] International law also recognises that implicit in indigenous peoples' right to self-determination is the right to effective participation and consultation in relation to any measures that impact on them.[89] The right to self-determination also embodies the 'freely expressed will and desire' of a people.[90] Consequently for indigenous peoples, the standard that has crystallised as the basis for effective consultation and participation in the context of development in their territories is FPIC.[91]

Fundamental to a people's right to self-determination is their ability to chart their own destiny. FPIC, which provides for the right to reject projects or measures that directly impact on a people and thereby enable them to exercise control over their destiny, flows directly from this aspect of the right to self-determination. FPIC therefore is premised on and essential for the operationalisation of the right to self-determination. In recognition of this the PFII and experts have described FPIC as 'a substantive framework' that is integral to indigenous peoples' rights to lands and resources[92] and central to the exercise of their right to self-determination with respect to developments affecting them.[93] FPIC, while of particular significance to issues pertaining to control over lands, territories and natural resources,

[86] Daes (n 45) para 8: '[I]t has become clear that meaningful political and economic self-determination of indigenous peoples will never be possible without indigenous peoples' having legal authority to exercise control over their lands and territories.'

[87] Ibid, para 17.

[88] Emphasis added. This qualification that resources are inclusive of those on and within lands is in line with the provisions of the Declaration. These provisions do not make any distinction between subsoil and non-subsoil resources and as such the use of the term 'resources' within the Declaration is inclusive of both.

[89] See F MacKay, Compilations of UN Treaty Body Jurisprudence Volumes I, II and III Covering the Years 1993–2008, Forest Peoples Programme available. See also Programme of Action of the Second International Decade of the World's Indigenous People, Objective (ii).

[90] ICJ Western Sahara Advisory Opinion (n 50).

[91] The HRC has stated that effective participation in the decision-making process 'requires ... the free, prior and informed consent of the members of the community' *Poma Poma v Peru* (n 55) Para 7.6.

[92] PFII, Report of the International Workshop on Methodologies (n 52) para 41.

[93] P Tamang, Indigenous Expert, 'An Overview of the Principle of Free, Prior and Informed Consent and Indigenous Peoples in International and Domestic Law and Practices Contribution', PFII Workshop on FPIC, UN Doc PFII/2004.WS.2/8.

is also essential for the realisation of other self-determination rights.[94] Reflective of this is the fact that references to FPIC in the Declaration are broad in scope and extend to such areas as redress for the taking of cultural, intellectual, religious and spiritual property[95] and the requirement to obtain FPIC 'before adopting and implementing legislative or administrative measures that may affect' indigenous peoples.[96]

Within the context of rights to lands, territories and resources the Declaration explicitly requires FPIC in four contexts. First, it is required prior to any relocation of indigenous peoples from their lands or territories.[97] Secondly, FPIC must be obtained prior to the storage or disposal of hazardous materials in their lands or territories.[98] Thirdly, the Declaration affirms that indigenous peoples have a right to redress wherever 'lands, territories and resources, which they have traditionally owned or otherwise occupied or used … have been confiscated, taken, occupied, used or damaged without their free, prior and informed consent'.[99] Finally, Article 32 addresses the contentious issue of development projects that impact on indigenous peoples' lands, territories and resources. It states that:

1. Indigenous peoples have the right to determine and develop priorities and strategies for the development or use of their lands or territories and other resources.
2. States shall consult and cooperate in good faith with the indigenous peoples concerned through their own representative institutions in order to obtain their free and informed consent prior to the approval of any project affecting their lands or territories and other resources, particularly in connection with the development, utilization or exploitation of mineral, water or other resources.
3. States shall provide effective mechanisms for just and fair redress for any such activities, and appropriate measures shall be taken to mitigate adverse environmental, economic, social, cultural or spiritual impact.

The first paragraph of Article 32 contextualises the requirement for FPIC which is articulated in the second paragraph. It frames FPIC as a

[94] WGIP Standard-Setting Legal Commentary (n 52) para 33. See also 'Statement to the Third session of the UN Expert Mechanism on the Rights of Indigenous Peoples Presentation under Agenda Item 3 Cathal Doyle on behalf of University of Middlesex Department of Law & Philippines Indigenous Peoples Links'. Available at www.docip.org

[95] Art 11. This provision is in line with developments requiring FPIC under the Convention on Biological Diversity see Draft Protocol on Access to Genetic Resources and the Fair and Equitable Sharing of Benefits Arising from their Utilization to the Convention on Biological Diversity. UN Doc UNEP/CBD/COP/10/5/Add.4, Page 16.

[96] Art 19.

[97] Art 10.

[98] Art 29.

[99] Art 28.

prerequisite for the realization of a self-determined development path premised on control over lands and resources.[100] Viewed from this perspective FPIC is integral to the right to self-government and autonomy, being not only necessary to prevent unwanted developments, but also essential in ensuring that indigenous peoples shape developments by and for themselves. Consequently, FPIC is required for 'any project affecting their lands or territories and other resources'. This differs from the FPIC protections afforded in Articles 10 and 29 in two significant ways. On the one hand, the focus of Article 32 is limited to projects, whereas Articles 10 and 29 are not subject to this restriction. On the other hand, Article 32 does not link the requirement for FPIC to specific impacts of projects, and in this regard its scope is broader than that of Articles 10 and 29.

In summary, Article 32 places FPIC at the core of indigenous peoples' right to development. It requires FPIC for all projects affecting indigenous peoples, and does not place any limitations on FPIC in relation to either the type of project or its potential impact. It does, however, place special emphasis on projects that involve the 'development, utilization or exploitation of mineral, water or other resources'. The wording 'any such activities' in paragraph 3 would appear to imply that it should be read in the light of paragraph 2, and not interpreted separately as justifying the pursuit of activities without meeting the requirement for FPIC.[101] Instead, it makes clear that even where FPIC has been given, there is a duty on the state to ensure that appropriate redress and mitigation measures are provided for.

Article 32 also requires that states consult with indigenous peoples 'in good faith' through their 'own representative institutions'. Article 33 states that indigenous peoples have the right to 'determine the structures and to select the membership of their institutions in accordance with their own procedures'. Taken together these articles address one of the most common issues encountered by indigenous peoples in consultations with states and companies where the requirement to obtain FPIC has been recognised: that of portraying individuals amenable to the interests of these external entities, but who are not selected according to the community's procedures, customs or traditions, as being representative of the community.[102] A short overview of the content of the principle of FPIC

[100] This affirmation is consistent with indigenous peoples' right to development recognized in Article 23 and the right to self-determination under Article 3. See C Doyle & J Gilbert Indigenous Peoples and Globalization: From "Development Aggression" to "Self-Determined Development" in European Yearbook on Minority Issues Special Focus: Contemporary Challenges of Globalization (EURAC, Bolzano/Bozen, forthcoming)

[101] Article 28 addresses such situations requiring redress for taking or use of resources without FPIC.

[102] This was a consistent theme that emerged from regional consultations held with indigenous peoples in the Philippines in preparation for the ICERD indigenous peoples

or, as it is often interchangeably referred to, the right to FPIC, is provided in the following paragraph.

FPIC, in the context of development projects, requires that good faith consultation processes with indigenous peoples be free from all external manipulation, coercion and intimidation; that the affected indigenous peoples be notified that their consent will be sought sufficiently in advance of the approval, or commencement, of any activities; and that there be full disclosure of information regarding all aspects of a potential project in a manner that is accessible and understandable to the indigenous people. Finally, indigenous peoples can approve or reject a project or activity. This decision to approve or reject should be based on the consensus of all indigenous people affected and be reached though their traditional decision-making processes and representative institutions in accordance with their customary laws and practices. Consent may be required at multiple phases during the consultation and negotiation processes and throughout the projects lifecycle. If consent is given following good faith negotiations it should result in a legally binding agreement that ensures equitable benefit sharing arrangements. Effective grievance mechanisms spanning the entire project lifecycle, including any post-project impacts, should be guaranteed. FPIC therefore establishes the processes for consultation and negotiations that have to be followed and imposes a requirement that the outcome of these processes be recognised and upheld. Both the process and outcome components of FPIC are necessary to ensure indigenous peoples' effective participation in the decision-making process.

While literature elaborating on the content and meaning of FPIC exists, work remains to be done in terms of assessing the mechanisms, measures and conditions required to ensure its meaningful implementation in practice in accordance with the right to self-determination.[103] Such analysis and any conclusions drawn should be based on the actual experiences of indigenous communities and reflect their perspectives.[104]

shadow report, July–August 2008 (on file with authors). The issue of representation was addressed in *Saramaka People v Suriname* (n 43) para 164: '[T]he question of whether certain self-identified members of the Saramaka people may assert certain communal rights on behalf of the juridical personality of such people is a question that must be resolved by the Saramaka people in accordance with their own traditional customs and norms, not by the State or this Court in this particular case.'

[103] F MacKay, 'Indigenous Peoples' Right to Free, Prior and Informed Consent and the World Bank's Extractive Review' (2004) 4 *Sustainable Development Law and Policy* 43–65. Forest Peoples Programme, an organisation focused on forest peoples' rights, has published numerous reports on FPIC, including analyses of its implementation in a number of states. Numerous submissions were made to the World Commission on Dams regarding FPIC: see www.dams.org.

[104] The Tebtebba Foundation has conducted a number of such studies on the implementation of the FPIC in the Philippines (on file with the authors). The authors participated in consultation in relation to a number of FPIC processes conducted in the Philippines as part

Objections to the Inclusion of FPIC in the Declaration: A Right of Veto?

The inclusion of the requirement for FPIC in the Declaration, given its potentially profound implications for control over and access to resources, was inevitably going to be contentious.

As the requirement to obtain consent implies respecting the right to say 'no', one of the key contentious issues raised by certain states revolved around the notion of a 'right to veto'. Objections to the inclusion of a requirement to obtain FPIC came primarily from the four countries that voted against the adoption of the Declaration, namely New Zealand, the United States, Australia and Canada. These same countries are home to most of the world's transnational mining companies, many of which have operations or interests in indigenous territories either at home or abroad. The position of New Zealand, the United States and Australia with regard to FPIC is laid out in joint statements submitted to the PFII and the Human Rights Council: '[I]t is our firm position that there can be no absolute right of free, prior, informed consent that is applicable uniquely to indigenous peoples and that would apply regardless of circumstances.'[105] They further stated that giving a 'veto' to particular sub-groups of the population was not a position that a democratic government could accept.[106] Canada also objected to the use of the concept of FPIC in the Declaration, which it argued could be interpreted as 'giving a veto to indigenous peoples over many … development proposals … which concern the broader population and may affect indigenous peoples'.[107] During the drafting process these states made unsuccessful attempts to weaken the requirement for FPIC by proposing that the operative verb 'obtain' be changed to 'seek', in relation to FPIC.

A requirement to obtain indigenous peoples' consent in relation to development projects in their territories is now firmly enshrined within the normative framework of indigenous peoples' rights. At present however there appears to be some divergence of opinion within the human rights regime in relation to the situations which trigger this

of the preparation of the 2009 Philippines ICERD Indigenous Peoples Shadow Report see http://www2.ohchr.org/english/bodies/cerd/cerds75.htm

105 Statement of Peter Vaughn to the PFII, Representative of Australia, on behalf of Australia, New Zealand and the United States of America, on Free, Prior and Informed Consent, 22 May 2006, New Zealand Ministry of Foreign Affairs and Trade. http://www.australiaun.org/unny/soc_220506.html

106 Note verbale dated 2 August 2006 from the Permanent Mission of Australia to the United Nations Office at Geneva addressed to the Office of the United Nations High Commissioner for Human Rights, see UN Doc A/HRC/2/G/1 (24 August 2006).

107 Canada's position on the United Nations Draft Declaration on the Rights of Indigenous Peoples, 29 June 2006, http://www.ainc-inac.gc.ca/ap/ia/pubs/ddr/ddr-eng.asp.

requirement.[108] These opinions can be broadly grouped into two categories. The first is aligned with the view of many indigenous peoples and holds that FPIC is required for any project or activity affecting their lands, territories and resources or their well-being. The second, which also requires respect for FPIC, holds that it is only absolutely essential when there is a potential for a profound or major impact on the property rights of an indigenous people or where their physical or cultural survival may be endangered.[109]

The first position is premised on the fact that consent is an integral part of the right to self-determination. This implies that indigenous peoples have a right to determine if any projects that directly impact on them may or may not proceed. The outcomes envisaged are 'consent', 'no consent' or 'conditional consent', where consent is given contingent on certain binding conditions.[110] In putting forward this argument, indigenous peoples have acknowledged that this exercise of their right to self-determination must be consistent with respect for the right to self-determination of others in the state.[111]

FPIC, viewed from the legal perspective of indigenous peoples' rights to self-determination and to permanent sovereignty over the natural resources located in their territories, could be seen as a compromise between two antagonistic international norms. It allows states to attempt to reconcile the apparently irreconcilable, namely indigenous peoples' inherent right to natural resources under the principle of permanent sovereignty with states' claims to sovereignty over these same resources

[108] On the one hand the requirements of Art 32 of the Declaration that FPIC be obtained for 'any project' and CERD's General Comment XXIII requirement that 'no decisions that impact on the rights and interests of indigenous peoples be taken without informed consent' do not place any explicit limitations on when FPIC should be sought. On the other hand the Inter-American Court in case of the *Saramaka People v Suriname* (n 43) and the Special Rapporteur on Fundamental Freedoms and Human Rights of Indigenous Peoples have suggested that where the basic well-being or physical or cultural survival of the community is not at risk or where a project does not have a 'major impact', consent may not be an absolute condition for pursuing the project. See Report of the Special Rapporteur Annex 1 (n 64).

[109] According to the Saramaka judgement 'survival' 'must be understood as the ability of the [indigenous or tribal people] to "preserve, protect and guarantee the special relationship that [they] have with their territory", so that "they may continue living their traditional way of life, and that their distinct cultural identity, social structure, economic system, customs, beliefs and traditions are respected, guaranteed and protected' see Inter-American Court of Human Rights case of the Saramaka People v Suriname Judgment of August 12, 2008 (Interpretation of the judgment on preliminary objections, merits, reparations, and costs) para 37.

[110] See statement of Alberto Saldamando on behalf of the International Indian Treaty Council (IITC) under Agenda Item 3, Study on Indigenous People's right to participate in decision-making to the EMRIP at its 3rd session July 2010 www.docip.org

[111] Statement of Mattias Ahren on behalf of the Arctic Council under Agenda Item 3, Study on Indigenous People's right to participate in decision-making to the EMRIP 3rd session July 2010 www.docip.org

under doctrines, such as the Regalian doctrine, which are upheld by most states where natural resource extraction occurs.[112] This perspective is closely aligned with the position of many indigenous peoples—that FPIC be required for 'any' projects that impact on their control over these resources. Also supporting this position is the fact that it would appear to be consistent with the ordinary meaning of the term 'obtain consent' used in the Declaration when considered in the context of its recognition of indigenous peoples' right to self-determination and its acknowledgement of historical injustices, 'preventing them from exercising, in particular, their right to development in line with their needs and interests'.[113]

The second position holds that the extent of the requirement to obtain consent is a function of the degree of impact of the proposed activity. Under this interpretation provisions of the Declaration are not absolute and therefore limitations can be placed on the exercise of indigenous peoples rights, including their rights to self-determination and FPIC. Any such restrictions to the enjoyment of rights must however satisfy a number of criteria.[114] This approach envisages the consent requirement articulated in the Declaration as varying on a case by case basis,[115] ranging from an ILO Convention 169 style 'consultation with the objective of consent' requirement for measures or projects with minor impacts, to a strict 'obligation to obtain consent' for those with potentially major impacts or threatening the physical or cultural survival of a people. Under this interpretation of when FPIC is required it could be argued that, in the context of projects in their territories, the Declaration already identifies certain circumstances in which FPIC is always essential. Those explicitly mentioned are 'the development, utilization or exploitation of mineral, water or other

[112] In common law jurisdictions ownership of surface generally implies ownership of subsoil resources. In most other jurisdictions ownership of subsoil resources is claimed by the state. For an analysis of the issue of the Regalian doctrine versus Ancestral Domains which include subsoil resources and the associated requirement to obtain FPIC in the Philippines, see AT Pagayatan and FJ Victoria (eds), *A Divided Court, A Conquered People? Case Materials from the Constitutional Challenge to the Indigenous Peoples' Rights Act of 1997* (Quezon City, Legal Rights and Natural Resources Centre Inc, Kasama sa Kalikasan LRC-KSK, Friends of the Earth-Philippines, 2001). For a related discussion, arguing that indigenous lands were always private property and never public lands, see M Leonen, 'Weaving Worldviews: Implications of Constitutional Challenges to the Indigenous Peoples' Rights Act of 1997' (2000) 10 *Philippines Natural Resources Law Journal* 3–44.

[113] Declaration on the Rights of Indigenous Peoples, preamble. Art 31 of the Vienna Convention on the Law of Treaties (1969) requires that the ordinary meaning of the words in a treaty be interpreted 'in their context and in light of its object and purpose'. This criterion could also be used for interpreting the provisions of the Declaration.

[114] Saramaka Interpretation (n 109) paras 34 & 35: notes that the Court under its jurisprudence Article 21 requires that restrictions must be 'a) previously established by law; b) necessary; c) proportional, and d) with the aim of achieving a legitimate objective in a democratic society' and in addition restrictions must not amount 'to a denial of their traditions and customs in a way that endangers the very survival of the group and of its members'.

[115] Saramaka interpretation (n 109) para 42.

resources',[116] 'relocation',[117] 'disposal of any hazardous materials',[118] and the taking of 'cultural, intellectual, religious and spiritual property'.[119] This position could be used as a counter argument to the objections raised by New Zealand, Australia and the United States to FPIC on the grounds that it 'would apply regardless of circumstances'.

From an implementation perspective, basing the requirement to obtain FPIC on the possible impact of a project raises the question of who determines the potential impact on the well-being of a community or its property rights. Indigenous peoples' complaints in relation to natural resource extraction are generally targeted at states. Leaving the matter of determining the impact of these projects to the state, and consequently the decision as to whether FPIC is required or not, would therefore appear to change little in practice and is unlikely to be readily accepted by indigenous peoples. This view is reflected by the fact that indigenous peoples are working at national, regional and international levels, in conjunction with the PFII, to develop their own framework of indicators for monitoring their well-being.[120] If the principles underlying the development of this framework are to be respected, then the logical conclusion is that indigenous peoples should be the ones to decide under which circumstances FPIC is required.

Finally, the case for limiting or denying the requirement for FPIC is frequently based on the argument that indigenous peoples do not have an absolute right to 'veto' projects that are deemed to be in the public interest.[121] However, it is important to bear in mind that in the context of extractive projects this public interest argument is strongly contested and are rarely, if ever, substantiated.[122] Furthermore, international and

[116] Art 32.
[117] Art 10.
[118] Art 29.
[119] Art 11.
[120] Indicators of Well-being, Poverty and Sustainability Relevant to Indigenous Peoples February 2008, UN Doc E/C.19/2008/9. For additional material on indicators relevant for Indigenous Peoples see http://www.tebtebba.org/index.php?option=com_docman&task=cat_view&gid=53&Itemid=27
[121] This argument on behalf of some states and the extractive industry as a basis for denying a veto right can be traced back to discussions on the revision of ILO Convention 107 in 1986. See International Labour Conference, Partial Revision of the Indigenous and Tribal Populations Convention, No 107 (1957) Provisional Record 36, 75th session, 19.
[122] International empirical studies questioning the macro economic benefits of mining include JD Sachs and AM Warner, *Natural Resource Abundance and Economic Growth* (Cambridge, MA, Harvard Institute for International Development, 1997); JD Sachs and AM Warner, 'The Curse of Natural Resources' (2001) 45 *European Economic Review* 827–38; RM Auty, *Resource Abundance and Economic Development: Improving the Performance of Resource-Rich Countries* (United Nations University World Institute for Development and Economic Research, 1998); TM Power, *Digging to Development: A Historical Look at Mining and Economic Development. An Oxfam America Report*, September 2002. The concerns raised in these studies regarding the limited benefits accruing to developing countries from resource extraction are

regional human rights bodies and national courts have cautioned states against infringement of indigenous peoples' rights on the basis of national development and public interest.[123] An interpretation of the Declaration that justifies derogations from the requirement to obtain FPIC on the basis of such arguments could therefore lead to a shift in the burden of proof away from the state and onto indigenous peoples in a manner that is incompatible with the spirit and intent of the Declaration.

The Potential Impact of FPIC in the Declaration on Non-State Actors

Along with states, the extractive industry, international financial institutions (IFIs) and investors have a major role to play in the realisation of FPIC in practice.[124] The economic imperatives facing developing countries, in the context of a global development model that promotes foreign direct investment (FDI) and bilateral investment agreements, can dictate the legislative protection these states afford to indigenous peoples vis-a-vis the interests of transnational corporations, including mining companies.[125] In keeping with this prescription for development, some international bodies, states, investors and mining companies are arguing that the realisation of the Millennium Development Goals (MDGs) and poverty alleviation can be achieved through increased FDI in the extractive sector. This linking of the extractive industry and FDI to the MDGs should place an even greater onus on all involved to ensure adherence to the highest human rights standards, including the standards articulated

exacerbated in many countries by generous tax incentives to entice foreign investment, high levels of corruption associated with the sector and the potential long-term impacts on other economic sectors such as agriculture, fisheries and tourism.

[123] HRC *Lansman v Finland* (n 58); CERD has held that the exploitation of resources for national development 'must be exercised consistently with the rights of indigenous and tribal peoples' Suriname CERD/C/64/CO/9/Rev.2, Para 15 (2004); the Vienna Declaration and Programme of Action, adopted by the World Conference on Human Rights on 25th June 1993, Part I, at para. 10. UN Doc. A/CONF.157/23, 12th July 1993 affirms that 'development may not be invoked to justify the abridgement of internationally recognised human rights'; See also Canadian Supreme Court case *R v Sparrow* [1990] 1 S.C.R. 1075.

[124] The NGO community and UN system also have an important role to play in the implementation of FPIC in their activities. The United Nations Development Group Guidelines on Indigenous Peoples issued in February 2008 to assist the UN system in mainstreaming indigenous peoples' rights accords the principle of FPIC a central position.

[125] Regarding impacts on legislation see E Caruso et al, 'Synthesis Report' in *Extracting Promises: Indigenous Peoples, Extractive Industries & the World Bank* (Baguio City, Tebtebba Indigenous Peoples International Centre for Policy Research and Education & Forest Peoples Programme, 2005). See also Tujan and Guzman (n 48). On agreements between host countries and companies see especially the Report of the Special Representative on the issue of human rights and transnational corporations and other business enterprises, *Protect, Respect and Remedy: A Framework for Business and Human Rights*, UN Doc A/HRC/8/5 (2008) para 35.

in the Declaration. Failure to do so could result in an untenable position whereby the realisation of the MDGs, which should benefit indigenous peoples, becomes contingent on violations of their rights.[126]

The World Bank Group has, to date, failed to include FPIC as a requirement in its policies pertaining to indigenous peoples, despite strong recommendations that it do so emerging from two major international reviews it had commissioned, one on dams and the other on the extractive industry.[127] Instead the Bank has opted to include what it terms Free Prior Informed Consultation (FPICon) resulting in broad community support (BCS). The Bank's own Compliance Advisor/Ombudsman (CAO) has expressed concern in relation to the 'ambiguity' of the Bank's 'determination of BCS'.[128] This insistence on FPICon rather than FPIC has been strongly criticised by non-governmental organisations, indigenous peoples and the Eminent Person responsible for the Extractive Industry Review.[129] The implications of the adoption of the Declaration on the World Bank's polices, however, remain to be seen. As a specialised agency of the United Nations it is coming under pressure to respect the rights and principles contained in the Declaration and to uphold its obligations under Article 41 to 'contribute to the full realization of the Declaration' and Article 42 to 'promote respect for and full application

[126] C Doyle, 'Indigenous Peoples and the Millennium Development Goals: Sacrificial Lambs or Equal Beneficiaries?' (2009) 13 *International Journal of Human Rights* 44. See also United Nations Conference on Trade and Development (UNCTAD) World Investment Report 2007, *Transnational Corporations, Extractive Industries and Development,* which focuses on FDI in the extractive sector and suggests that it may help with the realisation of the MDGs but fails to mention the requirement for FPIC when addressing impacts on or participation of indigenous peoples.

[127] World Commission on Dams, www.dams.org, and 'Striking a better balance Volume 1 The World Bank Group and Extractive Industries The Final Report of World Bank Extractive Industry Review' December 2003 http://irispublic.worldbank.org/85257559006C22E9/All+Documents/85257559006C22E985256FF6006843AB/$File/volume1english.pdf.

[128] 'IFC's Policy and Performance Standards on Social and Environmental Sustainability and Disclosure Policy, Commentary on IFC's Progress Report on the First 18 Months of Application', Office of the Compliance Advisor/Ombudsman (CAO) IFC and MIGA, World Bank Group, Advisory Note, 17 December 2007.

[129] F MacKay, 'The Draft World Bank Operational Policy 4.10 on Indigenous Peoples: Progress or More of the Same?' (2005) 22 *Arizona Journal of International and Comparative Law* 81. See also E Salim, 'Business as Usual with Marginal Change: EIR Final Comment on the WBG Management Response to the EIR', Jakarta, 22 July 2004, in *Extracting Promises* (n 101) 340–50. Indigenous peoples and their support organizations have criticized BCS as being inconsistent with their right to self-determination see statement by Cathal Doyle on behalf of Indigenous Peoples Links (PIPLinks); the Forest Peoples Programme (FPP); the Asian Indigenous Peoples Pact (AIPP); the Foundation for Aboriginal and Islander Research Action (FAIRA); Russian Association of Indigenous Peoples of the North (RAIPON); Organizacions de Naciones y Pueblos Indigenas en Argentina (ONPIA) and Middlesex University Department of Law under Agenda Item 4 to the 3rd session of the EMRIP 2010. www.docip.org

of the provisions of this Declaration'.[130] The Banks private sector arm, the International Financial Corporation (IFC) initiated a review of its performance standards in 2009 and identified FPIC as one of four 'key operation topics'.[131] However, absence of any clear evidence to support its position, and despite repeated demands in consultations for the incorporation of FPIC into its performance standards, the IFC continues to hold that its current standard of FPICon is 'functionally equivalent' to FPIC.[132] In doing so it refuses to accept its responsibility to respect international human rights law as it pertains to indigenous peoples and is increasingly isolated among other IFI's.[133]

The European Bank for Reconstruction and Development's (ERBD) Environmental and Social Policy, issued in May 2008, 'recognises the principle, outlined in the UN Declaration on the Rights of Indigenous Peoples, that the prior informed consent of affected Indigenous Peoples is required for the project-related activities'. It requires clients who propose to develop natural resources commercially in indigenous peoples' lands to 'enter into good faith negotiation with the affected communities of Indigenous Peoples, and document their informed participation and consent as a result of the negotiation'.[134] The Asian Development Bank safeguard policy issued in July 2009 includes a requirement to obtain FPIC.[135] However, the ADB policy includes a definition of consent as 'broad community support' which is incompatible with the requirement that it be obtained in a manner that respects indigenous customs and traditions. The policy also places limitations on when the requirement for consent applies.[136]

[130] Statement to EMRIP ibid. See also reports of consultations held in Manila, Washington DC and Brussels in 2010 and Turkey 2009 where demands were made that the IFC policy be updated to include FPIC, reports available at http://www.ifc.org/ifcext/policyreview.nsf/Content/Resources#P2Summaries

[131] 'Progress Report on IFC's Policy and Performance Standards on Social and Environmental Sustainability, and Policy on Disclosure of Information Review and Update Process' International Finance Corporation (14 April 2010) paras 34 and 35 and Annex A 'Review and Update of IFC's Sustainability Framework: Overview of Key Issues'.

[132] Ibid, 26.

[133] Apart from the African Development Bank all Regional IFI's have to some degree addressed the issue of FPIC in their policies.

[134] European Bank for Reconstruction and Development (EBRD), Environmental and Social Policy, issued May 2008, page 50, http://www.ebrd.com/pages/about/principles/sustainability/policy.shtml. There appears to be some ambiguity in the EBRD definition of consent with a footnote in the policy linking it to involvement in, rather than authorisation of, a project. It states: 'Consent refers to the process whereby the affected community of Indigenous Peoples arrive at a decision, in accordance with their cultural traditions, customs and practices as to whether to become involved in the proposed project.'

[135] Asian Development Bank, Safeguard Policy Statement July 2009.

[136] Ibid para 33. The policy restricts the requirement for FPIC to projects involving 'commercial development of natural resources within customary lands under use that would impact the livelihoods or on cultural, ceremonial, or spiritual uses of the lands that define the identity and community of Indigenous Peoples'.

The Inter-American Development Bank (IDB) adopted its current policy on indigenous peoples prior to the adoption of the Declaration in 2006. It mirrors ILO Convention 169's requirement that consultation must have the objective of achieving agreement or consent.[137] In line with the IFC reasoning the IDB states that, while it has not included FPIC in its policy, 'it has included the equivalent—good faith negotiation—for special cases (proactive projects and projects with significant impact)'.[138] This statement would appear to imply that the IDB acknowledges that good faith negotiations include the right of indigenous communities to say 'no' to such projects. Importantly following the IACHR's *Saramaka v Suriname* ruling, FPIC is effectively required under the IDB policy, which identifies 'applicable legal norms' as including 'international jurisprudence of the Inter-American Court of Human Rights'.[139] In addition to banks, investors also play a significant role in funding extractive projects. Increasing demand from customers for ethical investment options has resulted in some investors advocating for respect of indigenous peoples rights and making attempts to encourage extractive companies to obtain FPIC.[140] However such initiatives are rare, with most policies in this sector driven, at best, by the standards produced by and for extractive industry bodies themselves.

The International Council for Minerals and Metals (ICMM) is the body that represents many of the major companies in the global mining industry. Despite making promises in discussions with indigenous peoples to include FPIC in its standards, it failed to do so.[141] Instead it only recommends that companies 'seek broad community support' for their projects, a position which is even weaker than that of the World Bank. The ICMM argues that 'practical implementation of FPIC presents significant challenges for government authorities as well as affected companies as the concept is not well defined and with very few exceptions, is not

[137] Inter-American Development Bank Operational Policy on Indigenous People (OP-765) and Strategy for Indigenous Development (GN -2387-5), July 2006.

[138] UN Doc E/C.19/2008/4/Add.10, Permanent Forum on Indigenous Issues, Information Received from the United Nations System and other Intergovernmental Organizations, Inter-American Development Bank, 7 February 2008.

[139] Inter-American Development Bank Operational Policy (n 137), 19.

[140] Ethical Funds Company, 'Sustainability Perspectives Winning the Social License to Operate Resource Extraction with Free, Prior, and Informed Community Consent', February 2008, https://www.ethicalfunds.com/SiteCollectionDocuments/docs/FPIC.pdf see also 'Improving Vedanta Resources' governance of responsible business practices' Experts in Responsible Investment Solutions (EIRIS) July 2010 and Robert Kropp 'Investors Urge US to Support Rights of Indigenous Peoples' Sustainability Investment News July 30, 2010 http://www.socialfunds.com/news/article.cgi?sfArticleId=3003

[141] ICMM Position Statement, *Mining and Indigenous Peoples*, released May 2008. The statement did not recognise the requirement to obtain FPIC but did commit ICMM members to participating 'in national and international forums on indigenous peoples' issues, including those dealing with the concept of free, prior and informed consent. See www.icmm.com. See also Moody (n 48) 10–11.

enshrined in local legislation'[142] However, the fact that FPIC is enshrined in legislation in a number of countries, in some cases for over a decade, and an increasing number of voluntary agreements pertaining to its implementation exist in other sectors, belies this claim.[143] The ICMM argument also ignores the fact that pressure exerted by the mining industry on governments in developing countries contributes to their reluctance to enact legislation pertaining to the implementation of FPIC in the first place.[144] Furthermore, it is ethically, and arguably legally, questionable not to uphold a principle of international human rights law on the ground that it has not yet been enshrined in local legislation.[145] It is to be hoped that the adoption of the Declaration and associated developments in international human rights law will eventually result in a revision of the ICMM's and its member's positions vis-a-vis FPIC. Doing so would arguably be in the industry's own long-term interest.[146]

The Future of FPIC and its Implications for the Declaration's Implementation

Overall, when considering the potential future impact of the requirement to obtain FPIC in the Declaration it is important not to lose sight of its historical and contemporary context. Historical pacts between indigenous

[142] Forest Peoples Programme and Association of Saramaka Authorities, *Free, Prior and Informed Consent: Two Cases from Suriname* (FPIC Working Papers, Forest Peoples Programme, Moreton-in-Marsh, March 2007) 16, www.forestpeoples.org/documents/law_hr/fpic_suriname_mar07_eng.pdf. See also Mining and Indigenous Peoples Issues Roundtable: Continuing a Dialogue between Indigenous Peoples and Mining Companies. IUCN-ICMM Dialogue on Mining and Biodiversity Sydney, Australia' 30–31 January 2008, 7.

[143] See generally Forest Peoples Programme, *Free, Prior and Informed Consent and the Roundtable on Sustainable Palm Oil: A Guide for Companies* (Forest Peoples Programme, Moreton-in-Marsh, October 2008). See also M Colchester and M Farhan Ferrari, *Making FPIC Work: Challenges and Prospects for Indigenous People* (Forest Peoples Programme, June 2007), providing an overview of experiences of FPIC in Suriname, Guyana, Peru, Peninsular Malaysia, Indonesia, Papua New Guinea and the Philippines.

[144] For example in Australia pressure from the mining industry resulted in the weakening of the consent requirement in the 1976 Northern Territories Land Rights Act see http://www.nlc.org.au/html/land_act_changes.html.

[145] The International Financial Institution (IFC) notes in its advice to companies on complying with ILO Convention 169 states that: 'There may also be circumstances where private sector companies' actions could influence or compromise the State's implementation of its obligations under international agreements, such as Convention 169'. See 'ILO Convention 169 and the Private Sector: Questions and Answers for IFC Clients', IFC World Bank Group, March 2007.

[146] Even ignoring the legal and moral obligations incumbent on companies to respect indigenous peoples' rights, strong arguments can be made as to why respecting the principle of FPIC may be beneficial to the industry in relation to its reputation and its capacity to ensure meaningful community engagement and maximise the prospect of long-term project viability. For an example of such an argument see World Resource Institute, *Development without Conflict: The Business Case for Community Consent*, May 2007, pdf.wri.org/development_without_conflict_fpic.pdf.

peoples themselves, and subsequently between indigenous peoples and states, show that consent has long been a basic principle in agreements involving indigenous peoples. Unfortunately, history also shows that where such agreements existed states have failed to respect them, invariably to the detriment of indigenous peoples. The re-emergence of the requirement to obtain indigenous peoples' consent over recent decades is undeniable. It can be traced from the relatively limited requirement under ILO Convention 169 to obtain consent in relation to relocation, through to CERD's 1997 interpretation of ICERD in its General Comment XXIII as requiring states parties to obtain indigenous peoples' informed consent in relation to all 'decisions that directly impact on their rights and interests', and up to the FPIC obligations articulated in the Declaration in light of its recognition of indigenous peoples right to self-determination. These provisions of the Declaration requiring FPIC are now informing international law, as evidenced by decisions of the HRC, the IACHR, the ACHPR and national Courts, the analysis of Special Rapporteurs, and the growing number of cases involving failure to obtain FPIC that are being considered by CERD under its Early Warning Urgent Action procedure.

In state practice, there currently exist varying degrees of recognition of FPIC, ranging from states that deny any requirement for FPIC to states that have enshrined it in legislation or have considered affording it constitutional protection. Even within the human rights regime, while there is clear acknowledgement of the necessity of FPIC to ensure the well-being of indigenous peoples, there exists some divergence of opinion as to when it should be mandatory. While these divergent opinions and practices might look like inconsistencies within the human rights regime, they may be more appropriately seen as reflective of an evolution along the spectrum of participative rights towards a consensus on a principle of, or right to, FPIC that effectively protects the well-being of indigenous communities in a manner that is consistent with their right to self-determination.[147] This evolution involves a shift in the established balance of power and will, as a result, occur at different rates in differing contexts. Nevertheless, despite any apparent inconsistencies, a clear trend is emerging within the international human rights regime toward recognition of the requirement for FPIC in line with what has been agreed upon with the adoption of the Declaration.

Finally, while FPIC is often referred to as a principle, it might more appropriately be conceived of as a right. Many, if not most, indigenous

[147] B Clavero, 'The Indigenous Rights of Participation and International Development Policies' (2005) 22 *Arizona Journal of International and Comparative Law* 41 suggests that the existing spectrum of consent related obligations, ranging from mere consultation to veto rights, indicate that international law is in a 'transitional phase' with regard to indigenous peoples' participation.

peoples hold this view.[148] They see FPIC as an inherent right of indigenous peoples, without which the rights to self-determination, lands, territories, resources and development can be rendered effectively meaningless. Denial of FPIC implies that control over decisions pertaining to their lands and resources, and by extension over their futures, is taken from them. Consultation with indigenous peoples is essential. However, consultations and negotiations without a requirement for consent freezes existing power relations and leaves indigenous peoples with no leverage to influence the outcome of decision-making processes. States, global financial institutions and transnational extractive corporations currently hold this decision-making power and are clearly reluctant to share it with indigenous peoples. In this sense, indigenous peoples' struggle for what they regard as their right to FPIC is perhaps best conceived in terms of Shivji's conceptualisation of human rights when he argues that:

> seen as a means of struggle, 'right' is therefore not a standard granted as charity from above but a standard-bearer around which people rally for struggle from below. By the same token the correlate of 'right' is ... power/privilege where those who enjoy such power/privilege are the subject of being exposed and struggled against.[149]

FPIC seen in this light is a powerful tool in indigenous peoples' struggle to alter longstanding discriminatory power equations. To ensure its effective implementation indigenous peoples will have to continue to rally and demand respect for this right to FPIC in all fora available to them. The adoption of the Declaration is a reflection of the adeptness of indigenous peoples in terms of getting their rights recognised. The extent to which FPIC is implemented in practice will be a measure of how successful they are in ensuring that they are upheld.

CONCLUSION

Some states have in the past maintained that the Declaration is only 'aspirational...with political and moral force but not legal force'.[150] However, this limited conception of the Declaration fails to appreciate its true significance. A more appropriate and realistic conception of the Declaration holds that it is an integral part of the evolving normative framework

[148] Repeated statements referring to a right to FPIC have been made by indigenous communities at the PFII, the former WGIP, and the Experts Mechanism on the Rights of Indigenous Peoples www.docip.org. See also WGIP Standard-Setting Legal Commentary (n 52).

[149] IG Shivji, *The Concept of Human Rights in Africa* (London, Council for the Development of Economic and Social Research in Africa, 1989) 71.

[150] Statement by Mr Hill on behalf of Australia. Report of the General Assembly 61st session UN Doc A/61/PV.107 (2007), 12.

of indigenous peoples' rights. The Declaration is in fact reflective of, and contributes to, the evolution of this normative framework pertaining to the recognition of indigenous rights. It attempts to address the fragmentation of the existing human rights regime by consolidating the rights this regime has recognised as pertaining to indigenous peoples into a single framework specific to them. However, it does not purport to be all-encompassing. Rather, acknowledging its place within the normative human rights framework, it provides space for evolution which may impact on those rights. The Declaration also lays out a roadmap for the future realisation of indigenous peoples' rights. It does so by providing a comprehensive, yet flexible, rights-based framework for the engagement of states, corporations, developmental and UN agencies with indigenous peoples. This framework is premised on the principles of self-determination, FPIC and the recognition of indigenous peoples' collective rights to their lands, territories and resources. While unambiguous in its requirement of adherence to these principles as the basis and minimum standard for engagement with indigenous peoples, the Declaration avoids being overly prescriptive as to the mechanics of how this engagement should occur in specific contexts. An example of this is the Declaration's instruction to states to establish and implement processes, in conjunction with, and ensuring the participation of, indigenous peoples, to adjudicate indigenous peoples' rights pertaining to their lands, territories and resources while ensuring that due respect and consideration is given to their customs, traditions, laws and land tenure systems. This need for the recognition of indigenous peoples' customs and land tenure systems identified in the Declaration is in line with recent developments within the international human rights regime calling for the recognition of indigenous peoples' customary laws as sources of law and for greater recognition of the cultural rights of indigenous peoples, including the maintenance of their traditional customary land tenure systems.

Following its adoption the human rights regime has proceeded to acknowledge the importance of the Declaration as a component of the normative framework of indigenous peoples' rights. Recent decisions emerging from national and regional courts citing the Declaration and its provisions on, inter alia, land rights and FPIC bear testimony to its pivotal and evolving role within this normative framework. Complementary developments within the international human rights regime such as CERD's increased emphasis on the rights and principles articulated in the Declaration, particularly FPIC, should assist indigenous peoples in their effort to ensure that the rights articulated in the Declaration are realised in practice, and states in understanding their obligation to facilitate this.

In terms of land, territory and resource rights, the Declaration is consistent with the existing body of international law and is sufficiently precise to give rise to identifiable and practicable rights and obligations and attract broad international support. Overall, within the current framework of international law regarding indigenous peoples' rights to lands, territories and resources, the Declaration has to be seen and accepted as a threshold reflecting the minimum standard of international law in this area. Over six decades have passed since the adoption of the Universal Declaration on Human Rights. Given the unprecedented influence this document has had on legal systems throughout the world it is worth highlighting that a declaration is a call to adopt universal accepted minimum standards of protection on which a system can then be developed. This is how international human rights law has evolved, and it is how indigenous peoples' rights will evolve. Hence, the affirmation of rights to lands, territories and resources in the Declaration does not represent the end, but rather the beginning, of a process of implementation. Operationalising FPIC and establishing adjudication mechanisms that respect indigenous peoples' customary laws and land tenure systems are tangible examples of how this implementation process must proceed.

The Declaration therefore sets the minimum threshold on which the future system of protection at the international, regional, national and local levels ought to be based. Viewed from the past and looking towards the future, the real revolution behind the Declaration is arguably the affirmation by states that they are not the only entities entitled to title to territory; that they do have to recognise and uphold the inherent rights of indigenous peoples which preceded the creation of the state. Consequently, control over lands, territories and resources does not lie exclusively with the government of a country; indigenous peoples have fundamental rights to ownership, use and control over their lands, territory and resources.

13

The Controversial Issue of Natural Resources: Balancing States' Sovereignty with Indigenous Peoples' Rights

STEFANIA ERRICO

INTRODUCTION

IN HIS 2003 report on the impact of large-scale development projects, the former UN Special Rapporteur on the situation of human rights and fundamental freedoms of indigenous people, Rodolfo Stavenhagen, highlighted that, as a consequence of the implementation of major development projects, numerous communities are being 'uprooted, evicted or resettled with little or no regard to their actual needs and rights', frequently by means of 'organized violence intended to intimidate, harass and make them comply with decisions taken by outside interests without or explicitly against their consent'.[1]

Very often, and increasingly so, the communities adversely affected by these development projects, especially large-scale exploitation of natural resources, are indigenous communities. This situation is commonly ascribed to the fact that indigenous peoples' traditional lands currently represent a large proportion of those 'under-developed regions' to which the attention of national States and private investors is being directed for the purpose of extracting natural resources, establishing plantations or industrial plants, and building dams in the name of the 'national interest' in development.[2] The extent of this phenomenon is possibly even greater in those countries that, due to pressures of public expenditure and foreign

[1] Report of the Special Rapporteur on the situation of human rights and fundamental freedoms of indigenous people (R Stavenhagen), UN Doc E/CN.4/2003/90, 21 January 2003, para 69.

[2] Ibid, para 7.

debt, view the possibility of granting concessions for the exploitation of minerals or timber to transnational corporations as the only viable option to ensure their economic growth.[3]

Several studies have shown that, in the context of the realisation of development projects and other extractive activities, indigenous peoples' rights are—to say the least—frequently disregarded. As a result, their physical and cultural survival as well as their traditional social organisation is being seriously undermined, sometimes in an irreversible manner.[4] Indigenous representatives have repeatedly pointed out that 'indigenous interests are seen as opposed to the interests of the State'.[5] As one might expect, the tensions are especially sharp when it comes to control over natural resources.

The UN Declaration on the Rights of Indigenous Peoples recognises the right of indigenous peoples to own, use, develop and control natural resources. Article 26(2), states that

> indigenous peoples have the right to own, use, develop and control the lands, territories and *resources* that they possess by reason of traditional ownership or other traditional occupation or use, as well as those which they have otherwise acquired.[6]

The long and laborious negotiations behind this provision are testament to the delicacy of this issue.[7] The principle of State sovereignty over natural resources and the goals of national development need to find a balance

[3] See *Transnational Investments and Operations on the Land of Indigenous Peoples*, Report of the Centre on Transnational Corporations, UN Doc E/CN.4/Sub.2/1994/40, 15 June 1994, para 15.

[4] In this sense, see eg the case studies presented in *Transnational Investments*, ibid, and in the Report of the Special Rapporteur (n 1). Note also that on 8 August 2008 the new UN Special Rapporteur on the situation of human rights and fundamental freedoms of indigenous people, S James Anaya, denounced, for example, the abuses suffered by the members of the Charco la Pava community in Panama, in connection with the execution of the Hydroelectric Project CHAN 75. See UN Media Centre, 'Expert on Indigenous Peoples Denounces Human Rights Violations against the Charco la Pava Community in Panama', 8 August 2008, www.ohchr.org.

[5] See UN Working Group on Indigenous Populations, Review of Developments pertaining to the Promotion and Protection of Human Rights and Fundamental Freedoms of Indigenous Peoples—Principal Theme: Indigenous Peoples and their Right to Development, Including their Right to Participate in Developments Affecting Them, UN Doc E/CN.4/Sub.2/AC.4/2001/2, 20 June 2001, para 10.

[6] United Nations Declaration on the Rights of Indigenous Peoples, adopted by the UN General Assembly on 13 September 2007, UN Doc A/61/67, Annex, 7 September 2007 (emphasis added).

[7] See, for all the reasons for delaying the adoption of the Declaration by the General Assembly as spelled out in the Report to the President of the General Assembly on the consultations on the Draft Declaration on the Rights of Indigenous Peoples, submitted on 13 July 2007 by the 'facilitator', the Permanent Representative of the Philippines to the United Nations in New York, HE Hilario G Davide, Jr, www.un.org/ga/president/61/follow-up/indigenous.shtml.

with the recognition of indigenous peoples' rights. This chapter will try to shed some light on the content of indigenous peoples' right to natural resources by juxtaposing the language finally adopted in the relevant provisions of the Declaration, in the light of their drafting history, with current international, regional and national practice regarding the issue. Besides helping clarify the scope of the provision, the reference to current practice seems appropriate in the light of Article 45 of the Declaration, which states that 'nothing in this Declaration may be construed as diminishing or extinguishing the rights indigenous peoples have now or may acquire in the future'.

The following sections will first examine indigenous peoples' right to natural resources vis-a-vis States' power to dispose, in particular, of subsoil resources. We will then consider the role of the State as a 'duty-bearer' in order to highlight the specific obligations that accompany States' sovereignty over natural resources and their decision-making power with regard to the planning and implementation of development projects. Having explored this background, the chapter will turn to describe indigenous peoples' right to consultation, participation and free, prior and informed consent as restrictions on States' freedom to dispose of natural resources. Next, we will refer briefly to the possible repercussions that the recognition of indigenous peoples' right to self-determination may have for States' power to dispose of the natural resources located in indigenous peoples' lands, especially in relation to indigenous peoples' right to control their own development path. The chapter will conclude with some final remarks.

INDIGENOUS PEOPLES' RIGHTS TO NATURAL RESOURCES

Natural Resources and Traditional Lands

Prior to the adoption of the UN Declaration on the Rights of Indigenous Peoples, the right of such peoples to natural resources, for example the right to use and manage these resources, had already been recognised in other international instruments, either in a specific and autonomous provision, as in the case of the ILO Convention concerning Indigenous and Tribal Peoples in Independent Countries of 1989 (Convention 169)[8] and the draft American Declaration on the Rights of Indigenous

[8] Art 15 of ILO Convention 169 provides: 'The rights of the peoples concerned to the natural resources pertaining to their lands shall be specially safeguarded.' ILO, Convention concerning Indigenous and Tribal Peoples in Independent Countries, adopted 27 June 1989 and entered into force 5 September 1991. To date, the Convention has been ratified by 20 States (Argentina, Bolivia, Brazil, Chile, Colombia, Costa Rica, Denmark, Dominica, Ecuador, Fiji, Guatemala, Honduras, Mexico, Nepal, Netherlands, Norway, Paraguay, Peru, Spain, and the Bolivarian Republic of Venezuela).

Peoples,[9] or in the context of a broader call for the recognition of indigenous peoples' rights over their traditional lands, as in the case of the UN Committee on the Elimination of Racial Discrimination's (CERD's) General Recommendation 23 on Indigenous Peoples.[10]

With regard to the provision set out in Convention 169, the Guide to the Convention acknowledges that '[t]his is an especially difficult provision, and it is drafted in terms which are not always specific because it has to apply to many different national situations'.[11] It goes on to explain that '[e]xactly what this right consists of will have to be defined within each national legal system, within the *land rights* that these peoples have, and within their capacity to exercise their rights'.[12] A link is thus established between the right to natural resources and the regime concerning land rights. It should be noted that even in those cases where the right of indigenous peoples over natural resources is incorporated in an autonomous norm, a reference is inevitably made to indigenous peoples' traditional lands. Thus, Convention 169 refers to 'natural resources pertaining to their lands'.[13] Similarly, the draft American Declaration speaks of 'recursos naturales en sus tierras'.[14]

The relationship between rights over lands and rights over resources has clearly been illustrated in the decisions of the Inter-American institutions. In the *Awas Tingni* case, the Inter-American Court of Human Rights found that the State of Nicaragua had violated the property right of indigenous peoples to their traditional lands, as covered by Article 21 of the American Convention on Human Rights, because, among other things, it had granted licences to third parties for the exploitation of various resources (ie timber) situated in the lands of the Awas Tingni community.[15] A similar position

[9] According to Art XVIII, para 4: 'Indigenous peoples have the right to an effective legal framework for the protection of their rights with respect to the natural resources on their lands, including the ability to use, manage, and conserve such resources; and with respect to traditional uses of their lands, interests in lands, and resources, such as subsistence.' See Organization of American States (OAS), Proposed American Declaration on the Rights of Indigenous Peoples, adopted by the Inter-American Commission on Human Rights on 26 February 1997, OEA/Ser.L/V/II.95, doc 7, rev.

[10] The General Recommendation of CERD follows, in fact, the same pattern as the UN Declaration. It calls upon States parties 'to recognize and protect the rights of indigenous peoples to own, develop, control and use their communal lands, territories and resources'. See CERD, General Recommendation 23 on Indigenous Peoples, UN Doc A/52/18, Annex 8, 18 August 1997, para 5.

[11] M Tomei and L Swepson, *Indigenous and Tribal Peoples: A Guide to ILO Convention No 169* (Geneva, International Labour Office, 1996) 19.

[12] Ibid, emphasis added.

[13] See n 8 above.

[14] See n 9 above.

[15] *Mayagna (Sumo) Awas Tingni Community v Nicaragua* (Series C No 79) [2001] IACHR 9 (31 August 2001) para 153: '[T]he Court believes that, in light of Article 21 of the Convention, the State has violated the right of the members of the Mayagna Awas Tingni community to the use and enjoyment of their property, every time that … it has granted concessions to third parties to exploit the property and the resources located in an area which could

was subsequently taken by the Inter-American Commission in the 2004 Report concerning *Maya Indigenous Communities of the Toledo District v Belize* with regard to the analogous provision included in Article XXIII of the American Declaration on the Rights and Duties of Man.[16] In its recent decision in the case of *Sarakama People v Suriname,* the Court made the connection between rights over land and rights over resources even more explicit by stating that 'the right to use and enjoy their territory would be meaningless in the context of indigenous and tribal communities if said right were not connected to the natural resources that lie on and within the land'.[17]

In order to understand the reasons underlying this statement, it is useful to recall that the protection of indigenous peoples' rights of ownership and use of their traditional lands is closely related to the need to preserve the social, cultural and economic integrity of these peoples.[18] However, such integrity cannot be truly guaranteed unless the possibility of using the resources located in the traditional lands and territories of indigenous peoples is also ensured so that they are able to continue performing their traditional activities, healing practices and spiritual rituals. In fact, the UN Human Rights Committee has acknowledged that 'culture manifests itself in many forms, including a particular way of life associated with the use of land resources, especially in the case of indigenous peoples'.[19] Significantly, the Inter-American Court has also expressly affirmed that 'the cultural and economic survival of indigenous and tribal peoples, and their members, depends on their access [to] and use of the natural resources in their territory'.[20] The UN Declaration itself recognises, in

correspond, fully or partially, to the lands which must be delimited, demarcated and titled' (author's translation).

[16] *Maya Indigenous Communities of the Toledo District—Belize,* Case 12,053, Inter-American Commission on Human Rights, Report No 40/04 (merits decision of 12 October 2004) para 194.

[17] *Case of the Saramaka People v Suriname* (Series C No 172) [2007] IACHR 5 (28 November 2007) para 122.

[18] In the words of the former UN Special Rapporteur, José Martinez Cobo, there exists a 'deeply spiritual special relationship between indigenous peoples and their lands as basic to their existence as such and to all their beliefs, customs, traditions and culture'. See José R Martinez Cobo, *Study of the Problem of Discrimination Against Indigenous Populations: Vol V, Conclusions, Proposals and Recommendations,* UN Doc E/CN.4/Sub.2/1986/7/Add.4. On the relationship of indigenous peoples to their lands, see also E-I Daes, *Indigenous Peoples and their Relationship to Land—Final Working Paper Prepared by the Special Rapporteur,* Sub-Commission for the Promotion and Protection of Human Rights, UN Doc E/CN.4/Sub.2/2001/21, 2001, 11 June 2001.

[19] UN Committee on Human Rights, General Comment XXIII on the Rights of Minorities (Art 27), UN Doc CCPR/C/21/Rev.1/Add.5, 8 April 1994, para 7.

[20] *Saramaka People v Suriname* (n 17) para 120. See also *Yakye Axa Indigenous Community v Paraguay* (Merits, Reparations and Costs), IACHR, judgment of 17 June 2005, Series C No 125 (2005), para 137; *Sawhoyamaxa Indigenous Community v Paraguay* (Preliminary Objections, Merits, Reparations and Costs), IACHR, judgment of 29 March 2006, Series C No 125 (2005), para 121.

Article 25, that indigenous peoples have a 'distinctive spiritual relationship' with both their traditional lands and resources.[21]

The considerations above suggest that the recognition of a 'right to natural resources' in favour of indigenous peoples has implications that go beyond the mere application of common principles regulating property regimes. Indigenous peoples must be entitled to the same rights over the natural resources existing in their lands as any other owner would be entitled under the national laws regulating property regimes.[22] However, the cultural repercussions connected to the disposal of natural resources in the case of indigenous peoples give a different dimension to their right to natural resources that should be explored.

This conclusion is reinforced by the fact that the UN Declaration has the objective of protecting 'peoples' and their cultural distinctiveness. To this end, the preamble to the Declaration stresses the urgent need to respect and promote the *inherent* rights of indigenous peoples, 'especially their rights to their lands, territories and resources' as they derive from 'their political, economic and social structures and from their cultures'. Accordingly, Article 26(3) of the Declaration affirms that the recognition of indigenous peoples' right to their traditional lands and resources 'shall be conducted with due respect to the customs, traditions and land tenure systems of the indigenous peoples concerned'.[23] This entails the recognition of rights over natural resources in favour of indigenous peoples whenever their traditional land tenure systems and customs include such rights. Indigenous peoples are accordingly entitled 'to own, use, develop and control'[24] these resources.

This line of reasoning seems to be reflected in the decision of the Constitutional Court of South Africa in the case of *Alexkor Ltd and The Republic of South Africa v The Richtersveld Community*.[25] In this case, the Court found that the Richtersveld community had a right of communal ownership

[21] In addition, Art 20 of the Declaration states that indigenous peoples have the right 'to be secure in the enjoyment of their own means of subsistence and development, and to engage freely in all their traditional and other economic activities'.

[22] In this sense, see SJ Anaya, 'Indigenous Peoples' Participatory Rights in Relation to Decisions about Natural Resource Extraction' (2005) 22 *Arizona Journal of International and Comparative Law* 17.

[23] On this point the case law of the Inter-American Court of Human Rights and of the Inter-American Commission on Human Rights is again extremely interesting. In the *Awas Tingni* case (n 15) at para 151 the Court affirmed that '[i]ndigenous peoples' customary law must be especially taken into account for the purpose of this analysis'. As for the Commission, it declared that 'the property rights of indigenous peoples are not defined exclusively by entitlements within a state's formal legal regime, but also include that indigenous communal property that arises from and is grounded in indigenous custom and tradition'. See *Maya Indigenous Communities* (n 16) para 117.

[24] See Art 26 of the UN Declaration.

[25] *Alexkor Ltd and the Republic of South Africa v The Richtersveld Community*, Constitutional Court of South Africa, CCT 19/03, 14 October 2003.

under indigenous law over the land in dispute. It then specified that '[t]he content of that right included the right to exclusive occupation and use of the subject land by members of the Community. The Community had the right to use its water, to use its land for grazing and hunting and *to exploit its natural resources, above and beneath the surface.*'[26] Accordingly, the Court concluded that the Ritchtersveld community 'held ownership of the subject land *under indigenous law*, which *included the rights to minerals* and precious stones',[27] and it thus ordered that the right to ownership of the land in dispute, including its minerals and precious stones, should be reinstituted to the Richtersveld Community.[28] Similarly, in *Delgamuukw v British Columbia*,[29] the Supreme Court of Canada considered that aboriginal title encompasses natural resources, including mineral resources.[30]

However, as will be revealed in the next section, there may exist a conflict between the provisions concerning the use of resources incorporated into indigenous customs and those included in national laws. In particular, despite the decisions referred to above, it seems that the recognition of indigenous peoples' rights to natural resources encounters a major limitation with regard to subsoil resources.

Surface versus Subsoil Resources

In her study on *Indigenous Peoples' Permanent Sovereignty over Natural Resources*, former UN Special Rapporteur Erica-Irene Daes affirmed that

> the developments during the past two decades in international law and human rights norms in particular demonstrate that there now exists a developed legal principle that indigenous peoples have a collective right to the lands and territories they traditionally use and occupy and that this right includes the right to use, own, manage and control the natural resources found within their lands and territories.[31]

As to the kinds of resources to which this right would extend, she spelled out that

> [t]hese resources can include air, coastal seas, and sea ice as well as timber, minerals, oil and gas, genetic resources, and all other material resources pertaining to indigenous lands and territories.[32]

[26] Ibid, para 62 (emphasis added).
[27] Ibid, para 102 (emphasis added).
[28] Ibid, para 103.1(a).
[29] *Delgamuukw v British Columbia* [1997] 3 SCR 1010.
[30] Ibid, para 122.
[31] Commission on Human Rights, *Indigenous Peoples' Permanent Sovereignty over Natural Resources*, Final Report of the Special Rapporteur (Erica-Irene Daes), UN Doc E/CN.4/Sub.2/2004/30, 13 July 2004, para 39.
[32] Ibid, para 42.

However, she promptly admitted that the issue concerning subsurface resources was an extremely contentious one. Indeed, indigenous customs and national laws may diverge considerably when it comes to subsoil resources.

Regarding aboriginal title, in the recent judgment delivered by the High Court of Australia in *Northern Territory of Australia v Arnhem Land Aboriginal Land Trust*,[33] Kirby J admitted that the national legislature can 'qualify, diminish or abolish' legal interests connected with aboriginal title, provided that it does so 'clearly and expressly'.[34] In an earlier decision concerning the case *Commonwealth v Yarmirr*,[35] the High Court stated that when common law and native title rights are inconsistent, the common law will prevail.[36] Illustrative in this regard is the decision of the Federal Court of Australia in *Attorney General of the Northern Territory v Ward*,[37] in which the Court found that the claimants' native title right 'to use and enjoy the land and waters *in accordance with their traditional laws and customs*' encompasses 'the right to hunt on the land, to gather and use the *natural resources* of the land such as food, medicinal plants, wild tobacco, timber, stone and resin, and to have access to and use of natural water on the land'.[38] At the same time, however, the Court specified that native title does not cover minerals and petroleum.[39] It will be useful to recall here that the Aboriginal Land Rights (Northern Territory) Act 1976 reserves the rights relating to all minerals to the Commonwealth and the Northern Territory.[40]

Equally significant is the position taken by the Supreme Court of the Philippines when it was confronted with the delicate problem of reconciling the constitutional provision affirming the State's ownership of natural resources[41] with the provision of the Indigenous Peoples Right Act recognising indigenous peoples' right 'to develop lands and natural resources'.[42] The conclusion reached by the Court was that the Act should be interpreted narrowly as encompassing only the right to surface resources.[43]

[33] *Northern Territory of Australia v Arnhem Land Aboriginal Land Trust* [2008] HCA 29.
[34] Ibid, para 69.
[35] *Commonwealth v Yarmirr* [2001] HCA 56.
[36] Ibid, para 42.
[37] *Attorney General of the Northern Territory v Ward* [2003] FCA 283.
[38] Ibid, para 5(a) (emphasis added).
[39] Ibid, para 7.
[40] Aboriginal Land Rights (Northern Territory) Act 1976, www.austlii.edu.au/au/legis/cth/consol_act/alrta1976444/s12.html.
[41] 1987 Constitution of the Republic of the Philippines, Art 12(2).
[42] Republic Act No 8371, Indigenous Peoples Rights Act of 1997, adopted 29 October 1997, s 7(b).
[43] See Asian Development Bank, *Indigenous Peoples/Ethnic Minorities and Poverty Reduction: Philippines* (Manila, 2002) 16.

Similar provisions can be found in the constitutions and legislation of most States worldwide. In this regard, it has been noted that '[s]uch legal regimes have a distinct and extremely adverse impact on indigenous peoples, because they purport to unilaterally deprive the indigenous peoples of the subsurface resources that they owned prior to colonial occupation and the creation of the present State'.[44] It has also been underscored that 'indigenous peoples were not participants in the process of adopting State constitutions and cannot be said to have consented to the transfer of their subsurface resources to the State'.[45] On this point, S James Anaya has acknowledged that 'when indigenous land tenure systems encompass subsoil resources and therefore conflict with the state property regime, the result is unclear'.[46]

However, as will be seen below, international, regional and national practice suggest that, at present, States do retain ownership of subsoil resources and, in practice, this poses a limit to indigenous peoples' right to 'own, use, develop and control' the resources located in their lands. The UN Declaration, in our view, confirms this interpretation. Both Convention 169 and the draft American Declaration, while recognising indigenous peoples' right to use, manage and conserve the natural resources pertaining to their lands, explicitly contemplate the case in which the State retains ownership of mineral or subsurface resources.[47] In the same vein, the recently adopted Operating Guidelines on the Indigenous Peoples Policy of the Inter-American Development Bank make indigenous peoples' interests in subsurface resources subject to the 'relevant norms of the country'.[48]

The decision of the Supreme Court of Belize in the conjoined cases of *Maya Village of Conejo* and *Maya Village of Santa Cruz v Belize* is highly important in this context.[49] In these cases the Court, on the one hand, declared that Maya indigenous peoples 'hold, respectively, collective and individual rights in the lands and *resources* that they have used and occupied *according to Maya customary practises*'.[50] On the other, it acknowledged that the Government could issue concessions for resource exploitation, including mining, provided that various conditions were met.[51] The

[44] Final Report (n 31) para 43.

[45] Ibid.

[46] Anaya (n 22) 16.

[47] See, respectively, Art 15 para 2, and Art XVIII para 5.

[48] Inter-American Development Bank, *Operating Guidelines on the Indigenous Peoples Policy*, 6 October 2006, p 34.

[49] *Aurelio Cal and the Maya Village of Santa Cruz v Attorney General of Belize; and Manuel Coy and Maya Village of Conejo v Attorney General of Belize*, (Consolidated) Claim Nos 171 & 172, 2007, Supreme Court of Belize (18 October 2007).

[50] Ibid, para 136(a) (emphasis added).

[51] Ibid, para 136(d)(iv). Discussed below.

Inter-American Court of Human Rights followed this pattern in *Sarakama People v Suriname*.[52] Faced with the provision in the Constitution of Suriname conferring ownership of natural resources on the State, the Court affirmed that indigenous peoples have the right to 'those natural resources traditionally used and necessary for their very survival, development and continuation of such people's way of life'.[53] Like the Supreme Court of Belize, it however admitted the possibility that States may grant concessions for the exploration and extraction of natural resources in indigenous lands, on condition that—once again—particular requirements are fulfilled.[54] Similarly, the Ley Orgánica de Pueblos y Comunidades Indígenas of Venezuela links, under Article 53, the right of indigenous peoples to use the resources located in their lands to their performing traditional activities and their development. Article 54 then regulates separately the exploitation of 'recursos natural de propriedad de la Nación' situated in indigenous lands.[55]

What does the UN Declaration say in this regard? As previously noted, it does not specify what are the resources which indigenous peoples have the right 'to own, use, develop and control' pursuant to Article 26. In order to shed some light on this provision, it is useful to look at its drafting history. Article 26 of the draft declaration, approved in 1994 by the Sub-Commission on Prevention of Discrimination and Protection of Minorities, read:

> Indigenous peoples have the right to own, develop, control and use the lands and territories, including the total environment of the lands, air, waters, coastal seas, sea-ice, flora and fauna and other resources which they have traditionally owned or otherwise occupied or used. This includes the right to the full recognition of their laws, traditions and customs, land-tenure systems and institutions for the development and management of resources, and the right to effective measures by States to prevent any interference with, alienation of or encroachment upon these rights.[56]

In 1995 this draft was sent to the UN Commission on Human Rights for consideration prior to submission to the Economic and Social Council and the General Assembly. However, the process stalled precisely because of concerns surrounding, among other things, the provisions of the Declaration concerning control over the natural resources existing in the traditional lands of indigenous peoples.

[52] See n 17 above.
[53] Ibid, para 122.
[54] Ibid, paras 125ff. Note also that in its 2004 Concluding Observations on Suriname, CERD stated that Suriname's rights pertaining to natural resources, as recognised in the Constitution, 'must be exercised consistently with the rights of indigenous and tribal peoples' (UN Doc CERD/C/64/CO/9/Rev.2, 12 March 2004, para 11).
[55] Ley Orgánica de Pueblos y Comunidades Indígenas, 8 December 2005.
[56] UN Doc E/CN.4/Sub.2/1994/2/Add.1.

During the debates leading to the 1994 draft, the indissoluble link between the preservation of the life and culture of indigenous peoples and control over their lands and resources was repeatedly emphasised.[57] Not only was the deprivation of natural resources 'as basic as water or natural food'[58] deplored, but several indigenous representatives also pointed out that 'in order for land rights to be meaningful, they ought to include *indigenous control* of natural *resources, subsoil* as well as surface'.[59] On more than one occasion, reference was made to the devastating consequences of the extraction of subsoil resources on indigenous peoples' lives.[60] The need to accommodate the issue of natural resources along with other questions led to the creation in 1995 of a specific forum—the Working Group on the Draft Declaration—where negotiations between States and indigenous representatives could take place.[61] Within this new framework, States voiced their concerns.

Australia, for example, made it clear that 'ownership of minerals, petroleum and certain other resources was vested in the Crown and the exploitation and use of such resources was governed by legislation', while acknowledging, at the same time, that native title could include a range of rights also relating to the enjoyment of natural resources.[62] New Zealand stressed that indigenous peoples' right to maintain their special relationship with their traditional lands and resources 'must be balanced by the need for the Government to own and regulate resources in the interests of all citizens'.[63] Similarly, the representative of Canada stated that it was 'critical to find a language which reconciles the interests of indigenous peoples in land and resources, and the rights of States'.[64] The governmental delegate of Venezuela underlined that 'natural resources are under the control of the State'.[65]

On the other hand, indigenous representatives made various attempts at introducing into the text of the Declaration an express reference to subsoil resources. At a certain point during the negotiations a new Article 25 circulated, stipulating that

> Indigenous peoples have the right to maintain and strengthen their distinctive spiritual and *material* relationship with the lands [,] [or] territories, waters and coastal seas and other resources [including the total environment of the lands,

[57] See UN Doc E/CN.4/Sub.2/1983/22, 23 August 1983, para 46.
[58] Ibid.
[59] UN Doc E/CN.4/Sub.2/1984/20, 8 August 1984, para 114 (emphasis added).
[60] See eg UN Doc E/CN.4/Sub.2/1995/24, 10 August 1995, paras 88ff.
[61] The Working Group on the Draft Declaration was established by the UN Commission on Human Rights in 1995 by Res 1995/32.
[62] UN Doc E/CN.4/2000/84, 6 December 1999, para 92.
[63] Ibid, para 93.
[64] UN Doc E/CN.4/2001/85, 6 February 2001, para 108.
[65] Ibid, para 110.

> air, waters, coastal seas, sea ice, flora and fauna and other *surface and subsurface resources*] ...[66]

Likewise, a new paragraph was suggested within Article 30 of the 1994 draft which read: 'Indigenous peoples have rights to the possession, ownership and control of *surface and subsurface* resources within their traditional lands and territories.'[67] None of these attempts succeeded, however, as many governmental delegations were strongly opposed to keeping this language in the text.[68] Nor did attempts at retaining in the final text the adjective 'material' before the reference to the relationship with lands, territories and resources prove victorious.[69] Conversely, efforts to have the adjective 'their' inserted before 'resources' in what is now Article 32 of the Declaration seemed initially to have some chance of success. In fact, the draft Declaration as it was approved in 2006 by the Human Rights Council provided that:

> States shall consult and cooperate in good faith with the indigenous peoples concerned through their own representative institutions in order to obtain their free and informed consent prior to the approval of any project affecting their lands or territories and other resources, particularly in connection with the development, utilization or exploitation of *their* mineral, water or other resources.[70]

This version of Article 32 thus qualified mineral resources as *theirs*—that is, as belonging to indigenous peoples. However, as we know, in order for the Declaration to be approved by the General Assembly this reference was eventually removed. The deletion of the adjective 'their' in Article 32 in fact represents one of the nine amendments to the 2006 draft which were necessary to ensure the adoption of the Declaration by the General Assembly in 2007.[71] The Steering Committee of the global Indigenous Peoples' Caucus endorsed adoption of the Declaration incorporating the nine amendments, including the one concerning natural resources.

In the light of its drafting history, it is believed that there is indeed very little room left for arguing that the Declaration differentiates itself from the general practice denying indigenous peoples control over subsoil

[66] UN Doc E/CN.4/2004/81, 17 January 2004 (emphasis added). See also UN Doc E/CN.4/2004/WG.15/CRP.4, 12 October 2004, 32.

[67] UN Doc E/CN.4/2004/WG.15/CRP.4, ibid, 37.

[68] See UN Doc E/CN.4/2005/89, 28 February 2005, para 33. In the 2004 study on *Indigenous Peoples' Permanent Sovereignty over Natural Resources* (n 31) Special Rapporteur Daes recommended that 'Articles 25 and 26 of the draft [declaration] should include an express reference to subsurface resources' (para 71).

[69] Compare the text of Article 25 in UN Doc E/CN.4/2005/89/Add.2 with the text finally approved. Note that the adjective 'material' was included in the 1994 draft.

[70] See Human Rights Council Resolution 2006/2, Art 32 (emphasis added).

[71] S Errico, 'The UN General Assembly Adopts the Declaration on the Rights of Indigenous Peoples' (2007) 10(19) *ASIL Insight*, 9 October.

resources. Nonetheless, much caution is needed on this point since the denial of indigenous peoples' control over subsoil resources does not mean that these peoples are deprived of *all* rights with regard to the subsoil resources existing in their lands and territories. On the contrary, as will be illustrated in the following sections, the State has specific obligations towards indigenous peoples and, correspondingly, indigenous peoples have precise rights in connection with the exploitation of these resources, which the Declaration endorses.

THE STATE AS SOVEREIGN AND 'DUTY BEARER'

The obligations that States have towards indigenous peoples in connection with the exploitation of natural resources seem to be perfectly in line with the modern development of international law, which stresses more and more the association that exists between the sovereignty of States and their responsibilities. The State is not only a 'sovereign'; it is clearly also a 'duty-bearer'. This proves to be especially true in the context of natural resources, as the principle of States' permanent sovereignty over them[72] has to be reconciled with various specific duties that States hold towards their citizens.[73] These developments in fact represent an interesting background against which we can analyse the specific obligations that States have towards indigenous peoples. A good starting point is the General Assembly's Declaration on the Right to Development, which defines the right to development as 'an inalienable human right by virtue of which every human person and all peoples are entitled to participate in, contribute to, and enjoy economic, social, cultural and political development, in which all human rights and fundamental freedoms can be fully realized'.[74] It also declares that the right to development 'implies the full realization of the right of peoples to self-determination, which includes, subject to the relevant provisions of both International Covenants on Human Rights, the exercise of their inalienable right to full sovereignty over all their natural wealth and resources'.[75] The primary responsibility for creating conditions favourable to the development of peoples and individuals is placed on States.[76] In particular, the Declaration emphasises the duty of States 'to formulate appropriate national development policies that aim at

[72] See Declaration on Permanent Sovereignty over Natural Resources, GA Res 1803 (XVII), 14 December 1962.

[73] See generally N Schrijver, *Sovereignty over Natural Resources: Balancing Rights and Duties* (Cambridge University Press, 1997).

[74] Declaration on the Right to Development, UN Doc A/RES/41/128, 4 December 1986, Art 1(1).

[75] Ibid, Art 1(2).

[76] Ibid, preamble.

the constant improvement of the well-being of the *entire population* and of *all individuals*, on the basis of their active, free and meaningful participation in development and in the fair distribution of the benefits resulting therefrom'.[77] The Declaration thus seems to suggest that if States hold sovereignty over the natural resources located in their territories, it follows that they cannot 'freely' dispose of them since people's right—all people's right—to development would come into play as a limit and, at the same time, as a justification for States' decision-making power with regard to natural resources.

This reading seems to be mirrored in the views expressed by CERD in its concluding observations on Nigeria in 2005. Concerned about the adverse effects on local communities flowing from large-scale exploitation of natural resources in the Delta Region, the Committee spelt out that 'along with the right [of the State] to exploit natural resources there are specific, concomitant obligations towards the local populations, including effective and meaningful consultations'.[78] On another occasion, noting the complaints made by indigenous and tribal peoples of Suriname about the deleterious effects of natural-resource exploitation on their environment, health and culture, the Committee clarified that 'development objectives are no justification for encroachments on human rights'.[79] On the contrary, respect for human rights should guide development processes. Accordingly, the Committee has thus recommended that the State 'investigate and monitor the impact of the work of mining companies, including foreign ones' on the enjoyment of fundamental human rights.[80] Similarly, the UN Committee on Economic, Social and Cultural Rights (CESCR) has recommended that the State implement legislative and administrative measures to avoid violations of rights by transnational companies.[81]

A similar concern is echoed in the practice of the UN Human Rights Committee, which has pointed out that if, on the one hand, '[a] State

[77] Ibid, Art 2(3) (emphasis added).

[78] CERD, Concluding Observations on Nigeria, UN Doc CERD/C/NGA/CO/18, 1 November 2005, para 19.

[79] CERD, Concluding Observations on Suriname, UN Doc CERD/C/64/CO/9, 12 March 2004, para 15.

[80] See CERD, Concluding Observations on Panama, UN Doc CERD/C/304/Add.32, 23 April 1997, para 23. Taking note of the adverse effects of economic activities connected with the exploitation of natural resources, CERD has also called on States to take appropriate legislative or administrative measures to prevent acts of transnational corporations registered in their territories which negatively impact on the enjoyment of human rights abroad and explore ways to hold these transnational corporations accountable. See Concluding Observations on Canada, UN Doc CERD/C/CAN/CO/18, 25 May 2007, para 17. See also Concluding Observation on the United States, UN Doc CERD/C/USA/CO/6, 8 May 2008, para 30.

[81] UNCESCR, Concluding Observations on Ecuador, UN Doc E/C.12/1/Add.100, 7 April 2004, para 35.

may understandably wish to encourage development or allow economic activity by enterprises', on the other hand, the scope of its freedom is to be assessed in light of the obligations it has undertaken with regard to human rights, including the right to enjoy one's culture under Article 27 of the Covenant on Civil and Political Rights.[82] In this sense, it is worth noting that the World Bank Extractive Industries Review[83] identified three 'enabling conditions' that would make extractive industries projects compatible with the World Bank's goals of sustainable development and poverty reduction. One of these 'enabling conditions' was represented precisely by 'respect for human rights'.[84] In fact, experience suggests that a failure to respect this basic condition will bring about an uneven distribution of the costs and benefits related to the exploitation of natural resources where the negative burden will fall, for the major part, on poor local communities.[85]

In the same vein, the Inter-American Commission on Human Rights in the case of the *Maya Indigenous Communities of the Toledo District v Belize*[86] recognised that 'development activities must be accompanied by appropriate and effective measures to ensure that they do not proceed at the expense of the fundamental rights of persons who may be particularly and negatively affected, including indigenous communities'.[87] The African Commission on Human and Peoples' Rights in the *Ogoni People* case,[88] referring to certain activities carried out by multinational corporations in the territory of Nigeria, underscored that such activities may contribute in positive way to the State's development solely on condition that the latter is 'mindful of the common good and the sacred rights of individuals and communities'.[89] Equally interesting is the Vienna Declaration (1993) which, once more, highlighted that 'the lack of development may not be invoked to justify the abridgement of internationally recognized human rights'.[90]

[82] UN Committee on Human Rights, *Ilmari Lansman v Finland*, UN Doc CCPR/C/52/D/511/1992, 26 October 1994, para 9(4).

[83] This was an initiative set in motion in 2001 by the former President of the World Bank Group, James Wolfensohn, in response to public pressure calling on the institution to cease funding for oil, gas and mining sector investments. Its aim was to focus on the World Bank Group's engagement in the extractive sector.

[84] According to the Extractive Industries Review, the other two 'enabling conditions' are: 'pro-poor and corporate governance, including proactive planning and management to maximize poverty alleviation through sustainable development', and 'much more effective social and environmental policies'. See Executive Summary of the Review, 1.

[85] Ibid.

[86] See n 16 above.

[87] Ibid, para 150.

[88] *Social and Economic Rights Action Center and Center for Economic and Social Rights v Nigeria*, Communication No 155/96, 2001.

[89] Ibid, para 69.

[90] UN Doc A/CONF.157/23, 25 June 1993, para 10.

All these considerations have led to the adoption of the so-called human-rights based approach to development. This approach aims at integrating the norms and principles of the international human rights system into development programmes and projects.[91] In particular, it is said to have 'the human being at its center',[92] and to be concerned with how 'development outcomes are brought about, and not simply on achieving outcomes themselves'.[93] It focuses on 'accountability of the duty-holders (mainly national or local government, but also others), and participation of the rights-bearers, such as indigenous peoples'.[94] Such an approach thus stresses the need to respect human rights in the implementation of development projects, including the exploitation of natural resources, especially with regard to those segments of the population that may be particularly affected.

If development has to go hand in hand with respect for human rights, so does States' power to dispose of natural resources. This power is, in fact, instrumental in pursuing the goal of national development. It is suggested that this understanding is reinforced by the current 'multidimensional' interpretation of the concept of 'poverty' which no longer defines poverty in terms of insufficient income to buy a minimum basket of goods and services, but, rather, regards it more broadly as a lack of basic capabilities to live in dignity. According to CESCR, poverty may be defined as 'a human condition characterized by sustained or chronic deprivation of the resources, capabilities, choices, security and power necessary for the enjoyment of an adequate standard of living and other civil, cultural, economic, political and social rights'.[95] In these terms, poverty constitutes a denial of human rights and, therefore, poverty eradication policies and development strategies should be based upon international human rights in order to be more effective and meaningful.[96]

It follows that if the State bears sovereignty over the natural resources of a country, it is also accountable for development policies implemented

[91] See UN Working Group on Indigenous Populations, *Review of Developments* (n 5) para 6.

[92] See *Engaging Indigenous Peoples in Governance Processes: International Legal and Policy Frameworks for Engagement*, UN workshop on 'Engaging the Marginalized: Partnerships between Indigenous Peoples, Governments and Civil Society', Background paper prepared by the Secretariat of the UN Permanent Forum on Indigenous Issues, Division for Social Policy and Development/UN Department of Economic and Social Affairs, International Conference on Engaging Communities, Brisbane, Australia, 15 August 2005, para 6.

[93] Ibid.

[94] Ibid.

[95] See 'Poverty and the International Covenant on Economic, Social and Cultural Rights', statement adopted by the Committee on Economic, Social and Cultural Rights on 4 May 2001, UN Doc E/C.12/2001/10, para 8.

[96] In the same vein, see the *European Consensus on Development* adopted jointly by the European Council, Parliament and Commission, OJ C46/1, 24 February 2006, para 11.

in that country and, in this context, it is thus called upon to ensure that these policies benefit the whole population and the communities that are indirectly or directly affected and do not undermine the enjoyment of their human rights. Precisely in order to ensure that development policies benefit the whole population, current international, regional and national practice suggest that the State has a duty to ensure that the population participate[97] in the planning and execution of development projects as well as in the benefits flowing from them.

In the *Ogoni People* case, for instance, the African Commission on Human and Peoples' Rights held that Article 21 of the African Charter on Human and Peoples' Rights, enshrining the right to dispose of national wealth and natural resources, had been violated precisely because

> the State party should not act arbitrarily in exercising the right to freely dispose of its wealth and natural resources. The non-participation of the Ogoni people and the absence of any benefit accruable to them in the exploitation of the oil resources by the Nigerian government and the oil companies were undoubtedly contrary to Article 21 of the Charter.[98]

Additionally, with regard to peoples' right to economic, social and cultural development, as laid down in Article 22 of the African Charter, the Commission affirmed that this right is an 'inalienable Human Right by virtue of which every human person is entitled to participate in, contribute to and enjoy the economic, social, cultural and political development of the society'.[99]

From an empirical point of view these considerations are confirmed and strengthened by the abovementioned World Bank's Extractive Industries Review and the Report of the World Commission on Dams.[100] On the whole, both reports highlight that without the effective participation of the communities involved in the various stages of realisation of development projects, the adverse effects of such projects on the communities will outstrip by far any potential benefit, in contrast with the objective of poverty

[97] On the issue of participation in natural resource development see DN Zillman, AR Lucas and GR Pring, *Human Rights in Natural Resource Development—Participation in the Sustainable Development of Mining and Energy Resources* (Oxford University Press, 2002).

[98] See C Nwobike, 'The African Commission on Human and Peoples' Rights and the Demystification of Second and Third Generation Rights under the African Charter: *Social and Economic Right Action Center (SERAC) and the Center for Economic and Social Rights (CESR) v Nigeria*' (2005) 1 *African Journal of Legal Studies* 129.

[99] Resolution on the African Commission on Human and Peoples' Rights, ACHPR/RPT/6th, Annex 3, reproduced in Report of the African Commission's Working Group on Indigenous Populations/Communities. See ACHPR/Res.65 (XXXIV), Resolution on the Adoption of the 'Report of the African Commission's Working Group on Indigenous Populations/Communities', 20 November 2003.

[100] The World Commission on Dams was called to review large dam projects. Its report was published in 2000 and provided guidelines for sustainable dam development fully recognising indigenous peoples' right to free, prior and informed consent.

reduction that these projects ultimately have. Even earlier, in 1987, the Brundtland Report, referring to the situation of marginalised communities, highlighted that 'a more careful and sensitive consideration of their interests is a touchstone of a sustainable development policy'.[101] Bearing these considerations in mind, this chapter examines the obligations of States, and the correlative rights of indigenous peoples, which the UN Declaration incorporates in relation to the exploitation of natural resources.

STATES, INDIGENOUS PEOPLES, AND THE EXPLOITATION OF NATURAL RESOURCES

It is the author's view that the final compromise reached between indigenous peoples and States with regard to the issue of subsoil resources is summarised in Article 32 of the Declaration and moves within the orbit of the principle of participation. In fact, participation is one of the fundamental principles underlying the Declaration.[102] Article 5 asserts that indigenous peoples have the right to participate fully in the 'political, *economic*, social and cultural life of the State'.[103] Article 18 spells out that they have the right 'to participate in decision-making in matters which would affect their rights, through representatives chosen by themselves in accordance with their own procedures'. Article 19 proclaims that States 'shall consult and cooperate in good faith with the indigenous peoples concerned through their own representative institutions in order to obtain their free, prior and informed consent before adopting legislative or administrative measures that may affect them'. It is thus more than reasonable to expect that the principle of participation also applies to the specific issue of the exploitation of natural resources, notably of subsurface resources.

Indeed, given the conclusion reached above that the right of indigenous peoples to own, use, develop and control natural resources contemplated in Article 26 of the Declaration is bound to be interpreted fairly narrowly, restricting its meaning exclusively to surface resources, the provisions of the Declaration embracing the principle of participation and consultation are of vital importance for indigenous peoples' cultural and physical survival. Article 32(2) of the Declaration reads as follows:

> States shall *consult* and cooperate in good faith with the indigenous peoples concerned *through their own representative institutions* in order to obtain their free

[101] The Brundtland Report was released in 1987 by the World Commission on Environment and Development. See S Jentoft, H Minde and R Nilsen, *Indigenous Peoples, Resource Management and Global Rights* (Delft, Eburon Publishers, 2003) 22.

[102] S Errico, 'The Draft UN Declaration on the Rights of Indigenous Peoples: An Overview' (2007) 7 *Human Rights Law Review* 241.

[103] Emphasis added.

> and informed consent prior to the approval of any project affecting their lands or territories and other resources, particularly in connection with the development, *utilization or exploitation of mineral*, water or other resources.[104]

It goes on to state in paragraph 3 that

> States shall provide effective mechanisms for just and fair redress for any such activities, and appropriate measures shall be taken to mitigate adverse environmental, economic, social, cultural or spiritual impact.

In other words, Article 32 acknowledges the possibility that the State will undertake extractive activities in indigenous lands and territories but, at the same time, establishes various conditions that must be fulfilled, ie indigenous peoples must be consulted through their representative institutions prior to these initiatives being approved (we will deal with the matter of free, prior and informed consent in the following section). This approach is in line with current international, regional and national practice concerning indigenous rights. Nevertheless, several useful elements can be drawn from these sources that will enrich our interpretation of this provision of the Declaration and help us to understand its practical implications.

In the event that the State retains ownership of mineral or subsoil resources, ILO Convention 169, at Article 15(2), sets out that

> governments shall establish or maintain procedures through which they shall *consult* these peoples, with a view to ascertaining whether and to what degree their interests would be prejudiced, before undertaking or permitting any programmes for the exploration or exploitation of such resources pertaining to their lands. The peoples concerned shall wherever possible *participate in the benefits of such activities*, and shall *receive fair compensation for any damages* which they may sustain as a result of such activities.[105]

In relation to this provision, the Tripartite Committee of the ILO Governing Body[106] has stated that when 'differing interests and points of view are at stake such as the economic and development interests represented by the hydrocarbon deposits and the cultural, social and economic interests of the indigenous peoples situated in the zones where those deposits are situated', then the principles of consultation and participation which inform this provision of the Convention require that 'the parties involved seek to establish a dialogue allowing them to

[104] Emphasis added.

[105] Emphasis added.

[106] Under Art 24 of the ILO Constitution, workers' and employers' organisations are entitled to submit 'representations' alleging violations of articles of ILO Conventions on the part of a State. The representation is examined by a Tripartite Committee, ie a committee composed of one governmental representative, one employers' representative and one workers' representative, appointed by the ILO Governing Body.

find appropriate solutions in an atmosphere of mutual respect and full participation'.[107]

In this regard, Article 15 of the Convention should be read together with Article 6 establishing the minimum requirements to be met when consulting indigenous peoples. First, such consultations shall take place 'through appropriate procedures and in particular through their representative institutions'. Second, they shall be carried out 'in good faith and in a form appropriate to the circumstances'. Finally, it is specified that these consultations shall be undertaken 'with the objective of achieving agreement or consent to the proposed measures'. As clarified by the Tripartite Committee of the ILO Governing Body, in order for consultations to be effective, 'sufficient time must be given to allow the country's indigenous peoples to engage *their own decision-making processes* and participate effectively in decisions taken in a manner consistent with their cultural and social traditions'.[108] It is worth noting that Article 7 of the Convention requires that States assess, in cooperation with indigenous peoples, the social, spiritual, cultural and environmental impact on them of planned development activities. Further, the ILO Committee of Experts on the Application of Conventions and Recommendations has pointed out that this provision of the Convention covers not just the case of a project being implemented in the traditional lands of indigenous peoples, but also the case of a project having an impact on the 'life' of the community. It has thus affirmed that 'a project for exploration or exploitation in the immediate vicinity of lands occupied or otherwise used by indigenous peoples, or which directly affects the interests of such peoples, would fall within the scope of the Convention'.[109]

A similar provision is incorporated in the draft American Declaration on the Rights of Indigenous Peoples. Article XVIII(5), referring to State ownership of natural resources, affirms that

> In the event that ownership of the minerals or resources of the subsoil pertains to the state or that the state has rights over other resources on the lands, the governments must establish or maintain procedures for the *participation* of the peoples concerned in determining whether the interests of these people would be adversely affected and to what extent, before undertaking or authorizing any program for planning, prospecting or exploiting existing resources on their lands. The peoples concerned shall *participate in the benefits of such activities*, and shall receive *compensation*, on a basis not less favourable than the standard of international law *for any loss* which they may sustain as a result of such activities.[110]

[107] See ILO Governing Body, 282nd session, November 2001, representation under Article 24 of the ILO Constitution, GB.282/14/2, para 36.

[108] ILO Governing Body, 282nd session, November 2001, representation under Art 24 of the ILO Constitution, Colombia, GB.282/14/3, para 79 (emphasis added).

[109] CEACR: Individual Observation concerning Indigenous and Tribal Peoples Convention, 1989 (No 169) Guatemala (ratification: 1996, published: 2007) para 5.

[110] Emphasis added.

This provision is linked to Article XXI, which requires that decisions concerning the realisation of plans or projects affecting indigenous peoples' rights or living conditions are subject to indigenous peoples' consent and their informed and free participation. Article XXI also calls on States to take necessary measures to ensure that indigenous peoples' preferences are recognised and that no plan, programme or proposal that could have harmful effects on those peoples is adopted.

Equally relevant for the purposes of the present analysis are General Comment No 23 of the UN Human Rights Committee[111] and CERD's General Recommendation 23,[112] as well as the practice of both bodies. Regarding the former, it should be recalled that the UN Human Rights Committee has maintained that the right to cultural integrity protected by Article 27 of the Covenant on Civil and Political Rights also covers 'a way of life which is closely associated with territory and use of its resources'.[113] Prior to the adoption of the General Comment, the Committee had already pointed out that 'the rights protected by Article 27, include the right of persons, in community with others, to engage in economic and social activities which are part of the culture of the community to which they belong'.[114] It should be noted here that the Committee has emphasised that the protection of this right may require the adoption of measures to ensure 'the *effective participation* of members of minority communities in decisions which affect them'.[115] In line with this orientation, the Committee has deemed that the legality of mining and logging activities with respect to Article 27 of the Covenant should be evaluated in light of two different criteria: the 'sustainability' of the activity in relation to the culture of indigenous communities that will be affected by these initiatives,[116] and the 'participation' of the indigenous communities concerned in the decision-making process with regard to projects to be carried out in their lands.[117] Thus, in the Committee's view, 'the acceptability of measures that affect or interfere with the culturally significant economic activities of a minority depends on whether the members

[111] Above, n 19.

[112] Above, n 10.

[113] Above, n 19, para 3(2).

[114] *Ominayak and the Lake Lubicon Band v Canada*, CCPR/C/38/D/167/1984 (1990), para 32(2).

[115] Ibid, para 7 (emphasis added).

[116] The Committee has, in fact, considered that '[m]easures whose impact amounts to a denial of the right are incompatible with the obligations under Article 27'. However, 'measures that have a certain limited impact on the way of life and the livelihood of persons belonging to a minority will not necessarily amount to a denial of the rights under Article 27'. See *J Lansman v Finland*, CCPR/C/58/D/671/1995, 22 November 1996, para 10.3.

[117] See eg *Ilmari Lansman v Finland* (n 82) paras 9.4ff. See also *J Lansman v Finland*, ibid, paras 10.3ff. See generally P Thornberry, *Indigenous Peoples and Human Rights* (Manchester University Press, 2002) 167ff.

of the minority in question have had the opportunity to participate in the decision-making process in relation to these measures and whether they will continue to benefit from their traditional economy'.[118] Accordingly, when examining the periodic report of Chile, the Committee reiterated that:

> When planning actions that affect members of indigenous communities, the State party must pay primary attention to the *sustainability* of the indigenous cultures and way of life and to the *participation* of members of indigenous communities in decisions that affect them.[119]

Likewise, in its concluding observations on Canada, the Committee stressed that the State

> should consult with the [Lubicon Lake] Band before granting licences for economic exploitation of the disputed land, and ensure that in no case such exploitation jeopardizes the rights recognized under the Covenant.[120]

As far as CERD is concerned, it is worth noting that, in its General Recommendation 23 on Indigenous Peoples, the Committee recommended that States 'provide indigenous peoples with conditions allowing for a *sustainable development* and social development *compatible with their cultural characteristics*'[121] and ensure that 'no decisions directly relating to their rights and interests are taken without their informed consent'.[122] It is suggested that such decisions encompass those decisions concerning the realisation of development projects and, in particular, the exploitation of subsoil resources.

The previous section of this chapter underscored the general orientation of the Committee according to which States' decision-making power with regard to natural resources is accompanied by specific obligations towards the local population, notably the obligation to ensure that the latter are consulted. The same approach is followed with regard to indigenous peoples. For instance, in its Concluding Observations on Guatemala of 2006, the Committee noted with concern that the Ministry of Energy and Mines had granted mining licences to concession enterprises and regretted that

[118] See *Apirana Mahuika v New Zealand*, UN Doc CCPR/C/70/D/547/1993, 15 November 2000, para 9.5.

[119] CCPR, Concluding Observations on Chile, UN Doc CCPR/C/79/Add.104, 30 March 1999, para 22.

[120] See UN Doc CCPR/C/CAN/CO/5, 20 April 2006, para 9. Similarly, in its Concluding Observations on Thailand, the Committee declared that '[t]he State party should guarantee the full enjoyment of the rights of persons belonging to minorities that are set out in the Covenant, in particular with respect to the use of land and natural resources, through *effective consultations with local communities*'. UN Doc CCPR/CO/84/THA, 8 July 2005, para 24 (emphasis added).

[121] Above, n 10, para 4(c) (emphasis added).

[122] Ibid, para 4(d).

'indigenous peoples [had not been] consulted or informed'.[123] With regard to Suriname, while noting the principle set forth in the Constitution according to which natural resources are the property of the nation and must be used to promote economic, social and cultural development, the Committee clearly affirmed that 'this principle must be exercised consistently with the rights of indigenous and tribal peoples'.[124] Among these rights, the Committee also identified the right to an 'equitable sharing of benefits' to be derived from the exploitation of natural resources.[125]

Interesting considerations have also been developed by CESCR. The Committee has requested that the State 'consult and seek consent of the indigenous people concerned prior to the implementation of natural resources-extracting projects ... affecting them',[126] or, in a more specific way, 'prior to the implementation of timber, soil or subsoil mining projects ... affecting them'.[127]

Turning to the Inter-American system, for the moment[128] it is sufficient to recall that the Inter-American Commission on Human Rights has repeatedly demanded that

> all projects to build infrastructure or exploit natural resources in the indigenous area or that affect their *habitat* or culture [are] processed and decided on with the *participation* of and *in consultation* with the peoples interested, with a view to obtaining their *consent* and possible *participation in the benefits*.[129]

The Commission has also made clear that the participation of indigenous peoples in decision-making concerning development projects affecting them, including exploitation projects, entails the involvement of their 'representantes indígenas'.[130] It has further specified that '[t]he State

[123] CERD, Concluding Observations on Guatemala, UN Doc CERD/C/GTM/CO/11, 15 May 2006, para 19. See also Concluding Observations on Suriname, UN Doc CERD/C/DEC/SUR/5, 18 August 2006, para 2.

[124] CERD, Concluding Observations on Suriname, UN Doc CERD/C/64/CO/9, 12 March 2004, para 11.

[125] CERD, Concluding Observations on Ecuador, UN Doc CERD/C/62/CO/2, 21 March 2003, para 16. See also Concluding Observation on the United States, UN Doc CERD/C/USA/CO/6, 8 May 2008, para 29.

[126] CESCR, Concluding Observations on Ecuador, UN Doc E/C.12/1/Add.100, 7 June 2004, para 35.

[127] CESCR, Concluding Observations on Brazil, UN Doc E/C.12/1/Add.87, 23 May 2003, para 58. See further Concluding Observations on Colombia, UN Doc E/C.12/1/Add.74, 30 November 2001, para 12; and Concluding Observations on Canada, UN Doc E/C.12/CAN/CO/5, 19 May 2006, para 38.

[128] See the next section.

[129] Second Report on the Human Rights Situation in Peru, ch X, 'The Rights of Indigenous Communities', OEA/Ser.L/V/II.106 Doc 59 rev, 2 June 2000, para 39.5 (emphasis added).

[130] See Report on the Human Rights Situation in Ecuador, ch IX, 'Human Rights Issues of Special Relevance to the Indigenous Inhabitants of the Country', OEA/Ser.L/V/II.96 Doc 10 rev 1, 24 April 1999, recommendations.

should also ensure that such exploitation does not cause irreparable harm to the religious, economic or cultural identity and rights of the indigenous communities'.[131]

As for the Inter-American Court of Human Rights, its recent judgment in *Saramaka People v Suriname*[132] is extremely interesting for the purpose of this section. The Court spelled out that:

> in order to guarantee that restrictions to the property rights of the members of the Saramaka people by the issuance of concessions within their territory does not amount to a denial of their survival as a tribal people, the State must abide by the following three safeguards: First, the State must ensure the *effective participation* of the members of the Saramaka people, *in conformity with their customs and traditions*, regarding any development, investment, exploration or extraction plan (hereinafter 'development or investment plan') within Saramaka territory. Second, the State must guarantee that the Saramakas will receive a *reasonable benefit* from any such plan within their territory. Thirdly, the State must ensure that no concession will be issued within Saramaka territory unless and until independent and technically capable entities, with the State's supervision, perform a *prior environmental and social impact assessment*. These safeguards are intended to preserve, protect and guarantee the special relationship that the members of the Saramaka community have with their territory, which in turn ensures their survival as a tribal people.[133]

Regarding the consultation procedure, the Court affirmed that 'the State has a duty to actively consult with said community according to their customs and traditions'.[134] In particular, it pointed out that '[t]hese consultations must be in good faith, through culturally appropriate procedures and with the objective of reaching an agreement'. Moreover, the State 'should take account of the Saramaka people's traditional methods of decision-making'.[135]

At the European level, the advisory committee charged with monitoring the implementation of the European Framework Convention for the Protection of National Minorities (Council of Europe Advisory Committee) has provided some interesting indications on the issue of State–indigenous interaction vis-a-vis the exploitation of natural resources. In its Second Opinion on Finland, the Committee stressed the existence of a 'clear obligation' to pursue economic activities affecting indigenous communities' lands and territories in a manner that protects their right to cultural identity.[136]

131 See Third Report on the Human Rights Situation in Colombia, ch X, 'The Rights of Indigenous Peoples', OEA/Ser.L/V/II.102 Doc 9 rev 1, 26 February 1999, para 58.4.

132 Above, n 17.

133 Ibid, para 129 (emphasis added).

134 Ibid, para 133.

135 Ibid.

136 Council of Europe Advisory Committee, Second Opinion on Finland, ACFC/OP/II(2006)003, 20 April 2006, para 55.

To this end, it is of paramount importance that the communities concerned are consulted and can provide their viewpoint on the impact that may potentially flow from the implementation of the project on their culture and life. Consequently, referring to the case of Saami indigenous peoples, the Committee declared that:

> it is essential that Saami are given an effective possibility to participate in the decision-making concerning other types of land-use in the region concerned, including in the territories administered by the State, in order to ensure that initiatives concerning forestry, tourism and other spheres are carried out in a manner that does not threaten the maintenance or development of reindeer herding or other aspects of Saami culture.[137]

It is also worth mentioning the EU Council of Ministers' resolution of 1998, 'indigenous peoples within the framework of the development cooperation of the Community and Member States', which provides that indigenous peoples have the right to choose their own development path, including objecting to projects in their traditional areas. Such an affirmation was reiterated in 2002 by the European Commission, which specified that the EU interprets the resolution as equivalent to the right to free, prior and informed consent.[138]

As regards Africa, we have illustrated in previous sections the position taken by the African Commission in the *Ogoni People* case according to which States' power to dispose of natural resources should be balanced with the human rights of the groups affected.

Reference should also be made to the various international development institutions' policies on indigenous peoples, beginning with the new policy adopted by the World Bank.[139] Its 2005 Operational Policy on Indigenous Peoples makes the financing of any project affecting indigenous peoples conditional upon their free, prior and informed consultation resulting in 'broad community support to the project'.[140] It also establishes that indigenous peoples must receive 'social and economic benefits that are culturally appropriate' from the implementation of projects affecting them.[141]

[137] Council of Europe Advisory Committee, First Opinion on Sweden, ACFC/INF/OP/I(2003)006, 25 August 2003, para 32.

[138] See, UN Permanent Forum on Indigenous Issues, An Overview of the Principle of Free, Prior and Informed Consent and Indigenous Peoples in International and Domestic Law and Practices, PFII/2004/WS.2/8, para. 22. In this respect, see also European Union, *Second Northern Dimension Action Plan 2004–06*, 18 October 2003, http://ec.europa.eu/external_relations/north_dim/index_en.htm.

[139] See S Errico, 'The World Bank and Indigenous Peoples: The Operational Policy on Indigenous Peoples (OP 4.10) between Indigenous Peoples' Rights to Traditional Lands and to Free, Prior, and Informed Consent' (2006) 13 *International Journal on Minority and Group Rights* 367.

[140] World Bank, Operational Policy on Indigenous Peoples (OP 4.10), adopted 20 May 2005, para 1.

[141] Ibid.

In the same vein, the policy on indigenous peoples of the Asian Development Bank (ADB) provides, among other things, that the ADB's interventions affecting indigenous peoples should '(i) be consistent with the needs and aspirations of affected indigenous peoples; (ii) be compatible in substance and structure with affected indigenous peoples' cultures and social and economic institutions; [and] (iii) be conceived, planned, and implemented with the informed participation of affected communities'.[142] Furthermore, the policy states that indigenous peoples should 'benefit equitably from the interventions'.[143]

Likewise, the Inter-American Development Bank's policy on indigenous peoples[144] states that in the case of projects relating to natural resource extraction, 'prior consultation mechanisms to safeguard the physical, cultural, and economic integrity of the affected people' should be set up. It also provides for fair compensation for any damage these peoples might suffer as a result of such a project, and, 'whenever possible, participation in project benefits'.[145]

Additionally, United Nations Development Programme (UNDP) policy on indigenous peoples[146] fosters the full participation of indigenous peoples in development processes and the incorporation of indigenous perspectives in development planning and decision-making.[147]

Looking at the national experience, several examples of application of the principle of consultation and participation of indigenous peoples in relation to the exploitation of natural resources can be found. Illustrative is the Constitution of Brazil, which, while affirming in Article 176 the principle of the State's ownership of subsoil resources, then specifies, at Article 231, that:

> The exploitation of hydraulic resources, including energy potential, as well as the prospecting and extraction of mineral resources in indigenous lands can only be carried out upon authorisation of the National Congress, after hearing the communities affected, who should be guaranteed participation in the results of the extractive activities, in accordance with the law. (author's translation) [148]

[142] Asian Development Bank, 'Policy on Indigenous Peoples', adopted April 1998 and incorporated into the ADB Operations Manual 2004, revised 2006 (OM Section F3/BP, 25 September 2006), para 8.

[143] Ibid, para 6.

[144] Inter-American Development Bank, 'Operational Policy on Indigenous Peoples', 22 February 2006, OP-765.

[145] Ibid, para 4.4(b).

[146] *UNDP and Indigenous Peoples: A Policy of Engagement* (2001).

[147] Ibid, para 27.

[148] Constitution of Brazil, Art 231(3), as reproduced in 'Authorities and Precedents in International and Domestic Law for the Proposed American Declaration on the Rights of Indigenous Peoples', Inter-Am OEA/Ser.L/V/II.110, Doc 22 (2001). 'El aprovechamiento de los recursos hidráulicos, incluido el potencial energético, la búsqueda y extracción de las riquezas minerales en tierras indígenas sólo pueden ser efectuadas con autorización del

Similarly, the Constitutions of Venezuela[149] and Ecuador,[150] legislation on indigenous peoples of the Philippines[151] and Taiwan,[152] Bolivian legislation on minerals,[153] the Nunavut Agreement in Canada,[154] the Home Rule Act of Greenland,[155] and the Estatuto de Autonomia de las Regiones de la Costa Atlantica of Nicaragua.[156]

Congreso Nacional, oídas las comunidades afectadas, quedándoles asegurada la participación en los resultados de la extracción, en la forma de la ley'.

[149] According to Art 120 of the Constitution of the Bolivarian Republic of Venezuela, 'the exploitation of natural resources located in indigenous habitats by the State shall be carried out without damaging the cultural, social and economic integrity of indigenous peoples, and it is subject to the prior information and consultation of the respective indigenous communities' (author's translation). The procedure of consultation is then regulated in the Ley Orgánica de Pueblos y Comunidades Indígenas.

[150] Pursuant to Art 84(5) of the Constitution of Ecuador, 'the State shall recognise and guarantee, in conformity with the Constitution and the law, respect for public order and human rights, the following collective rights of indigenous peoples: ... 5. To be consulted about plans and programmes for prospecting and exploiting non-renewable resources located in their lands which can affect them environmentally and culturally; to participate in the benefits resulting from these projects, as far as possible, and to receive compensation for any social and environmental damages affecting them' (author's translation).

[151] s 57 of the Indigenous Peoples Rights Act 1997 of the Philippines (Republic Act No 8371) states that non-indigenous parties can carry out extractive activities in the ancestral domains of indigenous peoples on condition that 'a formal and written agreement is entered into with the ICCs/IPs [Indigenous Cultural Communities/Indigenous Peoples] concerned or that the community, pursuant to its own decision making process, has agreed to allow such operation'. See also s 7(b).

[152] The Indigenous Peoples Basic Law of Taiwan of 5 February 2005 establishes that the Government or private actors 'shall consult indigenous peoples and obtain their consent or participation, and share with indigenous peoples benefits generated from land development, resource utilization, ecology conservation and academic research in indigenous peoples' regions'.

[153] The Ley de Hidrocarburos (Law No 3058 of 17 May 2005) stipulates that, prior to undertaking any extractive activities concerning hydrocarbons, indigenous peoples must be consulted through their representative institutions. By Supreme Decree No 29033 of 18 February 2007 specific regulations were enacted regarding the procedure for participation and consultation of indigenous peoples in relation to hydrocarbon exploitation taking place in their lands.

[154] The preamble to the Nunavut Land Claims Agreement explicitly states that one of the objectives of the negotiations conducted by the Inuit People and the Government of Canada was 'to provide for certainty and clarity ... of rights for Inuit to participate in decision-making concerning the use, management and conservation of land, water and resources'. Art 27 of the Agreement then specifies that prior to undertaking exploration activities for petroleum and other resources in the Nunavut Settlement Area, the Government and the proponent shall consult the Designed Inuit Organization (DIO).

[155] Pursuant to s 8 of the Greenland Home Rule Act enacted on 29 November 1978, preliminary study, prospecting and the exploitation of natural resources are to be regulated by agreement between the Government and the Home Rule authorities.

[156] Law No 28 of 1987 regulating the scope of autonomy accorded to the Regions of the Atlantic Coast of Nicaragua provides that the exploitation of minerals and other resources located in the Autonomous Regions of the Atlantic Coast shall take place according to agreements to be signed between the Central Government and the Regional Government with a view to ensuring that local communities benefit in just proportion from the extractive activities.

Finally, it should be noted that the approach embraced by the UN Declaration is receiving increasing attention from private actors, notably multinational corporations, as they have started to consider the establishment of consultation mechanisms as a precious means of reducing the costs and risks with which their investments might be faced in the event of local protests against their activities. As highlighted by the report of the Centre on Transnational Corporations regarding transnational investments and operations on the lands of indigenous peoples,[157] 'TNCs' performance was chiefly determined by the quantity and quality of indigenous peoples' participation in decision-making'.[158] Thus, it has been remarked that 'environmental and social costs are already part of the economic equation for mining companies: increased instability translates into higher operating costs'.[159] In this regard, it is interesting to note that the International Finance Corporation (IFC) of the World Bank Group[160] recently released Performance Standard 7 on Indigenous Peoples, which establishes various requirements to be met by IFC clients when a project affects indigenous peoples, including the duty 'to establish and maintain an ongoing relationship with the Indigenous Peoples affected by a project throughout the life of the project' and 'to foster good faith negotiation with and informed participation of Indigenous Peoples when projects are to be located on traditional or customary lands under use by the Indigenous Peoples'.[161]

To sum up, the UN Declaration, while conceding that States can dispose of subsoil resources located in indigenous lands, also establishes a specific framework within which any extractive activity must be carried out. In line with current practice, the Declaration requires that States engage with indigenous peoples and thus provides that indigenous peoples have the right to be consulted effectively in connection with projects involving exploitation of natural resources to be carried out in their lands. This consultation shall involve indigenous peoples' representative institutions and shall take place through a procedure which must be respectful of their own decision-making mechanisms. Although not expressly indicated in the Declaration, current practice also suggests that indigenous peoples have the right to participate in the benefits deriving from the implementation of said projects.

[157] See n 3 above.

[158] Ibid, para 20.

[159] See G Whiteman and K Mamen, *Meaningful Consultation and Participation in the Mining Sector? A Review of the Consultation and Participation of Indigenous Peoples within the International Mining Sector* (Ottawa, North-South Institute, 2002) 42.

[160] The International Finance Corporation is the branch of the World Bank Group financing private sector enterprises in developing countries.

[161] Performance Standard 7 on Indigenous Peoples, 30 April 2006, para 2. See also para 9.

As a matter of fact, only through consultation with the indigenous communities affected will it be possible to assess whether and to what extent a project will impact on them and accordingly take the necessary measures to address the adverse effects as well as to ensure that the communities eventually benefit from the implementation of the project. Furthermore, as shown in the following section, the safeguarding of indigenous peoples' cultural integrity seems to come into play as a parameter to be taken particularly into account before making decisions on the realisation of such activities. In this respect, it should be remarked that the preamble to the Declaration explicitly acknowledges that '*control* by indigenous peoples over developments affecting them and their lands, territories and resources will enable them to maintain and strengthen their institutions, cultures and traditions, and to promote their development in accordance with their aspirations and needs'.[162] In the case under consideration, 'control' on the part of indigenous peoples is ensured through the requirement for their '*free, prior and informed consent* prior to the approval of any project affecting their lands and territories and other resources, particularly in connection with the development, utilization or exploitation of mineral ... resources'.[163] This will be analysed further in the next section.

The Right to Free, Prior and Informed Consent[164]

The explicit recognition of indigenous peoples' right to free, prior and informed consent in the UN Declaration represents a noticeable advancement in the field of indigenous peoples' rights given the uncertainty that seems to surround the issue. It was at the centre of intense debates during the revision of the World Bank's policy on indigenous peoples. As the reader may be aware, the Extractive Industries Review commissioned by the World Bank itself pointed out that recognition and implementation of the right of affected people to free, prior and informed consent is a necessary condition for extractive projects to be successful in contributing to the World Bank' s mandate of poverty reduction. Nonetheless, in its Legal Note on Indigenous Peoples,[165] the World Bank's Legal Department

[162] Emphasis added.

[163] Art 32 (emphasis added).

[164] The principle of free, prior and informed consent is viewed as a fundamental part of the human rights-based approach to development. It is also considered to be closely linked to indigenous peoples' rights to self-determination and to traditional lands, territories and resources.

[165] Legal Note on Indigenous Peoples, 8 April 2005, submitted to the Board of Executive Directors, 10 May 2005, www.worldbank.org/indigenous.

maintained that only the principle of consultation with and participation of indigenous peoples on decisions affecting them could be deemed an 'emerging principle of international law'.[166] By contrast, the view was expressed that no conclusive evidence could be found with regard to indigenous peoples' right to free, prior and informed consent. In fact, the only binding instrument on indigenous peoples' rights, namely ILO Convention 169, makes no mention of it, with the exception of the provision on relocation in Article 16. And yet, the reference to the 'objective of achieving agreement or consent' attached to the consultation procedure in Article 6 of the Convention should not be overlooked. Furthermore, consistent practice on the issue can be traced, to which the Declaration will now contribute.

In its General Recommendation on Indigenous Peoples, for instance, CERD exhorts States to ensure that no decisions directly relating to the rights of indigenous peoples and interests are taken without their informed consent.[167] In its Concluding Observations on Ecuador, the Committee clarified that 'merely consulting these communities prior to exploiting the resources falls short of meeting the requirements set out in the Committee's general recommendation ... The Committee therefore recommends that the *prior informed consent* of these communities be sought ...'.[168] On more than one occasion, the Committee has affirmed the principle in general terms, that is, with regard to any decisions which may affect indigenous peoples' right to traditional lands.[169]

For its part, CESCR, in noting that the traditional lands of indigenous peoples had been reduced or occupied without their consent by timber, mining and oil companies at the expense of the exercise of their culture, urged the State to 'seek the consent of indigenous peoples concerned prior to the implementation of timber, soil or subsoil mining projects'.[170] Similarly, in its 2008 Concluding Observations on Panama under Articles 1 and 27 of the Covenant on Political and Civil Rights, the UN Human

[166] Ibid, para 28.

[167] See n 10 above, para 4(d).

[168] CERD, Concluding Observations on Ecuador, UN Doc CERD/C/62/CO/2, 21 March 2003, para 16 (emphasis added).

[169] See CERD, Concluding Observations on Australia, UN Doc CERD/C/AUS/CO/14, 14 April 2005, paras 11, 16; Concluding Observations on Guatemala, UN Doc CERD/C/GTM/CO/11, 15 May 2006, para 19; Concluding Observations on India, UN Doc CERD/C/IND/CO/19, 5 May 2007, para 19. See also the following decisions: Suriname: Decision 1(67), Early Warning and Urgent Action Procedure, UN Doc CERD/C/DEC/SUR/4, 18 August 2005, para 4; Suriname: Decision 1(69), Early Warning and Urgent Action Procedure, UN Doc CERD/C/DEC/SUR/3, 18 August 2006, para 2.

[170] CESCR, Concluding Observations on Colombia, UN Doc E/C.12/Add.1/74, 30 November 2001, paras 12, 33. See also Concluding Observations on Ecuador, UN Doc E/C.12/1/Add.100, 7 June 2004, paras 12, 35; Concluding Observations on Brazil, UN Doc E/C.12/17Add.87, 23 May 2003, para 58.

Rights Committee expressed its concern at the 'absence of a process of consultation to seek the prior, free and informed consent of communities to the exploitation of natural resources in their territories'.[171]

Analogous considerations have been developed by the Inter-American institutions. In this regard, it is worth recalling that the Inter-American Court of Human Rights, in the case of *Mayagna (Sumo) Awas Tingni Community v Nicaragua*,[172] found Nicaragua responsible for violating the right to property protected under Article 21 of the American Convention owing, in part, to *unilateral* concessions granted in relation to lands that were the subject of the communal property right of the Awas Tingni people. More explicitly, in the case of *Saramaka People v Suriname*, the Court considered that 'regarding large-scale development or investment projects that would have a major impact within Saramaka territory, the State has a duty, not only to consult with the Saramakas, but also to obtain their free, prior, and informed consent, according to their customs and traditions'.[173] As for the Inter-American Commission, it has repeatedly pointed out that *fully informed consent* on the part of the indigenous community is required whenever the State intends to make decisions relating to their traditional lands, 'such as the granting of concessions to exploit the natural resources of indigenous territories'.[174] Equally, in its Report on the Human Rights Situation in Colombia it recommended that the State should ensure that exploitation of natural resources on indigenous lands is preceded by 'appropriate consultations and ... consent from the affected indigenous communities'.[175] Additionally, it should be noted that the draft American Declaration on the Rights of Indigenous Peoples enshrines the principle of free, prior and informed consent in Article XXI.[176]

[171] HRC, Concluding Observations on Panama, UN Doc CCPR/C/PAN/CO/3, 17 April 2008, para 21.

[172] See n 15 above.

[173] See n 17 above, para 134.

[174] See *Maya Indigenous Communities* (n 16) para 142. See also *Mary and Carrie Dann v United States*, Case 11, 140, Inter-American Commission on Human Rights, Report No 75/02 (merits decision of 27 December 2002) para 130.

[175] See Third Report on the Human Rights Situation in Colombia (n 131) para 58.4. See also Second Report on the Human Rights Situation in Peru (n 129) para 39.5, according to which 'all projects to build infrastructure or exploit natural resources in the indigenous area or that affect their *habitat* or culture is processed and decided on with the participation of and in consultation with the peoples interested, with a view to obtaining their consent and possible participation in the benefits'.

[176] Art XXI(2) reads as follows: 'Unless exceptional circumstances so warrant in the public interest, the states shall take necessary measures to ensure that decisions regarding any plan, program or proposal affecting the rights or living conditions of indigenous peoples are not made without the free and informed consent and participation of those peoples, that their preferences are recognized and that no such plan, program or proposal that could have harmful effects on those peoples is adopted.'

Likewise, the UN Sub-Commission on the Promotion and Protection of Human Rights, which deals with transnational corporations and other business enterprises, has affirmed the need for respect of the principle of free, prior and informed consent of indigenous peoples affected by development projects.[177] A similar orientation, as was illustrated in previous sections, can be found within the EU following the 1998 Council of Ministers' resolution on 'indigenous peoples within the framework of the development cooperation of the Community and Member States'. In fact, the 2006 document *The European Consensus on Development* emphasises that 'the key principle for safeguarding indigenous peoples' rights in development cooperation is to ensure their full participation and the free and prior informed consent of the communities concerned'.[178] The same position was taken in the recent Spanish Strategy Paper for Cooperation with Indigenous Peoples,[179] and in the UNDP policy on indigenous peoples.[180]

At the national level, besides various relevant provisions incorporated into national legislation,[181] it is worth mentioning the recent decision of the Supreme Court of Belize in the cases of *Maya Village of Conejo* and *Maya Village of Santa Cruz v Belize*,[182] in which the Court subjected the possibility of undertaking extractive activities in indigenous lands to the condition that the communities affected had given their informed consent.[183] But what does the recognition of indigenous peoples' right to free, prior and informed consent entail in practice? According to the Report of the International Workshop on Methodologies regarding Free, Prior and Informed Consent and Indigenous Peoples,[184] the common understanding of the concept of free, prior and informed consent is this:

[177] Commentary on the Norms on the Responsibilities of Transnational Corporations and Other Business Enterprises with Regard to Human Rights, UN Doc E/CN.4/Sub.2/2003/38/Rev.2, para 10(c).

[178] See n 96 above, para 103.

[179] See Spanish Strategy Paper for Cooperation with Indigenous Peoples, www.maec.es.

[180] See n 146 above.

[181] See eg the Indigenous Peoples Rights Act of the Philippines (n 42) s 57, referring to the need to enter into a 'formal agreement' with the indigenous community concerned. See also Law No 28 of 1987 regulating the scope of autonomy accorded to the Southern and Northern Regions of the Atlantic Coast of Nicaragua (available in the databank of the Inter-American Development Bank at www.iadb.org//sds/ind/index_ind_e.htm), which provides that the exploitation of minerals and other resources located in the Atlantic regions is subordinated to the agreement signed between the Central Government and the Regional Government. See further the Home Rule Act of Greenland in Denmark, laying down, at Art 8, that the exploitation of natural resources must be regulated by agreement between the Government and the Home Rule authorities. The text of the Home Rule Act can be found at http://www.stm.dk/_p_12712.html.

[182] See n 49 above.

[183] Ibid, para 136(d).

[184] See Report of the International Workshop on Methodologies regarding Free, Prior and Informed Consent and Indigenous Peoples, 17–19 January 2005. The Workshop was convened in accordance with Economic and Social Council decision 2004/287 of 22 July

> *Free* should imply no coercion, intimidation or manipulation; *Prior* should imply that consent has been sought sufficiently in advance of any authorization or commencement of activities and that respect is shown for time requirements of indigenous consultation/consensus processes; *Informed* should imply that information is provided that covers (at least) the following aspects: a) Nature, size, pace, reversibility and scope of any proposed project or activity; b) Reason(s) for or purpose of the project and/or activity; c) The duration of the above; d) The locality of areas that will be affected; e) A preliminary assessment of the likely economic, social, cultural and environmental impact, including potential risks and fair and equitable benefit-sharing in a context that respects the precautionary principle; f) Personnel likely to be involved in the execution of the proposed project (including indigenous peoples, private sector staff, research institutions, government employees and others); g) Procedures that the project may entail; *Consent*.[185]

The Report also underlines that the principle of free, prior and informed consent entails the establishment of a 'dialogue allowing them [ie the parties] to find appropriate solutions in an atmosphere of mutual respect in good faith, and full and equitable participation'.[186] It further indicates that '[t]his process *may* include the option of withholding consent'.[187]

During the negotiations leading to the adoption of the Declaration, the exact meaning to be attached to the expression 'free, prior and informed consent' was widely debated, especially in relation to the so-called right of veto. The difficulties encountered in having the expression inserted into the Declaration arose out of several governments'objections to the use of the world 'consent' as 'it would give indigenous people a right of veto'.[188] On more than one occasion, governmental delegates made their support for this wording conditional upon the clarification of its meaning since it 'had been identified by some speakers as giving indigenous peoples a right of veto', which States did not seem willing to recognise.[189]

It is thus not clear whether the right to free, prior and informed consent, as incorporated in the Declaration, ultimately confers on indigenous peoples the right to veto the undertaking of extractive activities on their lands. In all likelihood, the reply will be 'no' if one considers the objections raised by governments during the negotiations specifically

2004, following a recommendation of the Permanent Forum on Indigenous Issues at its 3rd session. It was designed to provide a general overview of the current understanding or understandings of the principle of free, prior and informed consent as a methodological issue.

185 Ibid, para 46.

186 Ibid, para 47.

187 Ibid *(emphasis added)*.

188 See Report of the Working Group on the Draft Declaration, UN Doc E/CN.4/1996/84, 4 January 1996, para 81.

189 See Report of the Working Group on the Draft Declaration, UN Doc E/CN.4/1997/102, 10 December 1996, para 227. See also para 273.

concerning the issue, along with more general arguments put forward to defend State control of subsoil resources. It should also be recalled that a similar possibility was denied during the negotiations leading to ILO Convention 169. What the Declaration thus requires is that authentic negotiations between the parties concerned do take place in order to find an agreed solution prior to the implementation of any project. Nevertheless, even in the absence of a right of veto on the part of indigenous peoples, considering the broad context of the Declaration that we have described above, it can be argued that in the case of a project which will have a severe impact on indigenous communities, States' obligation to safeguard cultural diversity[190] and to protect indigenous peoples' cultural and physical integrity will come into play as a constraint to the realisation of the project.

The preamble to the Declaration recognises that 'the diversity and richness of civilization and cultures' constitute 'the common heritage of mankind'. Accordingly, Article 8 of the Declaration proclaims that States shall prevent 'any action which has the aim or the *effect* of depriving [indigenous peoples] of their integrity as distinct peoples, or of their cultural values'.[191] Additionally, Article 20, affirming indigenous peoples' right 'to be secure in the enjoyment of their own means of subsistence and development and to engage freely in all their traditional and other economic activities', should not be overlooked.

In light of the above, it is suggested that the criterion of 'sustainability' of a project vis-a-vis the culture of the indigenous peoples affected—which is commonly resorted to by the UN Human Rights Committee—can also be applied when interpreting the UN Declaration. This claim is strengthened by the fact that such an approach is not confined to the practice of the UN Committee. For example, the Inter-American Court of Human Rights, when dealing with the issue of possible restrictions on the right to property in *Yakye Axa Indigenous Community v Paraguay*, spelled out that

> the States must take into account that indigenous territorial rights encompass a broader and different concept that relates to the collective right to survival as an organized people, with control over their habitat as a necessary condition for reproduction of their culture, for their own development and to carry out their life aspirations.[192]

Accordingly, in *Saramaka People v Suriname*,[193] the Court maintained that the State could restrict indigenous peoples' right to use their lands

[190] On this aspect, see in particular the 2005 UNESCO Convention on the Protection and Promotion of the Diversity of Cultural Expressions and the 2001 Universal Declaration on Cultural Diversity.

[191] Emphasis added.

[192] *Yakye Axa v Paraguay* (n 20) para 146.

[193] See n 17 above.

and resources for the purpose of issuing concessions for the exploration and extraction of natural resources only if it did not 'deny their survival as a tribal people'.[194]

Likewise, in the *Nibutani Dam* case,[195] the Sapporo District Court of Japan, confronted with the Government's project to build a dam in the south-western part of Hokkaido, firstly noted that '[t]he affected interest in the present case is an Ainu person's right to enjoy his people's own culture, which is guaranteed by Article 27 of the International Covenant' since '[t]he Nibutani region is a sacred homeland for the indigenous Ainu people'. Then, it held that the Government's decision to expropriate Ainu land was illegal because '[w]hen considering projects with such negative effects on Ainu cultural rights, the Government ought to give the utmost consideration to these rights'. By contrast, in the case at hand, the Government had 'unreasonably underestimated and disregarded the Ainu's cultural values'.[196]

Finally, it is worth noting that the former UN Special Rapporteur, Erica-Irene Daes, in her study of indigenous peoples' permanent sovereignty over natural resources, found that States' power to confiscate resources for public purposes must be exercised 'in a manner that fully respects and protects all the human rights of indigenous peoples'. According to Daes, this entails that the States cannot exercise this power when 'to do so could destroy the future existence of the indigenous culture and society and possibly deprive them of its means of subsistence'.[197]

SELF-DETERMINED DEVELOPMENT: SOME OVERALL CONSIDERATIONS

This survey would not be complete without at least a mention to another relevant issue, namely the possible repercussions that the recognition of indigenous peoples' right to self-determination may have for States' power to dispose of the natural resources located in indigenous peoples' lands, especially in relation to indigenous peoples' right to determine their own development path. The Declaration recognises the right of indigenous peoples to self-determination.[198] It also specifies that in exercising this right, indigenous peoples have the right to autonomy in matters relating to their internal or local affairs. The 1994 draft once indicated that these matters

[194] Ibid, para 128.

[195] *Nibutani Dam* case, 18 March 1997. The text of this decision is reproduced in T Tsunemoto, 'Rights and Identities of Ethnic Minorities in Japan: Indigenous Ainu and Resident Korean' (2001) 2 *Asia-Pacific Journal on Human Rights and the Law* 127–29.

[196] Ibid.

[197] *Indigenous Peoples' Permanent Sovereignty over Natural Resources* (n 31) para 61.

[198] Errico (n 102).

would encompass economic activities, land and resource management, as well as environmental issues,[199] but such a provision no longer figures in the Declaration. Nonetheless, it is worth noting that the preamble to the Declaration expressly refers to indigenous peoples' 'right to development in accordance with their own needs and interests'. Accordingly, Article 32 states that indigenous peoples have the right 'to determine and develop priorities and strategies for the development or use of their land or territories and other resources'.[200] Similarly, Article 20, as previously mentioned, recognises the right of indigenous peoples 'to be secure in the enjoyment of their own means of subsistence and development'.

It has been highlighted that 'meaningful … economic self-determination of indigenous peoples will never be possible without indigenous peoples' having the legal authority to exercise control over their lands and territories'.[201] In fact, during the negotiations prior to the Declaration, the interrelation between the two elements was repeatedly underscored.[202] In this respect, it is interesting to note that the UN Human Rights Committee has spelled out the relationship between the right to self-determination, as enshrined in Article 1(2) of the Covenant, and the exercise of control by indigenous peoples over their resources and lands. In its Concluding Observations on Canada in 1999,[203] the Committee emphasised that the right to self-determination entails indigenous peoples' free disposal of their natural wealth. Additionally, it observed that unilateral extinguishment of indigenous peoples' rights to land and resources contravenes Article 1(2). Similarly, in connection with Article 1(2) of the Covenant, in 2002, the Committee admonished Australia that it should 'take the necessary steps in order to secure for indigenous inhabitants a stronger role in decision-making over their traditional lands and natural resources'.[204] Likewise, CESCR, recalling the right to self-determination, has urged the Russian Federation to ensure that indigenous peoples are not deprived of their means of subsistence.[205]

In the same vein, the UNDP policy on indigenous peoples embraces the notion of 'self-determined development', that is, 'a concept of

[199] See UN Doc E/CN.4/Sub.2/1994/2/Add.1, Art 31.

[200] A similar concept is mirrored in Art 7 of the ILO Convention and Art XXI of the draft American Declaration on the Rights of Indigenous Peoples.

[201] See *Indigenous Peoples' Permanent Sovereignty over Natural Resources* (n 31) para 8.

[202] See eg Report of the Working Group on the Draft Declaration, UN Doc E/CN.4/1997/102, 10 December 1996, para 246; and Report of the Working Group on the Draft Declaration, UN Doc E/CN.4/2003/92, 6 January 2003, para 19.

[203] See Concluding Observations of the Human Rights Committee on Canada, UN Doc CCPR/C/79/Add.105, 7 April 1999.

[204] See Concluding Observations of the Human Rights Committee on Australia, UN Doc A/55/40, 24 July 2002, paras 506–08.

[205] CESCR, Concluding Observations on the Russian Federation, UN Doc E/C.12/1/Add.94, 12 December 2003, para 39.

development that incorporates indigenous peoples' own aspirations, spirituality, culture, social and economic aims'.[206] Similarly, the Spanish Strategy Paper for Cooperation with Indigenous Peoples refers to indigenous peoples' right 'to create their own model and processes of social economic, political and cultural development'.[207] But, in order for indigenous peoples to be in a position to determine their own development model, a prerequisite seems to be that they must effectively control their lands and resources so as to be able to decide how to utilise them. However, as has rightly been observed, '[t]his opens up the possibility of a conflict between the two forms of self-determination coexisting within the same State. The majority of the population may want to extract valuable natural resources from land owned or traditionally occupied by indigenous peoples, while the latter may invoke their right to self-determination to oppose such development. ... [I]t is perhaps not surprising that no legal guidelines exist on how to deal with this conflict'.[208]

CONCLUSION

The interests and rights of indigenous peoples are often perceived as standing in opposition to the interests of the State and the goals of national development and economic growth of the country. Naturally, tensions are especially apparent when it comes to the issue of control over the natural resources situated in indigenous peoples' lands. Against this background stands Article 26 of the UN Declaration, which recognises indigenous peoples' right to own, use, develop and control natural resources.

The drafting history of the Declaration, together with current international, regional and national practice, suggests that the recognition of indigenous peoples' right to natural resources encounters a major limitation with regard to subsoil resources, as States normally retain ownership of such resources. Nevertheless, this chapter has highlighted that while conceding that States can dispose of subsoil resources located in indigenous lands, the Declaration establishes, in Article 32, a specific framework within which any extractive activity must be carried out. In line with current practice, the Declaration requires that States engage with indigenous peoples and thus provides that indigenous peoples have the right to be consulted effectively in connection with projects relating to exploitation of natural resources to be carried out in their lands. This consultation shall involve indigenous peoples' representative institutions and shall

[206] See n 146 above, para 30.
[207] See n 179 above.
[208] H Quane, 'The Rights of Indigenous Peoples and the Development Process' (2005) 27 *Human Rights Quarterly* 666.

take place through a procedure which must be respectful of indigenous peoples' decision-making mechanisms. Although not expressly indicated in the Declaration, current practice also suggests that indigenous peoples have the right to participate in the benefits deriving from the implementation of the aforementioned projects.

Furthermore, the chapter has underscored that the explicit recognition of indigenous peoples' right to free, prior and informed consent in the Declaration represents a noticeable advance in the field of indigenous peoples' rights. As to the exact meaning to be attached to this expression, given the objections raised by governments during the negotiations specifically concerning the issue and the more general arguments put forward to defend State control of subsoil resources, it does not seem likely that the Declaration provides indigenous peoples with the right to veto extractive activities in their lands. However, it can be argued that in the case of a project which will have a severe impact on indigenous communities, States' obligation to safeguard cultural diversity and to protect indigenous peoples' cultural and physical integrity will come into play as an obstacle to the realisation of the project. In particular, the criterion of 'sustainability' of a project vis-a-vis the culture of the indigenous peoples affected should be applied to the interpretation of the Declaration. Finally, the chapter showed that the recognition of indigenous peoples' right to self-determination might have some repercussions in terms of States' power to dispose of the natural resources located in indigenous peoples' lands, especially in relation to indigenous peoples' right to determine their own development path.

Although it is too early to draw conclusions as to the practical impact of the Declaration, recent practice shows that its provisions can actually exert considerable influence when it comes to the protection of indigenous peoples' rights over natural resources. In considering, under Article 5 of the International Convention for the Elimination of All Forms of Racial Discrimination, activities, including logging and mining, that were carried out in areas of spiritual or cultural significance to Native Americans, CERD expressly recommended that 'the declaration be used as a guide to interpret the State party's obligations under the Convention relating to indigenous peoples'.[209] Moreover, the provisions of the Declaration regarding natural resources have been referred to, for instance, by the Inter-American Court of Human Rights in its decision in *Saramaka v Suriname* and by the Supreme Court of Belize in the case of *Maya v Belize* to guide and uphold the conclusions they reached in favour of indigenous peoples' rights.

[209] CERD, Concluding Observation on the United States of America, UN Doc CERD/C/USA/CO/6, 8 May 2008, para 2.

14

Indigenous Rights and the Right to Development: Emerging Synergies or Collusion?

JOSHUA CASTELLINO

INTRODUCTION

THE HUMAN RIGHTS movement has been successful in bringing a rights-based approach to the fore, and in highlighting the importance of the need to guarantee the rights of all. However, this success is tempered by an inevitable and crucial qualification: indigenous peoples. Despite the best statement of principle, they lie at the bottom of the socio-economic hierarchy in most societies around the world in terms of being able to gain access to the fruits of such rights.[1] For the purpose of this paper the term 'indigenous peoples' will be understood along the lines proposed by José Martinez Cobo. Thus:

> Indigenous communities, peoples and nations are those which, having a historical continuity with pre-invasion and pre-colonial societies that developed on their territories, consider themselves distinct from other sectors of the societies now prevailing in those territories or parts of them. They form at present non-dominant sectors of that society and are determined to preserve, develop and transmit to future generations their ancestral territories, and their ethnic identity, as the basis of their continued existence as peoples, in accordance with their own cultural patterns, social institutions and legal systems.[2]

[1] See Report of the Special Rapporteur on the situation of human rights and fundamental freedoms of indigenous people, UN Doc E/CN.4/2003/90, 21 January 2003, paras 69–70. For a general and recent global analysis of the vulnerabilities of minorities and indigenous peoples see [various authors] *State of the World's Minorities* (London, Minority Rights Group International, 2008) which focused on events between 2006-2008 and their impact on minorities and indigenous peoples.

[2] José Martinez Cobo (former Special Rapporteur to the UN Sub-Commission on Prevention of Discrimination and Protection of Minorities), *Study on the Problem of Discrimination against Indigenous Populations*, UN Doc E/CN.4/Sub.2/1986/Add.4.

This definition is problematic for several reasons that are beyond the scope of this paper.[3] However, it is clear that indigenous peoples, minorities and others in vulnerable positions, such as women and children, have in common their shared experience of discrimination and lack of access to the fruits of human rights law. There remain fundamental differences in the de jure statement of equality and the de facto situations facing indigenous peoples and others. While there are gross differences in terms of the extent to which they can enjoy their civil and political rights, the more fundamental differences lie in the extent to which they enjoy economic, social and cultural rights. However, rather than this being the focus of human rights law, conceptual difficulties over justiciability and ideology have meant that these issues are relegated to a lower level,[4] while civil and political rights regimes are further strengthened.[5] It has been clear from the outset, as stated in the 1948 Universal Declaration of Human Rights, that human rights are indivisible. However, the intervening years have succeeded in dividing these rights, starting with the separation of human rights into two separate Covenants, as against the one envisaged at the start of negotiations to create a global, legally binding standard of human rights. More recently, economic and social rights have begun to develop at global level once again with a further articulation of the substance of the right to food, the right to education and other socio-economic rights.[6]

Irrespective of the healing of the rift between what used to be labelled as 'first generation' and 'second generation' rights, there are still fundamental questions to be answered before collective rights like the right to development can begin to empower those most in need of its prom-

[3] For discussion of the terms 'indigenous peoples' and 'minority' and the implications of the constituent individuals who fall under this label see P Ramaga, 'The Bases of Minority Identity' (1992) 14 *Human Rights Quarterly* 409; T Makkonen, *Identity, Difference and Otherness: The Concepts of 'People', 'Indigenous People' and 'Minority' in International Law* (University of Helsinki, 2000); JR Valentine, 'Toward a Definition of National Minority' (2004) 32 *Denver Journal of International Law and Policy* 445; V Van Dyke, 'Human Rights and the Rights of Groups' (1974) 18 *American Journal of Political Science* 725; EJ Mitnick, 'Three Models of Group-Differentiated Rights' (2004) 35 *Columbia Human Rights Law Review* 215; JE Oestreich, 'Liberal Theory and Minority Group Rights' (1999) 21 *Human Rights Quarterly* 108; P Jones, 'Human Rights, Group Rights and Peoples' Rights' (1999) 21 *Human Rights Quarterly* 80.

[4] See eg the views voiced in the context of the tepid Asian Values Debate, as contained in J Castellino and E Domínguez Redondo, *Minority Rights in Asia: A Comparative Legal Analysis* (Oxford University Press, 2006) 11–25. In the more specific context of indigenous peoples this has also led to questioning of the value of this term in the Asian context. See B Kingsbury, '"Indigenous Peoples" in International Law: A Constructivist Approach to the Asian Controversy' (1998) 92 *American Journal of International Law* 414.

[5] For more on this issue of justiciability see M Sepúlveda Carmona, *The Nature of Obligations under the International Covenant on Economic, Social and Cultural Rights* (Antwerp, Intersentia, 2003).

[6] For an articulation of this vision see M Robinson, 'Advancing Economic, Social and Cultural Rights: The Way Forward' (2004) 26 *Human Rights Quarterly* 868.

ise of providing fair opportunity and access for all.[7] Perhaps the most fundamental of these, from an indigenous perspective, is whether indigenous peoples' right to development can ever be upheld through the articulation of legally binding standards.[8] Positivists argue that such an articulation constitutes the only way in which rights can be realised; but the practical experience of more than 60 years of codified civil and political rights suggest that lack of access to the law itself is an inhibitor of empowerment. It is in this context that this essay seeks to unpack the 'value-added' dimension of the Declaration on the Rights of Indigenous Peoples ('the Declaration') within the context of development.

There is the further difficulty in that even if these standards are embraced by all governments, will the de facto structures that exist within societies allow for a more even distribution of socio-economic resources? Discussions about resources are inevitably controversial: when these resources are contended on historical grounds the tension is palpably increased. Further, in a more individualised, market-driven competitive society, is adequate attention likely to be paid to the needs of those who start this competition in a disadvantaged position? It could be argued that, in keeping with these difficulties, the task of ever more codification at the international level is a distraction from the real challenge: namely the implementation of basic rights for the entirety of the human population, particularly mindful of those who may be vulnerable. In this light, the effort spent in agreeing the Declaration should not be underestimated, especially in terms of the opportunity cost of the lack of such efforts in other pursuits.[9]

Another related question is one concerning international institutions: namely, the segment of international society that is responsible for addressing the socio-economic rights of indigenous peoples. From within the United Nations, it is clear that the United Nations Development Programme (UNDP) has the mandate to address general issues of 'underdevelopment'. This has enabled the UN, in the name of solidarity and international cooperation, both technical and non-technical, to seek to ensure the spread of development from north to south. The UNDP has survived through generous endowments of wealthy States based on the principle of concern for ways in which it can provide communities with

[7] For a recent book that examines the context of development from the perspective of corporate see D Aguirre, *The Human Right to Development in a Globalized World* (Dartmouth, Ashgate, 2008).

[8] This discussion has been taking place to some extent in the context of the Convention on Biological Diversity adopted in Rio de Janeiro, Brazil on 5 June 1992, and Art 8(j) in particular. In this context, the *Akwé: Kon Voluntary Guidelines* should be considered particularly relevant. See www.cbd.int/doc/publications/akwe-brochure-en.pdf.

[9] For more on this discussion see C Tennant, 'Indigenous Peoples, International Institutions and the International Legal Literature from 1945–1993' (1994) 16 *Human Rights Quarterly* 1.

the basic necessities of 'normal' life. While it has done sterling work in many situations, it has clearly not succeeded in eradicating poverty, as its own annual Human Development Index reports conclusively demonstrate. In addition, the Millennium Promise articulated in the Millennium Development Goals (MDGs) specifically seeks to build a system by which human achievement can be measured against targeted outcomes.[10] This is a welcome approach in the context of development: it could reveal the extent to which goals are being met. From an indigenous peoples' perspective, however, it is worrying since sheer nationwide macro-measurements are not necessarily going to reflect the state of indigenous rights.

This essay begins by briefly sketching the contours of the right to development in human rights law, examining its applicability to indigenous peoples. It is clear that there is an 'implementation gap' between the soft laws that exist on development, and the plight of indigenous peoples. The second section examines the context of the Declaration and poses the simple question as to the extent to which the Declaration could potentially address this gap. The conclusion posits the question as to whether the Declaration will lend greater synergy to the task of realising the right of development for indigenous peoples.

INDIGENOUS PEOPLES, HUMAN RIGHTS LAW AND THE RIGHT TO DEVELOPMENT

It could be argued that the failure to agree a binding universal standard protecting indigenous peoples at an international level is a significant lacuna that haunts the international regime of human rights.[11] The modern regime of human rights law was built as part of the international community's response to the events of World War II where Jews and other minorities were subject to the ultimate crime: genocide, based on their membership of a group. Yet, the issue of minority rights, while at the centre of the human rights agenda, has never had a universal legally binding standard.[12] With indigenous peoples, the neglect runs significantly deeper,

[10] For an interesting analysis of these goals see J Vandemoortele, 'Are the MDGs Feasible?' (2003) *UNDP Development Policy Journal* 1. For a human rights perspective, see E Domínguez Redondo and C Doyle (eds), 'Special Issue: The Millennium Development Goals, Minorities and Indigenous Peoples' (2009) 13 *International Journal of Human Rights* 29.

[11] See J Castellino, 'The Protection of Minority and Indigenous Peoples' Rights: A Comparative Temporal Analysis' (2010) 17(3) *International Journal of Minority and Group Rights* 393.

[12] The exception to this was the complex system that existed under the League of Nations system. For more see J Stone, 'Procedure under the Minorities Treaties' (1932) 26 *American Journal of International Law* 502; and J Kunz, 'The Present Status of the International Law for the Protection of Minorities' (1954) 48 *American Journal of International Law* 282. It is worth

and, as Barsh has highlighted, the movement from accepting indigenous peoples as subjects rather than objects of law was probably one of the first real steps towards accepting this shared identity as a ground on which discrimination occurred.[13] The traditional position advanced by human rights law has been to argue that minorities could be better protected by ensuring that their human rights were protected through the general human rights measures.[14] Thus neither the Declaration on the Rights of Ethnic, Linguistic and National Minorities[15] nor the Declaration on the Rights of Indigenous Peoples[16] create binding legal obligations on the international community.[17]

Each of the existing core human rights treaties, on the other hand, impose implementation and reporting obligations on States, monitored through the submission of regular periodic reports that are scrutinised by special bodies set up by the treaties themselves.[18] These reports contain materials submitted by State governments indicating their performance against each of the obligations contained in the treaties.[19] However, since the data presented is not often disaggregated by group identity,

emphasising that the protection envisaged did not extend to indigenous peoples. For an interesting account of the attempt by indigenous peoples to get a hearing at the League of Nations see L Malezer, 'Permanent Forum on Indigenous Issues: Welcome to the Family of the UN' in J Castellino and N Walsh (eds), *International Law and Indigenous Peoples* (Leiden, Brill, 2005) 67.

[13] See RL Barsh, 'Indigenous Peoples and the UN Commission on Human Rights: A Case of Immovable Object and the Irresistible Force' (1996) 18 *Human Rights Quarterly* 782; and 'Indigenous Peoples in the 1990s: From Object to Subject in International Law?' (1994) 7 *Harvard Human Rights Journal* 33.

[14] This is reflected in the failure to codify specific standards for minority rights protection in the creation of the United Nations, despite its founding driver being the experience of minorities during World War II. It could be argued that those in favour of the new regime were aware of the failure of the previous specific legal mechanism for the protection of minorities under the League of Nations, and were keen to avoid this route.

[15] Adopted by GA Res 47/135, 18 December 1992.

[16] Adopted by GA Res A/RES/61/295, 13 September 2007.

[17] This view is at odds with that expressed by Anaya, who argues that the Declaration is part of customary international law. The view of this author is more circumspect on the basis that the Declaration reflects compromise language on several articles, and it remains to be seen whether it would merit consistent State practice and opinio juris globally to cross the threshold into customary international law. For more on the Anaya argument see 'The Human Rights of Indigenous Peoples, in Light of the New Declaration, and the Challenge of Making Them Operative: Report of the Special Rapporteur on the situation of human rights and fundamental freedoms of indigenous people', papers.ssrn.com/sol3/papers.cfm?abstract_id=1242451. This commentary takes on additional gravitas in view of the author's role as Special Rapporteur on the situation of human rights and fundamental freedoms of indigenous people.

[18] For general reading on this system see P Alston and J Crawford (eds), *The Future of UN Human Rights Treaty Monitoring* (Cambridge University Press, 2000). See also O Hathaway, 'Do Human Rights Treaties Make a Difference?' (2002) 111 *Yale Law Journal* 1870.

[19] State reports to the various mechanisms are available on the website of the Office of the High Commissioner for Human Rights at www.ohchr.org/EN/HRBodies/Pages/HumanRightsBodies.aspx.

it can prove difficult to understand the extent to which the fruits of protection are becoming accessible to all within the State. In addition, the failure to codify a specific right to development means that the right has to be mainly extrapolated from the mandate under the Committee on Economic, Social and Cultural Rights.[20]

The 'right' to development itself has not been codified. Instead it remains in a soft law instrument similar to the Declaration on the Rights of Indigenous Peoples.[21] The Declaration on the Right to Development stresses that development

> is a comprehensive economic, social, cultural and political process, which aims at the constant improvement of the well-being of the entire population and of all individuals on the basis of their active, free and meaningful participation in development and in the fair distribution of benefits resulting therefrom …[22]

It further emphasises that:

> 1. The right to development is an inalienable human right by virtue of which every human person and all peoples are entitled to participate in, contribute to, and enjoy economic, social, cultural and political development, in which all human rights and fundamental freedoms can be fully realized.
> 2. The human right to development also implies the full realization of the right of peoples to self-determination, which includes, subject to the relevant provisions of both International Covenants on Human Rights, the exercise of their inalienable right to full sovereignty over all their natural wealth and resources.[23]

Based on this articulation, the right to development arguably consists of five specific pillars:

a. full sovereignty over natural resources;[24]
b. the right to self-determination;[25]
c. full participation in processes aligned with development;[26]

[20] It could be argued that support for the normative framework of the right to development as applicable to indigenous peoples could also be extrapolated from joint Art 1 (on self-determination) of the International Covenant on Civil and Political Rights and the International Covenant on Economic, Social and Cultural Rights (1966); General Comment 23 of the Committee for the Elimination of Racial Discrimination, and the Convention for Biological Diversity (1992). However, it would nonetheless be fair to argue that the primary framework for the right to development is located with the codification of socio-economic rights.

[21] For more on the right to development, its history and associated concepts see S Marks, 'The Human Right to Development: Between Rhetoric and Reality' (2004) 17 *Harvard Human Rights Journal* 137.

[22] Preamble, Declaration on the Right to Development, GA Res 41/128, Annex, 41 UN GAOR Supp (No 53) at 186, UN Doc A/41/53 (1986).

[23] Declaration on the Right to Development, Art 1.

[24] Ibid, Art 1(2).

[25] Ibid.

[26] Ibid, Art 2.

d. equality of opportunity;[27] and
e. the creation of conditions conducive to the achievement of human rights.[28]

In addition, one of the other key components that is clearly articulated in the Declaration is the principal responsibility for engaging in activities that will further development. In the words of the Declaration: 'States have the primary responsibility for the creation of national and international conditions favourable to the realization of the right to development.'[29]

The importance of the State's role is further elaborated in the Declaration in its seeking cooperation from other States to achieve development,[30] its obligation to act individually and collectively,[31] to take all necessary measures for implementation at national level,[32] to consider the right to development as indivisible,[33] and to take urgent action in the face of flagrant violations of rights.[34] Though a soft law, and now dated instrument, it could be argued that this Declaration built on previous attempts in this regard[35] to enshrine the importance of development at the heart of the focused attention of the international community. Along with the famous report *Our Common Future*, published in 1987 under the auspices of the United Nations World Commission on the Environment and Development via the stewardship of former Norwegian Prime Minister Gro Harlem Brundtland,[36] the issue of development finally took a more prominent position in world politics. Today,

> The right to development is the closest legal manifestation of the rights of marginalized people to participate in development. It is a representation in law, universally recognized by the international community of the political demands for a rights based equitable development programme ... Its political and moral importance is no longer in question.[37]

[27] Ibid, Art 1(1), and implied in Art 2(2) and (3).

[28] As contained in ibid, Art 1(1). Paraphrased from the explanation under 'Right to Development' on the website of the Office of the High Commissioner for Human Rights, http://www.ohchr.org/EN/Issues/Development/Pages/DevelopmentIndex.aspx.

[29] Declaration on the Right to Development, Art 3(1).

[30] Ibid, Art 3(3).

[31] Ibid, Art 4(1).

[32] Ibid, Arts 8(1) and 10.

[33] Ibid, Art 9.

[34] Ibid, Art 5.

[35] See eg Declaration on Social Progress and Development, GA Res 2542 (XXIV), 24 UN GAOR Supp (No 30) 49, UN Doc A/7630 (1969) and Declaration on the Use of Scientific and Technological Progress in the Interests of Peace and for the Benefit of Mankind, GA Res 3384 (XXX), 30 UN GAOR Supp (No 34) 86, UN Doc A/10034 (1975).

[36] See *Our Common Future: The World Commission on Environment and Development* (Oxford University Press, 1987), adopted by GA Res 42/187, 11 December 1987.

[37] D Aguirre and I Pietropaoli, 'Gender Equality, Development and Transitional Justice: The Case of Nepal' [2008] *International Journal of Transitional Justice* 1.

The MDGs offer a different approach to more traditional human rights law, mainly since they consist of a series of distinct targets with measurable indicators of progress.[38] Thus the eight elaborated goals[39] are broken down into a further 18 targets[40] which are viewed through the lens of 48 recommended indicators of progress[41] towards the targets and goals. Five of these specific indicators require the disaggregation of data by sex (especially in the context of Goal 3). However, there is no requirement for disaggregated data on the grounds of ethnicity or other identifiers, and as a result the occurrence of some of the phenomena among indigenous peoples and other vulnerable groups remains difficult to track.[42] As stated by MacDougall:

> Without this kind of data, the impact of MDG strategies on different groups cannot be measured accurately. A marginalized ethnic or religious minority group [or indigenous people] may be experiencing increased levels of poverty as resources are diverted to meet the needs of the 'less poor'; in the absence of disaggregated data, this negative impact may go unnoticed.[43]

According to MacDougall, the four key issues from a minority rights perspective that are important could consist of i) the right to exist; ii) the right to non-discrimination; iii) the right to cultural identity; and iv) the right to participate in public life.[44] According to her, each of these four rights is in principle catered for the in the MDGs, though in each instance there is a

[38] For more on the MDGs see the official website at www.un.org/millenniumgoals.

[39] These are: (i) End Poverty and Hunger; (ii) Universal Education; (iii) Gender Equality; (iv) Child Health; (v) Maternal Health; (vi) Combat HIV/AIDS; (vii) Environmental Sustainability; and (viii) Global Partnerships.

[40] For instance, the three targets for eradicating poverty and hunger consist of: Target 1: Halving the proportion of people whose income is less than $1 a day (1990 and 2015); Target 2: Achieving full and productive employment and decent work for all, including women and young people; and Target 3: Halving the proportion of people who suffer from hunger (1990 and 2015).

[41] For instance, the five indicators attached to the eradication of poverty and hunger are: 1. Proportion of population below $1 (1993 PPP) per day (World Bank); 2. Poverty gap ratio [incidence × depth of poverty] (World Bank); 3. Share of poorest quintile in national consumption (World Bank); 4. Prevalence of underweight children under five years of age (UNICEF-WHO); and 5. Proportion of population below minimum level of dietary energy consumption (FAO).

[42] An earlier report of the then Special Rapporteur on the situation of human rights and fundamental freedoms of indigenous people, Rodolfo Stavenhagen, highlighted the importance of engaging with various actors in terms of the debate on development and its impact on indigenous peoples. See Report of the Special Rapporteur on the situation of human rights and fundamental freedoms of indigenous people, UN Doc E/CN.4/2003/90, 21 January 2003.

[43] See G McDougall, *Achieving the Millennium Development Goals (MDGs) for Minorities: A Review of MDG Country Reports*, Report of the independent expert on minority issues, submitted to the Human Rights Council, UN Doc A/HRC/4/9/Add.1, 2 March 2007, para 36 with the author´s insertion in parenthesis.

[44] Ibid.

need to link them better, as will be raised in the conclusion to this paper.[45] These four rights can clearly be extrapolated to the situation of indigenous peoples, with the additional factor of the necessary link between indigenous communities and their territory identified as an additional issue.[46]

The fundamental question of concern to those interested in the rights of indigenous peoples remains simple: Does the concept of 'development', whether articulated in the human rights instruments or the MDGs, offer an adequate vehicle for the furtherance of the rights of indigenous peoples? Overall several MDG reports acknowledge that indigenous peoples and minorities face higher rates of poverty than other segments of the population. There are several reasons for this, usually tracing back to the historical exclusion of indigenous peoples from the development of the State. Most States around the world have been dominated by a majority who have, at various points in time, sought to subjugate the Other with a view to harnessing and buffeting their own status within the State. The particular land dimension germane to indigenous communities and identities has been a further spur to excluding them from the emerging States growing on their territories.

Reversing this trend is a significant challenge. At the outset it requires strong political will on the part of governments, which, in many instances, continue to adopt policies that seek to ensure their dominance. However, even in cases where there is strong political will seeking to address inequalities in society along the traditional identity fault-lines, there are deep structural problems to overcome.[47] These include physical problems, such as the lack of infrastructure and investment in regions dominated by indigenous peoples,[48] and, worse, zealous exploitation of resources from indigenous territories without the prior informed consent of the communities and, as a result, not to their benefit.[49] Unequal and unjust land rights regimes remain a fundamental source of difficulty and have resulted in many indigenous peoples living as second class citizens in their own homelands, with a severe paucity of access to

[45] UN Doc A/HRC/4/9/Add.1 Table, 13.

[46] Of course, it could be argued that right to exist includes the issue of land and territorial rights for indigenous peoples; however, owing to its fundamental important to indigenous peoples, an explicit reference to this issue is more appropriate.

[47] This is best demonstrated in the context of New Zealand, where positive processes that are providing rights to the Maori are still struggling to overcome the differential in privilege between the Maori and the Parekha (settlers). For more see J Castellino and D Keane, *Minority Rights in the Pacific: A Comparative Legal Analysis* (Oxford University Press, 2009) 98.

[48] Such as in the Northern Territory of Australia, ibid, ch 2.

[49] See eg the Early Warning Measures and Urgent Procedures mechanism of CERD, www2.ohchr.org/english/bodies/cerd/early-warning.htm.

social services, health, education, housing and other key socio-economic indicators.

In addition, the persistent exclusion of indigenous peoples from decision-making processes means that these groups are disadvantaged in terms of the manner in which they can access ostensibly evolved systems:[50] inevitably, the few who manage to access the regime of global rights do so with a high degree of trepidation and suspicion. This is less a reflection of the growing skills and expertise of indigenous advocates, and rather a statement of the extent to which such skills result directly from being able to engage at an international rather than national level. For many indigenous peoples, engaging at this level remains far from their daily contexts, and as a result they fail to benefit from the considerable skills that their more internationalised compatriots possess. In addition, in most instances, irrespective of governmental policy, indigenous peoples face levels of discrimination that continue to impact negatively on their situation. This discrimination is clearly an 'overarching factor' that can

> decrease access to health, education, financial credit, housing and employment—each compounding the likelihood of living in poverty. Due to a lack of disaggregated data, the inequalities experienced by minorities usually are invisible in public policy discourses, where minorities also often lack a strong political voice.[51]

According to the overview presented by MacDougall, positive action taken in reporting on the MDGs includes:

- publishing disaggregated data on poverty;
- undertaking baseline studies on the experiences of poverty by minorities (and indigenous peoples);
- adopting national strategies to reduce poverty for the poorest minorities (and indigenous peoples); and
- using affirmative action policies to increase public employment opportunities for minorities (and indigenous peoples).[52]

However, irrespective of the manner in which the discourse on development has grown, the following can be offered as a concrete list of concerns as to its direct relevance to indigenous peoples:

1. Development, as defined by a given indigenous community, remains fundamental to the protection and promotion of their rights. It is the one concept that brings together a series of aspirations and rights

[50] For a particularly stark example of this in the context of Australia under the previous Howard regime see Castellino and Keane (n 47) 48, which discusses the disbanding of the elected body of Aboriginal and Torres Strait Islander Commissioners.
[51] MacDougall Report (n 42) para 44.
[52] Ibid. See Box 5 'Good Practice on Poverty Reduction'.

that communities have, and which, to a certain extent, have been historically denied to them, especially in the colonial context and its aftermath, which resulted in independence for various states, though not for indigenous peoples.[53]

2. The identification of the State as the key implementer of the right has placed the burden of responsibility upon States; however, the lack of binding obligations has made this obligation difficult to enforce.
3. As a consequence, the fundamental problem with the right to development, has been its poor implementation, leaving a significant gap between political rhetoric and implementation on the ground.

The last is perhaps the most crucial aspect that hinders the efficacy of this potentially important tool for the empowerment of indigenous peoples. In this context of implementation ILO Convention 169,[54] which creates binding obligations, has been considerably more useful. It is particularly well formulated in this context, and provides a flavour of what would be needed in a binding document before it could be called upon by communities. Article 7, focused on development, states:

> 1. The peoples concerned shall have the right to decide their own priorities for the process of development as it affects their lives, beliefs, institutions and spiritual well-being and the lands they occupy or otherwise use, and to exercise control, to the extent possible, over their own economic, social and cultural development. In addition, they shall participate in the formulation, implementation and evaluation of plans and programmes for national and regional development which may affect them directly.
> 2. The improvement of the conditions of life and work and levels of health and education of the peoples concerned, with their participation and co-operation, shall be a matter of priority in plans for the overall economic development of areas they inhabit. Special projects for development of the areas in question shall also be so designed as to promote such improvement.
> 3. Governments shall ensure that, whenever appropriate, studies are carried out, in co-operation with the peoples concerned, to assess the social, spiritual, cultural and environmental impact on them of planned development activities. The results of these studies shall be considered as fundamental criteria for the implementation of these activities.
> 4. Governments shall take measures, in co-operation with the peoples concerned, to protect and preserve the environment of the territories they inhabit.[55]

[53] For further discussion of 'sustainable development' from an indigenous perspective see S Kinane, 'Indigenous Sustainability: Rights, Obligations and a Collective Commitment to Country' in Castellino and Walsh (n 12) 159.

[54] Convention (No 169) titled as 'Concerning Indigenous and Tribal Peoples in Independent Countries' was adopted on 27 June 1989 by the General Conference of the International Labour Organization at its 76th session, entered into force 5 September 1991.

[55] See ILO Convention 169, Art 7.

One of the key drawbacks to this Convention remains the low rate of ratification.[56] It is clear, however, that adoption of such a standard at the international level would make a material difference to the extent to which the right to development and its impact on indigenous peoples could feature more prominently in national governmental plans. Any new formulation on development ought to build on Article 7 if it is to add value to indigenous communities' thrust for implementation of this right. It is now germane to address whether the Declaration on the Rights of Indigenous Peoples bridges this fundamental gap.

THE DECLARATION ON THE RIGHTS OF INDIGENOUS PEOPLES AND THE RIGHT TO DEVELOPMENT

The passage of the Declaration through the United Nations system was problematic, and it came as a surprise to many when the General Assembly finally passed the Declaration on 13 September 2007. While the discussions leading up to the final text were tedious and met with with several setbacks, it is clear that the issue of 'development' was at the forefront of the discussion at all times. The preamble to the Declaration recognises not only its importance, but also its context:

> *Concerned* that indigenous peoples have suffered from historic injustices as a result of, inter alia, their colonization and dispossession of their lands, territories and resources, thus preventing them from exercising, in particular, their right to development in accordance with their own needs and interests ...[57]

This is followed by some indication of what the right to development could be seen as entailing:

> *Recognizing* the urgent need to respect and promote the inherent rights of indigenous peoples which derive from their political, economic and social structures and from their cultures, spiritual traditions, histories and philosophies, especially their rights to their lands, territories and resources ...[58]

However, the Declaration recognises the emerging synergy between the right to development and its relevance to indigenous peoples, which is expressed in another section of the preamble, thus:

> *Recognizing* and reaffirming that indigenous individuals are entitled without discrimination to all human rights recognized in international law, and that

[56] Only 20 states have so far ratified this convention: Argentina, Bolivia, Brazil, Chile, Colombia, Costa Rica, Denmark, Dominica, Ecuador, Fiji, Guatemala, Honduras, Mexico, Nepal, the Netherlands, Norway, Paraguay, Peru, Spain, and Venezuela.

[57] Preamble, United Nations Declaration on the Rights of Indigenous Peoples, adopted by GA Res 61/296, 13 September 2007.

[58] Ibid.

> indigenous peoples possess collective rights which are indispensable for their existence, well-being and integral development as peoples ...[59]

In studying the Declaration it could be argued that the term 'development' is used in at least four specific contexts:

(a) In the context of the promotion of indigenous identity: as given in Article 7 (distinct identity); Article 8 (removals); Article 10 (relocations); Article 11 (culture); Article 12 (religion); Article 13 (historical treatment); Article 14 (educational systems); Article 15 (media); Article 16 (cultural heritage and traditional knowledge); and Article 36 (cross-border identities).
(b) In the context of support for indigenous institutions: Article 5 (right to distinctive institutions); Article 20 (appropriate political, economic and social institutions); Article 27 (creation of appropriate institutional remedies); and Article 34 (appropriate institutional structures).
(c) In the context of the environment: Article 24 (health); Article 25 (land rights); and Article 29 (rights regarding conservation).
(d) In the context of self-determination: Article 3 (right to self-determination); Article 4 (right to autonomy); Article 18 and 19 (free, prior and informed consent); Article 21 (socio-economic rights); Article 23 (determination of priorities); Article 26 (land and resource rights); Article 28 (right to effective remedies); and Article 32 (determination of priorities and strategies for development).

For the purposes of this essay, the 'right to development' will be examined in the context of the general provision on self-determination, defined as the process through which:

(i) 'a people may ... freely determine their political status and freely pursue their economic, social and cultural development', and
(ii) 'may, for their own ends, freely dispose of their natural wealth and resources without prejudice to any obligations arising out of international economic co-operation, based upon the principle of mutual benefit, and international law. In no case may a people be deprived of its own means of subsistence'.[60]

The provisions most directly concerned with the right to development as understood in classic terms are Articles 20 and 21. Thus:

> 1. Indigenous peoples have the right to maintain and develop their political, economic and social systems or institutions, to be secure in the enjoyment

[59] Ibid.

[60] See joint Art 1, International Covenant on Civil and Political Rights and International Covenant on Economic, Social and Cultural Rights.

of their own means of subsistence and development, and to engage freely in all their traditional and other economic activities.

2. Indigenous peoples deprived of their means of subsistence and development are entitled to just and fair redress.[61]

And:

1. Indigenous peoples have the right, without discrimination, to the improvement of their economic and social conditions, including, inter alia, in the areas of education, employment, vocational training and retraining, housing, sanitation, health and social security.
2. States shall take effective measures and, where appropriate, special measures to ensure continuing improvement of their economic and social conditions. Particular attention shall be paid to the rights and special needs of indigenous elders, women, youth, children and persons with disabilities.[62]

In addition, Article 23 is of particular importance:

> Indigenous peoples have the right to determine and develop priorities and strategies for exercising their right to development. In particular, indigenous peoples have the right to be actively involved in developing and determining health, housing and other economic and social programmes affecting them and, as far as possible, to administer such programmes through their own institutions.

Thus the 'right to development' as iterated in this Declaration could be identified as consisting of the following basic contours:

(a) the determination by the group of its socio-economic, cultural, civil and political future;
(b) the determination by the group of its priorities and strategies for the future to be able to actualise its determination under point (a) above;
(c) the determination by the group of the necessary institutions and regimes to be able to guarantee that its vision can be translated into reality.

This 'development' can then be conceptualised as occurring in the specific context of (a) land rights;[63] (b) the environment,[64] and (c) the signing of agreements through which non-indigenous can establish relationships with indigenous peoples concerning issues related to socio-economic rights.[65]

It needs to be emphasised that this articulation of the right to development is a clearer enunciation of the extent to which the right has salience

[61] United Nations Declaration on the Rights of Indigenous Peoples, Art 20.
[62] Ibid, Art 21.
[63] Ibid, Arts 25 and 26.
[64] Ibid, Arts 24, 25 and 29.
[65] Especially in the context of free, prior and informed consent: ibid, Arts 18 and 19.

to indigenous peoples than can be found in other international instruments. By focusing on specific contexts, actors and relationships, and particular actions, the Declaration makes a more coherent case for the right to development than has previously been articulated in any document of this nature at a universal level. Thus while earlier drafts of the Declaration may have been more forthright in terms of their insistence on aspects of land rights and self-determination, in the specific context of the right to development the final document appears to have been relatively less affected by the discussion processes around the text. More than anything else, this probably reflects a shared consensus at the international level regarding the importance of the right to development and its specific application to indigenous peoples. This contrasts with the more qualified views that are visible in several States' approaches to the question of self-determination.

Nonetheless, as established in the first section of this paper, one of the significant gaps in the discourse remains the implementation of the right. The Declaration clearly makes several important points about implementation but, without the driver of creating binding legal obligations upon States,[66] the rights remain mere aspirations. One possible route towards securing implementation is the extent to which a legal document articulates remedies that would be available in the context of a failure to implement. The most relevant of these are articulated as the right to establish means of redress including restitution and compensation, physical or monetary;[67] the obligation to take all appropriate measures, including legislative measures, in conjunction and consultation with indigenous peoples;[68] and the establishment of processes designed to guarantee prompt decisions through fair procedures that are particularly reflective of indigenous customary law.[69]

The two obvious doubts that remain with these remedies are arguably applicable to every right articulated in the Declaration. Namely, are these remedies enough? Are they likely to result in improved implementation? Finally, what is the 'value-added' element that the Declaration brings to the discussion of indigenous rights in the specific context of development? These questions are addressed in the concluding section of this paper.

[66] As commented on below, it remains premature to address the Declaration's status in customary international law without a lack of consistent state practice and opinio juris across the world. While it is clear that national systems are becoming more cognisant of indigenous rights, the practice remains inconsistent. In addition, it is the view of this author that customary international law is formed from below to above, ie from State practice to international law, and not the other way around.

[67] UN Declaration on the Rights of Indigenous Peoples, Art 28.

[68] Ibid, Art 38.

[69] Ibid, Art 40.

CONCLUSION: EMERGING SYNERGIES OR COLLISION?

It is clear that, by virtue of various measures, indigenous peoples remain, with other vulnerable communities, at the bottom of national socio-economic and political hierarchies. In this context the articulation of a right to development could potentially have been a key conceptual milestone in the improvement of the rights of these communities. By linking the socio-economic with the political, the discourse of development seemed the ideal vehicle by which to promote the rights of communities that have been marginalised throughout recent history. For a long time though, 'development' meant different things to different audiences: articulated by southern States, it was a call for fairer and more equitable socio-economic engagements in global society to benefit the State as a whole, not necessarily its component communities, and rarely its indigenous communities. Viewed from the perspective of multinational corporations, this enabled access to resource-rich parts of the globe at low thresholds or even deferential conditions, due to the potential of job creation and foreign direct investment. Viewed from the perspective of indigenous communities however, it held the promise of self-realisation and self-determination while delivering the reality of a new form of vulnerability as policies and entities converged upon the resources incumbent in their ancestral homelands.

The commentary framed above in the context of the value of the Declaration on the Rights of Indigenous Peoples is equally applicable to the soft-law standard of the Declaration on Development. It was an important milestone in signalling international intent, but needed several other events to occur before it had an impact on the global psyche. The invisibility of the economic, social and political status of indigenous peoples in evidence in many MDG reports suggests that new ideas do not always evolve to benefit indigenous peoples effectively.[70] This invisibility means that data specifically disaggregated on indigenous peoples or minorities remains difficult to unearth, and this acts as a further barrier to a thorough understanding of the actual socio-economic situation in countries with regard to its more vulnerable groups. Thus it is difficult

[70] The Independent Expert on Minorities, Gay McDougall, reviewed a sample of 50 state reports and selected Poverty Reduction Strategy Papers submitted to the World Bank and found that only 19 of these reports made any mention of ethnic or linguistic minorities. The range of countries reviewed was broad: Afghanistan, Bangladesh, Belize, Bhutan, Bolivia, Botswana, Brazil, Bulgaria, China, Denmark, Dominican Republic, Ecuador, Ethiopia, Finland, Honduras, Hungary, Indonesia, Iran, Kazakhstan, Kenya, Kosovo, Lao, Lebanon, Malaysia, Mexico, Namibia, Nepal, Netherlands, Nicaragua, Nigeria, Norway, Occupied Territories of Palestine, Pakistan, Peru, Philippines, Romania, Rwanda, Senegal, South Africa, Sudan, Sweden, Switzerland, Tanzania, Thailand, Turkey, Uganda, United Kingdom, Uruguay, Venezuela, and Vietnam.

to track the extent to which overall progress towards the goals is being reflected along the traditional fault-lines in society.

There are several key questions in terms of determining the extent to which the Declaration could make a potential contribution vis-a-vis indigenous rights to development, namely: What is the opportunity cost of this Declaration and what is the value of internationalising the plight of indigenous peoples in the context of the right to development? Secondly, what is likely to be the impact of the Declaration on the right to development at the domestic level? Thirdly, who are the custodians of the Declaration and to what extent can they be instrumental in creating momentum towards its implementation and/or articulation as a set of legally binding obligations upon States?

The first question essentially stems from the varied discussions about the role of standard setting. Clearly the Declaration is a first universal attempt to formulate an internationally accepted benchmark of indigenous rights. That has immense value in and of itself and needs to be emphasised. Further, the issue of development is inevitably transnational in nature, and thus confining it to the national theatre is unlikely to result in the articulation of an appropriate standard in an increasingly globalised world. Yet the cost of arriving at the Declaration has been significant, involving outlays of resources over a considerable period of time, mainly on the part of indigenous communities who have struggled to follow its trajectory due to limited resources and the long-drawn-out process. Against this, while the process has been frustrating, and the rewards relatively slim, it has served to shore up the identity of indigenous peoples within the UN system, and made them a significant lobby. It has also arguably played a role in creating the momentum for the establishment of the Permanent Forum on Indigenous Issues (PFII)[71] and in safeguarding the other international offices focused on indigenous peoples, such as the UN Special Rapporteur and the Working Group. However, from the perspective of indigenous peoples, the value of internationalising issues probably lies in:

(a) being able to contribute to an overarching system of law that could compel States to recognise their rights via international law;
(b) creating a mechanism for complaint at the international level that could address cases on an issue-by-issue basis; and
(c) being recognised as a collective community and gaining access to international decision-making processes.

[71] For more on the PFII and its discussions relating to development see P Tamang, 'An Overview of the Principle of Free, Prior and Informed Consent and Indigenous Peoples in International and Domestic Law and Practices', Doc PFII/2004/WS 2/8, United Nations Permanent Forum on Indigenous Issues, Workshop on Free, Prior and Informed Consent, New York, 17–19 January 2005.

The most significant success in terms of the Declaration would lie in point (c), with relative failures for (a) and (b). In the specific context of the right to development, a more significant impact is the extent to which indigenous peoples were able to emphasize the importance of their right of development, to an audience consisting transnational corporations, inter-governmental agencies, donors and other stakeholders.

It could be argued that the opportunity cost of this engagement was the removal of sustained pressure at the domestic level as the limited resources available to the communities came under pressure from following the circuitous route through which the Declaration came into existence. Advocates could argue that for many communities the 'national' stage was never likely to yield any results due to the intransigent attitudes of particular governments. While this may be true of some States, it is unlikely to be true for the vast majority. It does seem that the international community is preoccupied with the creation of standards and that arguably a greater impact could be achieved through a more concerted focus on implementation. The analogy that could be called upon is a community that meets regularly to create an ever more specific set of rules to contain a problem rather than tackling it directly. Of course, with the Declaration having arrived on the international landscape the issue of cost can be conveniently forgotten, and some would suggest that pointing to the cost is to be unnecessarily negative about the process. There remains no way of analysing whether the cost incurred in passing this Declaration is greater than other efforts that may have been made in its lieu that directly tackle the issue of development.

This leads to the second question as to the impact of the Declaration at the national level. From a study of the extent to which the domestic legal systems of many States in the world accommodate indigenous and minority rights,[72] it would be difficult to see any immediate positive impact from the passage of this Declaration in domestic law. The general trend in terms of the manner in which national policies are framed suggests that they become concerned about international standards only when they have reached the threshold of becoming legally binding, and even then the concern can be inconsistent. The other routes toward creating an impact then tend to be through the media and concerted campaigning; or through courts of law where a particularly creative barrister is met by a sympathetic judge. In both cases the opportunities for these vehicles being appropriated for use by indigenous peoples and their advocates

[72] This study is currently being conducted by the author and others and is ongoing. The results of the first two regional studies are contained in *Minority Rights in Asia: A Comparative Legal Analysis* (n 4), and *Indigenous Peoples and Minorities in the Pacific: A Comparative Legal Analysis* (n 47). Subsequent volumes will study the Middle East, Africa and Latin America.

remain limited. As a result, despite the excitement about the Declaration within the international community, the impact, especially in terms of the right to development, could be limited for a long while to come.[73]

The final question that is raised is the issue of the custodians of this Declaration. Like every human rights declaration or treaty adopted under the auspices of the United Nations, the custodians are considered as being 'the people'. It is through their actions that declarations and treaties come alive, and through their efforts that they remain central to national debates. For the right to development to be actualised a few key actors would be required to engage in a serious way with its provisions. The relevant agencies upon whom this burden of custodianship would fall would include the specific offices created under the United Nations to address indigenous peoples' rights: including the UN Special Rapporteur, the Working Group on Indigenous Peoples and the PFII. In addition, it would need support from other offices and procedures that overlap with indigenous peoples, such as the UN Special Rapporteur on development and the Special Representative of the Secretary General on Human Rights and Transnational Corporations and Other Business Enterprises.[74] It would also need the fundamental support of UNDP, UNICEF and those working on MDGs who have a significant national presence. Finally, it would need support from key stakeholders outside the United Nations, such as the International Labour Organization, the Bretton Woods institutions, and other global and regional development banks. It is clear that it is only through such concerted support that the Declaration could make a positive and real contribution to the right to development of indigenous peoples. Without that support it is likely to be a rhetorical quest that promises aspirations without a delivery mechanism for their realisation.

In that sense, the conclusion offered by the current Special Rapporteur, S James Anaya, in his report on the Declaration can be endorsed:

> The United Nations Declaration on the Rights of Indigenous Peoples represents an authoritative common understanding, at the global level, of the minimum content of the rights of indigenous peoples, upon a foundation of various sources of international human rights law … the Declaration does not attempt to bestow indigenous peoples with a set of special or new human rights, but rather provides a contextualized elaboration of general human rights principles and rights as they relate to the specific historical, cultural and social circumstances of indigenous peoples.[75]

[73] For instance, in the recently completed study cited above at n 47, the authors felt that there was no impact from the passage of the Declaration in domestic law, and therefore did not include a specific section addressing this.

[74] Mandate ratified in Human Rights Council Resolution 8/7 (2008).

[75] Report of the Special Rapporteur on the situation of human rights and fundamental freedoms of indigenous people, UN Doc A/HRC/9/9, 11 August 2008, paras 85–86.

The report goes on to enunciate the role of States in making the Declaration operative, the central role of the specialised UN agencies, and the importance of indigenous peoples and civil society participation.[76] From the perspective of the lesser codified right to development, it will take all of this, and in addition a concerted decision on the part of States to make socio-economic and collective rights truly operational at the national level.

[76] Ibid, paras 87–90.

15

Taking Cultural Rights Seriously: The Vision of the UN Declaration on the Rights of Indigenous Peoples

ELSA STAMATOPOULOU

Dear Teacher,

I am worried about my child being in your class. You see, my daughter is a person of culture ... In numerous ways, she is like any young girl sitting in your classroom, yet, art, spirit, and culture are inextricably intertwined. She very naturally blends these aspects in her heritage. She has several dolls that reflect her darker skin, eyes and hair. Her pretend play includes making a sweat lodge, singing songs, saying prayers, dressing up the dolls in hand-crafted regalia, and having a feast, complete with miniature foods. How will these natural connections be continued? When she collects gifts from nature, she offers tobacco to the Earth Mother. How will she reconcile this practice when signs in your school say, 'No tobacco products'. Will she still have her cultural voice when she leaves your classroom?

Excerpt from a letter sent by Claudia Fox Tree to her daughter's teacher[1]

INTRODUCTION

FEW WOULD DOUBT, by listening to indigenous people's presentations at the UN since the 1980s, that indigenous peoples' human rights concerns were about both their cultural and physical survival as peoples, those two aspects also being inextricably linked to the right to self-determination and the right to lands, territories and natural resources. Since the early days of the UN Working Group on Indigenous Populations (WGIP) through to today's sessions of the UN Permanent Forum on Indigenous Issues (UNPFII), indigenous leaders have spent a considerable amount of time explaining to the world the specificities

[1] nativeamericanresources.blogspot.com/2007/08/letter-to-my-childrens-teacher.html.

of their cultures, including their legal systems, customs, languages, spirituality, world views, concepts of economic, social, cultural and political development, traditional knowledge systems and other aspects of their ways of life that form the basis of their collective sense of who they are and what their vision is for the future. Year in and year out, during the drafting of the UN Declaration on the Rights of Indigenous Peoples ('the Declaration'), indigenous Elders and other indigenous representatives from all parts of the world spared no effort in describing, for example, the special spiritual, moral and material relationship of indigenous peoples to their ancestral land, the concept of community ownership of the land, and various traditional systems of governance. It has also been a common occurrence at UN meetings that indigenous languages are spoken by the leaders at the beginning of their speeches to mark the significance of language to identity and that, following indigenous cultural protocol, recognition of the indigenous peoples of the land where the meeting is held is expressed.[2] Indigenous peoples have also come to the UN wearing traditional costume, exhibiting their art and sharing music, dance, stories, film and other aspects of their traditional and contemporary cultural expressions.

At the same time, indigenous peoples have brought to the UN numerous allegations of systemic discrimination and systematic violations of their cultural rights, including the non-recognition and even suppression of indigenous languages, the prohibition of access to their spiritual and religious sites, the banning of their traditional cultural expressions in public, the marginalisation they face when wearing their traditional clothes, the economic exclusion they suffer because they are culturally distinct, the lack of access to traditional occupations for subsistence, such as hunting and fishing, the lack of access to the country's education system, curricula and mass media that would both allow indigenous persons to benefit from mainstream education and make indigenous cultures known to the rest of the population, the pillaging of their cultural heritage, both tangible and intangible, the patenting of their traditional knowledge without their free, prior and informed consent, and the marginalisation and suffocation of their traditional systems of governance and law. Indigenous voices at the UN debates on the Declaration clearly articulated that the suppression of identity and culture is a denial of human dignity that must be addressed within the human rights framework.

It is therefore understandable that the Declaration is imbued with an affirmation of the cultural rights of indigenous peoples, as collectivities

[2] The annual sessions of the PFII in New York, for example, are always opened by the spiritual chief of the Onondaga Nation, who speaks in the Onondaga language, with interpretation provided in the six official UN languages.

and as individuals. Cultural rights are reflected in at least 17 of the 46 articles of the Declaration and the word 'identity' is mentioned in Article 2 (the right to be free from any discrimination based on indigenous origin or identity) and Article 33 (the right of indigenous peoples to determine their own identity or membership in accordance with their customs and traditions). The word 'culture' or 'cultural' is mentioned no fewer than eight times in the preamble and 16 times in the articles of the declaration (Articles 3, 5, 7, 11, 12, 14, 15, 16, 31, 32, 36). Significantly, around 15 of the 46 articles deal with governance and participation in a democratic polity, in other words they are crucial process and substantive rights via which the culture and identity of indigenous peoples will have an impact in the public sphere, in relations with the state.

In this essay I will first provide a brief historical perspective on the path towards recognition of the cultural rights of indigenous peoples and will outline what these rights are in light of international instruments, including the Declaration, and the case law and practice of international bodies. I will then go on to discuss the significance and role of cultural rights protection and promotion in mending historical injustices.[3]

HISTORICAL PERSPECTIVE

The recognition of indigenous peoples' cultural human rights in the Declaration and its significance in international law, policy and relations can be better understood by examining the interface of identity, culture and diversity in the UN era.

The Drafting History of Article 27 of the Universal Declaration of Human Rights

States' resistance to the recognition of cultural rights predates the emergence of indigenous peoples' rights on the UN's agenda. One of the most significant difficulties in dealing with cultural rights is that these rights have evoked, for various governments, a scary spectrum of group identities and group rights that they feared could threaten the 'nation' state and territorial integrity. The drafting history of Article 27 of the Universal Declaration of Human Rights (UDHR) is telling. Article 27 states:

1. Everyone has the right freely to participate in the cultural life of the community, to enjoy the arts and to share in scientific advancement and its benefits.

[3] This essay draws in part on E Stamatopoulou, *Cultural Rights in International Law: Article 27 of the Universal Declaration of Human Rights and Beyond* (Leiden, Martinus Nijhoff, 2007).

2. Everyone has the right to the protection of the moral and material interests resulting from any scientific, literary or artistic production of which he is the author.

Article 27, through the inclusion of the word 'the' before 'cultural life' and 'community', does not present a commitment to diversity and pluralism, assuming somehow that cultural participation will take place in the 'one' culture of the 'nation-state'. The question about the inclusion of rights of minorities did arise, as was to be expected, in the very first session of the Commission on Human Rights in 1948. In the minds of the drafters of the UDHR, 'protection of minorities' would normally 'include both protection from discrimination and protection against assimilation' and in particular protection of ethnicity and language—since other elements of minorities' protection were covered by other articles of the Declaration.[4]

The text originally debated provided for the right of persons belonging to ethnic, linguistic or religious minorities to establish and maintain schools and cultural and religious institutions and to use their own language in the press, in public assembly and before the courts and other authorities of the state. However, this language was never adopted. It is overwhelming to realise that these cultural rights have remained burning demands and rallying points for indigenous peoples and minorities to date.

The drama of the debate on cultural rights, which encompassed the debate on minority rights, had another angle as well. It was connected with the Convention on the Prevention and Punishment of the Crime of Genocide (Anti-Genocide Convention) that was being drafted by the UN General Assembly's Sixth Committee simultaneously with the Universal Declaration of Human Rights, then in preparation by the Third Committee. There was a proposal during the drafting of the Anti-Genocide Convention to include, in the definition of genocide, the intent to destroy, in whole or in part, cultural groups, as well as 'national, ethnical, racial or religious' groups, in other words to include 'cultural genocide' along with 'physical or biological' genocide. The proposed Article 3 in the Anti-Genocide Convention read as follows:

> In this Convention genocide also means any deliberate act committed with the intent to destroy the language, religion or culture of a national, racial or religious group on grounds of national or racial origin or religious belief such as: 1. Prohibiting the use of the language of the group in daily intercourse or in schools, or the printing and circulation of publications in the language of the group; 2. Destroying, or preventing the use of, libraries, museums, schools,

[4] J Morsink, *The Universal Declaration of Human Rights: Origins, Drafting and Intent* (Philadelphia, University of Pennsylvania Press, 1999) 270.

historical monuments, places of worship or other cultural institutions and objects of the groups.[5]

The proposal on cultural genocide in the context of the Anti-Genocide Convention at the Sixth Committee of the UN General Assembly was finally put aside, and, as mentioned above, the Universal Declaration of Human Rights did not include reference to minority rights either.[6]

The tumultuous history of Article 27 may well explain much of the silence on cultural rights over the decades, to the extent that the original reasons for resisting them for minorities and indigenous peoples still remain for many states. But in today's interconnected world of greater expectations for democracy and rising cultural identities, avoiding the subject of respect for cultural rights can only lead to frustrations in society and the instigation of conflict. In fact, states have learnt hard lessons and are gradually opening up to cultural rights recognition and implementation.

How States' Positions Changed over Time and Why

In the case of indigenous peoples, the change in the positions of states over time has been dramatic. While stories of political and cultural resistance of indigenous peoples to colonialism, domination and exploitation at the local level abound, these did not always find resonance at the international level, in particular at the United Nations. After the WWII era, questions of ethnicity and minorities were viewed with suspicion, and even the UN expert body established in 1946 for this purpose, the Sub-Commission on Prevention of Discrimination and Protection of Minorities, was essentially prevented for years from adequately doing its work on minority issues by its parent bodies, including the Commission on Human Rights, until after the end of the Cold War, in the later 1980s and early 1990s.

However, in addition to historical reasons—at state and regional levels—that are beyond the purview of this essay, there is something else that clearly distinguished the UN minority-related agenda from the UN indigenous peoples-related agenda. And this distinguishing factor has been the transformation of local struggles into international ones, through

[5] Ibid, 371, fn 45.

[6] It is interesting to note that the United States presented the sole strong opposition to the minority-related article, claiming that minorities were a European issue and there was no reason to reflect the matter in the UDHR. The USA was subsequently joined by Canada and Latin American countries, while Australia declared that it had opted for the principle of assimilation. One wonders whether the colonial histories of mass extermination and oppression by those countries of their indigenous peoples may have had a bearing on the positions taken by them at the UN in 1948.

the creation of an international indigenous peoples' movement and its dynamic interface with the United Nations.[7] There has never been such an international movement on the part of minorities.

From the side of states, we note a differentiation of their positions vis-a-vis indigenous peoples over the years. In the earlier days, in the 1970s, when gross violations of human rights were brought up in the UN human rights bodies, including mass killings in Guatemala, states viewed the issue of indigenous peoples mostly as a humanitarian one, one of 'kindness' so to speak, to disappearing civilisations in the final process of assimilation. One could therefore observe some degree of permissiveness on the part of states in UN processes; that is, states allowed the birth of exceptional, unprecedented and extensive participatory procedures for indigenous peoples, which, in turn, increased the number of indigenous representatives at the UN as well as their overall political impact. In recent years, political changes sweeping through Latin America, from Mexico, with the Zapatista movement,[8] to Guatemala, with the peace accords, to Bolivia with an indigenous Aymara President, have brought indigenous peoples to the fore. The final years of negotiations on the UN Declaration on the Rights of Indigenous Peoples reflected this new reality and thus, the recognition of cultural rights in international human rights law has now surfaced, both in terms of individual cultural rights and in terms of group cultural rights.

CULTURAL RIGHTS OF INDIGENOUS PEOPLES

The Declaration refers explicitly to collective rights as well as to rights of individuals. At least 17 of the 46 articles are about cultural rights; in fact, one can find the cultural rights angle in each article of the Declaration: the right of indigenous peoples and individuals to be free from any kind of discrimination, in particular that based on indigenous origin or identity (Article 2); the right to self-determination, by virtue of which indigenous peoples should freely determine their political status and freely pursue their economic, social and cultural development (Article 3); the right to maintain and strengthen their distinct cultural institutions, while retaining their rights to participate fully, if they so choose, in the cultural life of the state (Article 5); the collective right to live as distinct peoples (Article 7); the right not to be subjected to forced assimilation or destruction of their culture, including mechanisms of prevention and redress (Article 8); the

[7] For an account of this, see E Stamatopoulou, 'Indigenous Peoples and the UN: Human Rights as a Developing Dynamic' (1994) 16 1 *Human Rights Quarterly* 58–81.

[8] The world can still recall the declarations of the mysterious *Sub-Commandante* Marcos, whose supreme leader was no other than a council of indigenous Elders.

right to belong to an indigenous community or nation in accordance with the traditions and customs of the community or nation concerned (Article 9); the right to practise and revitalise their cultural traditions and customs and to receive redress for cultural, intellectual, religious and spiritual property taken without their free, prior and informed consent (Article 11); the right to manifest, practise, develop and teach their spiritual and religious traditions, customs and ceremonies, to maintain, protect and have access to their religious and cultural sites, to use and control their ceremonial objects and to have their human remains repatriated (Article 12); the right to revitalise and transmit to future generations their histories, languages, oral traditions and philosophies, and to designate their own names for communities, places and persons; and the obligation of states to ensure that indigenous peoples can understand and be understood in political, legal and administrative proceedings (Article 13); the right to establish and control their education systems and institutions providing education in their own language and in a manner appropriate to their cultural methods of learning and teaching; and the right to have access, when possible, to an education in their own culture and provided in their own language (Article 14); the right to have the dignity and diversity of their cultures reflected in all forms of education and public information (Article 15); the right to establish their own media in their own languages and have equal access to all forms of non-indigenous media (Article 16); the right to their traditional medicines and to maintain their health practices (Article 24); the right to maintain, control, protect and develop their cultural heritage, traditional knowledge and traditional cultural expressions, as well as the manifestations of their sciences, technologies and cultures, including human and genetic resources, seeds, medicines, knowledge of the properties of fauna and flora, oral traditions, literatures, designs, sports and traditional games and visual and performing arts; they also have the right to,maintain, control, protect and develop their intellectual property over such cultural heritage, traditional knowledge and traditional cultural expressions (Article 31); the right to determine their own identity or membership in accordance with their customs and traditions (Article 33); the right to promote, develop and maintain their institutional structures and their distinctive customs, spirituality, traditions, procedures and practices and, in case they exist, juridical systems or customs in accordance with international human rights standards (Article 34); the right of indigenous peoples divided by borders to maintain and develop contacts, relations and cooperation across borders (Article 36).

Comparing the above-mentioned cultural rights to those that the advocates of minorities wanted to include in the UDHR and the Convention on the Prevention and Punishment of the Crime of Genocide, we note that the Declaration has indeed covered what some were hoping to include in 1948, and has even gone beyond that. Part of the reason for this is that international human rights law has been dynamic and developing over the decades through standard-setting and international practice. Another factor is, as mentioned above, a certain political 'permissiveness' on the part of states, namely that states were willing to allow for the recognition of 'harmless' cultural rights for what they saw at that time, some 40 years ago, as dying cultures or disappearing civilisations in the final stages of assimilation. Finally, another important factor is the birth and dynamism of the international indigenous peoples' movement that has eloquently claimed cultural human rights. The elements of the cultural rights of indigenous peoples, even if not always explicit, have been captured in the texts of human rights instruments preceding the Declaration, as well as in the case law and practice of international human rights treaty bodies and other international bodies. It should be pointed out that, before the adoption of the Declaration in 2007, international human rights bodies covered indigenous peoples' cultural rights by using, in some cases, the analogy to minority rights, as can be seen through an examination of the practice and case law of those bodies.

There are no formal international definitions of the terms 'minorities' and 'indigenous peoples' and these categories overlap in international practice, especially in terms of the need to establish non-discrimination towards them. However, there is an accepted distinction between these two terms, although it is not always clearly articulated. Indigenous peoples, to use one distinction, are in some cases majorities, as in Guatemala and Bolivia, or are majorities in the areas which they have traditionally inhabited. Indigenous peoples have a special spiritual relation to the land which is linked to both their physical and cultural survival as indigenous.[9] International Labour Organization Convention 169 on Indigenous and Tribal Peoples, in Article 1, states the following in lieu of a definition:

> This Convention applies to:
>
> (a) tribal peoples in independent countries whose social, cultural and economic conditions distinguish them from other sections of the national community, and whose status is regulated wholly or partially by their own customs or traditions or by special laws or regulations;

[9] The distinction between indigenous peoples and minorities has been affirmed on various occasions at the international level. Among them is a paper prepared in 1985 by Judge Jules Dechenes, Canadian Expert of the UN Sub-Commission on Prevention of Discrimination and Protection of Minorities (see E/CN.4/Sub.2/1985/31). This was also the case at a 1989 UN seminar on the effects of racism and racial discrimination on the social and economic relations between indigenous peoples and states (E/CN.4/1989/22, para 40). On 24 October 1991, United Nations Day, the Home Rule Parliament of Greenland, which is the most advanced indigenous autonomous regime globally, adopted a resolution reiterating the distinction between indigenous peoples and minorities (quoted in 'Status and Rights of the James Bay Crees in the context of Quebec's Secession from Canada', submission to the Commission on Human Rights, February 1992, 63).

> (b) peoples in independent countries who are regarded as indigenous on account of their descent from the populations which inhabited the country, or a geographical region to which the country belongs, at the time of conquest or colonization or the establishment of present day boundaries and who, irrespective of their legal status, retain some or all of their own social, economic, cultural and political institutions.
>
> Self-identification as indigenous or tribal shall be regarded as a fundamental criterion for determining the groups to which the provisions of this Convention apply.

The Declaration thus does not contain any new cultural human rights, but restates, in one systematic text, human rights contained in previously adopted international instruments and confirmed through the case law of international bodies. Some of these provisions and cases will be mentioned below, as the brevity of this essay does not allow an exhaustive review.[10]

The texts of international legal instruments provide various elements of recognition of the individual and collective aspects of cultural rights, including those of indigenous peoples. Article 27 of the 1966 International Covenant on Civil and Political Rights (ICCPR) provides for the right of persons belonging to ethnic, linguistic or religious minorities 'in community with the other members of their group' to enjoy their own culture, to profess and practise their own religion, and to use their own language.

Other international instruments are also vocal about the cultural rights of minorities and indigenous peoples. The 1990 Copenhagen Document of the Conference on the Human Dimension of the CSCE (Conference for Security and Co-operation in Europe, later renamed OSCE), in paragraph 32, provides a series of rights including that persons belonging to national minorities have the right freely to express, preserve and develop their ethnic, cultural, linguistic or religious identity and to maintain and develop their culture in all its aspects, free of any attempts of assimilation against their will. This concept is also included and developed in the 1995 Framework Convention for the Protection of National Minorities adopted by the Council of Europe, where nine articles refer to the cultural rights of persons belonging to minorities, namely Articles 4, 5, 6, 9–12, 14 and 17. The 1992 United Nations Declaration on the Rights of Persons Belonging to National or Ethnic, Religious and Linguistic Minorities similarly states that 'persons belonging to minorities may exercise their rights, including those set forth in the present Declaration, individually as well as in community with other members of their group, without any discrimination'. The 1989 Convention on the Rights of the Child, in Article 30, similarly

[10] For a comprehensive account of existing instruments and case law, see Stamatopoulou (n 3) 4.

recognises that 'in those states in which ethnic, religious or linguistic minorities or persons of indigenous origin exist, a child belonging to such a minority or who is indigenous shall not be denied the right, in community with other members of his or her group, to enjoy his or her own culture, to profess and practise his or her own religion, or to use his or her own language'.

The 1966 UNESCO Declaration of the Principles of International Cultural Cooperation states in Article 1 that each culture has dignity and value which must be respected and preserved, that every people has the right and duty to develop its culture and that, in their rich variety and diversity, and in the reciprocal influence they exert on one another, all cultures form part of the common heritage belonging to all mankind. In 2001, UNESCO adopted an extraordinary instrument, the Universal Declaration on Cultural Diversity. Article 2 states:

> In our increasingly diverse societies, it is essential to ensure harmonious interaction among people and groups with plural, varied and dynamic cultural identities as well as their willingness to live together. Policies for the inclusion of all citizens are guarantees of social cohesion, the vitality of civil society and peace. Thus defined, cultural pluralism gives policy expression to the reality of cultural diversity. Indisociable from a democratic framework, cultural pluralism is conducive to cultural exchange and to the flourishing of creative capacities that sustain public life.

Article 4 of the Declaration, entitled 'Human Rights as Guarantees of Cultural Diversity', states:

> The defense of cultural diversity is an ethical imperative, inseparable from respect for human dignity. It implies commitment to human rights and fundamental freedoms, in particular the rights of persons belonging to minorities and those of indigenous peoples. No one may invoke cultural diversity to infringe upon human rights guaranteed by international law, nor to limit their scope.

The African Charter on Human and Peoples' Rights has set out guidelines requiring states to take specific measures for the promotion of cultural identity and the awareness and enjoyment of the cultural heritage of national ethnic groups and minorities and indigenous sectors of the population.[11] ILO Convention 169 on Indigenous and Tribal Peoples (Article 2) spells out the duty of states to promote 'the full realization of the social, economic and cultural rights of these peoples with respect for their social and cultural identity, their customs and traditions and their institutions'.

[11] African Commission on Human Rights, 'General Guidelines regarding the Form and Contents of Reports to be submitted by States Members regarding the meaning, scope and weight of "the rights of peoples" recognized by Articles 17(2), 19 to 20 of the Charter', 1990, pp 417–18.

Human Rights Committee

In 1994, the Human Rights Committee enriched the understanding of the cultural rights of minorities and indigenous peoples by adopting an important General Comment on Article 27 of the ICCPR.[12] The Committee underlines that the enjoyment of these rights 'does not prejudice the sovereignty and territorial integrity of a State party. At the same time, one or other aspect of the rights of individuals protected under that article—for example, to enjoy a particular culture—may consist in a way of life which is closely associated with territory and use of its resources. This may particularly be true of members of indigenous communities constituting a minority'.[13] In the case of indigenous peoples such traditional activities may include fishing or hunting and the right to live in reserves protected by law. In examining states parties' reports the Committee has been thorough in its monitoring of cultural rights of minorities, in particular linguistic rights,[14] cultural autonomy in terms of cultural institutions, as well as consultation regarding traditional means of livelihood,[15] threats to indigenous cultures from logging, mining and delays in demarcation of traditional lands,[16] and protection of sites of religious or cultural significance.[17]

The case law of the Human Rights Committee under the Optional Protocol to the Covenant has reflected the above-mentioned interpretation of Article 27 and has made pronouncements regarding (a) use of land and resources in a way that will respect the culture of a minority or indigenous group, (b) the possible limitations of such rights of the group by other development concerns in the area, (c) the requirement of consultation by the state with the minority group concerned by a decision that may affect its use of the land and resources, and (d) the issue of the sensitive limits between the cultural rights of a member of a group and what the group perceives as its own cultural rights. Some of the important cases of the Committee in this regard include *Mahuika et al v New Zealand*,[18] *Ominayak v Canada*,[19] the *Lansman et al v Finland* cases of 1994[20]

[12] General Comment No 23, CCPR/C/21/Rev.1/Add.5.

[13] Para 3.2.

[14] Eg A/56/40, para 79(5), where the Committee welcomes Uzbekistan's language policy whereby education at all levels is offered in 10 languages, including the languages of the minority groups.

[15] Eg A/55/40, para 75, where the Committee notes positively the transfer of certain cultural institutions to the Saami in Norway as well as full consultation with the Saami in matters affecting their traditional means of livelihood.

[16] Eg A/55/40, para 379 regarding Guyana.

[17] Eg A/55/40, para 510 regarding Australia.

[18] A/56/40, Volume I, Annex X, A (Communication No 547/1993).

[19] CCPR/C/60/D/549/1993/Rev. 1, Communication No. 549/1993.

[20] CCPR/C/52/D/511/1992, Case No 511/1992.

and 1996,[21] *Francis Hopu and Tepoaitu Bessert v France*,[22] *Lovelace v Canada*,[23] and *Kitok v Sweden*.[24]

The Committee has been analytical and creative in protecting indigenous peoples' cultural rights, and a case in point is *Francis Hopu and Tepoaitu Bessert v France*. Long before the adoption of the Declaration and its recognition, as part of cultural rights,[25] of the right to the repatriation of human remains with the corresponding obligation of states to enable this through fair, transparent and effective mechanisms developed in conjunction with indigenous peoples concerned (Article 12), the Committee eloquently described the parameters of indigenous identity. The Committee was dealing with a complaint against the planned destruction of a burial site of an indigenous community in Polynesia. The Committee observed that the objectives of the Covenant require that the term 'family' be given a broad interpretation so as to include all those comprising the family as understood in the society in question (Polynesians in Tahiti, French Polynesia). The Committee accepted the applicants' claim that their ancestors are an essential element of their identity and play an important role in family life and thus burial grounds play an important role in the authors' history, culture and life. It concluded that the construction of a hotel complex on a burial site constituted a violation of the right to family and privacy, in violation of Articles 17, paragraph 1, and 23, paragraph 1. The Committee did not invoke Article 27 in this case, since France has made a reservation declining to accept the applicability of Article 27 to France. In individual opinions, several members of the Committee regretted that they could not apply Article 27, which is clearly relevant in this case in terms of the need for the state to respect the cultural values of the community.

Considerable progress has been made in state practice on the subject of repatriation of human remains to indigenous peoples. Since 2003, in the United States alone, more than 2,000 culturally sensitive items—including human remains and affiliated funerary objects—have been returned to

[21] CCPR/C/58/D/671/1995, Case No 671/1995.

[22] CCPR/C/60/D/549/1993/Rev.1, Communication No 549/1993.

[23] A/36/40, Annex 7(G) (1998).

[24] A/43/40, Annex 7(G) (1988).

[25] NB Rossoff, 'Integrating Native Views into Museum Procedures' in L Peers and AK Brown (eds), *Museum and Source Communities: A Routledge Reader* (London, Routledge, 2003) 72–79. For the cultural significance of the return of human remains, see also E Barkan, *The Guilt of Nations: Restitution and Negotiating Historical Injustices* (Baltimore, Johns Hopkins University Press, 2000) 187–201. In my work at the United Nations, indigenous peoples' representatives have told me painful stories of indigenous communities forcibly uprooted who had to carry with them the remains of their ancestors to the place they were relocated. In one case, the same indigenous community was forcibly removed twice and had to twice unbury and rebury the human remains of their ancestors, who were part of the community's identity, spirituality, history and culture.

their descendants and places of origin, in accordance with the Native American Graves Protection and Repatriation Act (NAGPRA).

Organization of American States

The Organization of American States has also upheld the norm of the survival of indigenous peoples as distinct cultures.[26] In the case concerning the indigenous peoples of Nicaragua, the Inter-American Commission on Human Rights cited Nicaragua's obligations under Article 27 of the ICCPR and found that the special protections accorded to the indigenous peoples for the preservation of their cultural identity should extend to the aspects linked to livelihood, which includes, among other things, their relation to their ancestral and communal lands.[27] In the case of the Yanomami of Brazil, the Commission again invoked Article 27, stating that 'international law at its present state recognizes … the right of ethnic groups to special protection of their use of their own language, for the practice of their own religion, and, in general, for all those characteristics necessary for the preservation of their cultural identity'.[28]

In the groundbreaking 2001 decision of *Awas Tingni v Nicaragua*,[29] the Inter-American Court of Human Rights recognised that the relation of indigenous peoples with their lands is the basis of their cultural and spiritual life as well as their economic survival. The Court declared that for indigenous peoples, their land base is indispensable for the preservation of their cultural heritage and its transmission to future generations; thus the state has an obligation to establish laws and other mechanisms for the demarcation and issuance of property titles to the community

[26] The discussion of OAS is based on SJ Anaya, *Indigenous Peoples in International Law*, 2nd edn (Oxford University Press, 2004) 101.

[27] OAS Doc OEA/Ser.L/V/II.62, doc 10 rev 3 (1983); OAS Doc OEA/Ser.L/V/II.62, doc 26(1984) (Case No 7964 (*Nicaragua*)), quoted in Anaya, ibid.

[28] Case No 761 (Brazil), Inter-American Commission Res No 12/85 (5 March 1985); Annual Report of the Inter-American Commission on Human Rights, 1984–1985, OAS Doc OEA/Ser.L/V/II.66, doc 10, rev 1, at 24, 31 (1985), quoted in Anaya (n 26) 261.

[29] *Mayagna (Sumo) Awas Tingni Community v Nicaragua* (Series C No 79) [2001] IACHR 9 (31 August 2001). Para 149 reads: 'Given the characteristics of the instant case, some specifications are required on the concept of property in indigenous communities. Among indigenous peoples there is a communitarian tradition regarding a communal form of collective property of the land, in the sense that ownership of the land is not centered on an individual but rather on the group and its community. Indigenous groups by the fact of their very existence, have the right to live freely in their own territory; the close ties of indigenous people with the land must be recognized and understood as the fundamental basis of their cultures, their spiritual life, their integrity, and their economic survival. For indigenous communities, relations to the land are not merely a matter of possesion and production but a material and spiritual element which they must fully enjoy, even to preserve their cultural legacy and transmit it to future generations.'

members in accordance with the c.ommunity's customary law, values and customs.[30]

Practice of International Human Rights Treaty Bodies in Examining State Reports

In addition to its case law, the Human Rights Committee has been thorough in its monitoring of cultural rights of minority and indigenous groups. The Committee has paid particular attention to linguistic rights,[31] cultural autonomy in terms of cultural institutions as well as consultation regarding traditional means of livelihood,[32] the obligation of the state to provide protection from threats to indigenous cultures by logging, mining and demarcation of indigenous lands,[33] and protection of sites of religious or cultural significance.[34]

The Committee on Economic, Social and Cultural Rights has shown interest, among other areas, in the lack of opportunities for education of minorities in their own languages,[35] non-discrimination in national legal frameworks,[36] and the need for steps to be taken to safeguard the cultural identity and heritage of ethnic groups.[37]

The Committee on the Elimination of Racial Discrimination has systematically focused on linguistic rights of minorities, indigenous peoples and migrants in education as well as in the media.[38] It has also paid attention to the following other aspects of cultural rights related to groups: use of minority languages in administration[39] and health services,[40] measures

[30] The link between culture and traditional use of land and natural resources is also evident in many efforts at the national level. An eloquent account of the case of the Kalash people of Pakistan is given in S Hussain and S Zaman, 'Land, Culture and Identity: The Case of the Kalasha' in V Tauli-Corpuz and J Carino (eds), *Reclaiming Balance: Indigenous Peoples, Conflict Resolution and Sustainable Development* (Bagui City, Tebtebba Foundation, 2002) 267–91.

[31] Eg A/56/40, para 79(5), where the Committee welcomes Uzbekistan's language policy whereby education at all levels is offered in 10 languages, including the languages of the minority groups.

[32] Eg A/55/40, para 75, where the Committee notes positively the transfer of certain cultural institutions to the Saami in Norway as well as full consultation with the Saami in matters affecting their traditional livelihood.

[33] Eg A/55/40, para 379 regarding Guyana.

[34] Eg A/55/40, para 510 regarding Australia.

[35] Eg E/2000/22, para 231 regarding Bulgaria.

[36] Eg E/1998/22, para 79 regarding Zimbabwe.

[37] Eg E/1997/22, para 209 regarding Guinea.

[38] Eg A/44/18, para 51 regarding France, para 64 regarding Mexico, para 89 regarding Venezuela, para 113 regarding Poland, para 145 regarding Norway, para 193 regarding Niger; A/48/18, para 75 regarding Algeria, para 116 regarding Sudan, para 185 regarding Poland, para 519 regarding Yugoslavia and para 523 regarding Bulgaria.

[39] Eg A/45/18, para 133 regarding Czechoslovakia.

[40] Eg A/46/18, para 234 regarding Australia.

for regaining linguistic and cultural identity,[41] preservation of cultural identity of minorities,[42] policies to ensure that tribal people live according to their original customs,[43] prevention of the illegal export of indigenous art,[44] promotion of multicultural training for teachers,[45] enactment of legal provisions to preserve the existence, culture and traditions of minorities,[46] teaching the history of different ethnic groups and cultures at schools,[47] concern over budget cuts in mother tongue education,[48] concern over assimilation,[49] concern over different levels of protection for different groups,[50] ensuring the participation of indigenous people in decisions affecting lands, culture and traditions,[51] concern over the lack of statistical and qualitative data on the demographic composition of the population,[52] cultural autonomy,[53] and regional cultural development.[54]

In conclusion, human rights treaty bodies have shown a keen interest in the cultural rights of groups through case law and through the specific questions they have raised in examining state party reports on the implementation of the human rights treaties, and in this way they have helped to clarify the concept of cultural rights. The elements that the treaty bodies have focused most closely on are language rights, cultural participation and cultural autonomy, education of the broader society about the cultures of minorities and indigenous peoples, protection of minority cultural heritage, and protection of certain economic activities of indigenous groups closely linked to their cultural preservation and development. Other normative elements of cultural rights regarding groups emerge from the overall letter and spirit of human rights instruments and work of the treaty bodies on other aspects of human rights, such as the right to choose which culture or cultures to participate in.

The area of indigenous cultural heritage and traditional knowledge and its protection and development, according to the traditional owners' protocols and wishes, is a rich and complex field that the brevity of this essay does not permit me to go into. Suffice it to say that close to 15 intergovernmental entities deal with traditional knowledge issues, from both a normative and

[41] Eg A/51/18, para 111 regarding Hungary.
[42] Eg A/48/18 para 113 regarding Poland.
[43] Eg A/45/18, para 73 regarding Bangladesh.
[44] Eg A/45/18, para 246 regarding New Zealand.
[45] Eg A/45/18, para 273 regarding the Byelorussian SSR.
[46] Eg A/46/18, para 68 regarding the Ukrainian SSR.
[47] Eg A/46/18, para 101 regarding Burundi.
[48] Eg A/46/18, para 214 regarding Sweden.
[49] Eg A/46/18, para 136 regarding Ecuador.
[50] Eg A/48/18, para 431 regarding Germany.
[51] Eg A/50/18, paras 490–92 regarding El Salvador.
[52] Eg A/51/18, para 43 regarding Colombia.
[53] Eg A/51/18, para 111 regarding Hungary.
[54] Eg A/53/18, para 405 regarding Morocco.

a commercial perspective, demonstrating the huge trade and economic interests of states and the private sector. The Declaration on the Rights of Indigenous Peoples clearly highlights the human rights norms that must inform the actions of the state as well as the private sector.[55]

The Borders between Individual and Group Cultural Rights

The Declaration outlines the borders between individual and group cultural rights by clearly placing its norms within the overall normative framework of internationally recognised human rights. Article 34 states that

> Indigenous peoples have the right to promote, develop and maintain their institutional structures and their distinctive customs, traditions, procedures and practices and, in the case where they exist, juridical systems or customs, *in accordance with internationally recognized human rights standards.*[56]

Article 46 of the Declaration states:

> 2. In the exercise of the rights enunciated in the present Declaration, human rights and fundamental freedoms of all shall be respected. The exercise of the rights set forth in this Declaration shall be subject only to such limitations as are determined by law and in accordance with international human rights obligations. Any such limitations shall be non-discriminatory and strictly necessary solely for the purpose of securing due recognition and respect for the rights and freedoms of others and for meeting the just and most compelling requirements of a democratic society.
> 3. The provisions set forth in this Declaration shall be interpreted in accordance with the principles of justice, democracy, respect for human rights, equality, non-discrimination, good governance and good faith.

This means that an indigenous people or community must respect the human rights of individuals within it. In addition, a group cannot oblige an individual within it to exercise his/her rights as an indigenous person; in other words a group cannot impose indigeneity on an individual. This is a matter of choice. The duties that an indigenous community would require of its members must comply with international human rights standards. It is well known that indigenous leaders who participated in the

[55] For a discussion of indigenous cultural heritage and traditional knowledge, see amongst others F Lenzerini, 'Indigenous Peoples' Cultural Rights and the Controversy over Commercial Use of their Traditional Knowledge' in F Francioni and M Scheinin (eds), *Cultural Human Rights* (Leiden, Martinus Nijhoff, 2008) 119–51. See also Stamatopoulou (n 3) 207–25; and E-I Daes, *Protection of the Heritage of Indigenous Peoples: Final Report of the Special Rapporteur*, E/CN.4/Sub.2/1995/26.

[56] Emphasis added.

negotiations at the United Nations during the drafting of the Declaration over the years were well aware of and agreed to this principle early on.

International bodies, through their case law, have also been at pains to delineate the borders between the individual and the group in the case of cultural rights. One such border between the individual and the group is that an individual within an indigenous people is free to exercise or not to exercise her/his rights as an indigenous person—in other words, the cultural autonomy of the individual is recognised. The indigenous group/community/collectivity must respect the internationally recognised human rights of its members or other persons or groups in its midst.

Human rights treaty bodies have considered on a case-by-case basis the permissible limitations of individual cultural rights when they conflict with imputed rights of the collectivity. Under general human rights principles, such limitations would need to be duly justified and remain in force for the duration strictly necessary. Limitations on the individual's cultural rights vis-a-vis the group may be imposed only when the survival and welfare of the group are threatened and only for as long as the situation of threat persists.

Information and educating the Wider Society

The state should take measures to inform and educate the wider society about indigenous peoples. This particular obligation has been underlined by various UN bodies, including the UN Permanent Forum on Indigenous Issues and the Special Rapporteur on the human rights and fundamental freedoms of indigenous people.[57] The obligation to inform and to educate has emerged from the assumption that non-discrimination policies must be supported by a participatory and informed civil society. The role of the media has been repeatedly stressed in terms of combating racism and discrimination vis-a-vis indigenous peoples and minorities. Indigenous communities should have access to mainstream media and the media should refrain from exploiting or sensationalising their heritage. Policies should encourage the presentation of indigenous cultures in mainstream media and the world of the arts. School curricula and textbooks should teach understanding and respect for the heritage of indigenous peoples.[58] In order to spread this concept to the wider society, policies should, for

[57] See respectively A/60/270 containing the plan of action of the Second International Decade of the World's Indigenous People, and E/2005/43, paras 47, 48, 50 and 52.

[58] E/CN.4/1998/6/Add, paras 50 and 52: 'Journalists should respect the privacy of indigenous peoples in particular concerning traditional religions, cultural and ceremonial activities, and refrain from exploiting and sensationalizing indigenous peoples' heritage ... Educators should ensure that school curricula and textbooks teach understanding and

example, support the translation of literature from indigenous languages into the majority languages.

Multiculturalism does not entail the coexistence of various cultures as separate entities that happen to exist and develop independently within the state; neither does international law.[59] The interaction in a state between indigenous and non-indigenous populations, particularly in terms of educating and informing the latter about indigenous histories and cultures, should not be a cloak that hides assimilationist strategies; it should form part of a genuine effort to create not just tolerance, but an appreciation of indigenous peoples' cultures and to strengthen human solidarity.

Obligations of the State

The state and its agents have an obligation to respect the freedom of indigenous persons and indigenous peoples to participate freely in cultural life, to assert their cultural identity, and to express themselves culturally in the way they choose. In other words, the authorities must not interfere with this freedom unless certain circumstances, mentioned below, are present. The state, as part of the regular discharge of its police and justice functions, must also protect the right to participate in cultural life from infringement by third parties, whether they are individuals, groups or corporations, domestic or foreign. Indigenous peoples' rights form part of the human rights regime and, given the prohibition by human rights law of practices that contravene internationally recognised human rights, states should promote awareness of such problems and adopt preventive and corrective policies conducive to the elimination of such practices. Obviously, for such measures to have an effect, they have to be designed with the full and effective participation of indigenous peoples and be culturally sensitive, following the standards of the UN Declaration on the Rights of Indigenous Peoples. Particularly relevant to this issue are Article 3 on self-determination, including cultural development, Article 33 on the right to determine one's own identity, and Articles 34 and 46 mentioned above in the discussion of the borders between individual and group cultural rights.

The principles of non-discrimination and equality must guide the state's actions, in its obligations regarding the cultural rights of indigenous peoples.

respect for indigenous peoples' heritage and history and recognize the contribution of indigenous peoples to creativity and cultural diversity.'

[59] A Xanthaki, *Indigenous Rights and United Nations Standards: Self-Determination, Culture and Land* (Cambridge, Cambridge University Press, 2007) 22.

The state must establish laws and policies regarding non-discrimination in the enjoyment of cultural rights. Equality, however, may not amount to forced assimilation. The right to non-discrimination has evolved to entail not only the principle that equal cases be treated equally, but also that different cases be treated differently.[60]

Every state faces limitations of financial resources in the fulfillment of human rights however, this is not an excuse for the state's inaction in this area. This is equally true when it comes to the state's obligations regarding cultural rights. The state has the obligation to take steps, to the maximum of available resources, to fulfil conditions and correct circumstances that will allow the full enjoyment of cultural rights. The state is permitted to take special positive measures, that is, affirmative action measures, to secure the advancement of indigenous peoples. Such positive actions for the fulfilment of cultural rights, in terms of the provision of resources, subsidies etc, must be guided by the principle of non-discrimination. If the state does not have adequate resources to respond to its obligation, it should explore the possibility of international assistance and cooperation. The concept of positive measures is well enshrined in the International Convention on the Elimination of All Forms of Racial Discrimination and other human rights instruments. Defining the parameters of the obligation to fulfil is no easy matter. For example, Article 1, paragraph 4 of the International Convention on the Elimination of All Forms of Racial Discrimination speaks of 'special measures for the *sole* purpose of securing *adequate* advancement of certain racial or ethnic groups or individuals requiring such protection as may be necessary in order to ensure such groups or individuals *equal* enjoyment of human rights and fundamental freedoms'.[61] In other words, the parameters of positive measures are defined in terms both of duration and of nature: they should last up to the moment of achieving equality and end after that point in time and they should not be general, but tailored to the circumstances of a specific group, and, in the case of indigenous peoples, should be the result of effective consultations with them and their free, prior and informed consent.

Article 2 of the Declaration states that indigenous peoples and individuals are free and equal to all other peoples and individuals and have the right to be free from any discrimination, in particular discrimination based on their indigenous rights or identity. Article 8 explicitly provides for the right of indigenous peoples and individuals not to be subjected

[60] M Ahren, 'Protecting Peoples' Cultural Rights: A Question of Properly Understanding the Notion of States and Nations?' in Francioni and Scheinin (n 55) 115. Ahren's essay provides an overview and analysis of legal doctrine regarding the right to self-determination underpinning the cultural rights of indigenous peoples, in their collective aspect.

[61] Emphasis added.

to forced assimilation or destruction of their culture, and stipulates a list of state obligations for the prevention and redress of violations of this right. Article 9 prohibits any discrimination that may arise in terms of the exercise by indigenous peoples or individuals of their right to belong to an indigenous community or nation, in accordance with the tradition or custom of the community or nation concerned. In many articles the Declaration includes the obligation of the state to take effective measures to remedy and redress situations where indigenous peoples' rights have been negatively affected, such as for forced assimilation and destruction of culture (Article 8) and for violations of cultural, intellectual and spiritual property (Article 11(2)); furthermore, the state must ensure through the provision of interpretation or other appropriate means that indigenous peoples can understand and be understood in political, legal and administrative proceedings (Article 13(2)). Also explicit in terms of targeted measures as part of the obligations of the state are Articles 20(2) (indigenous peoples deprived of their means of subsistence and development are entitled to just and fair redress) and 32(3) (the state shall provide effective mechanisms for just and fair redress for the development or use of indigenous peoples' lands, territories and other resources, and appropriate measures to mitigate adverse environmental, economic, social, cultural or spiritual impact). The Declaration explicitly connects indigenous peoples to international development cooperation and the corresponding obligations of the states in which indigenous peoples live as well as of bilateral or multilateral donors. Indigenous peoples have the right to access financial and technical assistance from states and through international cooperation, for the enjoyment of the rights contained in the Declaration (Article 39). The organs and specialised agencies of the UN system and other intergovernmental organisations are to contribute to the full realisation of the provisions of the Declaration through the mobilisation, inter alia, of financial cooperation and technical assistance (Article 41). The state should also respect special cultural rights of indigenous peoples related to the continuation of certain economic activities linked to the traditional use of land and natural resources, such as hunting and fishing. The Declaration recognises the right of indigenous peoples to self-determination and that 'by virtue of that right they freely determine their political status and freely pursue their economic, social and cultural development' (Article 3). The recognition of the right to self-determination and the breadth of its application, as well as the recognition of the right to lands, territories and natural resources, constitute the main pillars of the Declaration that underpin most other rights recognised in the Declaration, including cultural rights. However, the concept of recognising the right of indigenous peoples to continue to pursue specific traditional economic activities linked to their cultures is not new and in fact predates the adoption of the Declaration. There is rich case law of the

Human Rights Committee under the Optional Protocol to the ICCPR[62] as well as the General Comment adopted by the Committee on Article 27 of the Covenant dealing with minorities[63] mentioned above. Similarly, the famous Inter-American Court of Human Rights case of *Awas Tingni*, also mentioned above,[64] links the cultural rights of indigenous peoples with the right to continue to pursue certain traditional economic occupations linked to land and natural resources.

States should create the conditions of respect for indigenous peoples' right to pursue their cultural development through their own institutions, through which indigenous peoples will participate in the definition, preparation and implementation of cultural policies that concern them. The state must consult indigenous peoples concerned via democratic and transparent processes, respecting indigenous governance structures. The Declaration places major emphasis on promoting indigenous peoples' full and effective participation in all matters that concern them, as well as their right to remain distinct and to pursue their own visions of economic and social development. Starting with the recognition of the right of indigenous peoples to self-determination, 15 of the 46 articles of the Declaration are about indigenous peoples' participation, through their governance structures, in all decisions that will affect their lives. This of course includes decisions affecting the protection and development of their cultures.

CONCLUSION

The UN Declaration on the Rights of Indigenous Peoples is a major instrument through which humanity will protect and promote the survival and well-being of indigenous peoples and the cultural diversity of the world. The Declaration also constitutes the boldest recognition of ethnicity in international law and international relations, through the angle of human rights.

A difficult and painful issue that can be addressed through respecting cultural rights on the part of the state is that of remedying historic injustices. Groups claim cultural rights as collective rights vis-a-vis the majority society, with corresponding obligations, both negative and positive, which are necessary to preserve and develop the cultural integrity of the group, often in order to remedy historical injustices.[65] The fact of

[62] See eg *Mahuika et al v New Zealand* (n 18); *Länsman et al v Finland* (nn 20 and 21); *Kitok v Sweden* (n 24).

[63] General Comment No 23, CCPR/C/21/Rev.1/Add.5.

[64] See text at n 29.

[65] Anaya (n 26) 102 finds that in the case of indigenous peoples the norm of cultural integrity has developed remedial aspects in light of their historical and continuing vulnerability.

past injustice does not necessarily lead to an automatic legal obligation to remedy all those injustices, but it is clear that the state and society have to find mechanisms to deal with such injustices.

Since every society is unique in its history, culture and political circumstances, there do not seem to exist easy or homogenous answers to such questions. Key, however, is whether or not the descendants of groups to whom historic injustices were done continue to suffer discrimination, marginalisation and disempowerment at the hands of the dominant society-which is represented by the state. International legal thinking has contributed to solutions by addressing the concept of continuing violations of human rights, that is, injustice that stems from far back but the effects of which still continue in the present, by promoting positive measures to deal with past discrimination, by developing concepts of truth commissions and transitional justice, and, of course, by establishing imprescriptibility for crimes against humanity and gross and systematic violations of human rights and humanitarian law. The International Law Commission has defined 'continuing act' as a single act extending over a period of time and of a lasting nature; an act which proceeds unchanged over a given period of time: in other words an act which, after its first occurrence, continues to exist as such and not merely in its effects and consequences.[66] The Human Rights Committee has defined a continuing violation as an affirmation, after the entry into force of the Optional Protocol to the ICCPR, by act or by clear implication, of the previous violations of the state party.[67] At the national level, truth commissions and formal apology have been ways of dealing with past injustices and human rights violations.[68]

[66] Report of the ILC on its 28th session, A/31/10, 3 May–23 July 1976, para 21, Official Records of the General Assembly, 31st session, Supplement No 10.

[67] *Simunek v Czech Republic*, Case No 516/1992, para 6.4, 54th session.

[68] The United States, for example, adopted the Apology Bill (Public Law 103-150, signed by President Bill Clinton) on 28 November 1993, to acknowledge the 100th anniversary of the 17 January 1893 overthrow of the Kingdom of Hawai'i, and to offer an apology to Native Hawaiians on behalf of the United States. The preamble to the Bill states, inter alia, that the long-range economic and social changes in Hawai'i over the nineteenth and early twentieth centuries have been devastating to the population and to the health and well-being of the Hawaiian people and that the Native Hawaiian people are determined to preserve, develop and transmit to future generations their ancestral territory, and their cultural identity in accordance with their own spiritual and traditional beliefs, customs, practices, language, and social institutions. Section I states, inter alia, that the United States Congress acknowledges the historical significance of the illegal overthrow of the Kingdom of Hawai'i which resulted in the suppression of the inherent sovereignty of the Native Hawaiian people; apologises to Native Hawaiians on behalf of the people of the United States, and expresses its commitment to acknowledge the ramifications of the overthrow of the Kingdom of Hawai'i, in order to provide a proper foundation for reconciliation between the United States and the Native Hawaiian people. Although the road to such reconciliation seems still to be a long one, some useful steps have been taken, such as the establishment of the Office of Hawaiian Affairs (publication of Hawaian Affairs, Apology Bill; see also www.oha.org). In 2008, both

Attention by the state to cultural rights, through laws, policies and budgets, can have real moral and practical effects in society. It can enhance public respect for the identity of indigenous peoples and their communities, and even motivate action to mend historic injustices meted out to these communities by the majority population, as well as build positive inter-cultural relations. Since cultural rights impact so deeply on identities, even symbolic acts can have a significant impact in society and set the stage for more positive changes, changes that go beyond symbolism and moral aspects of policy to material demands that some cultural rights entail, such as language rights or the continuation of a number of traditional occupations linked to land and natural resources.

The three UN mechanisms specific to indigenous peoples, namely the Permanent Forum on Indigenous Issues, the Special Rapporteur on the human rights and fundamental freedoms of indigenous people and the Expert Mechanism on Indigenous Peoples' Rights, should continue and strengthen the integration of indigenous peoples' cultural rights in their respective work—in fact, they should lead in this field.

A welcome development in this area has been the adoption, in 2009, by the Committee on Economic, Social and Cultural Rights of its General Comment on Article 15, paragraph 1 (a) on the right of everyone to participate in cultural life, which also refers to the cultural rights of indigenous peoples.[69]

In this era where colonialism and crimes against humanity are outlawed and respect for human rights is the prevalent moral paradigm, it cannot be permissible to extinguish cultural groups, whether this happens through physical extermination, systematic oppression and discrimination, expropriation, forced removal or forced assimilation. Given the link between peace and human rights, the UN human rights Special Rapporteurs and treaty bodies could become 'peace ambassadors' for cultural rights and show how cultural rights policies could prevent or respond to various conflicts affecting indigenous peoples and dominant societies.

In the discussions on development at the UN, indigenous peoples put forward their paradigms of development that are often quite different from the current dominant paradigm, and correspond to various indigenous world views and cultures. Concepts such as well-being and self-determined development are preferred by indigenous peoples[70] and the UNPFII devoted the special theme of its 9th session in 2010 to 'indigenous

Australia and Canada issued apologies to generations of indigenous peoples who had suffered harm in boarding schools established by those states.

[69] E/C.12/GC/21

[70] *Vivir bien* is what the Bolivian indigenous peoples use (in their languages of course). Victoria Tauli-Corpuz, Chairperson of the PFII, often uses the term 'self-determined development'.

peoples' development, with culture and identity: articles 3 and 23 of the United Nations Declaration on the Rights of Indigenous Peoples'.[71] Whether states and the international community pursue the Millennium Development Goals or the overall international development goals or the human rights-based approach to development that is now followed by the UN as a methodology, they must take into account the cultural rights of indigenous peoples, including the use of culturally sensitive indicators,[72] implement genuine and effective processes of participation of indigenous peoples through their governance structures, and conduct cultural impact assessments before projects and programmes are decided.

A great gap that remains to be filled is that between the needs of indigenous communities for funding to support cultural projects, such as community museums, and the availability of resources for such projects. It is time for funders to realise that cultural projects of this kind are far from a luxury. They can contribute immensely to the morale and overall economic and social well-being of indigenous peoples and their communities, especially for groups long marginalised and discriminated against. UN country teams (UNCTs) should advocate and support programmes aimed at enhancing the availability of ethnically disaggregated accurate and reliable data. While assessing the situations of indigenous peoples, UNCTs should take into consideration their special social, cultural, political and historical contexts along with statistical data. UNCTs should support and/or undertake programmes aimed at capacity building of their own staff and of indigenous peoples so as to enable them to participate and contribute in programme formulation and to take ownership of programme implementation.[73]

The adoption of the UN Declaration on the Rights of Indigenous Peoples, with its historic, moral, political and legal implications, has already unleashed a tremendous potential for change in terms of states accepting and celebrating diversity. For example, in 2007 Bolivia adopted

[71] E/2010/43, paragraphs 4 to 35.

[72] The UNPFII and its secretariat have led, in cooperation with indigenous organisations and other UN agencies, various efforts aimed at creating culturally sensitive indicators of well-being, poverty and sustainability of indigenous peoples. A global synthesis report on 'Indicators of Well-being, Poverty and Sustainability Relevant to Indigenous Peoples' was presented by Victoria Tauli-Corpuz to the 7th (2008) session of the PFII, Doc E/C.19/2008/9; see www.un.org/esa/socdev/unpfii.

[73] A major development in 2008 was the adoption by the UN Development Group (UNDG is a UN executive committee bringing together all the UN system organisations, funds and programmes working on development) of the UNDG Guidelines on Indigenous Peoples' Issues for UN country teams. The Guidelines aim at implementing the Declaration on the Rights of Indigenous Peoples and a human rights-based approach that is culturally sensitive. Capacity-building of UN staff in the field is part of the Action Plan to roll out these Guidelines. For the text of the Guidelines, see www.un.org/esa/socdev/unpfii. A Resource Kit on Indigenous Peoples' Issues has also been produced by the Secretariat of the PFII to facilitate programme officers (the Resource Kit is also accessible through the abovementioned website).

the Declaration as a law of the country and, in 2008, Guatemala and Ecuador approved legislative reforms recognising the existence of indigenous peoples and the nature of the states as pluricultural. In the case of Ecuador, the new constitution also recognised Quechua and Shuar as official languages, in addition to Spanish. Also in 2008, Australia and Canada issued apologies to indigenous peoples, while Japan recognised the Ainu as the indigenous peoples of the country. The optimism that the Declaration inspires is about humanity preserving its cultural diversity, where indigenous peoples will play a central role as the custodians of living and dynamic cultures.[74]

The ultimate test of the Declaration's impact will obviously be proven in practice, in terms of how states and indigenous peoples as well as the UN system and the rest of the international community use and implement it. But to those who say that the Declaration is difficult to implement because 'it is just a Declaration and not a treaty' or 'because it goes too far in the rights it proclaims' I would say this: The manner in which the Declaration was adopted by the United Nations gives it a different status from that of other international declarations. Essentially, the Declaration was the result of negotiations between indigenous peoples and states under the mediation of the United Nations. The length of the negotiations, more than 20 years, the tremendous diplomatic efforts of states and indigenous peoples to reach agreement and the goal of consensus that underpinned the negotiations until the very last minute illustrate the special status of this Declaration—which provides checks and balances for the possibility of implementation at the national level. The human rights contained in the Declaration are not new, but are established in other pre-existing sources of international law, whether normative instruments, jurisprudence, international practice and custom or reputable academic writings. The Declaration sets high standards and has an ambitious vision in terms of what justice is in today's world—and so do the other international human rights instruments. The high standards of the Universal Declaration of Human Rights, of the International Convention on the Elimination of All Forms of Racial Discrimination, of the two International Covenants and of other instruments are not arguments for devaluing them; rather they galvanise the efforts of civil society, states, the intergovernmental system and others to strive towards the implementation of those standards. And the same, we expect, will be the case with the Declaration.

As the UN Permanent Forum on Indigenous Issues states in its General Comment on Article 42 of the Declaration, the purpose of the Declaration

[74] For a discussion of the impact of indigenous cultural perspectives on the Declaraion see E-I Daes, *Indigenous Peoples: Keepers of our Past—Custodians of our Future* (Copenhagen, International Work Group on Indigenous Affairs, 2008).

is to constitute the legal basis for all activities on indigenous issues. The Declaration is the most universal, comprehensive and fundamental instrument on indigenous peoples' rights.[75]

What the member states of the UN did not achieve in 1948, while preparing the Universal Declaration of Human Rights and the Convention on the Prevention and Punishment of the Crime of Genocide, they were able to accomplish in 2007, by adopting the UN Declaration on the Rights of Indigenous Peoples and boldly recognising indigenous peoples' cultural rights—namely their human right to exist as peoples and as cultures. The cultural rights of indigenous peoples constitute a major path to mending the hurt of historical injustices committed against indigenous peoples, building bridges among indigenous and non-indigenous communities and fostering inclusive, pluricultural democratic states.

[75] UN Permanent Forum on Indigenous Issues, Report on its 8th session (18–29 May 2009), Economic and Social Council Official Records, Supplement No 23 (E/2009/43), Annex. See in particular paras 6–13 entitled 'The legal character of the Declaration'. The report is available at www.un.org/indigenous.

16

The UN Declaration on the Rights of Indigenous Peoples and Collective Rights: What's the Future for Indigenous Women?

ALEXANDRA XANTHAKI

INTRODUCTION

THE ADOPTION OF the Declaration on the Rights of Indigenous Peoples has undoubtedly been a major event in international law. Its importance lies, I believe, on three grounds: first, and most importantly, the instrument provides indigenous peoples around the world with long-awaited protection of their rights. Although ILO Conventions 107 and 169 have recognised a range of rights for indigenous peoples—and in some cases have gone further than the Declaration—their small number of signatories has always limited the basis of their protection and ultimately their effect. The Declaration is able to have an impact on a wider scale. Secondly, the process of adoption of the Declaration was unique; never before has the development and adoption of a human rights instrument been driven so much and so successfully by the interested party, the transnational indigenous movement. The third element that substantiates the importance of this Declaration is the impact it has on the standards of international human rights law: it contributes significantly to the clarification and evolution of standards in several areas of international law. Although many of its provisions crystallise non-controversial rights for indigenous peoples, several provisions recognise rights that, even though conforming to current norms of international law, have not been explicitly included in general human rights instruments or have not been widely accepted.

COLLECTIVE RIGHTS

There seems to be no better example of this effect of the Declaration than the case of collective rights. A long-standing claim of indigenous peoples, collective rights have always been an important pillar of the Declaration. Following several state attempts to restrict their recognition, the final version of the Declaration maintained its emphasis on collective rights, albeit in a more diluted version than the various drafts. The text recognises the rights of indigenous peoples to self-determination, to decide on their membership, to establish their own separate systems and institutions, and to wide consultation and participation in matters that affect them. It also includes a wide range of land rights, including rights relating to traditional activities, to natural resources, and to the development and management of indigenous land rights. Collective intellectual property rights and rights to redress for past injustices are also included in the final version of the text.

The inclusion of such strong collective rights represents an evolution of international law standards. During the deliberations over the text, several states argued that collective rights were not even part of current international law standards. Even though the Chairperson of the Commission Drafting Group stated in 2002 that he had 'not heard any intervention that could be interpreted as denying the existence of collective rights as such',[1] a few states had indeed doubted their existence in international law. For example, in 2003 'the representatives of the United States, the United Kingdom and France all … remained concerned about the possible confusion between individual and collective rights'.[2] More lucidly, the representative of Australia stated that 'the concept of a collective right was not recognized in domestic or international legal systems at present'.[3] France also stated that 'collective rights did not exist in international human rights law, and therefore [France] had reservations with regard to those articles that aimed to establish collective rights'.[4] Following the adoption of the Declaration, Japan and the UK also proclaimed that they did not 'accept the concept of collective rights in international law'.[5] The main problem that states had with these articles was their collective nature, and debates were difficult and controversial. Other states recognised the existence of collective rights, but feared that

[1] See Report of the Working Group established in accordance with Commission on Human Rights Resolution 1995/32, UN Commission on Human Rights (2002), UN Doc E/CN.4/2002/98, para 37.

[2] See Report of the Working Group established in accordance with Commission on Human Rights Resolution 1995/32, UN Commission on Human Rights (2003), UN Doc E/CN.4/2003/92, para 67.

[3] Ibid, para 39.

[4] See Report of the Working Group established in accordance with Commission on Human Rights Resolution 1995/32, UN Commission on Human Rights (1997), UN Doc E/CN.4/1997/102, para 108.

[5] Statement made by the United Kingdom, UN General Assembly, 61st session, 107th plenary meeting, UN Doc A/61/PV.107, p 21; also see Statement made by Japan, ibid, p 20.

their inclusion would lead to a weakening of the respective individual rights.[6] One 'solution' repeatedly suggested by the USA was the adoption of a language similar to the UN Declaration on the Rights of Persons belonging to National or Ethnic, Religious and Linguistic Minorities, whereby persons may enjoy human rights individually, and these may be exercised individually or in community with others.[7] Such language would lower the level of protection offered by international law on indigenous rights, as both ILO Conventions 107 and 169 already recognised a wide range of indigenous collective rights. Furthermore, the adoption of language that emphasised individual rights would nullify the raison d'être of the Declaration.

The adoption of a Declaration with a substantially collective element put arguments and doubts to rest. The Declaration supplements the human rights foundation system of standards and clearly reinforces the existence of collective rights within this system. Of course, contrary to states' arguments, the Declaration did not *add* collective rights to the human rights system; their recognition was in line with the existing system. Earlier texts such as the Genocide Convention, the UN Charter and the (1970) ECOSOC Resolution 1503 on gross violations of human rights[8] all include collective elements without recognising collective rights. In subsequent texts, the collective element becomes more prominent. The 1969 International Convention on the Elimination of All Forms of Racial Discrimination recognises special measures for the advancement of 'ethnic groups'[9] and imposes obligations on states and public institutions not to racially discriminate against 'groups of individuals'.[10] The United Nations Declaration on Rights Belonging to National or Ethnic, Religious or Linguistic Minorities aims at protecting the identity and existence of minorities.[11] More recently, the Rio Declaration has recognised the role 'of indigenous people and their communities and other local communities' in environmental management and development and states' obligation to recognise and support their 'identity, culture and interests'. The monitoring mechanisms and other supporting bodies of all the above texts have over the years greatly advanced the idea of collective rights.[12] Clear recognition of collective rights can be found in the African

[6] See UN Doc E/CN.4/1997/102, paras 108–13.

[7] Ibid, paras 103–29; also see E/CN.4/1999/82, para 49.

[8] Resolution 1503 (XLVIII) of the Economic and Social Council on Procedure for dealing with communications relating to violations of human rights and fundamental freedoms.

[9] Article 1.4.

[10] Article 2.1.

[11] UN Declaration on the Rights of Indigenous Peoples, Art 1.

[12] H Ketley, 'Exclusion by Definition: Access to International Tribunals for the Enforcement of the Collective Rights of Indigenous Peoples' (2001) 8 *International Journal on Minority and Group Rights* 331.

Charter on Human and Peoples' Rights[13] and in both ILO conventions on indigenous rights. Finally, very few commentators will nowadays doubt the incorporation of the 'third generation rights' into the human rights system; these rights, including the right to self-determination, the right to development, the right to peace, the right to co-ownership of the common heritage of the mankind, the right to a healthy environment and the right to the culture of humankind, are all fundamentally collective rights.

States have not been the only ones to oppose collective rights; some authors have also doubted the desirability of these rights.[14] One of the arguments against the recognition of collective rights has focused on the moral standing of the group: according to this view, groups cannot be right holders because they have no morally significant interests. The indigenous paradigm has proven this to be a weak argument. The Declaration, a statement of states' values and beliefs, is full of references that recognise the value of indigenous groups. Paragraph 31 of the preamble notes that 'indigenous peoples possess collective rights which are indispensable for their existence, well-being and integral development as peoples'. Paragraph 10 of the preamble recognises the political, economic and social structures of indigenous groups, while paragraph 12 welcomes 'the fact that indigenous peoples are organising themselves for political, economic, social and cultural enhancement'. Therefore, the Declaration seems to back up Jones' statement that 'it is simple nonsense—nonsense upon stilts—to suppose that, if we treat individual persons as the ultimate units of moral concern, that must prevent us from taking full account of the communal dimensions of their lives'.[15]

Another traditional argument against collective rights is that their recognition is not needed, as individual rights enhance the development and flourishing of minority groups.[16] It has been suggested that most collective rights are essentially reducible to individual rights of the members of the group; the same result can be achieved through individual rights,[17]

[13] Arts 20, 22 and 24 for collective rights and Art 29 for the duties of the individual towards her group.

[14] A Kuper, *The Reinvention of Primitive Society: Transformations of a Myth* (London, Routledge, 2005); Y Tamil, 'Against Collective Rights' in C Joppke and S Lukes (eds), *Multicultural Questions* (Oxford University Press, 1999) 158; also see discussion in M Seymour, 'Rethinking Political Recognition' in A Gagnon et al (eds), *The Conditions of Diversity in Multinational Democracies* (Montreal, Institute for Research of Public Policy, 2003) 59.

[15] P Jones, 'Individuals, Communities and Human Rights' (2000) 26 *Review of International Studies* 199, 215.

[16] A Buchanan, 'Assessing the Communitarian Critique of Liberalism' (1989) 99 *Ethics* 852, 862.

[17] J Donnelly, 'Human Rights' in J Dryzek, B Honig and A Phillips (eds), *Oxford Handbook of Political Theory* (Oxford University Press, 2006) 601.

for example through the individual right to association.[18] Again, the indigenous peoples debate reduces the value of this argument. During the two decades of deliberations over the Declaration, it became clear that providing indigenous peoples with a system of individual rights would fail to protect them from the main violations of their human rights, because these include violations of a collective nature, towards indigenous communities as a group. Land rights, for example, do not have the same value as individual rights as they do as collective ones. If rights to indigenous lands are recognised as individual rights, then indigenous individuals can sell parcels of what is the homeland of the indigenous community.[19] One could argue that it is the free choice of any individual to sell his land; however, those rights are recognised to the individual because of his membership to the indigenous group and would not have been recognised as such otherwise. Ultimately, an individual system of protection would fail to redress the disrespect indigenous communities have experienced in relation to their identities. Insistence on such a system would put the maintenance and coherence of a liberal, individualistically perceived system of human rights above the needs of indigenous peoples around the world. Koskenniemi has recently warned against attempts to focus on the possible incoherence of international law, as they seem 'to assume that international law is an intellectual discipline that would (or should) pay much regard to logical problems'.[20] Indeed, insisting on an individualistic system of protection for indigenous peoples merely on the basis that collective rights do not fit with a prescribed version of liberalism would ignore the needs of these communities all over the world for the sake of intellectual coherence. It would mean submitting human rights to the oppression of a western jurisprudential viewpoint; and ultimately, this would not serve the quest for global justice.

The recognition of collective rights in the Declaration is important for indigenous peoples, but can also be of paramount importance to other sub-national groups. If the recognition of collective rights is seen as a natural progression of standards of international law, then the Declaration paves the way for the recognition of collective rights for minority groups. Jones supports the recognition of collective rights in the following two cases: first, when the title to a good has a collective form that cannot be divided into a number of rights held individually by the members of the group; and second, when the claim of the individual is not adequate to

[18] C Kukathas, 'Are there Any Cultural Rights?' (1992) 20 *Political Theory* 5.

[19] See eg S Hutt, 'If Geronimo was Jewish: Equal Protection and the Cultural Property Rights of Native Americans' (2003) 24 *Northern Illinois University Law Review* 527.

[20] M Koskenniemi, 'The Politics of International Law—20 Years Later' (2009) 20 *European Journal of International Law* 7, 8.

substantiate a right.[21] Jones gives as an example the right of minorities not to have their sacred sites desecrated, a right also pertinent to indigenous communities. This right, he notes, cannot be perceived as an individual right, as the sacred site is a special property of the group and desecration violates a right possessed by this group. The right of minorities to use their own language, he suggests, also cannot be seen as an individual right, as it involves rights that can only be exercised collectively. He uses the example of the minority individual's claim to have official documents in the minority language. The cost of realising such a right, which would include the translation to the minority language of administrative documents, court proceedings, tax forms and road signs, would exceed the benefit gained by the individual; however, the group's claim to such right can be substantiated as the benefits experienced by the group would justify the cost of realising the right.[22] Unfortunately, international standards have not yet accepted a collective right to language; the UN Declaration on the Rights of Minorities still recognises rights to 'members of minorities'. As Thornberry suggests, the limited collective dimension of the Declaration on Minorities 'represents a *via media* between the rights of individuals and full collective rights'.[23] The recognition of collective rights in the Declaration can act as a force to push for the recognition of minority rights as collective rights.

An obstacle to this may be the approach that indigenous rights are a 'special case', and therefore 'an emerging exception' to the otherwise individual focus of human rights.[24] Several states have pushed for the adoption of this approach in an attempt to stop any future 'spillage' of rights recognised to indigenous peoples into other sub-national groups. For example, in explaining its position on the adoption of the Declaration, the United Kingdom made the point that the right to indigenous self-determination is 'to be separate and different from the existing right of all peoples to self-determination in international law',[25] making a distinction between the indigenous right and the right for all others. More genuine seem the reasons why some commentators have also pushed for viewing indigenous rights as a special case: they believe that current international law cannot accommodate indigenous rights and restore their inherent rights. Charters argues that 'confining indigenous peoples' rights to extended interpretations of existing hard law instruments' rather

[21] Jones (n 13) 211–14.

[22] Ibid.

[23] P Thornberry, 'The UN Declaration on the Rights of Persons Belonging to National or Ethnic, Religious and Linguistic Minorities: Background, Analysis, Observations and an Update' in A Philips and A Rosas (eds), *Universal Minority Rights* (Leiden, Martinus Nijhoff, 1995) 13, 54.

[24] Donnelly (n 15).

[25] Statement made by the United Kingdom (n 5) 21.

than viewing these rights as 'emergent sui generis type norms, presents, ultimately, conceptual problems for the development of fairer indigenous peoples' rights norms into the future'.[26] She is convinced that current international law cannot accommodate indigenous rights; instead of trying to fit 'a square peg in a round hole',[27] she urges us to look at these issues more 'critically' and treat indigenous rights as a sui generis case.

It remains to be seen whether approaching the question of indigenous peoples as a 'special case' would help their rights. It seems to me that it may prevent them from being part of the whole human rights construction, with the values, principles and guarantees that this carries. I am also not sure that this would be consistent with the indigenous repeated insistence that their rights do not create new standards, hence their rights fall within existing current international law. In essence, indigenous peoples want to be recognised as equal partners in the evolution of the state, the evolution of the society and—why not?—the evolution of international law. Rather than being outsiders or on the periphery, they have in fact managed to become a cog in the machine that pushes forward international law. I am not sure why indigenous peoples would want to change direction.

CONFLICTS BETWEEN COLLECTIVE AND INDIVIDUAL RIGHTS: THE CASE OF INDIGENOUS WOMEN'S RIGHTS

Another important argument against collective rights relates to the conflicts that arise between collective and individual rights. During the deliberations that preceded adoption of the Declaration, several states expressed fears that the recognition of indigenous collective rights may restrict individual rights. For example, the USA noted:

> characterising a right as belonging to a community, or collective, rather than an individual, can be and often is construed to limit the exercise of that right (since only a group can invoke it), and thus may open the door to the denial of the right to the individual. This approach is consistent with the general view of the United States, as developed by its domestic experience, that the rights of all people are best assured when the rights of each person are effectively protected.[28]

[26] C Charters, book review of Alexandra Xanthaki, *Indigenous Rights and UN Standards: Self-Determination, Culture and Land*, (2009) 9 *Human Rights Law Review* 509, 516.

[27] Ibid, 517.

[28] See USA Delegation comments on section 1 of the draft declaration during the 1995 UN Working Group on Indigenous Populations (on file with the author). Similar comments are included in 'Consideration of a Draft United Nations Declaration on the Rights of Indigenous Peoples: Information received from Governments', United States of America, UN Commission on Human Rights, UN Doc E/CN.4/1995/WG.15/2/Add.1, paras 10–12.

Some authors have also noted that collective rights may lead to the oppression of indigenous individuals by their groups.[29] So far, academic literature has not looked at the rights of indigenous women from this perspective in any depth. The challenges that indigenous women face *outside their communities* have been discussed by the UN Special Rapporteur on indigenous issues, and indigenous women's rights vis-a-vis the state has been discussed in the Permanent Forum on Indigenous Issues. The Forum has

> expressed its concern about the multiple forms of discrimination experienced by indigenous women, based on gender and race/ethnicity, and the complex problems stemming from this discrimination. In addition, globalization presents new challenges and problems for indigenous women in many parts of the world. Indigenous women's roles have eroded due to the compounding factors of loss of natural resources and depletion of the ecosystems, their transformation into cash economies, changes in local, social and decision-making structures, and their lack of political status within States.[30]

However, little discussion has taken place with regard to the particular challenges that indigenous women face *within their communities.* Stereotypes, pre-determined roles for women and harmful practices negatively affect indigenous women around the world in a way similar that they affect non-indigenous women. In his 2007 annual report, Professor Yakin Ertürk, Special Rapporteur on violence against women, noted:

> [I]dentity politics and cultural relativist paradigms are increasingly employed to constrain in particular the rights of women. Essentialized interpretations of culture are used either to justify violation of women's rights in the name of culture or to categorically condemn cultures 'out there' as being inherently primitive and violent towards women. Both variants of cultural essentialism ignore the universal dimensions of patriarchal culture that subordinates, albeit differently, women in all societies and fails to recognize women's active agency in resisting and negotiating culture to improve their terms of existence.[31]

It is fair to say that the negative impact of some indigenous practices and stereotypes on indigenous women has been seen as a taboo by some

Similar views were expressed in the 1998 Working Group on Indigenous Populations; see Draft Report of the Working Group established in accordance with Commission on Human Rights Resolution 1995/32, Commission on Human Rights, UN Doc E/CN.4/1998/WG.15/CPR.1, para 40. In the same meeting, Japan and Sweden were also very negative about the establishment of collective rights.

[29] Kukathas (n 16) 113; also J Donnelly, 'Cultural Relativism and Universal Human Rights' (1984) 6 *Human Rights Quarterly* 400, 410–13.

[30] Report of the 3rd Session of the Permanent Forum on Indigenous Issues, UN Doc E/C.19/2004/23, para 3.

[31] 'Intersections between Culture and Violence against Women', Report of the Special Rapporteur on violence against women, its causes and consequences (Yakin Ertürk), UN GAOR, Human Rights Council, 4th session, UN Doc A/HRC/4/34 (2007), para 68.

indigenous activists and scholars; as Radcliffe confirms, 'gender issues remain secondary to the cultural politics of the indigenous movements, where the persistence of a complimentary dual model of gender underpins a traditional and symbolic role for indigenous women'.[32] Although viewing the experiences of indigenous women as a unified whole would be erroneous,[33] they are often, like women in many other communities, seen as carrying the honour of the community and, as such, they are encouraged to suffer in silence and put the 'wider rights of the community' above their own rights. For example, the Aboriginal Justice Inquiry of Manitoba identified bias in favour of the male partner in indigenous domestic abuse situations and criticised chiefs and councils for being unwilling to address the plight of women suffering abuse at the hands of their husbands.[34] Communities are reluctant to discuss issues of abuse and illiberal practices affecting women beyond their boundaries.

An issue that complicates matters further is the fact that States have indeed used indigenous women's rights as an argument to restrict or deny control of indigenous communities over their affairs. As mentioned earlier, during the process leading to the adoption of the Declaration, the relevant fora often heard states focusing on the possible violations that individuals could suffer at the hands of group power. Therefore, it is not without reason that indigenous activists have been reluctant to discuss the challenges that indigenous women face within their communities. In addition to the reluctance of activists to become engaged in these issues, some indigenous scholars have also been shying away from these issues, as they see the feminist discourse as 'inauthentic, un-indigenous and in other ways deeply problematic for indigenous peoples'.[35] It is argued that often Indigenous feminists have to challenge not only 'patriarchy within native communities, but also white supremacy and colonialism within mainstream white feminism'.[36] There have on occasions been differences in the agendas of feminist movements and indigenous women's movements; for example, the 1995 Fourth World Conference of Women in Beijing saw a 'contradictory and often conflictual relationship between

[32] S Radcliffe, 'Indigenous Women, Rights and the Nation-State in the Andes' in N Craske and M Molyneux (eds), *Gender and the Politics of Rights in Latin America* (New York, Palgrave, 2002) 149, 162.

[33] D Vinding, *Indigenous Women: The Right to a Voice,* IWGIA Document No 88 (Copenhagen, IWGIA, 1999).

[34] Report of the Aboriginal Justice Inquiry of Manitoba, Vol 1: *The Justice System and Aboriginal People* (1991), ch 13, 482–85.

[35] J Green, 'Indigenous Feminism' in J Greene (ed), *Making Space for Indigenous Feminism* (Canada, Zed Books, 2007) 14, 15.

[36] A Smith, 'Indigenous Feminism without Apology' 58 (2006) *New Socialist*. This issue can be found at http://www.newsocialist.org.

feminist organisations and female indigenous representatives',[37] as indigenous women were pushing for a different agenda from the feminists.

Moreover, some Indigenous scholars see the issue of oppression of women from within their cultures as irrelevant to indigenous societies, as they argue that sex-based oppression does not relate to tribal cultures, but derives from Western colonial influences[38] and stems from the hierarchical nature of Western society and its valuing of all opposites as good or bad. Indeed, since time immemorial some indigenous communities have placed a high value on women in their communities and women have enjoyed more respect and more power than non-indigenous in their communities.

The history of the Declaration on the Rights of Indigenous Peoples reflects the reluctance to touch upon issues related to women's rights.[39] Article 44 (initially Article 43) reads that 'all the rights and freedoms herein are equally guaranteed to male and female indigenous individuals'; however, this article was never really discussed in depth during the elaboration of the Declaration and was the focus of very little attention. Indigenous female representatives repeatedly said, when asked informally, that this was not the forum to discuss the issue. In addition to Article 44, Article 22 asks for particular attention to be paid to the rights and special needs of women and for special measures to ensure that indigenous women enjoy protection against all forms of violence and discrimination. This was a welcome addition to the final text.

On occasions, United Nations monitoring bodies have tried to touch on these issues. For example, in its 2006 Concluding Observations on Canada, the Human Rights Committee (HRC) expressed its concern about the discriminatory effects of the Indian Act against aboriginal women and their children in matters of reserve membership and matrimonial property on reserve lands and urged the state to seek solutions with the informed consent of the indigenous people. The HRC also stressed that 'balancing collective and individual interests on reserves to the sole detriment of women is not compatible with the Covenant'.[40] Also, the Permanent Forum on Indigenous Issues has repeated that 'the natural gender balance must be reinstated in culturally appropriate ways, within indigenous societies and beyond'[41] and special meetings for indigenous women now take place on the side of the annual sessions of the Permanent Forum.

[37] Radcliffe (n 30) 164.

[38] M Sunder, 'Piercing the Veil' (2003) 112 *Yale Law Journal* 1399, 1430; also A Smith, *Conquest: Sexual Violence and American Indian Genocide* (New York, South End Press, 2005) 18, 139.

[39] M Davies, 'The Globalization of International Human Rights Law, Aboriginal Women and the Practice of Aboriginal Customary Law' in M Cain and A Howe (eds), *Women, Crime and Social Harm* (Oxford, Hart Publishing, 2007) 137.

[40] Concluding Observations of the Human Rights Committee: Canada (2006), UN Doc CCPR/C/CAN/CO/5, para 22.

[41] Report of the 3rd Session of the PFII (n 28) para 3.

Article 9 of the Declaration recognises the right of indigenous individuals 'to belong to an indigenous community or nation, in accordance with the traditions and customs of the community or nation concerned', but specifies that 'no discrimination of any kind may arise from the exercise of such a right'. The historical discrimination that women of minority and majority groups alike have suffered is further highlighted in the UN Declaration on the Elimination of Violence against Women: in its preamble, the Declaration states that 'violence against women is a manifestation of historically unequal power relations between men and women, which has led to domination over and discrimination of men against women'. Discrimination against women, both direct and indirect, is also prohibited by Article 1 of the Convention on the Elimination of All Forms of Discrimination against Women (CEDAW). Article 2(f) urges States to take all necessary measures 'to modify and abolish existing laws, regulations, customs and practices which constitute discrimination against women'.

Many such practices and roles that affect indigenous women derive not from indigenous cultures as such, but from colonialism,[42] or are just attitudes that have developed among indigenous—and non-indigenous—persons. Violence against indigenous women, sexual assaults, and stereotypical roles of women seem to fall in this category. It is easy for the states to criticise these practices and to request their elimination from indigenous and non-indigenous communities; however, the states also have international obligations in this respect. Article 5 of CEDAW urges states to 'modify the social and cultural practices of conduct of men and women, with a view to achieving the elimination of prejudice and customary and all other practices which are based on the idea of the inferiority or the superiority of either of the sexes or on stereotyped roles for men and women'. States have to look at the causes and take measures to help the community eliminate such acts and perceptions. These measures certainly include socio-economic measures that would improve the situation of these communities, and measures to reverse feelings of non-worth developed over generations of colonialism. In the wider context the apology of Canada for the residential schools and of Australia for the Stolen Generations were viewed by some as measures falling in the latter category. Of course, in deciding the measures that will eliminate such underlying causes, the indigenous groups—and more specifically the indigenous women—affected by this must have the first say. The Declaration is clear that indigenous peoples must have control over the matters that affect them.

[42] For the link between colonialism and current violations of indigenous women's rights, see DA Mihesuah, 'Colonialism and Disempowerment' in *Indigenous American Women, Decolonization, Empowerment, Activism* (Lincoln, University of Nebraska Press, 2003) 41.

Unfortunately, sometimes such acts and perceptions derive from practices and beliefs inherent in cultures. Any revisions of cultural practices or decisions on how to assert the rights of indigenous women must first come from the indigenous group itself. Furthermore, deciding on the future of any practice that affects indigenous women must lie primarily with the indigenous women of the group, and this choice must be real. Richards has noted that 'even when indigenous women are physically present at debates about human rights, their unique positions are frequently marginalised by those who set the terms of discussion'.[43]

This is not the whole truth though. Often, indigenous communities have active indigenous female leaders and signs of women's involvement in debates on human rights are positive; the process leading to the Declaration and the successful transnational indigenous movement have brought to the light several strong indigenous women who were protagonists in this process and are assertive about the changes that need to take place in their own cultures. For example, Indigenous Asian Women has noted in the Baguio Declaration of the second Asian Indigenous Women's Conference:

> We accept the challenge and responsibility to address cultural renewal and revitalization to promote gender-sensitive values and structures within our communities. We note with concern that some modern changes in our traditional social, cultural and political institutions and practices have led to a loss of values and codes of behaviour which uphold gender-sensitive structures and roles, while accepting our responsibility to change other customary laws and practices which oppress indigenous women. We will speak up against abusive treatment of indigenous women in the name of custom and tradition.[44]

Elimination of all discriminatory acts and perceptions against indigenous women has to occur through dialogue primarily within the group. Who represents whom in this process of dialogue and change is fundamental. Ensuring full participation and real representation is a difficult task, and possibly one in which general rules do not always apply. Kukathas has pointed out the differences and conflicts of interests that may exist within any group. He notes that when elites are confronted with modernisation, they often develop distinct interests from the masses and in some cases they abuse the masses for personal ends.[45] Ensuring a multiplicity of voices, through political bodies, pressure groups, consultative bodies and party political influence, accepting the unstructured nature of this

[43] P Richards, 'The Politics of Gender, Human Rights, and Being Indigenous in Chile' (2005) 19 *Gender and Society* 199, 202.

[44] Baguio Declaration of the 2nd Indigenous Asian Women's Conference submitted in the 3rd session of the PFII (n 28).

[45] Kukathas (n 16).

process, and encouraging vulnerable members of communities, in this case women, to speak up can only create hope that the dialogue will be inclusive.[46]

It is important that the indigenous women of the group reach their decisions about the future of a practice without inappropriate interference. Unfortunately, as mentioned earlier, women who have the courage to criticise their communities are sometimes seen as betraying the indigenous cause and their authenticity as indigenous is questioned.[47] Similarly, it is important to respect their final decision, even if this goes against the 'feminist ideal', rather than label them as victims of culturally generated false consciousness in need of liberation.[48] Friedman sets a three-step test to determine whether individuals within groups are making their decision freely. First, they must 'be able to choose among a significant and morally acceptable array of alternatives'. Second, they must 'be able to make their own choices relatively free of coercion, manipulation, and deception'. And third, they must 'have been able to develop, earlier in life, the capacities needed to reflect on their situations and make decisions about them'.[49]

To this end, the vision of the Declaration that accepts the multiplicity of cultural frameworks that the indigenous individual enjoys is important: the Declaration views the indigenous individual as an individual and a member of the indigenous group; but also as a member of the state, other cultures and categories (for example women) and, of course, the world community; these loyalties are not seen as antagonistic, but as complimentary.[50] Hence, preambular paragraph 3 views all cultures as part of the common heritage of humankind. Article 5 recognises the right of indigenous individuals both to the indigenous systems and to the state system, and Article 33 specifies that indigenous peoples have the right to determine their own membership without this acting as an obstacle to obtaining state citizenship. Article 14 recognises the right of indigenous individuals both to the indigenous educational system and to language as well as the national educational system. In addition, Articles 21 and 22 recognise other specific categories of indigenous individuals, including elders, women, youth, children, and persons with disabilities.

[46] JT Levy, 'Sexual Orientation, Exit and Refuge' in A Eisenberg and J Spinner-Halev (eds), *Minorities within Minorities: Equality, Rights and Diversity* (Cambridge University Press, 2005) 172.

[47] S MacIvor et al, 'Women of Action' in Greene (ed) (n 33) 241.

[48] B Parekh, 'A Varied Moral World' in SM Okin, J Cohen, M Howard and MC Nussbaum (eds), *Is Multiculturalism Bad for Women?* (Princeton University Press, 1999) 69.

[49] M Friedman, *Autonomy, Gender, Politics* (Oxford University Press, 2003) 188.

[50] For more on this model see A Xanthaki, 'Multiculturalism and International Law: Discussing Universal Standards' (2010) 32 *Human Rights Quarterly* 21, 40.

This model emphasises common characteristics, rather than the possible conflicts that may occur. If these characteristics are seen not as antagonistic, but as complementary of each other within the same society that respects and celebrates the differences among groups, and if interaction among the various cultures is encouraged, it will be easier to instigate change. If the indigenous group is open to influence from several other frameworks, conflict can be resolved through a process of re-evaluation of the cultural practices by the group itself. The Declaration does not view indigenous cultures as stilted, but as evolving elements that influence and are influenced by other cultures. Being open to influence from both her own and other groups allows the indigenous woman to reach an informed decision.

At the same time, indigenous women must be able to choose to exit the group, should they feel restricted by its cultural values and practices. Kukathas places a lot of weight on the individual's right to exit, provided that the individual has an open market society to enter.[51] It is interesting to note that although Article 9 of the Declaration recognises the individual right to belong to an indigenous group, it does not explicitly also recognise the right of an individual not to belong to a group. Still, general instruments are clear on this: CERD Recommendation VIII (1990) notes that identification as a member of a particular group will depend on self-identification; this was repeated most recently in CERD Recommendation 32 (2009). The Human Rights Committee has also ruled that the individual can be considered a member of an indigenous group irrespective of whether the state sets other criteria for such state recognition.[52] Also, Recommendation 1201 (1993) of the Parliamentary Assembly of the Council of Europe proclaims that 'membership of a national minority is a matter of free personal choice', while Article 3 of the Framework Convention on National Minorities recognises that the 'every person belonging to a minority shall have the right to choose to be treated or not to be treated as such and no disadvantage shall result from this choice'. Although Article 9 does not repeat such a guarantee, the indigenous individual can protect himself from the group through Article 1 of the Declaration, which protects rights and freedoms gained 'under international human rights law'. In addition, all provisions recognising the need for prohibition of discrimination on the basis of race and ethnicity ensure that the individual will not feel under pressure to hide his or her ethnic identity and membership.

Unfortunately, the right to exit is not always adequate for the protection of indigenous women against oppressive methods of groups, as the basic conditions that would ensure such a right, also included in Friedman's

[51] Kukathas (n 16) 133–34.

[52] *Lovelace v Canada*, UN Human Rights Committee, Communication No R.6/24 (1981), para 14.

three-step test, are not present. If an indigenous woman has been denied respect for her identity, education, literacy, and the right to learn about the world outside the group, she does not really have 'a substantial freedom to leave because she lacks the preconditions' (knowledge and experience) to make 'a meaningful choice'.[53] Equally importantly, the right to exit puts the onus on the indigenous woman. It is the woman who has to leave and abandon her membership and group.[54] Ultimately, such a solution seems to sidetrack the problem as it maintains 'a systematic and structural problem'[55] within the indigenous group. For these reasons Spinner-Halev sets some minimal standards, similar to the Friedman test, that are needed to ensure that exit really is an option. According to him, 'these standards include freedom from physical abuse, decent health care and nutrition, the ability to socialize with others, a minimal education … and a mainstream liberal society'.[56] Unfortunately, these conditions are far from being fulfilled in many indigenous communities. As mentioned by the Permanent Forum, indigenous women 'often lack access to education, health care and ancestral lands, face disproportionately high rates of poverty and are subjected to violence, such as domestic violence and sexual abuse, including in the contexts of trafficking and armed conflict'.[57] The implementation of the Declaration pushes for the realisation of these conditions and in this way contributes to the improvement of the situation of indigenous women around the world. If these conditions are improved, then indigenous women will also be protected from becoming victims of persistent discrimination from within the group. In other words, contrary to their statements during the elaboration of the Declaration, the crucial role for States seems not to be in preventing any recognition of collective rights, but in contributing in the process of eliminating the conditions that perpetuate violations of indigenous women's rights.

Difficult dilemmas arise for the international human rights system when the group is not open to other influences or for whatever reason has taken the decision to continue the practice that affects women's rights. Also challenging is the situation where indigenous women consent to a group practice that deprives them of the core of their rights. Can

[53] W Kymlicka, 'The Rights of Minority Cultures: Reply to Kukathas' (1992) 20 *Political Theory* 140, 143.

[54] SM Okin, '"Mistresses of their Own Destiny": Group Rights, Gender, and Realistic Rights of Exit' (2002) 112 *Ethics* 205.

[55] M Malik, 'The Branch on which we Sit: Multiculturalism, Minority Women and Family Law' in A Diduck and K O'Donovan (eds), *Feminist Perspectives on Family Law* (Oxford, Routledge, 2006) 211, 215–16.

[56] J Spinner-Halev, 'Autonomy, Association and Pluralism' in Eisenberg and Spinner-Halev (n 44) 160.

[57] 'Indigenous Women: Analysis prepared by the Secretariat of the Permanent Forum on Indigenous Issues', UN Doc E/C.19/2009/8 (2009), para 1.

this consent validate the practice? Should the international community intervene and violate the indigenous group's control over the matters that affect them? Or should it stand by and continue to accept violations of human rights because the individual or the group in question refuses to acknowledge them? Coomaraswamy has noted that 'fighting prejudice against underprivileged groups while struggling for women's empowerment goes to the heart of the modern dilemma between the universalism of human rights and the particularity of cultural experience'.[58]

James Anaya believes that any assessment of a cultural practice must accord a certain deference to the group's 'own interpretive and decision-making processes in the application of universal human rights norms, just as states are accorded such deference'.[59] This would confirm the respect that the international community has for the indigenous group and its belief in the group's ability to solve any issue that occurs. However, most commentators disagree with this view and believe that in these cases individual rights must prevail over collective rights.[60] Madhavi Sunder urges the state's or international community's interference; she notes that many 'women argue that their governments—and the international human rights community—have improperly deferred to traditionalists and so-called cultural leaders' interpretations of private laws without taking proper account of modernising views'.[61]

Even though UN bodies have not often referred to these dilemmas, particularly as the monitoring mechanisms focus on states rather than groups, in general, some references appear to support the triumph of individual rights over collective rights in such cases. Also, the Universal Declaration on Cultural Diversity reads: 'No one may invoke cultural diversity to infringe upon human rights guaranteed by international law, nor to limit their scope.' This seems to imply a pre-determined hierarchy whereby individual rights always prevail over group rights. In 2001 the Commission on the Status of Women emphasised that multicultural approaches could reinforce 'existing power relations [between men and women] in marginalized communities', implying that in this case women's rights must prevail.[62]

[58] R Coomaraswamy, 'Identity Within: Cultural Relativism, Minority Rights and the Empowerment of Women' (2002) 34 *George Washington International Law Review* 483, 484.

[59] SJ Anaya, 'International Human Rights and Indigenous Peoples: The Move Towards the Multicultural State' (2004) 21 *Arizona Journal of International and Comparative Law* 13, 26.

[60] See eg R Alexy, 'Individual Rights and Collective Goods' in C Nino (ed), *The Ethics of Human Rights* (Oxford University Press, 1991) 163. Also MC Nussbaum, *Sex and Social Justice* (Oxford University Press, 1999), who is in favour of individual rights, *if* a choice has to be made. See also SM Okin, 'Feminism and Multiculturalism: Some Tensions' (1998) 108 *Ethics* 661.

[61] Sunder (n 36).

[62] 'Gender Perspective Needed in Development of Policies to Counter Racial Discrimination, Commission on Status of Women Told', Press Release, Commission on the Status of Women (2001), UN Doc WOM/1278.

Recent 'contextual justice theories' put forward by Parekh and Joseph Carens have discussed this dilemma.[63] Such theories aim to reconcile universal egalitarian principles of justice with claims based on identities and collectivities. Although framed within liberalism, contextual justice theories do not view universal principles—such as personal autonomy—as overriding principles that have to be accepted as they are, but suggest that adjustments may be needed in order to ensure that these principles accommodate collective identity claims. Adjustments must be tailored to the particular circumstances of each context. Some feminist authors have also agreed that to move away from universal claims on equality and to focus on a particular, 'western' understanding of equality would be detrimental to feminism; such foundations must be accepted albeit with a critical eye.[64] Therefore, in the case of indigenous communities, human rights foundations have to be respected, but seen within their cultural context.

Human rights law seems to endorse approaches that work towards the accommodation of conflicting human rights: one has to keep in mind that there is no hierarchy among human rights, apart from the non-derogable rights. Any conflicts between rights, principles and norms are generally solved on an ad hoc basis, after taking into account various considerations. Indeed, a pre-determined triumph of individual rights over collective rights would seem to be a rather simplistic solution, one that creates more problems than it solves. A system that recognises indigenous collectivities in the public sphere up to the point where these cultures are inconsistent with the dominant culture does not seem appropriate. A pre-determined hierarchy would ignore the indigenous voices pushing for collective rights, because of the perceived inconsistency of collective rights with western liberal theories. Such a direction would only harm the faith that indigenous peoples have put in international law for the protection of their rights.[65] The major challenge for the human rights system is to implement a fair way of preserving the core values of both individual autonomy and collective control.[66]

[63] B Parekh, *Rethinking Multiculturalism: Cultural Diversity and Political Theory*, 2nd edn (London, Palgrave, 2005); JH Carens, *Culture, Citizenship and Community: A Contextual Exploration of Justice as Evenhandedness* (Oxford University Press, 1999). See also AM Robinson, 'Would International Adjudication Enhance Contextual Theories of Justice? Reflections on the UN Human Rights Committee, *Lovelace, Ballantyne* and *Waldman*' (2006) 39 *Canadian Journal of Political Science* 271.

[64] S Benhabib, 'Subjectivity, Historiography, and Politics' in S Benhabib, J Butler, D Cornell, N Fraser and L Nicholson (eds), *Feminist Contentions: A Philosophical Exchange* (New York, Routledge, 1995) 107, 118.

[65] P Thornberry, *Indigenous Peoples and Human Rights* (Manchester University Press, 2002) 63.

[66] A Eisenberg, 'Context, Cultural Difference, Sex and Social Justice' (2002) 35 *Canadian Journal of Political Science* 613, 624.

The Declaration confirms the more ad hoc method of solving such conflicts by insisting that indigenous rights are firmly within the wider human rights system and, as such, subject to the same restrictions as other human rights. Preambular paragraph 1 links the Declaration with the 'purposes and principles of the Charter of the United Nations', while Article 1 links the text with the Charter, the UN Declaration on Human Rights and international human rights law. Article 46 notes that in exercising the rights contained within the Declaration, 'human rights and fundamental freedoms of all shall be respected. The exercise of the rights set forth in this Declaration shall be subject only to such limitations as are determined by law, and in accordance with international human rights obligations.' In making these decisions, the UN bodies have insisted on specific principles. In *Lovelace*,[67] *Kitok*[68] and *Länsman*,[69] the Human Rights Committee asked for evidence of a reasonable and objective justification for the prevalence of one right over the other; consistency with human rights instruments; the necessity of the restriction; and proportionality. It is argued that the complete neglect of one right—be it collective or individual—for the safe realisation of the conflicting right would in most cases violate the principle of necessity.[70]

Finally, the Declaration urges conflicts of rights to be 'interpreted in accordance with the principles of justice, democracy, respect for human rights, equality, non-discrimination, good governance and good faith'.[71] Hence, the Declaration highlights the existence of 'a wider circle', common values that are more or less common for the whole of humanity; Erin Kelly calls this 'international public reason'.[72] International public reason stems from the belief that the international community operates 'as a society of societies, with its own public culture and conception of public reason'[73] and is expressed in international decisions, including treaties, customary law, general principles, and soft law. Common values include the principle of non-derogation of some rights, such as the right to life and prohibition of torture; and also include *the core* of human rights, the essence of each human right. No cultural practices and beliefs can violate these values and no real adjustment can be made to these rights. This is clearly the position that the UN bodies have taken. Hence, 'family violence and abuse, [including] forced marriage, dowry deaths,

[67] Communication No 24/1977; Views in UN Doc A/36/40 (1981).
[68] Communication No 195/1985; Views in UN Doc A/43/40 (1988).
[69] Communication No 511/1992; Views in UN Doc A/50/40 (1995).
[70] For further discussion of these cases see Thornberry (n 63) 154–60.
[71] Art 46.
[72] E Kelly, 'Justice and Communitarian Identity Politics' (2001) 35 *Journal of Value Enquiry* 71.
[73] Ibid, 90.

[and] acid attacks' have been identified as unacceptable, irrespective of their being cultural practices.[74] These practices should be eliminated, even if they are viewed as an expression of particular cultures.

CONCLUSION

The Declaration on the Rights of Indigenous Peoples confirms the existence of collective rights in international law and hopefully puts an end to perceptions that the current international human rights system includes only individual rights. Apart from indigenous peoples, this recognition can also benefit other sub-national groups, if the case of indigenous peoples is not singled out as a special case. Arguments against the implementation of indigenous collective rights have focused on the possible conflicts arising with individual rights, and in particular women's rights. Several of the provisions of the text provide guidance concerning the resolve of these conflicts. It is accepted that the collective rights recognised are part of the human rights system; hence, notwithstanding their importance, when these rights violate women's rights, the indigenous group—with the active participation of the women of the group—should re-consider and re-evaluate such practices and stereotypes. As long as the latter do not attack non-derogable rights or the core of women's rights, and assuming this is what indigenous women choose, indigenous control over the group's values must be respected. At the same time, the Declaration emphasises the need for interaction and mutual influence of indigenous and non-indigenous societies and evolution of cultures. The Declaration presents a vision of indigenous societies where control over matters that affect them co-exists with dialogue both within and outside the community. It is up to indigenous peoples themselves and states to follow and implement this vision in a way that is consistent with human rights. States' particular responsibility is to improve the pre-conditions necessary to enable indigenous women and indigenous groups more generally to decide which such practices and perceptions will change, and to ensure that they have the adequate tools to change them. Measures for the improvement of indigenous socio-economic conditions, reversal of the effects of colonialism and respect for indigenous cultures are important in supporting such re-evaluations within those groups.

[74] 'Violence against Women', General Recommendation 19, UN Commission on the Elimination of Discrimination against Women (1992), UN Doc A/47/38, para 11. See also Declaration on the Elimination of Violence against Women (1993), UN Doc A/RES/48/104.

17

Community Rights to Culture: The UN Declaration on the Rights of Indigenous Peoples

JOHANNA GIBSON

THE DELIBERATE OMISSION of minority rights from the Universal Declaration of Human Rights (UDHR) is suggested to be the basis for the fundamental tension between individual and group rights. This historical background is critical to contemporary discussions of community rights to culture, particularly in the context of traditional cultural expressions and knowledge, as well as in the context of genetic and natural resources. With respect to traditional community knowledge and rights to culture, this primacy of the individual is potentially limiting. This paper examines international developments in the protection of traditional and indigenous knowledge, and the complex and, at times, discordant relationship between human rights protection and traditional communities. It will consider the impact of that original omission in the UDHR in the context of contemporary discussions of group rights and the right to culture, and the protection of community knowledge as part of the conditions necessary for an individual member of a minority to access that right. Indeed, perhaps the architecture for group rights to culture is necessarily the prerequisite for an individual's effective cultural participation.

Land and rights to land are necessarily relevant to community knowledge not only directly, with respect to access and management of resources, but also indirectly in terms of the knowledge embedded in the land and in the identity derived from the connection to land and nature. Indeed, legal frameworks governing native title claims and rights to lands have been invoked as possible mechanisms for the protection of cultural practices associated with the land. However, the success of such claims has been limited to date.

While the need to facilitate access to land as a resource for food and agriculture is clearer in international law, less attention is paid to land as a mechanism for the transmission of knowledge including that of traditional cultural expressions. In this respect, there may be some interaction between land rights and individual human rights to cultural life, in that the land itself may emerge as a mechanism for realising an individual's right to culture and to benefit from one's creative output.[1] Indeed, the recent Sixth Session of the UN Permanent Forum on Indigenous Issues (PFII) took as its theme 'Territories, Lands and Natural Resources' with its recommendations identifying distinct links between land and cultural rights:

> Land is the foundation of the lives and cultures of indigenous peoples all over the world. This is why the protection of their right to lands, territories and natural resources is a key demand of the international indigenous peoples' movement and of indigenous peoples and organizations everywhere. It is also clear that most local and national indigenous peoples' movements have emerged from struggles against policies and actions that have undermined and discriminated against their customary land tenure and resource management systems, expropriated their lands, extracted their resources without their consent and led to their displacement and dispossession from their territories. Without access to and respect for their rights over their lands, territories and natural resources, the survival of indigenous peoples' particular distinct cultures is threatened.
>
> Land rights, access to land and control over it and its resources are central to indigenous people throughout the world, and they depend on such rights and access for their material and cultural survival. In order to survive as distinct people, indigenous people and their communities need to be able to own, conserve and manage their territories, lands and resources.[2]

The question is not that of whether tradition as such may be the subject matter of a human right, but whether indigenous and traditional groups will be able to realise the right to benefit in a culturally relevant and appropriate way if that mechanism of tradition is not sustained. Interference with traditional practices relating to the land may be argued as unjustifiable interference with individual human rights. In that traditional relationships to knowledge and cultural expression generally speaking are articulated upon a relationship to the land, land ownership or guardianship is thus instrumental in recognising interests and achieving relevant and effective protection of traditional cultural expression:

> The image is associated with a place on Rirratjingu land called Yalangbara (which is at Port Bradshaw south of Yirrkala) and represents the events associated with the Djangkawu that took place there. My rights to use this image arise by virtue of my membership of the land owning group. The right to use the image is one of the incidents arising out of land ownership … Aboriginal art allows our relationship with the land to be encoded, and whether the production

[1] International Covenant on Economic, Social and Cultural Rights (ICESCR), Art 15.1(c).
[2] PFII, Report of the Sixth Session, 14–25 May 2007, E/2007/43; E/C.19/2007/12, pp 2–3.

> of artworks is for sale or ceremony, it is an assertion of the rights that are held in the land. The place, Yalangbara, and the particular story of the Djangkawu associated with it do not exist in isolation. They are part of a complex or 'dreaming track' stretching from the sea off the east coast of Arnhem Land through Yalangbara, across the land to the west of Ramingining and Milingimbi.[3]

Stewardship of the land thus gives rise to the traditional right to knowledge, and the use and dissemination of knowledge is characterised upon this relationship to the land. Significantly, relevant access to the land appears to be tied to the fundamental right provided in Article 27 of the International Covenant on Civil and Political Rights (ICCPR): 'In those States in which ethnic, religious or linguistic minorities exist, persons belonging to such minorities shall not be denied the right, in community with the other members of their group, to enjoy their own culture, to profess and practise their own religion, or to use their own language.' Land is a critical and contested zone in interpretations of the right to self-determination and indeed in the meaningful realisation of that right for indigenous people.[4] The UN Declaration on the Rights of Indigenous Peoples[5] articulates this relationship between land and knowledge as the mechanism by which to give effect to the right to self-determination—not as alienable property but as cultural archive, narrating and preserving the historical and cultural stories of the community through the land.

WHAT IS TRADITIONAL COMMUNITY KNOWLEDGE?

> The impetus for the creation of artwork remains important in ceremony, and the creation of artwork is an important step in the preservation of important traditional customs. It is an activity which occupies the normal part of the day-to-day activities of the members of my tribe and represents an important part of the cultural continuity of the tribe.[6]

Identification of knowledge holders depends upon a suitable concept of community as a legal actor. A suitable mechanism by which to identify,

[3] Banduk Marika, Indigenous Australian artist, speaking about the painting *Djanda and the Sacred Water Hole*, quoted in T Janke, *Minding Culture: Case Studies on Intellectual Property and Traditional Cultural Expressions* (Geneva, WIPO, 2003) 11.

[4] Land was raised as one of the more controversial areas over two decades of negotiations leading to the Declaration on the Rights of Indigenous Peoples (GA Res 61/295), 13 September 2007. In an official fact sheet, the PFII refers to the significance of the dialogue and the long negotiations, identifying land as one of the areas of intense debate. See PFII, Frequently Asked Questions: Declaration on the Rights of Indigenous Peoples, www.un.org/esa/socdev/unpfii/documents/faq_drips_en.pdf.

[5] Declaration on the Rights of Indigenous Peoples, adopted by General Assembly Resolution 61/295, 13 September 2007.

[6] Indigenous artist Mr Bulun, quoted in C Golvan, 'Aboriginal Art and Copyright: The Case for Johnny Bulun Bulun' (1989) 11(10) *European Intellectual Property Review* 346, 348.

negotiate with and return benefits to the community is necessary notwithstanding the legal framework within which that knowledge is being navigated. Of fundamental importance, interests of cultural and social integrity and indeed dignity, cultural identity, and political and economic interests are common throughout the groups involved. The relationship between the cultural diversity and identity of the group, and the integrity of the knowledge and its management, arguably underpins the entire body of development in the area of traditional knowledge.[7] Knowledge is produced and maintained, not as an end or a product in itself, but, rather, as part of the cultural activity and sustainability of a particular traditional and indigenous group.

A second unifying aspect for the communities involved is the actual exploitation of the resources outside the community. This includes cases of actual removal (for example: genetic resources and the bioprospecting for plants and related medicinal and agricultural knowledge; removal of cultural artefacts) or removal through cultural transformation (for example, the diminution of cultural value in a symbol through offensive use). Indeed, it is useful to recognise the practice of appropriation of resources in the context of colonial imperialism. This historical context has been identified as significant not only within legal practice but also by anthropologists and archaeologists advising upon appropriate and effective mechanisms for negotiation with communities.

Finally, there are common issues in the creation of rights in harvested or appropriated knowledge without reference to the context in which that knowledge was obtained. In other words, the ethical context for appropriation can be relevant not only to the creation of intellectual property rights (with international discussions considering prior informed consent and disclosure of origin as mandatory criteria), but also in recognising the autonomy of communities and achieving effective and successful negotiation and mediation with communities to the benefit of all parties.

COMMUNAL 'OWNERSHIP' AND CUSTOMARY PRINCIPLES OF ACCESS

The dominant discourse on traditional knowledge and its management is inextricably bound to notions of self-determination, cultural diversity and cultural identity: 'Late twentieth-century cultural politics make it impossible to separate issues of identity from claims to the ownership

[7] T Janke, '"Berne, Baby, Berne": The Berne Convention, Moral Rights and Indigenous Peoples' Cultural Rights' (2001) 5(6) *Indigenous Law Bulletin* 14.

of resources.'[8] This includes arguments, particularly in North America, for privacy as a property mechanism for the protection of traditional and indigenous relationships to cultural resources. But the application of privacy is quite limited in most circumstances.[9] More usually the concerns of indigenous and traditional groups are framed as battles of self-determination, (a group self or identity, as it were) constructed upon the issue of dominion over resources.[10] Therefore, human rights doctrine continues to provide an oversight for the negotiation of community knowledge through various legal frameworks and contexts.

The diversity of traditional and indigenous communal structures converges in the importance of familial, kinship and initiatory ties with respect to resources.[11] This is distinct from proprietary relationships to resources, but certainly does not preclude the relevance of commercialisation of resources for communities in ways compatible with the customary management of those communities. In other words, commercialisation is often relevant to such groups, but is in possible deference to earlier rights within customary systems of managing that knowledge.

Furthermore, rejection of 'ownership' as such undermines community knowledge claims in that it constructs such knowledge as natural, authorless, ownerless and part of the common heritage, in ways comparable to scientific and colonial imperialism of the eighteenth and nineteenth centuries. Therefore, the assumption of communal or shared ownership on the part of traditional communities is often an inappropriate simplification of customary systems and knowledge management.[12]

COMMUNAL PRINCIPLES OF IDENTITY

> The clan is like a cluster of trees which, when seen from afar, appear huddled together, but which would be seen to stand *individually* when closely approached.[13]

[8] M Strathern, *Property, Substance and Effect: Anthropological Essays on Persons and Things* (London, Athlone, 1999) 134.

[9] MF Brown, *Who Owns Native Culture?* (Cambridge, Harvard University Press, 2003) 38.

[10] See Indigenous Peoples Council on Biocolonialism (IPCB), 'CBD's International Regime: Indigenous Activist Organizations Call for No Access Zones to Genetic Resources and Indigenous Knowledge', Press Release, 4 February 2004.

[11] J Leach, 'Land, Trees and History: Disputes Involving Boundaries and Identities in the Context of Development' in L Kalinoe and J Leach (eds), *Rationales of Ownership: Transactions and Claims to Ownership in Contemporary Papua New Guinea* (Wantage, Sean Kingston, 2004) 42–56. See further the critique of property models undertaken by Rosemary Coombe in *The Cultural Life of Intellectual Properties: Authorship, Appropriation and the Law* (Durham, Duke University Press, 1998).

[12] See the critique of 'communal rights' in the context of Papua New Guinean communities in Strathern (n 8) 3.

[13] Akan Proverb, quoted in K Gyekye, *An Essay on African Philosophical Thought: The Akan Conceptual Scheme*, rev edn (Philadelphia, Temple University Press, 1995) 158.

The critical relationship between knowledge and community, and between communalism and individual cultural identity, underpins arguments for specific treatment of traditional knowledge outside the conventional intellectual property framework:

> If one is by nature a social being, and not merely an atomized entity, then the development of one's full personality and identity can best be achieved only within the framework of social relationships that are realizable within a communal social system. That is to say, the conception and development of an individual's full personality and identity cannot be separated from his or her role in the group.[14]

In this way, the traditional community management of knowledge, according to customary systems, is intimately linked to issues of cultural diversity, individual dignity and self-determination. In traditional and indigenous philosophies of communalism, as discussed in the previous section, the individual dignity and identity is derived from community membership. Indeed, this is one of the many reasons why suggestions of incorporation and other systems of hierarchising proprietary management are never entirely relevant to the protection of community knowledge. A community is managed by all its members, whereas a corporation displaces that engagement to nominated directors, in defiance of the differentiated management beyond simple linear corporate streams. Therefore, at stake are not only the possible group rights of communities, but also the individual rights to take part in cultural life and to benefit from creative output in the context of communal expression.[15]

CHALLENGES FOR HUMAN RIGHTS PRINCIPLES

The application of an international human rights framework to community knowledge is not necessarily seamless. Most importantly, the ability of human rights doctrine to deal with cultural groups remains uncertain in this area of legal scholarship. Nevertheless, human rights principles present significant potential for oversight of the negotiation of traditional knowledge within various legal frameworks:

> The imbalances in the intellectual property law system have been created and are sustained by established mechanisms of accessing the modern economic space and power. Indigenous and local people often experience insecure resource tenure, are financially weak, and lack institutional arrangements to safeguard their property rights. Thus, the issues extend to fundamental and more complex questions of human rights of the peoples.[16]

[14] Gyekye, ibid, 161.
[15] ICESCR, Art 15.1(c).
[16] J Mugabe, *Intellectual Property, Traditional Knowledge and Genetic Resources: Policy Options for Developing Countries*, WIPO & the National Intellectual Property Association of Bulgaria,

Criticism for neglecting the duty of respect for cultural diversity has been made throughout the literature on the construction of culture within human rights discourse.[17] Whether articulated through minority rights or indigenous rights, respect for cultural diversity is the fundamental obligation at the centre of the discourse on genetic resources, traditional knowledge and traditional cultural expressions. In this context, the varying approaches to group rights are problematic, and the disjunction between individual human rights and the interests of traditional and indigenous communities has genuine impact.

(a) Minority Rights

Although some commentators argue that minority rights are indeed human rights,[18] their development in international law is nevertheless built upon an original and deliberate omission of minority rights from the UDHR. This omission is premised on the notion that the right to 'culture' can be achieved by the individual and through individual human rights. Indeed, this presumes a uniform community as 'collective' as distinct from the highly differentiated groups involved, and potentially neglects the achievement of individual rights to identity and dignity through membership of the community, as discussed earlier.

Similarly, Article 27 of the ICCPR emphasises the 'individual' agent in human rights law: '… persons belonging to such minorities shall not be denied the right, in community with the other members of their group, to enjoy their own culture, to profess and practise their own religion, or to use their own language.' Although this provision appears to acknowledge the concept of group cultural rights they are articulated through the language of individual rights.

The UN Declaration on the Rights of Persons Belonging to National or Ethnic, Religious and Linguistic Minorities (Declaration on Minorities)[19] also maintains a similar construction of rights as individual and not as group rights. The very title itself—'Persons Belonging to'—makes clear that this Declaration concerns individual rights as distinct from recognising any rights in minorities as groups.[20]

International Conference on Intellectual Property, the Internet, Electronic Commerce and Traditional Knowledge, 29–31 May 2001 (WIPO/ECTK/SOF/01/3.1), 16.

[17] J Tully, *Strange Multiplicity: Constitutionalism in an Age of Diversity* (Cambridge University Press, 1995).

[18] J Morsink, 'Cultural Genocide, the Universal Declaration, and Minority Rights' (1999) 21(4) *Human Rights Quarterly* 1009, 1053–60.

[19] Declaration on the Rights of Persons Belonging to National or Ethnic, Religious and Linguistic Minorities, adopted by General Assembly Resolution 47/135 of 18 December 1992.

[20] See discussion of the debate concerning the title in HJ Steiner and P Alston (eds), *International Human Rights in Context: Law, Politics, Morals* (Oxford, Clarendon Press, 1996) 1297.

Access to cultural rights as individuals who belong to a minority group may be relevant to community knowledge in this context. Article 2 of the Declaration on Minorities provides for these individual rights to culture:

1. Persons belonging to national or ethnic, religious and linguistic minorities (hereinafter referred to as persons belonging to minorities) have the right to enjoy their own culture, to profess and practise their own religion, and to use their own language, in private and in public, freely and without interference or any form of discrimination.
2. Persons belonging to minorities have the right to participate effectively in cultural, religious, social, economic and public life.

Despite this emphasis on individual human rights, the state's obligation to maintain the circumstances necessary for an individual citizen to enjoy basic human rights may necessitate the protection of community knowledge as part of the circumstance necessary for an individual member of a minority to enjoy basic human rights to culture, as provided in Article 4:

1. States shall take measures where required to ensure that persons belonging to minorities may exercise fully and effectively all their human rights and fundamental freedoms without any discrimination and in full equality before the law.
2. States shall take measures to create favourable conditions to enable persons belonging to minorities to express their characteristics and to develop their culture, language, religion, traditions and customs, except where specific practices are in violation of national law and contrary to international standards.
3. States should take appropriate measures so that, wherever possible, persons belonging to minorities may have adequate opportunities to learn their mother tongue or to have instruction in their mother tongue.
4. States should, where appropriate, take measures in the field of education, in order to encourage knowledge of the history, traditions, language and culture of the minorities existing within their territory. Persons belonging to minorities should have adequate opportunities to gain knowledge of the society as a whole.
5. States should consider appropriate measures so that persons belonging to minorities may participate fully in the economic progress and development in their country.

A further motivation for those striving for international consensus on protection within the World Intellectual Property Organization (WIPO), Intergovernmental Committee on Intellectual Property and Genetic Resources, Traditional Knowledge and Folklore (IGC) is arguably the vulnerability of minorities within international human rights discourse. In particular, it is subject to ongoing debate whether there is any corresponding positive duty toward cultural diversity in that process.[21] However, most significantly, the question of group rights is a persistent challenge for recognition of traditional community 'authorship' and management.

(b) Indigenous Rights as Group Rights

Arguments for group rights in the context of indigenous human rights have been rejected as unnecessary (because individual human rights are sufficient) or simply outside the framework of human rights (on the basis of their collective nature).[22] However, the collective qualities of indigenous interests and rights continue to be emphasised by indigenous people when it comes to the development of international standards with respect to indigenous rights.

Notably, and in distinct contrast to the Declaration on Minorities, the Declaration on the Rights of Indigenous Peoples emphasises collective interests in its very own name. As discussed previously, the use of 'Persons Belonging to' in the full title of the Declaration on Minorities establishes that such rights are recognised as rights of the individual belonging to a minority, rather than minorities themselves. On the other hand, the UN Declaration clearly establishes its scope as that of indigenous rights as individual, group or collective rights. This emphasis on the collective nature of indigenous rights is continued throughout the UN Declaration.

Although the UN Declaration is not legally binding, its adoption by the General Assembly is nevertheless a significant influence in international standard-setting with respect to indigenous rights. Most importantly, Resolution 143 of the 42nd General Assembly (1987), 'Human Rights in the Administration of Justice', establishes an overarching commitment to human rights principles in the establishment of standards. This has been interpreted as an intention to harmonise standard setting in international fora, such that the preparation and adoption of any instrument in one forum of the UN must necessarily give effect to human rights instruments in the UN system. The intergovernmental committee discussions currently underway within WIPO, as a UN specialised agency, are therefore interpreted as necessarily bound by the principles of the recently adopted UN Declaration.

Furthermore, the negotiation of the UN Declaration is part of the historic significance of this instrument, being a genuine negotiation between

[21] See eg the report of the recent Fifteenth Session of the IGC, WIPO/GRTKF/IC/15, 12 February 2010.

[22] P Thornberry, *Indigenous Peoples and Human Rights* (Manchester University Press, 2002) 3–6.

the states and the beneficiaries of the instrument. Indigenous people were direct participants in the process and a pre-condition of its adoption by the UN General Assembly was its acceptance by a united indigenous peoples' caucus. The general agreement was that states would not pass a document that was not supported by the indigenous peoples themselves:

> Kofi Annan, UN Secretary General, has made a point of his mission in the last two terms, to 'democratize' the way the UN goes about its work. That is, leadership is firmly in the hands of the member states, as represented by their delegations, and that other voices—non-governmental voices, specialist voices, indigenous voices—also contribute valuable information in the fora of this institution. Here, in the development of this Declaration, is a case in point. We can all use this process as a model.[23]

(c) Right to Self-Determination

The principle of self-determination first appeared in the Charter of the United Nations,[24] and subsequently in common Article 1 of the International Covenant on Civil and Political Rights (ICCPR) and the International Covenant on Economic, Social and Cultural Rights (ICESCR) and in several other international instruments.[25] Despite this controversy and dissensus on group rights, the right to self-determination remains particularly relevant to community knowledge and is emphasised by indigenous peoples. Nevertheless, treatments of the right to self-determination have been inconsistent in international human rights law and scholarship.[26] However, the United Nations bodies regularly recognise the right on the part of existing states, adding weight to the right as a principle of international customary law.[27] Indeed, these provisions of

[23] C Mokhiber, Officer in Charge, New York Office of the High Commissioner for Human Rights, Panel on the United Nations Declaration on the Rights of Indigenous Peoples, 4 November 2006.

[24] UN Charter, Arts 1(2) and 55.

[25] Declaration on the Granting of Independence to Colonial Countries and Peoples, Arts 1, 2, 4 and 7, adopted by General Assembly Resolution 1514(XV); Declaration on Principles of International Law concerning Friendly Relations and Co-operation among States in Accordance with the Charter of the United Nations, Arts 1 and 3, adopted by General Assembly Resolution 2625(XXV), 24 October 1970, confirmed in 2003 in 'Promotion of Peace as a Vital Requirement for the Full Enjoyment of All Human Rights by All', Commission on Human Rights Resolution 2003/61, adopted 24 April 2003.

[26] R Falk, 'The Right of Self-Determination under International Law: The Coherence of Doctrine Versus the Coherence of Experience' in W Danspeckgruber and A Watts (eds), *Self-Determination and Self-Administration* (New York, Lynne Rienner, 1997) 47, 61.

[27] The Commission on Human Rights has voted in favour of the Palestinian people's right to self-determination, reinforcing the right within the United Nations system. See eg the adoption of Resolution E/CN.4/2004/L.8 at the 44th meeting of the Commission on Human Rights, 8 April 2004.

the UN Declaration were emphasised at the recent intergovernmental committee meeting in Geneva in the last week of February 2008.[28]

The relevance of the right to indigenous peoples is evident in its emphasis in the UN Declaration, but the right is not necessarily effective in the protection of community knowledge if the traditional management of resources is seen as challenging national interests.[29] Given that the link between international trade and intellectual property is one of the driving pressures on the work of the WIPO IGC,[30] it is unclear whether self-determination would be subjugated to questions of trade in the context of community knowledge.[31]

Notwithstanding these provisions for the right to self-determination, the problems of identifying those entitled to self-determination and indeed the nature of the principle itself persist, particularly in the context of traditional and indigenous communities. Again, the historical background clarifies its application, with some arguing that the right is applicable only in the context of decolonisation and is thus diminishing in relevance.[32]

The UN Declaration explicitly rejects this distinction. The recent adoption of the UN by the United Nations 61st General Assembly[33] comes more than 20 years after its production was first agreed in 1985 at the 4th Session of the WGIP. A working paper was tabled at the 6th Session of the WGIP, in 1988, with the final text agreed in the 11th Session, 1993. The draft was adopted by the Sub-Commission on Prevention of Discrimination and Protection of Minorities the following year and submitted to the Commission on Human Rights,[34] remaining in draft form until 2007.

Although the adoption of the Declaration on the Rights of Indigenous Peoples by the General Assembly is encouraging, as already mentioned the instrument is nevertheless non-binding and may have little immediate impact at the national level, given the historically almost uniform reluctance to adopt the text for 14 years. Indeed, this could be in part

[28] All documents from the 12th Session of the WIPO Intergovernmental Committee on Intellectual Property and Genetic Resources, Traditional Knowledge and Folklore are available at www.wipo.int/meetings/en/details.jsp?meeting_id=14802.

[29] S Wright, *International Human Rights, Decolonisation and Globalisation: Becoming Human* (London, Routledge, 2001) 153–54.

[30] WIPO/RT/LDC/1/14 (29 September 1999) para 10. See also WIPO/GRTKF/IC/4/8 (30 September 2002) 9.

[31] F Kirgis, 'The Degrees of Self-Determination in the United Nations Era' (1994) 88 *American Journal of International Law* 304.

[32] H Charlesworth and C Chinkin, *The Boundaries of International Law: A Feminist Analysis* (Manchester University Press, 2000) 152.

[33] Four countries voted against its adoption: Australia, New Zealand, Canada and the United States.

[34] Resolution 1994/45, 26 August 1994.

attributed to persistent 'colonial' suspicions of secession based upon the discourse of colonisation and race.[35] These anxieties regarding the recognition of self-determination can be seen in the interventions of those states voting against adoption: Australia, Canada, New Zealand and the United States. For example, Robert Hill (Australia) was reported as stating the following:

> Regarding the nature of the Declaration, he said it was the clear intention of all States that it be an aspirational Declaration with political and moral force, but not legal force ... The Australian Government had long expressed its dissatisfaction with the references to self-determination in the Declaration, he said. Self-determination applied to situations of decolonization and the break-up of States into smaller states with clearly defined population groups. It also applied where a particular group with a defined territory was disenfranchised and was denied political or civil rights. The Government supported and encouraged the full engagement of indigenous peoples in the democratic decision-making process, but did not support a concept that could be construed as encouraging action that would impair, even in part, the territorial and political integrity of a State within a system of democratic representative Government.
>
> On lands and resources, he said the Declaration's provisions could be read to require recognition of indigenous rights to lands without regard to other legal rights existing in land, both indigenous and non-indigenous.[36]

Arguably, however, the development of the concept of self-determination has continued beyond its foundations in nationalism and territorial capacity. Indeed, the notion of cultural self-determination is particularly relevant in the context of community knowledge and with respect to current developments in rights to culture and cultural diversity.

(d) Right to Cultural Self-Determination

Developments in minority rights to culture and participation have led to development of the concept of so-called third-generation rights to self-determination—the rights of internal cultural self-determination. Arguably, cultural self-determination will be somewhat more significant in the context of community knowledge in that it is specifically dealing with the rights of participation and culture fundamentally related to questions of traditional cultural expression and knowledge.[37] Internal

[35] Wright (n 29) 137–38.

[36] United Nations 61st Session of the General Assembly, Plenary 13 September 2007, GA/10612.

[37] Carlos Correa notes that the protection of traditional knowledge is compatible with accessing the right to self-determination, where such protection gives the community control over resources: C Correa, *Protection and Promotion of Traditional Medicine: Implications*

self-determination is explained as 'forms of self-government and separateness within a state rather than separation (so called 'external' self-determination) from the state'.[38] International self-determination therefore indicates customary self-government within the nation-state according to the general political structure of that state.

The Declaration on Minorities is relevant to internal self-determination, despite no explicit reference to self-determination in the text. Nevertheless, it sets out the principles underlying internal self-determination. However, again, the most significant and relevant text is that of the recently adopted UN Declaration, which emphasises and clarifies the right to internal self-determination regardless of the loss of territory and other pressures on the displacement and disenfranchisement of groups.[39]

(e) Cultural Relativism

Calls for sui generis protection on cultural bases have also been criticised as problematic cultural relativism.[40] Indeed, the history of cultural relativism is largely borne out of a rejection of the universalising tendencies of human rights discourse.[41] It is this universalist momentum which is similarly criticised by indigenous and traditional groups when examining the impact of intellectual property standards and frameworks upon traditional knowledge and cultural expressions. These same groups have reiterated the need for sui generis approaches if the spirit of the UN Declaration is to be realised and the right to self-determination of indigenous groups to be realistically fulfilled.

Article 4 of the Declaration on Minorities, discussed earlier, is especially relevant in the context of community knowledge, encompassing the relationship of knowledge to the facilitation of the circumstances in which the cultural values and practices pertaining to that knowledge are possible.

Nevertheless, Article 4(2) provides that the obligation does not arise where the expression of cultural characteristics would be contrary to national law and international standards.

for Public Health in Developing Countries, South Centre-Department of Essential Drugs and Medicines Policy of the World Health Organization, 2002. Correa suggests that '[s]uch control may be an element of self-determination and collective cultural sovereignty' (45).

38 Steiner and Alston (n 20) 1249.

39 See further the discussion in CE Foster, 'Articulating Self-Determination in the Draft Declaration on the Rights of Indigenous Peoples' (2001) 12(1) *European Journal of International Law* 141.

40 Steiner and Alston (n 20) 366–68. See further Thornberry (n 22) 7.

41 JK Cowan et al, 'Setting Universal Rights' in JK Cowan et al (eds), *Culture and Rights: Anthropological Perspectives* (Cambridge University Press, 2001) 27.

> States shall take measures to create favourable conditions to enable persons belonging to minorities to express their characteristics and to develop their culture, language, religion, traditions and customs, except where specific practices are in violation of national law and contrary to international standards.

In this sense, the nature of the qualification of culture is especially important. This is particularly relevant when considering gross violations of human rights, where an extreme form of cultural relativism may suggest that interference with such violations would be unwarranted. What is important is an appreciation of the culture at stake not as an undifferentiated product, but as a dynamic and social process. Cultural characteristics, cultural values and cultural practices thereby articulate aspects of the overarching achievement of the expression of culture.

This is precisely the position taken by the Special Rapporteur to the Sub-Commission on Prevention of Discrimination and Protection of Minorities at the 51st Session. On the impact of traditional practices on the health of women and female children, the Third Report stated: 'The Special Rapporteur feels it is essential to act with tact and patience, bringing the communities concerned to understand that their cultural values are not to be confused with cultural practices, and that the practices can be changed without adversely affecting the values as such.'[42]

In this regard, current scholarship on cultural identity and cultural diversity is immediately pertinent not only to the clarification of group rights in respect of knowledge, but also with respect to the nature of 'culture' within key human rights documents themselves. As Patrick Thornberry, member of the UN Committee on the Elimination of Racial Discrimination (CERD), explains, it is not always possible to partition values and practices in this way: 'If a particular practice is bound up intimately with a language, view of the world, creation myth, religious observance and social practice, it cannot easily be "detached" or "severed" from "the body politic".'[43] An understanding of the mechanics of cultural diversity within human rights law is therefore an essential part of community knowledge frameworks.

CULTURAL DIVERSITY AND CULTURAL RIGHTS

Article 15(1) of the ICESCR obliges the state to recognise the right of every person 'to take part in cultural life' as well as a right on the part of each person 'to benefit from the protection of the moral and material interests

[42] Sub-Commission on Prevention of Discrimination and Protection of Minorities, 51st Session, *The Implementation of the Human Rights of Women: Traditional Practices Affecting the Health of Women and the Girl Child*, E/CN.4/Sub.2/1999/14, p 17.

[43] Thornberry (n 22) 424.

resulting from any scientific, literary or artistic production of which he is the author' (right to benefit).[44] In a sense, the complete text of Article 15 encompasses not only the contribution to culture on the part of the individual, but also the sense of participation and 'benefit' flowing back to the individual:

1. The States Parties to the present Covenant recognize the right of everyone:
   (a) To take part in cultural life;
   (b) To enjoy the benefits of scientific progress and its applications;
   (c) To benefit from the protection of the moral and material interests resulting from any scientific, literary or artistic production of which he is the author.
2. The steps to be taken by the States Parties to the present Covenant to achieve the full realization of this right shall include those necessary for the conservation, the development and the diffusion of science and culture.
3. The States Parties to the present Covenant undertake to respect the freedom indispensable for scientific research and creative activity.
4. The States Parties to the present Covenant recognize the benefits to be derived from the encouragement and development of international contacts and co-operation in the scientific and cultural fields.

In this sense, intellectual property rights provide the mechanism by which individuals access their right to benefit. However, whether such rights are relevant in the context of community knowledge holders is an important aspect of the impact of this provision on developments in other international arenas, including the WIPO IGC.

In the preamble to the 2001 UNESCO[45] Universal Declaration on Cultural Diversity,[46] 'culture' is defined as 'the set of distinctive spiritual, material, intellectual and emotional features of society or a social group', encompassing 'in addition to art and literature, lifestyles, ways of living together, value systems, traditions and beliefs'. The reference to 'distinctive' indicates observable characteristics, values and practices which

[44] International Covenant on Economic, Social and Cultural Rights, adopted and opened for signature, ratification and accession by General Assembly Resolution 2200A (XXI) of 16 December 1966, entered into force 3 January 1976, in accordance with Art 27.

[45] United Nations Educational, Scientific and Cultural Organization. UNESCO is one of the original specialised agencies of the United Nations, established by its Constitution adopted in London on 16 November 1945. The purpose of the agency, as set out in the Constitution, is 'to contribute to peace and security by promoting collaboration among the nations through education, science and culture in order to further universal respect for justice, for the rule of law and for the human rights and fundamental freedoms which are affirmed for the peoples of the world, without distinction of race, sex, language or religion, by the Charter of the United Nations'.

[46] Universal Declaration on Cultural Diversity, 2 November 2001, (2002) 41 ILM 57.

distinguish the individual or group,[47] both marking out membership and facilitating membership through recognition. Further, the 2001 Declaration notes that culture is intrinsically linked to questions of 'identity and social cohesion, and the development of a knowledge-based economy'. From this, the importance of cultural diversity is clear, with diversity being valuable in and of itself to the broader society. Article 1 affirms cultural diversity as 'the common heritage of humanity': 'As a source of exchange, innovation and creativity, cultural diversity is as necessary for humankind as biodiversity is for nature. In this sense, it is the common heritage of humanity and should be recognized and affirmed for the benefit of present and future generations.'[48]

Returning to the discussion of Article 15, the UN Committee on Economic, Social and Cultural Rights 19th Session appears to emphasise cultural diversity as a value in and of itself: 'Article 15 of the Covenant could serve as an important antidote to the tendency to homogenize and iron out differences and diversity.'[49]

In this context, the value of that diversity is translated into real conditions of societal benefit. In the general discussion of the right to education, one speaker drew explicit links between cultural diversity and the right to education (Article 13):

> Mr Meyer-Bisch stressed that if a country did not enjoy the necessary financial resources to implement the right to education for all, it had the obligation to accept assistance from partners. He emphasized, though, that it was mainly the political price of the right to education for all, rather than resource mobilization, that frightened many Governments, since implementing the right to education presumed the provision of other, concomitant cultural rights, such as linguistic freedom, minority rights, cultural identity and access to cultural properties. The right to education could not be ensured without taking into consideration its important cultural dimensions. The right to education could be implemented more efficiently only by adopting more complex approaches than was currently the case, based on the recognition of all cultural rights.[50]

[47] Thornberry (n 22) 195.

[48] Universal Declaration on Cultural Diversity (n 46) Art 1.

[49] Committee on Economic, Social and Cultural Rights, Report on the Eighteenth and Nineteenth Sessions, 27 April–15 May 1998; 16 November–4 December 1998, Economic and Social Council, E/1999/22; E/C.12/1998/26, 4 December 1998, para 483.

[50] Ibid, para 482. See further the Report of the Committee on Conventions and Recommendations, 162nd Session, 162/EX/53/Rev, 10 October 2001. On Item 5.3 (on the synthesis of State Reports as part of the permanent system of reporting on education): 'A number of Member States emphasized that, in light of the present world situation and the recent events of 11 September, education for peace, human rights and democracy and the elimination of racism and prejudice is of utmost importance as it concerns directly the future of our societies, and should be at the very heart of the discussions during the 31st session of the General Conference. They stressed that today culture and cultural diversity should be taken into account when reinforcing education for peace, human rights and democracy.' This link is reinforced by the 2001 decision of the 162nd Session Executive Board of UNESCO to

In other words, relevant and meaningful access to cultural rights on the part of all citizens (and thus, the consequent diversity in cultural expression) provides the fundamental circumstances for aspects of human development, including effective and successful education. Thus, cultural diversity has a genuine economic dimension.[51]

COMMUNITY AND CUSTOMARY LAW

Customary law may be understood as the cohering organisation of community and a necessary mechanism for the sustainability of cultural integrity and identity, cultural diversity and participation in cultural life. The governance of resources according to traditional customary laws embodies the responsibility to tradition described earlier.

Customary law is the inviolable and integral law of a community established over the history of that community, critical to its identity, binding its members, and therefore also identifying and cohering the community: 'Customary laws and protocols are central to the very identity of many Indigenous, local and other traditional communities.'[52] Indeed, the legitimacy of the community inheres in its responsibility to custom and tradition as realised in the observation and practice of its laws: 'Maintaining customary laws and protocols can therefore be crucial for the continuing vitality of the intellectual, cultural and spiritual life and heritage of many communities.'[53]

Literally, customary law narrates tradition. The appropriation and reproduction of knowledge in ways contrary to traditional forms of governance and management will be contrary to pre-existing customary law. Therefore, there is a potential conflict of laws between customary law and other legal systems that may form the basis for limits to the exercise of the latter in certain circumstances.

establish the Joint Expert Group UNESCO (CR)/ECOSOC (CESCR) on the monitoring of the right to education, Paris, 27 November 2001, 162 EX/Decisions.

[51] This link between cultural diversity and economic and other conditions of value is also set out in the 2005 UNESCO Convention on the Protection and Promotion of the Diversity of Cultural Expressions. Art 2, 'Guiding Principles', states, 'Since culture is one of the mainsprings of development, the cultural aspects of development are as important as its economic aspects' (para 5: Principle of the complementarity of economic and cultural aspects of development). Further, in para 6 (Principle of sustainable development): 'Cultural diversity is a rich asset for individuals and societies. The protection, promotion and maintenance of cultural diversity are an essential requirement for sustainable development for the benefit of present and future generations.'

[52] World Intellectual Property Organization (WIPO), Issues Paper (Unofficial Draft Version 3.0), Customary Law and the Intellectual Property System in the Protection of Traditional Cultural Expressions and Knowledge, p 5.

[53] Ibid.

This is related to what has been termed the principle of locality, explained by the Chairperson-Rapporteur of the WGIP, Dr Erica-Irene Daes, as meaning 'every people's territory is unique and has its own laws'.[54] In other words, national governments cannot legislate with respect to traditional and indigenous knowledge, but must give effect to and enforce local customary laws. Dr Daes suggests that the basis for this principle can be found in the International Labour Organization (ILO), Indigenous and Tribal Peoples Convention[55] and in the Convention on Biological Diversity (CBD).[56] However, it can be seen that it is strongly linked to cultural self-determination and to the rights to culture and participation.

PUBLIC DOMAIN AND COMMUNITY-BASED DOCUMENTATION

The management of knowledge according to customary principles is directly relevant to concerns regarding the concept of the 'public domain'. This contested principle is not only relevant to the character of traditional knowledge within intellectual property frameworks, it is also, in and of itself, a site of negotiation over the very different and often conflicting approaches to knowledge. The 'public domain' is not irrelevant in a traditional context and indeed customary systems of managing knowledge often incorporate mechanisms which might be identified as a type of 'public domain', further demonstrating the important role of customary law in identifying appropriate framework for traditional knowledge protection.

As well as a site of conflict, the ideology and legal concept of the 'public domain' is of particular significance for community knowledge in that much of the effort for protection within intellectual property systems has relied upon defensive protection and utilisation of the public domain. However, this trend toward defensive protection has been criticised by indigenous and traditional groups, not only as an unnecessary delivery of community knowledge out of the management of the community, but also as a concept contrary to pre-existing community laws with respect to the governance of that knowledge:

> There is no public domain in traditional knowledge ... Even knowledge shared and used widely does not fall into the public domain. When knowledge is shared, it is shared among those who are trusted to know their roles and responsibilities in using the knowledge ... Misuse, even when used by others outside of the tribe, or by tribal members who are outside of the

[54] E-I Daes, *Defending Indigenous Peoples' Heritage: Protecting Knowledge. Traditional Resource Rights in the New Millennium*, Keynote Address, Union of British Columbia Indian Chiefs, 23–26 February 2000, 5.

[55] C169 Indigenous and Tribal Peoples Convention, 27 June 1989, (1989) 28 ILM 1382.

[56] Convention on Biological Diversity, 5 June 1992, 1790 UNTS 79.

> control of customary authority, can cause severe physical or spiritual harm to the individual caretakers of the knowledge or their entire tribe from their failure to ensure that the Creator's gifts are properly used. For this reason, misappropriation and misuse is not simply a violation of 'moral rights' leading to a collective offense, but a matter of cultural survival for many Indigenous peoples.[57]

Therefore, intentional documentation and publication of community knowledge is not without weakness, not the least of which is the actual conflict with the needs and interests of community knowledge holders.[58] In this way, mechanisms to ensure the status of community knowledge as knowledge in the public domain (such as prior art databases,[59] digital libraries,[60] and the concept of *domaine public payant*[61]) continued to be emphasised as effective and logical mechanisms for protecting community knowledge.[62] This defensive approach has been rejected

[57] Statement by the Tulalip Tribes of Washington on Folklore, Indigenous Knowledge, and the Public Domain, 9 July 2003. WIPO Intergovernmental Committee on Intellectual Property and Genetic Resources, Traditional Knowledge and Folklore, Fifth Session, Geneva, 5–17 July 2003.

[58] Nevertheless, defensive protection has emerged as the dominant mechanism within the IGC, in the context of dissensus on the need for sui generis rights.

[59] For example, note the Traditional Ecological Knowledge Prior Art Database of AAAS, which has met with much criticism. See also the discussion of traditional knowledge as prior art in M Ruiz, *The International Debate on Traditional Knowledge as Prior Art in the Patent System: Issues and Options for Developing Countries*, Trade-Related Agenda, Development and Equity (TRADE) Occasional Papers, Paper No 9, Geneva, South Centre, 2002.

[60] For example, the Traditional Knowledge Digital Library (TKDL) for Indian systems of medicine has met with both positive (see N Sen, 'TKDL: A Safeguard for Indian Traditional Knowledge' (2002) 82(9) *Current Science* 1070) and negative reactions (see D Sharma, 'Digital Library Another Tool for Biopiracy', mindfully.org, 29 May 2002; and KS Jayaraman, 'Biopiracy Fears Cloud Indian Database', *Science and Development Network*, 5 December 2002). For more on the TKDL see Commission on Intellectual Property Rights, *Integrating Intellectual Property Rights and Development Policy* (London, 2002) 81. See the extensive report on databases and registers undertaken for the UNU-IAS in M Alexander et al, *The Role of Registers and Databases in the Protection of Traditional Knowledge: A Comparative Analysis* (Tokyo, 2003). See also, for a discussion of concerns regarding documentation and misappropriation, V Tauli-Corpuz, 'Biodiversity, Traditional Knowledge and Rights of Indigenous Peoples', IPRs Series No 5, International Workshop on Traditional Knowledge, 21–23 September 2005, UN Department of Economic and Social Affairs, Division for Social Policy and Development, Secretariat of the Permanent Forum on Indigenous Issues, PFII/2005/WS.TK/5.

[61] The *domaine public payant* (paying public domain) involves the collection of funds from those seeking access to the knowledge within. Such funds would ordinarily be directed towards programmes within the communities of the traditional knowledge holders involved. See the discussion in D Gervais, 'Traditional Knowledge: A Challenge to the International Intellectual Property System', Fordham University Conference on International Intellectual Property Law & Policy, New York City, 20 April 2001, 13. See also G Dutfield, *Protection, Traditional Knowledge and Folklore: A Review of Progress in Diplomacy and Policy Formulation*, UNCTAD/ICTSD Capacity Building Project on Intellectual Property Rights and Sustainable Development, October 2002, 34.

[62] D Downes, 'Using Intellectual Property as a Tool to Protect Traditional Knowledge: Recommendations for Next Steps', CIEL Discussion Paper, November 1997. See also the discussion in AR Chapman, 'Approaching Intellectual Property as a Human Right' (2001) 35(3) *Copyright Bulletin* 4.

by indigenous and traditional groups as contrary to opportunities for relevant self-governance and self-determination with respect to that knowledge. In a recent Joint Statement to the 23rd session of the Working Group on Indigenous Populations,[63] the Indigenous World Association and Indigenous Media Network raised several concerns about the concept of the public domain and about the articulation of protection through the application of public and private databases:

> [W]e stress that there are striking similarities between seizing our territories and the taking of our knowledge by defining it as part of the public domain. Both are based on the notion that they constitute *res nullius*, the property of no one, and can be treated as such. Placing our knowledge into the public domain turns it into a freely available resource for commercial utilization. Thus, it also creates the pre-condition for using non-indigenous Intellectual Property Rights (IPR) regimes to patent 'inventions' based upon our knowledge ... We therefore strongly reject the application of the public domain concept to any aspect that relates to our cultures and identities, including human and other genetic information originating from our lands and waters.[64]

Once again, the links between contemporary community knowledge debates and colonialism are relevant to the question of the legitimacy (or lack of legitimacy) for such approaches. While defensive approaches are an aspect of mechanisms of protection, they risk an ongoing paternalism and persistent historicising of the value of knowledge.

CONCLUSION: LOCAL CUSTOMARY LAW AND INTERNATIONAL FRAMEWORKS

Indigenous and traditional groups have called for sui generis protection that recognises the customary laws of communities: 'Our existing protection systems are legitimate on their own right and any new mechanisms for protection, preservation and maintenance of traditional knowledge and associated biological resources must respect and be complementary to existing systems and not undermine or replace them.'[65] At the 12th

[63] Commission on Human Rights, Sub-Commission on the Promotion and Protection of Human Rights, Working Group on Indigenous Populations.

[64] Indigenous World Association and Indigenous Media Network, Joint Statement, Commission on Human Rights, Sub-Commission on the Promotion and Protection of Human Rights, Working Group on Indigenous Populations, 23rd session, 18–22 July 2005. Review of Developments pertaining to the Promotion and Protection of the Rights of Indigenous Peoples, including their Human Rights and Fundamental Freedoms: Principle Theme, 'Indigenous Peoples and the International and Domestic Protection of Traditional Knowledge', item 4(b) of the provisional agenda, 13 July 2005, E/CN.4/Sub.2/AC.4/2005/CRP. 3.

[65] Indigenous Peoples Council on Biocolonialism, Collective Statement of Indigenous Peoples on the Protection of Indigenous Knowledge, agenda item 49(e): Culture. PFII, Third Session, New York, 10–21 May 2004.

Session of the WIPO IGC in February 2008, advocates of sui generis protection argued that the passage of the UN Declaration provides significant support and foundation for this approach.

The basis for the recognition of customary law can be found in several international instruments and sources with respect to distinct issues,[66] resulting in a multilateral justification for deference to customary law with respect to community knowledge as identified in those separate and operable issues. Although this amounts to recognition of customary law in each case, these disparate approaches may undermine the potential for cooperation within the WIPO IGC in the form of sui generis protection.

Significantly, however, the creation and exercise of conventional intellectual property rights may be subject to pre-existing customary laws and communal rights of the relevant community. Such rights may indeed impact upon the exercise of intellectual property rights (including the exclusion of non-traditional use) with repercussions for failure to observe these pre-existing laws. Indeed, membership of various intellectual property conventions does not oblige an intellectual property holder to act contrary to other laws. For example, in the context of Article 17 of the Berne Convention, the WIPO IGC notes that 'in the event that customary laws were to be recognized for this purpose by a country's laws, copyright does not entitle or oblige a traditional artist to act contrary to his or her customary responsibilities'.[67] Nevertheless, the relevance of such provisions necessarily rests upon the national government's recognition of customary laws, which is in doubt given the history of the troubled passage of the UN Declaration. Indeed, it rests upon the significance vested in the principle of locality and its current development within international law.

[66] Regard for customary law is set out in several international instruments, including ILO Convention 169, Art 8, which refers explicitly to customary law, and builds upon ILO Convention 107 on Indigenous and Tribal Populations, which makes similar provision in Art 7. The right to self-determination, is provided for in the ICCPR and ICESCR in Art 1 of each instrument, the Declaration on the Right to Development in the preamble, and Arts 1 and 5; and the Vienna Declaration on Human Rights and Programme of Action in Art 2. The United Nations Draft Declaration on the Rights of Indigenous Peoples is explicit in Art 9.

[67] WIPO/GRTKF/IC/4/3 (20 October 2002), 23.

Section D

Regional Perspectives

18

The Inter-American System and the UN Declaration on the Rights of Indigenous Peoples: Mutual Reinforcement

LUIS RODRÍGUEZ-PINERO

INTRODUCTION

THE AMERICAN REGION has played a major role in the configuration of the modern international regime on the rights of indigenous peoples. From the 1940s, American republics—and Latin American countries in particular—were the locus of conceptual reflection and policy innovation that set the basis for this regime, including the adoption of the first modern international instrument concerning specifically indigenous peoples, International Labour Organization (ILO) Convention 107.[1] Throughout the 1990s, Latin America regained international leadership in the affirmation of indigenous peoples' rights, with a massive ratification of a new ILO instrument, Convention 169,[2]

[1] International Labour Organization (ILO) Convention concerning the protection and integration of indigenous, tribal and semi-tribal populations in independent countries (No 107), adopted 26 May 1957 by the General Conference of the ILO at its 40th session, entered into forced 2 June 1959. An account of the historical role of Latin American countries in the articulation of the modern international legal regime concerning the rights of indigenous peoples can be found in L Rodríguez-Piñero, *Indigenous Peoples, Postcolonialism, and International Law: The ILO Regime (1919–1989)* (Oxford University Press, 2005). See also L Rodríguez-Piñero, 'La internacionalización de los derechos indígenas en América Latina: ¿el fin de un ciclo?' in S Martí i Puig (ed), *Pueblos indígenas y política en América Latina* (Barcelona, Bellaterra-Cidob, 2007). For the evolution of international policy paradigms regarding indigenous peoples during the 20th century, see generally R Nizen, *The Origins of Indigenism: Human Rights and the Politics of Identity* (Berkeley, California University Press, 2004); C Tennant, 'International Institutions and the International Legal Literature from 1945–1993' (1994) 16 *Human Rights Quarterly* 7.

[2] ILO Convention concerning indigenous and tribal peoples in independent countries (No 169), adopted 27 June 1989 by the General Conference of the ILO at its 76th session, entered into force 5 September 1991.

which prompted a wave of constitutional and legal reform under the paradigm of a new 'multicultural constitutionalism'.[3] A similar leading role was taken on by Latin American countries in the last phases of the standard-setting process leading to the adoption of the UN Declaration of the Rights of Indigenous Peoples ('the Declaration'), as well as ensuing discussions regarding its implementation.[4]

Over the course of the last decade, the Inter-American human rights system, the regional human rights system of the Organization of American States (OAS), has followed suit and reinforced international and domestic developments concerning the rights of indigenous peoples in the region. In so doing, the jurisprudence of the system's two major bodies, the Inter-American Commission and the Court, have become a point of reference at the international level concerning the elaboration of the minimum content of indigenous peoples' rights in key areas, starting with the definitive endorsement of indigenous collective rights in the Court's decision in *Awas Tingni*.[5] This jurisprudence has in turn provided a major source of authority for ongoing discussions concerning the adoption of an OAS instrument on the rights of indigenous peoples, a regional counterpart to the Declaration.

The objective of this chapter is to analyse the impact of the adoption of the Declaration on the action of the Inter-American human rights system in relation to the rights of indigenous peoples. The chapter first reviews the jurisprudence of the Inter-American human rights bodies with a

[3] For a discussion of the paradigm of 'multicultural constitutionalism', see D Lee Van Cott, *The Friendly Liquidation of the Past: The Politics of Diversity in Latin America* (University of Pittsburgh Press, 2002). Other works of reference on the recognition of indigenous peoples' rights in Latin American include W Assies, G Van de Haar and AJ Hoekema (eds), *The Challenge of Diversity: Indigenous People and Reform of State in Latin America* (Amsterdam, Thela Thesis, 2001); B Clavero, *Ama llunku, Abya Yala, constituyencia indígena y código ladino por América* (Madrid, Centro de Estudios Políticos y Constitucionales, 2000); B Clavero, *Derecho indígena y cultura constitucional en América Latina* (Mexico, Siglo XXI Editores, 1994); R Sieder (ed), *Multiculturalism in Latin America: Indigenous Rights, Diversity and Democracy* (London, Palgrave, 2002); R Stavenhagen, *Derecho indígena y derechos humanos en América Latina* (Mexico City, Instituto Interamericano de Derechos Humanos and El Colegio de México, 1988); R Stavenhagen and D Iturralde (eds), *Entre la ley y la costumbre: El derecho consuetudinario indígena en América Latina* (Mexico City, Instituto Indigenista Interamericano, Instituto Interamericano de Derechos Humanos, 1990). The regional dimension of the indigenous movement in Latin America is explored in A Brysk, *From Tribal Village to Global Village: Indian Rights and International Relations in Latin America* (Palo Alto, Stanford University Press, 2000).

[4] United Nations Declaration on the Rights of Indigenous Peoples, adopted by General Assembly Resolution 61/295 on 13 September 2007. A complete account of the final period of negotiations leading to the adoption of the Declaration can be found in M Åhrén, 'The UN Declaration on the Rights of Indigenous Peoples—How was it Adopted and Why is it Significant?' (2007) 4 *Gáldu Čála—Journal of Indigenous Peoples' Rights* 84.

[5] *Awas Tingni Mayagna (Sumo) Community v Nicaragua* (Merits, Reparations and Costs), judgment of 31 August 2001, IACHR, Series C, No 79 (2001).

view to identifying the interaction between this jurisprudence and the Declaration's human rights standards. The chapter goes on to provide an analysis of the first decision by the Inter-American Court following the formal adoption of the Declaration, *Saramaka v Suriname*, identifying the potential role of the OAS system in operationalising indigenous rights norms. By way of conclusion, the chapter examines the parallel articulation of the Inter-American jurisprudence and the standard-setting process at the OAS level concerning an American Declaration on the Rights of Indigenous Peoples, as well as the prospects of this process following the adoption of the UN instrument.

THE '*AWAS TINGNI* EFFECT'

The bodies of the Inter-American human rights system, including the Inter-American Commission, which performs monitoring functions with regard to Member States of OAS, and the Inter-American Court, with adjudicatory powers in relation to those Member States that have accepted its jurisdiction,[6] have elaborated in recent years a fairly advanced jurisprudence regarding the rights of indigenous peoples.[7] This jurisprudence has tackled issues particularly relevant to indigenous peoples under various provisions of two major normative instruments of the system, the 1948 American Declaration on the Rights and Duties of Man, and the 1969 American Convention on Human Rights ('the American Convention').[8]

[6] For general overviews of the legal and institutional framework of the Inter-American human rights system, see generally DJ Harris and S Livingstone (eds), *The Inter-American System of Human Rights* (Oxford, Clarendon Press, 1998); H Faúndez Ledesma, *El sistema interamericano de protección de los derechos humanos* (San José de Costa Rica, Instituto Interamericano de Derechos Humanos, 1992).

[7] See SJ Anaya and RA Williams, Jr, 'The Protection of Indigenous Peoples' Rights over Lands and Natural Resources under the Inter-American Human Rights System' (2001) 15 *Harvard Human Rights Journal* 33; F Mackay, *A Guide to Indigenous Peoples' Rights in the Inter-American Human Rights System* (Copenhagen, IWGIA, 2002); I Madariaga Cuneo, 'Los derechos de los pueblos indígenas y el sistema interamericano de derechos humanos' (2005) 22 *Arizona Journal of International and Comparative Law* 53; JM Pasqualucci, 'The Evolution of International Indigenous Rights in the Inter-American Human Rights System' (2006) 6 *Human Rights Law Review* 1; L Rodríguez-Piñero, 'El sistema interamericano de derechos humanos y los pueblos indígenas' in M Berraondo (coord), *Pueblos indígenas y derechos humanos* (Bilbao, Universidad de Deusto, 2006). An institutional review of the case law and resolutions of the Inter-American Commission (IACHR) relevant to the rights of indigenous peoples was published in 2000, as a special report of the Commission. See IACHR, *The Human Rights Situation of the Indigenous People in the Americas*, OAS Doc OEA/Ser.L/V/II.108, Doc 62 (20 October 2000).

[8] American Declaration on the Rights and Duties of Man, adopted at the 9th International American Conference in Bogotá (Colombia), April 1948; American Convention on Human Rights, adopted 22 November 1969 in San José de Costa Rica, Inter-American Specialized Conference on Human Rights, entered into force 22 November 1978.

While the situation of indigenous peoples in the Americas has been on the agenda of the Inter-American Commission on Human Rights since the early 1970s,[9] it was only following the Inter-American Court's landmark decision in *Awas Tingni*, in 2001, that a distinct body of jurisprudence regarding indigenous peoples' rights began to take shape. The *Awas Tingni* case originated with the Nicaraguan Government's grant of a logging concession to a transnational company in lands traditionally used and occupied by the small indigenous community of Awas Tingni, without consulting the community and without its consent. The legal argument raised in this case was Nicaragua's claim that, in the absence of a formal title deed, the community had no formal entitlement over their traditional lands.[10] The community's lead counsel, the current UN Special Rapporteur on the situation of human rights and fundamental freedoms of indigenous people, S James Anaya, successfully argued that the right to property under the American Convention should also uphold indigenous title as emanating from indigenous customary law.[11] The Court endorsed

[9] As early as 1972, the Inter-American Commission adopted a resolution on the issue of 'Special Protection for Indigenous Populations. Action to Combat Racism and Racial Discrimination', where it affirmed that 'for historical reasons and because of moral and humanitarian principles, special protection for indigenous populations constitutes a sacred commitment of the states'. Quoted in IACHR (n 7) 21–25. For a critical review of the early activities of the IACHR with regard to indigenous peoples, see S Davis, 'Land Rights and Indigenous Peoples: The Role of the Inter-American Commission on Human Rights' (1988) *Cultural Survival Report* no 29.

[10] For an overview of the proceedings in the *Awas Tingni* case and an analysis of the Court's jurisprudence in this case, see ML Acosta Castellón, *El derecho de los pueblos indígenas al aprovechamiento sostenible de sus bosques: El caso de la comunidad Mayangna (Sumo) de Awas Tingni* (Managua, URACCAN-Editarte, 2004); SJ Anaya and C Grossman, 'The *Case of Awas Tingni v Nicaragua*: A New Step in the International Law of Indigenous Peoples' (2002) 19 *Arizona Journal of International and Comparative Law* 8; M Berraondo, 'El caso Awas Tingi: una esperanza ambiental indígena' in F Gómez (comp), *El caso Awas Tingni: nuevos horizontes para los derechos de los pueblos indígenas* (Bilbao, Universidad de Deusto, 2003); M Davis, 'The Awas Tingni decision: *Case of the Mayagna (Sumo) Awas Tingni Community v The Republic of Nicaragua*' (2002) *Indigenous Law Bulletin* 43, www.austlii.edu.au/au/journals/ILB/2002/43.html; L Rodríguez-Piñero, 'El Caso Awas Tingni y la norma internacional de derecho de propiedad indígena' in F Mariño and Daniel Oliva (eds), *Avances en la protección de los derechos de los pueblos indígenas* (Madrid, Dykinson, 2004).

[11] The original petition before the IACHR, along with an analysis of the initial proceedings of the case, is reproduced in SJ Anaya, 'The Awas Tingni petition to the Inter-American Commission on Human Rights: Indigenous Lands, Loggers and Government Neglect in Nicaragua' (1996) 9 *St Thomas Law Review* 157. The complete collection of legal pleas to the Court and the transcripts of the hearing on the merits, along with other relevant documentation, is reproduced in (2002) 19 *Arizona Journal of International and Comparative Law*. The original documentation (in Spanish) can be found in Felipe Gómez (comp), *El caso Awas Tingni: nuevos horizontes para los derechos de los pueblos indígenas* (Bilbao, Universidad de Deusto, 2003). For additional background information and legal materials on the case, see SJ Anaya and ST Crider, 'Indigenous Peoples, the Environment, and Commercial Forestry in Developing Countries: The Case of Awas Tingni, Nicaragua' (1996) 18 *Human Rights Quarterly* 345; SJ Anaya and T Macdonald, 'Demarcating Indigenous Territories in Nicaragua: The Case of Awas Tingni' 19 *Cultural Survival Quarterly* 69; Anaya and Williams

this argument, finding Nicaragua in violation of the right to property and other related provisions of the American Convention. It ordered the State to compensate the community, including by demarcating and titling its traditional lands.[12]

The Court's obiter dicta in *Awas Tingni* provided the first comprehensive statement of indigenous peoples' rights in the Inter-American system. Mixing legal reasoning with a somewhat romanticised anthropological depiction of indigenous cultures, the Court affirmed that:

> Among indigenous peoples there is a communitarian tradition regarding a communal form of collective property of the land, in the sense that ownership of the land is not centered on an individual but rather on the group and its community. Indigenous groups, by the fact of their very existence, have the right to live freely in their own territory; the close ties of indigenous people with the land must be recognized and understood as the fundamental basis of their cultures, their spiritual life, their integrity, and their economic survival. For indigenous communities, relations to the land are not merely a matter of possession and production but a material and spiritual element which they must fully enjoy, even to preserve their cultural legacy and transmit it to future generations.[13]

The Court expressly grounded aboriginal land title on indigenous customary law, and linked it to a positive State obligation to recognise indigenous land tenure through demarcation: 'Indigenous peoples' customary law must be especially taken into account for the purpose of this analysis … As a result of customary practices, possession of the land should suffice for indigenous communities lacking real title to property of the land to obtain official recognition of that property, and for consequent registration.'[14]

The Court's judgment in *Awas Tingni* was unprecedented in many ways. It was the 'first legally binding decision by an international tribunal to uphold the collective land and resource rights of indigenous peoples by an international body with formal adjudicatory powers'.[15] Moreover, the decision was unprecedented in its elaboration of a canon of interpretation of the American Convention on Human Rights that comprises distinct standards for indigenous peoples.

As distinct to the International Covenant on Civil and Political Rights (ICCPR), the American Convention, drafted in the spirit of the most

(n 7) (a summary of an amicus brief presented to the Inter-American Court in this case); P Macklem and E Morgan, 'Indigenous Rights in the Inter-American System: The Amicus Brief of the Assembly of First Nations in *Awas Tingni v Republic of Nicaragua*' (2000) 22 *Human Rights Quarterly* 569.

[12] *Awas Tingni* (n 5) para 173.
[13] Ibid, para 149.
[14] Ibid, para 151.
[15] Anaya and Grossman (n 10) 2.

classic American liberal tradition, does not include any specific provision regarding the rights of minority groups or other specific segment of the population. In interpreting the Convention in the context of indigenous peoples, the Court does not have an easy entry-point as in Article 27 ICCPR (rights of persons belonging to national, religious or ethnic minorities), which has opened up the possibility of a specific body of interpretation by the Human Rights Committee with regard to indigenous peoples.[16] The limited language of the Convention, linked to a inherited civilistic legal culture of the Inter-American system, explains why the indigenous cases dealt with by the Commission prior to *Awas Tingni* were limited to violations of individual rights or, in more limited instances, to economic, social and cultural rights.[17] Such limited focus is reflected, for instance, in the Commission's hurried conclusions in the *Miskito* case, in the late 1980s, where the Commission concluded that: 'in the current status of international law the claim is supported only with respect to the preservation of their culture, practice of their religion and the use of their own language, but it does not include the right to self-determination or political autonomy.'[18]

In *Awas Tingni*, the Court reset the Inter-American system's approach to indigenous issues, gearing it towards an 'an evolutionary interpretation of international instruments for the protection of human rights'.[19] Through this 'evolutionary interpretation', the Court implicitly endorsed developing understandings in international and comparative law, to conclude that the Inter-American system should provide a particularised protection for the rights of indigenous peoples by reason of their social and cultural specificities. This approach allowed the Court in this case to interpret the right to property provision of the American Convention—couched in the most classic Western tradition of 'private property'—to incorporate the collective and cultural dimensions of indigenous communal property in a way that would surely have shocked the liberal minds of the Convention's original drafters.[20]

[16] On the jurisprudence of the Human Rights Committee regarding the rights of indigenous peoples under the International Covenant on Civil and Political Rights, see inter alia B Clavero, 'Lovelace Versus Canada: Indigenous Rights Versus Constitutional Culture' (1999) 10 *Law and Anthropology: International Yearbook of Legal Anthropology* 1; D McGoldrick, 'Canadian Indians, Cultural Rights and the Human Rights Committee' (1991) 40 *International and Comparative Law Quarterly* 658; M Scheinin, 'The Right to Self-Determination under the Covenant on Civil and Political Rights' in P Aikio and M Scheinin (eds), *Operationalizing the Right of Indigenous Peoples to Self-determination* (Åbo, Åbo Academy, 2000) 179–202.

[17] See in particular Report on the Situation of Human Rights of a Segment of the Nicaraguan Population of Miskito Origin, OEA/Ser.L/V.II.62, doc 10 rev 3 (29 November 1983); *Yanomami Community v Brazil*, Case No 7615, Decision No 12/85 (Merits) (5 March 1985).

[18] Miskito report, ibid, Conclusions, A.1.

[19] *Awas Tingni* (n 5) para 148.

[20] Anaya has advanced an interesting analysis of the wider implications of the *Awas Tingni* ruling in terms of the recognition of indigenous law as a constitutive part of legal

The Court's 'evolutionary' contextual interpretation of the Inter-American human rights instruments to safeguard indigenous peoples' rights was subsequently endorsed by the Inter-American Commission in *Mary and Carrie Dann v United States,* a case involving the Western Shoshone claim over their traditional lands in the State of Nevada.[21] In interpreting the right to property provision of the American Declaration—as the concerned State is not a party to the American Convention—[22] the Commission referred to a perceived normative evolution regarding the rights of indigenous peoples in both international and domestic law. According to the Commission,

> a review of pertinent treaties, legislation and jurisprudence reveals the development over more than 80 years of particular human rights norms and principles applicable to the circumstances and treatment of indigenous peoples. Central to these norms and principles is a recognition that ensuring the full and effective enjoyment of human rights by indigenous peoples requires consideration of their particular historical, cultural, social and economic situation and experience.[23]

Within this evolution, the Commission identified in 'tandem' between the Inter-American system and 'developments in international human rights law more broadly',[24] applying the relevant human rights norms and principles applicable to indigenous peoples to the interpretation of the Inter-American human rights instruments.

By opening up the interpretation of the provisions of the Inter-American human rights instruments to specific standards applying to indigenous peoples, the *Awas Tingni* decision paved the way for the elaboration of a specific, distinct body of jurisprudence regarding indigenous peoples.

pluralistic systems in American societies. According to Anaya, the international recognition of indigenous rights in *Awas Tingni* and similar international legal rulings 'challenge previously dominant Western conceptions of the culturally homogenous and legally monolithic state', thus promoting a 'multicultural model'. SJ Anaya, 'International Human Rights and Indigenous Peoples: The Move Toward the Multicultural State' (2004) 21 *Arizona Journal of International and Comparative Law* 1.

[21] *Mary and Carrie Dann v United States,* Case 11,140, Report No 113/01, IACHR (2001). For a legal analysis of this case see Deborah Schaaf and Julie Fishel, 'Mary and Carrie Dann v United States at the Inter-American Commission on Human Rights: Victory for Indian Land Rights and the Environment' (2002) 16 *Tulane Environmental Law Journal* 175; D de Bakker, 'The Court of Last Resort: American Indians in the Inter-American Human Rights System: Why American Indians should Utilize Supranational Courts' (2004) 11 *Cardozo Journal of International and Comparative Law* 932.

[22] The IACHR takes the formal stand that it has a mandate to review the implementation of the American Declaration among OAS State members that have not ratified the American Convention, based on the argument that the declaration spells out the human rights obligations deriving from the OAS Charter. See D Cassell, 'Inter-American Human Rights Law, Soft and Hard' in D Shelton (ed), *Commitment and Compliance: The Role of Non-Binding Norms in the International Legal System* (Oxford University Press, 2003).

[23] *Dann* (n 21) para 125 (footnotes omitted).

[24] Ibid, para 127.

Following *Awas Tingni*, and prior to the adoption of the UN Declaration, the Court ruled in other three cases dealing with indigenous peoples' land rights[25] and one on political participation.[26] The Court also examined cases of massacres inflicted upon indigenous communities'[27] and it has elaborated on the State's positive duty to protect the right to life.[28] Through these various cases, the Court elaborated upon its own rules of reparation with regard to indigenous peoples, in particular in relation to the communitarian characteristics of indigenous societies and the need to provide reparation for the impact of human rights violations on indigenous cultures.[29] The Inter-American Commission has declared admissible

[25] See *Yakye Axa Indigenous Community v Paraguay* (Merits, Reparations and Costs), IACHR, judgment of 17 June 2005, Series C No 125 (2005); *Sawhoyamaxa Indigenous Community v Paraguay* (Preliminary Objections, Merits, Reparations and Costs), IACHR, judgment of 29 March 2006, Series C No 125 (2005); *Moiwana Community v Suriname*, IACHR, judgment of 15 June 2005, Series C No 124 (2005).

[26] *YATAMA v Nicaragua* (Preliminary Objections, Merits, Reparations and Costs), IACHR, judgment of 23 June 2005, Series C No 127 (2005). A detailed analysis of the Inter-American Court's jurisprudence in this case can be found in Maia Sophia Campbell, 'The Right of Indigenous Peoples to Political Participation and the Case of *YATAMA v Nicaragua*' (2007) 24 *Arizona Journal of International and Comparative Law* 499.

[27] *Masacre de Plan de Sánchez* (Guatemala) (Merits), IACHR, tudgment of 24 April 2004, Series C No 105 (2004). The case regarded the massacre of least 88 members of the indigenous Mayan community of Plan de Sánchez by the Guatemalan armed forces. Similarly, *Moiwana* (n 25) had its origins in the extrajudicial execution of members of the Maroon Moiwana Community by the Suriname military, resulting in the Community fleeing from their traditional lands.

[28] The positive duty of the State to prevent the loss of human life was first elaborated by the Court in *Sawhoyamaxa* (n 25). In this case, children and elders belonging to the Community had died as a consequence of a lack of minimum sanitary and health conditions in which the Community lived as a result of the lack of access to its traditional lands. The Court, noting that the living conditions of the Sawhoxamaya Community had been known to State authorities, found a violation of the right to life (Art 4(1) American Convention), 'since it has not adopted the necessary positive measures within its powers, which could reasonably be expected to prevent or avoid risking the right to life of the members of the Sawhoyamaxa Community' (178). In his separate concurring opinion in this case, Judge Cançado Trindade expanded the meaning of the Court's ruling to include aspects of cultural identity. According to Cançado, '[t]he right to life is ... viewed in its close and unavoidable connection with cultural identity'. See Separate Opinion of Judge AA Cançado Trindade in the Case of *Sawhoyamaxa Indigenous Community v Paraguay* (29 March 2006), para 28.

[29] The first case in which the Court showed a notable multicultural sensitivity in relation to the issue of reparations actually preceded *Awas Tingni*. In *Aloeboetoe*, the Court took into account the cultural patterns of the Maroon society, organised in clans, in the calculation of the reparations resulting from the extrajudicial execution of Community members. See *Aloeboetoe et al v Suriname* (Reparations and Costs), IACHR, judgment of 10 September 1993, Series C No 15 (1993), paras 55–66. This multicultural approach to reparations has been reinforced and expanded in subsequent cases, including the collective entitlement to reparations in relation to the material and immaterial harm suffered by indigenous communities as a result of the violation of their land rights (starting in *Awas Tingni*, n 5); and the State's duty to repair the loss of indigenous cultures, language and traditions as a result of human rights violations affecting their communitarian way of life (notably in *Masacre de Plan de Sánchez* (n 27) paras 50–111). A comprehensive review of the Inter-American Court's jurisprudence regarding reparations in cases of violations of the human rights of indigenous peoples can

many other cases dealing with the rights of indigenous communities and individuals, which in some instances had led to friendly settlements,[30] or, in cases in which the concerned State has not ratified the American Convention, to final reports on the merits.[31] In addition, both the Court and the Commission have granted provisional or precautionary measures on behalf of indigenous communities and individuals in circumstances of urgent necessity or when required to preserve the status quo of cases under examination.[32]

In the few years since *Awas Tingni* was heard, the Inter-American system has developed from an inauspicious legal avenue for indigenous peoples to a point of reference worldwide in conceptual legal developments regarding indigenous rights. The Inter-American system has not only surpassed other regional human rights systems, it has also outshined the incipient jurisprudence of UN treaty bodies. Moreover, the '*Awas Tingni* effect' has had a lasting impact within the institutional structure of the Inter-American bodies, and particularly that of the Inter-American Commission, now a major point of reference for the promotion and protection of indigenous rights in the region.

THE IMPACT OF THE UN DRAFT DECLARATION

The articulation of the Inter-American jurisprudence on indigenous peoples cannot be sufficiently explained without reference to the influence of the process of drafting of the UN Declaration on the Rights of Indigenous Peoples. Together with ILO Convention 169—ratified by most Latin American countries—the draft declaration operated as a major authoritative source in an 'evolutionary interpretation' of the American Convention

be found in G Citroni and KI Quintana, 'Reparations for Indigenous Peoples in the Case Law of the Inter-American Court of Human Rights' in F Lenzerini (ed), *Reparations for Indigenous Peoples: International and Comparative Perspectives* (Oxford University Press, 2008) 317.

[30] See eg *Enxet Lamenxay and Kayleyphapopyet (Riachito) Indigenous Communities v Paraguay* (Friendly Settlement), Report No 90/99, Case 11,713 (29 September 1999); *Mercedes Julia Huentenao Beroiza et al v Chile* (Friendly Settlement), Report No 30/34, Petition 4617/02 (11 March 2004). On the friendly settlement procedure in cases involving violations of the rights of indigenous peoples, see Rodríguez-Piñero (n 7) 175–77.

[31] See, in particular, *Dann* (n 21); *Mayan Indigenous Communities of the Toledo District Toledo v Belize* (Merits), IACHR, Report No 40/04, Case 12,053 (12 October 2004).

[32] See, inter alia, *Awas Tingni Mayagna (Sumo) Indigenous Community v Nicaragua* (Provisional Measures), IACHR, Resolution of 9 September 2002 (the provisional measures were granted in the phase of implementation of the Court's decision in this case, n 5); *Sarayaku Indigenous People* (Provisional Measures), IACHR, Resolution of 6 July 2004; *Sarayaku Indigenous People* (Provisional Measures), IACHR, Resolution of 17 June 2005. The case of *Sarayaku* is analysed in I Madariaga Cuneo, 'Los derechos de los pueblos indígenas y el sistema interamericano de derechos humanos' (2005) 22 *Arizona Journal of International and Comparative Law* 53, 59–61.

that reflects developing normative understandings concerning the rights of indigenous peoples. Even in its draft form, the human rights principles and standards enshrined in the American declaration have informed the normative practice of the Inter-American human rights bodies, signalling a relation of mutual reinforcement with a great deal of potential for the effective implementation of the Declaration following its adoption.

While not directly cited in the *Awas Tingni* decision, the UN draft declaration was a major source in the Court's interpretation of evolving international understandings of the minimum content of indigenous peoples' rights. Conscious of the path-breaking character of its decision, the Court grounded its construction of indigenous land rights in a combination of anthropological authority and domestic constitutional provisions.[33] It also took pains to combine the language of individual rights with the obvious collective implications of its indigenous land rights jurisprudence.[34] However, it is clear that this jurisprudence evokes some of the key elements of the then draft declaration, including the collective, cultural and spiritual dimensions of the relationship between indigenous peoples and their traditional lands;[35] the recognition of indigenous customary law as a source of entitlements within the State's legal system; and the State's positive duty to protect indigenous land tenure, including by demarcation and titling.[36]

The normative debt of the UN draft declaration in the *Awas Tingi* decision was acknowledged in the individual concurring opinion of Judge Sergio García Ramírez, which cited the draft declaration as an authoritative statement of the evolution of international law concerning indigenous peoples' rights. According to García Ramírez, it set 'the standards that the international juridical community is to observe in matters bearing upon

[33] *Awas Tingni* (n 5) para 148 ('it is the opinion of this Court that Article 21 of the Convention protects the right to property in a sense which includes, among others, the rights of members of the indigenous communities within the framework of communal property, which is also recognised by the Constitution of Nicaragua'); ibid, para 150 (citing the right to indigenous property provisions of the Autonomy Statute of the Regions of the Atlantic Coast of Nicaragua); ibid, para 153 ('it is the opinion of the Court that, pursuant to Article 5 of the Constitution of Nicaragua, the members of the Awas Tingni Community have a communal property right to the lands they currently inhabit').

[34] Ibid, para 149 ('Among indigenous peoples there is a communitarian tradition regarding a communal form of collective property of the land, in the sense that ownership of the land is not centred on an individual but rather on the group and its community'). Cf ibid, para 150 ('*the members* of the Awas Tingni Community have a communal property right to the lands they currently inhabit') (emphasis added).

[35] UN Declaration on the Rights of Indigenous Peoples (n 4) Art 25 ('Indigenous peoples have the right to maintain and strengthen their distinctive spiritual relationship with their traditionally owned or otherwise occupied and used lands, territories, waters and coastal seas and other resources').

[36] Ibid, Art 26(3) ('States shall give legal recognition and protection to these lands, territories and resources. Such recognition shall be conducted with due respect to the customs, traditions and land tenure systems of the indigenous peoples concerned').

indigenous peoples and the members of their communities'.[37] As evidence of the normative convergence between the jurisprudence elaborated in *Awas Tingni* and the draft declaration, the Judge cited expressly the draft's provisions safeguarding indigenous traditional land tenure.[38]

The Inter-American Court's jurisprudence on land rights was further elaborated in two parallel cases regarding the Enxet people in Paraguay, *Yakye Axa* and *Sawhoyamaxa*.[39] Unlike *Awas Tingni*, the two Enxet cases dealt with situations of involuntary loss of traditional indigenous lands, subsequently owned by private parties. The need to address a conflict of property interests led the Court to restate its indigenous land rights jurisprudence. As summarised by the Court in *Sawhoyamaxa v Paraguay*:

> 1) traditional possession of their lands by indigenous people has equivalent effects to those of a state-granted full property title; 2) traditional possession entitles indigenous people to demand official recognition and registration of property title; 3) the members of indigenous peoples who have unwillingly left their traditional lands, or lost possession thereof, maintain property rights thereto, even though they lack legal title, unless the lands have been lawfully transferred to third parties in good faith; and 4) the members of indigenous peoples who have unwillingly lost possession of their lands, when those lands have been lawfully transferred to innocent third parties, are entitled to restitution thereof or to obtain other lands of equal extension and quality.[40]

This restatement of indigenous land rights post-*Awas Tingni* is fully consistent with, and elaborates upon, the affirmation of indigenous rights over lands, territories and natural resources under the then draft declaration. Notably, the Court's emphasis on the persistent entitlement to reparation in cases in which indigenous peoples have been involuntarily deprived of their traditional lands echoes the strong remedial thrust of the Declaration, which affirms indigenous peoples' right to redress 'for the lands, territories and resources which they have traditionally owned or otherwise occupied or used, and which have been confiscated, taken, occupied, used or damaged without their free, prior and informed consent'.[41]

The Inter-American Court's jurisprudence has also tackled other issues relevant to the standards included in the draft declaration. In *YATAMA*, a case that dealt with the exclusion of an indigenous political party from participating in Nicaraguan local elections, the Court elaborated upon

[37] See Concurring opinion of Judge Sergio García Ramírez on the judgment on the merits and reparations of the case *Awas Tingni Mayagna (Sumo) Indigenous Community* (2001), para 7.

[38] Ibid, para 8 (citing the land rights provisions of the 'Draft Declaration on Discrimination against Indigenous Peoples [*sic*], prepared by the United Nations Economic and Social Council's Sub-Commission on Prevention of Discrimination and Protection of Minorities').

[39] See n 25 above.

[40] *Sawhoyamaxa* (n 25) para 128.

[41] UN Declaration on the Rights of Indigenous Peoples (n 4) Art 28(1).

the implications of the individual right to political participation under the American Convention in the context of indigenous peoples.[42] Various provisions of the draft declaration were used in the Commission's legal arguments.[43] While not expressly citing the draft declaration, the Court's legal construction in the *YATAMA* decision is fully consistent with the Declaration's dual affirmation of indigenous peoples' right to autonomy (Article 4) and to participate in State decision-making structures (Article 5). Thus, the Court held that indigenous peoples' right to participation included their right to 'participate directly and proportionately to their population in the conduct of public affairs, *and also* to do this from within their own institutions and according to their values, practices, customs and forms of organization'.[44]

In *Sawhoyamaxa*, the Court found violations of the right to life of the indigenous community concerned as a result of Paraguay's failure to provide 'the necessary positive measures within its powers, which could reasonably be expected to prevent or avoid risking the right to life' of members of this landless indigenous community, particularly with regard to children.[45] This is consistent with, and elaborates upon, the State's obligations to 'be secure in the enjoyment of their own means of subsistence and development', as affirmed in the final Declaration, as well as to adopt special measures in relation to the protection of indigenous children.[46]

The Court has further developed a fairly sophisticated jurisprudence concerning reparations in cases of violations of indigenous peoples' rights. This includes, for instance: the collective nature of reparations in the case of violations of the rights of indigenous communities and individuals; the call for reparations that are consistent with indigenous peoples' rights and cultural values and promote the revitalisation of cultures and language in cases in which these have been negatively affected by State action; and restitution of or compensation for indigenous lands lost without the consent of the peoples concerned.[47] The Court's elaboration of the requirements for reparations in the context of violations of indigenous peoples' rights corresponds again with the remedial prescriptions of the Declaration, particularly with regard to indigenous cultural traditions and identities.[48]

[42] See n 26 above.

[43] *YATAMA* (n 26) para 179(e).

[44] Ibid, para 225 (emphasis added).

[45] *Sawhoyamaxa* (n 25) para 178.

[46] UN Declaration on the Rights of Indigenous Peoples (n 4) Art 21(2) ('Particular attention shall be paid to the rights and special needs of indigenous elders, women, youth, children and persons with disabilities); Art 22(2) ('States shall take measures, in conjunction with indigenous peoples, to ensure that indigenous women and children enjoy the full protection and guarantees against all forms of violence and discrimination').

[47] See Citroni and Quintana (n 29).

[48] Cf UN Declaration on the Rights of Indigenous Peoples (n 3) Art 11(2) ('States shall provide redress through effective mechanisms ... with respect to their cultural, intellectual,

In resorting, either directly or indirectly, to the standards set forth in the draft declaration, the Inter-American human rights bodies have taken a significant stance concerning the binding force of the Declaration—at least for the States members of the Inter-American system—which is particularly relevant to ongoing debates concerning its legal status.[49] Both the Court and the Commission have promoted an intuitive reading of the UN Declaration as an authoritative statement of the international common understanding of the content of the rights of indigenous peoples in modern international law, irrespective of the legal status of the Declaration as a 'non-binding' instrument, in the certainly revisable established discourse.[50] Moreover, the use of the Declaration's standards by the Inter-American bodies as a proof of established State practice reinforces the argument, advanced by some authors, that some of the key provisions of the UN Declaration on the Rights of Indigenous Peoples are constitutive or reflect international customary norms.[51]

AFTER THE DECLARATION: *SARAMAKA V SURINAME*

Whilst the UN draft declaration operated as an indirect source of authority in the Inter-American Court's jurisprudence, the final adoption of the instrument paved the way for a more explicit and creative usage of the Declaration. This was evident in the Court's decision in *Saramaka*

religious and spiritual property taken without their free, prior and informed consent or in violation of their laws, traditions and customs'); Art 12(2) ('States shall seek to enable the access and/or repatriation of ceremonial objects and human remains in their possession through fair, transparent and effective mechanisms developed in conjunction with indigenous peoples concerned').

[49] The implementation of the UN Declaration was the focus of James Anaya's first report to the Human Rights Council in his official capacity as Special Rapporteur. See Report of the Special Rapporteur on the situation of human rights and fundamental freedoms of indigenous people (S James Anaya), UN Doc HRC/9/9 (15 August 2008). The issue is also explored in L Rodríguez-Piñero, 'Where Appropriate: Monitoring/Implementing Indigenous Peoples' Rights under the Declaration' in C Charters and R Stavenhagen (eds), *Making the Declaration Work: The Significance of the Declaration on the Rights of Indigenous Peoples* (Copenhagen, International Work Group for Indigenous Affairs, 2010).

[50] For a discussion of the legal status of the UN Declaration, see B Clavero, *Nota sobre el alcance del mandato contenido en el artículo 42 de la Declaración sobre los derechos de los pueblos indígenas y el mejor modo de satisfacerlo por parte del Foro Permanente para las Cuestiones Indígenas*, UN Doc E/C.19/2008/CRP.6 (26 March 2008); B Clavero, *Task of the Permanent Forum on Indigenous Issues in light of the Binding Nature and with a view to Furthering the Effectiveness of International Human Rights Law*, Paper presented the International Expert Group Meeting on the Role of the United Nations Permanent Forum on Indigenous Issues in the Implementation of Article 42 of the United Nations Declaration on the Rights of Indigenous Peoples (New York, 14–16 January, 2009), UN Doc PFII/2009/EGM1/4 (2009).

[51] For an authoritative reading of the standards of the UN Declaration as a reflection of existing international customary norms, see SJ Anaya and S Wiessner, 'OP-ED: The UN Declaration on the Rights of Indigenous Peoples: Towards Re-empowerment', *Jurist: Legal News and Research* (3 October 2007).

v Suriname, published only a few months after the formal adoption of the Declaration by the General Assembly.[52] The lessons to be drawn from this case go beyond the framework of the Inter-American system, signalling the crucial role that international bodies are called upon to play in the operationalisation of the Declaration's standards in specific contexts.

The Saramaka people are not indigenous to Suriname. A community of the so-called *Maroons*, they are descended from the African population that was forcefully brought to the country in colonial times, and have preserved their distinct cultures and identities and have developed a distinct relation to their lands. In this case, as in previous ones concerning Suriname,[53] the Court identified the Maroons as a 'tribal people' and applied to them the same standards of protection afforded to indigenous peoples.[54]

The *Saramaka* case involved a typical situation of exploitation of natural resources in traditional indigenous or tribal lands under concessions granted by the State. The factual elements of the case required that the Court examine the two most controversial issues regarding indigenous peoples' rights: first, the question of indigenous property over natural resources as deriving from their right to the land; and second, the right to free, prior and informed consent (FPIC) in connection to the exploration and exploitation of natural resources in indigenous territories.

Regarding the first question, the Inter-American Court elaborated a special test regarding the limitation of indigenous property rights as the result of the exploitation of natural resources in their traditional territories. Thus, according to the Court,

> in order to guarantee that restrictions to the property rights of the members of the Saramaka people by the issuance of concessions within their territory does not amount to a denial of their survival as a tribal people, the State must abide

[52] See *Saramaka People v Suriname* (Preliminary Objections, Merits, Reparations, and Costs), IACHR, judgment of 28 November 2007, Series C No 172 (2007). The decision was subsequently subject to the Court's interpretation upon the request of the State of Suriname: see *Saramaka People v Suriname* (Interpretation of the Judgment on Preliminary Objections, Merits, Reparations, and Costs), IACHR, judgment of 12 August 2008, Series C No 185 (2008). An analysis of the case can be found in L Brunner, 'The Rise of Peoples' Rights in the Americas: The *Saramaka People* Decision of the Inter-American Court of Human Rights' (2008) 7(3) *Chinese Journal of International Law* 699.

[53] See *Moiwana* (n 25); *Aloeboetoe* (n 29).

[54] According to the Court, 'the members of the Saramaka people make up a tribal community whose social, cultural and economic characteristics are different from other sections of the national community, particularly because of their special relationship with their ancestral territories, and because they regulate themselves, least partially, by their own norms, customs, and/or traditions'. *Saramaka* 2007 (n 52) para 84. This passage of the Court's decision notably recalls the text of ILO Convention 169, Art 1(a) of which characterises tribal peoples as groups 'whose social, cultural and economic conditions distinguish them from other sections of the national community, and whose status is regulated wholly or partially by their own customs or traditions or by special laws or regulations'.

> by the following three safeguards: First, the State must ensure the effective participation of the members of the Saramaka people, in conformity with their customs and traditions, regarding any development, investment, exploration or extraction plan ... within Saramaka territory. Second, the State must guarantee that the Saramakas will receive a reasonable benefit from any such plan within their territory. Thirdly, the State must ensure that no concession will be issued within Saramaka territory unless and until independent and technically capable entities, with the State's supervision, perform a prior environmental and social impact assessment. These safeguards are intended to preserve, protect and guarantee the special relationship that the members of the Saramaka community have with their territory, which in turn ensures their survival as a tribal people.[55]

This Court's special test reflects the obvious normative influence of the provisions of both the UN Convention and ILO Convention 169—despite the fact that the concerned State, Suriname, is not a party to the Convention—implicitly endorsing the two instruments as a common normative framework for indigenous peoples' rights in the Western Hemisphere. Departing from the more restrictive characterisation of indigenous title in *Awas Tingni*, the Court used the concept of indigenous territory, widely defined as the area on which indigenous peoples depend for their 'survival' as peoples and with which they maintain a 'special relationship'.[56] The concept of territory, which underlines the cultural dimensions of indigenous land property interests, is a direct borrowing from both the Convention and the Declaration. The acrid controversy around the use of the term in the drafting of the two instruments paved the way for its unproblematic use by an international court. Similarly, the three related procedural safeguards of participation, benefit-sharing and impact assessment correspond to specific provisions enshrined in the ILO Convention and in the Declaration.[57]

The procedural safeguard of indigenous participation led the Court to address the issue of FPIC, in what constitutes a particularly interesting example of how a broad affirmation of indigenous rights under the

[55] *Saramaka* 2007 (n 52) para 129.

[56] Cf UN Declaration on the Rights of Indigenous Peoples (n 4) Art 25 ('Indigenous peoples have the right to maintain and strengthen their distinctive spiritual relationship with their traditionally owned or otherwise occupied and used lands, territories, waters and coastal seas and other resources'); Convention 169 (n 2) Art 13(1) ('governments shall respect the special importance for the cultures and spiritual values of the peoples concerned of their relationship with the lands or territories ... which they occupy or otherwise use').

[57] See UN Declaration on the Rights of Indigenous Peoples (n 4) Art 32(2) (right to consultation in relation to development projects); Art 32(3) (right to effective mechanisms for redress and mitigation of development activities); Convention 169 (n 2) Art 6(1) (right to consultation in relation to development projects); Art 7(3) (duty to perform social impact development studies); Art 15(2) (right to participate in the benefits deriving from resource development projects).

Declaration may require operationalisation in order to accommodate conflicting rights and interests in real-life situations. The right to FPIC in relation to development projects is affirmed in Article 32 of the Declaration in the following terms:

> States shall consult and cooperate in good faith with the indigenous peoples concerned through their own representative institutions in order to obtain their free and informed consent prior to the approval of any project affecting their lands or territories and other resources, particularly in connection with the development, utilization or exploitation of mineral, water or other resources.[58]

FPIC was one of the most controversial issues in the drafting process at the UN, and some of the States that abstained or voted against the Declaration actually voiced concern at the affirmation of FPIC understood as a 'right to veto'.[59] On the indigenous rights-advocacy side, FPIC has often been depicted as a step beyond the right to consultation enshrined in ILO Convention 169, seen—not without empirical evidence—as a mere formality in which indigenous peoples have no effective voice.

Facing these two opposing, seemingly irreconcilable views, the Court provided in *Saramaka* a remarkable attempt to operationalise the rights to consultation and to FPIC on the basis of the level of impact of development practices over indigenous peoples' rights. In this connection, the Court developed the argument that the effective participation of indigenous peoples requires 'consultations … in good faith, through culturally appropriate procedures and with the objective of reaching an agreement'.[60] Additionally, the Court argued,

> regarding large-scale development or investment projects that would have a major impact within Saramaka territory, the State has a duty, not only to consult with the Saramakas, but also to obtain their free, prior and informed consent, according to their customs and traditions.[61]

The Court explicitly grounded this argument in Article 32 of the Declaration. As additional authoritative sources, the Court cited the report of the former UN Special Rapporteur, Rodolfo Stavenhagen, on large-scale development projects in indigenous lands, as well as CERD's Concluding Observations on Ecuador.[62]

The Court's decision in *Saramaka* constitutes an interesting example of a practical operationalisation of the right to FPIC that is not contradictory to the right of consultation enshrined in Article 6 of Convention 169.

[58] UN Declaration on the Rights of Indigenous Peoples (n 4) Art 32(2).

[59] The discussions around FPIC in the negotiations leading to the final adoption of the Declaration are analysed in Åhrén (n 4) 118–19.

[60] *Saramaka* 2007 (n 52) para 133.

[61] Ibid, para 134.

[62] Ibid, fnn 135–36.

Rather, the Court drew a continuum between consultation and consent in which the latter is required as a reinforced procedural requirement in cases of major developmental impacts, which should be determined on a case-by-case basis. This conclusion implicitly calls for the establishment of institutional and regulatory frameworks to enforce indigenous peoples' right to consultation/consent with regard to developments projects, which, despite clarification of the applicable standards, are still lacking in the vast majority of countries in the American region.

In what constitutes a remarkable example of the influence of the Inter-American jurisprudence in the wider international regime regarding indigenous peoples, the Inter-American Court's approach to FPIC has subsequently been echoed in the activities of the current UN Special Rapporteur on the situation of human rights and fundamental freedoms of indigenous people, James Anaya. Upon the request of the President of the Constituent Assembly, Anaya visited Ecuador in May 2008 to provide input into the constitution-making process in that country, in which the chapter on indigenous collective rights had become a major barrier to reaching a final agreement within the Assembly. One of the most controversial issues in this discussion was precisely the strong demand on the part of indigenous organisations that the right to FPIC should be explicitly included in the new constitutional text.

In his written comments submitted to the Government of Ecuador following his visit,[63] the Special Rapporteur cited the UN Declaration, the ILO Convention and the *Saramaka* decision to support his conclusion that international human rights law did not vest indigenous peoples with an absolute right to FPIC in relation to all State action with a potential impact on them. Resorting to a reasoning similar to that of the Inter-American Court in *Saramaka*, Anaya argued that international human rights law guarantees indigenous peoples a general right to participation and consultation—a remedial right stemming from the lack of participation of indigenous peoples in decision-making structures—that only in special cases may require the consent of the peoples concerned. According to the Special Rapporteur,

> States have a firm obligation to undertake consultations with indigenous peoples before adopting measures that may directly affect their interests, and those consultations should be aimed at reaching a consensus concerning those measures ... But, what happens if consensus is not reached after a good

[63] See 'Observaciones del Relator Especial sobre la situación de derechos humanos y libertades fundamentales de los indígenas acerca del proceso de revisión constitucional en el Ecuador', reproduced in Report of the Special Rapporteur on the situation of human rights and fundamental freedoms of indigenous people (S James Anaya), Addendum: Summary of Cases transmitted to Governments and Replies Received, UN Doc A/HRC/9/9/Add.1, Annex 1 (15 August 2008).

> faith procedure in which the indigenous party had participated fully and adequately? In general terms, in virtue of the principle of indigenous peoples' self-determination, as well as for practical reasons, the State should not proceed with a project that affects directly an indigenous community without their consent. However, this does not imply an absolute veto power. [Only] [i]n those situations in which the [proposed] measure may have substantial impacts that may endanger the basic physical or cultural well-being of the indigenous community concerned, [does the State have] the duty not to adopt a measure without the community concerned, as affirmed by the Inter-American Court of Human Rights in the *Saramaka v Suriname* case.[64]

Anaya further linked the *Saramaka* decision to two specific provisions of the UN Declaration, which actually limit the applicability of FPIC to State measures with a major impact on indigenous peoples' livelihoods: namely, forced removal,[65] and storage or disposal of hazardous materials/militarisation of indigenous areas. In other cases of exploitation of natural resources, Article 32 of the Declaration call upon States to 'cooperate' with a view to obtaining indigenous peoples' FPIC. Beyond this minimum standard, concludes Anaya, nothing precludes the possibility that 'the new Constitution of Ecuador may affirm ... more advanced rights of consultation and participation in decisions affecting them'.[66]

The final political deal struck between the Ecuadorian indigenous movement and the ruling political party eventually excluded the issue of FPIC from the constitutional discussion, relegating it to further legislative development. Yet, the new Ecuadorian Constitution explicitly incorporates, as also suggested by Anaya, an entry-point for the rights affirmed in the UN Declaration and other instruments upholding indigenous peoples' rights.[67]

The Court's decision in *Saramaka* shows how the jurisprudence of the Inter-American human rights system interacts with the standards set forth in the Declaration to uphold the rights of indigenous peoples. While the human rights principles and concepts of the draft declaration had a bearing in the articulation of this jurisprudence since the early 2000s, the formal adoption of the Declaration has now opened a window of opportunity for more direct interaction, one in which the Inter-American

[64] Ibid, paras 39–40 (unofficial translation; footnotes omitted).

[65] UN Declaration on the Rights of Indigenous Peoples (n 4) Art 10 ('No relocation shall take place without the free, prior and informed consent of the indigenous peoples concerned and after agreement on just and fair compensation and, where possible, with the option of return').

[66] Report of the Special Rapporteur (n 63) para 41 (unofficial translation).

[67] See Political Constitution of Ecuador (2008), Art 57 (upholding the rights of 'indigenous municipalities, communities, peoples and nationalities' according to 'the Constitution, and the covenants, conventions, declarations and other international human rights instruments') (unofficial translation).

human rights bodies can actually advance new interpretations of the Declaration's standards in specific contexts. As shown in *Saramaka*, the Inter-American system may, and surely will, become a significant locus for the operationalisation of the Declaration, with normative effects that go beyond the system's regional framework.

TOWARDS AN AMERICAN DECLARATION ON THE RIGHTS OF INDIGENOUS PEOPLES

The assumption of the UN Declaration's standards in the practice of the Inter-American human rights bodies constitutes a powerful sign of support for ongoing discussions at the OAS level aimed at the eventual adoption of a specific legal instrument regarding the rights of indigenous peoples in the Western Hemisphere. Since the inception of discussions regarding a draft American Declaration on the Rights of Indigenous Peoples, the standard-setting experience at the UN level has operated as an inevitable point of reference, in both procedural and substantive terms. This interaction is a further reflection of the mutually reinforcing relationship that exists between the UN and the OAS human rights protection systems with regard to indigenous peoples, and, further, of the capacity of the Inter-American system to contribute to produce new, complementary understandings of international standards regarding indigenous rights.

Initiatives towards the adoption of an Inter-American instrument concerning the rights of indigenous peoples run parallel to the standard-setting process at the UN level. As early as 1989, soon after the adoption of ILO Convention 169 and with the prospects of the 1992 continental celebration, the OAS General Assembly requested that the Inter-American Commission prepare 'a juridical instrument relative to the rights of Indian peoples'.[68] The celebration went by with no substantial advance towards the achievement of this goal, though, due to a lack of political drive on the part of Member States. It was only in 1997, four years after the UN Working Group on Indigenous Populations had issued the first draft of the UN Declaration, that the Inter-American Commission made public a 'proposed American declaration on the rights of indigenous peoples'.[69]

As distinct from the UN process, the Commission's text was not the outcome of a participatory process comparable to that of the Working Group, but rather, in the most classical Latin American Indigenist tradition, the

[68] OAS General Assembly Resolution AG/RES.1022 (XIX-O/89): 'Reports of the Inter-American Commission on Human Rights' (18 November 1989), para 13.

[69] Proposed American Declaration on the Rights of Indigenous Peoples, adopted by the Inter-American Commission on Human Rights on 26 February 1997 at its 1333rd session, 95th Regular Session, OAS Doc CP/doc.2878/97 corr 1.

outcome of a series of internal consultations and meetings of experts, coupled with piecemeal consultations with indigenous peoples at the local level.[70] The same non-participatory approach was initially followed by the OAS General Assembly, when in 1999 it established a Working Group of the OAS Permanent Council to consider the Commission's text, composed exclusively of State members and with only limited participation of indigenous peoples' organisations.[71]

This starting point was however a *faux pas*. Mirroring the example of the discussions on the UN draft declaration at the Commission on Human Rights, indigenous organisations of the Americas strongly demanded a re-routing of the process to include the broad participation of indigenous peoples in the discussion of the OAS draft. A working agreement was eventually reached in 2001, with the involvement of representatives of the Indigenous Caucus in the Permanent Council's Working Group practically on an equal footing with State delegations, coupled with the establishment of a voluntary fund to facilitate the participation of indigenous representatives.[72] The year 2003 marked a purported 'final phase' of the negotiations in the quest for consensus on the draft declaration, on the basis of the consolidated text prepared by the Chair of the Working Group, including the outcomes of the Working Group's negotiations to date.[73] A stage of 'final revision', still ongoing at the time of this writing, was inaugurated in 2006, with a new methodology that circumscribes the Working Group's discussions to the controversial wording included in an updated text.[74]

[70] A summary of the meetings and consultations organised by the Inter-American Commission in relation to the Draft American Declaration can be found in Report on the First Round of Consultations concerning the Future Inter-American Legal Instrument on Indigenous Rights, reproduced in *Annual Report of the Inter-American Commission on Human Rights 1992–93*, ch V(6), OAS Doc OEA/Ser./L/V/II.83, doc 14 corr 1 (12 March 1993); *Annual Report of the Inter-American Commission on Human Rights 1996*, ch V(6), OAS Doc OEA/Ser./L/V/II.95, doc 7 rev (14 March 1997), ch 4.

[71] OAS General Assembly Resolution AG/RES.1610 (XXIX-O/99): 'Proposed American Declaration on the Rights of Indigenous Populations' (7 June 1999). The Resolution called upon the Working Group of the Permanent Council to 'provide for appropriate participation in its efforts by representatives of indigenous communities, so that their observations and suggestions *may be considered*' (para 3) (emphasis added).

[72] See OAS General Assembly Resolution OEA/Ser.P AG/RES.1780 (XXXI-O/01) (5 June 2001): 'American Declaration on the Rights of Indigenous Peoples', paras 3–4.

[73] OAS General Assembly Resolution AG/RES.1919 (XXXIII-O/03) (10 June 2003): 'American Declaration on the Rights of Indigenous Peoples', para 4(a). The Chair's proposal is reproduced in *Consolidated Text of the Draft Declaration Prepared by the Chair of the Working Group*, OAS Doc OEA/Ser.K/XVI, GT/DADIN/doc.139/03 (17 June 2003).

[74] See *Procedure for Promptly Concluding the Negotiations in the Quest for Points of Consensus of the Working Group to Prepare the Draft American Declaration on the Rights of Indigenous Peoples*, OEA/Ser.K/XVI, GT/DADIN/doc.246/06 rev 7 (27 November 2006). The latest version of the negotiation text can be found in *Record of the Current Status of the Draft American Declaration on the Rights of Indigenous Peoples (Outcomes of the Eleventh Meetings of Negotiations*

In a context of stalemate in the negotiations at the UN Commission, the inauguration of the OAS standard-setting process was initially perceived as an easier one than that of the UN, leading to the swift adoption of a formal instrument which could in turn make an important contribution to the UN process. Valid arguments supported this initial prospect. First, as compared to the UN, the countries of the Americas shared common histories and similar legal approaches to indigenous issues, crystallised particularly throughout the 1990s with the massive ratification of ILO Convention 169 and subsequent legal reforms in the Latin American region. Second, as discussed, the active involvement of the Inter-American human rights bodies in the field of indigenous rights has contributed to the emergence of shared normative understandings regarding the human rights principles and norms applicable to indigenous peoples in the Americas.

Initial expectations seemed to be thwarted as the sessions of the OAS Working Group proceeded. Some of the countries that eventually took the hardest stand against the UN Declaration, including the United States, Canada and, initially, a number of Latin American countries (such as Brazil and Colombia), firmly opposed the American draft with the same level of vehemence. The institutional culture at the OAS, demanding consensus in the adoption of regional normative instruments, gave more power to the position of the States opposed to the Draft American Declaration, which in turn prompted new suspicions and desertions among the Latin American group.

The unpredicted acceleration of the UN standard-setting process had an important impact on the OAS process, which, opposite to what could initially have been expected, actually lowered the interest in reaching a consensus with regard to the American Declaration. The adoption, first, of the text of the draft Declaration by the Human Rights Council in 2006, and the eventual endorsement of the instrument by the General Assembly in 2007, had, in the words of the Chair of the OAS Working Group, a 'strong and crucial impact on the course of the reflection process' regarding the American Declaration.[75] The adoption of the Declaration, with the negative votes of Canada and the United States, actually posed an important dilemma to the OAS process. With the standards of the UN Declaration providing a working normative threshold, some voices, both governments and indigenous representatives, started to question the relevance

in the Quest for Points of Consensus, held by the Working Group), OAS Doc OEA/Ser.K/XVI, GT/DADIN/doc.334/08 (18 April 2008) (hereinafter 'Draft American Declaration').

[75] Note from the Chair of the Working Group to Prepare the Draft American Declaration on the Rights of Indigenous Peoples (Presented at the Committee Meeting of October 25, 2007), OAS Doc OEA/Ser.G, CP/CAJP-2545/07 (25 October 2007) 2.

of adopting an instrument that, faced with the strong opposition of Canada and the United States, could eventually lower those standards.

In late 2006, however, the dilemma was quickly resolved. At the Working Group's 10th session, possibly influenced by the massive Latin American support for the UN Declaration at the Human Rights Council, the United States changed its strategy regarding the OAS process, issuing a 'general reservation to all the text under discussion'.[76] Canada took a similar stand, suggesting a 'fundamental shift' in the Working Group's methodology: 'a shift from negotiating specific text to exploring in detail the underlying issues through discussion of, among other things, relevant State and indigenous experiences, practices and policies.'[77]

In November 2007, a special meeting was held at OAS headquarters 'to engage in a process of reflection regarding the Draft American Declaration on the Rights of Indigenous Peoples', including a specific focus on the implications of the adoption of the UN Convention in this process.[78] The wording of the final Declaration that emanated from the meeting is particularly illustrative of an emerging political consensus:

> The majority of States and all of the indigenous representatives supported the use of the UN Declaration as the baseline for negotiations and indicated that this represented a minimum standard for the OAS Declaration. Accordingly, the provisions of the OAS Declaration have to be consistent with those set forth in the United Nations Declaration. Moreover, the OAS Declaration should expand on the general concepts of the United Nations Declaration by addressing the

[76] *Tenth Meeting of Negotiations in the Quest for Points of Consensus (La Paz, Bolivia—April 23–27, 2007): Statement of the United States*, OEA/Ser.K/XVI, GT/DADIN/INF.31/07 (23 April 2007) 2. Following this general reservation, the United States Government formally announced that 'it would not join in any text that might be approved or otherwise appear in the Current Status of the Draft American Declaration on the Rights of Indigenous Peoples arising from the Tenth Meeting of the Working Group and in the Report of the Chair', ibid. Furthermore, the United States tabled a set of proposed 'Principles on the Rights of Indigenous Peoples' that could be adopted by the OAS General Assembly independently of the Draft American Declaration. See *Tenth Meeting of Negotiations in the Quest for Points of Consensus (La Paz, Bolivia—April 23–27, 2007): Proposals by the United States*, OEA/Ser.K/XVI, GT/DADIN/doc.295/07 corr 1 (27 April 2007). The principles have not been further considered by the Permanent Council's Working Group, and have been the object of severe criticism by indigenous organisations. See *Concerns of the National Chief of the Assembly of First Nations of Canada on Recently Published Documents of the Working Group*, OEA/Ser.K/XVI, GT/DADIN/doc.308/07 (27 June 2007) 2 (depicting the principles as reflecting the 'reactionary positions of the United States').

[77] *Canada's Statement to the Working Group to Prepare the Draft American Declaration on the Rights of Indigenous Peoples, April 14, 2008*, reproduced in *Record of the Current Status of the Draft American Declaration on the Rights of Indigenous Peoples, Eleventh Meeting of Negotiations in the Quest for Points of Consensus (Washington, DC, United States—April 14–18, 2008)*, OAS Doc OEA/Ser.K/XVI, GT/DADIN/doc.334/08 rev 2 (10 December 2008) 21 (hereinafter *Report of the OAS WG 2008*).

[78] *Report of the Chair on the Meeting for Reflection on the Meetings of Negotiations in the Quest for Points of Consensus (Washington, DC, United States—November 26–28, 2007)*, OAS Doc OEA/SER.K/XVI, GT/DADIN/doc.321/08 (14 January 2008) 1.

particular characteristics of the indigenous peoples of the Americas, while at the same time filling in any gaps or regulatory lacunae in those areas that were insufficiently addressed in the United Nations Declaration.[79]

Unsurprisingly, the delegations from Canada and the United States branched out from this common consensus, stating that 'they could not accept the UN Declaration text as the starting point or minimum outcome for these negotiations'.[80] Both countries explicitly detached themselves from the search for a consensus regarding the Draft American Declaration, reserving their final—predictably negative position—to the moment of its eventual adoption.[81]

While the self-imposed exclusion of Canada and the United States from the process has been criticised as a sort of 'pre-emptive veto on the consensus [being built] with the great majority of States and representatives of Indigenous peoples',[82] it has effectively contributed to unblocking the discussion regarding the American Declaration, and, at the time of writing, the prospects of its final adoption by the OAS General Assembly are certainly good. This does not necessarily mean, however, that the adoption will be a swift one. One of the arguments tabled by the Chair of the Working Group on the Draft American Declaration to justify the 'added value' of the instrument vis-a-vis the UN Declaration and therefore justify its formulation was the possibility that the former may include 'distinctive topics' that are not covered by the latter.[83] The topics currently under discussion include the situation of urban indigenous populations; indigenous migrants; environmental conservation; and access to social services.[84] The tardy incorporation of this additional raison d'être into the American Declaration will possibly involve an additional delay to the final adoption of the instrument, and, arguably, also a diluting of the international political momentum that ensued following the adoption of the UN Declaration.

[79] Ibid, 4.

[80] Ibid.

[81] As bluntly stated by the Canadian Government representative: '[I]f true consensus [is] not our shared goal, then Canada [will] have to fundamentally review its participation in, and support for, future negotiations ... We are formally reserving our position on the final text under negotiation. We will no longer actively negotiate or table text. We will, however, continue to be present and will occasionally speak about Canadian experience and perspectives.' *Canada's Statement* (n 77) 21. Similarly, the United States declared that it would not 'join in any text that might be approved or otherwise appear in the Chair's rolling text'. *Statement of the United States, 11th Meeting of Negotiations in the Quest for Points of Consensus on the draft Inter-American Declaration on the Rights of Indigenous Peoples*, reproduced in *Report of the OAS WG 2008* (n 77) 22.

[82] 'Response of the Indigenous Peoples' Caucus of the Americas, April 15, 2008,' reproduced in *Report of the OAS WG 2008* (n 77) 26.

[83] *Document of the Chair on Proposals Regarding Work for the Special Meeting*, OAS Doc OEA/Ser.K/XVI, GT/DADIN/doc.357/08 rev 1 corr 1 (24 November 2008) 7.

[84] Ibid, 8–9.

In terms of content, several provisions of the Draft American Declaration clearly evidence the jurisprudence of the Inter-American system, evolving, as discussed above, in parallel to the OAS standard-setting process. The Court's *Awas Tingni* decision and subsequent jurisprudence regarding collective land rights, for instance, is echoed in the provisions regarding indigenous land and resource rights, including the affirmation of indigenous peoples' 'right to legal recognition of the various and particular modalities and forms of property, possession and ownership of their lands and territories' as well as the related State duty to 'establish the special regimes appropriate for such recognition, and for their effective demarcation and titling'.[85] Moreover, the Draft American Declaration is obviously influenced by the content of ILO Convention 169, and, of course, of the UN Declaration, sometimes to the point of literal transplantation.[86]

A comparative analysis of the UN Declaration and the Draft American Declaration, as it currently stands, indeed reveals a number of important commonalities.[87] While the UN text is long, repetitive and somewhat ill-structured, the OAS draft displays a high level of concreteness and internal organisation. The Draft American Declaration further incorporates a number of significant innovations with regard to the UN Declaration. Thus, for example, the American draft incorporates a definition of its scope of application, a rather unproblematic issue in the Americas which became however strategically excluded from the negotiations at the UN level.[88] The relative convergence of American constitutional systems has further allowed the inclusion of a wide recognition of the 'multiethnic and multicultural' character of American States, now a common denominator in Latin American multicultural constitutionalism.[89]

[85] Draft American Declaration (n 74) Art XXIV(2).

[86] For some examples of the transplantation of the ILO Convention, see ibid, preamble, para 6(2) (recalling 'the international achievements in recognizing the rights of indigenous peoples and, in particular, the International Labour Organization's Convention concerning Indigenous and Tribal Peoples in Independent Countries [Convention No 169]'); Art I(2) (self-identification of indigenous peoples as a 'fundamental criterion' for determination of the scope of application of the Declaration); Art XXIV (affirming indigenous peoples' right to 'maintain and strengthen the distinctive spiritual, cultural, and material relationship to their lands, territories and resources'); Art XXIV(1) (affirming the right to the 'recognition of their property rights and ownership rights with respect to the lands and territories that they historically occupy, as well as the use of the lands to which they have traditionally had access for carrying out their traditional activities and for sustenance').

[87] A comparative analysis of the provisions of the UN Declaration and those of the Draft American Declaration can be found in *Table Comparing the Draft American Declaration on the Rights of Indigenous Peoples and the United Nations Declaration on the Rights of Indigenous Peoples*, OAS Doc OEA/Ser.K/XVI, GT/DADIN/doc.317/07 rev 1 (14 March 2008). *See* also *Authorities and Precedents in International and Domestic Law for the Proposed American Declaration on the Rights on Indigenous Peoples*, OEAS Doc OEA/Ser.L/V/II.110 Doc 22 (1 March 2001).

[88] Draft American Declaration (n 74) Art I.

[89] Ibid, Art II.

Of particular relevance are a number of substantive provisions in areas not covered, or insufficiently regulated, by the UN Declaration. This is the case, for instance, with the specific OAS draft standards concerning the situation of peoples in 'voluntary isolation' or 'initial contact', an issue of specific concern for countries sharing borders in the Amazon and the Chaco, and which has started to gain relevance in domestic and bilateral policies.[90] The Draft American Declaration further incorporates an explicit affirmation of the State's duty to recognise 'fully the juridical personality of indigenous peoples',[91] in a way that is consistent with recent pronouncements of the Inter-American Court.[92] Also consistent with the Court's multicultural sensitivity with regard to indigenous forms of social organisation—particularly evident in the area of reparations—the American Declaration incorporates a specific safeguard for the 'indigenous family', including various forms of 'extended family ... matrimonial union, filiations, descent, and family name'.[93] Possibly the best comparative advantage of the American draft vis-a-vis the UN Declaration's standards is its complete regulation of indigenous customary law and justice systems. While the issue is only incidentally tackled by the UN Declaration, as part of its wide recognition of indigenous peoples' right to 'promote, develop and maintain their institutional structures',[94] the Draft American Declaration incorporates a fairly complete regulation of the issue, including the recognition of jurisdictional functions of indigenous authorities;[95] the full recognition and application of indigenous law in internal matters;[96] and the formal incorporation of indigenous law and jurisdiction within the State legal and institutional framework.[97]

[90] Ibid, Art XXVI.

[91] Ibid, Art XI.

[92] The issue of the recognition of legal personality to indigenous communities was first tackled by the Court in *Saramaka v Suriname*. In this case, the Court acknowledged that the Saramaka were in a position of vulnerability 'in so far as they lacked the juridical capacity to collectively enjoy the right to property and to challenge before domestic courts alleged violations of such right'. *Saramaka* (n 52) para 174. The Court therefore ordered the State to 'establish ... the judicial and administrative conditions necessary to ensure the recognition of [the Saramaka's] juridical personality, with the aim of guaranteeing them the use and enjoyment of their territory ... as well as the rights to access to justice and equality before the law'. Ibid.

[93] Draft American Declaration (n 74) Art XVI(1).

[94] Ibid, Art XXXIV.

[95] Ibid, Art XXI(1) (recognising 'the [competence] of the authorities of indigenous peoples to exercise [jurisdictional functions] in their territories in accordance with their own standards, institutions and procedures').

[96] Ibid, Art XXI(2) ('The indigenous law and legal systems shall be recognized and respected by the national [and international] legal systems').

[97] Ibid, Art XXII(1) ('The States shall facilitate the inclusion, within their national and regional organizational structures, as appropriate, of the traditional institutions and practices of the indigenous peoples, in consultation with and with the consent of said peoples').

The thematic differences between the UN Declaration and the American Declaration will probably widen if the OAS standard-setting process continues to evolve in the direction of incorporating new topics as 'added value' for the American instrument. While this updating of the indigenous rights agenda ensues, the OAS text still contains a number of controversial provisions on which consensus has yet to be reached.[98] In this and other issues, both the UN Declaration and the jurisprudence of the Inter-American human rights bodies will continue to act as a minimum threshold that will prevent a deterioration in existing standards.

CONCLUSIONS

The drafting and final adoption of the UN Declaration has been a major influence in the gradual emergence of a specific set of standards regarding the rights of indigenous peoples within the Inter-American human rights protection system. These standards, which respond to the common human rights challenges that indigenous peoples face throughout the Americas, have been elaborated through the case law of the two major Inter-American human rights bodies in their interpretation of instruments of general applicability, as well as through the process of a specific normative instrument regarding the rights of indigenous peoples in the Americas.

A review of the case law of the Inter-American Court and Commission over the last decade suggests that the drafting process of the UN Declaration has played a major role in the articulation of a specific body of jurisprudence regarding indigenous peoples' rights. As an authoritative statement of evolving normative understanding concerning the rights of these peoples in international law, the Declaration's standards have been a critical point of reference in the Inter-American jurisprudence with regard to issues of particular importance for indigenous peoples. This includes, though not exclusively, the crucial issue of indigenous land and resource rights, starting in *Awas Tingni*, and beyond.

[98] In a recent evaluation of the Draft American Declaration, the OAS Department of International Law classified as 'difficult texts' the following provisions: Art III (right to self-determination); Art IV (territorial integrity); Art XX (right to autonomy and self-government); Art XII (right to cultural identity including restitution of cultural heritage); Art XV (indigenous spirituality, including protection of sacred sites and prohibition of religious conversion); Art XVIII (right to healthy environment, including the prohibition of establishing protected areas without indigenous peoples' consent); Art XXIV (right to land, territory and resources); Art XXVI (indigenous peoples in voluntary isolation, including their right to 'remain in that condition'); Art XXVIII (protection of cultural heritage and intellectual property). See *Classification of Provisions that could Facilitate Consensus*, OAS Doc OEA/Ser. K/XVI, GT/DADIN/doc.329/08 rev 2 (22 August 2008) 14–20.

The continuous influence of the UN standard-setting process on the articulation of the Inter-American jurisprudence concerning the rights of indigenous peoples has effectively established a relation of mutual reinforcement between those standards and the regional human rights protection regime, a relation that has now become explicit following the formal adoption of the UN Declaration. The utilisation of the Declaration's standards by the Court in *Saramaka v Suriname*, which will surely be replicated in future cases, is an important example of the kind of normative action required to operationalise those standards in the practice of international human rights bodies. *Saramaka* shows indeed that the human rights norms and principles affirmed in the Declaration can, and should, be interpreted in specific contexts to advance evolutionary interpretations of existing human rights instruments of general applicability in the specific context of indigenous peoples, while at the same time contributing to construct novel normative understandings on the content and scope of those norms and principles.

The jurisprudence of the Inter-American human rights bodies has been influential, as has been the UN Declaration, in the standard-setting process inaugurated in 1989 at the OAS regarding the drafting of the American Declaration on the Rights of Indigenous Peoples. Moreover, the adoption of the UN Declaration has actually been a trigger in ongoing negotiations between States and indigenous peoples leading to the final adoption of the American Declaration. When formally adopted, the American Declaration will play a symbolic role in signalling the political commitment of the OAS regional system to the promotion and protection of indigenous rights. The eventual adoption of the American Declaration will further mark the end of a decades-long process of standard-setting at the international level concerning the rights of indigenous peoples, a process that steered the efforts of international and domestic actors, including indigenous peoples' organisations, almost to the point of fatigue. With the final adoption of the American Declaration, those efforts may eventually be redirected to the implementation of the standards affirmed therein, a task in which the Inter-American human rights system is called upon to continue playing a leading role, both inside and outside the Americas.

19

The UN Declaration on the Rights of Indigenous Peoples in Africa: The Approach of the Regional Organisations to Indigenous Peoples

RACHEL MURRAY

INTRODUCTION

IN JANUARY 2007 the African Union (AU) adopted a Decision which sets out the central concerns of many African states regarding the concept of indigenous peoples' rights and helps explain why the UN Declaration on the Rights of Indigenous Peoples was not initially adopted by the UN General Assembly in November 2006. The AU's attitude was in contrast to the position adopted by its human rights body, the African Commission on Human and Peoples' Rights (African Commission), and the focus of its Working Group on Indigenous Populations/Communities, which had spent some time considering these issues. Despite the African Group and African states being initially unaware of the Working Group's work on the subject, in a remarkable demonstration of the impact of a clear policy by the African Commission on Human and Peoples' Rights and the political sway it can hold with states when necessary, its pressure convinced them to change their minds, eventually leading to the successful adoption of the UN Declaration by the General Assembly in September 2007.

Overall, the approach of the African Commission to the concept of indigenous peoples and its progressive stance is not due to the Commission itself adopting a proactive strategy on the issue, but a reaction to opportunities presented by the setting up of the Working Group composed of both Commissioners and experienced non-governmental organisations (NGOs). The Working Group on Indigenous Populations/Communities is perhaps the clearest example of what can go right with such a body before the African Commission and an indication of the impact that it can truly have at a political level. This is not the case with all of the working groups,[1] and this particular group owes its success in part to the commitment of a key NGO with long-standing expertise in this area, the International Work Group for Indigenous Affairs (IWGIA). This NGO, with individual experts from various indigenous peoples, backed by considerable and constant funding and the support of a few key Commissioners, some of whom were unlikely champions, led to the African Commission spearheading developments on the continent in relation to indigenous peoples' rights.

This chapter will examine the attitude of the AU and the African Commission towards indigenous peoples and the UN Declaration in particular. As will be shown, it was the continuous, gentle persuasion on the part of key individuals and NGOs that eventually led to the African Commission agreeing to examine the issue in greater depth and to the African states changing their minds and supporting the adoption of the UN Declaration.

CONVINCING THE AFRICAN COMMISSION TO CONSIDER THE ISSUE

Despite the African Charter on Human and Peoples' Rights (ACHPR), with its broad collection of peoples' rights in Articles 19–24, providing ample opportunity for discussion of the concept of indigenous peoples, it took some sustained persuasion on the part of a group of NGOs and individuals to persuade the African Commission of the need to pay attention to such peoples. Although some states had referred to their treatment of indigenous people as early as 1996 in statements before the African Commission or in the examination of their state reports,[2] the item did not appear on the agenda of the African Commission until its 25th session in May 1999.[3] As a follow-up to the conference in Arusha in January of that year,[4] Commissioner Barney Pityana introduced the item, encouraging the African Commission to become involved in the 'major international drive' to adopt a declaration on indigenous peoples and because the issue of ethnic minorities had implications for conflict. The Arusha conference, among other

[1] See BTM Nyanduga, 'Working Groups of the African Commission and their Role in the Development of the African Charter on Human and Peoples' Rights' in MD Evans and R Murray (eds), *The African Charter on Human and Peoples' Rights: The System in Practice, 1986–2006*, 2nd edn (Cambridge University Press, 2008) 379.

[2] Eg Cameroon, 20th session of the African Commission, October 1996; see report of session (on file with the author); Zimbabwe, 21st session, April 1997; see report of session (on file with the author).

[3] Agenda of the 25th Ordinary Session, 26 April–5 May 1999, Twelfth Activity Report of the African Commission on Human and Peoples' Rights, 1998–1999, AHG/215 (XXXV), item 8(j) under 'promotional activities'.

[4] IWGIA Conference on Indigenous Peoples in Africa, Arusha, Tanzania, 1999, www.iwgia.org/sw579.asp.

things, specifically requested 'adequate representation of hunter-gatherer communities in all contexts and in particular that all relevant hunter-gatherer communities be represented in any relevant national or international body that may be established'.[5] Importantly, however, it addressed specific recommendations to the African Commission itself, noting that despite indigenous peoples being a human rights issue, the African Commission had so far not considered this matter and that this was a 'neglect of its mandate' under the African Charter.[6] It called on the African Commission to encourage all NGOs concerned with indigenous affairs to seek observer status with the Commission; that the issue be included as an item on the agenda of the Commission's sessions; that the African Commission set up a working group; and that it consider whether local remedies should be exhausted when submitting a case to the Commission.

Commissioner Barney Pityana picked up on these recommendations and presented them to the session of the African Commission, although he specifically asked that the Commission ignore the last request regarding the exhaustion of domestic remedies. The discussion that followed at the session centred mostly around the derogatory nature of the term 'indigenous'. The Commissioners concluded by calling on Commissioner Pityana to prepare a paper for further discussion at the subsequent sessions.

The paper presented by Commissioner Pityana to the 26th session of the Commission in November 1999 addressed many of the concerns that would be raised by the AU nearly a decade later when it dealt with the UN Declaration. These included recognition that given the colonial context, and the way in which state boundaries were drawn in Africa, 'indigenous peoples were not necessarily minorities' if one looked at them as a collective. In addition, the context in which the African Charter was written, its reference to 'peoples' rights' in its title and its provisions reflected the need to include not the nation-state, but 'tribal communities'.[7] It also outlined difficulties faced by the UN, ILO and others in drafting a definition of 'indigenous peoples'. Further, it noted that African states had not taken part in discussions on the draft declaration at the UN and that many denied that indigenous peoples exist on the continent.[8] The report then recommended that a sub-commission of the African Commission be established,[9] composed of an 'equal number

[5] Arusha Resolutions, ibid, para 18.3.

[6] Ibid, para 21.

[7] Situation of Indigenous Peoples in Africa, 26th Session of the African Commission, 1–15 November 1999, DOC/OS(XXVI)/130.

[8] Ibid, para 21.

[9] Rule 28(1) of the Commission's Rules of Procedures provides: 'The Commission may during a session, taking into account the provisions of the Charter, establish, if it deems it necessary for the exercise of its functions, committees or working groups, composed of the members of the Commission and send them any agenda item for consideration and report.'

of experts from the indigenous community and other African experts in international law and social science', and that it report regularly to the African Commission on policy proposals.[10]

After some internal discussion, continued gentle lobbying by NGOs and the influence of Commissioner Pityana, at the 28th session in November 2000 the African Commission adopted a resolution agreeing to set up a Working Group of Experts on the Rights of Indigenous Populations/ Communities in Africa composed of two Commissioners and two African experts in the field.[11] This Working Group was to:

- Examine the concept of indigenous populations/communities in Africa;
- Study the implications of the African Charter on Human and Peoples' Rights and the well being of indigenous populations/communities especially with regard to:
  - the right to equality (Articles 2 and 3)
  - the right to dignity (Article 5)
  - protection against domination (Article 19)
  - self-determination (Article 20) and
  - the promotion of cultural development and identity (Article 22);
- Consider appropriate recommendations for the monitoring and protection of the rights of indigenous populations/communities.[12]

Although the Working Group would not produce its report for another three years, the willingness of the Commission to consider this issue in-depth prompted the rights of indigenous peoples to be raised in other areas of the Commission's work. For example, at the 29th session, during the examination of the Article 62 state report of Namibia, various questions were asked with regard to the government's treatment of the San and Himba people and these came from Commissioners who were not members of the Working Group. The Concluding Observations further urged the government to 'urgently introduce measures that adequately address the situation of vulnerable groups such as the San and Himba so as to enable such groups to enjoy the rights under the Charter on the basis of equality with other groups in the country'.[13] The 29th session also heard from NGO representatives on the item more generally and it was at this session that various 'representatives' of indigenous peoples came to speak to the Commission and made statements during the public sittings. These included individuals noting the situation of

[10] See above, n 7, para 22.

[11] Resolution on the Rights of Indigenous Populations/Communities in Africa, November 2000, ACHPR/Res.51(XXVIII) 00.

[12] Ibid, para 3.

[13] Concluding Observations on Namibia, 29th session of the African Commission, April–May 2001. See also, in relation to the treatment of pygmies in Congo, Concluding Observations on Congo, 29th session of the African Commission, April–May 2001.

the pygmies in Central Africa, Hadazbe and hunter-gatherers in East Africa, Tuareg and others in West Africa, and groups such as the Berber in North Africa.

The benefit of creating a working group over a Special Rapporteur, which had up until that stage been the preferred choice of the Commission, was that it enabled the NGO and individuals to influence directly Commission policy and yet ensure that their work, through the assistance and involvement of Commissioners, obtained the African Commission's stamp of approval. The establishment of this Working Group came at a time when the African Commission had had its fingers burnt by the failure of some of its own members as Special Rapporteurs to deliver on their mandates.[14] Working groups were seen, at that stage at least, as an interim solution which could avoid some of the pitfalls of Special Rapporteurs. Over time, however, the model of the Working Group has been duplicated and has proved particularly effective and useful.[15]

There was some initial discussion about the composition of the Working Group and whether those individuals who had been attending the sessions so far had been appointed to the Working Group in their individual capacity as experts or as representatives of peoples' rights organisations. In the end, quite rightly, the former approach appears to have been adopted, thus avoiding difficulties of any claims that there was 'representation' by the specific individuals of certain indigenous peoples.

In 2003 the Working Group produced its first comprehensive report.[16] This document, although relatively modest in terms of its analysis, was a breakthrough at the level of the African Commission for its indication by an African organisation of the marginalisation and human rights abuses suffered by indigenous people on the continent and its willingness to use the term to refer to groups such as hunter-gatherers[17] and pastoralists,[18] among others.[19]

[14] See R Murray, 'The Special Rapporteurs in the African System' in Evans and Murray (n 1) 344.

[15] See Nyanduga (n 1).

[16] Report of the African Commission's Working Group on Indigenous Populations/Communities submitted in accordance with the Resolution on the Rights of Indigenous Populations/Communities in Africa, adopted by the African Commission on Human and Peoples' Rights at its 28th Ordinary Session, 2003 (hereinafter 'Working Group Report').

[17] The Report lists these as: the Batwa/Pygmies of the Great Lakes Region, the San of Southern Africa, the Hadzabe of Tanzania, and the Ogiek of Kenya.

[18] The Report lists these as: the Pokot of Kenya and Uganda; the Barabaig of Tanzania; the Maasai of Kenya and Tanzania; the Samburu, the Turkana, the Rendille, the Orma, and the Borana of Kenya and Ethiopia; the Karamojong of Uganda; the Touareg of West and Central Africa; the Fulani of Mali, Burkina-Faso and Niger; the Mbororo of Cameroon and West Africa; the Ogoni of Nigeria; and the Berber of North Africa.

[19] Working Group Report (n 16) 8–10.

Since then the Working Group has produced an Advisory Opinion in May 2007,[20] in response to the AU's Decision several months previously, and various reports on visits it has made to states, as well as undertaking research projects and holding seminars.[21] As at September 2010 it is composed of three Commissioners and six additional individual experts.[22] Commissioners continue to ask questions of states during the examination of their Article 62 reports.[23]

One might have expected, therefore, given these developments at the level of the AU's human rights body, that African states and the AU would have had the way smoothed for them in the adoption of the UN Declaration on the Rights of Indigenous Peoples. However, due to the distance that is often maintained between the African Commission on Human and Peoples' Rights on the one hand and the other AU organs on the other, the latter did not seem to be aware of the former's developments in this field. Furthermore, there was a general lack of engagement on the part of African states with the UN Declaration drafting process.[24] As a result, when it came to the consideration of the UN Declaration by states parties at the UN and then at the AU, African states and the AU made no reference to the African Commission resolutions, the Working Group or its report. When the UN Human Rights Council adopted the Declaration in June 2006 a number of African states voted in favour of the Declaration,[25] but of those states that abstained, half of them were from Africa.[26] The difficulties experienced by some African states emerged at the General Assembly in November 2006 when Namibia suggested a resolution which would defer adoption of the Declaration until further discussions had taken place. The African Group listed its concerns regarding the Declaration in an Aide Memoire issued in November 2006 and the

[20] For discussion of this Advisory Opinion see below.

[21] See 23rd Activity Report of the African Commission on Human and Peoples' Rights, 2008, EX.CL/446(XIII), 42–43; and Presentation of the Chairperson of the Working Group on Indigenous Populations/Communities, Inter-sessional period between 41st and 42nd Ordinary Session, www.iwgia.org.

[22] The members of the Working Group are: Commissioner Musa Ngary Bitaye—Chairperson; Commissioner Soyata Maiga; Commissioner Mumba Malila; Ms Marianne Jensen; Mr Mohammed Khattali; Ms Naomi Kipuri; Mr Kalimba Zepharin; Dr Albert Barume; and Mr Melakon Tegegn. 23rd Activity Report of the African Commission on Human and Peoples' Rights, EX.CL/446 (XIII), para 10(e).

[23] See M Jensen, *IWGIA Report. The 43rd Ordinary Session of the African Commission on Human and Peoples' Rights, Swaziland, 7–22 May 2008*, www.iwgia.org.

[24] See W van Genugten, 'The African Move Towards the Adoption of the 2007 Declaration on the Rights of Indigenous Peoples: The Substantive Arguments behind the Procedures', Paper prepared for the Committee on the Rights of Indigenous Peoples of the International Law Association, 1 March 2008; C Morel, 'Defending Human Rights in Africa: The Case for Minority and Indigenous Rights' (2004) 1 *Essex Human Rights Review* 54.

[25] Eg Cameroon, South Africa and Zambia.

[26] Algeria, Ghana, Morocco, Nigeria, Senegal and Tunisia.

issue was then discussed at the AU Summit in January 2007, at which the Assembly adopted a Decision. This Decision, whilst expressing 'full support and solidarity with indigenous peoples of the world', and the need for a united front from Africa, set out a number of 'questions' that needed addressing:

(a) the definition of indigenous peoples;
(b) self-determination;
(c) ownership of land and natural resources;
(d) establishment of distinct political and economic institutions; and
(e) national and territorial integrity.[27]

At the 41st session of the African Commission in May 2007, several months after the adoption of the Decision by the AU, the African Commission adopted an Advisory Opinion addressing the concerns of the AU.[28] This Advisory Opinion dealt with each of the points of the AU Resolution in turn, highlighting the work that the Working Group had already carried out. It is worth examining the underlying issues, as reflected in the AU Decision, as they represent the difficulties that African states seem to have had with the UN Declaration and the concept of indigenous peoples in general.

Sovereignty

The Decision of the AU of 2007 displays a central concern with protection of sovereignty in the context of the territorial integrity of the state which is perceived as being threatened by granting indigenous peoples such rights, exacerbated by the historical colonial connotations that the term represented to many. As will be discussed further below, the notion of self-determination in this 2007 Decision is seen by the AU only in its external context, namely secession, and not internally. The traditional focus by African states on their sovereignty features prominently in this Decision. The AU Decision clearly reiterates the previous pledge by the former OAU 'to respect borders existing on their achievement of national independence' and 'reaffirms the United Nations General Assembly

[27] Decision on the United Nations Declaration, Assembly/AU/Dec.141 (VIII), para 6.

[28] Advisory Opinion of the African Commission on Human and Peoples' Rights on the United Nations Declaration on the Rights of Indigenous Peoples, adopted by the African Commission on Human and Peoples' Rights at its 41st ordinary session in May 2007 held in Accra, Ghana, 2007.

Resolution 1514 (XV) of 14 December 1960 concerning the Declaration on the granting of independence to colonial countries and peoples'.[29]

Sensibly, in its Advisory Opinion, the African Commission approached this issue carefully and noted that it had

> interpreted the protection of the rights of Indigenous Populations *within the context of a strict respect for the inviolability of borders and of the obligation to preserve the territorial integrity of State Parties*, in conformity with the principles and values enshrined in the Constitutive Act of the AU, the African Charter on Human and Peoples' Rights ... and the UN Charter.[30]

The African Commission and the AU have always guarded the sovereignty of African states parties to the AU and former OAU, from threats posed to the territorial integrity of states both internally and externally: 'The Commission is of the strong belief that such interests would better be protected within the confines of the territories of the Respondent States.'[31]

The Concept of Self-Determination

The concerns expressed by the AU in its Decision on the UN Declaration reflect an understanding of the notion of self-determination as focusing on external self-determination,[32] namely secession and independence:

> The principle of self-determination only applies to peoples under colonial and/or foreign occupation ... Implicitly recognising the rights of indigenous peoples to self determination ... can be misrepresented as conferring a unilateral right of self-determination and possible secession upon a specific subset of the national populace, thus threatening the political unity and the territorial integrity of any country.[33]

Indeed, the UN Declaration itself, while referring to the right to self-determination in its preamble, provides in Articles 3, 4 and 5:

> Article 3
>
> Indigenous peoples have the right to self-determination. By virtue of that right they freely determine their political status and freely pursue their economic, social and cultural development.

[29] Decision on the United Nations Declaration on the Rights of Indigenous Peoples, Assembly/AU/Dec.141 (VIII), paras 2 and 4.

[30] Advisory Opinion (n 28) para 6.

[31] Communication 227/99, *DRC v Burundi, Rwanda and Uganda*, Twentieth Activity Report of the African Commission on Human and Peoples' Rights, Annex IV, para 77.

[32] K Knop, *Diversity and Self Determination in International Law* (Cambridge University Press, 2002).

[33] Draft Aide Memoire, African Group, United Nations Declaration on the Rights of Indigenous Peoples, 9 November 2006, New York, para 3.1, www.iwgia.org.

Article 4

Indigenous peoples, in exercising their right to self-determination, have the right to autonomy or self-government in matters relating to their internal and local affairs, as well as ways and means for financing their autonomous functions.

Article 5

Indigenous peoples have the right to maintain and strengthen their distinct political, legal, economic, social and cultural institutions, while retaining their right to participate fully, if they so choose, in the political, economic, social and cultural life of the State.

Indeed, it was this concern that led to the insertion of an additional sentence in Article 46(1) of the UN Declaration, enabling it to be adopted by the UN General Assembly in September 2007.[34] This read: 'nothing in this Declaration may be interpreted as implying for any State, people, group or person any right to engage any activity or to perform any act contrary to the Charter of the UN', an approach underlined by the African Commission in its Advisory Opinion.[35]

The narrow view of AU is surprising given that the former OAU and AU have often recognised, in many of their resolutions and decisions over the years, that the right to self-determination can be recognised not just in the external context, but internally as well. The OAU/AU has moved from considering self-determination to apply in a decolonisation context, to a position where they also recognise the concept of self-determination as encompassing a prohibition against unconstitutional changes of government,[36] and an understanding that a democratic state requires institutions that reflect the will of the people, suggesting some recognition of autonomy within existing state boundaries. The African Commission has similarly recognised self-determination as being able to be exercised 'in any of the following—independence, self-government, local government, federalism, co-federalism, unitarism or any other form of relations that accords with the wishes of the people but fully cognizant of other recognised principles such as sovereignty and territorial integrity. The Commission is obliged to uphold the territorial integrity of Zaire, a member of the OAU and a party to the African Charter on Human and Peoples' Rights.'[37]

[34] S Errico, 'The UN Declaration on the Rights of Indigenous Peoples is adopted: An Overview' (2007) 7 *Human Rights Law Review* 756, 757–58.

[35] Advisory Opinion (n 28) paras 17 and 18.

[36] See Decision on the Unconstitutional Changes of Government in Africa, AHG/Dec.150 (XXXVI), Thirty Third Ordinary Session in Harare, Zimbabwe, June 1997. See also Declaration on the Framework for an OAU Response to Unconstitutional Changes in Government, AHG/Decl.5 (XXXVI).

[37] Communication 75/92, *Katangese Peoples' Congress v Zaire*, Eighth Annual Activity Report of the African Commission on Human and Peoples' Rights, Annex VI, paras 4 and 5.

Furthermore, in several decisions it held that Article 20(1) of the African Charter and the right of a people to self-determination has a close relationship with Article 13 and the right of individuals to participate freely in government through chosen representatives.[38] Thus, unconstitutional changes of government violate both provisions: '[T]he right of a people to determine their "political status" can be interpreted as involving the right of Nigerians to be able to choose freely those persons or party that will govern them. It is the counterpart of the right enjoyed by individuals under Article 13.'[39] The annulment of a free and fair election violated 'this right of the Nigerian people' under Article 20(1) of the Charter.[40]

However, on only one occasion has the African Commission suggested any divergence from this view. In Communication 75/92, *Katangese Peoples' Congress v Zaire*,[41] concerning requests by the Katangese People that the Commission recognise their right to be independent from Zaire, the Commission held that 'in the absence of concrete evidence of violations of human rights to the point that the territorial integrity of Zaire should be called to question and in the absence of evidence that the people of Katanga are denied the right to participate in government as guaranteed by Article 13(1) of the African Charter, the Commission holds the view that Katanga is obliged to exercise a variant of self-determination that is compatible with the sovereignty and territorial integrity of Zaire'.[42] This seems to suggest that there may be two occasions on which self-determination which impacts on the sovereignty and territorial integrity of Zaire may be called into question: where there are violations of human rights 'to the point that the territorial integrity of Zaire should be called into question', and where 'the people of Katanga are denied the right to participate in government as guaranteed by Article 13(1)', that is, an element of participation or potentially autonomy. As Cynthia Morel and Clive Baldwin note, 'this paragraph does strongly imply [that] if human rights violations against a people were to reach a certain level, the Commission would recognise that that people had a right to independence, presumably as the only way that they could enjoy their right to self-determination in practice'.[43] The African Commission has

[38] Art 13(1) reads: 'Every citizen shall have the right to participate freely in the government of his country, either directly or through freely chosen representatives in accordance with the provisions of the law.'

[39] Communication 102/93, *Constitutional Rights Project and Civil Liberties Organisation v Nigeria*, Twelfth Activity Report of the African Commission on Human and Peoples' Rights, Annex V, para 52.

[40] Ibid, para 53.

[41] Eighth Annual Activity Report of the African Commission on Human and Peoples' Rights, Annex VI.

[42] Ibid, para 6.

[43] C Morel and C Baldwin, 'Group Rights' in Evans and Murray (n 1) 244, 259.

never, however, gone beyond this in its consideration of self-determination and has instead focused primarily on self-determination as an internal concept.

Besides this one statement, the African Commission as well as the OAU/AU have consistently upheld the principle of *uti possidetis*, as reflected in an early Declaration of the OAU which 'solemnly declares that all Member States pledge themselves to respect the frontiers existing on their achievement of national independence'.[44] Despite recognition of Palestinian claims to self-determination,[45] the African regional institutions have clearly rejected secessionist claims that impact on the territory of existing African states.[46] As the African Commission's Working Group states in its report, 'Self-determination of peoples must therefore be exercised within the inviolable national boundaries of the state with due regard to the sovereignty of the nation-state'.[47]

Similarly, the African Commission has focused less on the notion of self-determination in the context of indigenous peoples, and more on their marginalisation and discrimination, which can then be addressed by greater participation in the state structures, structures that may have to be provided separately where necessary.[48] This is a line also taken by the AU in its African Charter on Democracy, Elections and Governance,[49] which contains amongst its objectives the recognition of the importance of popular participation,[50] not just 'through universal suffrage as the inalienable right of the people',[51] but also expressly requiring states to 'respect ethnic, cultural and religious diversity, which contributes to strengthening democracy and citizen participation'.[52] The requirement that states 'adopt legislative and administrative measures to guarantee the rights of

[44] Resolution on the Intangibility of Frontiers, AHG/RES.16(I), July 1964.

[45] Eg Executive Council, Decision on Palestine and the Middle East, January 2007, EX.CL/Dec.326 (X).

[46] See R Murray, *Human Rights in Africa: From the OAU to the African Union* (Cambridge University Press, 2004) ch 1; and I Enemo, 'Self-Determination as the Fundamental Basis of the Concept of Legitimate Governance under the African Charter on Human and Peoples' Rights' in EK Quashigah and OC Okafor (eds), *Legitimate Governance in Africa* (The Hague, Kluwer Law International, 1999) 403.

[47] Working Group Report (n 16) 54.

[48] Eg states should take measures 'to achieve the full realization of the right of everyone to receive compulsory and free education, including special provisions relating to specific groups such as … children belonging to linguistic, racial, religious or other minorities, and children belonging to indigenous sectors of the population'. Guidelines for State Periodic Reports, Second Annual Activity Report of the African Commission on Human and Peoples' Rights, Annex X, para 48.

[49] Adopted at the Eighth Ordinary Session of the Assembly of Heads of State and Government of the AU, Addis Ababa, 30 January 2007. As at August 2010 this has 3 states have ratified and 29 signed the Charter.

[50] Ibid, Art 2(10).

[51] Ibid, Art 4(2).

[52] Ibid, Art 8(3).

women, ethnic minorities, migrants, people with disabilities, refugees and displaced persons and other marginalized and vulnerable social groups'[53] introduces important obligations in respect of indigenous peoples' ability to influence decision-making.

It is this requirement to provide additional structures for participation of certain groups that characterises the stance adopted by the OAU/AU.[54] As the Assembly of Heads of State and Government decided in Algiers in 1999, democratic institutions within states should be

> representative of our peoples and receiving their active participation would further contribute to the consolidation of modern African states underpinned by the rule of law, respect for the fundamental rights and freedoms of the citizens and the democratic management of public affairs.[55]

The Concept of Indigenous Peoples in Africa

As early discussions at the sessions of the African Commission illustrated, the stumbling block to more substantial discussions was around the terms 'indigenous' and 'autocthone', which were seen as derogatory. As the Working Group on Indigenous Populations/Communities itself noted:

> We also recognise the concern of those who feel that the term 'indigenous peoples' has negative connotations in Africa as it has been used in derogatory ways during European colonialism and also been misused in chauvinistic ways by some post-colonial African governments.[56]

The AU reiterated this approach in its Decision of 2007, which affirmed that 'the vast majority of the peoples of Africa are indigenous to the African continent'.[57] It is this traditional approach to the notion of peoples' rights, namely with regard to who is constitutes a 'people' in the context of claiming these rights, that is reflected by the African states: 'the absence of a definition of indigenous peoples in the text creates legal problems for the implementation of the Declaration. It is therefore important that the Declaration's jurisdictional clause defining the rights holder should be included in the text.'[58] A lack of legal definition would also

[53] Ibid, Art 8(1).
[54] To 'promote citizen participation in the development process through appropriate structures'. African Charter on Popular Participation, Art 30.
[55] Algiers Declaration, AHG/Decl.1 (XXXV).
[56] Working Group Report (n 16) 61.
[57] Decision on the United Nations Declaration on the Rights of Indigenous Peoples, Assembly/AU/Dec.141 (VIII), para 7.
[58] Aide Memoire of African Group, New York, 9 November 2006, para 2.1, www.iwgia.org/sw21505.asp.

'create tension among ethnic groups and instability between sovereign states'.[59]

Yet as the African Commission's Working Group stated, it was unwilling to try to find definitions of the term 'indigenous peoples'. Neither was it necessary, as some Commissioners had previously recommended, to look to other wording or using the term 'minorities' as this would detract from the standards that were being developed internationally. The Working Group believed that the term 'indigenous peoples' was an

> internationally recognised term by which to understand and analyse certain forms of inequalities and suppression such as the ones suffered by many pastoralists and hunter-gather groups and others in Africa today and by which to address their human rights sufferings.[60]

Whilst it is understandable that the African Commission saw the need to refer to 'indigenous populations/communities' rather than 'indigenous people' in its 2003 Report and in some parts of its Advisory Opinion, in order to appease those who found the term problematic at the level of the Commission, this rather undermines this argument. The introduction of these new terms potentially adds another category to 'peoples', 'indigenous peoples' and 'minorities', unless one can see 'populations/communities' as being temporary and having no legal basis. Indeed, the latter seems to be the approach of the African Commission, which, now that the concept of indigenous peoples has gained acceptance among its members, refers more often to 'indigenous peoples' rather than 'indigenous populations/communities'.

Neither was the Commission, either in its 2003 Report or in its Advisory Opinion responding to the AU Decision, willing to set out a definition of an indigenous people, referring simply to the need for 'characteristics' and stating that 'no single definition can capture the characteristics of indigenous populations'.[61] Further, 'indigenous populations' 'does not mean "first inhabitants" in reference to aboriginality as opposed to non-African communities or those coming from elsewhere'.[62] The Report of the Working Group had set out the characteristics of indigenous populations/communities as follows:

> [T]heir cultures and ways of life differ considerably from the dominant society and … their cultures are under threat in some cases to the extent of extinction. A key characteristic for most of them is that the survival of their particular way of life depends on access and rights to their traditional land and the natural resources thereon. They suffer from discrimination as they are being regarded as

[59] Ibid, para 2.2.
[60] Working Group Report (n 16) 61.
[61] Advisory Opinion (n 28) para 10.
[62] Ibid, para 13.

> less developed and less advanced than other more dominant sectors of society. They often live in inaccessible regions, often geographically isolated and suffer from various forms of marginalization, both politically and socially. They are subject to domination and exploitation within national political and economic structures that are commonly designed to reflect the interests and activities of the national majority. This discrimination, domination and marginalization violate their human rights as peoples/communities, threaten the continuation of their cultures and ways of life and prevent them from being able to genuinely participate in deciding on their own future and forms of development.[63]

The Advisory Opinion followed this up with a list of 'constitutive elements or characteristics':

(a) self-identification;
(b) a special attachment to and use of their traditional land whereby their ancestral land and territory have a fundamental importance for their collective physical and cultural survival as peoples;
(c) a state of subjugation, marginalization, dispossession, exclusion or discrimination because these peoples have different cultures, ways of life or modes of production than the national hegemonic and dominant model.[64]

As the Report of the Working Group indicated, such groups can claim not only individual rights but also the peoples' rights of the African Charter. Indeed, in the rest of its jurisprudence, the African Commission has been unwilling to provide a definition of 'people', instead using the term to apply to a variety of different groups including the population of a state,[65] ethnic groups[66] and indigenous peoples.

The willingness to, for example, permit more autonomy or separate structures for indigenous peoples reflects a focus on 'accommodation' on the part of the AU and African Commission, which differs from the 'integration' approach taken by the UN.[67] As Will Kymlicka notes, the UN's 'official position is surprisingly simple: '"indigenous peoples" have a right

[63] Working Group Report (n 16) para 4.1.
[64] Advisory Opinion (n 28) para 12.
[65] Eg Communication 227/99, *DRC v Burundi, Rwanda and Uganda* (n 31).
[66] For example, in its Report on the Fact-Finding Mission to the Republic of Sudan in the Darfur Region the African Commission referred to individuals from the 'Fur, Marsalit, and Zaggawa ethnic groups, who are indigenous to the Darfur region'. Twenty-Second Activity Report of the African Commission on Human and Peoples' Rights, EX.CL/364 (XI), Annex III, para 3. Later on, however, it refers to them simply as 'ethnic groups', 'tribes', 'pastoralist tribes' and 'tribal groups of African origin', eg at paras 101, 102 and 118.
[67] J McGarry, B O'Leary and R Simeon, 'Integration or Accommodation? The Enduring Debate in Conflict Regulation' in S Choudhry (ed), *Constitutional Design for Divided Societies: Integration or Accommodation* (Oxford University Press, 2008), with accommodation aiming to provide separate institutions for particular groups, and integration including those groups within existing institutions.

to accommodation, whereas "minorities" have a right to integration'.[68] As the African Charter does not refer to 'minorities', the African Commission and its Working Group have not spent much time considering the distinction between the terms 'indigenous people' and 'minority'.[69] Unlike international law, which Kymlicka argues 'treats the distinction between indigenous peoples and national minorities as a categorical one, with enormous implications for the legal rights each type of group',[70] a distinction which is 'morally dubious and conceptually unstable',[71] the African Commission has not taken this approach and has often used the terms interchangeably.[72] A group claiming rights before the African Commission does not have to make a choice as to whether it identifies itself as a 'minority' or an 'indigenous people' as the African Commission has applied individual and peoples' rights to a variety of different entities.[73] What the African Commission has done, which the UN has not, is to say that those belonging to groups may be able to claim both individual and collective rights within the Charter, rather than saying that indigenous peoples have a particular set of rights. Thus, those members of a 'minority' can claim peoples' rights as well as individual rights. As the African Commission's Working Group stated in its 2003 report with respect to the distinction between 'minority' and 'indigenous people': 'It is thus important to apply a flexible approach that is based on concrete analysis of the human rights issues at stake.'[74]

This does not necessarily reflect the view that it is the fact that the minorities and indigenous peoples may make different claims and demands that distinguishes them: 'what distinguishes these groups is the nature of their political demands: simply put, minorities and national minorities demand cultural security; peoples demand recognition of their right to self-determination, or self-government.'[75]

[68] W Kymlicka, 'The Internationalization of Minority Rights' (2008) 6 *International Journal of Constitutional Law* 1, 23.

[69] See, however, in relation to the UN, UN ECOSOC, Commission on Human Rights, Sub-Commission on the Promotion and Protection of Human Rights, Working Paper on the Relationship and Distinction between the Rights of Persons belonging to Minorities and those of Indigenous Peoples, prepared by Asbjorn Eide and Erica-Irene Daes, UN Doc E/CN.4/Sub.2/2000/10, 19 July 2000.

[70] Kymlikca (n 68) 15.

[71] Ibid, 16.

[72] See eg Resolution on the Adoption of the Report of the African Commission's Working Group on Indigenous Populations/Communities, 34th session, November 2003.

[73] In Communication 299/05, *Anuak Justice Council v Ethiopia*, the complainants alleged discrimination against members of the Anuak indigenous people in Ethiopia, including killings, disappearances, torture, arbitrary detention, displacement and property destruction. Interestingly, although referring to the Anuak as an 'ethnic indigenous minority', the complainant alleged violations only of the individual rights in the African Charter, not peoples' rights. Arts 4, 5, 6, 12, 14 and 18, Twentieth Activity Report, Annex IV, para 12 of the decision.

[74] Working Group Report (n 16) 67.

[75] S Wheatley, *Democracy, Minorities and International Law* (Cambridge University Press, 2005) 124.

This more flexible approach avoids some of the difficulties experienced by the UN. Indeed, groups from Africa which previously may have presented themselves as minorities at the level of the UN are now presenting themselves as indigenous peoples, as there is a sense that this will provide them with better rights at that level.[76]

Control over Land and Natural Resources

In its Aide Memoire the Group of African States argued that control of land and natural resources was the responsibility of the state and the provision in the UN Declaration that indigenous peoples have rights to such was 'unworkable in the context of the countries concerned'.[77] This was reflected in earlier declarations from the OAU, where it stated that it would 'defend vigorously, continually and jointly the African countries' inalienable sovereign rights and control over their natural resources',[78] as long as this was 'for the economic benefit of African people'.[79]

In contrast to this intractable position, what the OAU/AU has done on numerous occasions is to recognise the importance of protecting the rights of 'local communities' within the context of 'indigenous knowledge', calling, for example, on states to 'take into account the rights of local communities' and 'develop and implement land tenure policies'.[80] Therefore, although prior to the adoption of the Decision on the UN Declaration at the Summit in January 2007 the AU had spent little time considering the issue of indigenous peoples, a search through its previous resolutions and declarations reveals a concern with protecting 'indigenous knowledge'. Thus, while earlier decisions of the OAU referred to 'indigenous' as black Africans (in the context of South Africa)[81] and the people of the Western Sahara 'under Spanish administration',[82] it consistently referred to the need to protect 'indigenous knowledge' and cultural heritage in the context of intellectual property rights and biodiversity. On many of these occasions it is clear that what is being talked about is not the knowledge of all Africans, but the knowledge of specific groups of Africans whom

[76] See Kymlicka (n 68) 17.

[77] Aide Memoire (n 58) para 7.0.

[78] African Declaration on Co-operation, Development and Economic Independence, 10th Ordinary Session AHSG, 25 May 1973, A.8.

[79] OAU Declaration on the Issues of the Law of the Sea, CM/St.11(XXI).

[80] African Convention on the Conservation of Nature and Natural Resources, EX/CL/50 (III), revising previous Convention, adopted July 2003, Article 6(4). As at the time of writing, this Convention has received eight ratifications.

[81] Assembly of Heads of State and Government, Resolution on South Africa, AHG/Res.124 (XX), November 1984.

[82] Council of Ministers, Resolution on the Sahara under Spanish Domination, CM/Res.301 (XXI), May 1973.

many in international human rights law would consider to be indigenous. As Article 17 of the AU's Convention on the Conservation of Nature and Natural Resources provides:

> 1. The Parties shall take legislative and other measures to ensure that traditional rights and intellectual property rights of local communities including farmers' rights are respected in accordance with the provisions of this Convention.
> 2. The Parties shall require that access to indigenous knowledge and its use be subject to the prior informed consent of the concerned communities and to specific regulations recognizing their rights to, and appropriate economic value of, such knowledge.
> 3. The Parties shall take the measures necessary to enable active participation by the local communities in the process of planning and management of natural resources upon which such communities depend with a view to creating local incentives for the conservation and sustainable use of such resources.[83]

Similarly, the African Commission has suggested that Article 21 of the African Charter, which provides that '[a]ll peoples shall freely dispose of their wealth and natural resources. This right shall be exercised in the exclusive interest of the people. In no case shall a people be deprived of it', should be seen in its historical context:

> The origin of this provision may be traced to colonialism, during which the human and material resources of Africa were largely exploited for the benefit of outside powers, creating tragedy for Africans themselves, depriving them of their birthright and alienating them from the land. The aftermath of colonial exploitation has left Africa's precious resources and people still vulnerable to foreign misappropriation. The drafters of the Charter obviously wanted to remind African governments of the continent's painful legacy and restore co-operative economic development to its traditional place at the heart of African Society.[84]

Permitting the exploitation of oil in the Ogoni area of Nigeria, the population of which the African Commission has recognised as being an indigenous people,[85] through giving 'the green light to private actors, and the oil Companies in particular, [has had a devastating effect on] the well-being of the Ogonis. By any measure of standards, its practice falls

[83] Ibid. Similarly, Art 12(3): 'The Parties shall promote the establishment by local communities of areas managed by them primarily for the conservation and sustainable use of natural resources.'

[84] Communication 155/96, *Socio Economic Rights Action Centre and Centre for Social and Economic Rights v Nigeria*, Fifteenth Annual Activity Report of the African Commission on Human and Peoples' Rights, 2001–02, Annex V, para 56.

[85] See n 18.

short of the minimum conduct expected of governments, and therefore, is in violation of Article 21 of the African Charter.'[86]

Status of the Declaration: Soft and Hard Law

What is also of interest is the approach taken by the African Group to the legal status of the UN Declaration, technically a non-legally binding document.[87] The Aide Memoire of the African Group specifically addresses the legal nature of the UN Declaration and stresses the importance of examining its content now, despite it being soft law. This is based on two elements. First, 'for the common people in the street of Africa there is no difference between a politically non-binding Declaration and a Treaty. What is important to them would be the fact that Governments or the United Nations have committed themselves to specific actions.'[88] Secondly, it provides for legal obligations that states have to abide by anyway, either because 'after adoption the Declaration would form part of international customary law and Member States would be expected to abide by it'[89] or '[m]ember states must be concerned about how they can give concrete meaning to the Declaration. If it is envisaged that there would be legal and constitutional implications arising from the adoption of the Declaration then the time to address such matters is before and not after adoption.'[90]

One might think that these statements illustrate some fundamental misunderstandings about the nature of soft law documents and overly optimistic views on the status of any UN Declaration. However, the line between hard and soft law in international human rights law is one that is not easily drawn.[91] The Aide Memoire suggests that in voting for the Declaration states are binding themselves legally to implement its provisions. UN declarations can become customary international law, in whole or in part, through acquiring the various elements of state practice and opinio juris.[92] It is of course highly unlikely that a document as controversial as this one can obtain such a status on its adoption. Similarly, it is not correct to state that simple adoption of

[86] Communication 155/96 (n 84) para 58.

[87] See A Boyle and C Chinkin, *The Making of International Law* (Oxford University Press, 2007).

[88] Aide Memoire (n 58) para 9.2.

[89] Ibid, para 9.3.

[90] Ibid.

[91] Boyle and Chinkin (n 87).

[92] See J Kammerhofer, 'Uncertainty in the Formal Sources of International Law: Customary International Law and Some of its Problems' (2004) 15 *European Journal of International Law* 523; C Chinkin, 'The Challenge of Soft Law: Development and Change in International Law' (1989) 38 *International and Comparative Law Quarterly* 850.

the Declaration will mean that it becomes part of customary international law. However, the UN Declaration itself in Article 38 provides that 'states in consultation and cooperation with indigenous peoples, shall take the appropriate measures, including legislative measures, to achieve the ends of this Declaration'. As van Genugten notes: 'its mandatory language—"shall"—means that states not living up to this wording are doing more than simply neglecting a political statement'.[93] Indeed, other states that voted against the Declaration referred to its legal status as one of the reasons for them doing so,[94] and case law from one jurisdiction at least subsequent to the adoption of the Declaration suggests that it is seen, if not in whole then in part, as containing 'principles of general international law'.[95]

It is to be welcomed that African states saw the Declaration as carrying such legal force as to require implementation in their own legal systems once it had been adopted, and we must be hopeful, now that it has been adopted, that states can be held to account under the Declaration.

CONCLUDING OBSERVATIONS: DEALING WITH A LACK OF JOINED-UP THINKING BETWEEEN THE ACHPR AND AU

Although not unusual,[96] the history behind the approach of the African Group at the UN, the AU resolution on the matter and the ACHPR's reaction to it illustrate once more the lack of attention paid by other AU organs to the work of the African Commission and, conversely, the inability or failure of the African Commission itself to publicise and promote what it is doing. On a more positive note, it also reveals that once the African Commission does engage with the AU it can wield considerable influence.

As seen above, although the AU paid little attention to indigenous peoples, either in the negotiations under the draft declaration at the UN or in its own resolutions and decisions, until faced with the adoption of the UN Declaration, there is some evidence of support for the concept of indigenous peoples in a less politically fraught environment. It is particularly striking that while a few months later the AU would adopt the decision it did on the UN Declaration, in November 2006 in the context of the First Africa-South America Summit, the AU Assembly of Heads of State and Government in its concluding Declaration underlined its commitment to human rights and expressly 'reaffirm[ed] the importance of

[93] van Genugten (n 24) 10.

[94] See GA/10612, 'General Assembly Adopts Declaration on Rights of Indigenous Peoples', 13 September 2007; see also van Genugten, ibid, 10–11.

[95] Supreme Court of Belize, Claim No 171 of 2007; see van Genugten (n 24) 11.

[96] See Murray (n 46).

protecting indigenous peoples' rights as accepted by our countries within the UN System and other relevant regional organizations'.[97]

Similarly, the important statements made by the African Commission and its Working Group on Indigenous Populations/Communities were clearly not common knowledge at the AU. Indeed, the AU's Decision in 2007 made no reference to the African Commission's Working Group's Report and findings and seemed to have no idea of its existence or the work it had carried out.

At the 41st session of the African Commission in May 2007 NGOs were initially unclear as to how to respond and how to get the African Commission to discuss the issue. It was suggested that the AU Declaration did provide language which enabled the Commission to put itself forward as providing some solution to the deadlock. Therefore NGOs lobbied the Commission to adopt, innovatively, an Advisory Opinion on the issue. This was the first time the Commission had adopted such a document, and arguably it gives more clout than a standard resolution would have done.

Armed with this Advisory Opinion and the Working Group's Report, certain members of the African Commission, its Working Group and other individuals[98] then lobbied African states to inform them of this important African position. Their efforts led to the UN Declaration eventually being adopted by the General Assembly in September 2007. At its 42nd session the African Commission extended the mandate of the Working Group for a further two years until November 2010,[99] and adopted a Communiqué[100] welcoming the adoption of the UN Declaration by the General Assembly, noting that no African state voted against its adoption and stressing that 'the UN Declaration … is in line with the position and work of the African Commission on indigenous peoples' rights'.

The above history illustrates the potential for creative thinking on human rights issues at the regional level but also the importance of ensuring that the approach to indigenous peoples is integrated across the entire regional institutional structure. That the delay in terms of the adoption of the UN Declaration could perhaps have been avoided if the African states had taken more note of the work of their own human rights body

[97] Declaration of the First Africa-South America Summit, 30 November 2006, para 15, www.africa-union.org.

[98] As IWGIA note, 'indigenous experts' visited some African governments in Cameroon, Central African Republic, Congo and Burundi, a number of experts visited New York to meet with various African embassies and roundtable and other events were organised. See www.iwgia.org/sw21505.asp.

[99] Resolution on the Composition and Renewal of the Mandate of the Working Group on Indigenous Populations/Communities in Africa, ACHPR/Res.123 (XXXXII) 07.

[100] Communiqué on the UN Declaration on the Rights of Indigenous Peoples, 28 November 2007, www.achpr.org. The Communiqué was adopted by the Resolution on the United Nations Declaration on the Rights of Indigenous Peoples, ACHPR/Res.121 (XXXXII) 07.

at an earlier stage, if there had been more joined-up thinking between the various elements of the AU, and if the African Commission itself had been more proactive in engaging the political organs, are lessons to be drawn from this analysis. In the end the African Commission and its Working Group did convince the African states to change their minds, and this does illustrate the potency of reasoned opinion and discussion of a contentious issue from the region's own human rights body. It is this sense of ownership over an issue that is so important to the AU and the African Commission, and if the latter seeks to engage fully with its political organs in the AU then, as the history of the Declaration shows, this African opinion will be more influential than any outside force.

20

Reflections on the UN Declaration on the Rights of Indigenous Peoples: An Arctic Perspective

DALEE SAMBO DOROUGH

INTRODUCTION

REACHING BACK IN time to the days of random and strange contact with Arctic explorers, a gulf existed between Inuit and others. In many parts of our circumpolar territory, this remains true. Even tracing back to the formative years of the Inuit Circumpolar Council (ICC) in the mid-1970s, one can clearly identify the contours of this gulf and our early efforts to define our relations with others. However, through Inuit political organising and Inuit diplomacy, we have been generally successful at not only defining, but continuously re-defining our relations with others. Indeed, the very fact that our communities have been divided by nation-state boundaries thrust us into the world of international relations despite our long-standing blood relations across these borders.

The ICC and its representatives Aqqaluk Lynge, Hjalmar Dahl, Henriette Rasmussen and numerous other Inuit colleagues associated with the ICC have all provided me the opportunity to become engaged in Inuit diplomacy directly. For over three decades, the work of this organisation has increased Inuit knowledge, political leadership and insights. Formally organised in 1977 in Barrow, Alaska, the goals of the ICC are as follows: to strengthen unity among Inuit of the Circumpolar region; to promote Inuit rights and interests on the international level; to ensure and further develop Inuit culture and society for both the present and future generations; to seek full and active participation in political, economic and social development in our homelands; to develop and encourage long-term policies which safeguard the Arctic environment; and to work for international recognition of the human rights of all indigenous peoples.

In a global sense, the intersection of Inuit aspirations and international relations has afforded us the opportunity to raise awareness about the issues faced by our peoples and to demonstrate the legitimacy of Inuit perspectives in the context of international human rights law and in particular, the United Nations Declaration on the Rights of Indigenous Peoples ('the Declaration'). This brief essay intends to provide an Arctic perspective of the significance of the Declaration and its future implementation in our lands and territory, which span from the Russian Far East to Alaska, Canada and Greenland. The Inuit territory is vast and there is much diversity. Let me make two caveats: first, I cannot speak for all Inuit; and second, this essay does not aim to be an exhaustive survey of every aspect of concern to Inuit, but rather an attempt to emphasise the positive developments and to provide a balanced perspective on some of the outstanding issues facing Inuit.

THE IMPORTANCE OF THE DECLARATION TO THE INUIT

One of the earliest initiatives of the ICC was to draft and adopt a set of Arctic policy principles, which was essentially a set of standards that the world community, and in particular those nation-states and private interests keen on having a presence in the Arctic, must recognise and respect. One of the crucial themes of the final document, entitled *Principles and Elements for a Comprehensive Arctic Policy*,[1] was the full, effective and direct role that Inuit must play in promoting and protecting our distinct culture, our unique environment, and our traditions and values. As the title suggests, the document is comprehensive, addressing issues ranging from the right of self-determination to peace and security, and from scientific research to environmental protection to Inuit elders and youth.

Simultaneous with the ICC's preparation of the Arctic Policy, the Declaration was being drafted by the UN Working Group on Indigenous Populations (WGIP). Due to these concurrent debates and dialogue, we were able to intensify or amplify our fundamental organisational objectives as well as influence many provisions of the Declaration's final text as adopted by the UN General Assembly.[2] Among other articles, an explicit

[1] *Principles and Elements for a Comprehensive Arctic Policy*, Inuit Circumpolar Conference, 1992. The initial draft was prepared in 1983 and refined through Inuit debate and dialogue until its final adoption at the 1992 ICC General Assembly held in Inuvik, NWT, Canada. See www.inuit.org.

[2] From 1982 to 2007, the ICC participated in the Working Group on Indigenous Populations (WGIP), which forwarded their text to the then Sub-Commission on Prevention of Discrimination and Protection of Minorities, which subsequently adopted the draft UN Declaration in Resolution 1994/45 of 26 August 1994 as an annex, UN Doc E/CN.4/1995/2, E/CN.4/Sub.2/1994/56, 105 (1994). The text was then transmitted to the Commission on Human Rights and subsequently to its successor, the Human Rights Council. The ICC maintained its participation throughout the HRC consideration as well as in the Third Committee and, finally, the General Assembly.

example of this was the inclusion of the term 'sea-ice' in Article 26 of the WGIP draft declaration.[3] Despite the overall cost of participating in this UN human rights standard-setting process, the ICC recognised the importance of the Declaration as a tool to advance our concerns within our particular geopolitical region and beyond. Therefore, we maintained a constant presence and participation in all the relevant human rights standard-setting sessions of the UN.[4]

Aside from the adverse impacts of the Cold War, throughout the elaboration of the Declaration, a wide range of developments within the Arctic were happening at a very fast pace. Threats to Inuit whaling activities emerged within the context of the International Whaling Commission;[5] low-level test flights were being initiated throughout the Canadian Arctic and sub-Arctic;[6] the mass drowning of thousands of caribou in Northern Quebec[7] (later attributed—although still disputed—to flooding initiated by Hydro Quebec and their massive, complex hydroelectric system affecting the Caniapiscau River); the 1986 Chernobyl disaster; offshore lease sales in the Chukchi and Beaufort Seas; and dumping of radioactive waste into the Arctic Ocean by the former USSR, to name a few. In addition, the growth and strengthening of Inuit political leadership and institutions as reflected by the development of the North Slope Borough (1972), the James Bay and Northern Quebec Agreement (1975), the Greenland Home Rule Government (1979) and the Inuvialuit Final Agreement (1984) were taking place as well. And often, the negotiations and final results of these processes were not entirely equitable or comprehensive, especially when held up against the standards ultimately embraced by the ICC's Arctic Policy Principles. In the context of these dramatic political and legal processes as well as the adverse environmental, social and cultural impacts upon Inuit communities, the benefits that could be derived from

[3] Art 26 of the WGIP *draft* UN Declaration read: 'Indigenous peoples have the right to own, develop, control and use the lands and territories, including the total environment of the lands, air, waters, coastal seas, sea-ice, flora and fauna and other resources which they have traditionally owned or otherwise occupied or used. This includes the right to the full recognition of their laws, traditions and customs, land-tenure systems and institutions for the development and management of resources, and the right to effective measures by States to prevent any interference with, alienation of or encroachment upon these rights.' Unfortunately, the term was removed in the final text of the Declaration.

[4] In addition to the Declaration work, the ICC participated in the 1988 and 1989 revision process of ILO Convention 107 on Indigenous and Tribal Populations.

[5] In the mid-1970s, the International Whaling Commission extended its regulations to Inuit whaling activity in Alaska and voted to ban the subsistence take of whales by the Inuit of Alaska's north and northwest coast.

[6] A 1983 agreement between Canada and the United States allowed cruise missile low-level test flights to take place over certain corridors throughout Northern Canada, including Goose Bay, Northwest Territories and Labrador.

[7] Letter from the Publisher, *Sports Illustrated*, 15 October 1984; and S Verhovek, 'Power Struggle', *New York Times*, 12 January 1992.

an international human rights instrument specifically addressing our fundamental rights can be easily identified.

Upon implementation of the Declaration, the standards elaborated may help to counterbalance the asymmetrical nature of negotiations over land claims provisions otherwise shaped by colonisation and the imposition of western legal perspectives. This counterbalance of international legal weight is sorely needed in the context of indigenous peoples and their efforts to promote and protect their rights. To a large extent, this was the overall objective of the Declaration process: to help reverse the tide of colonisation. One of the other important features of the Declaration is the fact that it is universal, yet it ensures the expression of our distinct cultural context. Indeed, the concept of 'cultural context' is significant in order to reinforce the positive purposes of international human rights instruments.[8] Our Arctic regional and cultural particularities and conditions require the manifestation of every right in a fashion unique to our circumstances. The UN Charter itself recognises that regional organs and arrangements were anticipated by the United Nations in order to accommodate regional differences.[9] This sentiment is also captured by one of the preambular paragraphs of the Declaration which recognises different circumstances and national and regional particularities.[10] Furthermore, the overarching nature of human rights creates a more navigable terrain by which all of the positive and negative developments in the Inuit world can be coupled or decoupled, engaged or disengaged dependent upon the desired outcome as expressed through the Inuit exercise of the right to self-determination. And, through self-determination we can hopefully transcend the narrowing gulf between Inuit world perspectives and those of others.

THE RIGHT OF SELF-DETERMINATION

In relation to this fundamental collective human right, the language of the Declaration is clear. Fortunately, indigenous peoples were successful

[8] HJ Steiner and P Alston, *International Human Rights in Context: Law, Politics, Morals* (Oxford University Press, 1996) 374, which includes 'American Anthropological Association, Statement on Human Rights' (1947) 49 *American Anthropologist* 539: 'Today the problem is complicated by the fact that the UN Declaration must be of worldwide applicability. It must embrace and recognize the validity of many different ways of life.'

[9] Charter of the United Nations, Ch VIII.

[10] The new preambular paragraph reads: '*Recognizing* also that the situation of indigenous peoples varies from region to region and from country to country and that the significance of national and regional particularities and various historical and cultural backgrounds should be taken into consideration'. This is a major improvement on the text originally circulated in the Commission on Human Rights Working Group on the Draft Declaration (WGDD). This new language allows for the play of the important principle of universality of human rights and the significance of international law.

in safeguarding the original WGIP text and fending off state attempts to diminish or qualify this primordial right in the context of indigenous peoples through language that emerged much later in this long debate. The text, upon careful review, is in fact consistent with international law and does not import any of the idiosyncratic views of those states that were operating solely on the basis of 'unfounded fears'. In this regard, Inuit have acknowledged the positive role of Denmark (Greenland), Norway and Finland in our collective debates over the right to self-determination.[11]

It is worth taking a few paragraphs to highlight some of the relevant language of the Declaration concerning the right of self-determination. The opening preambular paragraph states:

> *Guided* by the purposes and principles of the Charter of the United Nations, and good faith in the fulfilment of the obligations assumed by States in accordance with the Charter

This paragraph provides an important contextual, foundational clause that is relevant to every provision of the Declaration. The reference to 'purposes and principles of the Charter' is extremely helpful. Article 1 of the Charter emphasises the need:

> To maintain international peace and security, and to that end: to take effective collective measures for the prevention and removal of threats to the peace, and for the suppression of acts of aggression or other breaches of the peace, and to bring about by peaceful means, and in conformity with the principles of justice and international law, adjustment or settlement of international disputes or situations which might lead to a breach of the peace;
>
> *To develop friendly relations among nations based on respect for the principle of equal rights and self-determination of peoples*, and to take other appropriate measures to strengthen universal peace;
>
> To achieve international co-operation in solving international problems of an economic, social, cultural, or humanitarian character, *and in promoting and encouraging respect for human rights and for fundamental freedoms for all without distinction as to race, sex, language, or religion;*[12]

This language is critical in the context of interpretation of all of the Declaration's provisions, including the amendments to Article 46 (discussed below), which were made in the closing hours of debate in Geneva, and especially so when bolstered by the language of preambular paragraphs 17 and 18:

> *Bearing in mind* that nothing in this Declaration may be used to deny any peoples their right to self-determination, exercised in conformity with international law

[11] In the last few years of the WGDD (and certainly not thereafter), it should be acknowledged that Canada did play a useful role in relation to self-determination.

[12] Emphasis added.

> *Convinced* that the recognition of the rights of indigenous peoples in this Declaration will enhance harmonious and cooperative relations between the State and indigenous peoples, based on principles of justice, democracy, respect for human rights, non-discrimination and good faith

State 'obligations' (referred to in the first preambular paragraph of the Declaration) include those relating to the right of all peoples to self-determination in common Article 1 of the two International Covenants. Also, in Article 56 of the UN Charter, Member States have pledged to cooperate with the United Nations to achieve the purposes set out in Article 55. Article 55(c) of UN Charter provides:

> With a view to the creation of conditions of stability and well-being which are necessary for peaceful and friendly relations among nations based on *respect for the principle of equal rights and self-determination of peoples*, the United Nations shall promote:
>
> ....
>
> c. *universal respect for, and observance of, human rights and fundamental freedoms for all without distinction as to race, sex, language, or religion.*[13]

Therefore, when read in the context of the whole Declaration and other relevant international instruments, the interpretation of 'territorial integrity' in Article 46(1) must be exactly the same as what presently exists in international law—namely, that the right to self-determination may be balanced by the principle of territorial integrity if certain conditions are met (see the Friendly Relations Declaration[14]). As affirmed in Article 45, nothing in the Declaration can be construed to diminish the rights that indigenous peoples have now. Therefore, 'territorial integrity' in Article 46(1) cannot be applied to restrict indigenous rights in any way that is not consistent with the meaning of this term in existing international law.

The reference is an indirect way of stating what ICC representatives argued during sessions of the Commission on Human Rights Working Group on the Draft Declaration (WGDD), that states do not need a reference to territorial integrity, because the whole of the Friendly Relations Declaration is an interpretive document of the UN Charter (especially its elaboration of the right to self-determination). Throughout our efforts to maintain the text of the Declaration, we persisted in our argument that states could not impose any discriminatory double standards in the context of indigenous peoples' right of self-determination. In this way, the reference to equality, made elsewhere in the Declaration (eg Article 2),

[13] Emphasis added.

[14] UN Declaration of Principles of International Law Concerning Friendly Relations and Co-operation among States in Accordance with the Charter of the United Nations.

strengthens or serves as positive reinforcement of the equal application of the right of self-determination of peoples as understood in international law.

The amended preambular paragraph 16[15] was also helpful. Among other provisions, the Vienna Declaration reinforces the duty to respect human rights, the principle of universality of human rights and the important inter-related and indivisible nature of human rights. In addition, the Vienna Declaration goes a step further and acknowledges situations of 'colonial' domination in the context of the right of indigenous peoples to self-determination.[16]

Article 46 is a highly important balancing article in the context of indigenous peoples and the exercise of the right to self-determination, affirming the full nature of this right. On the face of it, one might erroneously presume that the reference to territorial integrity applies to the whole Declaration and thereby restricts a range of rights. However, it is crucial to read these provisions in the context of, and not in isolation from, all other provisions of the Declaration. Article 45 of the Declaration bears specific significance, as it ensures that our rights cannot be diminished:

> Nothing in this Declaration may be construed as diminishing or extinguishing the rights indigenous peoples have now or may acquire in the future.

Furthermore, the significance of equal rights of indigenous peoples as reflected in Articles 1 and 2 must be stressed. Article 1 affirms that

> Indigenous peoples have the right to the full enjoyment, as a collective or as individuals, of all human rights and fundamental freedoms as recognized in the Charter of the United Nations, the Universal Declaration of Human Rights and international human rights law.

[15] '*Acknowledging* that the Charter of the United Nations, the International Covenant on Economic, Social and Cultural Rights and the International Covenant on Civil and Political Rights *as well as the Vienna UN Declaration and Programme of Action*, affirm the fundamental importance of the right of self-determination of all peoples, by virtue of which they freely determine their political status and freely pursue their economic, social and cultural development' (emphasis added).

[16] The Vienna Declaration and Programme of Action, A/CONF.157/23, 12 July 1993, para 2 states: 'All peoples have the right of self-determination. By virtue of that right they freely determine their political status, and freely pursue their economic, social and cultural development'. Para 5 of the Vienna Declaration references the universal nature of human rights: 'All human rights are universal, indivisible and interdependent and interrelated. The international community must treat human rights globally in a fair and equal manner, on the same footing, and with the same emphasis. While the significance of national and regional particularities and various historical, cultural and religious backgrounds must be borne in mind, it is the duty of States, regardless of their political, economic and cultural systems, to promote and protect all human rights and fundamental freedoms.'

The principle of equality is also specified in Article 2, as an operative paragraph that affirms that we are equal to all other peoples and further reinforces non-discrimination:

> Indigenous peoples and individuals are free and equal to all other peoples and individuals and have the right to be free from any kind of discrimination, in the exercise of their rights, in particular that based on their indigenous origin or identity.

Also, preambular paragraph 2 affirms that we are equal to all other people, including in the context of self-determination, by

> Affirming that indigenous peoples are equal to all other peoples, while recognizing the right of all peoples to be different, to consider themselves different, and to be respected as such.

Therefore, when read in context (as it must be), the language is clear concerning the restriction confined to the interpretation of territorial integrity as understood and presently exists in international law. The specific provisions and the expansive context set out by the language used are consistent with international law and have no additional meaning in the Declaration. When read in relation to Article 45, ultimately, the Declaration cannot amend or diminish existing international instruments and international law and, therefore, cannot diminish indigenous peoples' rights in this regard. As noted above, the opening preambular paragraph recalls the obligations of states bound by the UN Charter as well as the language of preambular paragraph 17. Furthermore, both International Covenants affirm the right[17] and the Friendly Relations Declaration elaborates upon its exercise and, as widely recognised, places conditions upon states in the event of denial of the right.

Finally, the amendments to Article 46(2) reinforce international law and its status in the context of indigenous human rights, making it necessary for states to show that any 'limitation' must be consistent with international law and cannot be arbitrary.[18] Again, the overall contextual framework provides important dimensions that help us to understand these critical provisions. Specifically, the first sentence requires that the 'human rights and fundamental freedoms of all shall be respected'. [Here, the

[17] International Covenant on Civil and Political Rights (1966), GA Res 2200 (XXI), 21 UN GAOR, Supp (No 16) at 49, adopted by the UN General Assembly 16 December 1966, entered into force 23 March 1976.

[18] Art 46(2) reads: 'In the exercise of the rights enunciated in the present Declaration, human rights and fundamental freedoms of all shall be respected. The exercise of the rights set forth in this Declaration shall be subject only to such limitations as are determined by law and in accordance with international human rights obligations. Any such limitations shall be non-discriminatory and strictly necessary solely for the purpose of securing due recognition and respect for the rights and freedoms of others and for meeting the just and most compelling requirements of a democratic society.'

use of the term 'of all' includes individual and collective human rights. Perfect example of the lack of final, technical review of the UNDRIP!] Any 'limitations' must be 'determined by law' as well as in the light of 'international human rights obligations'. They cannot be arbitrary or have the effect of undermining, impairing or diminishing the rights of indigenous peoples. Furthermore, 'any such limitations shall be non-discriminatory', and 'strictly necessary' for securing the rights of others and 'for meeting the just and most compelling requirements of a democratic society'. This is quite a range of restrictive conditions by which states may attempt to limit the human rights of indigenous peoples.

In light of the diverse conditions, circumstances and developments facing Inuit communities throughout the circumpolar region, the right to self-determination takes on a very important contextual framework for all existing and future indigenous/non-indigenous relations. In some regions, such as the Russian Federation, the right of self-determination must be affirmed, recognised and respected. In others, it must be assessed in light of existing political and legal arrangements, the universal, minimum standards embraced by the Declaration and dependent upon the distinct aspirations of the Inuit concerned. In the implementation of existing agreements, the matter of good governance and aspects of its relationship to human rights in the context of both indigenous and non-indigenous peoples will be better informed as well.

The increased understanding of the linkages and inter-relationship of human rights found in the Declaration will benefit Inuit in many ways, particularly through enhanced self-determination and the Inuit expression of it in land claim negotiations. Because of the urgent need to safeguard the Arctic environment, present and future land claims negotiations may be improved by referring to the Declaration's standards and the overall human rights-based approach that this instrument reflects. This is equally the case in relation to the specific provisions addressing lands, territories and resources.

RIGHTS TO LANDS, TERRITORIES AND RESOURCES

The range of political arenas that Inuit find themselves in and the multiplicity of conditions that face each region and community give rise to the need for a comprehensive assessment of political status, land rights and associated economic, social and cultural development. Despite the reality of Inuit presence in the Arctic and sub-Arctic, the modern Arctic rim nation-states have had a far greater interest in advancing their respective agendas of state sovereignty, national security and resource development. Though there have been important positive developments that have emerged in the Inuit context, the outstanding indigenous land claims and the related right of self-determination in the Russian Far East, the Alaska Native Claims Settlement Act of 1971, the various forms of 'public government' and land claim agreements in Canada, and the possible road to full independence in Greenland, are all relevant to the recently adopted Declaration. This range of northern examples highlights the need to address Inuit rights in comprehensive terms and in a manner consistent with existing and emerging international human rights law, in particular they should be reviewed in light of the Declaration.

In this regard, the relevant articles of the Declaration are those addressing consultation and participation (Article 18), free, prior and informed consent (Article 19), hunting and fishing rights (Article 20), self-determination (Article 3) and associated political rights (Articles 33 and 35), autonomy or self-government[19] (Article 4), treaties (Article 37), and land rights (Articles 25 and 26).

Russian Federation

In the case of the Russian Far East, as referenced above, the fact that there has been no substantive response to the appalling conditions facing the Siberian Yup'ik by the local and national authorities begs for an overall strategy to secure their rights and interests in relation to their traditional lands, territories and resources.[20] In the context of the Arctic Council, one Inuit expressed a saying in Russian that translates as 'he will hurry slowly. (It sounds like the Arctic Council.) But let me tell you: if it "hurries slowly", many of the aboriginal peoples of Russia will be at the point of disappearing.' This statement accurately characterises the situation facing the Inuit of Chuckchi Peninsula in the Russian Far East. There is an urgent

[19] It is important to note that the false dichotomy raised by states in the Declaration debates related to the use of the terms 'internal' and 'external' in relation to this provision. As consistently argued, indigenous peoples have already transcended internal or national borders simply by virtue of their involvement in the United Nations, Organization of American States, CBD, WIPO, etc. The long record of indigenous peoples' international engagement is just one example of their continuing external expression of autonomy. In addition, Art 36 of the Declaration addresses indigenous peoples and their relations across international borders and affirms the important external dimension of Art 4. Finally, preambular para 14 specifically makes reference to treaties 'in some situations' being 'matters of international concern, interest, responsibility and character'. Therefore, the character of autonomy or self-government cannot be limited, especially when the overall Declaration itself goes much further.

[20] To date, there has been no concrete or substantive recognition of their fundamental individual or collective rights as distinct peoples. The level of poverty as well as other socioeconomic indicators reflect marginalisation and neglect on the part of the national and local governments. See A Pika, J Dahl and I Larsen (eds), *Anxious North: Indigenous Peoples in Soviet and Post Soviet Russia*, IWGIA Document No 81 (1996).

need to implement the Declaration overall. At a minimum, those articles dealing with lands, territories and resources must be given full effect.

Post-Soviet relations with Inuit are a matter of domination by a non-indigenous minority in urban areas over the indigenous minority occupying their traditional, rural homelands. Russian government efforts to become more 'democratic' have actually resulted in them becoming more repressive, and especially so toward indigenous peoples. The ICC has engaged in efforts to assist our brothers and sisters in the Russian Far East. For many reasons, it has been difficult. The new political dynamics are overwhelming and difficult to unravel. The Inuit of the Russian Far East as well as all other 'small nations of the Russian North' face rapid industrialisation due to non-renewable resource exploitation. The Inuit do not have any measure of control over or direct participation in these initiatives.

In 2001, the Russian Federation adopted a law to establish permanent legal status for the territories traditionally used and inhabited by indigenous communities, the Federal Law on Territories of Traditional Nature Use or 'TTP', using a concept similar to the former Soviet idea of clan lands. Under this law, indigenous peoples would have a measure of control over the territories, and such lands and environment would be protected from adverse impacts of resource exploitation. However, to date, this law has not been implemented. In response to the lobbying and organising efforts of RAIPON[21] primarily, a range of working groups, commissions and much discussion has taken place, but no real protections have emerged nor has there been any demarcation of TTP lands.

With regard to actual land codes being amended, they have been 'revised in a spirit of economic liberalization and privatization', meaning that they can be bought and sold while ignoring the original 2001 concept of recognising indigenous land use under the TTPs. In the meantime, hydro-electric, mining, oil and gas development and other projects are moving forward with little or no indigenous participation, consultation, consent; let alone recognition of land rights. The only real possibility for measures to be altered is in the context of multinational corporations or international aid from entities, such as the World Bank and the ILO, which cite their standards and require that they be incorporated into development initiatives.

[21] The Russian Association of Indigenous Peoples of the North, Siberia and Far East (RAIPON) was created in 1990 at the First Congress of Indigenous Peoples of the North. They presently comprise 41 indigenous groups. They are organised as a public organisation whose objectives include 'protection of human rights, defense of the legal interests of indigenous peoples of the North, Siberia and the Far East, and the assistance in solution of environmental, social and economic problems, and the problems of cultural development and education'.

In relation to oil development, indigenous peoples demanded implementation of 'ethnological impact assessment' in addition to the environmental impact assessments. Such efforts have been met with opposition, while former President Putin commented that such work would slow down development.[22] The government is rushing to develop while delaying every effort to address the outstanding rights of the Inuit to their lands, territories and resources.

As the earlier quote suggested, the Russian Federation will 'hurry slowly'. The fact that the Russian Federation abstained during the UN General Assembly vote on the Declaration, purportedly on the basis of the need for more time and procedural concerns that disallowed their views to be taken seriously, their actions are regarded as another stalling tactic to defer any concrete action that might conflict with the 'new Russia'. Again, a serious, concerted effort to change the political and legal conditions must be launched. This task is extremely challenging due to the lack of financial resources, the very rural geographical locations as well as the agenda and powerful desires of the Russian Federation overall. Yet, if nothing is done, there is a very real possibility that the Inuit (among other small nations) of the Russian Far East may disappear.

United States (Alaska)

The discovery of oil on Alaska's north slope in 1968 prompted demands by Alaska Natives for the United States to address their outstanding legal claims to the territory. Recognising the surrounding legal issues that could be argued in favour of the Native peoples, the non-Native stakeholders determined that either legislation or a unilateral Act of Congress would optimise their interests. Throughout the crafting of legislation, there was minimal Alaska Native participation and no full and formal referendum, certainly not in the context of the current provision of consent as found in Article 19 of the Declaration. The final text of the Alaska Native Claims Settlement Act (ANCSA) of 1971 provided for 44 million acres of land (roughly 10 per cent of the original indigenous territory) and $962.5 million in exchange for lands lost. Rather than transferring indigenous lands and assets to traditional institutions, they were placed in the hands of profit-making corporations: 12 regional corporations and over 200 village corporations. The regional corporations retain subsurface rights to those lands conveyed to them as well as subsurface rights to those lands conveyed to the villages. There was no recognition of self-government or self-determination as affirmed in Articles 3 and 4 of the Declaration.

[22] Pika et al (n 17).

The Act provided for a 20-year time period (from 1971 to 1991) to create and increase capacity of the Alaska Native peoples responsible for the corporate operations. Those born on or before December 1971 who were one quarter Native blood or more were enrolled as shareholders in the corporations. During this period no transfer of land, no taxation, and no alienation of shares were allowed. In contrast, the language of Articles 20 and 33 (respectively) of the Declaration recognise the right of an indigenous people to 'maintain and develop their political, economic and social systems or institutions' and to 'determine their own identity or membership in accordance with their customs and traditions', both of which are important elements of the right to self-determination.

Moreover, despite the 1966 International Covenants, which state that '[i]n no case may a people be deprived of their own means of subsistence', the 1971 Act purportedly 'extinguished' hunting and fishing rights. Further, the Act purportedly 'extinguished' rights to all lands lost. The 20-year time period provisions essentially allowed for the exposure of lands and assets after 1991. There have been some successes, especially at the regional corporation level. However, there have been failures as well. In some cases, villages have actually disappeared. The ANCSA has been regarded by many as an act of social engineering and assimilation, and ultimately termination of the distinct status of Alaska native peoples.

At present, there is an urgent need for the Alaska Native community to re-examine the impact of the ANCSA, especially in light of the significant developments concerning international human rights law and the Declaration specifically. Alternatives exist and there appears to be a desire, especially amongst the younger generation 'disenfranchised' by the Act, to re-group or rise up in order to address the outstanding issue of self-determination and chart a course for genuine de-colonisation. In addition, the need to entrench hunting and fishing rights of the Inuit and other Alaska Natives must be dealt with. Finally, some provision for the return of lands to the traditional institutions in order to safeguard them from loss should be explored in order not to further disenfranchise Alaska's 'First Peoples'.

Canada

James Bay and Northern Quebec Agreement 1975

The James Bay and Northern Québec Agreement of 1975 is regarded as 'the first major agreement between the Crown and the native people in Canada since the numbered treaties of the 19th and early 20th centuries'.[23]

[23] See John A Price's contribution at www.thecanadianencyclopedia.com/index.cfm?PgNm=TCE&Params=A1ARTA0004098, later revised by Brian Craik.

The agreement was triggered by the 1971 announcement of a mega project to build a complex system of hydroelectric dams throughout the territory of the Cree and Inuit of Northern Quebec. To a large extent, the Agreement was modelled after the ANCSA and it involved not only the Cree and Inuit of Northern Quebec and the governments of Canada and Quebec, but also the Quebec Hydro-Electric Commission (Hydro-Quebec). The Agreement provided for 8,151 square kilometres for the Inuit (5,543 square kilometres for the Cree) and C$225 million to Makivik Corporation on behalf of the Inuit (and to the Cree Regional Authority).

In contrast to ANCSA, the Inuit and Cree were able to affirm exclusive harvesting rights throughout the lands transferred as well as over an additional 15,000 square kilometres of land. With regard to lands lost, this amounted to the remainder of the James Bay and Ungava territory. Fortunate for the Inuit and unlike ANCSA, provisions for the parties to re-visit the original Agreement were included. Because the matter of self-government and self-determination were not originally addressed in the 1975 agreement, discussions over the Nunavik Self-Government Political Accord ('the Accord') have been agreed upon, providing for a measure of self-government and self-determination. The Partnership Accord was agreed upon in 2005. This is an important new development as well as an example of how indigenous peoples have benefited from the development of international law and international human rights standards (and specifically the Declaration), and have been able to re-visit and re-define relations with others that are more consistent with their rights and aspirations. The synergy generated by the domestic debates concerning the right to self-determination in the context of the Canadian Supreme Court consideration of the Reference regarding Secession of Quebec[24] and its intersection with the international indigenous/state dialogue on Article 3 of the Declaration—largely initiated by the Grand Council of the Cree as well as the Inuit—informed both the local and global debates in a positive fashion.

Inuvialuit Final Agreement 1984 (IFA)

On the border with Alaska, the blood relatives and neighbours of Alaskan Inupiat were aware of the emergence of ANCSA and knew that they, too, should be organising and pressing for land claims. Coincidentally, not long after a 1973 meeting of Inuit leaders in Copenhagen, Denmark, the Committee for the Original People's Entitlement (COPE) was established

[24] Reference re Secession of Quebec, [1998] 2 SCR 217, in the matter of Section 53 of the Supreme Court Act, RSC, 1985, c S-26; and in the matter of a Reference by the Governor in Council concerning certain questions relating to the secession of Quebec from Canada, as set out in Order in Council PC 1996-1497, dated the 30th day of September, 1996.

to provide a united voice for the Inuvialuit of Canada to address land claims. In 1974, COPE began negotiations with the Government of Canada, which resulted in the Inuvialuit Final Agreement (IFA) in 1984. The Agreement provided for 90,600 square kilometres of land, including 12,980 square kilometres of subsurface mineral rights and $152 million. In addition to hunting and fishing rights secured by the IFA, the Inuvialuit have co-management roles in matters related to fisheries, wildlife and environmental impact through various joint boards and councils. However, self-determination and self-government were not addressed and the corporate model of ANCSA was generally replicated in the Inuvialuit context. The major distinctions between the Inuvialuit and ANCSA are that the Inuvialuit included negotiated provisions (rather than an Act of Congress or Parliament) and a full and formal referendum allowing for free, prior and informed consent, and it is an agreement rather than a 'settlement'. It also recognised hunting, fishing and gathering rights as well as joint management, and the status of the IFA is explicitly recognized within the context of Section 35 of the Canadian Constitution.

Some may attribute these marked distinctions between the IFA and ANCSA to the Canadian government and a greater sense of fairness as well as greater respect for human rights. However, at the same time, the legal developments emerging internationally may have been influential in the final outcome. At a minimum, the Inuvialuit had hindsight in their favour. They were able to scrutinise the terms of ANCSA by querying Alaska Native people as to the advantages and disadvantages of the Alaskan 'settlement'.

Nunavut 1993

The Nunavut Land Claims Agreement is the largest Aboriginal land claim settlement in Canadian history. When the Agreement was signed, legislation was also passed leading to the creation of a new Canadian territory called Nunavut on 1 April 1999. The new territory is a 'public government' serving both Inuit and non-Inuit in the form of a unicameral legislative assembly. However, provisions for a form of self-government for the Nunavut Inuit were included in the Agreement. Inuit have title to approximately 350,000 square kilometres of land and of this about 35,000 square kilometres include mineral rights. Inuit and government are represented equally in matters concerning wildlife management, resource management and environmental boards. Inuit rights to harvest wildlife on lands and waters throughout the Nunavut settlement area were also secured. A scheduled distribution of compensation over a 14-year period totals approximately $1.161 billion as well as revenue sharing from royalties generated by oil, gas and mineral development on Crown lands.

Unfortunately though, recently, the Canadian government has failed to uphold or respect the terms of the Nunavut Agreement. The formal submission of views by the Land Claims Agreement Coalition (Canada) in the context of the Universal Periodic Review of Canada by the UN Human Rights Council puts the matter in stark contrast to what might be generally deemed cooperative relations between the government of Canada and Inuit.[25] In this regard, the Inuit representatives of Nunavut initiated a lawsuit in 2006 against the government of Canada for failure to uphold the terms of this modern-day land claim agreement.[26] Other Inuit-based members of the Coalition include Makivik Corporation, Nunatsiavut Government, Nunavut unngavik Inc and the Inuvialuit Regional Corporation.[27]

However, in contrast to being used as 'human flag poles', the reality and terms of Nunavut as an autonomous territory is a significant development for Inuit, which may play a role in future questions of Canadian Arctic sovereignty. The combination of public government and provision for possible distinct Inuit government have led some to believe that 'devolution' of control to Nunavut will enhance the national government's assertions of sovereignty over the internal waters of the Canadian high Arctic.[28] In the event of any such enterprise as well as in relation to Nunavut Tunngavik Inc's ongoing lawsuit, the relevance of the Declaration is

[25] Universal Periodic Review of Canada, Submission of the Land Claims Agreements Coalition (LCAC) to the United Nations Human Rights Council, 8 September 2008, wherein the Coalition '[o]bserves that Canada has not adequately supported the full extent of modern treaties, and that its practice of ignoring the spirit and intent and broad objectives of these agreements is contrary to its human rights commitments and obligations'. See www.upr-info.org/IMG/pdf/LCAC_CAN_UPR_S4_2009_LandClaimsAgreementsCoalition_JOINT.pdf.

[26] 'Nunavut Tunngavik Inc Launches Land Claim Implementation Lawsuit', Canadian Bar Association website, 6 December 2006, www.cba.org/nunavut/main/sections_abor/news_2006-12-06.aspx. According to the Canadian Bar Association: 'Nunavut Tunngavik Inc filed a statement of claim against the Government of Canada today, asserting that the Government of Canada stands in violation of its contract and fiduciary obligations arising from the *Nunavut Land Claims Agreement* ... The assertions set forth in the claim include that the Crown has: failed to engage in good faith negotiations; failed to seek the agreement of Inuit with respect to the initiatives required to implement provisions and objectives of the claim; and unilaterally exercised its power over the appropriation of funds so as to erode, delay or minimize the scope and substance of the benefits promised to the Inuit.'

[27] Land Claims Agreement Coalition members include: the Council of Yukon First Nations (which represents land claim governments in the Yukon); Grand Council of the Crees (Eeyou Istchee), Gwich' in Tribal Council, Inuvialuit Regional Corporation, Kwanlin Dun First Nation, Makivik Corporation, Naspaki Nation of Kawawachikamach, Nisga'a Nation, the Nunatsiavut Government, Nunavut unngavik Inc, Sahtu Secretariat Inc, and the Tlicho Government.

[28] See generally S Arnold, Arnold, Samantha (2008), "Nelvana of the North: Traditional Knowledge and the Mythical Function of Canadian Foreign Policy," *Canadian Foreign Policy* 14 (Spring): 95-108.; and S Arnold and S Roussel, 'Expanding the Canada-US Security Regime to the North?', Paper presented at the Academic Roundtable 'Security Prospects in the High North: Geostrategic Thaw or Freeze?', Reykjavík, Iceland, 29–30 January 2009.

critical for Inuit, especially in terms of securing their distinct rights and interests throughout the entire region and pushing the envelope on every article that the Declaration has to offer.

Labrador 2005

In 1977, when the Inuit Circumpolar Conference General Assembly in Barrow, Alaska was being organised, the Labrador Inuit were preparing to pursue a land claims agreement with the Canadian government. After 27 years of effort, the Labrador Inuit Land Claims Agreement was adopted by referendum of the Labrador Inuit in December 2004. The Labrador Inuit now own 15,800 square kilometres of land as well as traditional use rights (including hunting, fishing, harvesting and social and ceremonial use) to 72,500 square kilometres of land and 48,690 square kilometres of sea. This agreement specifies Aboriginal self-government and like other Canadian Inuit agreements provides for a co-management role for Labrador Inuit. The Agreement also provides for C$130 million in compensation and an additional C$120 million for development of self-government.

It is interesting to note that partly because of developments at the international level (namely at the UN and the OAS) and partly due to the hindsight of the Labrador Inuit, this agreement addresses offshore areas in terms of water rights and the adjacent ocean zone extending to the limit of Canada's territorial sea as well as specifying Inuit self-government, rather than merely public government or a corporate structure. One cannot put this down to pure coincidence—it is certain that international developments were taken into consideration and incorporated into this Agreement. Such cooperative interaction and comprehensive recognition of indigenous rights and interests are needed in many other indigenous/non-indigenous arenas in a fashion that will ultimately promote and protect the human rights of the indigenous peoples concerned.

Denmark (Greenland)

Similar to the heightened political and legal developments amongst Inuit elsewhere, the 1979 establishment of the Home Rule Government in Greenland is another example of Inuit prompting the re-definition of relations with others. In enacting the Greenland Home Rule Act, the Kingdom of Denmark did in fact recognise Greenland as a distinct community within its 'Realm'. The Act provided for both legislative and executive branches of home rule government in Greenland, with powers to administer domestic affairs. The Act further recognised Inuit peoples' fundamental rights to the natural resources of Greenland. Natural resource exploitation is regulated by agreement between the Danish Government and the Greenland

Home Rule Government, with the important element of consent by both parties. The Act also recognised Greenlandic as the principal language, with Danish taught. In relation to international affairs, the Greenland Home Rule Government was subject to Danish obligations arising out of treaties in force and binding on Denmark. However, foreign relations, defence and national security were left to the Realm. Yet, Denmark has a commitment to dialogue and has referred to Greenland for comment in the event of direct or indirect impact of such foreign relations upon Greenland's interests. Furthermore, it was agreed that consultation would take place within the context of the legislation before the Council of the European Communities, which particularly affects Greenlandic interests, including capacity for Greenland Home Rule authorities to advance their own interests within the European Community.

One clear example of such a matter is the 2004 revised Agreement between the US and Denmark,[29] including the Home Rule Government of Greenland, to amend the 1951 Agreement pursuant to the North Atlantic Treaty concerning the defense of Greenland.[30] The Agreement focuses on the strategic role of Thule Air Base, defence areas in Greenland,[31] and the need for cooperation within NATO in ensuring North Atlantic security. The Agreement references the need to 'ensure due protection of the environment and hunting areas in Greenland' as well as the need to consult with the Home Rule Government regarding 'any significant changes to United States military operations or facilities in Greenland'.[32] Finally, the Home Rule Government 'may appoint a representative with whom the US commanding officer at Thule Air Base will consult on local affairs that affect the Home Rule Government of Greenland'.[33]

[29] Agreement between the United States and Denmark, including Greenland, amending and supplementing the agreement of 27 April 1951, as amended, concerning the defence of Greenland, with joint declarations, signed at Igaliku on 6 August 2004, entered into force 6 August 2004. With related joint declarations on environmental cooperation in Greenland, and economic and technical cooperation also signed in Iqaliku (Greenland) by the same three parties. See www.nanoq.gl.

[30] Defense of Greenland: Agreement Between the United States and the Kingdom of Denmark, 27 April 1951.

[31] Art 3(1)(b) reads: 'In the exceptional case of planned landings of military aircraft in Greenland outside airports, the Government of the United States consults with and informs the government of the Kingdom of Denmark, including the Home Rule Government of Greenland, in order to ensure due protection of the environment and hunting areas in Greenland.'

[32] Art 3(1)(c) reads: 'Consistent with the Defense Agreement, as amended herein, and the Memorandum of Understanding of March 13, 1991, and without prejudice to other relevant agreements and arrangements between the Parties, the Government of the United States will consult with and inform the Government of the Kingdom of Denmark, including the Home Rule Government of Greenland, prior to the implementation of any significant changes to United States military operations or facilities in Greenland.'

[33] Art 3(2)(a) reads: 'The Home Rule Government of Greenland may appoint a representative with whom the US commanding officer at Thule Air Base will consult on local affairs that affect the Home rule Government of Greenland …'

Another example of the extent of authority that the Greenland Home Rule Government enjoys is the EU Partnership Agreement.[34] In 2006, Greenland and the EU agreed on a comprehensive partnership for the sustainable development of Greenland. The Partnership Agreement is a political Declaration stating the parties' intentions to continue and expand their cooperation in various areas. The Declaration was made in recognition of the close historical, political, economic and cultural ties between Greenland and the EU. Essentially, the Agreement provides Greenland with approximately 25 million to support Greenland education programmes in exchange for fishing rights for the EU.

The most recent, dramatic news was the 25 November 2008 referendum, wherein 75.5 per cent of the Greenlandic electorate voted 'yes' to the question of pursuing independence and nationhood.[35] The 2008 referendum was the result of a comprehensive review and study undertaken by the Commission on Self-Government established by the Parliament in 2002. There is no doubt that the Greenland Home Rule Government, through its establishment of the Commission on Self-Government, reviewed all developments in international law concerning the right to self-determination and the Declaration text well before pursuing this referendum. This is a significant example of how Inuit have and will benefit from the reality of the Declaration. The self Government Act is now being implemented and has prompted debate over resource development and sovereignty. Either way, the future efforts of the Greenlandic Inuit to re-define and re-conceptualise their relations with others, in this case initially through self-government, but potentially through actual sovereignty and independence, can clearly be traced not only to their own political aspirations, but also to the work of Inuit at the international level.[36]

ARCTIC RIM STATES' POSITIONS

Though the Russian Federation stated that 'many of the provisions are appropriate and acceptable' and further made an express commitment to 'foster international cooperation in the promotion and protection of the rights of indigenous peoples', not surprisingly, the Russian Federation's primary concern was related to land and natural resources and associated provisions relating to compensation and redress. As noted earlier, the

[34] Council Decision on relations between the European Community on the one hand, and Greenland and the Kingdom of Denmark on the other, 9802/06 VL/cz, DG E II EN, Council of the European Union, Brussels, 20 June 2006 (OR.en) 9802/06, Greenland 3.

[35] Ministry of Foreign Affairs, Denmark, news release on referendum, www.ambprag.um.dk/nr/exeres/90374b68-bcca-4139-b538-614533ebcdd1.htm.

[36] Act on Greenland Self-Government, Act No 473 of 12 June 2009, uk.nanoq.gl/sitecore/content/Websites/uk,-d ,nanoq/Emner/Government/~/media/6CF403B6DD954B77BC2C33E9F02E3947.ashx (English translation).

primary struggle facing the Inuit and all other small nations of the north is specifically related to land and natural resources. Unfortunately, the key to responding to the promotion and protection of indigenous peoples' rights is for the Russian Federation to make a genuine *domestic* commitment to the promotion and protection of the rights of the Inuit as well as all other indigenous peoples. If in fact the Russian Federation view is that many of the Declaration's provisions are indeed appropriate and acceptable, perhaps the Inuit, in collaboration with other Arctic indigenous peoples, can create an opening for domestic dialogue that results in an affirmation of their fundamental human rights. This circumstance begs for a regional solution in the form of a human rights recourse mechanism substantially supported by other Arctic-rim nation-states.

With regard to the United States, their first claim concerning insufficient time to discuss the text collectively is wholly false. The US is one of the few states, dating back to the first session of the WGIP, that was consistently present, in force, throughout all of the debates and discussions concerning the Declaration. As the US itself notes, they had ample opportunity to discuss the text as 'an active participant throughout the long history of the negotiations'.[37] Unfortunately, they were also instrumental during inter-sessional periods in communicating with other nation-states to effectively block the collective work being done by other states, the Chairperson of the WGDD and representatives of indigenous peoples. Furthermore, their particular interests were to diminish standards that other states were willing to negotiate through the collective Provisional Adoption process,[38] ably chaired by the Government of Norway. Any efforts 'to undertake further work to generate a consensus text' would have meant allowing the US, Canada, Australia and New Zealand additional time to incite fear amongst other Human Rights Council members as well as drafting language down to the lowest possible denominator and based solely on unsubstantiated positions.

On the one hand the US government stated: 'we will continue our opposition to racial discrimination against indigenous individuals and

[37] Observations of the United States with respect to the Declaration on the Rights of Indigenous Peoples and USUN Press Release 204(07), 13 September 2007, as delivered, United States Mission to the United Nations; and Explanation of vote by Robert Hagen, US Advisor on the Declaration on the Rights of Indigenous Peoples, to the UN General Assembly, 13 September 2007.

[38] In the final phase of Commission on Human Rights consideration of the Declaration and prior to the establishment of the Human Rights Council, the Commission on Human Rights Working Group (CHRWG) instigated a series of small working groups to focus on either parts or provisions of the Declaration text. This exercise was aimed at the eventual adoption of Declaration arts on a 'provisional' basis. The Government of Norway took on the responsibility of chairing this series of meetings, which all took place in the context of the CHRWG.

communities';[39] and on the other hand, they were insisting upon a racially discriminatory prescription concerning the right of indigenous peoples to self-determination. They even went so far as to question whether indigenous peoples are 'peoples' in a tired attempt to deny the status of indigenous peoples in order to deny their right to self-determination. I refer to this as a 'tired attempt' because of the practice and early debates within the UN and the ILO, and the general milieu in which the discussion first came about.[40] At that time, the overarching state-driven initiative was an expression of their continuing practice of discrimination against indigenous peoples. For a more instructive view, even the US should have referred to their own reservations to the ratification of the International Covenant on Civil and Political Rights.[41] However, the most important point to make in regard to this discriminatory hold-over is the fact that a range of international instruments, including the Declaration, close the chapter on the matter by essentially prohibiting racial discrimination in the context of indigenous peoples. The approval of the Declaration by the General Assembly and the practice of UN specialised agencies supersedes this former prejudicial view.

The US has been attempting to suggest that the provisions concerning land and resource rights are 'unworkable' because they have erroneously interpreted them as being absolute rights.[42] When these specific provisions are read in context, though, it is clear that the competing rights and

[39] Explanation of vote by Robert Hagen (n 34).

[40] For example, it was utilised in the title of the WGIP, indicative of early concern about the political and legal implications of the term. Needless to say, because the term 'populations' was being employed in early United Nations documents and meetings, there were persistent statements made by indigenous peoples' representatives who objected to the use of the term 'populations'. Take, for example, the statement delivered by the author on behalf of the Inuit Circumpolar Conference to the 1989 WGIP session: 'Inuit and other indigenous peoples worldwide are not and have never been mere "populations"'. Many indigenous peoples' organisations refused to employ the term and referenced it by quotation marks in both written and verbal statements of opposition to it. Others informed the members that they would refer to the body only as the Working Group on Indigenous *Peoples*. It was not until the WGIP members resolved the issue of self-determination, that the term "indigenous peoples" was included in their version of the draft Declaration. In the ILO context, see Statement of the Inuit Circumpolar Conference to the ILO, 1989: 'We are not and have never been mere populations … the ILO revision process … would be severely undermined should the terminology of the Convention continue to depict us, the world's indigenous peoples, in inaccurate and inadequate terms.'

[41] The US reservation reads: '(1) That the Constitution and laws of the United States guarantee all persons equal protection of the law and provide extensive protections against discrimination. The United States understands distinctions based upon race, colour, sex, language, religion, political or other opinion, national or social origin, property, birth or any other status …' United Nations Treaty Collection (as of 5 February 2002), Declarations and Reservations (unless otherwise indicated, the declarations and reservations were made upon ratification, accession or succession. For objections thereto and declarations recognising the competence of the Human Rights Committee under Art 41, see hereinafter). See http://treaties.un.org/Pages/ViewDetails.aspx?src=TREATY&mtdsg_no=IV-4&chapter=4&lang=en.

[42] See explanation of vote by Robert Hagen (n 34).

interests of others have not been written out of the Declaration text. In particular, Article 46(2) clearly states:

> In the exercise of the rights enunciated in the present Declaration, human rights and fundamental freedoms of all shall be respected. The exercise of the rights set forth in this Declaration shall be subject only to such limitations as are determined by law and in accordance with international human rights obligations. Any such limitations shall be non-discriminatory and strictly necessary solely for the purpose of securing due recognition and respect for the rights and freedoms of others and for meeting the just and most compelling requirements of a democratic society.

The provisions are fair and balanced in this regard. Even the articles dealing with redress contemplate the fact that indigenous peoples' rights and those of others will be addressed in the context of competing rights and interests and not in absolute terms.

Furthermore, similar to the Government of Canada, the US government has suggested that the Declaration creates a 'veto' power that attaches solely to indigenous peoples by acknowledging free, prior and informed consent; this is equally unsubstantiated. Both states are exaggerating the implications of this language, while at the same time denying its value in relation to 'the spirit of partnership and mutual respect'.[43] In relation to the collective human rights, the US articulates a view that would essentially deny the rights of indigenous peoples to culture, language, oral history and traditions, repatriation, safeguards against genocide and assimilation, spirituality and religious traditions, and education—many of which are expressly recognised in the context of US domestic law. Finally, the US suggests that the Declaration is unworkable, because it does not contain a definition of indigenous peoples. Such a view distorts the diversity of the indigenous world as well as the important element of the rights of self-identification, the right to be different and to be respected as such and the need for states and the international community to take into account the multiple realities of indigenous peoples 'from region to region and from country to country'.

Having gained some insight into the range of Inuit experiences in the Canadian north, one can easily see that the Canadian government's position on the Declaration is entirely incongruent with and disconnected from reality. Despite the UN's consistent call for universal respect for human rights, the government of Canada had the audacity to state that the Declaration does not apply in Canada. One from the north might reply

[43] The preamble to United Nations Declaration on the Rights of Indigenous Peoples, final paragraph, reads: '*Solemnly* proclaims the following United Nations Declaration on the Rights of Indigenous Peoples as a standard of achievement to be pursued in a spirit of partnership and mutual respect'.

that the caribou and the polar bear do not stop at the border; and neither do human rights and the need for *universal* respect.

The position that the Declaration 'has no legal effect in Canada, and its provisions do not represent customary international law' is erroneous, as for some, even the use of the term 'Declaration' gives it a more 'solemn ring, and takes it closer to most important policy statements of the organised world community—into the vicinity of instruments such as the 1948 Universal Declaration of Human Rights'.[44] The fact that a range of indigenous human rights have been 'received' into the realm of customary international law cannot be disputed, especially by states like Canada (and the United States), as they recognised Inuit, Indian and Metis political institutions, engaged them as parties to contemporary or modern treaty negotiations and land agreements, and afforded them a range of legal protections for the rights embraced by such solemn accords (in the Constitution no less). As described in the Inuit context above, most of these contemporary agreements include measures for self-government and extensive responsibility by Inuit over their members and on their lands and territories. Furthermore, not only Canadian courts, but also regional courts and international human rights treaty bodies have contributed to the crystallisation of customary international law through their analysis, decisions and concluding and general observations specifically concerning indigenous peoples and their collective and individual human rights.

Recently, First Nations and indigenous organisations based in Canada and supported by indigenous peoples worldwide are applying intense pressure in the framework of the Human Rights Council Universal Periodic Review (UPR) in order to draw the necessary attention to Canada's shameful and disturbing position on the Declaration.[45] Let

[44] SJ Anaya and S Wiessner, 'The UN Declaration on the Rights of Indigenous Peoples: Towards Re-Empowerment' *Jurist Legal News and Research—Forum* (US) (3 October 2007), http://turtletalk.wordpress.com/2007/11/14/anaya-weissner-on-the-un-declaration/.

[45] Joint Submission 4 to the United Nations Human Rights Council in regard to the Universal Periodic Review concerning Canada submitted by the Grand Council of the Crees (Eeyou Istchee); Inuit Tapiriit Kanatami; Inuit Circumpolar Council—Canada; Union of British Columbia Indian Chiefs; Chiefs of Ontario; Atlantic Policy Congress of First Nations Chiefs Secretariat Inc; Québec Native Women Inc/Femmes Autochtones du Québec; Asia Indigenous Peoples Pact (AIPP); Indigenous Peoples of Africa Co-ordinating Committee (IPACC); Tebtebba (Indigenous Peoples' International Centre for Policy Research and Education); Saami Council; Cordillera Peoples Alliance; Kus Kurá SC (Costa Rica); Programa Indígena del Centro de Asistencia Legal Popular (Cealp); Corporación de Abogados Indígenas de Panamá (CAIP); Centro de Apoyo a las tierras nativas; First Peoples Human Rights Coalition; International Indigenous Women's Forum/Foro Internacional de Mujeres Indígenas—North America; Indigenous Peoples Rights Monitor—Philippines; Canadian Friends Service Committee (Quakers); KAIROS: Canadian Ecumenical Justice Initiatives; International Work Group for Indigenous Affairs (IWGIA); and Forest Peoples Programme, UN Document A/HRC/WG.6/4/CAN/3, Human Rights Council, Working Group on the Universal Periodic Review Fourth Session, Geneva, 2–13 February 2009.

us hope that the UPR process is not politicised and that the UN reform is genuinely manifested through this action hastily, because the issues facing the Inuit throughout the Arctic and sub-Arctic are in fact urgent.

On a positive note, the election of President Barack Obama has had a dramatic impact upon both domestic and international policy for the United States. For indigenous peoples throughout the United States, including the Inuit of Alaska, the potential for re-defining relations and giving full effect to the Declaration is now far greater than under the narrowly focused former US administration. President Obama appears to have a more sensitive view of the matter of discrimination and human rights generally, which will likely translate into a more comprehensive, principled role for the United States in dialogue at home as well as abroad.

CLAIMS OF SOVEREIGNTY IN THE ARCTIC AND THE URGENT NEED FOR IMPLEMENTATION OF THE DECLARATION

As recently as 7 November 2008, Inuit leaders met for two days at the 'Inuit Leaders Summit on Arctic Sovereignty' in Kuujjuaq, Northern Quebec, where they discussed the matter of Arctic sovereignty at length.[46] The Inuit leaders involved in this topical discussion recognised the complex nature of sovereignty anchored in international law with many overlapping elements. These leaders affirmed that within the Inuit context, the starting point must be the history and reality of Inuit use and occupation of Arctic lands and waters, and the need for Arctic-rim nation states to respect the human rights and roles of Inuit in all international discussions and commitments dealing with the Arctic. The issue of climate change and its impact on Inuit communities as well as the escalating speculation about how drastic reduction of ice coverage will open the Arctic waterways to increased shipping traffic and expedited oil and gas development have all been recognised.

In addition to addressing nation-state movements and the rights and interests of our own peoples and Inuit institutions (including Inuit controlled governments), Inuit are also aware of the need to assert their rights and interests in relation to the Arctic Ocean itself. The potential threats to the Arctic Ocean trigger the need to review the relevant provisions of the UN Convention on the Law of the Sea and possibly to pursue a distinct regime to deal with what appears to be the inevitable

[46] The final outcome of these discussions was 'A Circumpolar Inuit Declaration on Sovereignty in the Arctic', adopted on behalf of Inuit in Greenland, Canada, Alaska and Chukotka by the Inuit Circumpolar Council, April 2009. See www.itk.ca/circumpolar-inuit-declaration-arctic-sovereignty.

traversing of the Arctic Ocean. The need for a new perspective on the Convention on the Law of the Sea in light of international developments, especially in the context of the Declaration's elaboration of the human rights of indigenous peoples, must be taken into consideration by both Inuit and nation-states. One of the first critical elements of such a discussion is the need to affirm and recognise the distinct status and rights of the indigenous peoples of the circumpolar region, ranging from the small nations of the Russian Federation to the Inuit throughout Alaska, Canada and Greenland, to the Saami of northern Norway, Sweden and Finland.

A second critical element is the need to recognise the profound relationship that indigenous peoples of the Arctic Ocean coastal areas have with their respective lands, territories and resources. Similar to the position of Inuit in the context of the Declaration, Arctic-rim nation-state representatives must have a comprehensive understanding of the term 'territories'; it must be inclusive of the coastal land areas and shore fast sea ice as well as the offshore areas and the ocean itself, which have been traditionally used for millennia as the source of sustenance. Similar to the contextual framework and provisions of the Labrador Agreement, it must be widely recognised that the Inuit harvesting of whales, seals, walrus, migratory birds and other marine life not only relate to subsistence or traditional economies; it must be accepted that such harvesting activities are interrelated and indivisible from other social, cultural and spiritual dimensions of Inuit societies.

The international human rights developments, and in particular the Declaration, that emerged following the formal codification and eventual adoption of the UN Convention on the Law of the Sea (UNCLOS), are necessary benchmarks for determining the shortcomings of the UNCLOS provisions. Even a cursory review of the long list of participants engaged in the decades of drafting of UNCLOS will quickly show that despite their direct rights and interests in the Arctic Ocean, the Inuit, indigenous to the region, did not have any measure of direct, meaningful and effective participation in the preparation of its content. Such lack of participation, consultation and collaboration must be corrected in any future consideration and implementation of UNCLOS in the Arctic Ocean arena. This is even more essential in the face of the wide range of adverse impacts on this northern environment brought about by climate change.

Though some may argue that the UNCLOS provisions dealing with ice-covered areas are fast becoming irrelevant, they remain critical to indigenous peoples throughout the circumpolar region. Such provisions were never dealt with in a comprehensive fashion in the context of UNCLOS. Furthermore, indigenous peoples' interests were wholly ignored in terms of recognition of their distinct resource rights, which have now been affirmed by the Declaration. The matters of peaceful uses, peaceful purposes and collective security need to be scrutinised against the backdrop of the rights and interests of indigenous peoples and should not be seen in solely military terms. An expansive approach that goes beyond freedom of navigation and military and strategic interests would respond to the absence of adequate environmental protections and move us closer to global security. Here again, the Declaration would be extremely helpful in providing the human rights-based approach to peace and security, which we would all benefit from.

As previously argued by this author and other interested scholars[47], one potential path forward is the designation of the Arctic Ocean as a semi-enclosed sea, which would trigger important safeguards in response to the concerns and interests of many, including Arctic indigenous peoples. For example (and consistent with the interests of indigenous peoples and members of the Arctic Council), environmental protection, management and conservation of marine resources and marine scientific research are all matters of direct relevance.

The Arctic Council and initiatives such as the Arctic Environmental Protection Strategy have been good starting points. However, the Council does not go far enough in light of the political and international human rights developments, the expansion of interests, and the urgent issues facing Arctic indigenous inhabitants and each coastal nation-state. A new regime is needed to take into account the dramatic changes impacting this fragile ecosystem. Even the single issue of ice free navigation of the Arctic Ocean itself necessitates a comprehensive response and new regime that will effectively involve the Inuit as well as other stakeholders. Any such regime must include all Arctic indigenous peoples and must afford them full recognition of and respect for their fundamental human rights. Given the adoption of the Declaration as well as the existing Arctic Council regime and the role of Arctic indigenous peoples as permanent participants within the Council, there is ample opportunity to establish a human rights-based approach to a wide range of issues in a collective fashion. In response to this need and in recognition of the wide range of positive developments concerning Inuit rights, the ICC has already determined that an update of its own Arctic Policy Principles is necessary. Through such an exercise, a programme focused on human rights education of both Inuit and non-Inuit could be initiated. In this way, Inuit and others could strengthen both international and regional systems.

[47] See generally D S Dorough, 'Indigneous Peoples and the Law of the Sea: the Need for an Arctic Perspective' in D Vidas and W Østreng (eds) *Order for the Oceans at the Turn of the Century* (The Hague, Netherlands: Kluwer Law International, 1999).

CONCLUSIONS

Though the United States and Canada, as Arctic-rim countries, played a shameful role by escalating their attempts to diminish the standards contained in the Declaration in the final hours of its consideration by the UN, they ultimately did not succeed; their voices were expressions of a minority viewpoint. Unfortunately, the Russian Federation could not find a voice by which they could support the Declaration. In positive contrast, though, all other Arctic-rim countries of Denmark, Norway, Finland, Iceland and Sweden supported the Declaration.

The original objective of the United Nations was to 'give special attention to the evolution of standards concerning the rights of indigenous populations, taking account of both the similarities and the differences in the situations and aspirations of indigenous populations throughout the world'.[48] The overall process of negotiating the Declaration as well as its final adoption was often frustrating and painful. After reflecting upon the decades long involvement by indigenous peoples in this process one can safely say that the first two stages were largely successful. However, we are embarking upon a new stage. The implementation of the Declaration, through partnership, can bring about enhanced international cooperation on a wide range of issues among Arctic-rim countries. Such action should be pursued in light of the urgent issues facing not only the circumpolar region but the entire world.

We are now far from the days of random and strange contact with Arctic explorers. From this brief essay, one can deduce that the gulf that existed between Inuit and others has disappeared. The Inuit, through the ICC as well as through our diverse members, are clearly prepared to re-define our relations with others. We are prepared to do what is necessary through political organising and Inuit diplomacy to succeed in safeguarding our communities and our homelands, but we cannot do it alone; we can and must extend our hands. We hope that the Arctic-rim countries will do the same. In so doing, they must be prepared to acknowledge and implement the Declaration that we have all worked so hard to gain.

[48] Economic and Social Council Resolution 1982/34, mandate of the UN Working Group on Indigenous Populations to '[g]ive special attention to the evolution of standards concerning the rights of indigenous populations, taking into account both the similarities and the differences in the situations and aspirations of indigenous populations throughout the world'. The establishment of the WGIP is generally recognised as a substantive result of the conclusions and recommendations contained in the report of the Special Rapporteur to the Sub-Commission, Mr José R Martinez Cobo, entitled 'Study of the Problem of Discrimination against Indigenous Populations' (E/CN.4/Sub.2/1986/7 and Add.1–4).

21

The UN Declaration on the Rights of Indigenous Peoples: Recent Developments regarding the Saami People of the North

MALGOSIA FITZMAURICE

INTRODUCTION

THIS CHAPTER IS devoted to the Saami people of Northern Europe and Russia.[1] The essay will critically analyse regional developments in Northern Europe (Finland, Norway and Sweden). The main focus will be on the 2005 Norwegian Finnmark Act[2] and the 2005 Draft Saami Convention (a draft treaty between Finland, Norway and Sweden). These new developments will be assessed in the light of the 2007 UN Declaration on the Rights of Indigenous Peoples ('the Declaration') as well as in the light of other relevant international instruments, such as the 1989 ILO Convention 169 concerning Indigenous and Tribal Peoples in Independent Countries, to which Norway only is a party. The essay will also discuss the legal position of the Saami people in the legislation of the three Nordic States; this is necessary for a better understanding of the complicated legal and political issues arising for the Nordic States regarding the future signing and ratifying of the Draft Saami Convention.

[1] There is a voluminous body of literature on this subject; among recent publications see A Xanthaki, 'Indigenous Peoples' Rights in the Russian Federation: The Case of Numerically Small Peoples and the Russian North, and Far East' (2004) 1 *Human Rights Quarterly* 54–105. Note that (2001) 2–3 *International Journal on Minority and Group Rights* was devoted to the Saami. See also G Ulfstein, 'Indigenous Peoples' Right to Land' [2004] *Max Planck United Nations Yearbook* 1; HP Graver and G Ulfstein, 'The Saami People's Right to Land in Norway' (2004) 4 *International Journal on Minority and Group Rights* 337–77; M Åhrén, 'Indigenous Peoples' Culture-Customs, and Traditions and Customary Law: The Saami People's Perspective' (2004) 1 *Arizona Journal of International & Comparative Law* 63.

[2] Finnmarksloven [2005] AILR 54; 9(3) 87, <http://www.regjeringen.no/upload/BLD/The%20Finmark%20Act.pdf>.

Due to their progressive character, these developments (in particular the adoption of the text of the Draft Saami Convention) will potentially have an impact on the position of indigenous peoples in other countries too.

GENERAL REMARKS ON THE UN DECLARATION ON THE RIGHTS OF INDIGENOUS PEOPLES

At present, it appears that the Declaration is the most overarching and comprehensive instrument relating to indigenous rights. The drafting of the Declaration spanned a long period of time.[3] The final text is a comprehensive document, consisting of a preamble and 46 articles, and sets out the minimum standards for the survival, dignity and well-being of the indigenous peoples of the world (Article 43). The Declaration refers to indigenous peoples as the holders of collective and individual rights. Collective human rights and their relationship with individual rights remain contested issues of human rights law.

Special mention must be made of Articles 18 and 19, which differentiate between an indigenous right to participate in decisions that would affect them (Article 18) and an indigenous right to consent before States implement measures of a legislative or administrative character which may affect indigenous peoples (Article 19). Article 34 is also very important and has attracted criticism from both State delegations[4] and indigenous representatives[5] for explicitly limiting aspects of the right to self-determination and, in this manner, discriminating against indigenous peoples. Thornberry has noted that if the intention of the wording of Article 34 was to ensure that individual human rights are respected among collective rights, then the clause is too limited and it should clearly apply to all the rights in the Declaration. Self-determination is not specially devised to destroy all individual human rights.[6] In defining the relationship between the individual and the collective, indigenous peoples should use the language of international human bodies: necessity, proportionality, equity and balance of rights.[7]

[3] There were few substantial changes between the draft declaration and the adopted version. See on this S Errico, 'The UN Declaration on the Rights of Indigenous Peoples is Adopted' (2007) 4 *Human Rights Law Review* 756.

[4] Article 34 provides: 'Indigenous peoples have the right to promote, develop and maintain their institutional structures and their distinctive customs, spirituality, traditions, procedures, practices and, in the cases where they exist, juridical systems or customs, in accordance with international human rights standards.'

[5] UN Doc E/CN.4/Sub.2/1998/106, para 39.

[6] P Thornberry, *Indigenous Peoples and Human Rights* (Manchester University Press, 2002) 381.

[7] Ibid.

The general right to self-determination is proclaimed in Article 3 of the Declaration. The provision should be read in conjunction with Article 46, which links all the rights contained in the Declaration with the rights recognised in the UN Charter and specifies that limitations will only occur when determined by law and in accordance with international human rights obligations. Gilbert concludes that in light of Article 46, 'the right to self-determination will apply within the existing international human rights framework on self-determination for indigenous peoples', which includes the jurisprudence of the Human Rights Committee on Article 1 of the International Covenant on Civil and Political Rights (ICCPR).[8] According to Eide, the crucial addition of Article 46(1) significantly curtails the scope and significance of Article 3.[9]

Almost as contentious is the issue of indigenous peoples' collective land rights and rights to natural resources, which are of particular importance in relation to both the 2005 Finnmark Act and the 2005 Draft Saami Convention.[10] Article 8(2)(b) of the Declaration recognises the link between land rights and the existence and well-being of indigenous peoples.[11] Also, in line with ILO Convention 169, Article 26 recognises collective rights of indigenous peoples to land, natural resources and the environment.[12] However, Gilbert notes that unlike Article 14(2) of Convention 169, the Declaration does not include an obligation on States to make a clear land demarcation.[13] Further, Article 26 of the Declaration is not very clearly phrased: according to paragraph 1, 'indigenous peoples have the right to the lands, territories and resources which they traditionally owned, occupied or otherwise used and occupied', while paragraph 2 reads that 'indigenous peoples have the right to own, use, develop and control the lands, territories and resources that they possess by reason of traditional ownership or other traditional occupation or use, as well as those which they have otherwise acquired'. The initial version of

[8] J Gilbert, *Indigenous Peoples' Land Rights under International Law: From Victims to Actors* (Leiden, Martinus Nijhoff, 2006) 220.

[9] A Eide, 'Rights of Indigenous Peoples: Achievements in International Law during the Last Quarter of the Century' [2005] *Netherlands Yearbook of International Law* 211.

[10] See below.

[11] It states as follows: 'States shall provide effective mechanisms for prevention of, and redress for ... any action which has the aim or effect of dispossessing them of their lands, territories or resources ...'

[12] Art 26 is in accord with the findings of the Inter-American Cout of Human Rights (IACHR) in *Mayagna (Sumo) Awas Tingni Community v Nicaragua* (Series C No 79) [2001] IACHR 9 (31 August 2001) at para 148; see Gilbert (n 8) 85–155.

[13] Gilbert (n 8) 225. The same author observes that the Human Rights Committee interpreted in a 'dynamic' manner Art 27 of the ICCPR as obliging States to ensure, through demarcation of indigenous peoples' territories, effective protection of these territories. The IACHR in the *Awas Tigini* case (n 12) found that Nicaragua was in breach of Art 21 of the American Convention on Human Rights by reason of its failure to demarcate the land (225–26).

the article, which was not adopted by the Human Rights Council, only included lands 'which they traditionally owned or otherwise occupied or used', but the final version restricted the rights to lands 'they possess by reason of traditional ownership' in order to limit the scope to 'lands currently owned'.[14] Also, the nature of the right to lands, territories and resources that indigenous peoples have traditionally occupied (Article 26(1)) is not clear, and neither is it clear how they differ from rights of 'ownership, use, development and control' that are recognised in relation to indigenous lands that indigenous peoples currently possess (Article 26(2)).

Article 28 of the Declaration, regarding the right to redress, is equally confusing. The original draft Article 27 (which later became Article 28) included a right to restitution for lands which were taken from indigenous peoples in a discriminatory manner. In cases where restitution would be impossible, indigenous peoples were granted a right to compensation. However, this was disputed as raising the possibility of encroachment on third parties' rights; also, the basis of the right to compensation in international law was questioned, despite practice of the UN human rights bodies. In the final version Article 28 of the Declaration was retained, but phrased in terms of 'redress' rather than 'restitution'.[15] 'Redress' appears to be an overarching concept that includes restitution. Redress is provided for 'the lands, territories and resources which [indigenous peoples] have traditionally owned or otherwise occupied or used, and which have been confiscated, taken, occupied, used or damaged without their free, prior and informed consent' (Article 28(1)). Restitution is upheld as the fundamental principle and compensation is to be resorted to only where restitution is impossible. However, the special relationship of indigenous peoples with their land puts in doubt the appropriateness of financial compensation. A favoured method of compensation would be in the form of lands, territories and resources of equal quality, size and legal status (Article 28(2)). The compensation standard adopted in the Declaration is that of 'just, fair and equitable compensation'.

Notwithstanding its weaknesses, the Declaration is an important instrument. According to Panzironi, 'the UN Declaration remains a groundbreaking and remarkable tribute to a new generation of international consensus on indigenous peoples' rights both at the international and regional institutional level'.[16] Gilbert is of the view that despite certain lacunae, the Declaration is particularly important in furthering the

[14] Ibid.

[15] Ibid, 228.

[16] F Panzironi, 'Indigenous Peoples' Right to Self-Determination and Development Policy', unpublished doctoral thesis, University of Sydney, 2006, 63, ses.library.usyd.edu.au/bitstream/2123/1699/2/02whole.pdf.

development of 'a stronger corpus of laws on collective rights',[17] striking a good balance between individual and collective rights and instilling the idea that collective rights, which are requisite for the existence of indigenous peoples, and individual rights are not opposites.[18] This Declaration, although legally a non-binding document, is a long-awaited affirmation of the position of indigenous peoples as important actors in the contemporary world whose interests have to be taken into account by States, and a further indication that both States and indigenous peoples have to be engaged in a dialogue.

THE 2005 FINNMARK ACT[19]

The 2005 Finnmark Act regulates rights to land and natural resources in the northernmost county of Norway, which is called Finnmark and which covers 48,649 kilometres, an area larger than Denmark. The Act is of fundamental importance because land rights are notoriously difficult to prove in court proceedings.[20] It is the result of many historical events, as it was originally at the centre of a dispute over the Alta-Kautokeino hydro-electric power development. This dispute led to the establishment in 1980 of the Norwegian Saami Rights Committee. The first report of the Committee resulted in the adoption in 1988 of a new provision of the Norwegian Constitution, Article 110A on the Saami People; also, the 1997 report of the Committee regarding rights to land and natural resources in Finnmark formed the basis of the Finnmark Act.

THE FINNMARK ACT—THE GENERAL FRAMEWORK

The Finnmark Act (*Finnmarksloven*, 'the Act') is founded upon the principle that 95 per cent of the land in Finnmark will be under the common administrative regime, the *Finnamarkseiendommen/Finnmárkkuopmodat*, ie the Finnmark Estate. Until the entry into force of the Act all land was registered as the property of *Statskog SF* (State Enterprise, a State-owned company that administers State-owned land). Registered title to State land in Finnmark was transferred from *Statskog* to the Finnmark Estate (section 1 of the Act). The Act applies to real property as well as mineral and natural

[17] Xanthaki (n 1) 107 argues that 'certainly, the whole essence of the draft Declaration is the recognition of indigenous collective rights'.

[18] Gilbert (n 8) 226 and 229.

[19] Act of 17 June 2005 No 85 relating to Legal Relations and Management of Land and Natural Resources in the County of Finnmark (the Finnmark Act), Entered into force July 2006. (see n2)

[20] Xanthaki (n 1) 249.

resources in the county of Finnmark. The Act's provisions regulate in a completely novel manner the relationship between indigenous peoples and the State in relation to land rights and the use of natural resources. Its most fundamental feature is the extent of consultations with Saami Parliament over the management of uncultivated land and participation in the Finnmark Estate administration; this will be analysed below.

The Finnmark Estate is in principle a private landowner. The main principles of the Act are formulated in section 1 of the first chapter: 'the purpose of the Act is to facilitate the management of land and natural resources in the county of Finnmark in a balanced and ecologically sustainable manner for the benefit of the residents of the county and particularly as a basis for Saami culture, reindeer husbandry, use of non-cultivated areas, commercial activity and social life'. The scope of the Act is defined in section 2. It applies to real property and watercourses with natural resources in the county of Finnmark. On the shoreline, it applies as far out to sea as private rights of ownership extend. Section 3 regulates the relationship between international law and Finnmark. The Act shall apply within the limitations set in ILO Convention 169 and in compliance with the provisions of international law concerning indigenous peoples and minorities as well as agreements with foreign States concerning fishing in trans-boundary watercourses.

According to Chapter 1, section 4, the Saami Parliament may issue guidelines for assessing the effect of changes in the use of uncultivated land on Saami culture, reindeer husbandry and the use of non-cultivated areas, commercial activity and social life. The guidelines shall be approved by the Ministry. The Ministry shall examine whether the guidelines lie within the framework laid down in the first sentence of section 1 and whether they have been drawn up in an appropriate manner. In matters concerning changes in the use of uncultivated land, the State, the county and municipal authorities shall assess the significance such changes will have for Saami culture, reindeer husbandry, use of non-cultivated areas, commercial activity and social life. The guidelines of the Saami Parliament will be followed in the assessment of Saami interests pursuant to section 1.

Crucially, section 5 clarifies that through prolonged use of land and water areas, the Saami have collectively and individually acquired rights to land in Finnmark. However, in general, this Act does not interfere with collective and individual rights acquired by Saami and other peoples through prescription or immemorial usage. It also recognises the rights held by reindeer herders pursuant to the Reindeer Herding Act. In order to establish the scope and content of the rights held by anyone through prescription or immemorial usage or any other basis, a commission shall be established to investigate the issues and a special court to settle related disputes. Therefore, the Finnmark Estate will not change any existing rights either of the Saami or of other persons; a special Commission and a special court will be established to this end. Following an assessment of the Act by independent experts Graver and Ulfstein (see below), two new paragraphs, sections 6 and 7, were added to the Act; these uphold the status of the rights acquired by the Saami and other persons.

Chapter 2 sections 6 and 7 deal with the legal position and the structure of the Finnmark Estate. The Finnmark Estate is an independent legal entity in Finnmark which administers the land and natural resources that the Estate owns in compliance with the purpose and other provisions of the Act. It is governed by a board consisting of six persons, all residents in Finnmark: three elected by the Finnmark County Council and three elected by the Saami Parliament, each with a personal deputy. Among the members elected by the Saami Parliament, at least one board member and that person's deputy shall be representatives of reindeer husbandry. According to section 8, some preference will be given to female representatives of the Estate, in accordance with the Local Government Act. The Board is defined in section 9 as the body responsible for the management of the Finnmark Estate.

Section 10 is the heart of the Act as it concerns matters relating to, inter alia, changes in the use of uncultivated land and transfer of real property. In matters concerning changes in the use of uncultivated land, the Finnmark Estate must assess the significance of the change for Saami culture, reindeer husbandry, the use of non-cultivated areas, commercial activity and social life. In assessing this, the guidelines of the Saami Parliament pursuant to section 4 shall be followed. Decisions concerning changes in the use of uncultivated land require the support of at least four board members; otherwise, the matter may be considered by the Saami Parliament and will need the approval of the Saami Parliament and Finnmark County Council. If the Saami Parliament does not ratify the decision of the majority or does not consider the matter within a reasonable time, the collective majority of the board may demand that the Finnmark Estate place the matter before the King, who shall then decide whether the decision will be approved.[21] This provision does not apply to transfer of properties that have been partitioned by public division proceedings and that have been designated for development in plans pursuant to the Planning and Building Act or sites that have been parcelled out and developed.

The State may designate some areas of the Finnmark Estate as national parks, which may result in the prohibition or restriction of certain activities in these areas. However, compensation may be given to the Estate

[21] The Act contains separate provisions regarding uncultivated land which apply to Karasjok, Kautokeino, Nessby, Possanger and Tana municipalities.

and the use holders whose rights have been affected (section 19).[22] Finally, certain procedural rules regarding the matters concerning changes in the use of uncultivated land and transfer of property may result in a restriction on the legal status of the Estate as a private landowner (section 10). In general, as a private landowner, the Finnmark Estate will have to comply with the existing laws and regulations that govern the management of natural resources.

Access to renewable resources in Finnmark is regulated in sections 21–27 (Chapter 3) of the Act. Section 21 sets out the main principles relating to management. The Finnmark Estate manages the renewable resources on its land in compliance with the purpose of the Act and within the frameworks provided by the Wildlife Act, the Act relating to salmonids and fresh-water fish and other legislation. The Act urges that the diversity and productivity of nature is preserved and proclaims that all residents of Finnmark will be granted the right to exploit natural resources on the land belonging to the Estate, including hunting, fishing and cloudberry picking. Such a right is more extensive for residents of the area than for persons from outside Finnmark, who nevertheless are entitled to hunt and trap small game, fish and pick cloudberries for their own domestic use (section 25).[23] A permit is always required for hunting, fishing and trapping. Permits for fish for anadromous salmonids in the sea are preferably reserved for persons associated with primary industries in the area.

The enactment of the Act made it necessary to introduce certain amendments to other legislation in Norway, such as the Mining Act. Before undertaking any search for mineral deposits in Finnmark, the Estate, the Saami Parliament and the local reindeer husbandry board must be

[22] Land owned by *Finnmarkseiendommen* may be designated as national parks pursuant to the provisions of the Nature Conservation Act. When drafting rules on use, emphasis shall be placed upon the possibility of continuing traditional use. *Finnmarkseiendommen* and affected holders of rights of use may demand compensation for financial loss pursuant to the provisions of s 20b Nature Conservation Act.

[23] All residents of a municipality have the right to: fish for freshwater fish with nets; fish for anadromous fish with salmonids with fixed gear in the sea; gather eggs and down; fell deciduous trees for domestic fuel; cut peat for fuel and other domestic purposes; and remove deciduous trees for use in fence posts and poles for hay drying racks in the reindeer husbandry and agriculture industries. All residents of Finnmark have the right to: hunt big game; hunt and trap small game; fish in watercourses with a rod and line; pick cloudberries; remove timber for home crafts. Everyone (including persons resident outside Finnmark) is entitled to hunt and trap small game; access fish watercourses with a rod and line; and pick cloudberries for their own domestic use. It must be stated that in Rivers Tana and Neiden, the local population holds special rights to fishing on the basis of statutes, immemorial usage and local customs. The legal system of fishing in these watercourses negotiated with Finland shall be conducted with the Saami Parliaments, affected municipalities and holders of special rights to fishing in these rivers (s 27).

notified in writing. In assessing any application, the decisive factor will be Saami interests. The Saami Parliament, the county authority and the municipality shall be granted the opportunity to express their views regarding this matter. If both the Saami Parliament and the Estate object to the granting of the application, the matter shall be decided by the Ministry of Trade and Industry.

The following section, section 24, regulates special rights to local use:

> [I]ndividuals, or groups or persons who are associated with a rural district and whose livelihood is wholly or partly associated with the utilization of renewable resources in the vicinity of the rural district may for up to ten years at a time be assigned special rights by the municipality to utilize renewable resources … in specified areas of the municipality. When establishing the area and the specific conditions, the use traditionally made of the area by people associated with the rural district shall be taken into consideration. The area shall preferably constitute an uninterrupted area in the vicinity of the rural district.

The Estate may issue general rules concerning the procedures and assessment of matters pursuant to this section, which must all be consistent with the Public Administration Act; the Estate will also constitute the appeal body for decisions taken by the municipality. Section 28 regulates fishing in the Tana and Neiden watercourses, which is subject to a special regime. It must be noted that the Act does not cover fishing rights in saltwater, mining or oil rights.

Chapter 5 regulates the Finnmark Commission, which, according to the law, will investigate rights of use and ownership in respect of land to be taken over by the Finnmark Estate (Chapter 5, section 29). Appointed by the King, the Finnmark Commission will consist of a chairman and four other members. The chairman shall fulfil the requirements of the Courts of Justice Act regarding Supreme Court judges, while two other members will fulfil the requirements regarding district court judges. At least two members shall have links to Finnmark. The Finnmark Commission will establish the fields of investigation and decide the order of investigation. When so deciding, emphasis shall be placed on the possibility of a natural and appropriate delimitation of the field, legal and historical contexts and the need to clarify legal relations.

The Commission may restrict or extend a field after initiating the investigation and may omit to investigate rights, if the nature of the right or the basis on which it is founded renders the investigation inappropriate. Any investigation must be publicised, so that potential right holders can make themselves known; reindeer husbandry organisations and other representatives of user interests in the field concerned, the Saami Parliament, Finnmark County Council, the Finnmark Estate and affected municipalities are notified separately (Chapter 5, sections 30 and 31). All parties have the right to give an account of the actual circumstances and provide evidence significant to the Commission's deliberations. In order to safeguard the interests of the parties, the Finnmark Commission may appoint representatives from various interest groups to monitor the work of the Commission (section 32). After investigating a field, the Commission shall issue a report containing information about who are the owners of the land; what rights of use exist; and the circumstances on which the Commission has based its conclusions. The way the decision was reached will also be announced and grounds shall be given for the conclusions of both the majority and the minority. The Finnmark Estate will then assess the Commission's conclusions and, if they accept them, will take appropriate measures in relation to other parties' rights. Parties that are not in agreement with the Commission's conclusions, or that need assistance in ensuring that the conclusions are laid down in a binding agreement, may request the Finnmark Commission to mediate. The Act also establishes a special court (the Uncultivated Land Tribunal for Finnmark) to consider disputes concerning rights that arise after the Finnmark Commission has investigated a field.

THE ACT AND CURRENT STANDARDS OF INTERNATIONAL LAW

The Finnmark Act is a unique piece of legislation, which contains considerable protection of the Saami peoples' interests. The Act came into being following many direct consultations between Storting (the Norwegian Parliament) and the Saami Parliament and introduces a very complicated system of administration of land and natural resources in Finnmark led by the Finnmark Estate, the body that took over ownership from the State. The Finnmark Commission decides on rights to land and natural resources in this area, a notoriously daunting task. The most striking feature of the structure of the Finnmark Estate is Saami participation. The Finnmark Act will be supplemented by the new Mineral Resources Act and the Fisheries Act (the elaboration of which is now complete) and will require the collaboration of various ministries. It is very difficult to draw any conclusions as to its success at present, as the Finnmark Act entered into force in 2007 and the Finnmark Commission has just been set up. Similar arrangements are being discussed regarding the Saami areas outside Finnmark (the Hilogaland Estate). Thus far a report has been submitted by the Expert Group.

This Act endeavoured to incorporate the provisions of ILO Convention 169. Specifically, the Guidelines Concerning Procedures for Consultations between Central Government Authorities and the Saami Parliament were enacted to implement ILO Convention 169 and are consistent with its Article 6: the Act requires that the Saami people be consulted in matters that 'may affect them directly'. Indeed, the procedure set out in the

Act implements the State's obligation under international law to consult indigenous peoples; seeks to reach an agreement between central government and the Saami Parliament whenever a matter that affects them is being discussed; facilitates the development of a partnership between the State's authorities and the Saami Parliament; and seeks to develop an understanding of the situation and the developmental needs of the Saami community (Guideline 1). The Consultation procedures apply to the Government, ministries, directorates and other subordinate agencies in matters that may directly affect Saami interests and may include all ideal and material forms of Saami culture. Relevant concerns may include music, theatre, literature, art, media, language, religion, cultural heritage, intellectual property rights and traditional knowledge, place names, health and social welfare, day care facilities for children, land use, business development, biodiversity, etc (Guideline 2). Consultation with Saami Parliaments must take place in good faith with the aim of reaching agreement on proposed measures through mutual cooperation.

The 2005 Finnmark Act also follows many of the standards set out in the UN Declaration on the Rights of Indigenous Peoples.[24] As the rights granted by this Act relate mostly to land rights and natural resources, Article 26 of the Declaration is quite relevant. Although not very clearly drafted, Article 26(1) acknowledges rights of indigenous peoples relating to lands, territories and resources that they traditionally owned, occupied or otherwise used or acquired. Article 26(2) enumerates the types of rights that can be accrued by indigenous peoples in relation to the land: ownership, usage, development and control. These formulations are general and give little guidance to States whose populations have many conflicting interests, such as Norway. Unfortunately, the Finnmark Act is also rather vague in terms of the types of rights it grants. It may be argued that the Finnmark Act falls short of the standards of Article 26(3),[25] as it does not distinguish between the rights of indigenous and non-indigenous populations of Finnmark. Moreover, the 'land rights' approach was replaced by a right to partial administration of the region, which is not in the spirit of the Declaration and leaves open the issue of ownership rights over land and water, used by indigenous peoples on the basis of prescription and use since time immemorial. It must also be stated that if the right of self-determination for indigenous peoples is to be realised through control of land and free disposal of natural resources, the Finnmark Act does not comply with this aspect of the right.

[24] The right to self-determination will be analysed below.

[25] Art 26(3) provides: 'States shall give legal recognition and protection to these lands, territories and resources. Such recognition shall be conducted with due respect to the customs, traditions and land tenure systems of the indigenous peoples.'

The Finnmark Act does not grant any special rights to the Saami, as it remains 'ethically neutral'. Article 32(2) of the UN Declaration provides for consultations and cooperation in good faith with indigenous peoples in order to obtain their prior informed consent relating to the use of their lands and resources.[26] As observed above, the Finnmark Act provides for the establishment of the Finnmark Estate, which includes representatives of the Saami people. However, as Graver and Ulfstein observed,[27] the structure of voting in the Finnmark Estate is such that it may allow encroachment on Saami rights. We must be also mindful that the Saami Parliament guidelines—required in certain circumstances—are not binding and may be overruled by the Ministry. Therefore, it may be said that the Finnmark Act does not comply with the requirements set forth in the UN Declaration.

It would be an oversimplification to argue that the Finnmark Act regulates the administration of this area in its entirety. In fact, this Act is one among many (though it is admittedly the most important) which constitute an extremely complicated nexus of legal acts, which are still in force together with the Finnmark Act, including the Mining Act, the Forestry Act, the Nature Conservation Act, the Motor Traffic Act, the Tana River Salmon Fishing Act and the Wildlife Act. This plethora of legislative acts entails different levels of Saami participation, therefore excluding in many cases Saami self-management. Again, these aspects indicate that the Finnmark Act falls below the standards set by the 2007 Declaration. The Finnmark Commission, which will investigate existing rights of use and ownership, will take into account both Saami people's and non-Saami peoples' rights. Therefore, Saami rights are not secured. In conclusion, it may be said that the Finnmark Act takes Saami rights into account to a certain degree, but is not fully compliant with the 2007 Declaration.

THE 2005 DRAFT SAAMI CONVENTION

1. Introductory Remarks[28]

In 1986, the Saami Council together with the four countries in which the Saami live decided that they should jointly elaborate the Saami

[26] Art 32(2) provides: 'States shall consult and cooperate in good faith with the indigenous peoples concerned through their own representative institutions in order to obtain their free and informed consent prior to approval of any project affecting their lands or territories and other resources, particularly in connection with the development, utilisation of mineral, water or other resources.'

[27] See above.

[28] For in-depth analysis of the Draft Saami Convention see T Koivurova, 'The Draft Saami Convention: Nations Working Together' (2008) *International Community Law Review* 279–93;What's wrong with this ?and 'From High Hopes to Disillusionment: Indigenous Peoples'

Convention, whose purpose would be to strengthen the rights of the Saami as an indigenous people and to deal with the issue of national borders. In 1996, Finland, Norway and Sweden appointed a committee to investigate the need to draft a Saami Convention. In 1998, the Commission endorsed the project and recommended that an Expert Group be established for that purpose; this was done in 2002. That same year, the Expert Group started its work, which led to a 2005 Report consisting of the Convention and comments. Although the Draft Saami Convention was adopted with consensus among the members of the Expert Group, the covering letter stated that the Finnish members of the Group accepted with great difficulty Article 3 on self-determination, Chapter IV on land rights and Article 42 on reindeer husbandry as an exclusive right of the Saami people.

The Draft Saami Convention was finally signed by the governments of Finland, Norway and Sweden in 2005; it is arguably the most important event in terms of the development of Saami rights and one of the most important for indigenous rights at the international level. Although the Saami played a fundamental role in the drafting of the Convention, they are not a formal party to it. However, the entering into force of and any subsequent amendments to the Convention require the agreement of the Saami Parliaments.[29]

One of the most complex issues that arose during the drafting of the Convention was the position of the Saami of Russia on the Draft Convention, namely their inclusion in its scope. Arguments were presented for and against. The Expert Group argued that in essence the Convention was meant to be an exclusively Nordic one. However, it was felt that it would be desirable to establish the cooperation of the Saami in Russia, especially since any Russian Saami residing in the Nordic States would be covered by the Convention. Still, the Expert Group felt that negotiations with Russia would be very difficult. In the end, the idea of cooperation was abandoned, as it would have been to difficult to implement, considering Russia's general attitude to the question of indigenous peoples, evidenced by its abstention in voting on the adoption of the Indigenous Peoples Declaration.[30]

Struggle to (Re)Gain their Right to Self-Determination' (2008) 15 *International Journal on Minority and Group Rights* 1; M Åhrén, 'The Saami Convention' in M Åhrén, M Scheinin and JB Henriksen, 'The Nordic Convention: International Human Rights, Self-Determination and Other Central Provisions' (2007) 3 *Gáldu Čála—Journal of Indigenous Peoples' Rights* 8.

[29] See the contrary view that Russia should be a party in G Alfredsson, 'Minimum Requirements for New Nordic Saami Convention' (1997) 68 *Nordic Journal of International Law* 397.

[30] Koivurova, 'The Draft Saami Convention' (n 28) 284.

2. General Framework[31]

One of the most pertinent issues discussed by the Expert Group was the choice between a rights and a framework Convention, that is, whether the text would include concrete rights, directly implementable into the domestic legislation of each State, or just general principles, carrying only general obligations on States and very few concrete rights. The drafters of the Convention opted for the first option, a rights Convention that contains mostly concrete rights.[32] The text is divided into two preambular parts and one operative part. In the first preambular part, the governments lay down what they understand as the foundations of the Convention, while in the second preambular part the Saami Parliaments express their own views on the matter. The text adopts the stance that the Saami in the three Nordic States constitute 'one people residing across national borders and the Saami want to live as one people within the three states' (the Saami homeland is spread across four countries, an area called Sápmi). Therefore, the Convention addresses the Saami as one people, with one aspiration and one culture. The same part of the Convention also acknowledges the Saami's right to self-determination (see below) and the past injustices committed against them.

The preambular paragraphs also state that the Saami have rights to land and mineral and natural resources in the areas that constitute the Saami historical homeland. However, the Convention does not specify the exact character of these rights. Still, its preamble makes the connection with the historical 1751 Lapp Codicil, whose Additional Protocol regulated cross-border reindeer herding between Denmark-Norway and Sweden-Finland ('as a renewal and a development of Saami rights established through historical use of land that were codified in the Lapp Codicil of 1751').

Chapter 1 of the Convention sets forth the general rights of the Saami people. The objective of the Convention is 'to affirm and strengthen such rights of the Saami people that are necessary to secure and develop its language, its culture, its livelihoods and society, with the smallest possible interference of the national borders' (Article 1). The following articles set out what Article 8 specifies as minimum rights. Article 2 affirms that the Saami people are the indigenous peoples of Finland, Norway and Sweden, while the next article introduces the right to self-determination,

[31] English text of the Convention (unofficial translation), www.saamicouncil.net/includes/file_download.asp?deptid=2213&fileid=2097&file=Nordic%20Saami%20Convention%20(Unofficial%20English%20Translation).doc.

[32] Åhrén (n 28) s 3.2.

which will be discussed below. Article 4 defines the type of persons to whom the Convention is applicable as

> persons residing in Finland, Norway or Sweden that identify themselves as Saami and who: 1. have Saami as their domestic language or have at least one parent or grandparent who has or has had Saami as his or her domestic language; or 2. have a right to pursue Saami reindeer husbandry in Norway or Sweden; or 3. fulfil the requirements to be eligible to vote in elections to the Saami Parliament in Finland, Norway or Sweden; or 4. are children of a person referred to in 1, 2 or 3.

As Åhrén notes, the question of who is a Saami for the purposes of the Convention was one of the most complicated issues. The definition derives from the criteria used to determine who is eligible to vote in the Saami Parliament, expanded by the addition of the second element, namely: individuals who do meet the language criterion but are active in Saami reindeer husbandry shall be regarded as Saami persons under the Convention.[33]

A very interesting point is the provision on State responsibility, which is expanded to cover public bodies and Saami Parliaments (Article 5). According to Article 6, the Nordic States are obliged to 'establish conditions enabling the Saami people to secure and develop its language, its culture, its livelihoods and its society. States shall create favourable conditions for maintaining and developing the local Saami communities …' Further, States shall ensure the protection of Saami people and individuals against discrimination and will, if necessary, adopt special measures to realise the rights contained in the Draft Convention (Article 7). Åhrén observes that the language of this article explicitly proclaims the right of the Saami as a people—and not just as individuals—as having the right not to be subjected to discrimination.[34] Furthermore, States in cooperation with the Saami Parliaments will 'strive to ensure continued harmonisation of legislation and other regulation of significance for Saami activities across national borders' (Article 10). States will also implement measures to provide for the Saami's cultural needs, to enable them to pursue their economic activities across borders, including access to national cultural provisions (Article 11); implement measures for better access to education and medical and social services (Article 12); and enable Saami people to use their own symbols to indicate their 'status as distinct in three countries' (Article 13). Further, Article 23 obliges States to 'identify and develop the area within which the Saami people can manage its particular rights pursuant to this Convention and national legislation'.

The following chapters elaborate on some of the rights recognised above. Chapter 3 elaborates specific rights in relation to Saami language,

[33] Ibid, s 4.2.2.
[34] Ibid, s 4.2.5.

culture and education. Article 23 grants to the Saami full language rights to use, develop and pass on to future generations their language and their traditions as well as to ensure that knowledge and the wider dissemination of the Saami language. Again, States must take positive measures, including the use of Saami language in courts of law and in public matters, inside but also outside Saami areas (Article 24). States shall also create conditions conducive to an independent Saami media policy (Article 25) and will work towards the establishment of sound Saami education both within and outside Saami areas, including financing it (Article 26). States, in cooperation with the Saami Parliaments, must also create conditions favourable for research of Saami society, taking into account ethical rules that the Saami's status as an indigenous people requires (Article 28). States shall also promote knowledge of the Saami outside their society (Article 28) and ensure that health and social services within and outside Saami settlements are organised in a manner compatible with the Saami's linguistic and cultural background (Article 29). Article 30 ensures that Saami children and adolescents are granted the right to practise their culture and to preserve their identity. States must also support and respect the right of the Saami to manage their traditional knowledge and their cultural expression and ensure that it will be passed on future generations, and must undertake to ensure that when Saami culture is used commercially, Saami have some control and some share of the financial revenues. In general, States shall protect Saami culture against misuse (Article 31), and Saami heritage will be protected by law and cared for by the Saami Parliaments and relevant cultural institutions (Article 32). States also pledge the provision of economic and commercial conditions to secure and develop Saami culture (Article 33).

Chapter 4 of the Convention deals with the controversial issues of the traditional use of land, water and natural resources. The Saami members of the Expert Group treated the standards contained in ILO Convention 169 as a floor, not the ceiling;[35] this of course was not welcomed by all State representatives. Following negotiations, a compromise was reached; Articles 34–40 of the Convention draw from ILO Convention 169, but have been adjusted to fit the particular position of the Saami.[36] Article 34 differentiates between individual and collective ownership in the areas in which the Saami have enjoyed protracted use of land or water and proclaims their right to continue to occupy and use certain land or water areas for reindeer husbandry, hunting, fishing, or in whichever other ways they have traditionally been used, to the same extent as before. However, such use or occupation can be pursed by the Saami without

[35] Ibid, s 4.2.11.
[36] Ibid.

them 'being deemed to be the owners'. In the event of joint use of these areas by Saami and other users, the exercise of the rights by both shall be subject to mutual considerations on the nature of the competing rights. This is a formulation similar to Article 14(2) of Convention 169. The fact that Saami use of these areas is limited to the right of continued use to the same extent as before shall not prevent the forms of use from being adapted to new technical and economic developments. Also, it is noted that this article cannot be construed as to imply any limitation on the right to restitution of property that the Saami might have under national or international law. Article 35 states that the Saami rights deriving from this provision are entitled to effective protection by States, including the identification of the land and water areas that the Saami traditionally use, and the establishment of national procedures to examine questions concerning Saami rights to land and water, including financial support and judicial protection.

Article 35 urges States to introduce into domestic legislation efficient mechanisms and funds for Saami to pursue their claims in the courts. Article 36 regulates the use of natural resources. According to the first paragraph, particular protection shall be accorded to the rights of Saami to natural resources within such land or water areas as fall within the scope of Article 34; again this provision draws on Convention 169. Consideration will be given to continuing access to natural resources as is necessary to preserve traditional Saami knowledge and cultural expression. Prospecting or extraction of minerals or other sub-surface resources, or decisions concerning utilisation of other natural resources within such land or water areas that are owned or used by the Saami, will be based on prior State permits and subject to negotiations with the affected Saami and the appropriate Saami Parliament, when the matter falls within Article 16. Åhrén notes that paragraphs 2–4 of Article 36 are built on Article 27 of the ICCPR, as interpreted by the Human Rights Committee, and merged with the provisions on the Saami right to self-determination.[37] Prospecting for or extraction of natural resources will not be permitted if the activity substantially impedes Saami usage of the land and this usage is essential to Saami culture, unless the prior consent of the Saami Parliament and the affected Saami has been obtained. These provisions also apply to other forms of natural resource utilisation and to other forms of the use of nature in Saami areas, including activities such as forest logging, hydroelectric and wind power plants, construction of roads and recreational housing, military exercise activities, and permanent exercise ranges.

Special status is accorded to fjords and coastal areas (Article 38), while Articles 34–37 on water areas and use of water areas are also applicable

[37] Ibid.

to them. When allocating catch quotas as well as in other decisions relating to fish and other marine resources, due regard shall be had to Saami usage, however limited, and its importance to local Saami communities. The same provision applies if the use is reduced or has ceased owing to a reduction in marine resources in these areas (Article 39). Also, the Saami Parliaments shall have a right to exercise co-management and co-decision powers in the public management of the areas referred to in Articles 34 and 38. Finally, in cooperation with the Saami Parliaments, States shall actively protect the environment and ensure sustainable development in these areas (Article 40).

Chapter 4 relates to Saami livelihoods. Article 41 accords Saami livelihoods and the use of natural resources special protection to the extent that they constitute an important foundation of Saami culture. Article 42(1) explicitly acknowledges reindeer as a means of traditional livelihood and a fundamental cultural factor of the Saami people and proclaims that the Saami right to reindeer husbandry will be specifically protected by law. Åhrén explains that reindeer husbandry should not be seen as the only traditional means of livelihood or the sole means of identifying the Saami, especially as its importance differs in various Saami communities. In Norway and Sweden, reindeer husbandry is the exclusive right of the Saami; however in Finland, non-Saami people also enjoy this right. It is expected that Finland will promulgate the same legislation,[38] which will grant the Saami exclusive reindeer husbandry rights, having acknowledged Protocol No 3 of its Affiliation Agreement with the European Union concerning the Saami as an indigenous people. This article was one of the more problematic provisions in the Draft Saami Convention, in light of the reindeer husbandry legislation in Finland. The formulation of Article 42 of the Draft Saami Convention on reindeer husbandry was the only one acceptable to the representatives of the Finnish Government in the Expert Group.[39]

Article 43 regulates reindeer husbandry across national borders, another contentious issue. The right of the Saami to graze reindeer across national borders is based on custom. For example, at present, there is no agreement between Norway and Finland on cross-border herding activities. The provision specifies that if agreements exist between Saami villages (*samebyar*), *siidas* or reindeer grazing communities (*renbeteslag*) on the right to reindeer grazing, these will prevail and any dispute will be decided by an arbitration committee, whose modalities will be decided by the three Saami Parliaments. In the absence of any applicable agreement

[38] Ibid, s 4.2.12.

[39] M Scheinin, 'The Rights of an Individual and a People: Towards the Saami Convention' (2007) 3 *Gáldu Čála—Journal of Indigenous Peoples' Rights* 40–51.

between Saami villages (*samebyar*), *siidas* or reindeer grazing communities (*renbeteslag*), if a valid bilateral treaty regarding reindeer grazing exists, this will apply; otherwise any custom-based reindeer grazing right can be recognised by a court.

Finally, Chapter 6 contains rules concerning the implementation and development of the Convention. The Ministers in Finland, Norway and Sweden responsible for Saami affairs and the Presidents of the Saami Parliaments from each of these countries shall convene regularly and promote the Convention (Article 44). The Convention also establishes a Nordic Saami Convention Committee (Article 45) that will monitor implementation of the Convention, submit reports and proposals to the States, and deliver opinions in response to questions from individuals and groups. However, this Committee is neither a legal body nor a supervisory one. It will nevertheless be capable of receiving information from the public that can be used in its reporting activities.[40] States are obliged to make the provisions of the Convention directly applicable in national law (Article 46); therefore, the Saami can invoke their rights under the Convention within their national judicial systems. The Convention also includes provisions concerning the role of the Saami Parliaments, which are of great interest regarding the law of treaties. According to Article 48, after being signed, the Convention shall be submitted to the three Saami Parliaments for approval and will not be able to receive ratification until all three Saami Parliaments have given their approval (Article 49). Amendments to the Convention can only be made in cooperation with the three Saami Parliaments, and with respect for the provision set out in Article 48.

3. The Draft Saami Convention and the UN Declaration on Indigenous Rights

The Draft Saami Convention and the UN Declaration share many common features. Their general spirit is similar, as they both strive to prohibit discrimination against indigenous peoples. However, there are also several differences between the two, deriving in part from the special character of the Saami Convention, whose aim is to regulate one particular people, rather than to set universal standards. Thus, for example, Article 46(2) of the Declaration includes the stipulation that 'human rights and fundamental freedoms of all shall be respected' in the implementation of the Declaration. This provision created a certain degree of uncertainty as to what influence third party rights might have on the rights secured

[40] Koivurova in *ICLR* (n 28).

by the Declaration. On the contrary, the Draft Saami Convention does not include such a general provision, as the Expert Group elected not to address general issues, but rather to focus on specific problems.

Article 46(1) of the Declaration, which refers to the territorial integrity of States, has not been a particular focus of the Expert Group and hardly featured in their discussions. The article is rather succinctly formulated. The Expert Group came to the conclusion that the Saami right to self-determination does not include the right to secede from existing States and that such a right is not based on general international law. This view of the Expert Group, combined with Article 3 of the Draft Saami Convention, which stipulates that the right to self-determination is to be implemented pursuant to international law, and also combined with the Saami Parliaments' declaration in the preambular part of the Convention that the Saami people aspire to live as 'one people', 'took care of the territorial integrity issue in the Saami Convention'.[41]

The Draft Saami Convention contains no provisions directly addressing collective rights.[42] During the drafting of the Declaration the issue of collective rights proved to be very contentious. Indigenous peoples continuously argued for the recognition of the collective character of rights pertaining to them and insisted that collective rights are human rights and that they play a more fundamental role in relation to them than individual human rights.[43] This view was contested by some States, which continued to deny the existence of such rights. Åhrén describes the language used in Articles 1 and 2 of the Declaration, the result of a compromise between these two approaches, as 'constructively ambiguous'.[44] These articles appear to confirm that collective human rights in the Declaration are human rights, but their language leaves some room for a different interpretation 'by a non-objective and wicked enough lawyer'.[45] The Expert Group has not discussed the theoretical issue of collective rights. However, numerous provisions of the Convention referring to the Saami people rather than individuals clearly indicate that the Convention recognises collective rights. Still, Åhrén adopts a cautious view and notes that, compared to the UN Declaration, the Saami Convention contains more provisions referring to individual rights than collective rights. He also argues that the drafters of the Saami Convention have been more cautious when considering what rights are collective and what are individual and have found a better balance between these two types of rights. He writes:

[41] Åhrén (n 28) s 6.3.
[42] Ibid, s 6.2.
[43] Ibid.
[44] Ibid.
[45] Ibid.

> The UN Indigenous Declaration clearly contains a few provisions referring to the subject of the right as 'indigenous peoples', when it is difficult to understand the right addressed in the provision as being anything but individual in nature. Indeed, the UN Indigenous Declaration on a few occasions even proclaims that 'indigenous peoples have the individual right to ...' Such provisions do nothing but create confusion around what is the exact nature of the rights the UN Indigenous Declaration proclaims, and could potentially be harmful since they render it less clear to what extent the UN Indigenous Declaration acknowledges collective right proper.[46]

Åhrén observes, however, that other provisions of the Saami Convention are less far-reaching than the UN Declaration. For example, Article 9 of the Saami Convention on Saami custom is narrowly conceived. The UN Declaration addresses indigenous customary law in a more adequate manner in its Article 5, which enunciates indigenous peoples' right to retain and strengthens their legal system. Pursuant to Article 34, they also have the right to develop and maintain their juridical systems and customs.[47] Another such example is that of the repatriation of human remains, found in Article 12(1) of the UN Declaration. Article 32 of the Saami Convention does not address this issue, as it does not have any bearing on the Saami. As Åhrén explains, there are few Saami remains, as unfortunately, during the nineteenth and early twentieth centuries, many such remains were used in 'scientific' research that was conducted to prove the superiority of the non-Saami population over the Saami people. The Expert Group could not agree on a common stand and, as a result, the issue was not addressed in the Convention.[48] A further serious issue which is not addressed fully in the 2005 Draft Saami Convention is the restitution of lost lands, recognised in Article 28 of the Declaration. This issue was left for discussion towards the end of the drafting of the Convention and was included only upon the insistence of the Saami members of the Expert Group. Unfortunately, the State-appointed members of the Expert Group were not particularly willing to pursue this issue. Eventually, a compromise was reached, evidenced in the form of Article 34, which affirms the right of the Saami people to restitution and the right to non-traditional natural resources, as relevant in the Saami context; the text specifies that these matters will be solved later and does not offer any concrete solutions. However, as Åhrén argues, Article 34 paras 1, 3 and 4 'should not be construed to limit any right the Saami, under international law and national law, might have to restitution of traditional lands and waters taken without their consent'.[49]

[46] Ibid; see too fn 93.
[47] Ibid, s 4.2.4.
[48] Ibid, s 4.2.11.
[49] Ibid, s 4.2.11.

CONCLUDING OBSERVATIONS ON THE SAAMI RIGHT TO SELF-DETERMINATION

The Draft Saami Convention is a pioneering international law instrument regarding the protection of indigenous peoples.[50] From an international law point of view, it implements the very controversial Articles 14 and 15 of ILO Convention 169 and is mostly in conformity with the UN Declaration on the Rights of Indigenous Peoples as regards indigenous livelihoods and their relationship with the land and natural resources. Although the Draft Saami Convention is not perfect, Åhrén is of the view that, if accepted, it will open a new political chapter in the relationship between the Saami and the non-indigenous populations of Finland, Norway and Sweden.[51] However, in the event of non-entry, 'it will set a very poor precedent for the future'.[52] The fate of the Convention is still undecided. It was submitted for comments to the Saami people (but not Saami institutions), various NGOs and national authorities. Reactions have been very varied: the Saami were positive and non-Saami national authorities offered support. However, public authorities representing forestry and mining (thus threatened by the Saami right to pursue traditional livelihoods), municipalities and county administrative boards in the Saami areas, particularly in Finland, were against its adoption. Also, the Ministry of Environment in Finland disagreed on the formulation of Article 3 of the Draft Convention on self-determination and its relationship to the general structure of the governance system in Finland. According to the Ministry, there is a disparity between section 2(1) of the Constitution (which states that the powers of the State are vested in the people and represented by the Parliament) and section 121(4) of the Convention, which provides that in their region the Saami people are granted linguistic and cultural self-government. The issue at hand is how the question of the Saami's self-determination as a people relates to the rights already granted by the Constitution.[53] Further attempts to find an acceptable solution failed and at present the three Governments further discuss the Draft Convention individually, a situation which Åhrén finds absurd.[54] He notes: 'the Saami Convention—louder than any person, institution or text before it—poses a question to Finland, Norway and Sweden; will they allow the Saami' issues to be continuously politicised, or will they finally adopt a Saami policy based on the principle of non-discrimination, respect for human rights and the rule of law?'[55] Åhrén

[50] Koivurova in *ICLR* (n 28).
[51] Åhrén (n 1) s 7.
[52] Ibid.
[53] Koivurova, 'From High Hopes to Disillusionment' (n 28) 18.
[54] Ibid.
[55] Ibid.

hopes for the second option, especially when all three States were staunch supporters of the UN Indigenous Declaration.

The Declaration includes in Article 4 the right to internal self-determination.[56] The Article 4 formulation is neither revolutionary nor innovative in its approach. In fact, it is formulated in a familiar manner, which does not encroach on the classic state-centred definition as regards the issue of indigenous peoples' right to self-determination. However, Article 4 has to be assessed and viewed in relation to other articles of the Declaration, which constitute an indirect expression of the right to self-determination, that is the various elements of the definition of the right to self-determination. These should be viewed holistically, not in isolation.[57] Although they guarantee a fairly broad scope of rights, 'the terms of the relationship giving effect to these provisions are not established'.[58] The Declaration fails to direct States on how to establish a governance framework so as to create 'the terms and the legal procedures according to which the relationship between states and indigenous autonomous entities would be regulated'.[59]

Actually, the text of the 2005 Finnmark Act raises doubts as to its underlying principle of self-determination. In Scheinin's view,[60] the Finnmark Act is not in accordance with Articles 1 and 27 of the ICCPR, as several aspects of this Act do not constitute an expression of the right to self-determination. The Finnmark Estate was established contrary to Saami wishes, exclusively through Norwegian legislation. It is a mixed (Saami and non-Saami) body, in which Saami do not have a decisive role. This body is vested with powers that decide on issues with a direct impact on Saami livelihood. Therefore, it is in conflict with the fundamental precepts of the right to self-determination of indigenous peoples, that is, their right to design their own structures and to regulate the use of land and natural resources. The Finnmark Act appears also to conflict with Article 27 ICCPR, whose priorities are effective participation by indigenous peoples and sustainability of their economy, rather than the mere settling of land ownership. The Observations of the Human Rights Committee regarding the Saami position in Norway, Sweden and Finland have indeed referred to the role of the Saami in decision-making regarding measures affecting their livelihood, natural environment and means of subsistence, and have recommended their broader involvement in the

[56] Art 4 of the Declaration provides: 'Indigenous peoples, in exercising their right to self-determination, have the right to autonomy of self-government in matters relating to their internal and local affairs, as well as ways and means for financing their autonomous functions.'

[57] Arts 8, 12–14, 19–21, 23.

[58] Panzironi (n 16) 87.

[59] Ibid.

[60] Scheinin (n 38) 15–16.

management of natural resources. The Committee has pointed out the resource dimension of the right to self-determination and has asked Norway to report on the Saami people's right to self-determination under Article 1 of the Covenant, including paragraph 2 of that article.[61] Contrary to the Finnmark Act, as mentioned earlier, Article 3 of the 2005 Draft Saami Convention[62] treats the Saami in the Nordic States as being one indivisible people who enjoy the right to self-determination. The extent of the right to self-determination was a focus of extensive discussion during the drafting of the Convention. Very different and conflicting views were presented. Some argued that only States and peoples with a colonised past can conclude treaties and qualify as 'peoples' under international law and that indigenous peoples are not 'peoples' within the meaning of international law and at most qualify to be granted the right to internal self-determination within existing States. Others, including three members of the Expert Group, argued that indigenous peoples have a right to self-determination which is not restricted to internal self-determination, but also includes external self-determination. These views were based mainly on the interpretation of Article 1 ICCPR by the Human Rights Committee, an interpretation that, according to some, treated indigenous peoples as included within the scope of Article 1 of the ICCPR. They also interpreted Article 3 of the Draft Convention as including the right to external self-determination for the Saami, which included according to them the right of participation in various international fora and in intergovernmental affairs but excluded secession, except in very exceptional circumstances.

The Expert Group concluded that without doubt the Saami people constitute 'a people' entitled to the right to self-determination. Åhrén argues that this statement precludes claims that indigenous self-determination is a *sui generis* right, rather than of the kind falling under the general rules on international law.[63] He further argues that this right also encompasses the right of the Saami people to determine their own natural resources. The issue of the implementation of the right to self-determination was brought up repeatedly in the discussions of the Expert Group. The Draft Saami Convention approached this issue by introducing the so-called

[61] Concluding Observations of the Human Rights Committee on Finland, UN Doc CCPR/C/79/Add.91 (1998); Concluding Observations on Norway, UN Doc CCPR/C/79/Add.112 (1999); Concluding Observations on Sweden, UN Doc CCPR/CO/74/SWE (2002). See also B Henriksen, 'Oil and Gas Operation in Indigenous Peoples' Lands and Territories in the Arctic: A Human Rights Perspective' (2006) 4 *Gáldu Čála—Journal of Indigenous Peoples' Rights* 34.

[62] Providing: 'As a people, the Saami has the right to self-determination in accordance with the rules and provisions of international law and this Convention, the Saami people has the right to determine its own economic, social and cultural development and to dispose of its natural resources for its own benefit.'

[63] Åhrén (n 1) s 4.2.3.

sliding scale, providing the Saami with varying degrees of influence over decision-making processes depending on the importance of the decision to the Saami. Such decision-making powers vary from exclusive decision-making competence to the right to be informed and briefed only in matters which affect the Saami people.[64]

Article 14(3) of the Draft Convention further incorporates the Saami right to self-determination, as it stipulates that in each of the Contracting States the Saami Parliament represents the Saami population. Article 14(3) provides all Saami Parliaments with such decision-making and participatory rights as enable them to contribute effectively to realising Saami people's right to adopt independent decisions on all matters that national or international law prescribes. Article 15 transfers general powers (jurisdiction) to the Saami Parliaments to make such decisions. They may conclude agreements with national, regional and local entities concerning cooperation with regard to the strengthening of Saami culture and Saami society.

Article 16 states that on matters of importance to the Saami, negotiations with the Saami Parliaments will precede any decision by the public authority. These negotiations must take place sufficiently early to enable the Saami to exert real influence on both the proceedings and the outcome. States parties must not engage in or allow any activities that could damage Saami culture, livelihoods or society, without the consent of the Saami Parliaments. In matters that affect Saami people in a non-significant manner, the State must consult with the Saami Parliaments (Article 17(2)). Furthermore, the Saami Parliaments are entitled to be represented in governmental committees and similar bodies when such bodies deal with matters that are of concern to the Saami people (Article 17(1)).

Article 19 of the Draft Convention appears to contain an element of the external right to self-determination: 'The Saami Parliaments shall represent the Saami on intergovernmental matters. States shall also promote Saami representation in international institutions and Saami participation in international meetings.' Article 20 confirms that the Saami can form such joint organisations as the Saami Parliamentarian Council. Koivurova finds it surprising that the Saami were not accorded full treaty-making capacity. The lack of such a provision was probably the result of strong views on this subject on the part of Norwegian and Finnish representatives during the negotiations, who argued that only States have such powers.[65] Article 21 stresses that States will respect and, when necessary, will consult with the Saami Parliaments, as well as with Saami villages,

[64] Ibid.
[65] Koivurova, 'From High Hopes to Disillusionment' (n 28) 14.

reindeer herding cooperatives and other local Saami representatives. In addition, according to Article 9 of the Draft Saami Convention on Saami legal customs, States shall show due respect for the Saami people's conceptions of law, legal traditions and customs and shall investigate whether such customs exist and, if so, consider them when elaborating legislation in Saami areas. Due consideration shall also be paid to Saami legal customs in the application of law. However, as Åhrén notes, the provision gives non-Saami authorities the power to decide to what extent they will acknowledge and apply Saami custom; this weakens the right to self-determination as set out in the Draft Convention.[66]

A general assessment of the provisions of the Draft Convention indicates that it grants to the Saami very wide rights, enabling them to develop self-identification through participatory and cultural rights, including land rights and rights relating to natural resources. It encompasses both internal and external aspects of the right to self-determination. Therefore, it may be said that it comes closer than other international instruments to embodying the standards of self-determination of indigenous peoples as recognised in the UN Declaration. Indeed, the Draft Convention may prove very useful in terms of the future status of transnational indigenous peoples, due to the involvement of the Saami Parliaments in the drafting of the Convention and the recognition of the mutual willingness of all Saami across borders to regulate their livelihoods in a similar manner. Therefore, one member of the Executive Committee perceived the Draft Convention not as a treaty as such, but as a kind of 'social contract' between States and indigenous peoples sharing the same region.[67] It must be noted that the right to self-determination is based on ethnicity rather than on territory, which, as Åhrén observes, adds to the challenges of implementing it.[68]

The Draft Convention appears to pave the way for formal recognition of a future trans-border Saami nation, which in time will develop a joint Saami Parliament, with the possible participation of the Saami in Russia. It is envisaged that this body's main tasks will include all decision-making concerning Saami matters as well as their representation at the national and international levels. This body will secure to the Saami rights to their traditional lands, waters and sea areas and may even lead to the recognition of a common Saami homeland for the Saami people. Thus, the Saami—separated at present by borders—will be able to cultivate their culture in its totality.[69] The 2005 Draft Saami Convention appears to facilitate these goals.

[66] Åhrén (n 1) s 4.2.3.
[67] Ibid, p 14.
[68] Ibid, s 4.2.4.
[69] Ibid.

22

Between the Devil and the Deep Blue Sea: Indigenous Peoples as the Pawns in the US 'War on Terror' and the Jihad of Osama Bin Laden

JAVAID REHMAN

INTRODUCTION

THE PROCESS LEADING to the adoption of the United Nations (UN) Declaration on the Rights of Indigenous Peoples ('the Declaration') spanned almost a quarter of a century, corresponding to the emergence of the international indigenous peoples movement as a global development.[1] The adoption by the UN General Assembly of the Declaration is widely perceived as a triumph for indigenous peoples' rights worldwide. The text of the Declaration presents an acknowledgment of the affirmed position of indigenous peoples within international law. Many of the provisions contained in the Declaration already represent customary international law, thereby binding all States.[2] These provisions include, inter alia, 'the rights to life, physical and mental integrity, liberty and security of person' (Article 7); a right to self-determination, including the 'right to autonomy or self-government in matters relating to their internal and local affairs, as well as ways and means for financing their autonomous functions' (Article 4);[3] and arguably rights to 'lands, territories

[1] See P Oldham and MA Frank, '"We the Peoples …": The United Nations Declaration on the Rights of Indigenous Peoples' (2008) 24 *Anthropology Today* 4, 5.

[2] In the recent landmark decision in the Belize Supreme Court, the Court concluded that 'this Declaration, embodying as it does, general principles of international law relating to indigenous peoples and their lands and resources, is of such force that the defendants, representing the Government of Belize, will not disregard it'. *Aurelio Cal and the Maya Village of Santa Cruz v Attorney General of Belize; and Manuel Coy and Maya Village of Conejo v Attorney General of Belize*, (Consolidated) Claim Nos 171 & 172, 2007, Supreme Court of Belize (18 October 2007).

[3] See Art 3 of the Universal Declaration of Human Rights (UDHR), 10 December 1948, UN GA Res 217 A (III), UN Doc A/810 at 71 (1948); Art 6 of the International Covenant on Civil and Political Rights (ICCPR) (1966), adopted 16 December 1966, entered into force 23

and resources which [indigenous peoples] have traditionally owned, occupied or otherwise used or acquired' (Article 26(1)). These rights have been incorporated into international human rights law through treaty law as well as customary law; breaches of these rights amount to significant violations of the rights of indigenous peoples in international law.

Notwithstanding the fundamental nature of the aforementioned provisions of the Declaration, indigenous peoples continue to suffer gross violations of their rights. As this paper exemplifies, one unfortunate avenue by which the rights of indigenous peoples have been undermined is through their treatment as terrorists and as apparent threats to the security and integrity of the State. Although a historic feature, the prosecution of the US-led 'war on terror' has brought this practice back to the surface and has had a devastating impact on the plight of indigenous communities. This paper examines the position of the Pakhtuns and the Baluchis—indigenous peoples who straddle the tribal belt across Pakistan and Afghanistan. The chapter is divided into six sections. Following these introductory comments, there follows an overview of the position of indigenous peoples within South Asia, with particular reference to the Pakhtuns and Baluchis of Pakistan. We then move on to analyse the Pakistani State's treatment of these indigenous peoples and the State's official and perpetual categorisation of Baluchis and Pakhtuns as terrorists. The following two sections examine the implications of the US-led 'war on terror' for the indigenous Baluchis and Pakhtuns, and in so doing trace the path towards violation of the rights recognised in the UN Declaration of the Rights of Indigenous Peoples. The final section provides a number of concluding reflections with particular reference to the Declaration.

INDIGENOUS PEOPLES IN THE CONTEXT OF SOUTH ASIA

The term 'indigenous' is most difficult to define in the context of South Asia, not least because of its relative nature.[4] Many of the indigenous

March 1976, GA Res 2200A (XXI), UN Doc A/6316 (1966) 999 UNTS 171, (1967) 6 ILM 368; Art 2 of the European Convention on Human Rights (1950), signed in Rome 4 November 1950, entered into force 3 September 1953, 213 UNTS 221, ETS 5; Art 4 of the American Convention on Human Rights (1969), signed November 1969, entered into force 18 July 1978, OASTS Off Rec OEA/Ser.L/V/11.23, doc 21, rev (1979), (1970) 9 ILM 673; African Charter on Human and Peoples' Rights (1981), adopted 27 June 1981, entered into force 21 October 1986, OAU Doc CAB/LEG/67/3 Rev 5, (1982) 21 ILM 58. On the right to self-determination see Art 1 ICCPR. For useful analysis of the rights in the context of indigenous peoples see A Xanthaki, *Indigenous Rights and United Nations Standards: Self-Determination, Culture and Land* (Cambridge University Press, 2007); P Thornberry, *Indigenous Peoples and Human Rights* (Manchester University Press, 2002); SS Ali and J Rehman, *Indigenous Peoples and Ethnic Minorities of Pakistan: Constitutional and Legal Perspectives* (Oxford, Routledge-Curzon, 2001).

[4] For an overview of these issues see J Rehman, 'Indigenous Peoples at Risk: A Survey of Indigenous Peoples of South Asia' in BKR Burman and BG Verghese (eds), *Aspiring to*

peoples of South Asia, such as the Veddas of Sri Lanka, the Adivasis of India and Bangladesh, and the Sindhis, Baluchis and Pakhtuns of Pakistan, found themselves being colonised by powerful elements long before European western imperialist powers.[5] This relativity and slipperiness in the conception of 'indigenous' meant that in the transformation of the colonial world to a world of new nation-States, the term 'indigenous' was equated with those wanting independence from western imperialists or, as one author has appropriately put it, was based on 'pigmentational' or 'racial' sovereignty.[6] In the march towards independence from European colonisation, rights of indigenous peoples were overlooked.[7] In contemporary terms, the States of South Asia have maintained that the concept of 'indigenous' cannot be applied to their populations.[8] The official argument is that all peoples within their territorial boundaries are indigenous and therefore no distinction based on indigenousness can be maintained. Instead, as shall be examined using the case of Pakistan, partial recognition has been accorded through the concept of 'Tribal Areas'.[9] The non-ratification of ILO Convention 169 (1989) concerning Indigenous and Tribal Peoples in Independent Countries by Afghanistan, Pakistan,

Be: The Tribal, Indigenous Condition (Delhi, Konark, 1998) 72–121; J Rehman, 'International Law and Indigenous Peoples: Definitional and Practical Problems' (1998) 3 *Journal of Civil Liberties* 224–39; B Kingsbury, '"Indigenous Peoples" as an International Legal Concept' in R Barnes, A Gray and B Kingsbury (eds), *Indigenous Peoples of Asia* (Ann Arbor, Association for Asian Studies, 1993) 13–34.

5 For further articulation of the issues concerning specific indigenous peoples of South Asia see J Rehman and N Roy, 'South-Asia' in P Thornberry et al (eds), *World Directory of Minorities* (London, Minority Rights Group, 1997) 535–87; J Rehman, 'Minority Rights: South-Asia' in R Green et al (eds), *World Directory of Minorities and Indigenous Peoples* (London, Minority Rights Group, 2008), www.minorityrights.org/directory.

6 A Mazrui, 'Consent, Colonisation and Sovereignty' (1963) 11 *Political Studies* 36; M Promerance, *Self-Determination in Law and Practice: The New Doctrine at the United Nations* (Leiden, Martinus Nijhoff, 1982) 15–16. 'In the context of decolonization what matters is not the distinctiveness of a colonial people in relation to an ex-colonial people, but the identity of all the Colonial peoples in relation to the European rulers. Thus the definition of colonialism as subjugation to alien rule is of a very relative character, and its depend not on whether the ruler is alien, but on whether in being alien it is also European': A Rigo-Sureda, *The Evolution of the Right of Self-Determination* (Leiden, Sijthoff, 1973) 237.

7 'The consequence for the smaller groups of the transition from Empire to Statehood may be severe; inter-ethnic solidarity in the face of a common alien oppressor may be ruptured and replaced by a more intimate, local and knowing oppression.' P Thornberry, 'Self-Determination, Minorities and Human Rights: A Review of International Instruments' (1989) 38 *International and Comparative Law Quarterly* 867, 867.

8 According to Barsh, a leading authority on the subject, 'Bangladesh, Indonesia, the former Soviet China and India have maintained that there are no "indigenous" peoples in Asia, only minorities epitomising the former Soviet Ambassador Sofinsky's view before the Sub-Commission in 1985 that "indigenous situations only arise in the Americas and Australasia where there are imported populations" of Europeans'. R Barsh, 'Indigenous Peoples: An Emerging Object of International Law' (1986) 80 *American Journal of International Law* 369–85, 375. See also R Barsh, 'United Nations Seminar on Indigenous Peoples and States' (1989) 83 *American Journal of International Law* 599–604.

9 See Arts 246 and 247 of the Constitution of Pakistan (1973).

India and Bangladesh was based on the argument of its inapplicability to the populations of these States.[10] These assumptions were also prevalent during the drafting stages of the Declaration.[11] This helps to explain why upon the adoption of the draft declaration by the Human Rights Council on 29 June 2006, Pakistan, a member of the Council, voted in favour of the Declaration. Indeed, all South Asian States, save Bangladesh, voted in the United General Assembly for adoption of the Declaration on 13 September 2007.[12] Bangladesh was most fervent and also perturbed at the absence of a definition of 'indigenous' within the Declaration and hence abstained from voting in the Human Rights Council and the UN General Assembly.

The Pakhtuns and the Baluchis

The Pakhtuns are the main inhabitants of the mountainous areas that straddle the present day Pakistan-Afghanistan border.[13] The Pakhtuns currently occupy one-quarter to one-third of Afghanistan's territory and the North West Frontier Province (NWFP) of Pakistan. The Pakhtuns are speakers of Pashtu, an Indo-European language, in one of its two major dialects, Pashto (Pushto) or Pakhtu (Pukhktu). Of the estimated 21 million Pakhtuns of Pakistan, the vast majority inhabit the plains of

[10] 72 ILO Bulletin 59 (1989); 28 ILM 1382.

[11] Mr Ajai Malhotra from India noted that 'India had consistently favoured the rights of indigenous peoples, and had worked for the Declaration on the Rights of Indigenous Peoples. The text before the Council was the result of 11 years of hard work. The text did not contain a definition of "indigenous". The entire population of India was considered to be indigenous. With regards to the right to self-determination, this was understood to apply only to peoples under foreign domination, and not to a nation of indigenous persons. With this understanding, India was ready to support the proposal for the adoption of the draft Declaration, and would vote in its favour.' www.un.org/News/Press/docs/2007/ga10612.doc.htm.

[12] Bilal Hayee, the representative from Pakistan, was reported as stating that 'his country had voted in favour of the Declaration both in the Human Rights Council and in the Assembly. Although the Declaration did not define indigenous peoples, he hoped that its adoption would fulfil the aims of the International Decade for the rights of indigenous peoples and enable them to maintain their cultural identity, with full respect for their values and traditions.' For Mr Ajai Malhotra from India, 'while the Declaration did not define what constituted indigenous peoples, the issue of indigenous rights pertained to peoples in independent countries who were regarded as indigenous on account of their descent from the populations which inhabited the country, or a geographical region [to] which the country belonged, at the time of conquest or colonization or the establishment of present State boundaries and who, irrespective of their legal status, retained some or all of their socio-economic, cultural and political institutions.' www.un.org/News/Press/docs/2007/ga10612.doc.htm.

[13] Pathan is a Hindi term adopted by the British for Pakhtuns. See further O Caroe, *The Pathans: 550 BC–AD 1957* (Oxford University Press, 1976); K Ali, *A New History of India and Pakistan* (Karachi, Book Centre, 1992).

the NWFP, while a minority of 2.2 million live in the highlands of the semi-autonomous Federally Administered Tribal Areas (FATA).[14] Substantial numbers of Pakhtuns have settled in Baluchistan; up to 20 per cent of the total population of that province is comprised of Pakhtuns. Due to migration to urban areas there are probably over a million Pakhtuns living in greater Karachi. While the ancient proud history of the Pakhtuns is undoubted, their racial and ethnic composition is less clear. The tribes who lived in the area during the days of the Greek historians are believed to be part of the great Aryan horde that moved down from Central Asia a millennium earlier.[15] Over the centuries, the Greek, Persian, Turkish and Mongol invaders who passed through the region have added their blood.[16]

The Pakhtuns have an ancient history, culture and tradition often identified to the 'Pakti' kingdom as inscribed in the ancient works of Herodotus. The Pakhtun culture and tradition was firmly established between the tenth and fifteenth centuries. Pushto folklore was established and Pakhtun nationalism was subsequently reinvigorated by the lyrics of Khushal Khan Khuttak. Pakhtuns have a political history riddled with internal strife and unrest. Bitter internal feuds in the Pakhtun-dominated Afghan regimes provided an opportunity to many outsiders, and subsequently the British, to interfere and to divide the Pakhtuns themselves with the establishment of the Durrand Line in 1893.

Like the Pakhtuns, the Baluchis are also indigenous peoples native to the region that straddles the international borders of Pakistan, Afghanistan and Iran.[17] They are tribal pastoralists inhabiting the remote and hostile mountains and desert region of these border areas. According to popular Baluch legend, the Baluchis migrated northwards from Aleppo (in modern-day Syria) during the Arab conquests of the ninth century seeking pasture lands and fresh water, travelling through the southern shores of Caspian sea, and subsequently settling in what is now Iranian and Pakistani Baluchistan between the sixth and the fourteenth centuries.[18] The majority are found in the Baluchistan province of Pakistan, with smaller numbers in Iran and Afghanistan. There are a considerable number of Baluchis living outside their traditional homelands in other regions of these States as well as in the Gulf States. The Baluchis are not

[14] For a detailed analysis see Ali and Rehman (n 3) 44–58.

[15] See R Wirsing, *The Baluchis and Pathans* (London, Minority Rights Group, 1987).

[16] S Harrison, 'Ethnicity and the Political Stalemate in Pakistan' in A Banuaziz and M Weiner (eds), *The State, Religion and Ethnic Politics: Afghanistan, Iran and Pakistan* (Lahore, Vanguard Press, 1987) 271.

[17] S Harrison, *In Afghanistan's Shadow: Baluch Nationalism and Soviet Temptations* (New York, Carnegie Endowment, 1981) 10.

[18] Ibid, 10–12.

a homogenous group and are divided between the Sulemani or Eastern Baluchis in Iran, the Makrani or Western Baluchis in Pakistan and South West Afghanistan. The Brahuis of the central Kalat Plateau of Pakistani Baluchistan, speak the Brahui language. While the Brahui language is not related to Baluchi, it nevertheless has a heavy Baluchi admixture.[19]

Indigenous Peoples and the Constitutional Framework of Pakistan

The 'Tribal Areas' and tribal peoples of British India were accorded an unusual position during the colonial period. Unable to occupy or subjugate the warring and martial tribes, the British entered into a series of treaties with the indigenous tribes of the tribal belt. These treaty agreements made them territorially responsible for keeping peace with the government, and for protecting the means of communication passing through their areas, and in consideration thereof the tribal elders were assured payment of allowances by the government. On attaining independence in August 1947, successive governments of Pakistan continued with the pre-independence arrangement and did not shed this particular colonial legacy. The government executed fresh agreements with the tribal leaders and at the same time declared their territories to be an integral part of Pakistan. The tribal elders were assured that they would retain the position they had held in the pre-independence period, which consisted of receiving allowances in return for their pledge of loyalty to the government of Pakistan. Under the 1973 Constitution of the Islamic Republic of Pakistan, the Pakhtun and Baluchi peoples have been accommodated through the continuation of the scheme of 'Tribal Areas'.[20] Tribal Areas are defined in Article 246 of the Constitution as follows:

(a) 'Tribal Areas' means the areas in Pakistan which, immediately before the commencing day, were Tribal Areas, and includes

(i) the Tribal Areas of Baluchistan and the North-West Frontier Province; and

(ii) the former States of Amb, Chitral, Dir and Swat;

(b) 'Provincially Administered Tribal Areas' means

(i) The districts of Chitral, Dir and Swat (which includes Kalam), [the Tribal Area in Kohistan district,] Malakand Protected Area, the Tribal Area adjoining [Mansehra] district and the former State of Amb; and

[19] Wirsing (n 15) 4.

[20] See Ali and Rehman (n 3) 44–54; for the text of the Constitution of Pakistan see *Government of Pakistan, The Constitutions of Islamic Republic of Pakistan, 1973* (Karachi, Government of Pakistan Printing Press, 1973).

(ii) Zhob district, Loralai district (excluding Duki Tehsil), Dalbandis Tehsil of Chagai District and Marri and Bugti tribal territories of Sibi district; and

(c) 'Federally Administered Tribal Areas' includes

(i) Tribal Areas adjoining Peshawar district;

(ii) Tribal Areas adjoining Kohat district;

(iii) Tribal Areas adjoining Bannu district;

(iv) Tribal Areas adjoining Dera Ismail Khan district;

[(v) Bajaur Agency;

(va) Orakzai Agency;]

(vi) Mohmand Agency;

(vii) Khyber Agency;

(viii) Kurram Agency;

(ix) North Waziristan Agency, and

(x) South Waziristan Agency.

Article 247 of the Constitution of Pakistan reaffirms the separate legal status of the Tribal Areas, continuing the tradition of the colonial powers of simply 'containing' the 'unruly tribals', rather than extending to them the rights and privileges which are theirs as responsible and equal citizens of an independent country. The executive authority of the federation extends to the FATA, and that of the NWFP and Baluchistan to the Provincially Administered Tribal Areas (PATA). The President rules the Tribal Areas through his agent, the governor of the province where the particular Tribal Area is situated, and gives directions in this regard. No Act of Parliament applies to the FATA or any part of them, unless the President so directs, and no Act of Parliament or provincial assembly applies to the PATA, unless the governor of the province in which the Tribal Area is situated so directs, with the approval of the President. Thus, the President enjoys far-reaching legislative functions and powers in respect of making regulations for the peace and good governance of a Tribal Area or any part thereof. The President may also, at any time, by order, direct that the whole or any part of a Tribal Area shall cease to be a 'Tribal Area'; such an order may contain such incidental and consequential provisions as appear to the President to be necessary and proper. Such an order, however, may only be made after ascertaining the views of the people of the Tribal Area concerned, as represented in tribal *jirga* (an assembly of tribal elders that takes decisions by consensus), but in a manner considered appropriate by the President himself. Neither the Supreme Court nor a High Court can exercise any jurisdiction under the Constitution in relation to a Tribal Area, unless the Parliament by law provides otherwise. Since the

FATA were not part of the 'settled' areas of Pakistan, the normal civilian government does not function within their borders.

Several administrative, political and legal arrangements have been made in relation to the governance of the FATA: the Governor of the NWFP has been appointed agent to the President of Pakistan in the FATA and exercises immediate executive authority in these areas, while the Chief Secretary, Government of NWFP has been appointed head of the local administration of the FATA. The services of the provincial departments are utilised to meet the needs of the FATA within their respective spheres of jurisdiction. For this purpose, each Secretary of the provincial government acts as Secretary to the local administration, while the Finance Secretary acts as Financial Adviser to the agent of the President in respect of the FATA. Special cells created in the provincial government departments attend exclusively to the affairs of the FATA. The department at the federal level that coordinates these activities in the FATA is SAFRON. In actual terms, governance in the FATA is carried out through a political agent who utilises a number of measures in fulfilling this task; primarily though he relies on the 'cooperation' of the tribal leaders of the area.

The various mechanisms employed include the *Maliki*, *Lungi* and *Muhajib* allowances. *Maliki* is an allowance for the head(s) of a tribe and is hereditary, subject to 'good conduct' of the heir of the *malik* (head of the tribe) and approval of the government, whereas *Lungi* is a personal allowance for individual service and may be modified on the death of a *Lungi* holder. Finally, *Mawajib* allowances are those that are paid out to the entire tribe biannually. The main objective of these allowances is to maintain amiable political relations with the tribes, to bind them to the government of Pakistan by excluding other 'influences' and hence outside interference in the area. A further objective is to preserve law, order and security of life and property within the Tribal Areas and to keep mountain passes and roads open for trade and communications at all times. The essence of political control through the mechanisms described above is to maintain law and order in the Tribal Areas by enforcing tribal and territorial responsibility through accredited representatives of tribes, namely tribal *maliks* and elders who receive allowances. The system is designed to reinforce official influence and to implement development programmes.

The *maliks* and elders who receive allowances for a tribe/section are perceived as the political medium and are required to control and restrain their tribesmen from committing any act hostile or subversive to the State. The federal government's policies are implemented in the area through the *maliks* and elders. The federal government, in constitutional terms, is under an obligation to implement peaceful development programmes by helping to open up schools, dispensaries, roads and other development projects in the Tribal Areas.

PAKISTANI STATE PRACTICE AND CHARACTERISATION OF INDIGENOUS PEOPLES AS TERRORISTS

Throughout the historical trajectory of international terrorism, minorities and indigenous peoples have frequently been targeted.[21] Since time immemorial there have been sad tales of terrorism and violence against indigenous peoples. There are many examples of terrorism (eg in the form of horrifying massacres, torture and genocide) inflicted to eliminate indigenous elements.[22] Indeed, the essence of all forms of colonialism and in particular European colonialism was violent and intimidating; it terrorised indigenous peoples.[23] The British colonisers were not substantively different from other colonisers—they deployed the full panoply of manoeuvres and tactics, including using force to subjugate indigenous peoples and local communities. As noted above, however, the British were unsuccessful in their attempt to overpower the Pakhtuns and Baluchis through force. They thereby resorted to various treaty or other arrangements—the system was nevertheless exploitative and *mala fide*. As British imperial rule drew to an end, the Pakhtuns and Baluchis raised claims to independent Statehood. However, such aspirations on the part of the Pakhtun and Baluch nationalist movements were brutally repressed: it was convenient for the British and more importantly for the Indian nationalist movements (led by Mohammad Ali Jinnah's Pakistan Muslim League and Mohatmma Ghandhi's Indian Nationalist Party) to emphasise the principle of *uti possidetis*.[24] The principle was applied so far as Baluchis and Pakhtuns were concerned, thereby maintaining the territorial boundary as established by the British in 1893 (as the effective international border) separating Pakistan from Afghanistan.

Furthermore, and as noted already, despite the forcible annexation of indigenous territories within independent Pakistan, the inequitable and

[21] See J Rehman, *The Weaknesses in the International Protection of Minority Rights* (The Hague, Kluwer Law International, 2000); P Thornberry, *International Law and the Rights of Minorities* (Oxford, Clarendon Press, 1991); P Thornberry, *Minorities and Human Rights Law* (London, Minority Rights Group, 1991); M Weller (ed), *Universal Minority Rights: A Commentary on the Jurisprudence of International Courts and Treaty Bodies* (Oxford University Press, 2007); J Rehman, 'Minorities' in P Cane and J Conaghan (eds), *The New Oxford Companion to Law* (Oxford University Press, 2008) 791–93.

[22] 'Genocide has been committed against indigenous, Indian or tribal peoples in every regime in the world.' H Hannum, *Autonomy, Sovereignty and Self-Determination: The Accommodation of Conflicting Rights* (Philidelphia, University of Pennsylvannia Press, 1990) 74.

[23] L Kuper, *International Action against Genocide* (London, Minority Rights Group, 1984) 5; J Clinebell and J Thomson, 'Sovereignty and Self-Determination: The Rights of Native Americans under International Law' (1978) 27 *Buffalo Law Review* 669–714.

[24] The principle, in the end, could not be implemented fully; both Bengal and Punjab within British India had to be partitioned. See J Rehman, 'The Right to Physical Existence in International Law: A Case Study of Pakistan' (1998) 30 *Liverpool Law Review* (1998) 201–27.

exploitative British system of 'Tribal Areas' was retained. However, the Pakhtuns and Baluchis never accepted this border and nationalists have repeatedly pointed out that it divides 'peoples' with common traditions and history. It is clear that by 1946 (immediately prior to the partition of India) Mohammad Ali Jinnah, the founder of Pakistan, had a stranglehold on the affairs of the NWFP, and Pakhtun nationalists point to a denial of the right to self-determination.[25] A hastily organised referendum was conducted, but it was not representative of the wishes of the Pakhtuns since the people were not given the option of union with Afghanistan, and consequently it was boycotted by the major nationalist parties. It is equally clear that the creation of the Pakistani State was opposed by the political leaders of the Afghan State, who had consorted with the Indian National Congress before partition and believed that Afghanistan would gain the port of Karachi if the Pakistan movement failed.[26] The Afghan and Baluch leaders bitterly resented their forced entry into Pakistan. In the aftermath of the creation of Pakistan, Pakhtun nationalist leaders were condemned as terrorists and many of them were detained or imprisoned for demanding national self-determination.

Like the Pakhtuns, at the time of national independence (and notwithstanding considerable protests on the part of Baluchi nationalists) the Baluch territories were forcibly annexed into the new Pakistan. The newly established Pakistan government, relying upon the verdict of an appointed assembly of tribal elders, forcibly merged the whole of Baluchistan into Pakistan. The Baluchi were not consulted on the annexation of their territories and their tribal leaders consistently pointed to the unconstitutional nature of this merger. Baluchi nationalist leaders remained rebellious in the light of the Pakistan government's constitutional interference in what they regarded as their domestic affairs and, despite constant threats of coercion and use of force by respective Pakistan governments, it was not until 1955 that the rulers of the independent territories formally agreed to cede their states to Pakistan. In order to curb any outstanding dissent, the Pakistan authorities accused the Baluch and Pakhtun leaders of engagement in terrorism. In 1973, soon after the adoption of the Constitution of Pakistan, Baluchi nationalist leaders were accused of engineering secessionist movements and were incarcerated. During 1973–77 Baluchis were engaged in a long drawn-out political and military confrontation with the federal government led by Prime Minister Zulfiqar Ali Bhutto. Over 80,000 military were involved in an armed confrontation with 55,000

[25] See J Rehman, 'Self-Determination, State Building and the Mohajirs: An International Legal Perspective of the Role of the Indian Muslim Refugees in the Constitutional Developments of Pakistan' (1994) 3 *Contemporary South Asia* 111–29.

[26] See A Mohabbat, *Pakhtun National Self-Determination: The Partition of India and Relations with Pakistan*, unpublished PhD thesis, Saint Louis University, USA, 1979.

Baluchis. According to one authority, 'the Pakistan armed forces suffered about 8,000–10,000 casualties. The number of guerrillas and their casualties is not reliably known. Thousands of civilian Baluchis were killed in the military action and in the bombardments by Pakistan Armed forces and thousands migrated to Afghanistan or took refuge in Sind.'[27]

During the repressive military regimes of General Zia-ul-Haq between 1977 and 1988 and General Pervaiz Musharraf between 1999 and 2008, Pakhtun and Baluchi nationalism was brutally suppressed. While all segments of the society were denied the right to self-determination, indigenous peoples were particularly targeted over allegations of instigating secessionist movements. The indigenous lifestyles of the Baluchis and Pakhtuns were manipulated by the militarisation of the State and educational institutions and religious schools were politicised during General Zia's premiership to inject a virulent and intolerant interpretation of the *Shari'a*.[28]

INDIGENOUS PEOPLES OF PAKISTAN, THE 'WAR ON TERROR', AND THE *JIHAD* OF OSAMA BIN LADEN

International Conspiracies against Indigenous Peoples and the Road to the 'War on Terror'

The phrase 'war on terror' is associated with the United States' actions in response to the terrorist acts of 11 September 2001, which were allegedly masterminded by Osama Bin Laden from Afghanistan and executed by his footsoldiers in the US.[29] However, so far as the Pakhtuns of Afghanistan and the Pakhtuns of the NWFP are concerned, the 'war on terror' cannot be dissociated from the US military exercises that commenced in the immediate aftermath of the Soviet invasion of Afghanistan of 1979.[30] Following the invasion, the Tribal Areas of Pakistan became the headquarters of the *Jihadi* insurgent movement. At the same time, over three million Afghan refugees poured into the tribal or settled areas of Baluchistan and the NWFP.[31] The influx of such huge numbers made

[27] I Bolach, 'The Baluch Question in Pakistan and the Right to Self-Determination' in W-P Zingel et al (eds), *Pakistan in its Fourth Decade* (Hamburg, Deutshes Orient Institut, 1983) 188–209, 205.

[28] J Rehman, 'Minority Rights and the Constitutional Dilemmas of Pakistan' (2001) 19 *Netherlands Quarterly of Human Rights* 417–43.

[29] J Rehman and S Gosh, 'International Law, US Foreign Policy and Post-9/11 Islamic Fundamentalism: The Legal Status of the "War-on-Terror"' (2008) 77 *Nordic Journal of International Law* 87–103.

[30] Rehman 2000 (n 21) 213–14.

[31] See AN Nadery, 'Peace or Justice? Transitional Justice in Afghanistan' (2007) 1 *Interrnational Journal of Transitional Justice* 173–79.

extortionate and excessive demands on land resources and subsistence sources. Furthermore, these Afghan refugee camps were transformed into military zones, with the Pakistani military engaged in training operations for the so-called Afghan *Jihadis*. It was critical that the US discredit and defeat the Soviets in Afghanistan, and the Afghan Mujahedeen were equipped and trained to conduct military operations from within Tribal Areas of Pakistan. Saudi and US aid flowed into Tribal Areas to arm radical groups, and the culture of Islamic religious seminaries (*madrassas*) was transformed.

The period following Soviet invasion marked the emergence of Osama Bin Laden as a Mujahid as well as the establishment of Al-Qaeda in Afghanistan. The end of the Soviet period also marked the rise of a revolutionary *Shari'a*-implementation movement led by the Afghan Taliban.[32] The *madrassas* were turned into outlets of aggressive and revolutionary Islam: indigenous youth was inculcated towards radicalisation and extremism. The indigenous Pakhtun and Baluch cultures were transformed through heavy militarisation. The defeat of the Soviets in Afghanistan was a major success in the attainment of the United States' ultimate strategic goals—the demise of Communism and the break-up of the USSR. However, following Soviet withdrawal from Afghanistan, this collapsing State was left to its own devices: the Taliban of Afghanistan emerged as the ruling force, and enforced their intolerant brand of the *Shari'a* with complete and uncompromising rigour. The repression of the Taliban in Afghanistan ensured that millions of Afghan refugees made Tribal Areas their new homelands.

The indigenous Afghans of Afghanistan and Pakistan as well as the Baluchis were to suffer greatly following the terrorist attacks in the US in 2001.[33] The peoples of the tribal belt were not only subjected to the most devastating firepower of the US, NATO and Pakistani military, indigenous lifestyles, means of subsistence and livelihoods were systematically destroyed. Within four weeks of the 11 September 2001 terrorist attacks, the US, led by its coalition partners (most notably the United Kingdom), started a bombing campaign over Afghanistan. Relying on UN Security Council Resolutions 1368/2001[34] and 1373/2001,[35] as well as on

[32] See Minority Rights Group, 'Afghanistan Overview', www.minorityrights.org/5429/afghanistan/afghanistan-overview.html; N Jawad, *Afghanistan: A Nation of Minorities* (London, Minority Rights Group, 1992).

[33] D Price, 'Terror and Indigenous People: Terror without End', *Counterpunch*, 3 November 2001, www.counterpunch.org/price2.html.

[34] See Security Council Resolution S/RES/1368(2001) condemning the terrorist attacks of 11 September 2001 in New York, Washington DC, and Pennsylvania, USA, adopted by the Security Council at its 4370th meeting (12 September 2001).

[35] See Security Council Resolution S/RES/1373(2001) Threats to international peace & security caused by terrorist acts (Mandating the Formation of the Counter Terrorism Committee CTC), adopted by the Security Council at its 4385th meeting (28 September 2001).

customary international law, the US justified its military bombardment.[36] The United States' chief regional ally—Pakistan—rendered full military and intelligence support to the US in its military actions. The apparent rationale for such action was the removal of the Taliban, who according to the US administration had colluded with and supported Osama bin Laden in his terrorist plot. As a result of this US-led military operation, entitled 'Operation Enduring Freedom', the Taliban regime was removed.[37] The US military bombs were then aimed at the hills of Tora Bora, a huge cave complex near the Afghan city of Jalalabad. This range of caves was cited as the hiding place of Bin Laden and his remaining fighters. However, these US military operations were not restricted to specific targeted places, but covered various regions of Afghanistan and Pakistan. Recent years have witnessed attacks on civilian buildings, and religious and educational institutions, leading to the deaths of thousands of tribal people.

The allied aerial campaign, accompanied by evidence of indiscriminate bombardment and human casualties, presented an unfortunate development for peoples of the tribal belt.[38] As the war on terrorism gained momentum, indigenous communities were targeted not only in Afghanistan, but also in the tribal and settled areas of Pakistan. Hundreds of tribal people were forcibly removed; indeed, many were taken to torture cells or incarcerated. At the same time there was a considerable reaction to the US-led military actions, with the growth of extremism and militancy in these Tribal Areas.[39] Recent years have witnessed increasing support for the Taliban and Al-Qaeda, not only in Afghanistan but also in the northern areas of Pakistan. This growing militancy under the banner of Talabanisation is further endangering the physical existence of indigenous peoples and their cultures and values. While the scale of the US-led policies of kidnapping, detention, torture and rendition is yet to become fully evident,[40] abuses of the principles of international humanitarian law were apparent even at the start of the bombing campaign in October 2001.[41]

36 JNB Frank and J Rehman, 'Assessing the Legality of the Attacks by the International Coalition against Terrorism (ICAT) against Al-Qaeda and Taleban in Afghanistan: An Inquiry into the Self-Defence Argument under Article 51 of the United Nations Charter' (2003) 67 *Journal of Criminal Law* 415–30.

37 The initial name of this operation was 'Operation Infinite Justice'. This was however replaced for fear of provoking Muslim sentiments.

38 See Frank and Rehman (n 36) 415; M Herold, 'Counting the Dead: Attempts to Hide the Number of Afghan Civilians Killed by US Bombs are an Affront to Justice', *Guardian Unlimited*, 8 August 2002, www.guardian.co.uk/afghanistan/comment/story/0,11447,770999,00.html.

39 J Rehman, *Islamic State Practices, International Law and the Threat from Terrorism: A Critique of the 'Clash of Civilizations' in the New World Order* (Oxford, Hart Publishing, 2005) 226.

40 See Rapporteur Dick Marty, Council of Europe, Parliamentary Assembly, 16 Part II (June 2006), assembly.coe.int/Main.asp?Link=/CommitteeDocs/2006/20060606_Ejdoc162006PartII-FINAL.htm.

41 Rehman and Gosh (n 29) 97.

A more disturbing element emerging from the 'war on terror' was the decision of the US to transfer captured individuals from Afghanistan and from within Pakistan to Camp X-ray (and subsequently Camp Delta), a detention camp at the US naval base at Guantánamo Bay in Cuba.[42] Since October 2001 775 captives (including numerous Pakhtuns and Baluchis) have been sent to this base.[43] Incommunicado detention, torture, and inhuman and degrading treatment have been visited upon these individuals. Captivity in conditions described by Amnesty International as 'falling below minimum standards for humane behaviour' generated substantial criticism from international human rights agencies.[44] In February 2006, the UN, through its Special Rapporteur on torture, Manfred Nowak, heavily criticised the activities in the camp and called for its immediate closure.[45]

Political rhetoric aside, the first eighteen months of US administration under President Barak Obama hava proved disappointing. Upon taking office, President Obama committed the new administration to closing the detention facility by January 2010. This has not happened. Furthermore, there are likely to be substantial delays in this process: the administration is struggling to deal with issues surrounding the legal basis for those detained without charge and perhaps more significantly determination of appropriate jurisdictions for housing detainees once they are removed from Guantánamo. A disappointing feature of the new administration's policies has been the apparent 'U-turn' by President Obama over trials of Guantánamo detainees by the US military Commissions. Prior to being elected, Obama had condemned the military commissions system as being fundamentally flawed. However, in May 2009, he announced the recommencement of the trials of the Guantánamo detainees by the dreaded military commissions. As at September 2010, over 170 detainees remain Languishing at this detention centre. Amidst the quagmire of US domestic politics, a fair and objective treatment of the Guantánamo detainees appears a remote possibility.[46]

In the meantime, the treatment of detainees at Guantanamo and elsewhere, illustrates the disdain shown by the US and her partners in 'the war

[42] See E Katselli and S Shah, 'September 11 and the UK Response' (2003) 52 *International and Comparative Law Quarterly* 245, 250.

[43] J Steyn, 'Guantanamo Bay: The Legal Black Hole' (2004) 53 *International and Comparative Law Quarterly* 7.

[44] Cited in PA Thomas, '11 September and Good Governance' (2002) 53 *Northern Ireland Legal Quarterly* 366, 379.

[45] See United Nations, *Situation of Detainees at Guantánamo Bay*, UN Doc E/CN.4/2006/120 (15 February 2006), news.bbc.co.uk/1/shared/bsp/hi/pdfs/16_02_06_un_guantanamo.pdf; Manfred Nowak, *What Practices Constitute Torture? US and UN Standards* (2006) 28 *Human Rights Quarterly* 809.

[46] Philippe Naughton, 'President Obama to Restart Guantanomo Bay Military Tribunals', *Times online*, 15 May 2009, www.timesonline.co.uk/tol/news/world/us_and_americas/article6291650.ece.

on terror' for the accepted norms of international human rights law and international humanitarian laws, but also for the religious values of indigenous peoples as devout Muslims.[47] Examples of such humiliating exercises resulted in the apparent desecration of the Qur'an, forcing Muslim detainees to shave off their beards and perform sexual activities contrary to their religious beliefs.[48] The former Law Lord, Lord Steyn, in describing the practices at Guantánamo Bay 'as a monstrous failure of justice',[49] warned that 'the type of Justice meted out at Guantánamo Bay is likely to make martyrs of the prisoners in the moderate Muslim world with whom the West must work to ensure world peace and stability'.[50] This so-called 'war on terror' provided an excuse for the dictatorial and autocratic regime of President Musharraf to torture and violate the fundamental human rights of the Baluchi and Pakhtun tribal peoples.[51] The international community will remain tight-lipped so long as the Pakistan government continues to follow the political agenda set by the US administration.

THE UN DECLARATION ON THE RIGHTS OF INDIGENOUS PEOPLES AND ITS APPLICATION TO THE PAKHTUNS AND BALUCHIS

The Baluchis and Pakhtuns, despite comprising part of the global fraternity of indigenous peoples, have suffered from the cruelty, indifference and vagaries of international law. Continuing assertions of sovereignty and aggression in attempts to regain independent Statehood have incurred the wrath of the Pakistani State. Labelling them as anti-State, insurrectionist

[47] Katselli and Shah (n 42) 250; Steyn (n 43) 7.

[48] *Newsweek* magazine initially reported news of the desecration of the Holy Book (9 May 2005); subsequently there were attempts to retract this report: the damage to Muslim-West relations was nevertheless visible in international rioting and violence (resulting in at least 15 deaths in Afghanistan and other countries). See 'Newsweek Backs Off Quran Desecration Story', CNN, 15 May 2005, edition.cnn.com/2005/WORLD/asiapcf/05/15/newsweek.quran.

[49] J Steyn, 'In the Dock of Guantánamo Bay', 27th FA Mann Lecture, 30 November 2003, www.statewatch.org/news/2003/nov/17guantanamo.htm

[50] Steyn (n 43) 14.

[51] The US-led 'war on terror' also sanctified and licensed other regional dictators to terrorise and torture their citizens. An Amnesty International Report reinforces this point when it notes: 'The impact of the so called "war on terror" on human rights in the Gulf and the Arabian Peninsula has been profound and far reaching. Governments in the region and the US government have treated nationals and residents of the area with a disturbing disregard for the rule of law and fundamental human rights standards. The results have been mass arrests, prolonged detention without charge or trial, incommunicado detention, torture and ill treatment, strict secrecy surrounding the fate and whereabouts of some detainees, and apparent extra-judicial killings. These human rights violations have had profound effects not only on individual victims but also on their relatives and the general human rights situation in the region.' See Amnesty International, 'The Gulf and the Arabian Peninsula: Human Rights Fall Victim to the "War on Terror"' (22 June 2004) AI Index: MDE 04/002/2004, web.amnesty.org/library/Index/ENGMDE040022004?open&of=ENG-USA.

elements, successive federal governments have undermined Baluch and Pakhtun rights as most recently proclaimed in the Declaration.

Article 3 of the Declaration reaffirms the right of indigenous peoples to self-determination. It provides that '[i]ndigenous peoples have the right to self-determination. By virtue of that right, they freely determine their political status and freely pursue their economic, social and cultural development.' The 'internal aspect' of the right to self-determination is affirmed in Article 4, which provides that 'indigenous peoples, in exercising their right to self-determination, have the right to autonomy or self-government in matters relating to their internal and local affairs'.[52] The UN Committee on the Elimination of All Forms of Racial Discrimination has elaborated that the right of autonomy and self-governance entails a right to effective and informed choices on matters relating to internal affairs concerning indigenous communities.[53] The Pakhtuns and the Baluchis have been victims of a denial of their right to self-determination: they have been denied both autonomy and self-governance. As noted above, since the time of independence, successive federal governments have maintained the colonial stance of forcibly isolating indigenous peoples from the remainder of the Pakistani population under the pretext of establishing an autonomous status. However, this different status is in effect an attempt to deprive indigenous peoples of their fundamental rights to equality and genuine autonomy. Thus, under the Pakistan constitutional framework, tribal peoples have been denied the right to vote in national elections. In violation of Article 5 of the Declaration, they have been deprived of the right to participate in the 'political, economic, social and cultural life of the State'.

At the time of the creation of an independent Pakistan, the Pakhtun and Baluch territories were forcibly incorporated within the new State. Since 1947, the denial of the right to autonomy and self-governance for the indigenous Baluchis and Pakhtuns has been persistent and ceaseless. The majority of Pakhtun and Baluch grievances have stemmed from the denial of political and economic autonomy. Baluchistan has economic resources which successive federal governments have exploited without

[52] For further elucidation of 'internal' and 'external' aspects of self-determination see P Thornberry, 'The Democratic or Internal Aspect of Self-Determination with Some Remarks on Federalism' in C Tomuschat (ed), *Modern Law of Self-Determination* (Leiden, Martinus Nijhoff, 1993) 101–38.

[53] Australia, CERD/C/AUS/CO/14, 14 April 2005, para 11 (recommending that 'the State party refrain from adopting measures that withdraw existing guarantees of indigenous rights and that it make every effort to seek the informed consent of indigenous peoples before adopting decisions relating to their rights to land'); and USA, 14/08/2001, A/56/18, paras 380–407, para 400 (concerning 'plans for expanding mining and nuclear waste storage on Western Shoshone ancestral land, placing their land up for auction for private sale, and other actions affecting the rights of indigenous peoples'.

either due acknowledgement of Baluchistan's contribution to the national economy or recompense in monetary or financial terms.

This deprivation of their natural resources represents a core grievance of the Baluchis, who also point to a violation of the provisions of the Declaration. Natural gas deposits were found in the Sui area in 1953 and in Pirkoh in 1982.[54] The natural gas deposits of Baluchistan facilitate in very large measure the running of industries, factories and businesses, as well as for domestic usage all over Pakistan. Baluchi nationalists claim that the royalties received from these projects are next to negligible. In common with other indigenous peoples, the Baluchis also feel that their land and territory have been taken over by outsiders who are politically and economically more powerful. The federal government under the rule of former President Pervaiz Musharraf (1999–2008) had put forward plans to construct a deep seaport at Gwadar and establish road links with Afghanistan and Central Asia. The federal government's claim that these developments will bring greater prosperity to the people of Baluchistan are refuted by the Baluchi tribal leaders, who consider this to be a new variant of economic and political exploitation. National economic developmental arguments are frequently advanced by Asian States whilst exploiting the natural resources of indigenous communities. The Baluchi people continue to experience considerable displacement and erosion of their resources and lands at the dictates of military generals or bureaucrats officiating from Islamabad. The Declaration explicitly notes that '[i]ndigenous peoples shall not be forcibly removed from their lands or territories. No relocation shall take place without the free, prior and informed consent of the indigenous peoples concerned and after agreement on just and fair compensation and, where possible, with the option of return.'[55]

In order to enquire into the grievances and claims advanced by Baluchi leaders, former Prime Minister Chaudhary Shujaat Hussain on 23 September 2004 set up a special Parliamentary Committee (unanimously approved by both Houses of Parliament). The overall mandate of the Committee was 'to examine the current situation in Baluchistan and make recommendations thereon'.[56] The establishment of the committee, which was further sub-divided into two committees—one headed by Senator Wasim Sajjad and the other by Mushahid Hussain Syed—represented a positive step. Baluchi nationalist leaders were not invited to participate in the deliberations, nor was the consent of the Baluchis sought

[54] Rehman 2000 (n 21) 210.
[55] Art 10.
[56] Rehman, *World Directory on Minorities and Indigenous Peoples: Baluchis* (n 5), www.minorityrights.org/5626/pakistan/baluchis.html.

in any other respect. The two sub-committees presented a number of recommendations in March 2005 which included assurances on the part of the federal government to make payments of all arrears on gas royalties, to pledge greater investment to eliminate unemployment, poverty and under-development in the province, to withdraw Frontier constabulary and coastguards from the interior of Baluchistan, and to shift the head office of the Gwader Port Authority (GPA) from Karachi to Gwadar. None of these recommendations was taken further, either by former President General Pervaiz Musharraf or by the current President, Asif Ali Zardari; instead, reliance has been placed once again on coercive means such as arrests and detention of dissident Baluchi and Pakhtun nationalists.

Moreover, in 2005, Baluchi leaders presented a 15-point agenda to the government that included greater control of resources and protection for the Baluchi indigenous community.[57] The failure of the Government of Pakistan to consider this, coupled with the failure to implement the recommendations of the parliamentary sub-committee in 2006, created further resentment on the part of the Baluchi.[58] Speaking at the 61st session of the former Commission of Human Rights at Geneva in August 2005, Mehran Baluch, a prominent Baluchi leader, said: 'The forceful annexation of Baluchistan into Pakistan in 1948 and continued violation of human rights and absence of basic human dignity as well as the forced assimilation and integration programmes implemented by the Punjabi establishment has reached a crucial point where the Baluch existence is under threat.'[59]

Article 7 of the Declaration on the Rights of Indigenous Peoples provides as follows:

1. Indigenous individuals have the rights to life, physical and mental integrity, liberty and security of person.
2. Indigenous peoples have the collective right to live in freedom, peace and security as distinct peoples and shall not be subjected to any act of genocide or any other act of violence, including forcibly removing children of the group to another group.

As has been discussed in the preceding sections, unfortunate large-scale breaches of these rights have taken place during both the colonial and post-colonial periods. Since 11 September 2001, Baluch and Pakhtun indigenous peoples have been targeted and victimised as terrorists or Al-Qaeda operatives by the Pakistan and US military. Despite strong protests and

[57] 'Civil War Festers in Baluchistan', *Hindustani Times*, 3 April 2006.

[58] 'Balochistan: Jackboot Justice in Tribal Heartland' *Indigenous Issues* 27 January 2007.

[59] *Human Rights Situation in Baluchistan*, 61st session of the Commission on Human Rights (17 January and 14 March–22 April 2005), Agenda Item 14: Specific Groups and Individuals, (b) Minorities.

local opposition, such practices as arbitrary and enforced disappearances and so-called extra-ordinary renditions have continued. Notwithstanding the change of the US administration, the continued existence of detention centres at Bagram airbase in Afghanistan as well as Guantánamo Bay has seriously undermined the right to liberty and security of indigenous peoples of the tribal belt. Furthermore, US air attacks on Pakhtun Tribal Areas using drones have become a frequent occurrence, resulting in an incalculable loss of life.[60] The heavy-handed tactics deployed by the previous Musharraf government under the pretext of the 'war on terror' resulted in enormous human suffering within Baluchistan and the tribal belt surrounding the province. During the period 2005–08, the Pakistani military launched fully-fledged operations in the Baluch territories of Kohlu and Dera Bugti. The military have reportedly been using jet fighters and helicopter gun ships in its operations to attack suspected hideouts of combatant Marri and Bugti tribesmen in Kolhu and Dera Bugti respectively. According to the Human Rights Commission of Pakistan (HRCP), as many as 53 people were killed and 132 injured in military operations in Dera Bugti between the last week of December 2005 and 8 January 2006. Eighteen people, including 12 suspected members of the Baluchi armed opposition group and six security personnel, were reportedly killed on 11 January 2006. The murder of the leading Baluchi nationalist Mir Baluch Marri in November 2007 further aggravated the political situation. The immediate aftermath resulted in the deaths of 'at least 100 men, women and children. More than 200 houses and other buildings, including schools and clinics, have been bombed and burned to the ground. Many farm animals were also killed in the attacks, depriving already poor people of their livelihood. Faced with this state terrorism by the dictatorship of President Pervez Musharraf, thousands of Baluchi people have fled into the mountains to escape the military onslaught.'[61] There were also reports of extra-judicial killings of detainees by law enforcement agencies. The Pakistan government claimed that Baluchi and Pakhtun tribesmen were harbouring Al-Qaeda militants in the Tribal Areas of South Waziristan, a claim vigorously denied by the tribal people. The repressive nature of the 'war on terror' generated a considerable backlash amongst local tribal peoples. Some of the tribal leaders have galvanised opposition to the US and Pakistani military operations. During 2008–09, a new movement under the leadership of the Pakistani Taliban surfaced. The Pakistani

60 See 'US Airstrike Kills 30 in Pakistan', *New York Times*, 14 February 2009, www.nytimes.com/2009/02/15/world/asia/15pstan.html; 'US in New Missile Attack on Pakistan Territory', *The Telegraph*, 24 October 2008, www.telegraph.co.uk/news/worldnews/asia/pakistan/3249830/US-in-new-missile-attack-on-Pakistan-territory.html.

61 Pater Tatchell, 'Pakistan's Secret War in Baluchistan', *The Guardian*, 21 December 2007, www.guardian.co.uk/commentisfree/2007/dec/21/pakistanssecretwarinbaluch.

Taliban, who claim to be spiritually and religiously associated with the Afghani Taliban, declared the entire tribal belt a *Shari'a*-compliant zone. The strictest and most rigid Taliban interpretation has already resulted in the violation of rights of women and children. In the Swat district, which remains under the control of the Pakistani Taliban, girls' schools have been closed down or burnt out and thousands of local residents have fled in fear of their lives.[62] During the military dictatorships of General Zia-ul-Haq and General Pervaiz Musharraf, considerable militarisation of the Pakhtun territories took place. The official commencement of the 'war on terror' in October 2001 was accompanied by sustained military offensives in Pakhtun and Baluch homelands. As noted in the above analysis, since 9/11 and at the behest of the US administration, indigenous Pakhtuns are arbitrarily associated with the Taliban and Al-Qaeda—they are labelled as supporters and allies of *Jihadi* organisations and in light of this terrorist status have been hunted down and brutalised. Many Pakhtun leaders fled into neighbouring Baluch territories. The militarisation of the Pakhtun and Baluch homelands has been accompanied by a relentless campaign of bombardment by Pakistani military and the US drone attacks, leading to a substantial number of casualties. These activities clearly violate the provisions of Article 30 of the Declaration, according to which:

> [m]ilitary activities shall not take place in the lands or territories of indigenous peoples, unless justified by a relevant public interest or otherwise freely agreed with or requested by the indigenous peoples concerned [and] States shall undertake effective consultations with the indigenous peoples concerned, through appropriate procedures and in particular through their representative institutions, prior to using their lands or territories for military activities.

Another provision of special importance for the Pakhtun and Baluch peoples contained within Article 36 of the Declaration provides for 'the right to maintain and develop contacts, relations and cooperation, including activities for spiritual, cultural, political, economic and social purposes, with their own members as well as other peoples across borders'.[63] States must 'take effective measures to facilitate the exercise and ensure the implementation of this right'.[64]

Throughout their history the Pakhtuns and the Baluchis have been arbitrarily divided, a division confirmed by the Durrand Line of 1893 created by the British colonisers. Following the independence of British India, the

[62] 'Militants Raze Second Swat Girls' School', *The Daily Times*, 8 May 2008, www.dailytimes.com.pk/default.asp?page=2008%5C05%5C08%5Cstory_8-5-2008_pg7_9; 'Taliban Restrict Women's Education in Pakistan', *Independent on Sunday*, 18 January 2009, www.independent.co.uk/news/world/asia/taliban-restrict-womens-education-in-pakistan-1419199.html.

[63] Art 36(1).

[64] Art 36(2).

historical frontiers drawn by the Durrand Line were maintained, thereby splitting the Afghani Pakhtuns from the Pakistani Pakhtuns and the Pakistani Baluchis from the Afghani and Iranian Baluchis. This separation and control of borders has been maintained over the past 63 years since independence. The only exception to this strict border control was during the tumultuous period of Soviet invasion of Afghanistan when, with official US and Pakistan permission, the international border ceased to exist—the tribal belt became the primary route for the supply of ammunition supporting the Afghani *Jihad* and for the flow of refugees into the Tribal Areas. Millions of Afghans, who poured into Pakistan, have remained there ever since.

Also, Article 14 of the Declaration provides for the right of the indigenous peoples 'to establish and control their educational systems and institutions providing education in their own language, in a manner appropriate to their cultural methods of teaching and learning'.[65] For the indigenous Baluchis and Pakhtuns, manipulation of religious institutions has been sustained and rigorous. After the Soviet invasion of Afghanistan, many *madrassas* were, with official patronage and indeed the support of the Pakistani State, converted into *Jihadi* training camps, providing an extreme and aggressive interpretation of *Jihad*.

Following the events of 11 September 2001 and placing reliance on what he described as 'enlightened moderation', General Musharraf attempted to change this extremist trend. The Pakistan Madrassa Education (Establishment and Affiliation of Model Dini Madaris) Board Ordinance was enacted in November 2001 to reform the existing curriculum through the introduction of secular and science subjects.[66] The then government also announced that it would carefully review the admissions processes in *madrassas* and would prevent a sectarian bias amongst pupils and teachers. The events of 11 September 2001 intensified concerns over the role of *madrassas* in increased radicalisation and extremism. In its report submitted to the UN Counter-Terrorism Committee[67] in December 2001, the Pakistan government pledged to reform the *madrassas* as part of its overall strategy to curb international terrorism.[68] As part of this reform package, the Deeni Madaaris (Voluntary Registration and Regulation) Ordinance 2002 was introduced.[69] No new *madrassa* was to be established without

[65] Art 14(1).

[66] K Lakshman, '*Madrassa* Reform: A Habit of Deception' (2005) 4 *South Asia Intelligence Review* 12, www.satp.org/satporgtp/sair/Archives/4_9.htm.

[67] See UN Security Council Resolution 1373, adopted 28 September 2001.

[68] See Report of the Islamic Republic of Pakistan to the UNSC Counter Terrorism Committee on Implementation of UNSC Resolution 1373, S/2001/1310 (27 December 2001) 4.

[69] See International Crisis Group, *Pakistan: Madrasas, Extremism and the Military* (Asia Report No 36, 2002), p 25.

the permission of the local district authorities. Existing *madrassas* were asked to register with one of the five Religious Education Boards (*wifaq*).[70] The Ordinance imposed a ban on the preaching of sectarian hatred and the promotion of extremism. It also aimed to control the enrolment of foreigners without a valid visa and 'no-objection' certificates from the Ministry of the Interior. However, the new law was never properly enforced: of the estimated 12,000 *madrassas*, it is reckoned that most did not register, and none was forcibly closed.[71] In the aftermath of the 7 July 2005 bombings in the UK, General Musharraf decided to expel the 1,400 foreign nationals studying in *madrassas* and not to issue any visas to foreigners wishing to study in the future.[72] In August 2005, President Musharraf promulgated the Societies Registration (Amendment) Ordinance, affecting the status of 11,882 *madrassas*. The Ordinance was aimed at introducing a scheme of compulsory registration. However, by the end of 2005, only 278 of the several thousand *madrassas* in the NWFP had registered in accordance with the Ordinance, and even local officials took the position that 'there was no need for fresh registration for the already registered seminaries, as their conversion under the newly implemented law would be considered automatically'.[73] Furthermore, since the *madrassas* are not financially dependent on governmental *zakat* funds, many *madrassas* rejected an offer in 2006 to receive financial assistance under the Madrassas Reform Project and refused to fill in forms providing details of their annual financial breakdown. Aware of this financial independence of the *madrassas*, the federal government had already humiliatingly conceded on 26 August 2005 that it would not check or even comment on accounts submitted by the seminaries or seek details as to donors.[74] *Madrassas* have remained the subject of intense controversy. While unable to restore the historic liberal educational values of *madrassa* education, the government has consistently accused the indigenous communities, administrators and staff of preaching an extreme version of *Shari'a* (and *Jihad*). The government continues to perceive them as hotbeds of radicalisation and extremism. On 30 October 2006, a *madrassa* in the Tribal Area, Bajaur Agency bordering Afghanistan was attacked by Pakistan and US forces, resulting in the

[70] T Rahman, 'The Madrassa and the state of Pakistan' (Source: www.himalmag.com/the-Madrassa-and-the-state-of-Pakistan_nw1297.html); see also K Rahman and SR Bukhari, 'Pakistan: Religious Education and Institutions' (2006) 96 *The Muslim World* 323, 326.

[71] See www.state.gov/g/drl/rls/irf/2005/51621.htm.

[72] 'Madrassa: Foreigners Must Leave', BBC News, 29 July 2005, news.bbc.co.uk/1/hi/world/south_asia/4728643.stm.

[73] A Hassan 'Ulema Reject Registration law', Dawn.com, www.dawn.com/2005/08/31/top3.htm.

[74] See Lakhsman (n 66).

deaths of 82 people.[75] In July 2007, government forces removed *Jihadi* factions from the Red Mosque (*Lal Masjid*) in the centre of the Federal Capital, Islamabad. At the time of the governmental operation, there were several hundred inmates, including dozens of male *madrassa* students (and also women at the connected Jamia Hafsa *madrassa*). In this process of recapturing the Mosque, over 100 occupants were killed by the military, many of them *madrassa* students.

In the overwhelmingly religious socio-political environment of the Tribal Areas of Pakistan, *madrassas* continue to retain significant political significance. Over the past three decades, unfortunately, the character of the *madrassas* has been transformed. From educational institutions imparting indigenous cultural and religious educational values, *madrassas* have been politicised and militarised. In all this, General Musharraf's attempt to control the *madrassas* can be described at best as uncertain and at worst as 'a shambles'. [76]

F. CONCLUSIONS

The adoption of the UN Declaration on the Rights of Indigenous Peoples is a significant step towards standard-setting and the ultimate realisation of the rights of indigenous peoples. The Declaration, in its capacity as a UN General Assembly Resolution, is not a binding document per se. Nevertheless, a number of its provisions are of such a fundamental character that they represent customary international law and are therefore binding on all States. Despite the normative value of the provisions contained in the Declaration, their implementation represents a real challenge to the international community.

The present chapter has examined the plight of the Pakhtuns and the Baluchis—the indigenous communities of present-day Pakistan. This investigation has established that in the post-colonial period, indigenous peoples of South Asia have faced an oppressive, albeit localised, form of colonisation. There have been consistent denials of both the 'external' and 'internal' dimensions of the right to self-determination.[77] Since the commencement of the US-led 'war on terror', indigenous Baluchis and Pakhtuns have faced substantial threats to their right to life and liberty. In the political environment generated since September 2001, it seems unlikely that the international community will be prepared to defend the

[75] BBC News, 'Pakistan's Madrassa Raid "Kills 80"', news.bbc.co.uk/1/hi/world/south_asia/6097636.stm.

[76] International Crisis Group, *Pakistan: Karachi's Madrasas and Violent Extremism* (Asia Report No 130, Brussels, 2007) 1.

[77] See further Thornberry (n 52) 101–38.

Pakhtuns or the Baluchis. The domineering US-led political and media campaigns have tarnished the image of these tribal peoples: although a serious distortion of reality, they are increasingly portrayed as Al-Qaeda supporters or *Jihadis*. Whilst welcoming the adoption of the Declaration, members of the indigenous Pakhtun and Baluch communities lament the ineffectiveness of international law and the absolute lack of difference which the adopted Declaration has made to their plight. Practitioners of indigenous rights law and human rights law hope for a more effective monitoring system on the part of the UN. It is anticipated that, following the Declaration, the UN will move swiftly towards the adoption of a binding Convention on the rights of indigenous peoples. Whether any such instrument will in fact improve the lot of the Baluchis and Pakhtuns of Pakistan remains a matter of conjecture.

The United Nations Declaration on the Rights of Indigenous Peoples

Adopted by General Assembly Resolution 61/295 on 13 September 2007

The General Assembly,

Guided by the purposes and principles of the Charter of the United Nations, and good faith in the fulfilment of the obligations assumed by States in accordance with the Charter,

Affirming that indigenous peoples are equal to all other peoples, while recognizing the right of all peoples to be different, to consider themselves different, and to be respected as such,

Affirming also that all peoples contribute to the diversity and richness of civilizations and cultures, which constitute the common heritage of humankind,

Affirming further that all doctrines, policies and practices based on or advocating superiority of peoples or individuals on the basis of national origin or racial, religious, ethnic or cultural differences are racist, scientifically false, legally invalid, morally condemnable and socially unjust,

Reaffirming that indigenous peoples, in the exercise of their rights, should be free from discrimination of any kind,

Concerned that indigenous peoples have suffered from historic injustices as a result of, inter alia, their colonization and dispossession of their lands, territories and resources, thus preventing them from exercising, in particular, their right to development in accordance with their own needs and interests,

Recognizing the urgent need to respect and promote the inherent rights of indigenous peoples which derive from their political, economic and social structures and from their cultures, spiritual traditions, histories and philosophies, especially their rights to their lands, territories and resources,

Recognizing also the urgent need to respect and promote the rights of indigenous peoples affirmed in treaties, agreements and other constructive arrangements with States,

Welcoming the fact that indigenous peoples are organizing themselves for political, economic, social and cultural enhancement and in order to bring to an end all forms of discrimination and oppression wherever they occur,

Convinced that control by indigenous peoples over developments affecting them and their lands, territories and resources will enable them to maintain and strengthen their institutions, cultures and traditions, and to promote their development in accordance with their aspirations and needs,

Recognizing that respect for indigenous knowledge, cultures and traditional practices contributes to sustainable and equitable development and proper management of the environment,

Emphasizing the contribution of the demilitarization of the lands and territories of indigenous peoples to peace, economic and social progress and development, understanding and friendly relations among nations and peoples of the world,

Recognizing in particular the right of indigenous families and communities to retain shared responsibility for the upbringing, training, education and well-being of their children, consistent with the rights of the child,

Considering that the rights affirmed in treaties, agreements and other constructive arrangements between States and indigenous peoples are, in some situations, matters of international concern, interest, responsibility and character,

Considering also that treaties, agreements and other constructive arrangements, and the relationship they represent, are the basis for a strengthened partnership between indigenous peoples and States,

Acknowledging that the Charter of the United Nations, the International Covenant on Economic, Social and Cultural Rights and the International Covenant on Civil and Political Rights,2 as well as the Vienna Declaration and Programme of Action, affirm the fundamental importance of the right to self-determination of all peoples, by virtue of which they freely determine their political status and freely pursue their economic, social and cultural development,

Bearing in mind that nothing in this Declaration may be used to deny any peoples their right to self-determination, exercised in conformity with international law,

Convinced that the recognition of the rights of indigenous peoples in t his Declaration will enhance harmonious and cooperative relations between the State and indigenous peoples, based on principles of justice, democracy, respect for human rights, non-discrimination and good faith,

Encouraging States to comply with and effectively implement all their obligations as they apply to indigenous peoples under international instruments, in particular those related to human rights, in consultation and cooperation with the peoples concerned,

Emphasizing that the United Nations has an important and continuing role to play in promoting and protecting the rights of indigenous peoples,

Believing that this Declaration is a further important step forward for the recognition, promotion and protection of the rights and freedoms of indigenous peoples and in the development of relevant activities of the United Nations system in this field,

Recognizing and reaffirming that indigenous individuals are entitled without discrimination to all human rights recognized in international law, and that indigenous peoples possess collective rights which are indispensable for their existence, well-being and integral development as peoples,

Recognizing that the situation of indigenous peoples varies from region to region and from country to country and that the significance of national and regional particularities and various historical and cultural backgrounds should be taken into consideration,

Solemnly proclaims the following United Nations Declaration on the Rights of Indigenous Peoples as a standard of achievement to be pursued in a spirit of partnership and mutual respect:

Article 1

Indigenous peoples have the right to the full enjoyment, as a collective or as individuals, of all human rights and fundamental freedoms as recognized in the Charter of the United Nations, the Universal Declaration of Human Rights and international human rights law.

Article 2

Indigenous peoples and individuals are free and equal to all other peoples and individuals and have the right to be free from any kind of discrimination, in the exercise of their rights, in particular that based on their indigenous origin or identity.

Article 3

Indigenous peoples have the right to self-determination. By virtue of that right they freely determine their political status and freely pursue their economic, social and cultural development.

Article 4

Indigenous peoples, in exercising their right to self-determination, have the right to autonomy or self-government in matters relating to their internal and local affairs, as well as ways and means for financing their autonomous functions.

Article 5

Indigenous peoples have the right to maintain and strengthen their distinct political, legal, economic, social and cultural institutions, while retaining their right to participate fully, if they so choose, in the political, economic, social and cultural life of the State.

Article 6

Every indigenous individual has the right to a nationality.

Article 7

1. Indigenous individuals have the rights to life, physical and mental integrity, liberty and security of person.
2. Indigenous peoples have the collective right to live in freedom, peace and security as distinct peoples and shall not be subjected to any act of genocide or any other act of violence, including forcibly removing children of the group to another group.

Article 8

1. Indigenous peoples and individuals have the right not to be subjected to forced assimilation or destruction of their culture.
2. States shall provide effective mechanisms for prevention of, and redress for:
   (a) Any action which has the aim or effect of depriving them of their integrity as distinct peoples, or of their cultural values or ethnic identities;

(b) Any action which has the aim or effect of dispossessing them of their lands, territories or resources;
(c) Any form of forced population transfer which has the aim or effect of violating or undermining any of their rights;
(d) Any form of forced assimilation or integration;
(e) Any form of propaganda designed to promote or incite racial or ethnic discrimination directed against them.

Article 9

Indigenous peoples and individuals have the right to belong to an indigenous community or nation, in accordance with the traditions and customs of the community or nation concerned. No discrimination of any kind may arise from the exercise of such a right.

Article 10

Indigenous peoples shall not be forcibly removed from their lands or territories. No relocation shall take place without the free, prior and informed consent of the indigenous peoples concerned and after agreement on just and fair compensation and, where possible, with the option of return.

Article 11

1. Indigenous peoples have the right to practise and revitalize their cultural traditions and customs. This includes the right to maintain, protect and develop the past, present and future manifestations of their cultures, such as archaeological and historical sites, artefacts, designs, ceremonies, technologies and visual and performing arts and literature.
2. States shall provide redress through effective mechanisms, which may include restitution, developed in conjunction with indigenous peoples, with respect to their cultural, intellectual, religious and spiritual property taken without their free, prior and informed consent or in violation of their laws, traditions and customs.

Article 12

1. Indigenous peoples have the right to manifest, practise, develop and teach their spiritual and religious traditions, customs and ceremonies; the right to maintain, protect, and have access in privacy to their religious and cultural sites; the right to the use and control of their ceremonial objects; and the right to the repatriation of their human remains.
2. States shall seek to enable the access and/or repatriation of ceremonial objects and human remains in their possession through fair,

transparent and effective mechanisms developed in conjunction with indigenous peoples concerned.

Article 13

1. Indigenous peoples have the right to revitalize, use, develop and transmit to future generations their histories, languages, oral traditions, philosophies, writing systems and literatures, and to designate and retain their own names for communities, places and persons.
2. States shall take effective measures to ensure that this right is protected and also to ensure that indigenous peoples can understand and be understood in political, legal and administrative proceedings, where necessary through the provision of interpretation or by other appropriate means.

Article 14

1. Indigenous peoples have the right to establish and control their educational systems and institutions providing education in their own languages, in a manner appropriate to their cultural methods of teaching and learning.
2. Indigenous individuals, particularly children, have the right to all levels and forms of education of the State without discrimination.
3. States shall, in conjunction with indigenous peoples, take effective measures, in order for indigenous individuals, particularly children, including those living outside their communities, to have access, when possible, to an education in their own culture and provided in their own language.

Article 15

1. Indigenous peoples have the right to the dignity and diversity of their cultures, traditions, histories and aspirations which shall be appropriately reflected in education and public information.
2. States shall take effective measures, in consultation and cooperation with the indigenous peoples concerned, to combat prejudice and eliminate discrimination and to promote tolerance, understanding and good relations among indigenous peoples and all other segments of society.

Article 16

1. Indigenous peoples have the right to establish their own media in their own languages and to have access to all forms of non-indigenous media without discrimination.

2. States shall take effective measures to ensure that State-owned media duly reflect indigenous cultural diversity. States, without prejudice to ensuring full freedom of expression, should encourage privately owned media to adequately reflect indigenous cultural diversity.

Article 17

1. Indigenous individuals and peoples have the right to enjoy fully all rights established under applicable international and domestic labour law.
2. States shall in consultation and cooperation with indigenous peoples take specific measures to protect indigenous children from economic exploitation and from performing any work that is likely to be hazardous or to interfere with the child's education, or to be harmful to the child's health or physical, mental, spiritual, moral or social development, taking into account their special vulnerability and the importance of education for their empowerment.
3. Indigenous individuals have the right not to be subjected to any discriminatory conditions of labour and, inter alia, employment or salary.

Article 18

Indigenous peoples have the right to participate in decision-making in matters which would affect their rights, through representatives chosen by themselves in accordance with their own procedures, as well as to maintain and develop their own indigenous decision-making institutions.

Article 19

States shall consult and cooperate in good faith with the indigenous peoples concerned through their own representative institutions in order to obtain their free, prior and informed consent before adopting and implementing legislative or administrative measures that may affect them.

Article 20

1. Indigenous peoples have the right to maintain and develop their political, economic and social systems or institutions, to be secure in the enjoyment of their own means of subsistence and development, and to engage freely in all their traditional and other economic activities.
2. Indigenous peoples deprived of their means of subsistence and development are entitled to just and fair redress.

Article 21

1. Indigenous peoples have the right, without discrimination, to the improvement of their economic and social conditions, including, inter alia, in the areas of education, employment, vocational training and retraining, housing, sanitation, health and social security.
2. States shall take effective measures and, where appropriate, special measures to ensure continuing improvement of their economic and social conditions. Particular attention shall be paid to the rights and special needs of indigenous elders, women, youth, children and persons with disabilities.

Article 22

1. Particular attention shall be paid to the rights and special needs of indigenous elders, women, youth, children and persons with disabilities in the implementation of this Declaration.
2. States shall take measures, in conjunction with indigenous peoples, to ensure that indigenous women and children enjoy the full protection and guarantees against all forms of violence and discrimination.

Article 23

Indigenous peoples have the right to determine and develop priorities and strategies for exercising their right to development. In particular, indigenous peoples have the right to be actively involved in developing and determining health, housing and other economic and social programmes affecting them and, as far as possible, to administer such programmes through their own institutions.

Article 24

1. Indigenous peoples have the right to their traditional medicines and to maintain their health practices, including the conservation of their vital medicinal plants, animals and minerals. Indigenous individuals also have the right to access, without any discrimination, to all social and health services.
2. Indigenous individuals have an equal right to the enjoyment of the highest attainable standard of physical and mental health. States shall take the necessary steps with a view to achieving progressively the full realization of this right.

Article 25

Indigenous peoples have the right to maintain and strengthen their distinctive spiritual relationship with their traditionally owned or otherwise occupied and used lands, territories, waters and coastal seas and other resources and to uphold their responsibilities to future generations in this regard.

Article 26

1. Indigenous peoples have the right to the lands, territories and resources which they have traditionally owned, occupied or otherwise used or acquired.
2. Indigenous peoples have the right to own, use, develop and control the lands, territories and resources that they possess by reason of traditional ownership or other traditional occupation or use, as well as those which they have otherwise acquired.
3. States shall give legal recognition and protection to these lands, territories and resources. Such recognition shall be conducted with due respect to the customs, traditions and land tenure systems of the indigenous peoples concerned.

Article 27

States shall establish and implement, in conjunction with indigenous peoples concerned, a fair, independent, impartial, open and transparent process, giving due recognition to indigenous peoples' laws, traditions, customs and land tenure systems, to recognize and adjudicate the rights of indigenous peoples pertaining to their lands, territories and resources, including those which were traditionally owned or otherwise occupied or used. Indigenous peoples shall have the right to participate in this process.

Article 28

1. Indigenous peoples have the right to redress, by means that can include restitution or, when this is not possible, just, fair and equitable compensation, for the lands, territories and resources which they have traditionally owned or otherwise occupied or used, and which have been confiscated, taken, occupied, used or damaged without their free, prior and informed consent.
2. Unless otherwise freely agreed upon by the peoples concerned, compensation shall take the form of lands, territories and resources equal in quality, size and legal status or of monetary compensation or other appropriate redress.

Article 29

1. Indigenous peoples have the right to the conservation and protection of the environment and the productive capacity of their lands or

territories and resources. States shall establish and implement assistance programmes for indigenous peoples for such conservation and protection, without discrimination.

2. States shall take effective measures to ensure that no storage or disposal of hazardous materials shall take place in the lands or territories of indigenous peoples without their free, prior and informed consent.
3. States shall also take effective measures to ensure, as needed, that programmes for monitoring, maintaining and restoring the health of indigenous peoples, as developed and implemented by the peoples affected by such materials, are duly implemented.

Article 30

1. Military activities shall not take place in the lands or territories of indigenous peoples, unless justified by a relevant public interest or otherwise freely agreed with or requested by the indigenous peoples concerned.
2. States shall undertake effective consultations with the indigenous peoples concerned, through appropriate procedures and in particular through their representative institutions, prior to using their lands or territories for military activities.

Article 31

1. Indigenous peoples have the right to maintain, control, protect and develop their cultural heritage, traditional knowledge and traditional cultural expressions, as well as the manifestations of their sciences, technologies and cultures, including human and genetic resources, seeds, medicines, knowledge of the properties of fauna and flora, oral traditions, literatures, designs, sports and traditional games and visual and performing arts. They also have the right to maintain, control, protect and develop their intellectual property over such cultural heritage, traditional knowledge, and traditional cultural expressions.
2. In conjunction with indigenous peoples, States shall take effective measures to recognize and protect the exercise of these rights.

Article 32

1. Indigenous peoples have the right to determine and develop priorities and strategies for the development or use of their lands or territories and other resources.
2. States shall consult and cooperate in good faith with the indigenous peoples concerned through their own representative institutions in

order to obtain their free and informed consent prior to the approval of any project affecting their lands or territories and other resources, particularly in connection with the development, utilization or exploitation of mineral, water or other resources.

3. States shall provide effective mechanisms for just and fair redress for any such activities, and appropriate measures shall be taken to mitigate adverse environmental, economic, social, cultural or spiritual impact.

Article 33

1. Indigenous peoples have the right to determine their own identity or membership in accordance with their customs and traditions. This does not impair the right of indigenous individuals to obtain citizenship of the States in which they live.
2. Indigenous peoples have the right to determine the structures and to select the membership of their institutions in accordance with their own procedures.

Article 34

Indigenous peoples have the right to promote, develop and maintain their institutional structures and their distinctive customs, spirituality, traditions, procedures, practices and, in the cases where they exist, juridical systems or customs, in accordance with international human rights standards.

Article 35

Indigenous peoples have the right to determine the responsibilities of individuals to their communities.

Article 36

1. Indigenous peoples, in particular those divided by international borders, have the right to maintain and develop contacts, relations and cooperation, including activities for spiritual, cultural, political, economic and social purposes, with their own members as well as other peoples across borders.
2. States, in consultation and cooperation with indigenous peoples, shall take effective measures to facilitate the exercise and ensure the implementation of this right.

Article 37

1. Indigenous peoples have the right to the recognition, observance and enforcement of treaties, agreements and other constructive

arrangements concluded with States or their successors and to have States honour and respect such treaties, agreements and other constructive arrangements.

2. Nothing in this Declaration may be interpreted as diminishing or eliminating the rights of indigenous peoples contained in treaties, agreements and other constructive arrangements.

Article 38

States in consultation and cooperation with indigenous peoples, shall take the appropriate measures, including legislative measures, to achieve the ends of this Declaration.

Article 39

Indigenous peoples have the right to have access to financial and technical assistance from States and through international cooperation, for the enjoyment of the rights contained in this Declaration.

Article 40

Indigenous peoples have the right to access to and prompt decision through just and fair procedures for the resolution of conflicts and disputes with States or other parties, as well as to effective remedies for all infringements of their individual and collective rights. Such a decision shall give due consideration to the customs, traditions, rules and legal systems of the indigenous peoples concerned and international human rights.

Article 41

The organs and specialized agencies of the United Nations system and other intergovernmental organizations shall contribute to the full realization of the provisions of this Declaration through the mobilization, inter alia, of financial cooperation and technical assistance. Ways and means of ensuring participation of indigenous peoples on issues affecting them shall be established.

Article 42

The United Nations, its bodies, including the Permanent Forum on Indigenous Issues, and specialized agencies, including at the country level, and States shall promote respect for and full application of the provisions of this Declaration and follow up the effectiveness of this Declaration.

Article 43

The rights recognized herein constitute the minimum standards for the survival, dignity and well-being of the indigenous peoples of the world.

Article 44

All the rights and freedoms recognized herein are equally guaranteed to male and female indigenous individuals.

Article 45

Nothing in this Declaration may be construed as diminishing or extinguishing the rights indigenous peoples have now or may acquire in the future.

Article 46

1. Nothing in this Declaration may be interpreted as implying for any State, people, group or person any right to engage in any activity or to perform any act contrary to the Charter of the United Nations or construed as authorizing or encouraging any action which would dismember or impair, totally or in part, the territorial integrity or political unity of sovereign and independent States.
2. In the exercise of the rights enunciated in the present Declaration, human rights and fundamental freedoms of all shall be respected. The exercise of the rights set forth in this Declaration shall be subject only to such limitations as are determined by law and in accordance with international human rights obligations. Any such limitations shall be non-discriminatory and strictly necessary solely for the purpose of securing due recognition and respect for the rights and freedoms of others and for meeting the just and most compelling requirements of a democratic society.
3. The provisions set forth in this Declaration shall be interpreted in accordance with the principles of justice, democracy, respect for human rights, equality, non-discrimination, good governance and good faith.

Source: UN Permanent Forum on Indigenous Issues: www.un.org/esa/socdev/unpfii/en/declaration.html

Index

Note: UN Declaration on the Rights of Indigenous Peoples has its own entry, and is also referred to as the 'Declaration' in index headings.

Lightning Source UK Ltd.
Milton Keynes UK
UKOW01f0408111017
310778UK00004B/178/P